EXCELLENCE IN BUSINESS COMMUNICATION

SECOND EDITION

JOHN V. THILL
Chief Executive Officer
Communication Specialists of America

COURTLAND L. BOVÉE
Professor of Business Communication
C. Allen Paul Distinguished Chair
Grossmont College

McGraw-Hill, Inc.

New York	St. Louis	San Francisco	Auckland	Bogotá	Caracas
Lisbon	London	Madrid	Mexico	Milan	Montreal	New Delhi
Paris	San Juan	Singapore	Sydney	Tokyo	Toronto

*T*o Seib Adams and June Smith,
whom we salute for their excellence
as publishing professionals and
to whom we are deeply grateful
for their wisdom, commitment,
and friendship

NOTE TO STUDENTS

A study guide for this textbook can be obtained from college bookstores under the title *Study Guide, Excellence in Business Communication*, Second Edition, by John V. Thill and Courtland L. Bovée.

You can use the *Study Guide* throughout the course for reviewing the content of this textbook, for developing communication skills, and for increasing your knowledge of business communication. It is also an ideal aid when preparing for tests.

If the *Study Guide* is not in stock, ask the bookstore manager to order a copy from the publisher.

3 4 5 6 7 8 9 0 VNH VNH 9 0 9 8 7 6 5 4 3

ISBN 0-07-006867-4

This book was set in Century Expanded by York Graphic Services, Inc. The editors were Bonnie K. Binkert, Jim Nageotte, and Bob Greiner; the production supervisor was Al Rihner.
The cover was designed by Wanda Lubelska.
Von Hoffmann Press, Inc., was printer and binder.

Library of Congress Cataloging-in-Publication Data

Thill, John V.
    Excellence in business communication / John V. Thill, Courtland L. Bovée. — 2nd ed.
        p.   cm.
    Includes bibliographical references and indexes.
    ISBN 0-07-006867-4
    1. Business communication—United States—Case studies.
    I. Title.
HF5718.2.U6T45   1993
658.4′5—dc20   92-33421

INTERNATIONAL EDITION

Copyright © 1993. Exclusive rights by McGraw-Hill Inc. for manufacture and export. This book cannot be re-exported from the country to which it is consigned by McGraw-Hill. The International Edition is not available in North America.

When ordering this title, use ISBN 0-07-112945-6

written or spoken. Beyond that, you can convey a message by phone, computer, letter, memo, report, face-to-face exchange, or other medium. Ben & Jerry's executives use both face-to-face contact and package labels in addition to written reports, memos, and newsletters to get their message across.

The transmission channel and the medium you choose depend on the message you want to convey and on factors such as the location of your audience, the need for speed, and the formality of the situation. Let's say that you are trying to sell books. You might advertise in newspapers and magazines, put a sign in your store window, hire a door-to-door sales force, launch a direct-mail campaign, or solicit sales over the phone. Whichever approach you choose, the nature of the channel and the medium will influence the message. The wording of a newspaper ad should be, and usually is, different from the wording used in a face-to-face sales call.

The transmission channel and medium also affect what the receiver gets from the message. Watching a movie on television is different from watching it in a theater. Even though the movie is exactly the same, a theater offers no outside distractions, no commercials, and no lights. Likewise, reading a handwritten report is different from reading a perfectly typed copy of the same material. The paper, the binding, and the graphics of a document all influence its reception.

The choice of a transmission channel depends on the
- Message
- Audience
- Need for speed
- Situation

THE RECEIVER GETS THE MESSAGE

For communication to occur, the receiver has to get the message. If you send a letter, the recipient has to read it before she or he can understand it. If you're giving a speech, the people in the audience have to be able to hear you, and they have to be paying attention.

But physical reception is only the first step. The receiver also has to absorb the message mentally. In other words, the message has to be understood and stored in the receiver's mind. If all goes well, the message is interpreted correctly; that is, the receiver assigns to the words the same basic meaning as the sender intended and responds in the desired way.

THE RECEIVER REACTS AND SENDS FEEDBACK TO THE SENDER

Feedback is the final link in the communication chain. After getting the message, the receiver responds in some way and signals that response to the sender. The signal may take the form of a smile, a long pause, a spoken comment, a written message, or an action of some sort. Even a lack of response is, in a sense, a form of feedback.

Feedback is a key element in the communication process because it enables the sender to evaluate the effectiveness of the message. If your audience doesn't understand what you mean, you can tell by the response and refine the message. In business, many written messages are also designed to elicit a response of some sort. If that response indicates you have not made your point, you may want to repeat the communication cycle as often as necessary. However, you may find that you need to make some changes in the way you encode and transmit the message.

Estée Lauder credits the success of her skin-care company, in part, to her communication policy. She keeps herself open to input and feedback from everyone she deals with: customers, retailers, employees, suppliers, and managers.

HOW MISUNDERSTANDINGS ARISE

Although most acts of communication are at least partially successful, very few are perfect. Generally speaking, some meaning is lost as the message encounters various barriers along the pathway between sender and receiver. Such communication barriers can arise while the message is being developed, transmitted, received, or interpreted.

PROBLEMS IN DEVELOPING THE MESSAGE

Problems in formulating your message get communication off to a bad start.

The first potential source of trouble is formulation of the message. Problems involve indecision about message content, lack of familiarity with the situation or the receiver, emotional conflicts, or difficulty in expressing ideas. If you aren't successful at this point, the communication process starts out wrong and rapidly goes downhill.

Indecision about message content

Include only the information that is useful to the receiver, and organize it in a way that encourages its acceptance.

Communication often fails because the sender tries to convey everything that she or he knows about a subject. When a message contains too much information, it is difficult to absorb. So if you want to get your point across, you have to decide what to include and what to leave out, how much detail to provide, and what order to follow. If you try to explain something without first giving the receiver adequate background, you will create confusion. In addition, if you recommend actions without first explaining why they are justified, your message may provoke an emotional response that inhibits understanding.

Lack of familiarity with the situation or the receiver

Ask why you are preparing the message and for whom you are preparing it.

Creating an effective message is also difficult if you don't know how it will be used. Unless you know why a report is needed, you are forced to create a very general document, one that covers a little bit of everything. In the process, you are likely to leave out some important information and to include some irrelevant material.

Lack of familiarity with your audience is an equally serious handicap. You need to know something about the biases, education, age, status, and style of the receiver in order to create an effective message. If you were writing for a specialist in your field, for example, you could use technical terms that might be unfamiliar to a layperson. Or if you were addressing a lower-level employee, you might approach the subject differently than if you were talking to your boss.

Emotional conflicts

In business communication, try to maintain your objectivity.

Another potential problem in developing the message arises when the sender has conflicting emotions about the subject or the audience. Let's say that you've been asked to prepare a report recommending ways to improve the organization of your department. After analyzing the situation, you have come to believe that the best approach is to combine two positions. Unfortunately, this solution means eliminating the job of one of your close associates, and when the time comes to write your report, you find yourself apologizing for your recommendation. Even though you know your position is justified, you find you cannot make a convincing case.

Difficulty in expressing ideas

Lack of experience in writing or speaking can also prevent a person from developing effective messages. Some people may have a limited vocabulary or may be uncertain about questions of grammar, punctuation, and style. Or perhaps they are simply frightened by the idea of writing something or appearing before a group. Problems of this sort can be overcome, but only with some effort. The important thing is to recognize the problem and take action.

An inability to put thoughts into words can be overcome through study and practice.

Taking courses in communication at a college is a good first step. Some companies offer their own in-house training programs in communication; others have tuition reimbursement programs to help cover the cost of outside courses. Self-help books are another good, inexpensive alternative. Or you might prefer to join a club—Toastmasters or the League of Women Voters, for example—that provides opportunities for practicing communication skills in an informal setting.

PROBLEMS IN TRANSMITTING THE MESSAGE

Communication may also break down because of problems in getting the message from sender to receiver. The most obvious transmission problems are physical: bad connections, poor acoustics, illegible copy. Although defects of this sort (called "noise") seem trivial, they can completely block an otherwise effective message. For this reason, you should exercise as much control as possible over the physical transmission link. If you're preparing a written document, make sure that its appearance doesn't detract from your message. If you're delivering an oral presentation, choose a setting that permits the audience to see and hear you without straining.

Transmission of a message may be blocked by
- Physical factors
- Conflicting signals
- Too many transmission links

A more subtle transmission problem arises when two messages compete for the receiver's attention or when two messages have conflicting meanings. When two messages are transmitted at once, there is interference in the communication line, just as there is interference when two radio signals overlap. Both messages are garbled, and the receiver has trouble deciphering either one. A similar problem arises when two messages are contradictory. You should be aware that a conflicting message may also be conveyed nonverbally— a tone of voice, a wink, or a casual shrug may conflict with the words being spoken.

Perhaps the most troublesome transmission problem arises when the communication chain has too many links. Because everyone's mental map is different, some distortion is likely when messages are transferred from person to person. The original message is interpreted and retold differently by each person in the chain. By the time the message reaches the end of the line, it may only vaguely resemble the original version. The longer the chain, the bigger the problem.

PROBLEMS IN RECEIVING THE MESSAGE

Reception problems arise from
- Physical distractions
- Mental distractions

Like transmission problems, reception problems often have a physical cause. The receiver may be distracted by competing sights and sounds, an uncomfortable chair, poor lighting, or some other irritating condition. In some cases, the barrier may be related to the receiver's health. Hearing or visual impairment, or even a headache, can interfere with reception of a message. These annoy-

As corporate vice president of human resources at Avon Products, Marcia Worthing long ago recognized the impact of differing cultural backgrounds. Her solution was to institute cultural-sensitivity courses to help employees deal with the growing changes both in the customer base and in the work force.

Try to understand the other person's point of view, and be willing to change your mind if new information doesn't match your old perceptions.

ances generally don't block communication entirely, but they may reduce the receiver's concentration.

Perhaps the most common barrier to reception is simply lack of attention on the receiver's part. We all let our minds wander now and then, regardless of how hard we try to concentrate. People are especially likely to drift off when they are forced to listen to information that is difficult to understand or that has little direct bearing on their own lives. If they are tired or concerned about other matters, they are even more likely to lose interest.

PROBLEMS IN INTERPRETING THE MESSAGE

Although messages may get lost anywhere along the communication chain, the biggest potential trouble spot is the final link, where the message is interpreted by the receiver. Differences in background, vocabulary, and emotional state can all lead to misunderstanding.

Different backgrounds

When the receiver's life experience differs substantially from the sender's, communication becomes more difficult. For example, as Ben & Jerry's spreads across the nation, the two founders communicate with employees whose cultural backgrounds and communication expectations differ from region to region. Age, education, gender, social status, economic position, cultural background, temperament, health, beauty, popularity, religion, political belief, and even a passing mood can all separate one person from another and make understanding difficult. Figure 1.2 shows how shared experience contributes to shared meaning and understanding; the portion of each diagram where the circles overlap represents the level of understanding between sender and receiver.

Decoding a message to absorb its ideas is a complex process. Our ability to absorb information depends on our past experiences, and over time, each of us builds up a particular view of the world. Then when we learn something new, we try to fit it into our existing pattern. But if the new information doesn't quite fit, we are inclined to distort it rather than rearrange the pattern, or we pay more attention to some ideas than to others. Therefore, when we communicate with people who share similar experiences and expectations, much of what we say automatically fits into their mental framework. But when we encounter people with different backgrounds, what we say may be interpreted from an entirely different viewpoint. Communicating with someone from an-

FIGURE 1.2
How Shared Experience Affects Understanding

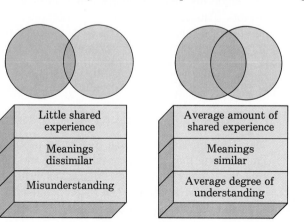

Little shared experience	Average amount of shared experience	Large amount of shared experience
Meanings dissimilar	Meanings similar	Meanings very similar
Misunderstanding	Average degree of understanding	High degree of understanding

other country is probably the most extreme example of how background may impede communication, and Chapter 17 details the problems and opportunities of intercultural communication.

Different interpretations of words

Our denotative (literal) and connotative (subjective) definitions of words may differ dramatically from those of other people.

Part of the problem in understanding messages is built into language, which uses words as symbols to represent reality. Nothing in the word *cookie* automatically ties it to the physical thing that is a cookie. We might just as well call a cookie a zebra. Language is an arbitrary code that depends on shared definitions. But there is a limit to how completely any of us can share the same meaning for a given word.

Even on the literal (denotative) level, words are imprecise. All of us who live in this culture generally agree on what a cookie is. But your idea of a cookie is a composite of all the cookies you have ever tasted or seen: oatmeal cookies, chocolate chip cookies, sugar cookies, vanilla wafers. Someone from a different background may have a different range of cookie experiences: meringues, florentines, spritz. You both agree on the general concept of *cookie*, but the precise image in your minds differs.

As anchor of NBC's "Evening News," Tom Brokaw addresses a nationwide audience daily. He must be careful to use words that mean the same thing to everyone, regardless of background or region of the country. Straightforward and simple is best, says Brokaw. Your chances of being misunderstood decrease if you are as accurate and specific as you can be.

On the subjective (connotative) level, the differences are even greater. Your interpretation of the word *cookie* depends partly on how you feel about cookies. You may have very pleasant feelings about them; you may remember baking them with your mother or coming home from school on winter afternoons to cookies and milk. Or you may be on a diet, in which case *cookie* will be an unpleasant reminder that you are too fat and must say no to all your favorite foods.

Obviously, the "fuzziness" of words is not an insurmountable problem. People manage to communicate with one another all the time, despite the limitations of language. But it's useful to remember that words by themselves don't mean anything. Their meanings depend on the ideas they evoke in people's minds, and no two minds are identical. Try to overcome differences in the interpretation of words by using the most specific and accurate language possible.

Different emotional reactions

A receiver may react either to the content of a message or to the relationship between sender and receiver that it implies.

Interestingly enough, one person may react differently to the same words on different occasions. A message that might be perfectly clear and acceptable in one situation can lead to confusion and hostility in another, depending on the emotional relationship between receiver and sender.

Every message contains both a content meaning, which deals with the subject of the message, and a relationship meaning, which suggests the nature of the interaction between sender and receiver. Communication can break down when the receiver reacts negatively to either of these meanings. When the boss says, "Get that monthly report on my desk by 5:00 tonight," the employee may become angry on two counts:

- The content of the message means work for the employee, perhaps under difficult circumstances.

- The wording of the message implies that the employee is a pawn lacking freedom and power.

Although in this case the receiver may understand the message perfectly, communication suffers because the receiver is reacting emotionally.

Roger Plummer is president of Ameritech Information Systems, which sells communications systems to business clients in five states. Plummer believes communication must bridge the gap between corporate philosophy and the individual. Although sometimes difficult to do, says Plummer, every employee must represent the company's view in all business communications.

SPECIAL PROBLEMS OF BUSINESS COMMUNICATION

Although all communication is subject to misunderstandings, business communication is particularly difficult. The material is often complex and controversial, and both the sender and the receiver may face distractions that divert their attention. Furthermore, the opportunities for feedback are often limited, making it difficult to correct misunderstandings. Unfortunately, when business communication goes awry, the consequences can be grave.

Complexity of the message

In business messages, you must communicate both as an individual and as a representative of an organization. Thus you must adjust your own ideas and style so that they are acceptable to your employer. In fact, you may be asked occasionally to write or say something that you disagree with personally. Let's suppose that you work in the personnel department as a recruiter for your firm. You have interviewed someone who you believe would make an excellent employee, but others in the firm have rejected this person's application. Now you are in the position of having to write a letter telling the candidate, in effect, "Sorry, we don't want you." That's a tough assignment.

Even when you agree with the message, you may have emotional reservations about expressing it. You may know that you are doing the right thing, that you have no choice but to fire this or that person or to cancel this or that program, but you would also rather avoid causing hardship or disappointment. Business is full of difficult decisions like these, decisions that affect people's lives.

Even in purely unemotional situations, you may be dealing with subject matter that is difficult to express. Imagine trying to write an interesting insurance policy or a set of instructions on how to operate a scraped-surface heat exchanger. These topics are dry, and making them clear and interesting is a real challenge.

On top of everything else, you may not know as much as you need to know about the purpose of or the audience for your message. Furthermore, you may be asked to prepare it under difficult conditions. You may be under time pressure, with two days to do a job that should take ten. You may be interrupted in the middle of your work. You may have to collaborate with other people and incorporate their ideas, regardless of whether they fit or not. You may be told to produce a document that looks professional but, at the same time, not to waste a lot of time and money. Moreover, you may have to revise your message time and again to please everybody in the chain of command.

Difficult conditions for transmission and reception

Assuming that you survive the ordeal of preparing the message, you still have to get through to your audience. In business, the filters between you and the receiver are many: Secretaries, assistants, receptionists, and answering machines line the path between you and your audience. Just getting through by telephone can take a week if you're calling someone who's protected by layers of gatekeepers. Worse yet, your message may be digested and distilled, and probably distorted, before it is passed on to the intended receiver. Those same gatekeepers may also translate, embellish, and augment the receiver's ideas before passing them on to you.

The complexity of messages relates to
- Your conflicts about the content
- The dry or difficult nature of the subject
- The difficult conditions you are working under

Transmission and reception of messages may be hindered by
- Numerous layers of message processors
- Interruptions from other message senders

When the message finally does reach the receiver, he or she may be unable to digest it in peace. Your message may have to compete with a variety of interruptions: The phone rings every five minutes, people intrude, meetings are called, crises arise. In short, your message rarely has the benefit of the receiver's undivided attention; it may be picked up and put down several times.

Differences between sender and receiver

Your biggest problem is the gulf between you and your receiver. In business, you often communicate with an unknown and unseen audience. Even when you know the other party, you may be separated by differences in function, status, age, or allegiance. These differences make communication very difficult indeed. The problem of communicating with someone who has a different frame of reference is twofold: You have to establish credibility with the other person and, at the same time, try to understand that person's needs and reactions.

Whether you're writing a letter, making a phone call, or meeting face-to-face, the first step is convincing the receiver to trust you. In some circumstances, you may have to overcome hostility. For example, if you're a customer service representative, you often have to pacify disgruntled customers. Building trust is a difficult problem, and the solution depends on your ability to "read" the other person. The approach you take with one individual might not work at all with another. If you're communicating by phone or face-to-face, you can glean something from the person's tone of voice, appearance, and replies. But if the only communication between you is the printed page, drawing meaningful conclusions about the other person is very difficult. Yet, as you know, unless you can develop a shared perspective with your audience, your message is likely to be misunderstood.

> Differences between sender and receiver are bridged by
> - Getting the other person to trust you
> - Sharing the other person's perspective

HOW TO IMPROVE COMMUNICATION

Think about the people you know. Which of them would you call successful communicators? What do these people have in common? The individuals on your list probably share five qualities:

> Effective communication requires perception, precision, credibility, control, and congeniality.

- *Perception.* They are able to predict how their message will be received. They anticipate your reaction and shape the message accordingly. They read your response correctly and constantly adjust to correct any misunderstanding.

- *Precision.* They create a "meeting of the minds." When they finish expressing themselves, you share the same mental picture.

- *Credibility.* They are believable. You have faith in the substance of their message. You trust their information and their intentions.

- *Control.* They shape your response. Depending on their purpose, they can make you laugh or cry, calm down, change your mind, or take action.

- *Congeniality.* They maintain friendly, pleasant relations with the audience. Regardless of whether you agree with them, good communicators command your respect and goodwill. You are willing to work with them again, despite your differences.

Look at your list of good communicators once more. Chances are, it's fairly short. When you think about it, effective communication is relatively rare.

What sets the effective communicators apart is their ability to overcome the main barriers to communication. They do this by creating their messages very carefully, minimizing noise in the transmission process, and facilitating feedback.

CREATE THE MESSAGE CAREFULLY

If you want the people in your audience to understand and accept your message, you have to help. You cannot depend on others to carry the communication ball; the burden is yours, not theirs.

Think about your purpose and your audience

The first step is to define your goal in communicating. Why are you sending your message? What do you want your audience to do or know as a consequence? Once you have answered these questions, you can begin to build a message to achieve your purpose. You must create a bridge of words that leads listeners or readers from their current position to your point. Before you can do this, of course, you have to know something about their current position. What do they know now, and what do they need to know? If you're addressing strangers, try to find out more about them; if that's impossible, try to project yourself into their position by using your common sense and imagination.

In general terms, your purpose is to bring the audience closer to your views.

Tell the audience what to expect

After you have defined your readers' or listeners' information needs, you can launch them on their journey toward the intended destination. As they travel, you must be their guide, providing them with a map of the territory they will cover. Tell them at the outset what they can expect to gain from the trip. Let them know the purpose of the message (thus helping them recognize the relationship among the ideas you hope to convey), and tell them what main points they will encounter on the way (so that they can organize them into a rational framework). Even if you do not want to reveal controversial ideas at the beginning of the message, you can still give receivers a preview of the topics you plan to cover.

Give your audience a framework for understanding the ideas you communicate.

By telling the members of your audience how to categorize the information in your message, you eliminate the discrepancy between your mental filing system and theirs. In addition, you make it easier for them to cope with the distractions that occur in most environments. If people know the basic framework of the message, they can pick it up and put it down without getting lost.

Use concrete, specific language

To make your message memorable
- Use words that evoke a physical, sensory impression
- Use specific details

Because business communication often involves difficult, abstract, and technical material, you must do something to help your audience understand and remember the message. The best way to do this is to balance the general concepts with specific illustrations. At the beginning, state the overall idea; then develop that idea by using vivid, concrete examples to help the audience visualize the concept.

The most memorable words are the ones that create a picture in the receiver's mind by describing colors, objects, scents, sounds, and tastes. Specific details can also be very vivid. For example, did you know that by the year 2000, the average car will be driven 22 years before it wears out?

Stick to the point

You can also help your audience by eliminating any information that doesn't directly contribute to your purpose. Many business messages contain too much material; in hopes of being thorough, the sender tries to explain everything there is to know about a subject. But most receivers don't need everything. All they need are a few pertinent facts, enough information to answer their questions or facilitate their decisions.

By keeping your messages as lean as possible, you make them easier to absorb. With few exceptions, one page is better than two, especially in a business environment where the receiver is bombarded by competing claims for attention. By eliminating unnecessary ideas, you focus the other person's thoughts on those few points that really matter.

> The key to brevity is to limit the number of ideas, not to shortchange their development.

You have to be careful, however, to develop each main idea adequately. You're better off covering three points thoroughly than eight points superficially. Don't rush the audience through a laundry list of vague generalities in the mistaken belief that you are being brief. If an idea is worth including, it's worth explaining.

Connect new information to existing ideas

The mind absorbs information by categorizing it into mental files. If you want the receiver to understand and remember new ideas, you have to indicate how those ideas are related to the files that already exist in her or his mind. When the connection with familiar concepts is lacking, the new material tends to get lost, to become mentally misplaced, because it doesn't fit into the receiver's filing cabinet.

> Tie the message to the receiver's frame of reference.

By showing the audience how new ideas relate to familiar ones, you increase the likelihood that your message will be understood correctly. The meaning of the new concept is clarified by its relationship to the old. The receiver already has a wealth of information on the subject; all she or he has to do is apply it to the new idea.

Connecting new ideas to existing ones also helps make the new concepts acceptable. Most of us approach anything unfamiliar with caution. When we discover that it's similar to something familiar, we become more confident. We pick it up, look it over more carefully, and then take it home with us.

Emphasize and review key points

Another way to help the audience is to call attention to the most important points of the message. You can do this with your words, your format, and your body language. When you come to an important idea, say so. This way, you wake people up; you also make it easier for them to file the thought in the proper place. Underscore key points by calling attention to them visually. Use headlines, bold type, and indented lists to emphasize major ideas. Reinforce the text of your message by using charts, graphs, maps, diagrams, and illustrations that will help your audience "see" the point. If you are delivering the message orally, use your body and voice to highlight important concepts.

> By highlighting and summarizing key points, you help the audience understand and remember the message.

Before you conclude your message, take a moment or two to review the essential points. Restate the purpose and then show how the main ideas relate to it. This simple step will help your audience remember the message.

In addition, because business audiences are frequently interrupted, it's a good idea to provide summaries at the ends of major sections of a long message as well as at the end of a document or presentation. Such summaries not only refresh people's memories but also help simplify the overall meaning of complex material.

MINIMIZE NOISE

Even the most carefully constructed message will fail to achieve results if it does not reach the receiver. To the extent possible, you should try to eliminate potential sources of interference that stand between you and your audience. The key to getting through to the receiver often lies in the choice of communication channels and media. You should choose the method that will most likely attract the receiver's attention and enable him or her to concentrate on the message.

The careful choice of channel and medium helps focus the receiver's attention on your message.

If a written document seems the best choice, try to make it physically appealing and easy to comprehend. Use an attractive, convenient format, and pay attention to such details as the choice of paper and quality of type. If possible, deliver the document when you know the reader will have time to study it.

If the message calls for an oral delivery channel, try to eliminate environmental competition. The location should be comfortable and quiet, with adequate lighting, good acoustics, and few visual distractions. In addition, you should think about how your own appearance will affect the audience. An outfit that screams for attention creates as much noise as a squeaky air-conditioning system. Another way to reduce interference, particularly in oral communication, is to deliver your message directly to the intended audience. The more people who filter your message, the greater the potential for distortion.

FACILITATE FEEDBACK

In addition to minimizing noise, you frequently need to give the receiver a chance to provide feedback. But one of the things making business communication difficult is the complexity of the feedback loop. If you're talking face-to-face with one other person, feedback is immediate and clear. But if you're writing a letter, memo, or report that will be read by several people, feedback will be delayed and mixed. Some of the readers will be enthusiastic or respond promptly; others will be critical or reluctant to respond. As a consequence, revising your message to take account of their feedback will be difficult.

When you plan a message, think about the amount of feedback that you want to encourage. Although generally useful, feedback reduces your control over the communication situation. You need to know whether your message is being understood and accepted, but you may not want to respond to comments until you have completed your argument. If you are communicating with a group, you may not have the time to react to every impression or question.

For this reason, think about how you want to obtain feedback, and choose a form of communication that suits your needs. Some channels and media are more compatible with feedback than others. For example, if you want to adjust your message quickly, you must talk to the receiver face-to-face or by phone. If feedback is less important to you, you can use a written document or give a prepared speech.

Make feedback more useful
by
- Planning how and when
  to accept it
- Being receptive to oth-
  ers' responses
- Encouraging frankness
- Using it to improve communication

Feedback is not always easy to get, even when you have chosen a transmission method that encourages it. In some cases, you may have to draw out
the other person by asking questions. If you want to know specific things, ask
specific questions. But also encourage the other person to express general
reactions; you can often learn something very interesting that way.

Remember too that in order to get feedback, you have to listen. Ben &
Jerry's executives spend more time listening than giving orders. But listening
is more difficult than you might think. We tend to let our minds wander and
miss important points, or we jump in too quickly with comments of our own so
that the other person doesn't have a chance to complete a thought. We make
the mistake of prejudging other people because we don't like the way they look
or because they represent an opposing group. Often we lack patience, objectivity, and understanding. We send signals, subconsciously perhaps, that we
don't value the other person's comments.

Regardless of whether the response to your message is written or oral, you
have to encourage people to be open if you want them to tell you what they
really think and feel. You can't say "please tell me what you think" and then
get mad at the first critical comment. So try not to react defensively. Your goal
is to find out whether the people in your audience have understood and accepted your message. If you find that they haven't, don't lose your temper.
After all, the fault is at least partially yours. Instead of saying the same thing
all over again, only louder this time, try to find the source of the misunderstanding. Then revise your message. If you keep trying, you'll achieve success
sooner or later. You may not win the audience to your point of view, but at
least you'll make your meaning clear, and you'll part with a feeling of mutual
respect.

SUMMARY

Effective communicators use both nonverbal and verbal signals to get their
messages across. Moreover, they pay as much attention to receiving information as they do to transmitting it.

Communication is a five-step process: The sender has an idea, the idea
becomes a message, the message is transmitted, the receiver gets the message, and the receiver reacts and sends feedback. Misunderstandings arise
when any part of this process breaks down.

Business communication is especially prone to misunderstandings because
the message is complex, conditions are difficult, and psychological or social
differences often separate the sender and receiver. To overcome communication barriers, think about your audience, let them know what to expect, use
vivid language, stick to the point, connect new ideas to familiar ones, emphasize and review key points, minimize noise, and provide opportunities for feedback.

ON THE JOB:
Solving a Communication Dilemma
at Ben & Jerry's Homemade

Communication—with employees, government officials,
customers, investors, and the public—plays a key role in
Ben & Jerry's success. Whether it's a company meeting, a

tour of the facilities, or involvement in various social and
environmental causes, the company energetically works to
get its messages across.

To begin with, the communicators at Ben & Jerry's never miss an opportunity to get their messages across to customers. For instance, packages and labels for most food products talk about great taste, healthy ingredients, and so on. Ben & Jerry's labels go a step further and talk about world peace, the environment, and other causes the company supports. Some products are even designed to convey messages. For example, a percentage of sales from Peace Pops goes to promoting world peace, and Rainforest Crunch is made with nuts from the South American rain forest (which both supports the native people directly and gives them a long-term financial incentive to nurture the forest instead of cutting it down). These products essentially become the transmission channel for Ben & Jerry's message.

Publicly owned companies are required to publish annual reports for their stockholders, and these reports are usually slick, glossy affairs that heap praise on the company's managers and employees. An annual report from Ben & Jerry's, on the other hand, is likely to be illustrated with whimsical drawings of cows, ice cream cones, and endangered species. The content can include such features as a "social audit," in which an outside observer assesses the company's success in meeting its social goals. Employees, investors, and other readers are left with no doubt about the company's orientation after reading one of these reports.

In addition to communicating with customers and stockholders, communicating with employees is crucial to the success of any business. At Ben & Jerry's, internal communication ranges from meetings in which all employees are encouraged to speak their minds about company policies and practices to the following formal mission statement (which was also published in the annual report):

- *Product Mission.* To make, distribute, and sell the finest quality all-natural ice cream and related products in a wide variety of innovative flavors made from Vermont dairy products.

- *Social Mission.* To operate the company in a way that actively recognizes the central role that business plays in the structure of society by initiating innovative ways to improve the quality of life in a broad community: local, national, and international.

- *Economic Mission.* To operate the company on a sound financial basis of profitable growth, increasing value for our shareholders and creating career opportunities and financial rewards for our employees.

This mission statement clearly communicates what the company's leaders consider important, and it gives every employee a framework in which to make decisions and take action. By communicating what the company is about and what it is supposed to accomplish, Cohen and Greenfield hope to keep their unusual business effort alive and well.

Your Mission: You've recently been appointed Ben & Jerry's first director of communications. This role covers both internal communications with employees and external communications with customers, suppliers, the news media, and the general public. You have three responsibilities: (1) developing guidelines and practices to help the company communicate more effectively, (2) helping individual employees and managers with specific communication problems, and (3) acting as the company's official voice (talking to reporters, welcoming tour groups, and so on).

In the following hypothetical situations, select the *best* choice from the available options. Keep in mind that in some of the situations, two or three options might be attractive, so you'll have to pick the best one carefully. In other situations, none of the options may look particularly strong, but you still need to pick the best one from the choices offered. In each situation, be sure to use good judgment and common sense to help identify the best answer.

1. A reporter from *The New York Times* is writing an article on fat and cholesterol in the American diet. She wants to know how Ben & Jerry's can claim to be so socially responsible when the company sells products that aren't exactly healthy. The article is running in tomorrow's editions, so the reporter doesn't have time to let you think about it and call back with an answer. Which is the best response?
   a. You know that anything you say might provoke a negative reaction, so you simply say, "I'm sorry; we don't comment on health-related issues."
   b. You know that you have to establish some credibility, and pretending that a steady diet of ice cream is acceptable is not the way to do that, so you say, "We don't encourage anyone to eat excessive amounts of ice cream. We do believe, however, that modest amounts of ice cream can be compatible with a generally healthy life-style that includes healthier foods and regular exercise."
   c. You want to take control of the conversation, so you tell her that "until we conduct our own research, we're not willing to accept without question the negative image that the medical profession has created for ice cream."
   d. You know that you can't control what your customers eat, so you say, "We can't be held responsible for our customers' health. After all, we make only ice cream, and people could have unhealthy eating habits that extend beyond dessert."

2. The manager of one of the production plants realizes that his communication skills are important, for several reasons: he holds primary responsibility for successful communication inside the plant, he needs to communicate with the managers who report to him, and his style sets an example for other managers. He asks you to sit in on face-to-face meetings for several days to observe any nonverbal messages that he may

be sending. You witness the following four habits; which do you think is the most negative?

a. He rarely comes out from behind his massive desk when meeting with people in his office; at one point he gave an employee a congratulatory hand-shake, and the employee had to lean way over his desk just to reach him.

b. When an employee hands him a report and then sits down to discuss it, he alternates between making eye contact and making notes on the report.

c. He is consistently pleasant, even if the person he is meeting is delivering bad news.

d. He interrupts meetings to answer the phone, rather than letting an assistant get the phone; then he apologizes to visitors for the interruption.

3. Say that a weak economy has forced the company to lay off 5 percent of its employees. Knowing that this is an emotionally charged issue, the company president asks you to recommend the best way to break the news to those who will lose their jobs.

a. Soften the blow by writing an article for the company newsletter, describing the plans to lay off 5 percent of the work force.

b. It is the responsibility of individual managers to tell the employees who report to them. However, the president should send a brief personal letter to all affected employees, noting their accomplishments and wishing them luck in finding new jobs.

c. The president owes it to the employees to meet with them individually and break the news.

d. On bulletin boards around the company, post a list of employees to be laid off.

4. The company's marketing manager, a man in his late forties, has come to you in a state of confusion and frustration. He has repeatedly told the people in his department that the company's new ad campaign should conjure images of the 1960s, as he says, "when hope was high that people could band together for world peace and people began to question the traditional ways of doing things." But his staffers, most of whom are young, energetic, and highly creative, seem unable to translate his ideas into ads with just the right feel. What do you think the problem is?

a. The younger people want to pursue ideas that relate more to people their own age; they are bored and frustrated by the manager's interest in things that happened so long ago.

b. The problem is fairly easy to understand: The manager and his younger employees don't have the same pool of shared experiences. Unlike the manager and his generation, the younger staffers aren't old enough to have lived through the 1960s as teenagers and young adults, so they can't possibly have the same feel for that time in U.S. history.

c. When the manager repeated his idea in an attempt to communicate what he wanted more clearly, the employees began to resent his treating them like children, so they've decided not to cooperate.

d. The idea is too complex to be communicated from one person to another.

5. At a recent companywide meeting, employees were told that shareholders have been pressuring company management to pay them a higher dividend and the board of directors has agreed. (Dividends are a portion of the company's profits set aside for shareholders; higher dividends mean less money is available for other purposes.) Then when employees returned to work, they found the latest issue of the company newsletter, in which an article by Jerry Greenfield asked employees to voluntarily cut their lunch periods to increase ice cream production so that more money can be given to charities. Which of the following best describes the effect of the two messages?

a. The two messages are compatible; shareholders will get more money from the existing profit margin, and charities will get more from the employees' working longer hours. You can't foresee any problems.

b. Employees will actually work less because they'll resent the shareholders' request for higher dividends.

c. Employees will begin to question the wisdom of the company's charitable contributions.

d. Confusion is the most likely result because the two messages basically conflict. Some employees are likely to think that their sacrifice of working longer for the same pay is going to benefit the shareholders.

6. The human resources manager is writing a letter to all employees explaining that health insurance is getting more expensive and that employees will have to pay 10 percent more for coverage (the company and the employees share the cost of coverage, and the company decides how much the employees have to pay). The manager asks you to read four possible openings for the letter; which would you recommend that she use?

a. "If you follow the news, you are certainly aware of the skyrocketing costs of health insurance, and those increases are now going to affect all of us here at Ben & Jerry's."

b. "You're probably aware of the increasing costs of health insurance, and we have been doing everything possible to keep your insurance payments from rising; unfortunately, we've reached a point where the company can no longer absorb all the increases by itself."

c. "Your health insurance premiums have increased by 10 percent, effective immediately."

d. "We're pleased to announce that the company has found a way to improve its profitability by de-

creasing the amount we spend on health insurance."[9]

QUESTIONS FOR DISCUSSION

1. Why does propping your feet on the desk while talking to someone transmit different messages in different situations?
2. Which party bears more responsibility for the outcome of communication, the sender or the receiver?
3. Some communication experts contend that good communication does not necessarily produce agreement between the parties. Do you agree or disagree? Why?
4. Is written communication or spoken communication more susceptible to noise?
5. Do you believe it is easier to communicate with members of your own sex? Why or why not?
6. "One of the things making business communication difficult is the complexity of the feedback loop." Show what this sentence means by giving some examples.

DOCUMENT FOR ANALYSIS

Read the following memo; then (1) analyze the strengths or weaknesses of each sentence and (2) revise the memo so that it follows this chapter's guidelines.

It has come to my attention that many of you are lying on your time cards. If you come in late, you should not put 8:00 on your card. If you take a long lunch, you should not put 1:00 on your time card. I will not stand for this type of cheating. I simply have no choice but to institute a time-clock system. Beginning next Monday, all employees will have to punch in and punch out whenever they come and go from the work area.

The time clock will be right by the entrance to each work area, so you have no excuse for not punching in. Anyone who is late for work or late coming back from lunch more than three times will have to answer to me. I don't care whether you had to take a nap or if you girls had to shop. This is a place of business, and we do not want to be taken advantage of by slackers who are cheaters to boot.

It is too bad that a few bad apples always have to spoil things for everyone.

EXERCISES

1. Observe a small group of people in the college cafeteria or lounge area. Closely examine the dress of each person to see what he or she is communicating. Start with such easily visible matters as color combinations and general styles. Then notice matters that are often ignored but contribute to a person's total appearance: shoes, jewelry, the presence or absence of a belt. Finally, include personal grooming (hairstyle and cleanliness). Select two members of the group and, without naming them, write a one- or two-paragraph description of what they are communicating about themselves. Remember that for this exercise, your job is not to judge their dress; rather it is to try to understand the image that, consciously or unconsciously, they present through their dress and grooming.
2. As the director of communications at Ben & Jerry's Homemade (see this chapter's On-the-Job simulation), you are responsible for organizing the public tours of the company's ice cream production facilities. You view these tours as another important opportunity to communicate Ben & Jerry's messages about the causes the company supports, in addition to promoting the company and its products. What would be the most important points that your tour guides should make in a five-minute introductory speech to groups of visitors?[10]
3. In conversations with three people, pay attention to the type of feedback each gives you. What are the main methods of feedback used by each person: gestures, nods, questions about what you said? How does the amount of feedback differ? Do you

adjust your communication in any way as a result of this feedback? How can this exercise help you become more responsive to others?

4. Think of a communication experience you have had recently. In a paragraph or two, identify the sender, message, transmission channel and medium, receiver, and feedback. Also identify any barriers that affected the communication.

5. Cultural background determines, in part, the mental images that words produce. Imagine three people: a 19-year-old man who grew up on a ranch in Idaho, a 19-year-old woman who grew up in an elegant Baltimore home, and a retired mechanic who has lived all his life in a working-class neighborhood of Chicago. Describe the differences in the images or feelings that the following nouns might call to mind for each of them:
   a. rose
   b. shotgun
   c. snake
   d. wealth
   e. education
   f. horse
   g. danger
   What have you learned in this exercise that will help you communicate more effectively in business?

6. Some business communicators supply too much information, which makes it difficult for the recipient to sort out the most important points. Here is the first draft of a memo written by a busy office manager to her immediate supervisor. Rephrase it so that it gets to the point more quickly and fits easily onto a half-sheet memo form.

I can't ever remember being so frustrated in my life! Here is what happened. I ordered six regional U.S. maps last week at $17 each against our office equipment budget, but Mr. Olson in purchasing said that I had to place the order against the office supplies budget because the maps cost less than $25 each. The problem is, of course, that we are going to be overspent this year in the office supplies budget, but we still have equipment money because we got such a good price on the terminals I ordered last month. Anyway, Olson and I went round and round about this. He wouldn't budge, and I couldn't budge, but I do see a possible way out of the dilemma. Do you think that I could put the order through again, this time for a single set of U.S. maps costing $102? You'll probably be hearing from Mr. Olson, so I wanted to alert you to the problem and get your advice. We do need the maps!

CHAPTER TWO

COMMUNICATING SUCCESSFULLY IN AN ORGANIZATION

After studying this chapter, you will be able to

- Explain how organizations use communication
- List the distinctions between formal and informal communication channels
- Describe how management style influences an organization's communication climate
- Identify the considerations involved in making ethical communication decisions
- Explain how companies manage the creation and distribution of messages
- Explain how companies prepare for handling communication in times of crisis
- Identify the communication skills you will need in your career

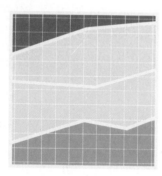

ON THE JOB:
Facing a Communication Dilemma at General Motors

Tuning Up Corporate Communication at the World's Biggest Automaker

Alvie Smith faced what must have been one of the world's largest communication challenges. His employer, General Motors, had made a lot of headlines in recent years with losses, layoffs, and restructurings; however, the problems were hardly new. For years, GM struggled with a top-heavy bureaucracy, a poorly motivated work force, an autocratic management style, and an ineffective process of communication between the many layers in its corporate hierarchy. The world's biggest automaker lost $726.5 million in 1980, and Japanese companies gained an unprecedented share of the U.S. market.

In response, top managers ordered a massive overhaul. They restructured GM's North American operations, built new plants, modernized others, made huge investments in advanced technology, reduced the number of nonproduction employees, and cut costs by $10 billion. But they made one serious omission: They neglected to communicate the company's new mission to GM employees.

As director of corporate communication, Alvie Smith was asked to muster employee support for the company's reorganization and to improve communication throughout the manufacturing giant. Smith faced a daunting challenge. How could he help GM's 60,000 middle managers become better communicators so that employees could understand and support the new mission? How could he tailor his communication program so that employees regained their trust in management and supported the company's goals? And what communication channels could he use to facilitate all organizational communication?[1]

THE COMMUNICATION CONNECTION

Alvie Smith
General Motors

Alvie Smith understands that an organization is a little society and that communication is the glue holding that society together, enabling it to function. Through the process of communication, the members of the organization exchange messages using a common system of symbols that result, at least to some degree, in shared meanings. Thus communication has two important functions in an organization: It enables people to exchange necessary information, and it helps set members of the organization apart from nonmembers.

Most organizations depend heavily on communication to accomplish their objectives. In fact, one study maintains that people in organizations spend 69 percent of their working day in one form of verbal communication or another—whether speaking, listening, writing, or reading.[2]

Impressive as this statistic may be, it understates the importance of communication because it fails to take into account nonverbal communication. Research suggests that people derive only 7 percent of the meaning of a spoken message from the sender's words. Tone of voice, facial expressions, and body language convey 93 percent of the meaning.[3] Taking these nonverbal messages into account, it would be fair to say that people communicate almost constantly.

When you stop to think about it, just about everything an organization does requires communication. Here are the organizational activities that rely on an exchange of views and facts:

Organizations rely on communication among employees at all levels to decide on and implement their goals.

- *Setting goals and objectives.* Most organizations have a variety of formal and informal objectives to accomplish. These goals are established by thinking and talking about them and then committing them to paper. The objective might be defined in terms of financial results, product quality, market dominance, employee satisfaction, or service to customers. But regardless of the goal, the fact that someone has thought about it and communicated it enables everyone to work toward a common purpose.

Managers make decisions by collecting facts and analyzing them, often with the help of lower-level employees; implementing these decisions requires communication between managers and others.

- *Making and implementing decisions.* To achieve their goals, people in business must make and implement many decisions. They must collect facts and evaluate alternatives, and they do so by reading, asking questions, talking things over with one another, and just plain thinking. Often their deliberations depend on reports that are prepared by others. Then once a decision has been made, it has to be implemented, and this requires more communication. Businesspeople have to explain what needs to be done and gain the support of people affected by the decision.

Keeping track of results requires the transmission of information from lower-level employees to management.

- *Measuring results.* As the decisions are translated into action, management needs to determine whether the desired outcome is being reached. Statistics on such factors as costs, sales, market share, productivity, employee turnover, and inventory levels are compiled. In larger companies, the data may be put together using a computerized management information system that prepares reports automatically. In smaller companies, management may obtain the required information through face-to-face contact with lower-level employees or in the form of hand-prepared memos or reports.

Organizations attract, train, motivate, and evaluate their employees by communicating with them.	■ *Hiring and developing staff.* If a company wants to hire someone, it must first advertise the opening, screen resumes, interview applicants, and eventually make a job offer. Then the new person must be introduced to the organization, instructed in the responsibilities of the position, and motivated to perform. As time goes on, the new employee must be given feedback on her or his performance, which involves more communication.
Both written and oral communication are essential to a company's interactions with customers.	■ *Dealing with customers.* All of an organization's interactions with customers involve communication in one form or another. Even the price tags on products are a form of communication. Sales letters and brochures, advertisements, personal sales calls, telephone solicitations, and formal proposals are all used to stimulate the customer's interest. Communication also plays a part in such customer-related functions as credit checking, billing, and handling complaints and questions.
Organizations rely on communication to obtain needed supplies at favorable prices and to attract investment capital.	■ *Negotiating with suppliers and financiers.* To obtain necessary supplies and services, companies develop written specifications that outline their requirements. They place orders for materials and bargain to get the best price. To arrange financing, they negotiate with lenders and fill out loan applications, or they sell stock to the public, which involves still more paperwork. Once they have obtained the necessary capital, they must keep their investors informed about the status of the business.
The production process is, in part, a communication process.	■ *Producing the product.* Getting an idea for a new product out of someone's head, pushing it through the production process, and finally getting the product out the door also require communication. Designers draw plans, marketing people conduct studies, and product managers develop sales campaigns. When the time comes for full-scale production, the company prepares a manufacturing plan. Supervisors get instructions and pass them on to production workers. As production gets under way, workers report any problems that arise. Records are kept regarding raw materials, inventory levels, and product quality. Finally, arrangements are made by phone or in writing for shipping the product. Similar steps are required when a company's product is a service such as accounting or air transportation.
Government regulation and services depend on a two-way flow of information.	■ *Interacting with regulatory agencies.* Communication also occurs between businesses and government. With input from companies and the public, government agencies establish rules and regulations that both protect companies and ensure that they operate in the general interest. Often, companies must then demonstrate their compliance with regulations by preparing reports that describe their efforts to meet such goals as cleaning up the environment or hiring women and minorities. Should a company fail to respond to government requirements, it may get an opportunity for further communication—in a court of law.

PATTERNS OF COMMUNICATION IN ORGANIZATIONS

Robert M. Beavers is senior vice president/zone manager at McDonald's Corporation. Having worked his way up from the bottom, he is now responsible for six regional offices: Phoenix, Denver, San Francisco, Sacramento, Los Angeles, and San Diego. He credits his success to good communication. No matter what the industry, says Beavers, it's communicating with people that makes the difference.

The formal flow of information follows the official chain of command.

Managers direct and control the activities of lower-level employees by sending messages down through formal channels.

Although all companies have to communicate in order to function, their approaches vary. These variations are not surprising when you consider the vastly different requirements organizations face. In a small business with only five or six employees, much information can be exchanged casually and directly. However, in a giant organization with hundreds of thousands of employees scattered around the world, transmitting the right information to the right people at the right time is a real challenge.

Some companies are better at communicating than others. At top-performing companies such as Procter & Gamble, Disney, IBM, and Microsoft, communication is a way of life. At IBM, for example, stands with big rolls of paper are placed throughout the building so that people can jot down their thoughts during informal discussions. At Microsoft, weekend retreats offer employees the opportunity to exchange ideas both formally and informally. Because managers in such companies communicate freely with employees, everyone develops a clear sense of mission, derived from a constant repetition of the organization's values. In these firms, management *is* communication.[4]

How do these companies achieve superior communication? What sets them apart from other organizations? To answer these questions, take a closer look at how communication occurs in organizations.

FORMAL COMMUNICATION CHANNELS

The official structure of an organization is typically depicted in a chart like the one in Figure 2.1 (see page 28). The chart summarizes the lines of authority within the company and depicts the formal hierarchy. Each box represents a link in the chain of command; each line represents a formal channel for the transmission of official information. (Employees also communicate informally, of course.) Information may travel down, up, and across the formal hierarchy.

Downward information flow

When a manager transmits information to a subordinate, communication is flowing downward. The message might take the form of a casual conversation or a formal interview between a supervisor and an individual employee, or it might be disseminated orally to a group through a meeting, workshop, or videotape. On other occasions, the message might be a written memo, training manual, newsletter, bulletin board announcement, or policy directive.

Although some companies make a point of letting management decisions be known, many employees are dissatisfied with both the quality and quantity of information they receive through official channels. In one survey of 2 million employees, almost half expressed a desire to be better informed. Employees at lower levels in the organization are particularly likely to feel out of touch with what's happening.[5]

The real problem may lie in the differing communication priorities of managers and employees. As Table 2.1 illustrates, employees are particularly curious about things that affect them personally (see page 29). They want to know how secure their jobs are, how their salary is determined, and when they'll get a raise. Often, this is the type of information that management prefers to keep confidential.

FIGURE 2.1
Formal Communication Network

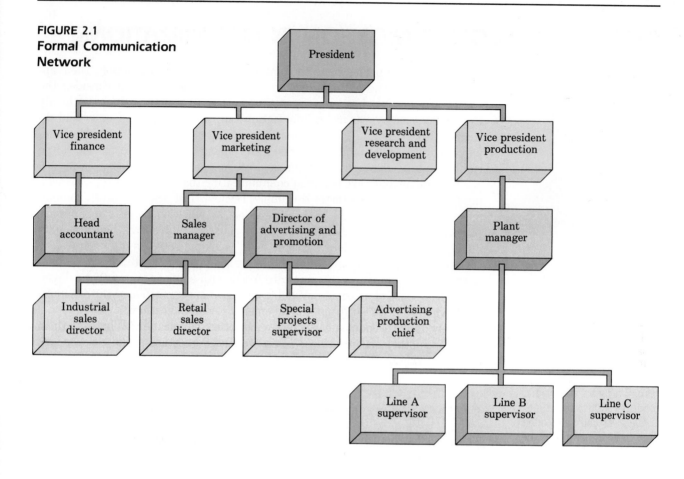

Upward information flow

From the organization's standpoint, upward communication is just as vital as downward communication. To solve problems and make intelligent decisions, management must learn what's going on in the organization. Because they can't be everywhere at once, executives depend on lower-level employees to furnish them with accurate, timely reports.

> Messages directed upward provide managers with the information they need to make intelligent decisions.

The danger, of course, is that employees will report only the good news. People are often afraid to admit their own mistakes or to report data that suggest their boss was wrong. Companies try to guard against the "rose-colored glasses" syndrome by creating reporting systems that require employees to furnish vital information on a routine basis. Many of these reports have a "red flag" feature that calls attention to deviations from planned results.

Other formal methods for channeling information upward include group meetings, interviews with employees who are leaving the company, and formal procedures for resolving grievances. In recent years, many companies have also set up systems that give employees a confidential way to get a message to top management outside the normal chain of command. If an employee has a problem or an idea that might be difficult to discuss with the person's immediate supervisor, he or she can talk to a neutral third party (sometimes called an ombudsman) who will consider the issue and see that appropriate action is taken without putting the employee in an awkward position.[6]

TABLE 2.1
Information Priorities of Employers and Employees

EMPLOYER RATING	TYPE OF INFORMATION	EMPLOYEE RATING
1	News about the company and its prospects for the future	2
2	Employee compensation, benefits, and service	3
3	Personal news	5
4	Company rules, policies, and programs	6
5	Promotions and opportunities for training and advancement	4
6	Social activities	7
7	Information that affects employees personally	1

Horizontal information flow

Official channels also permit messages to flow from department to department.

In addition to transmitting messages up and down the organization, the formal communication network also carries messages horizontally from one department to another. For example, the marketing director might write a memo to the production director, outlining sales forecasts for the coming period.

The amount of horizontal communication that occurs through formal channels depends on the degree of interdependence among departments. If the business requires coordinated action by its organizational units, horizontal communication may be frequent and intense. But if each department operates independently, official horizontal communication is minimal.

Limitations of formal communication channels

The formal communication network may limit lower-level employees' access to decision makers.

Although formal communication channels are essential in large organizations, they have drawbacks for both the company and the individual. From the standpoint of the individual, formal communication is often frustrating because it limits access to decision makers. In a big, formally structured organization, the only official way to communicate with people at higher levels is to go through one's immediate supervisor. Someone who has a sensational idea but whose boss doesn't agree is effectively stymied. Some people then try to go over the boss's head, but they risk endangering their future at that company and possibly their careers.

Each link in the communication chain is a potential source of blockage or distortion.

From the company's standpoint, the biggest problem with formal communication channels is the opportunity for distortion. Every link in the communication chain presents a chance for misunderstanding. By the time a message gets all the way up or down the chain, it may bear little resemblance to the original idea. As a consequence, people at lower levels may have only a vague idea of what top management expects of them, and executives may get an imperfect picture of what's happening lower down.

One way to reduce distortion is to decrease the number of levels in the organizational structure. The fewer the links in the communication chain, the less likely it is that misunderstandings will occur.[7] Generally speaking, bigger companies have more levels. But as Figure 2.2 illustrates, size does not necessarily force a company to have a hierarchy with many levels. By increasing the number of people who report to each supervisor, the company can reduce the

FIGURE 2.2
Organizational Structure and Span of Control

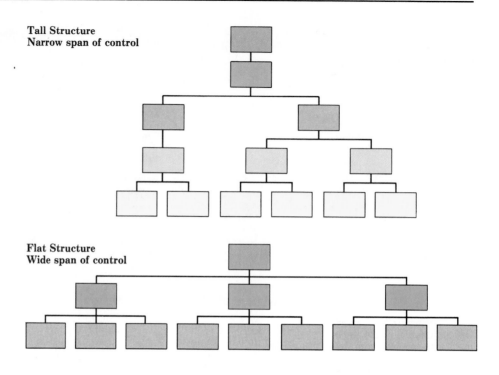

Tall Structure
Narrow span of control

Flat Structure
Wide span of control

number of levels in the organization and simplify the communication chain. In other words, a "flat" structure (with fewer levels) and a wider span of control (with more people reporting to each supervisor) are less likely to introduce distortion than are a "tall" structure and a narrow span of control.

Apart from being vulnerable to distortion, the formal communication chain has another potential disadvantage: Information may become fragmented. Unless management encourages horizontal communication and diligently practices downward communication, only the person at the very top can see the "big picture." People lower down in the organization obtain only enough information to perform their own isolated tasks. They don't learn much about other areas, and as a consequence, they cannot suggest ideas that cut across organizational boundaries. Their flexibility is limited by their lack of information. The solution is to make sure communication flows freely up, down, and across the organization chart.

INFORMAL COMMUNICATION CHANNELS

Formal organization charts illustrate how information is supposed to flow. In actual practice, however, lines and boxes on a piece of paper cannot prevent people from talking with one another. At one GM plant, managers encourage informal communication by providing information through the unofficial newsletter, which employees consider more effective than the official one.

However, every organization has one informal communication network—the "grapevine"—that supplements official channels. As people go about their work, they have casual conversations with their friends in the office. They joke and kid around and discuss many things: their apartments, their families, restaurants, movies, sports, other people in the company. Although many of these conversations deal with personal matters, business is often discussed as well. In fact, about 80 percent of the information that travels along the grapevine

Jack Welch started out in an engineering job in General Electric's plastics business. Now chairman and CEO, Welch believes GE must increase competitiveness and productivity. Thus he has declared war on what he sees as GE's excessive bureaucracy, and he encourages management to bypass formal communication channels and to communicate directly with employees.

pertains to business.[8] Furthermore, many employees rely on the grapevine as their main source of information about the organization.

Unfortunately, information gained through informal channels may be inaccurate. For example, most grapevines mix facts and assumptions. Party A knows a little bit and supposes a little bit more. Party B adds to that, and so it goes. By the time the information makes the rounds, between 10 and 30 percent of the facts will be distorted.[9] Nevertheless, sophisticated companies rarely try to eliminate the grapevine. Instead, they minimize its less desirable effects by making certain that the official word gets out. The best way to stop false rumors is to spread the truth as quickly as possible. Figure 2.3 illustrates a typical informal network, which is often the company's real power structure.

In every company, certain people seem to know everything, regardless of the position they officially fill. As a consequence, their role in the company's informal communication process is an active one. Also, unlike official channels, the informal network is in a constant state of flux. For example, for six or eight months someone might spend a good deal of time communicating with people from another department about a particular assignment; then, when the job is completed, this interaction might cease.

The informal network has its pluses. Peer-to-peer contact and interdepartmental interaction save the company a great deal of time. If two people from different departments need to work together to accomplish a task, it is often more efficient for them to talk directly to each other instead of passing messages through their bosses. And in an era when mergers, acquisitions, and

> Although the grapevine is a potential source of distortion, organizations can limit its negative effects by supplementing it with a free flow of official information.

> The informal communication network carries information along the organization's unofficial lines of activity and power.

FIGURE 2.3
Informal Communication Network

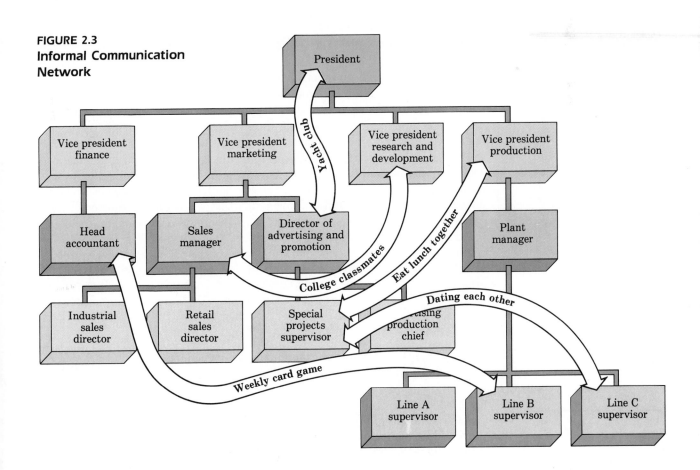

reorganization are the norm, the informal communication network often plays a particularly vital role. As organizations become more complex structurally, the formal lines of communication become increasingly cumbersome. Informal communication helps people continue to do their jobs effectively until the formal structure catches up with the changes.

THE INFLUENCE OF COMMUNICATION CLIMATE

Washington Post Company chairman Katherine Graham is a helpful, supportive manager who encourages communication. Such clues as her simple, tasteful office, with its soft lighting, neutral colors, and casual seating, help establish that role.

The organization's communication climate affects the quantity and quality of information that passes through the pipeline.

Setting up an effective network for transmitting information is important, but the best transmission links in the world won't do an organization much good if the information that flows through them is insufficient, unreliable, or ignored. When people are reluctant to report or to acknowledge the truth, the nature of the communication network is irrelevant.

An organization's communication climate is a reflection of its corporate culture—the mixture of values, traditions, and habits that give a place its atmosphere or personality. Companies like General Motors foster candor and honesty. Their employees feel free to confess their mistakes, to disagree with the boss, and to express opinions. Other companies tend to choke off the upward flow of communication, believing that debate is time consuming and unproductive.

For an example of how communication climate affects performance, consider the *Challenger* disaster. Months before the space shuttle went up in flames, engineers at Morton Thiokol wrote memos to executives warning of problems with the rubber O-ring seals, which ultimately failed. Morton Thiokol management apparently dismissed the warnings as being excessively cautious. Then, on the night before the fateful launch, Morton Thiokol engineers tried again to point out that the seals might fail in cold weather. They expressed their concerns directly to officials of the National Aeronautics and Space Administration (NASA) at the launch site and also to Morton Thiokol's top management. Again, their worries were dismissed as negative thinking. The next day, immediately before the launch, the NASA officials who had received the engineers' warnings didn't even mention the concerns to their bosses, despite the fact that NASA was debating postponement of the launch in light of the cold weather. Seven people died in a stunning disaster because bad news was unacceptable in NASA's "can-do," success-oriented culture, which established unspoken limits on the kind of information that could be transmitted.[10]

Many factors influence an organization's communication climate, including the nature of the industry, the company's physical setup, the history of the company, and passing events. However, two of the most important variables are the style of the top management group and the organization's code of ethics.

MANAGEMENT STYLE

The management style of top executives influences the organization's communication climate.

Experts on management describe four basic management styles, each associated with a unique communication climate:[11]

■ *Directive style.* Top managers make most of the decisions. The firm operates on the assumption that the workers cannot be trusted, that their overriding motive is to avoid work, that they lack initiative and responsibility, and that they must be told precisely what to do. In firms with this philosophy, communication is tightly controlled from the top, and people are discouraged from expressing their opinions. Top management limits the flow of information to employees and restricts communication between departments.

- *Coaching style.* Top executives still provide direction and tell lower-level employees what to do. However, management assumes that employees are members of the team, willing to do their share to accomplish the organization's goals. Management explains the rationale for decisions and listens to ideas and suggestions from below.

- *Supportive style.* Executives assume that employees are competent and motivated. Management establishes goals and plans but delegates much of the day-to-day decision making and problem solving to people at lower levels. Communication is a two-way street, flowing both up and down the hierarchy. Employees are free to establish their own informal communication channels.

- *Delegating style.* Top management allows employees to "run their own show." The chief executive provides broad direction but delegates responsibility for determining how tasks and goals are to be accomplished. Because employees are encouraged to solve their own problems, top management may become isolated and lose control of the organization's operations.

Today more and more companies are recognizing the value of an open communication climate.

The trend in management today is toward the styles that encourage an open communication climate. In this environment, managers spend more time listening than issuing orders. Workers offer suggestions, help set goals, and collaborate on solving problems.[12] However, some managers have trouble making the switch from a directive management style to a more participatory style. They accept the concept of participation but continue to restrict the flow of information.

COMMUNICATION ETHICS

Conflicting priorities pose ethical problems for an organization's communicators.

Although most organizations pay lip service to such virtues as honesty, courtesy, and moral integrity, doing the "right thing" is not as easy as it sounds. Corporations and their employees are often caught in moral dilemmas, trapped between conflicting loyalties.

Let's say you are the president of a company that is losing money. You have a duty to your shareholders to try to cut your losses. After looking at various options, you conclude that you will have to lay off 500 people immediately. You suspect that you may have to lay off another 100 people later on, but right now you need these 100 workers to finish a project. What do you tell them? If you confess that their jobs are shaky, many of them may quit just when you need them most. But if you tell them that the future is rosy, you will be stretching the truth. There are no easy answers to such questions. Between the clearly right and the clearly wrong lies a vast gray area, full of difficult ethical trade-offs.

Legal considerations

Laws provide ethical guidelines for certain types of messages.

One place to look for guidance is the law. If saying or writing something is clearly illegal, there is no dilemma: You obey the law. Human resource management is one problem area where the law provides a lot of answers. For example, people in organizations must be very careful to avoid doing or saying anything that might be interpreted as illegal discrimination. Advertising is another area regulated by laws, some of which prohibit unfair and deceptive trade practices. For example, companies should not make false or misleading promises about their products.

Regardless of whether a specific situation is covered by law, you should be aware of the legal implications of anything you say or write on the job. For better or for worse, we live in litigious times. That innocent memo for the files may well end up as evidence in court. So before you commit words to paper, ask yourself whether you would want to defend your remarks before a judge and jury.

Moral judgment

Although legal considerations will resolve some ethical questions, you and your organization will often have to fall back on your own judgment and principles in making communication decisions. Your organization may have a written code of ethics that outlines standards of conduct, or it may have well-established traditions that provide some guidance. If not, you might apply the Golden Rule: Do unto others as you would have them do unto you.

You might also want to ask yourself these questions when faced with a murky decision:

Ethical messages are well intentioned, honest, moral, professional, and kind.	■ *What effect will the message have?* Are you advocating something that will benefit others, or is your purpose potentially harmful?

■ *Is the message true?* In attempting to accomplish your objectives, have you stretched the facts or covered up important information? Have you distorted the evidence to improve your case? As long as everything you say is true, there is nothing wrong with accentuating the positive and minimizing the negative.

■ *Does the message appeal to good or bad values?* Are you using rational arguments and humanistic appeals? Or are you trying to persuade people by exploiting their baser motives?

■ *Does the message reflect the wishes of my organization?* Occasionally, your own views or communication style may conflict with the organization's. If that happens, remember that during the working day, you represent your employer.

■ *Is the message expressed in a tactful manner?* Although bluntness is occasionally appropriate, nine times out of ten it's better to be kind than inconsiderate. How much support for GM's strategies would Alvie Smith have gotten if he had tried to reach employees by saying something like, "You idiots are ruining this company!"

HOW COMPANIES MANAGE COMMUNICATION

Now that you've gained some insight into the nature of organizational communication, think for a minute about the logistics of moving all those messages, both within the organization and to and from the outside world. A few statistics may help you put the problem in perspective:

Debbie Fields, founder of Mrs. Fields Cookies, uses a chainwide interactive computer and electronic mail system to instruct store managers hourly on what to bake, to plan work schedules, and even to screen job applicants. The computer system makes it easy to maintain the two-way communication that is so necessary between store managers and headquarters.

- Americans create 30 billion documents a year at a cost of over $100 billion. Many of these documents are filed away, but 75 to 85 percent of the time we don't look at the information again.[13]

- U.S. companies waste $2.6 billion each year on unnecessary photocopies. Roughly one-third of the copies made are tossed into the trash.[14]

- Every year, a single division headquarters of a typical large corporation mails 9 million documents to the outside world. These documents include letters, memos, reports, brochures, news announcements, policy statements, product catalogs, and the like.[15]

And those are just the routine written messages. How many meetings are a waste of time? And how much effort is involved in handling messages in times of crisis? One begins to wonder whether companies are in business to produce products or words.

HANDLING ROUTINE MESSAGES

The volume of messages is greater in large organizations than in small ones, but all companies are concerned about holding down costs while maximizing the benefits of their communication activities. To a great extent, they expect managers to control communication efforts. Some of the measures that managers may take are to reduce the number of messages being produced, to make assignments and procedures clearer, to distribute communication responsibility more evenly, and to make writers and speakers better at their jobs.

Reduce the number of messages

Producing even a one-page letter takes time and resources, so the organization must be concerned with how many letters it sends out. The average cost of dictating, transcribing, and mailing a business letter is over $9;[16] the typical business letter, which contains only 190 words, takes eight minutes to dictate.[17] If a message must truly be put in writing, a letter is a good investment. But if a letter merely adds to the information overload, the message is probably better left unsent or handled in some other way—say, by a quick telephone call or a face-to-face chat.

Within the organization, many memos are superfluous, and many meetings are a waste of everyone's time. Thus even these types of communication should be evaluated. How long does the message need to be? Can it be conveyed over the telephone? Can the answer to a question posed in a memo simply be penciled onto the original memo? How many copies of a letter really need to be made? How many copies need to be filed? Can the information be conveyed more concisely with a standardized form, such as a sales report? A thrifty approach to questions like these will save the organization both time and money.

Organizations save time and money by sending only necessary messages.

Make instructions clearer

Communication breakdowns can be blamed on almost anyone, but managers have a special responsibility to make sure everyone knows what to do. The person who is passing out communication assignments must have a clear understanding of the organization's overall needs and goals together with a grasp of the purpose of a particular message. Only then can she or he fully explain the communicator's role.

The manager is responsible for making sure that employees understand their role in preparing messages.

Another aspect of this problem is a lack of follow-through. To keep everyone on course and to provide feedback about the developing message, managers should keep in touch with staff members throughout a project. Communicators also have a responsibility to seek clarification as the need arises.

Delegate responsibility

Managers should delegate some communication jobs to others.

Follow-through and feedback are helpful; breathing down people's necks is not. A manager should be able to trust others to do their assigned jobs. Imagine how much of the organization's time is wasted when a manager feels the need to redo every message in his or her own style.

Train writers and speakers

A person who can hold a pencil is not necessarily a good writer; someone with an attractive voice is not always able to explain something clearly to an audience. In fact, even writers and speakers with unusual natural talent need some sort of guided practice to become really good.

In-house training benefits even experienced communicators.

An organization would be well advised, therefore, to provide some sort of in-house training in communication skills for those who communicate on its behalf. Obviously, such training should cover at least the organization's style preferences and communication philosophies so that all can speak with one voice or as close to one voice as possible. Communicators may also need to brush up on their language and presentation skills.

One of the nice things about such training is the sense of pride and professionalism that it creates in those who go through the program. They do their jobs with confidence, so the organization operates more smoothly.

HANDLING CRISIS COMMUNICATION

Managing the day-to-day flow of messages is one thing, but the real test of an organization's communication skills comes in times of crisis. Consider the following situations (you may remember them from news stories):

- Your firm manufactures pain relievers. A woman dies after taking some of your capsules, and the police investigation reveals that the medicine is laced with cyanide. After several more deaths occur, it becomes clear that someone is tampering with your products.

- In separate incidents, consumers from 30 states report finding fragments of glass in your firm's jars of baby food. You investigate but can find no evidence to substantiate any of these claims. A thorough review of your manufacturing and distribution operations suggests that the problem simply does not exist.

The organizations that faced these events in real life, Johnson & Johnson and Gerber, each handled the crisis in its own way. Johnson & Johnson immediately recalled its Tylenol pain-reliever capsules and cooperated fully with the press and the police. Within months, the company reintroduced Tylenol in a tamper-proof form and recovered its position in the market. On the other hand, Gerber handled the negative publicity about glass fragments in baby food by maintaining silence. When the state of Maryland ordered retailers to remove the company's strained peaches from their shelves, Gerber fought back by

The way a company handles a crisis says a lot about its communication skills.

suing the state for $150 million. Although the suit is still pending, the publicity has subsided, and Gerber has resumed its position of leadership in the baby food market.[18]

The way an organization handles these one-time situations can have a profound impact on its future. If it copes well, it will not suffer and may even come out ahead. But if it fails to deal effectively with a crisis, its reputation and profitability will suffer.

Most crisis management plans adhere to one of two communication philosophies: (1) say nothing or (2) tell all and tell it fast. Both approaches can succeed, as the Gerber and Johnson & Johnson cases demonstrate. However, many public relations professionals favor Johnson & Johnson's approach of presenting the facts candidly and openly.[19] They advise companies to counteract rumors and panic by explaining problems to both the public and the employees. At the same time, companies should attack the source of the problem and bring it under control. The important thing is to remain calm. A deliberate, rational response inspires more confidence than a hasty statement that has to be corrected a few hours later.

Of course, all of this is easier said than done. When Exxon's supertanker *Valdez* ran into Bligh Reef in Alaska, 11 million gallons of oil were spilled, and 800 miles of Alaskan coastline were affected. Exemplifying what not to do in a crisis, Exxon neglected taking charge of the news flow, thus taking a beating from both the media and the angry public. Although Exxon will be dealing with the *Valdez* incident for years to come, many of its initial problems might well have been avoided had the company communicated more effectively during the crisis.[20]

HOW YOU CAN IMPROVE YOUR COMMUNICATION SKILLS

So far, this chapter has emphasized communication from the organization's viewpoint. But remember, communication is the link between the individual and the organization. Your ability to understand what is going on depends on your sensitivity as a communicator. Once you know the dynamics of communication within an organization, you can read between the lines to get an accurate picture of what is happening. At the same time, you can adjust your own messages, using the communication network to best advantage and tailoring your style to the organization's communication climate.

In addition, communication skills—the ability to read, write, listen, and speak—are highly prized by most employers. One survey asked, "In assessing an individual's chance of success in your company, how important do you think communication skills are, relative to other kinds of abilities?" About 85 percent of those surveyed replied that communication skills are extremely important.[21] Thus your communication skill, or lack of it, will have a profound impact on your success in the business world.

All jobs require communication skills of one sort or another.

Whether you're a secretary, a management trainee, an accountant, a salesperson, a financial analyst, a human resource specialist, chairman of the board, or something else entirely, you will need the ability to communicate effectively. Some jobs require greater communication skill than others, however. A salesperson needs to be an excellent communicator, and so does an advertising copywriter or a public relations specialist. But even if your job involves staring

BEHIND THE SCENES AT AMTRAK
Keeping an Image on Track

As Amtrak's director of government and public affairs, John Jacobsen must ensure that the company and its trains are portrayed favorably in motion pictures. You saw Amtrak in *Midnight Run*, *Rain Man*, and *Witness*. But you did not see the familiar silver trains with their red, white, and blue stripes in *Throw Momma from the Train* or in *Planes, Trains and Automobiles*.

Sue Martin, senior director of public affairs, manages Amtrak's relationships with its various external audiences. Her "public" includes the news and travel media, consumer groups such as the National Association of Railroad Passengers, travel industry organizations, riders, and the general public. Among these, "media relations get most of our time," she points out. "The press is a conduit to the general public, to existing and prospective travelers, and to elected officials. It is the easiest way to reach large numbers of people. And we can be proactive with the media, taking action to reach people rather than just reacting to events or inquiries."

Martin's work with the motion picture industry is a small but highly visible demonstration of how an organization communicates externally. Amtrak is the nation's only passenger railroad, and its trains and stations are much sought after for movie scenes. "Typically," says Martin, "producers come to Amtrak with a movie idea involving a train setting. They ask a lot of questions, and we discuss what we would be able to do for them."

Scripts are reviewed carefully by Jacobsen. "We refuse some scripts, perhaps because of the way a train employee is portrayed or the way a murder is staged." And Jacobsen will work with a producer to make a script acceptable. "*Witness*'s opening scene was originally set on a bus. But in order to keep the murder scene at Amtrak's 30th Street Station in Philadelphia, the producer agreed to replace the bus ride with a train trip through beautiful Pennsylvania Dutch country."

If a script portrays Amtrak positively, a meeting is set up with the producer and the Amtrak employees who will be involved: a station manager, for example, or someone in the operating department if the trains are involved. "We decide what's possible and what isn't," Jacobsen notes, "then negotiate a contract to cover all our costs—we can't use taxpayer money to make movies—and to indemnify Amtrak in an insurance policy." Once the contract and insurance are in place, the next step is filming. "A public affairs staff

through a microscope in a remote laboratory, you will sometimes need to work with other people. That means you will need to communicate. If you can do it well, you will have an advantage. You will be able to get what you need more quickly, your contributions to the organization will be more useful, and you will be rewarded accordingly. Among the specific skills required in business communication are

Seven communication skills are typically required in business.

- Reading
- Listening
- Engaging in casual conversation
- Interviewing
- Dealing with small groups
- Delivering speeches and presentations
- Writing letters, memos, and reports

member is on the scene to be sure the movie crew doesn't interfere with ongoing operations and to serve as liaison with others in the company." When completed, the movie serves Amtrak in two ways: Showing the trains or an interesting station to millions of movie-goers gives the railroad visibility, and charges to the producer generate revenues—$80,000 in a recent year.

In her work serving all Amtrak departments, Martin and her nine-member staff rely heavily on recognized, formal channels of communication to get the job done. "We are the communicators for the company. We help others plan, decide on strategy, and carry out public relations, whether it's crisis management, publicity, or marketing communications. We recently created a crisis-response workshop for field managers." Her staff helps Amtrak employees deal with the public, even exercising control over how and when employees speak with the media. Martin's department writes and edits such materials as press releases, columns for the on-train magazine (*Express*), and mailings to consumer groups. Informal communication also has a role, "but in public affairs work, informal channels are hard to manage."

Like Sue Martin, you may be called on to speak to outsiders on behalf of your company. When communicating with the public, your concern will be to create and distribute messages that, in Sue Martin's words, "help the public see that the corporation's interests are actually the public's interests."

APPLY YOUR KNOWLEDGE

1. Review the following list of events that Sue Martin's department might have to deal with: (a) Amtrak is planning the grand reopening of Union Station in Washington, D.C., (b) next month is the five-year anniversary of the most serious fatal accident involving an Amtrak train, (c) a writer for a widely circulated travel magazine is planning to travel around America by train to write a series of articles, and (d) a railroad historical society wants to launch an annual excursion over Amtrak's most historic routes. Which would be the most complex (requiring you to work with others in Amtrak or to draw on resources outside Amtrak)? Which would consume more of your time? Which would benefit Amtrak's public image the most? Justify your decisions.

2. A train en route from Chicago to Seattle has been trapped by an avalanche in a remote, mountainous region of Montana. Passengers include a United States senator, a famous football commentator known for his fear of flying, and a pregnant woman on her way to a life-saving medical procedure (which can only be performed in Spokane, Washington). Create a plan to manage press coverage of the event. What factors would you take into consideration? Which can you control? Which are out of your control? What can you do to offset those out of your control?

The extent to which you use each of these skills depends on where you work and what you do, but you should try to be competent in all of them "just in case."

| Focus on building skills in the areas where you've been weak. | Perhaps the best place to begin any improvement program is with an honest assessment of where you stand. All of us have developed some communication skills to a higher degree than others. Maybe you're a good listener, or maybe writing is your strong point. In the next few days, watch how you handle the communication situations that arise. Try to figure out what you're doing right and what you're doing wrong. Then, in the months ahead, try to focus on building your competence in areas where you need the most work. |

Establish some realistic goals for yourself. What do you hope to accomplish? What part do you think communication will play in your own career plans? How can you best prepare yourself?

| Set goals for improvement that are related to your career plans. | |

Perhaps the best way to improve your ability is to practice. People are not "born" writers or speakers. They become good at these things by doing them. Someone who has written ten reports is usually better at it than someone who has written only two reports. You learn from experience, and some of the most important lessons are learned through failure. Learning what *not* to do is just as important as learning what *to* do.

> Practice using all communication skills so that you can learn from your mistakes.

One of the great advantages of taking a course in business communication is that you get to practice in an environment that provides honest and constructive criticism. A course of this kind also gives you an understanding of acceptable techniques so that you can avoid making costly mistakes on the job. This book has been designed to provide the kind of communication practice that will prepare you for whatever comes along later in your career. Chapters 3, 4, and 5 explain how to plan and organize business messages and how to perfect their style and tone. These chapters are followed by ones that deal with specific forms of communication: letters and memos, proposals and reports, resumes and application letters, interviews and meetings, speeches and presentations. As you progress through this book, you will also meet many business communicators. Their experiences will give you insight into what it takes to communicate effectively on the job.

SUMMARY

Communication, the link between an organization and its members, is essential to the organization's major functions. When you understand how an organization communicates, you are equipped to become a productive member of the group. Communication also facilitates interactions among management, employees, customers, suppliers, financiers, and government officials. Occurring through both formal and informal channels, communication flows up and down the hierarchy, as well as across the lines of authority, and the communication climate is affected by the corporation's management style and ethics.

Given the volume of messages flowing into, around, and out of modern organizations, communication management has become an issue. In many organizations, managers are encouraged to limit the number of messages, clarify communication assignments, delegate responsibility for writing and speaking, and build employees' communication skills. Many organizations have also developed plans for communicating during times of crisis.

Regardless of where you work or what you do, communication will play a part in your career. By analyzing your strengths and weaknesses, setting realistic goals, and practicing various types of communication, you can improve your oral and written communication skills.

ON THE JOB:
Solving a Communication Dilemma
at General Motors

General Motors' top communicator, Alvie Smith, faced a mammoth task as his company entered the 1980s faltering under the attack of Japanese automakers with their well-built, fuel-efficient cars. GM's efforts to compete with Japanese cars produced a series of setbacks, and GM's top managers called for an unprecedented reorganization of the company to restore its competitive position. But their attempts misfired because they neglected to communicate their new vision and their reorganization goals to employees.

It's not too great an exaggeration to say that GM employees were in shock. As one GM manager observed, "We changed all of our cars. We downsized them twice, changed from rear-wheel drive to front-wheel drive, changed all the systems of the company, changed all the factories, and *then* told almost every employee in North America,

'You've got a new job.'" Employee attitude surveys revealed that employee loyalty was strained and that managers were alienated. Established lines of communication were disrupted, and worthwhile initiatives (such as new quality programs) were abandoned.

GM's size complicated the situation. GM is not merely the largest automaker in the world, it is the largest industrial corporation in the world. It has roughly three-quarters of a million employees and more than 200 plants in 33 countries. It has also struggled under the weight of a complex corporate hierarchy, with as many as 21 layers between the chief executive and the people on the assembly line. The fact that communication efforts were sometimes unsuccessful is not all that surprising.

So top managers called on Alvie Smith, director of corporate communication, to open new channels of communication and to marshal support for the sweeping reorganization. Smith quickly conducted a number of internal surveys. They revealed that one of GM's most serious problems was the "frozen middle"—the reluctance or inability of disaffected middle managers to communicate upward or downward. Even worse, GM management lacked credibility in the eyes of its employees. The employees didn't believe top managers when they described the extent of GM's losses and explained how the sweeping changes they advocated would solve GM's problems.

Smith understood that fostering communication through the many hierarchical layers was only the first step in mobilizing the entire corporation in support of the needed restructuring. Once he established lines of communication, he would have to train everyone at GM, from the assembly-line employee to the top manager, to be a better communicator.

Smith moved to improve communication between headquarters and the field. He beefed up established media (such as the company's monthly publication for employees and retirees, *GM Today*), and he started the bimonthly *GM Management Journal* to keep field managers informed about corporate thinking and strategy. He also experimented with new channels of communication.

Smith made extensive use of video. *Issue Update*, a six-program yearly video series for GM managers and supervisors, conveys the company's position on such issues as product quality, customer satisfaction, and target markets. Smith also compiled and distributed video highlights of a key top management conference. That tape left its viewers with no doubt about the serious nature of GM's problems.

Smith found that electronic media could also be used to promote direct contact between headquarters and the field. All GM locations have satellite receivers, and many conversations between corporate executives and field management are carried live on interactive satellite television. GM hooked up its 9,700 dealers to a new satellite system at the end of 1992, establishing what the company called the world's largest private satellite network.

Having improved two-way communication between headquarters and the field, Smith turned his attention to bolstering communication within each field office and factory. Plants and offices throughout GM were producing 350 employee newsletters, and Smith began by boosting their effectiveness. He encouraged their editors to improve the visual appeal, and he provided graphic and editorial materials to supplement local efforts. Smith also met with local managers to enlist their support for these publications.

Having gained their attention, Smith persuaded the local managers to improve their speaking skills. GM's own research revealed that the closer the information source was to the employee, the greater its relevance and credibility—and, therefore, its effectiveness. So Smith organized training workshops to improve the speaking skills of GM plant managers and to impress these executives with the importance of their role as the leading GM communicator in each location.

GM realized that effective employee communication is a fundamental part of good management and can contribute to an organization's performance. By 1989, GM's quality had indeed improved, but the company continued to lose market share. GM faces tough times in the 1990s. The firm reported a record $4.45 billion loss in 1991 and is again reorganizing to compete locally and globally. The communication lessons GM learned in the 1980s will surely play a major role in the company's strategy as it drives into the twenty-first century.

Your Mission: Robert Stempel, GM's chairman, has renewed GM's focus on car quality and cost reduction. Stempel is determined to enlist the support of all GM employees. As the newly appointed director of communication at GM's Saginaw division, your job is to encourage better communication within the division, between the division and people in other areas of GM, and between the division and the news media. In the following scenarios, pick the *best* option from the choices offered.

1. GM's renewed emphasis on product quality and innovation has spurred a lot of creative thinking throughout the company. Over the past few months, however, you've learned of numerous instances in which employees in other divisions had ideas that could have helped Saginaw, but no one in Saginaw heard about them. At the same time, you know that many of the ideas floating around Saginaw could help other divisions. Which is the best way to make sure that people can exchange ideas in a timely fashion?
   a. The company should install electronic mail throughout the organization so that every time someone has an idea, he or she can instantly transmit it to everyone else electronically.
   b. Formal and informal horizontal communication links are the best idea. For example, engine de-

signers across the company should have their own formal communication network so that they can regularly share and discuss new ideas.

c. GM should establish a corporate "idea sharing" policy, in which anyone with a useful new idea is required to report it to his or her supervisor. The idea then moves up the corporate ladder, and the people at the top make sure it gets distributed to everyone in the company.

d. You should install bulletin boards around the Saginaw facility so that people with new ideas can post their thoughts and people who need help can post requests for assistance.

2. Employees have grown to trust the division grapevine more than they trust formal communication from division management. Although the grapevine is usually accurate, a blatantly false rumor concerning the division's future has been circulating for several days. What's the first step you should take to handle this?

a. Identify the opinion leaders throughout the division—employees who are known to be good sources of inside information—and invite them to a private session with management. Explain why the rumor is false, giving them complete data on the issue. Ask them to share the information with their colleagues.

b. Publish a memorandum to all employees, insisting that the rumor is false and stating the facts.

c. Instruct all managers to tell their departments that the rumor is false.

d. Call a divisionwide meeting at which the general manager can explain the facts and publicly state that the rumor is false.

3. Assume that the overall performance of the shipping and receiving department at Saginaw is declining. The department manager says that too many of her employees are simply going through the motions and not really putting their hearts into their jobs. As one way of improving performance, she wants to send a memo to everyone in the department. Which of the following approaches would you recommend that she use?

a. Tell employees that the group's performance is not as good as it could be, and solicit their ideas on how things might be improved.

b. Threaten to fire the next employee you see giving less than 100 percent, even though you know company policy prevents you from actually doing so.

c. Ask employees to monitor each other and to report directly to the department manager any instances of laziness or carelessness.

d. Tell all employees that the department better shape up or heads are going to roll.

4. Communication within an organization can be as complex as the informal networks that link employees and managers or as simple as the instructional signs that are posted throughout the company's buildings. On a recent tour of a painting facility, you see the following four signs; which one communicates its point most clearly?

a. "If dangerous fumes are present, all employees must wear respirators"

b. "All employees must wear respirators while painting"

c. "All persons must wear respirators in this area at all times"

d. "WARNING: Dangerous fumes present while painting operations are under way"

5. Crisis communication is among your responsibilities, and at ten o'clock on a Sunday night, you have to swing into action. You receive a phone call from the plant manager, explaining that a minor explosion in production spilled about a thousand barrels of toxic metal-cleaning solution into a creek that runs by the facility. You know the media will find out soon, and you have to decide how to respond. Which of the following is the best approach?

a. To keep the media from exaggerating the extent of the spill, tell them that a "small amount" of chemicals was spilled and that you're not even sure whether the chemicals are dangerous or not.

b. Give the media full access to division managers, and provide them with a written description of the incident and of the company's efforts to clean up the spill. Tell them as much as you know about the possible dangers of such spills.

c. Distribute a written statement to the media that says simply, "Until further notice, the managers of the Saginaw Division of General Motors Corporation will be unavailable for public comment regarding the alleged chemical spill."

d. Distribute a written statement to the media that emphasizes the division's past record of safety and environmental consciousness. Talk about the Saginaw's recycling program, efforts to encourage employees to carpool, and so on; avoid any discussion of the chemical spill.[22]

QUESTIONS FOR DISCUSSION

1. Think about the various groups you belong to. What role does communication play in establishing your membership in each group?
2. Do you think that downward or upward communication is more important to an organization? Why?
3. As president of a company, what would you do if you discovered that employees were spending too much time talking to one another about outside activities and too little time doing their jobs?
4. Let's say you are a stockbroker. The amount of money that you and your company make depends on the amount of stock you buy and sell for your clients. The more they trade, the richer you become. From an ethical standpoint, you are justified in recommending that your clients buy or sell stocks when it's clearly to their advantage to do so. But what are the ethics involved in encouraging them to buy or sell stocks when it is not so clearly in their best interests? Where would you draw the line?
5. Some companies have a policy of limiting all memos to one page. Do you think this is a good idea? Why or why not?
6. Pick three jobs that you might like to have after you graduate. What communication skills do you think would be most important to you in these positions?

EXERCISES

1. Interview a businessperson on the following subjects:

   - What types of communication occur in his or her job?

   - How important are written communications to the person's company?

   - How important are oral communications to the person's company?

   Your instructor will tell you whether to report your results orally or in writing.
2. Think of two organizations you are familiar with. (If you have not worked for a company, think of large clubs you've belonged to.) For each organization, make a list of the means used for downward communication. Your lists should include methods used by top executives to inform individuals about the organization itself, organization policies, employee or member responsibilities, and so forth. How do the systems differ? Why do you suppose the two organizations have different systems? Which system is better? What are the effects of each organization's communication style on individuals? How could the organization improve its downward communication?
3. Choose two organizations you are familiar with (the same organizations you used in exercise 2, if you like). List the methods that each uses for upward communication. Your list should include all means by which people in the ranks convey information to those at higher levels, such as regular reports, meetings, and so on. Which of the two organizations seems to encourage more input from individuals? What methods might each of these organizations use to improve upward communication? Do you see any correlations between the quality of an organization's downward communication and the quality of its upward communication?
4. Which management style (directive, coaching, supportive, delegating) would be best for handling each of the following situations? Explain your choices.
   a. Training the staff to use all the features of a new phone system
   b. Planning the Christmas parties that will be held in each department of the local branch of a national insurance company
   c. Coordinating an annual inventory, using mainly temporary workers
   d. Conducting a twice-yearly sale in a large department store, which requires marking down nearly every item
   e. Putting together a $5 million promotional campaign for a new product, including advertising and publicity
5. Imagine that you are the manager of a clothing store. During the day, the following communication tasks arise. For which would you phone and for which would you write? Briefly explain your answers.
   a. You want to inform the placement office at the nearby college that you need a part-time sales-clerk.
   b. You have to turn down an applicant for an assistant manager position because she does not have sufficient experience in retail clothing.
   c. You want to announce a new line of pants to your steady customers.

d. You need to check on an order for two dozen shirts that should have arrived last week.

e. You want to congratulate one of your regular customers, whose job promotion was just announced.

f. You need to confirm details of an upcoming trade show.

6. As the director of communication at General Motors' Saginaw division (see this chapter's On-the-Job simulation), you're working hard to improve communication between employees and management. Write a one-page cover memo for a survey that is designed to identify communication problems (such as managers who don't take the time to explain things or employees who refuse to believe what managers say). Remember that some egos and reputations could get trampled by the survey answers, so write your memo with that in mind.[23]

■ PART TWO

THE WRITING PROCESS

PLANNING BUSINESS MESSAGES

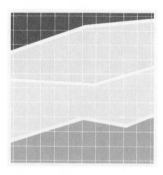

ON THE JOB:
Facing a Communication Dilemma at Mattel
The "Bimbo" with a Brain

Dressed in a zebra-striped bathing suit, she made her grand entrance in 1959, a curvaceous blonde with a mane of platinum hair. Though 34 years have passed, she's still one of America's hottest items. You know her. Her name is Barbie, and she's some doll.

Over the past three decades, the Mattel toy company has sold over 500 million of the petite 11-inch-tall Barbies—enough to circle the globe three and one-half times. Every two seconds, a cash register rings, and a new Barbie goes home with another youngster. In fact, 90 percent of all American girls between the ages of 4 and 10 own at least one Barbie; many also own her boyfriend Ken and a group of her girlfriends, not to mention her $200 dream house, her red Ferrari, her vacation hideaway, her horse, her cats, and her incredible, ever-expanding wardrobe. Barbie's appeal is practically universal. She appears in 67 countries around the world, modified in facial characteristics and clothing to suit local tastes: Asian Barbie, Greek Barbie, Icelandic Barbie, Peruvian Barbie . . .

Still, not everybody loves her. Feminists complain that Barbie is a materialistic bubblehead concerned only with possessions, popularity, and appearances. Susan Reverby, director of the women's studies program at Wellesley College, sums it up by saying that Barbie is a "bimbo." Reverby won't allow her own little girl to play with Barbie. "I don't want my daughter to think that being a woman means she has to look like Barbie and date someone like Ken," Reverby says.

The people at Mattel are sensitive to the criticism. Jill Barad, executive vice president of marketing and product development, has set out to redeem Barbie's reputation by giving her a career. Hailed by *Savvy* magazine as one of the most powerful women in corporate America, Barad herself is a role model for many women. She has tried to add a new dimension to Barbie's appeal by giving her not just one job, but many. After plunging into the work force in 1983 as an employee of McDonald's, Barbie has gone on to bigger and better things. She's been an astronaut, a surgeon, a veterinarian, an Olympic athlete, and the leader of a rock band.

And she has the clothes to prove it, which points up the communication dilemma that Jill Barad faces: sending a message that will satisfy both Barbie's critics and her faithful fans. The critics want Barbie to be a strong, serious woman with a social conscience—the type of person who volunteers at a settlement house for the homeless after putting in a ten-hour day on Wall Street. The fans want Barbie to be what she has always been—a popular, pretty girl who wears glamorous clothes and has fun all the time.

How can Jill Barad plan messages that will appease one group without upsetting the other? What consideration should she give her purpose? Her audience? How would planning an oral message differ from planning a written one?[1]

UNDERSTANDING THE COMPOSITION PROCESS

Mattel

Three steps are involved in preparing business messages: planning, composing, and revising.

Jill Barad's dilemma is not unique. In your own career, you will face a variety of business communication assignments. Some of them will be routine; others will require reflection and research. But regardless of the complexity of the task, you will employ the same basic process for preparing both written and oral messages:

1. *Planning.* During the planning phase, you think about the fundamentals of the message: your purpose in communicating, the audience who will receive your message, the main idea of your message, and the channel and medium you will use to convey your thoughts. You also decide on the organization of ideas and the tone you will adopt.

2. *Composing.* As you compose the message, you commit your thoughts to words, creating sentences and paragraphs and selecting illustrations and details to support your main idea.

3. *Revising.* Having formulated your thoughts, you step back to see whether you have expressed them adequately. You review the purpose and content of the message; its overall structure and tone; the choice of words; and details such as grammar, punctuation, and format.

This basic process varies somewhat with the situation, the communicator, and the organization.

In the remainder of this chapter, you'll learn about planning a message, which is the first phase of the composition process. Planning includes defining the purpose, analyzing the audience, establishing the main idea, and selecting the channel and medium. Chapter 4 discusses how to organize and compose the message; Chapter 5 deals with revision. Although all three chapters focus on the task of writing a message, remember as you read that many of the same issues are important in composing an oral message.

DEFINING YOUR PURPOSE

Pulitzer Prize-winning columnist William Safire writes political columns for *The New York Times*. When planning how to organize your thoughts in writing, says Safire, use a combination of your experience, intuition, and common sense.

The first step in planning a business message is to think about your purpose. Obviously, you want to maintain the goodwill of the audience and create a favorable impression for your organization, just as Jill Barad wants to please both Barbie's critics and her fans. But in every situation, you also have a particular goal you want to achieve. That purpose may be straightforward and obvious—such as placing an order—or it may be more difficult to define. When the purpose is unclear, it pays to spend a few minutes thinking about what you hope to accomplish.

WHY YOU NEED A CLEAR PURPOSE

Suppose that your boss has asked you to prepare a memo describing the company's policy on vacation time. This is a fairly broad topic. What should you say about it? Until you know what the memo is supposed to accomplish, you can't really do a very effective job of writing it. You need a purpose to help you make the following decisions about the message:

- *To decide whether to proceed.* Unnecessary messages can backfire, even if the material is dazzling. Like the little boy who cried "wolf!" once too often, you can rapidly use up your credibility by writing memos that merely fill up filing cabinets. So when you're tempted to fire off a message, pause to ask yourself, "Is this really necessary? Will it make a difference?" If you suspect that your ideas will have little impact, hold off. Wait until you have a more practical purpose.

- *To respond to the audience.* You need to consider the audience's motives. Why will they pay attention to the material? What do they hope to gain? Are their expectations compatible with your own? If not, both you and the audience will fail to get what you want.

The purpose of the message determines content, organization, style, tone, and format.

- *To focus the content.* Establishing a clear purpose will also help you focus the message. You should include only the information that is necessary to accomplish your objective. Everything else is irrelevant and should be eliminated. Even though the extraneous information may be interesting, it diverts the audience from the real point and reduces the impact of your message.

- *To establish the channel and medium.* Depending on your purpose, you will choose a channel (oral or written) for your message and then a medium within that channel. For example, if your purpose is to put together a company softball team, you may decide to use the written channel so that you can send the same message simultaneously to everyone in the office. Then you may decide that the appropriate medium is a casual memo.

COMMON PURPOSES OF BUSINESS MESSAGES

There are three *general* purposes common to business communication: informing, persuading, and collaborating with the audience. Figure 3.1 shows how

FIGURE 3.1
General Purposes of Business Messages

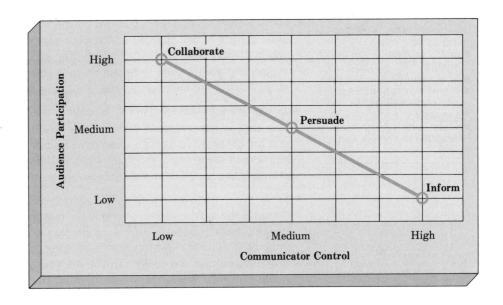

To determine the specific purpose, think of how the audience's ideas or behavior should be affected by the message.

As vice president of consumer market development for General Motors, Shirley Young is responsible for recommending ways to improve customer satisfaction as well as ways to enhance marketing effectiveness. Given such broad involvement, Young's business messages comprise all three common purposes: informing, persuading, and collaborating.

these general purposes affect communication. In addition, every presentation must accomplish a *specific* objective. To formulate this objective, ask yourself, "What should my audience do or think after reviewing this message?" Be as precise as possible in stating your purpose, and identify the individuals in the audience who should respond. Here are some examples:

GENERAL PURPOSE	SPECIFIC PURPOSE
To inform	To present last month's sales figures to the vice president of marketing
To persuade	To convince the vice president of marketing to hire more sales representatives
To collaborate	To help the personnel department develop a training program for new members of the sales staff

Sometimes you will want to accomplish several related things with the same message. For example, you might want to advance your own career while providing objective information about a business matter, or you might want to convince the audience to approve two decisions. When you find yourself facing twin goals, ask yourself whether they are compatible. Can both be accomplished with the same message? Even if one message can accommodate multiple goals, you must analyze how those goals are related and try to establish a priority. Focus on the more important one, especially if time or space is limited. And if one of the goals is personal, stress the business goal.

HOW TO TEST YOUR PURPOSE

Once you have established your purpose, pause for a moment to consider whether it is worth pursuing at this time. Ask yourself these questions:

Defer a message, or do not send it at all
- If the purpose is not realistic
- If the timing is not right
- If you are not the right person to deliver the message
- If the purpose is not acceptable to the organization

■ *Is the purpose realistic?* You can't expect to work miracles overnight. Most people resist change, and if your purpose involves a radical shift in action or attitude, you may have better luck going slowly. Instead of suggesting your whole program at once, consider proposing the first step. View your message as the beginning of a learning process.

■ *Is this the right time?* Timing is vital in transmitting any message. An idea that is unacceptable when profits are down, for example, may easily win approval when profits improve. If an organization is undergoing changes of some sort, you may want to defer your message until things stabilize and people can concentrate on your ideas.

■ *Is the right person delivering the message?* Even though you may have done all the work yourself, your boss may have a better chance of accomplishing results because of her or his higher status. If this is the case, let your boss deliver the message. Achieving your objective is more important than taking the credit. In the long run, people will recognize the quality of your work. Also bear in mind that some people are simply better writers or speakers than others. If the stakes are high and you lack

BEHIND THE SCENES AT ALLSTATE INSURANCE
Editing for Action: Fine Print that Insures Success

"My job is to help management create the future," says Patrick Williams. To carry out that heady challenge for his employer, Allstate Insurance Company, Williams edits one of the nation's top all-employee publications, *Allstate Now*. Part of the 85-member corporate relations department at the company's headquarters in Northbrook, Illinois, Williams plans his maga-paper (a magazine that's put out in an eight-page newspaper-size format) so that it plays a key role in helping employees participate in the Allstate story.

For Allstate's management, communicating with employees is critical to the future of the company. All employees must know where the company is going, what it is trying to achieve, and whether they are going to help it get there. Throughout the corporate relations department, therefore, the attitude is proactive—not telling people *what has happened* but helping people *make things happen*. For Williams, that means careful planning.

The planning actually begins at the highest level of the company. The board of directors meets annually with corporate relations management to formulate a communications policy for the coming year. They ad-

dress such issues as where Allstate is going, how communications can help the company get there, what issues the employees must understand to get the company there, and how management can help employees understand these issues. Working within the framework established at that meeting, Williams plans the articles that will appear in each monthly issue of *Allstate Now*.

Eight weeks before publication, Williams meets with his editorial board, which is made up of ten managers of Allstate's various departments, including law, planning, sales, underwriting, advertising, and human resources—the people who plan the future of the company and give it direction. Listening closely to learn what they think is ahead, Williams decides what Allstate employees will need to hear about. "On the other hand," he quickly points out, "it is equally important to listen to employees, my readers in the company, to learn their information needs. My job as editor is to bring these two groups together."

Every issue must include four articles, each demonstrating one of Allstate's "Four Commitments"—to customers, to community and society, to employees,

experience or confidence, you might want to play a supporting role rather than take the lead.

- *Is the purpose acceptable to the organization?* As the representative of your company, you are obligated to work toward the organization's goals. Let's say that you are a customer service representative who answers letters from customers and that you have received a truly abusive letter attacking your company unfairly. Your initial reaction might be to fire back an angry reply that defends the organization. But the management may prefer that you regain the customer's goodwill. Your response should reflect the organization's priorities.

ANALYZING YOUR AUDIENCE

Once you are satisfied that you have a legitimate and clear purpose in communicating, take a good look at your intended audience. Who are the members, what are their attitudes, and what do they need to know? The answers to these

and to being the best. Williams then has to consider whether the content is appropriate to the publication or whether it could be better communicated by others in a memo or at a meeting. He also asks himself whether the article is what his readers want: "Is the subject technical or financial? Is the article full of data to be digested? Is it new, important, complex, or controversial?" Finally, with all these factors in mind, Williams selects articles and plans their organization and approach by asking himself, "How will this story, its picture and headline, help the company and employees?" He does not ask whether the story is amusing or entertaining but, "Will it help the company and employees?"

Article creation and design come next. Photographs are decided on first because they have to be set up and shot. Meanwhile Williams and his staff interview the appropriate people. The format of the article is determined by its purpose. For example, a recent story covered changes at Allstate's parent company, Sears, and it was to convey both good news (the "every single day low prices" policy) and bad news (the end of employee discounts). The purpose of the article was to inform, reestablish trust, and allay fears. To accomplish that, Williams believed the readers needed to hear "the sound of another person's voice." Said Williams, "We chose to interview Sears merchandising group chairman and CEO Michael Bozic in a round-table setting, with 'typical' Allstate employees posing questions. . . . We wanted a voice, one

with authority, credibility, and humanity—someone willing to talk in person, not from the distance of a memo."

And the result of all that careful planning? Eight weeks after an editorial board discussion, 55,000 employees arrived on a Friday morning to find the latest issue of *Allstate Now* on their desks. When they finished reading it, they had been unobtrusively assured, through words and pictures, of their important place in creating Allstate's future.

APPLY YOUR KNOWLEDGE

1. As editor of *Allstate Now*, how would you plan to communicate the following future changes at Allstate as being in the best interests of the employees: (a) dropping the slogan "The Good Hands People," (b) selling Sears Tower in Chicago, (c) moving corporate headquarters from Illinois to Texas, (d) losing Allstate's president of 18 years to retirement, and (e) acquiring the home and auto insurance divisions of a major competitor?

2. With regard to planning articles for *Allstate Now*, list the advantages and disadvantages of the following changes: (a) The publication was expanded from 8 to 16 pages per issue. (b) It was published every two weeks instead of monthly. (c) It was published quarterly instead of monthly. (d) You got approval to use color photographs and a second color in the design.

questions will indicate something about the material you need to cover and the way you should cover it.

DEVELOPING AN AUDIENCE PROFILE

If you are communicating with someone you know well, perhaps your boss or a co-worker, audience analysis is relatively easy. On the other hand, if your audience is a group of strangers, you have to do some investigating and use common sense to anticipate their reactions.

Ask yourself some key questions about your audience:
- Who are they?
- What is their probable reaction to your message?
- How much do they already know about the subject?
- What is their relationship to you?

What is the size and composition of the audience?

Large audiences behave differently from small ones and require different communication techniques. For example, if Jill Barad were giving a speech to 500 people, she would have to limit the amount of audience participation; fielding comments from such a large audience could be chaotic. If she were writing a report for wide distribution, she might choose a more formal style, organization, and format than she would if the report were directed to only three or four people in her department.

Also, the larger the audience, the more diverse the members' education, status, and attitudes are likely to be. So you must look for the common denominators that tie the group together. At the same time, you often have to respond to the particular concerns of individuals. The head of marketing needs different facts about a subject than the head of production or finance needs. You should include a variety of evidence that touches on everyone's area of interest.

Who is the primary audience?

When several people will be receiving your message, try to identify those who are most important to your purpose. If you can reach these decision makers or opinion molders, the other members of the audience will fall into place. Ordinarily, those with the most organizational status are the key people, but occasionally someone will surprise you. A person in a relatively low position may have power in one or two particular areas.

What is the audience's probable reaction?

If you expect a favorable response with very little criticism or debate, you can be straightforward about stating your conclusions and recommendations. You can also use a bit less evidence to support your points. On the other hand, when you face a skeptical audience, you may have to introduce your conclusions and recommendations more gradually and provide more proof.

Also try to anticipate how the key decision makers will respond to specific points. From past experience, you may know that the boss is especially concerned about certain issues: profits, market share, sales growth, or whatever. By anticipating this bias, you can incorporate evidence in your presentation that will address these issues.

In the race against Nike for market share, Reebok International's founder and chairman, Paul Fireman, plans his advertising messages for specific audiences rather than trying to appeal to the entire shoe market at one time—he uses sniper shots, not shotgun blasts.

What is the audience's level of understanding?

If you and your audience do not share the same general background, you will have to decide how much you need to educate them. The trick is to provide the information they need without being pedantic or obvious. In general, you're better off explaining too much rather than too little, particularly if you're subtle about it. Members of the audience may get a bit impatient, but at least they will understand your message.

What is your relationship with the audience?

If you're an unknown, you will have to build the audience's confidence in you before you can win them to your point of view. The initial portion of your message will be devoted to gaining credibility. As you proceed, you will have to prove your points carefully because the audience will be judging your abilities as well as your information.

If you are communicating with a familiar group, your credibility will already be a given. You can get down to business immediately. However, you may have to overcome people's preconceptions about you. If they think of you as being a certain type, say, a "numbers person," they may question your competence in other areas. As you develop your message, you can overcome these prejudices by providing ample evidence on points outside your usual area of expertise.

Your status relative to the audience also affects the style and tone of your presentation. You address your peers differently than you do your boss; you use another tone when you're communicating with those who are lower in the hierarchy; and you handle a customer or supplier differently than you handle a co-worker.

Vary the tone and structure of the message to reflect your relationship with the audience.

SATISFYING THE AUDIENCE'S INFORMATION NEEDS

The key to effective communication is to determine your audience's needs and then respond to them. Try to tell people what they need to know in terms that are meaningful to them. Take the following five steps:

1. Find out what the audience wants to know.
2. Anticipate unstated questions.
3. Provide all the required information.
4. Be sure the information is accurate.
5. Emphasize ideas of greatest interest to the audience.

Find out what the audience wants to know

In many cases, the audience's information needs are readily apparent. For example, when Mattel's Jill Barad answers letters requesting information about Barbie, all she normally has to do is respond to the consumers' questions.

You will probably find, however, that some people are not particularly good at telling you what they want. For example, your boss might tell you, "Find out everything you can about the Polaroid Corporation, and write a memo on it." That's a pretty big assignment. Ten days later, you could submit a 25-page report only to have your boss say, "I don't need all this. All I wanted was their five-year financial record."

When you get a vague request, pin it down. One good approach is to restate the request in more specific terms. For example, you might respond to your boss by saying, "You want me to track down their market position by

Alfred F. Boschulte is vice president of carrier services for the NYNEX Service Company. Managing business relationships with more than 200 interexchange telecommunications carriers in New York and New England, Boschulte maintains that customer information needs must be anticipated; just meeting them is not enough.

product line and get sales and profit figures by division for the past five years, right?" Another way to handle a vague request is to get a fix on its priority. You might ask, "Should I drop everything else and devote myself to this for the next week?"

Asking a question or two forces the person to think through the request and define more precisely what is required. You can then provide that information more efficiently.

Anticipate unstated questions

It's also a good idea to try to think of information needs that your audience may not even be aware of. For example, suppose that your company has just hired a new employee from out of town and that you've been assigned to coordinate the person's relocation. At a minimum, you would write a welcoming letter describing your company's procedures for relocating employees. But with a little extra thought, you might decide to include some information about the city: perhaps a guide to residential areas, a map or two, brochures about cultural activities, and information on schools and transportation facilities. Although adding information of this sort lengthens your document, it creates goodwill.

> Include any additional information that might be helpful, even though the reader didn't specifically ask for it.

Provide all the required information

Once you've defined your audience's needs, you have to be certain to satisfy those needs completely. One good way to test the thoroughness of your message is to check it for what reporters call the five *w*'s and one *h*: *who, what, when, where, why,* and *how.*

> Make sure your document answers all the important questions.

You must take particular care to explain any action that you want to induce. Until readers get a clear picture of what they're supposed to do, they can't possibly do it. If you want them to send you a check for $5, tell them; if you want them to turn in their time cards on Friday by 3 P.M., spell it out. Don't be tactlessly blunt, but don't beat around the bush hoping to be subtle. If you want somebody to do something, be specific in stating your request. Cover all the essential points.

Be sure the information is accurate

In business, you have a special duty to check things before making a written commitment, especially if you are writing to someone outside the company. Your organization is legally bound by any promises you make, so be sure your company is able to follow through. Of course, honest mistakes are possible. You may sincerely believe that you have answered someone's questions correctly and later realize that your information was wrong. If that happens, contact the person immediately and correct the error. Most people will respect you for your honesty.

> Be certain that the information you provide is accurate and that the commitments you make can be kept.

Be accurate and double-check everything you write or say. Check first to be certain that the organization can meet any commitments you make involving other people. Then check again to be certain you have not made any errors of fact or logic. If you are using outside sources of information, ask yourself whether they are up-to-date and reliable. Review any mathematical or financial calculations. Check all dates and schedules. Examine your own assumptions and conclusions to be certain they are valid, and be alert to the sources of misunderstanding discussed in Chapter 1.

Emphasize ideas of greatest interest to the audience

Try to figure out what points will especially interest your audience, and then give these points the most attention.

Remember that various people will find some points in your communication more interesting and important than others. If you're summarizing a recent conversation you had with one of your company's oldest and best customers, the head of engineering might be interested in the customer's reaction to the design features of your product, whereas someone in the shipping department might be concerned about comments on delivery schedules. Pick out the points that will have the most impact on the reader, and emphasize those points.

If you don't know the audience, or if you are communicating with a group of people, you'll have to use your common sense to identify points of particular interest. Possibly such factors as age, job, location, income, and education will give you a clue to the person's interests. If you're trying to sell memberships in the Book of the Month Club, economy might be important to college students or retired people, and convenience might attract sales representatives or homemakers. Your main goal as a business communicator is to tell your audience what they need to know.

SATISFYING THE AUDIENCE'S MOTIVATIONAL NEEDS

Some types of messages have the purpose of motivating the audience to change beliefs or behavior. The problem for the communicator is that resistance occurs when people hear something that conflicts with their existing ideas. People sometimes reject the new information without even really listening.[2] They may selectively screen out threatening ideas or distort your message to fit their preconceived map of reality.

To prevent resistance, you must arrange your message so that the information will be as acceptable as possible. One approach is to use rational arguments presented in an objective tone. For example, if you're arguing that a loan applicant should reduce his existing debts before he borrows more, you might use cause-and-effect reasoning to prove your point: "Adding this amount to your current debt might endanger your credit standing." Or you could use an analogy to support your position: "A study of debt as a percentage of income suggests that this loan would put you over the safe limit." Presenting both sides of an argument is another rational approach that is often quite effective. For example, you could point out how both the bank and the individual might benefit if the loan were approved but then conclude your argument by stating the risks. Two-sided approaches like this increase the communicator's credibility and defuse the receiver's counterarguments.[3]

Rely mainly on reason to win your audience to your point of view, but don't overlook their underlying emotions.

Although appealing to reason is often the best approach, you might also try to convince the audience by appealing to people's emotions. For example, in attempting to sell a product, you might suggest that the item will enhance the customer's status or confer social acceptability. You can also build a convincing case by making the audience respect your honesty and fairness. This technique is frequently used in advertisements where an "expert" delivers the message. Readers accept the product because they trust the spokesperson.

Your credibility with an audience depends on their perception of your competence and integrity. People are more likely to believe you if they feel comfortable with you: if you have similar backgrounds or friends in common, if you wear the same style of clothes, enjoy the same sports, and aspire to the same goals. To establish rapport, you need to emphasize these common denominators.

SATISFYING THE AUDIENCE'S PRACTICAL NEEDS

Many business messages are directed toward people who are themselves in business—customers, suppliers, or co-workers. Regardless of where these people work or precisely what they do, they will receive your communication under distracting circumstances. Recent research on managerial work habits shows how fragmented a manager's day is:

- First-level supervisors are involved in at least 200 separate activities or incidents in an eight-hour day.

- Most activities are very brief. A study of supervisors shows one activity every 48 seconds.

- Another study of chief executives reports that periods of desk work average 10 to 15 minutes each.

- Responding to mail is a minor, routine part of a manager's day, taking less than 5 percent of her or his time. Most executives react to only about 30 percent of the mail they receive.[4]

Remember that your audience
- May have little time
- May be distracted
- May give your message low priority

In other words, many in your audience have very little time to devote to your message, so you should make your message as convenient as possible to grasp. Try to be brief. Generally speaking, a 5-minute talk is easier to follow than a 30-minute presentation, a two-paragraph letter is more manageable than one that's two pages long, and a two-page memo is more likely to be read than a ten-page report.

If your written message has to be long, make it easy for the reader to follow so that she or he can pick it up and put it down several times without losing the thread of what you're saying. For example, begin with a summary of key points, use plenty of headings, put important points in list format so that they will stand out, put less important information in separate enclosures or appendixes, and use charts and graphs to dramatize important ideas.

If you're delivering your message orally, be sure to give listeners an overview of the message's structure and then express your thoughts clearly and logically. You might also use flip charts, slides, or handouts to help listeners understand and remember key points.

DEFINING THE MAIN IDEA

The main idea is the "hook" that sums up why a particular audience should do or think as you suggest.

Once you've analyzed both your purpose and your audience, you're ready to deal with the basic question of how to achieve that purpose: What message will work best with this particular audience? Every business message can be boiled down to one main idea, regardless of the issue's complexity. One central point sums up everything, and this is your theme, your main idea. Everything else in the message either supports this point or demonstrates its implications.

A topic and a main idea are different, as Table 3.1 illustrates. The topic is the broad subject of the message. The main idea makes a statement about the topic—one of many possible statements—explaining your purpose in terms

TABLE 3.1
Topic, Purpose, and Main Idea

GENERAL PURPOSE	TOPIC	SPECIFIC PURPOSE	MAIN IDEA
To inform	Filing insurance claims	To teach customer service representatives how to file an insurance claim	Proper filing by employees saves the company time and money.
To persuade	Funding for research and development	To get top management's approval for increased spending on research and development	Competitors spend more than we do on research and development.
To collaborate	Incentive pay	To get the human resources and accounting departments to jointly devise an incentive system that ties wages directly to profits	Tying wages to profits will automatically reduce compensation costs in tough years while motivating employees to be more productive.

that the audience can accept. It has to motivate people to do what you want by linking your purpose with their own. When you're preparing a brief letter, memo, or meeting, the main idea may be pretty obvious, especially if you're dealing with simple facts that have little or no emotional content for the audience. In such cases, the main idea may be nothing more than "Here is what you wanted."

Finding the "angle" or "hook" becomes a bit more complicated when you are trying to persuade someone or when you have disappointing information to convey. In these situations, you have to look for a main idea that will establish a good relationship between you and your audience. What you're after is some point of agreement or common interest.

In longer documents and presentations, for which a large mass of material needs to be unified, establishing a main idea becomes still more challenging. You need to identify a generalization that encompasses all the individual points you want to make. For tougher assignments like these, you may need to take special measures to come up with a main idea.

USE BRAINSTORMING TECHNIQUES

When identifying the main idea requires creativity and experimentation, the best approach is to "brainstorm"; let your mind wander over the possibilities, testing various alternatives against your purpose, your audience, and the facts at your disposal. Various people use different approaches, and you have to experiment until you find a brainstorming method that fits your mental style.

■ *Storyteller's tour.* Turn on your tape recorder and pretend that you've just run into an old friend on the street. She says, "So, what are you working on these days?" Give her an overview of your message, focusing on your reasons for communicating, your major points, your rationale,

Some techniques for establishing the main idea:
- Storyteller's tour
- Random list
- FCR worksheet
- Journalistic approach
- Question-and-answer chain

and the implications for the message's recipient. Listen critically to the tape and then repeat the exercise until you are able to give a smooth, two-minute summary that conveys the gist of your message. This exercise should reveal your main idea.

- *Random list.* On a clean sheet of paper, list everything that pops into your head pertaining to your message. When you've exhausted the possibilities, study the list for relationships. Sort the items into groups as you would sort a deck of cards into suits. Look for common denominators; the connection might be geographic, sequential, spatial, chronological, or topical. Part of the list might break down into problems, causes, and solutions, another part into pros and cons. Regardless of what categories finally emerge, the sorting process will help you sift through your thoughts and decide what's important and what isn't.

- *FCR worksheet.* If your subject involves the solution to a problem, you might try using an FCR worksheet to help you visualize the relationships among your findings (F), your conclusions (C), and your recommendations (R). For example, you might find that you are losing sales to a competitor who offers lower prices than you do (F). From this, you might conclude that your loss of sales is due to your pricing policy (C). This conclusion would lead you to recommend a price cut (R). To make an FCR worksheet, divide a sheet of paper into three columns. List the major findings in the first column; then extrapolate conclusions and write them in the second column. These conclusions form the basis for the recommendations, which are listed in the third column. An analysis of the three columns should help you focus on the main idea.

- *Journalistic approach.* For informational messages, the journalistic approach may provide a good point of departure. The answers to six questions—who, what, when, where, why, and how—should clarify the main idea.

- *Question-and-answer chain.* Perhaps the best approach is to look at the subject from your audience's perspective. Ask yourself, "What is the audience's main question? What does the audience need to know?" Examine your answer to that question. What additional questions emerge? Follow the chain of questions and answers until you have replied to every conceivable question that might occur to the audience. This way, you should be able to pinpoint the main idea.

RESTRICT THE SCOPE

The main idea should be geared to the length of the message.

Whether the audience expects a one-page memo or a one-hour speech, you will have to select a main idea that can be developed within that framework. So once you have a tentative statement of your main idea, test it against the length restrictions that have been imposed for your message.

You can communicate only so much in a given number of words. What can be accomplished depends on several variables: the nature of the subject, the audience's familiarity with the topic, the listeners' receptivity to your conclusions, and your existing credibility. In general, presenting routine information to a knowledgeable audience that already knows and respects you takes fewer words. Building consensus about a complex and controversial subject takes longer, especially if the audience is composed of skeptical or hostile strangers.

Although the main idea of your message should be adjusted to fit the time or space available, the number of major points should not. Regardless of how long the message will be, you should stick with three or four major points—five at the very most. According to communication researchers, that's all your audience will remember.[5]

If you're delivering a long message, say, a 60-minute presentation or a 20-page report, the major points can be developed in considerable detail. If your message is brief, four minutes or one page, the amount of evidence you can present is restricted, which means that your main idea must be both easy to understand and easy to accept.

SELECTING THE CHANNEL AND MEDIUM

Business messages have to suit the occasion, or the message is ineffective. You can present your ideas in one of two basic channels: oral or written. Within these channels, you can vary the length, format, style, and tone in an almost infinite variety of ways to create the ideal vehicle for your message. The basic choice between speaking and writing depends on the purpose, the audience, and the characteristics of the two communication channels.

ORAL COMMUNICATION

The chief advantage of oral communication is the opportunity it provides for immediate feedback. This is the channel to use when your message is relatively simple, when you do not need a permanent record, and when you can assemble your audience conveniently and economically. The oral approach is also useful when you are presenting controversial information, because you can read the audience's reaction in their body language and adjust your message accordingly.

In general, use oral communication if your purpose is to collaborate with the audience.

Oral communication takes many forms, including unplanned conversations between two people, telephone calls, interviews, small group meetings, seminars, workshops, training programs, formal speeches, and major presentations. Chapters 15 and 16 explore these media in more detail.

In general, the smaller the audience, the more interaction among the members. If your purpose involves reaching a decision or solving a problem, you should select an oral medium geared toward a small audience. The program should be relatively informal and unstructured so that ideas can flow freely. Although a certain amount of planning should precede the meeting, the participants need not prepare a script or rehearse their remarks. Gatherings of this sort can be arranged quickly and economically.

At the opposite extreme are formal presentations to large audiences, which are common at events such as sales conventions, shareholder meetings, presentations to security analysts, and ceremonial functions. Often these major presentations take place in a big facility where the audience can be seated auditorium-style. The audiovisual aids are frequently elaborate as well: films, audio recordings, and multi-image slide shows. Because of the difficulty of coordinating all the audiovisual effects, the presentation must follow a carefully rehearsed plan. Long lead times, fancy equipment, a professional crew, and a big budget are required to stage one of these events. Their formality makes them unsuitable for collaborative purposes requiring audience interaction.

WRITTEN COMMUNICATION

Written messages also vary in formality. At one extreme are the scribbled notes that people use to jog their own memories; at the other extreme are elaborate, formal reports that rival magazines in graphic quality. But regardless of the degree of formality, written messages have one big advantage: They give the writer an opportunity to plan and control the message. A written format is called for when the information is complex, when a permanent record is needed for future reference, when the audience is large and geographically dispersed, and when immediate interaction with the audience is either unimportant or undesirable.

Although there are many specialized types of written communication, the most common media are letters, memos, and reports. Letters and memos are covered extensively in Chapters 6 through 9, reports in Chapters 10 through 12. In addition, Appendix B presents a detailed discussion of formats for business documents.

Letters and memos

With a few exceptions, most letters and memos are relatively brief documents, generally one or two pages. Memos, the "workhorses" of business communication, are used for the routine, day-to-day exchange of information within an

> Written communication increases the sender's control but eliminates the possibility of immediate feedback.

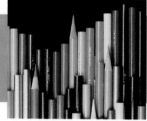

CHECKLIST FOR MESSAGE PLANNING

A. Purpose
- [ ] 1. Determine whether the purpose of your message is to inform, persuade, or collaborate.
- [ ] 2. Identify the specific behavior you hope to induce in the audience.
- [ ] 3. Make sure that your purpose is worthwhile and realistic.

B. Audience
- [ ] 1. Identify the primary audience.
- [ ] 2. Determine the size and composition of the group.
- [ ] 3. Analyze the audience's probable reaction to your message.
- [ ] 4. Determine the audience's level of understanding.
- [ ] 5. Evaluate your relationship with the audience.
- [ ] 6. Analyze the audience's informational, motivational, and practical needs.

C. Main Idea
- [ ] 1. Stimulate your creativity with brainstorming techniques.
- [ ] 2. Identify a "hook" that will motivate the audience to respond to your message in the way you intend.
- [ ] 3. Evaluate whether the main idea is realistic, given the length restrictions imposed on the message.

D. Channel and Medium
- [ ] 1. If your purpose is to collaborate, prepare an informal, relatively unstructured oral presentation to be given to a small group.
- [ ] 2. If you are celebrating an important public occasion, prepare a more formal speech to be given to a large audience.
- [ ] 3. If you need a permanent record, if the message is complex, or if immediate feedback is unimportant, prepare a written message.
  - [ ] a. Send a letter if your message is relatively simple and the audience is outside the company.
  - [ ] b. Send a memo if your message is relatively simple and the audience is inside the company.
  - [ ] c. Write a report if your message is objective and complex.

organization. Letters, which go to outsiders, perform an important public relations function in addition to conveying a particular message.

Letters and memos can be classified by purpose into four categories: direct requests; routine, good-news, and goodwill messages; bad-news messages; and persuasive messages. The purpose determines the organization of main points. Style and tone, however, are governed by the relationship between the writer and the reader.

The format for a letter depends on the traditions of the organization. Figure 3.2 is a typical example of a letter from the consumer relations department at General Mills. Memo format is somewhat different, as Figure 3.3 demonstrates. The body of a memo, especially a longer one, often includes headings and lists to call attention to important points and to make the information more convenient to readers. Introductions and transitions may be given less atten-

Letters and memos are organized according to their purpose; the relationship between writer and reader dictates their style and tone.

FIGURE 3.2
A Typical Letter

Irma Cameron uses letterhead enhanced with her name to give a personal touch.

The formal salutation indicates Irma's respect for a customer she doesn't know.

The body of the letter is brief but still includes a number of friendly remarks designed to maintain goodwill.

The signature also demonstrates a personal touch.

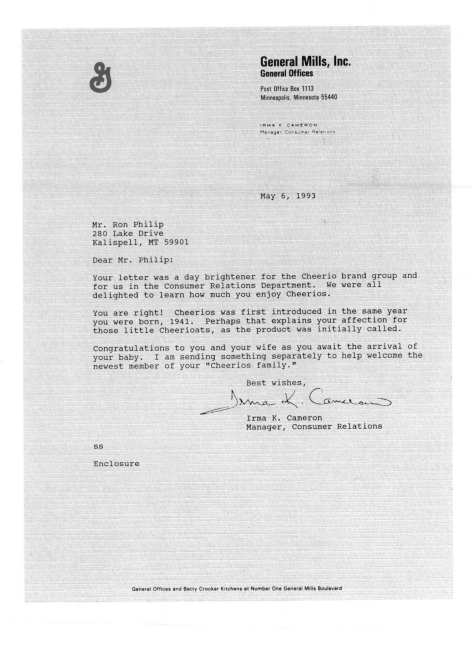

General Mills, Inc.
General Offices

Post Office Box 1113
Minneapolis, Minnesota 55440

IRMA K CAMERON
Manager, Consumer Relations

May 6, 1993

Mr. Ron Philip
280 Lake Drive
Kalispell, MT 59901

Dear Mr. Philip:

Your letter was a day brightener for the Cheerio brand group and for us in the Consumer Relations Department. We were all delighted to learn how much you enjoy Cheerios.

You are right! Cheerios was first introduced in the same year you were born, 1941. Perhaps that explains your affection for those little Cheerioats, as the product was initially called.

Congratulations to you and your wife as you await the arrival of your baby. I am sending something separately to help welcome the newest member of your "Cheerios family."

Best wishes,

Irma K. Cameron
Manager, Consumer Relations

ss

Enclosure

General Offices and Betty Crocker Kitchens at Number One General Mills Boulevard

FIGURE 3.3
A Typical Memo

Every memo is headed with four pieces of information—date, to, from, and subject—even when a plain sheet of paper is used.

The writer, Irma Cameron, states her business right away.

Direct phrasing may be used more frequently in memos than in letters, especially when a boss is telling an employee what to do.

Common courtesy never hurts.

General Mills, Inc.

INTRA-COMPANY CORRESPONDENCE

Copy to Carol Thomas At 4N

To   Mike Gamache   At 4N

From Irma Cameron   At 4N   Date 6/25/93

Subject 1993/1994 Human Resource Needs

We need to evaluate our human resource needs against anticipated growth in the volume of calls coming over our toll-free consumer service telephone lines.

Please compile a list of all General Mills products that currently carry the right toll-free phone number and another list of products expected to carry the number within this fiscal year.

The next step is to project call volume by month. I suggest that you use past history on call volume as well as our established volume-projection formulas for estimating the monthly totals.

Work with Carol to define our staffing needs. Use current individual productivity statistics as a guide, and take into account the impact of increased use of the toll-free phone number.

Please have this data ready for review on July 25. Let me know if you have any conflict in meeting this due date.

IC:ss
IC91J

tion in a memo than in a letter, because the writer and reader share a common frame of reference.

Reports and proposals

These factual, objective documents may be distributed either to insiders or to outsiders, depending on their purpose and subject. They come in many formats, including preprinted forms, letters, memos, and manuscripts. In length, they range from a few pages to several hundred. Generally, however, reports and proposals are longer than letters and memos, with a larger number of distinct components. Reports and proposals also tend to be more formal than letters and memos. But in reports and proposals, as in all forms of business communication, the organization, style, and tone depend on the message's purpose, on the relationship between writer and reader, and on the traditions of the organization. Thus the basic composition process is much the same for all.

Reports are generally longer and more formal than letters and memos, and they have more components.

SUMMARY

The process of preparing business messages consists of three basic steps: planning, composing, and revising. During the planning phase, you need to establish both the general and the specific purposes for your message and to decide whether your specific purpose is worth pursuing.

Also during the planning phase, you need to analyze the audience. Their information needs will help you decide on the content of the message; their motivational needs will help you organize your points in a convincing way. The audience's practical needs will guide your decisions regarding format.

Another step in the planning process is to establish the main idea of the message. The main idea summarizes what the audience should do or think as a result of your message and provides them with a rationale. By defining this idea, you provide direction for composing the message.

You also need to plan the channel of communication for your message. Oral communication gives you the opportunity to interact with the audience; written communication gives you a greater opportunity to plan and control your message. Within these two basic channels, you must select from alternative media such as speech versus presentation or letter versus report.

ON THE JOB:
Solving a Communication Dilemma at Mattel

Convincing the world that Barbie is more than just a bimbo is not an easy task, but Jill Barad is doing her best. This is a communication challenge that certainly takes plenty of planning and a good grasp of the audience's probable reaction.

Part of Barad's problem is that Mattel's purposes are mixed. On the one hand, the company wants Barbie to be a worthy role model for little girls, but on the other hand, Mattel wants to sell dolls and accessories—and that means that Barbie must retain her traditional appeal. After all, 500 million people have voted with their pocketbooks for the good old Barbie whose number-one priority is what to wear. As a businesswoman, Barad knows it would be risky to radically change Barbie's image; jeopardizing the doll's mystique could lead to a sharp drop in Barbie's popularity.

To a great extent, that mystique depends on Barbie's lack of a strong identity. Mattel intentionally says very little about Barbie's character because they want little girls to decide what Barbie is like. Her bland personality and her wide assortment of clothes and accessories allow for endless possibilities. Barbie can be whatever a child wants her to be.

Still, an image of Barbie emerges from a variety of messages—advertising, public relations events, and *Barbie* magazine, a glossy publication sent to 650,000 members of Barbie's fan club. The magazine describes Barbie's clothes and activities. In a recent issue, for example, Ken took Barbie out to dinner at a "sumptuous restaurant." For the occasion, Barbie chose her "ravishing new pink ruffled evening dress." Perhaps the strongest statement about Barbie's personality was a two-hour cartoon special, featuring her experiences with her all-girl rock band. But even there, Barbie's character remained a mystery. All she did on the show was sing and play music.

Although in many ways Mattel has reinforced the popular image of Barbie, the company has also tried to raise her consciousness a bit. In the mid-1970s, the firm surveyed mothers and asked them for their opinion of Barbie. Many responded that she lacked ambition and should get a job. According to Jill Barad, the public was delighted when

the company reacted by launching Barbie's career. Barbie is a better person now, according to Barad. She "*does* have talent and skills, and goes to work and makes money, and *that's* how she affords her car!"

In addition to giving Barbie a career, Mattel has introduced her to the civil rights movement. She has black, Asian, and Latino friends, and there are black and Latino versions of Barbie herself.

Mattel is also winning points for Barbie by emphasizing the doll's therapeutic value. Children's Hospital in Los Angeles uses Barbie to help youngsters who are going through an amputation. The hospital staff removes Barbie's arm or leg, fits her with an artificial limb, and gives her to the child as a gift. According to Ellen Zaman, director of patient family services, "It helps the children understand what will happen to them."

As a symbol of popular culture, Barbie has also gained a measure of respectability. Scholars write learned articles analyzing her significance. The Toy Manufacturers of America have acknowledged her unique place in the history of toys. The Smithsonian is sponsoring a special Barbie exhibit. And for her 30th birthday, a crowd of toy manufacturers, collectors, and fans assembled at Lincoln Center to pay tribute to America's number-one doll. Needless to say, Barbie wowed them in her rose gown, her pink feather boa, and her lavish earrings.

Your Mission: You have recently joined Mattel's marketing department as an administrative assistant to Jill Barad. One of your responsibilities is to respond to letters about Barbie. Your goal is to emphasize Barbie's positive qualities, to reinforce her popularity with youngsters, and to handle her critics as diplomatically as possible. Bearing these goals in mind, choose the *best* alternatives for handling the following correspondence:

1. You have received a letter from Alice Brown, a reporter for *Ms.* magazine, who is writing an article tentatively entitled "Barbie: Reflection or Molder of Contemporary Values?" Brown has asked you for in-

formation about the marketing campaign that Mattel has employed to create Barbie's image over the past 30 years. What should you do?

a. Search through the files, assemble as much information as possible, and send it off with a brief letter wishing Brown good luck with the article.

b. Consult Jill Barad to determine Mattel's policy about providing such information and to obtain guidance on how much effort to devote to responding.

c. Write Brown a letter asking for clarification of the request.

d. Draft a letter of reply and forward it to Barad for comments and approval.

2. You and Jill Barad are trying to decide how to respond to Brown's request. What should your purpose be?

a. The general purpose is to inform. The specific purpose is to provide Brown with a brief summary of the evolution of Mattel's marketing campaign for Barbie over the past 30 years.

b. The general purpose is to persuade. The specific purpose is to convince Brown that Barbie is a worthy role model for young girls and that the marketing campaign portrays Barbie as a socially aware, successful career woman.

c. The general purpose is to collaborate. The specific purpose is to work with Brown to develop an article that examines the evolution of Mattel's marketing campaign for Barbie.

3. Assume that your purpose is to convince Brown of Barbie's worthiness as a role model who is a socially aware, successful career woman. Does this purpose meet the tests suggested in the chapter?

a. Yes. The purpose is realistic. The timing is right. You are the right person to send the message. And the purpose is acceptable to the organization.

b. Although the purpose is good in several ways, it may not be realistic to expect Brown to accept Barbie as an admirable role model for young girls. Even though Barbie now has a career and some ethnic friends, her basic image has not changed a great deal.

c. The purpose is fine, but you are not the right person to send the message. Mattel's president should respond.

4. When planning your reply, what assumptions can you safely make about your audience?

a. The audience includes not only Alice Brown but also the readers of *Ms.* magazine. Given their feminist bias, the readers will probably be hostile to business in general and to Barbie in particular. They probably know virtually nothing about the toy business. Furthermore, they probably mistrust you because you are a Mattel employee.

b. Alice Brown will probably be the only person who reads the letter directly; she represents the primary audience, whereas the readers of her article are the secondary audience. Brown will be happy to hear from Mattel and will read the information with an open mind. As a journalist, Brown is probably intelligent and objective. However, she may not know a great deal about Mattel or about marketing. Although she is a stranger to you, she trusts your credibility as a Mattel spokesperson.

c. Alice Brown is probably the sole and primary audience for the letter. The fact that she is writing an article about Barbie suggests that she enjoyed playing with the doll as a child and that she knows a great deal about Barbie already. In all likelihood, she will respond positively to your reply and will trust your credibility as a Mattel representative.

d. Alice Brown may be an industrial spy working for a rival toy company. She will show your reply to the top people in your competitor's marketing department. They will analyze the information objectively and use it to improve their own marketing program at your expense.

5. Given the breadth of Alice Brown's request, what can you do to satisfy her information needs?

a. Put yourself in Brown's shoes and try to imagine what information would be most useful, given the title of the article.

b. Assume that Brown needs to know as much as possible about marketing Barbie, and based on your conversation with Jill Barad, send whatever information you can.

c. After touching base with your boss, write or call Brown to clarify the request.

d. Send only the information that portrays Barbie in a favorable light.

6. What appeal should you use to ensure that Brown will be objective in analyzing Mattel's approach to marketing Barbie?

a. Acknowledge that Barbie began life as a pretty teenager whose primary goal was to be popular; then show that Mattel has repositioned Barbie to reflect societal changes.

b. Let the facts speak for themselves. Provide a completely objective historical summary of Mattel's marketing campaigns for Barbie, using chronological order as the organizing principle.

c. Describe your own background, hitting on points you might have in common with Alice Brown. This will encourage her to trust you and view your response in a positive light.

d. Appeal to Brown's emotions by describing how Children's Hospital uses Barbie to help children who are facing an amputation.

7. Assume that your purpose is to inform Alice Brown that the approach to marketing Barbie evolved in response to societal changes. Which of the following main ideas best supports this purpose?
   a. Mattel's marketing department reports to a successful black woman who has improved Barbie's image with liberated women and ethnic minorities.
   b. Barbie has learned to dress for success in the world of work.
   c. In response to changes in society's values, Mattel has revised its marketing program to show Barbie as a strong, successful career woman who may be black, white, or Latino, and who has friends from many ethnic groups.
   d. Mattel keeps Barbie's personality a mystery so that children can use their own imaginations to create the Barbie of their dreams.

8. Which channel and medium of communication should you use in replying to Alice Brown?
   a. Call her on the phone to ask for clarification of her needs; then follow up with a letter report (4 to 20 pages, written in letter format).
   b. Call her on the phone, ask for clarification of her needs, and answer her while you have her on the line.
   c. Write a letter asking for clarification of her needs, and follow up with a letter report.
   d. Send a form letter used for replying to all inquiries about Barbie.[6]

QUESTIONS FOR DISCUSSION

1. What proportion of your time would you expect to spend on the three steps in the preparation process (planning, composing, and revising) for the following writing projects: (a) memo to a colleague, (b) report for the president's office, (c) letter to a client.
2. "An effective memo always has a single purpose." Do you agree? Why or why not?
3. How would the size of an audience affect your ability to communicate if you were (a) preparing a written message, (b) delivering a speech, (c) conveying information nonverbally?
4. What are some of the things a communicator might do to respond to the audience's practical needs?
5. What main idea might you try to develop in a one-page memo on cigarette smoking in the office? In a three-page memo?
6. Which channel and medium would you use to convince your boss, the director of planning, to reconsider the company's policy of requiring MBA degrees for all members of the planning staff?

EXERCISES

1. For each of the following communication tasks, write a statement of purpose (if you have trouble, try beginning with "I want to . . . "):
   a. A report to your boss, the store manager, about the outdated items in the warehouse
   b. A memo to clients about your plans to have a booth at an upcoming trade show
   c. A letter to a customer who has not made a payment for three months
   d. A memo to employees about the office's high water bills
   e. A phone call to a supplier to check on an overdue shipment of parts
2. Make a list of communication tasks you will need to accomplish in the next week or so (a job application, a letter of complaint, a speech to a class, an order for some merchandise, and so on). For each, determine a general purpose and a specific purpose.
3. List five messages that you have received lately, such as direct-mail promotions, letters, phone solicitations, and lectures. For each, determine the general purpose of the message and the specific purpose; then answer the following questions: Was the message well timed? Did the sender choose an appropriate channel and medium for the message? Was an appropriate person used for delivery of the message? Was the sender's purpose realistic?
4. For each communication task below, write brief answers to three questions: Who is the audience? What are the audience's general attitudes toward my subject? What does the audience need to know?
   a. A "final notice" collection letter from an appliance manufacturer to an appliance dealer, sent ten days before initiating legal collection procedures
   b. An unsolicited sales letter asking readers to purchase computer disks at near-wholesale prices
   c. An advertisement for peanut butter
   d. Fliers to be attached to doorknobs in the neighborhood, announcing reduced rates for chimney lining or repairs

e. A cover letter sent by a job applicant along with her resume

5. Rewrite the following message so that it includes all the information that the reader needs. (Make up any necessary details.)

I am pleased to offer you the position of assistant buyer at Marcus Industries at an annual salary of $15,500. I hope to receive notice of your acceptance soon.

6. As a member of Mattel's marketing department (see this chapter's On-the-Job simulation), you sent Alice Brown the information she requested on Barbie. You have just received a copy of her article. To your dismay, it is an extremely biased document. The article concludes that playing with Barbie encourages little girls to adopt harmful stereotypes and to value themselves in terms of their appearance and possessions. In her article, Brown acknowledges that Mattel has given Barbie a career and expanded her association with minorities; however, Brown argues that these changes are superficial and that Mattel made them only because of consumer pressure. She concludes the article by calling for a consumer boycott of Barbie. Plan your response: Determine your purpose, establish the main idea, and select the channel and medium of communication.[7]

After studying this chapter, you will be able to

- Identify the characteristics of a well-organized message
- Explain why organization is important to both the audience and the communicator
- Divide a main idea into subdivisions of thought, grouped into logical categories
- Arrange ideas in direct or indirect order, depending on the audience's probable reaction
- Compose a message using a style and tone that are appropriate to your subject, purpose, audience, and format
- Interest an audience in your message by using the "you" attitude

CHAPTER FOUR

ORGANIZING AND COMPOSING BUSINESS MESSAGES

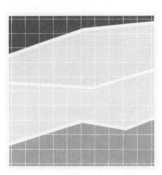

ON THE JOB:
Facing a Communication Dilemma at Drake Beam Morin
Putting a Silver Lining on the Pink Slip

"Layoffs Hit Executive Suite in Wake of Merger"; "Thousands of Jobs in Jeopardy as Economy Continues to Decline"; "Pink Slips Flow at Local Company Following Loss of Major Contract." When headlines like these predict doom and gloom for the employees of one or more companies, most people feel at least a moment of vicarious apprehension about losing their jobs. But at Drake Beam Morin, the country's largest outplacement firm, such bad news has a silver lining. When trouble strikes a company or an industry, outplacement executives see an opportunity to counsel those involved in the job termination process.

Outplacement services vary, but most of the leading firms like Drake Beam Morin provide help for both the managers involved in doing the firing and the people who are losing their jobs. Managers are taught to handle the legal and emotional complexities of the dismissal process; terminated employees get help in coping with rejection and finding new jobs.

Corporations and dismissed employees clearly derive both psychological and practical benefits from such programs; however, the price is steep. Outplacement firms typically charge 15 percent of the fired executive's total annual compensation. In most cases, the employer picks up the tab. So, if a company fires a manager who makes $100,000, providing the individual with outplacement service would cost $15,000.

Since many terminations are cost-cutting moves involving a substantial number of employees, corporations naturally think twice before buying outplacement services. More often than not, the corporation is already obligated by law to provide other termination benefits, such as severance pay, accrued vacation time, and extended insurance coverage. In reviewing a proposal from an outplacement firm, a corporate executive is therefore likely to ask, "Do we really need to spend a lot of extra money on outplacement counseling as well?"

Answering that question is a challenge. If you worked for Drake Beam Morin, what sort of letter could you write to stimulate an executive's interest in your service? How important will organization be to your letter? Will an outline help? What style will work best? How will the tone of your letter affect potential clients?[1]

THE NEED FOR *BEING WELL ORGANIZED*

Drake Beam Morin

Drake Beam Morin is not the only company facing such challenges. All business communicators must deal with the problem of developing a story, of finding a way to compress a multidimensional web of ideas into a linear message that proceeds point by point. Meeting the challenge is important: Research clearly demonstrates that people simply do not remember disassociated facts and figures.[2]

WHY SOME MESSAGES SEEM DISORGANIZED

Consider a letter sent to the customer service department of a department store in Mason City, Iowa:

My dad was in an accident last year, and he hasn't been able to work full-time, so we don't have as much money to spend as we used to. But my mom works as a clerk at the city hall, so we aren't destitute by any means. And soon my dad will be going back full-time.

My family has shopped at your store since I was a kid. It was smaller then, and it was located on the corner of Federal Avenue and 2nd N.W. My dad bought me my first bike there when I was six. I still remember the day. He paid cash for it. We always pay cash.

I have five brothers and sisters, and they need plenty of things. The cassette player that I bought for my sister Suzanne for Christmas has been a problem. We've taken it in for repairs three times in three months to the authorized service center, and my sister is very careful with the machine and hasn't abused it. She likes piano music. It still doesn't work right, and I'm tired of hauling it back and forth because I work at McDonald's after school and don't have a lot of spare time. I paid cash for the tape player.

This is the first time I've returned anything to your store, and I hope you'll agree that I deserve a better deal.

This letter displays the sort of disorganization that readers find frustrating. Here's a closer look at what's wrong:

<table>
<tr><td></td></tr>
</table>

Most disorganized communication suffers from problems with content, grouping, or sequence.

- *Taking too long to get to the point.* The writer wrote three paragraphs before introducing the topic: the faulty cassette player. She then waited until the final paragraph to state her purpose: She wants an adjustment.

- *Including irrelevant material.* The writer introduced extraneous information that has no bearing on her purpose or topic. Does it matter that the department store used to be smaller or that it was at a different location? And what difference does it make whether the writer works at McDonald's? Or whether Suzanne likes piano music?

- *Presenting ideas in illogical order.* The writer put some of the ideas in the wrong place. The grouping and sequence are illogical. The writer seems to be making six points: (1) her family has money to spend, (2) they are old customers, (3) they pay cash, (4) they buy many things at the store, (5) the cassette player doesn't work, and (6) the buyer wants an adjustment. Wouldn't it be more logical to begin with the fact that the machine doesn't work? And shouldn't some of these ideas be combined under the general idea that the writer is a valuable customer?

- *Leaving out necessary information.* The writer left out some important facts. The customer service representative may want to know the make, model, and price of the cassette player; the date on which it was purchased; the specific problems the machine has had; and whether the repairs were covered by the warranty. The writer also failed to specify what she wants the store to do. Does she want a new cassette player of the same type? A different model? Or her money back?

These four common faults are responsible for most of the organization problems you'll find in business communication.

WHY GOOD ORGANIZATION IS IMPORTANT

You might be asking yourself, "Does it really matter? Who cares whether the message is well organized, as long as the point is eventually made? Why not just let the ideas flow naturally and trust that the audience will grasp my meaning?" In general, the answer is simple: By arranging your ideas logically and diplomatically, you are able to satisfy the audience's informational, motivational, and practical needs. A well-organized message presents all the required information in a convincing pattern, with maximum efficiency.

Achieving good organization is a challenge sometimes. It's easier, however, if you know what good organization is. These four guidelines will help you recognize a well-organized message:

A message is well organized when all the pieces fit together in a coherent pattern.

- The subject and purpose must be clear.

- All the information must be related to the subject and purpose.

- The ideas must be grouped and presented in a logical way.

- All necessary information must be included.

A well-organized message helps the audience understand the message, helps the audience accept the message, saves the audience's time, and simplifies the communicator's job.

Helps the audience understand the message

The main reason for being well organized is to improve the chances that people will understand exactly what you mean.

By observing the four rules for organization, the writer of the previous letter can now be sure that the customer service department will understand the message:

I bought an Olympia Model 124 cassette player from your store on November 25, during your pre-Christmas sale, when it was marked down to $19.95. I didn't use the unit until Christmas because it was bought as a gift for my sister. You can imagine how I felt when she opened it on Christmas morning and it didn't work.

I took the machine to the authorized service center and was assured that the problem was merely a loose connection. The service representative fixed the machine, but three weeks later it broke again--another loose connection. For the next three weeks, the machine worked reasonably well, although the volume tended to vary at random. Two weeks ago, the machine stopped working again. Once more, the service representative blamed a loose connection and made the repair. Although the machine is working now, it isn't working very well. The volume is still subject to change without notice, and the speed seems to drag sometimes.

What is your policy on exchanging unsatisfactory merchandise? Although all the repairs have been relatively minor and have been covered by our six-month warranty, I am not satisfied with the machine. I would like to exchange it for a similar model from another manufacturer. If the new set costs more than the old one, I will pay the difference, even though I generally look for sale merchandise.

My family and I have shopped at your store for 15 years and until now have always been satisfied with your merchandise. We are counting on you to live up to your reputation for standing behind your products. Please let us hear from you soon.

This version meets the definition of a well-organized message. The main point is clear and is introduced early. All the information is directly related to the subject and purpose of the letter. The ideas are arranged in logical groups and presented in a logical sequence. And all necessary information is included. The result is a unified, coherent, and businesslike document that can be easily understood by the audience, thus satisfying the audience's need for information.

Helps the audience accept the message

Good organization also helps you get your ideas across without upsetting the audience.

Good organization pays off in another way too: It helps make your message more acceptable to your audience from a motivational standpoint. Let's say that you are the customer with the broken cassette player referred to earlier and that you got the following reply from Laura Hampton, a customer service representative at the department store:

Your letter has been referred to me for a reply. I'm sorry, but we are unable to grant your request for a cassette player. Our store does not accept returns on sale merchandise or on merchandise that was purchased over 30 days ago. Because you bought the machine on sale 3 months ago, we cannot help you. I suggest that you have it repaired before the warranty runs out.

We do hope that you will understand our position and that you will continue to shop at our store. As you said yourself, this is the first problem you've ever had with our merchandise.

How do you feel now?

Although Laura's letter appears at first glance to be logical enough, she has made no effort to select and organize her points in a diplomatic way. With greater care in choosing and presenting her ideas, Laura could have come up with something more acceptable, like the letter in Figure 4.1. Although this letter is still not likely to leave the customer totally satisfied, isn't the bad news a little easier to take?

FIGURE 4.1
Sample Letter Demonstrating the Importance of Good Organization

WAINWRIGHT'S DEPARTMENT STORE
660 Sixth Avenue, N.W.
Mason City, Iowa 50401
(515) 988-9900

March 15, 1993

Miss Evelyn Kittrell
Route 3, Hancock Highway
Clear Lake, IA 50401

Dear Miss Kittrell:

The letter begins with a neutral statement that the reader should not find objectionable.

Thank you for letting us know about your experience with the Olympia cassette player that you bought in November. It's important that we learn of unusual problems with merchandise we stock.

The refusal is stated indirectly and is linked with a solution to the reader's problem.

As you know, regularly priced merchandise returned to Wainwright's within 30 days is covered by the unconditional refund policy that has been our tradition for 22 years. But your machine is still covered by the manufacturer's warranty. Your needs will receive immediate attention if you write to

Ms. Bonnie Bendek
Olympia Manufacturing
P.O. Box 6671, Terminal Annex
Los Angeles, CA 90010

From experience, I know that the people at Olympia truly care about having satisfied customers.

The letter closes on an appreciative note and confidently assumes normal dealings in the future.

We too value your business, Miss Kittrell. Please don't miss our Tax Days sale in April, which will feature more of the low prices and high-quality merchandise that you've come to rely on.

Sincerely,

Laura Hampton
Customer Service

sb

As general manager of Ford's plastic products division, Ronald E. Goldsberry exemplifies the busy executive whose day is fragmented by such diverse activities as merger coordination, budget decisions, personnel problems, product decisions, and on and on. Goldsberry appreciates business messages that do not waste his time. He advises that you make sure the message is efficient, clear, and logical in organization.

Writers can soften refusals and leave a better impression by organizing messages diplomatically. They can also use good organization to enhance their credibility and add authority to their messages. In a recent survey of chief executives, 89 percent said that they interpret clear, well-organized writing as an indication of clear thinking.[3]

Saves the audience's time

In addition to being convincing, well-organized messages are efficient; they satisfy the audience's need for convenience. When a message is well organized, it contains only relevant ideas, so the audience doesn't have to waste time on information that is superfluous. Effective organization is the foundation of brevity. All the information in a well-organized message is in a logical place. The audience can follow the thought pattern without a struggle. And because the organization is clear and logical, members of the audience can save even more time, if they want to, by looking for just the information they need instead of reading everything.

Simplifies the communicator's job

Finally, being well organized is a good idea because it helps you get your message down on paper more quickly and efficiently. This is an important factor in business, where the objective is to get a job done, not to produce paper. In fact, when the chief executives in the survey mentioned earlier were asked what they would most like to improve about their own business writing, they mentioned speed of composition more often than any other factor.[4]

By thinking about what you're going to say and how you're going to say it before you begin to write, you can proceed more confidently. The draft will go more quickly because you won't waste time putting ideas in the wrong places or composing material you don't need. In addition, you can use your organizational plan to get some advance input from your boss so that you'll be sure you're on the right track *before* you spend hours working on a draft. And if you're working on a large and complex project, you can use the plan to divide the writing job among co-workers in order to finish the assignment as quickly as possible.

GOOD ORGANIZATION THROUGH OUTLINING

Basically, achieving good organization is a two-step process: First you define and group the ideas; then you establish their sequence with a carefully selected organizational plan.

DEFINE AND GROUP IDEAS

An outline or a schematic diagram will help you visualize the relationship among parts of a message.

Deciding what to say is the most basic problem that any business communicator has to solve. If the content is weak, no amount of style will camouflage that fact. But once you have decided on your main idea (using the techniques described in Chapter 3), you must develop it by grouping the supporting details in the most logical and effective way. You need to visualize how all the points fit together, and one way to do this is to construct an outline. Even if all you do is jot down three or four points on the back of an envelope, making a plan and sticking to it will help you cover the important details.

When you're preparing a long and complex message, an outline is indispensable because it helps you visualize the relationship among the various parts. Without an outline, you may be inclined to ramble. But with an outline to guide you, you can communicate in a systematic way, covering all the ideas necessary in an effective order and with proper emphasis. Following a plan also helps you express the transitions between ideas so that the audience will understand how your thoughts are related.

You're no doubt familiar with the basic alphanumeric outline, which uses numbers and letters to identify each point and indents them to show which ideas are of equal status. (Chapter 11 tells more about the various formats that can be used in this type of outlining.) But you may never have tried a more schematic approach, which illustrates the structure of your message in an "organization chart" like those depicting a company's management structure (see Figure 4.2). The main idea is shown in the highest-level box. Like a top executive, the main idea establishes the big picture. The lower-level ideas, like lower-level employees, provide the details. All the ideas are arranged into logical divisions of thought, just as a company is organized into divisions and departments.[5]

According to co-workers, Jane Pauley is a much better writer than most TV journalists—part of the reason for her success. Good organization is the key to good writing, says Pauley. Once you have defined the main idea, you decide how to break it down into logical pieces by considering your purpose and your subject matter.

Start with the main idea

The main idea is placed at the top of an organization chart to help you establish the goals and general strategy of the message. It summarizes two things: (1) what you want the audience to do or think and (2) the basic reason they should do it or think it. Everything in the message should either support this idea or explain its implications.

State the major points

In an organization chart, the boxes directly below the top box represent the major supporting points, corresponding to the main headings in a conventional outline. These are the "vice presidential" ideas that clarify the message by expressing it in more concrete terms.

To fill in these boxes, you break the main idea into smaller units. Generally, you should try to identify three to five major points. If you come up with more than seven main divisions of thought, go back and look for opportunities to combine some of the ideas. The big question is what to put in each box. Sometimes the choices are fairly obvious. But sometimes you may have hundreds of ideas to sort through and group together. In such situations, you should consider both your purpose and the nature of the material.

FIGURE 4.2
"Organization Chart" for Organizing a Message

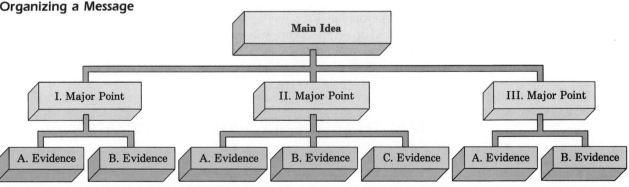

If your purpose is to inform and the material is factual, the groupings are generally suggested by the subject itself. They are usually based on something physical that you can visualize or measure: activities to be performed, functional units, spatial or chronological relationships, or parts of a whole. For example, when you're describing a process, the major supporting points are almost inevitably steps in the process. When you're describing a physical object, the vice-presidential boxes correspond to the components of the object. When you're giving a historical account, each box represents an event in the chronological chain.

When your purpose is to persuade or collaborate, the major supporting points may be more difficult to identify. Instead of relying on a natural order imposed by the subject, you need to develop a line of reasoning that proves your central message and motivates your audience to act. The boxes on the organization chart correspond to the major elements in a logical argument. Basically, the supporting points are the main reasons that your audience should accept your message.

Illustrate with evidence

The third level on the organization chart shows the specific evidence you will use to illustrate your major points. This evidence is the "flesh and blood" that helps your audience understand and remember the more abstract concepts. Let's say you're advocating that the company increase its advertising budget. To support this point, you could provide statistical evidence that your most successful competitors spend more on advertising than you do. You could also describe a specific case in which a particular competitor increased its ad budget and achieved an impressive sales gain. As a final bit of evidence, you could show that over the past five years, your firm's sales have gone up and down in unison with the amount spent on advertising.

> Each major point should be supported with enough specific evidence to be convincing but not so much that it's boring.

If you're developing a long, complex message, you may need to carry the organization chart (or outline) down several levels. Remember that every level is a step along the chain from the abstract to the concrete, from the general to the specific. The lowest level contains the individual facts and figures that tie the generalizations to the observable, measurable world. The higher levels are the concepts that reveal why those facts are significant.

The more evidence you provide, the more conclusive your case will be. If your subject is complex and unfamiliar, or if your audience is skeptical, you will need a lot of facts and figures to demonstrate your points. On the other hand, if the subject is routine and the audience is positively inclined, you can be more sparing with the evidence. You want to provide enough support to be convincing but not so much that your message becomes boring or inefficient.

Another way to keep the audience interested is to vary the type of detail. As you plan your message, try to switch from facts and figures to narration; add a dash of description; throw in some examples or a reference to authority; reinforce it all with visual aids. Think of your message as a stew, a mix of ingredients, seasoned with a blend of spices. Each separate flavor adds to the richness of the whole.

ESTABLISH SEQUENCE WITH ORGANIZATIONAL PLANS

Once you have defined and grouped your ideas, you are ready to decide on their sequence. You have two basic options:

FIGURE 4.3
Audience Reaction and
Organizational Approach

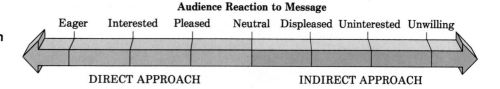

Audience Reaction to Message

Eager   Interested   Pleased   Neutral   Displeased   Uninterested   Unwilling

DIRECT APPROACH   INDIRECT APPROACH

- *Direct approach (deductive).* The main idea comes first, followed by the evidence.

- *Indirect approach (inductive).* The evidence comes first, and the main idea comes later.

These two basic approaches may be applied either to short messages (memos and letters) or to long ones (reports, proposals, and presentations). To choose between the two alternatives, you must first analyze your audience's likely reaction to your purpose and message.

Your audience's reaction will fall somewhere on the continuum shown in Figure 4.3. In general, the direct approach is fine when your audience will be receptive: eager, interested, pleased, or even neutral. If they will be resistant to your message—displeased, uninterested, or unwilling—you will generally have better results with the indirect approach. Drake Beam Morin would probably use the indirect approach in letters to potential clients.

Bear in mind, however, that each message is unique. You can't solve all your communication problems with a simple formula. If you're sending bad news to outsiders, for example, an indirect approach is probably best. On the other hand, you might want to get directly to the point in a memo to an associate, even if your message is unpleasant. The direct approach might also be the best choice for long messages, regardless of the audience's attitude, because delaying the main point could cause confusion and frustration. When planning your approach, just remember that the first priority in business communication is to make the message clear.

Once you have analyzed your audience's probable reaction and chosen a general approach, you can choose the most appropriate organizational plan:

- *Direct requests.* One of the most common types of business message is the most straightforward. Direct requests are used when the audience will be interested in complying or eager to respond. For example, if you are inquiring about products or placing an order, the recipient will usually want to comply and will welcome your request. Thus direct requests use the direct approach: They get straight to the point. This type of message is discussed in greater detail in Chapter 6.

- *Routine, good-news, and goodwill messages.* If you are providing routine information as part of your regular business, the audience will probably be neutral, meaning neither very pleased nor displeased. And if you are announcing a price cut, granting an adjustment, accepting an invitation, or congratulating a colleague, the audience will be pleased to hear from you. Thus routine, good-news, and goodwill messages use the direct approach. By starting off with the positive point, you put your audience in a good frame of mind and help make them receptive to whatever else you have to say. Also, this approach emphasizes the pleasing aspect of your message by putting it right up front, where it is the first thing

Use direct approach if the audience's reaction is likely to be positive, and use indirect approach if it is likely to be negative.

Direct requests get straight to the point because the audience usually wants to respond.

The direct approach is effective for messages that will either please the reader or cause no particular reaction.

recipients see. This type of message is discussed in more detail in Chapter 7.

- *Bad-news messages.* When the audience will be displeased about what you have to say, your challenge lies in being honest but kind. If, for example, you are turning down a job applicant, refusing credit, or denying a request for an adjustment, the audience will be disappointed. Thus the indirect approach is probably better to use. As long as you can be honest and reasonably brief, you're better off opening a bad-news message with a neutral point and putting the negative information after the explanation. Then if you can close with something fairly positive, you're likely to leave the audience feeling okay—not great, but not hostile either. When you're the bearer of bad tidings, that's often about all you can hope for. This type of message is discussed further in Chapter 8.

- *Persuasive messages.* When the audience really isn't very interested in your request or will be unwilling to comply without extra coaxing, persuasive messages are used, and the approach is indirect. If you write to ask for a favor, request an adjustment, collect a debt, or make a sale, the audience will initially resist. Although you might argue that people are likely to feel manipulated by the indirect approach, the fact remains that you have to capture people's attention before you can persuade them to do something. If you don't, there's really no way to get the message across. You also have to get your audience to consider with an open mind what you have to say; to do this, you have to make an interesting point and provide supporting facts that encourage the audience to continue paying attention. Once you have them thinking, you can introduce your real purpose. This type of message is discussed at greater length in Chapter 9.

Table 4.1 summarizes how each type of message is structured. In each organizational plan, the opening, the body, and the close all play an important part in getting your message across.

Most short messages can use one of the four basic organizational plans. But longer messages (namely, reports and presentations) require a more complex pattern to handle the greater mass of information. These patterns can be broken into two general categories: informational and analytical.

In general, the easiest reports and presentations to organize are the informational ones that provide nothing more than facts. Operating instructions, status reports, technical descriptions, and descriptions of company procedures all fall into this category.

Long informational messages have an obvious main idea, often with a descriptive or "how to" overtone. The development of subordinate ideas follows the natural breakdowns of the material to be explained. These subtopics can be arranged sequentially, chronologically, spatially, geographically, categorically, or in order of importance.

It is more difficult to organize analytical reports and presentations, which are designed to lead the audience to a specific conclusion. When your purpose is to collaborate with the audience in solving a problem or to persuade them to take a definite action, you have to choose an organizational plan that highlights logical arguments or focuses the audience's attention on what needs to be done. Your audience may respond in one of two ways to your material, and your choice of organizational plan should depend on the reaction you anticipate:

If you have bad news, try to put it somewhere in the middle, cushioned by other, more positive ideas.

Using the indirect approach gives you an opportunity to get your message across to a skeptical or hostile audience.

When your purpose is to inform, the major points are based on a natural order implied by the subject's characteristics.

When your purpose is to persuade or collaborate, the approach is analytical, with major points corresponding to logical arguments or to conclusions and recommendations.

TABLE 4.1 Four Organizational Plans for Short Messages

AUDIENCE REACTION	ORGANIZATIONAL PLAN	OPENING	BODY	CLOSE
Eager or interested	Direct requests	Begin with the request or main idea.	Provide necessary details.	Close cordially and state the specific action desired.
Pleased or neutral	Routine, good-news, and goodwill messages	Begin with the main idea or the good news.	Provide necessary details.	Close with a cordial comment, a reference to the good news, or a look toward the future.
Displeased	Bad-news messages	Begin with a neutral statement that acts as a transition to the reasons for the bad news.	Give reasons to justify a negative answer. State or imply the bad news, and make a positive suggestion.	Close cordially.
Uninterested or unwilling	Persuasive messages	Begin with a statement or question that captures attention.	Arouse the audience's interest in the subject. Build the audience's desire to comply.	Request action.

- If you expect your audience to agree with you, use a structure that focuses attention on conclusions and recommendations.

- If you expect your audience to be skeptical about your conclusions and recommendations or hostile toward them, use a structure that focuses attention on the rationale that supports your point of view.

You'll learn more about organizing longer messages in Chapter 12. For now, the important thing is to master the basics of structuring a message.

FROM OUTLINE TO FIRST DRAFT

Once you have completed the planning process, you are ready to begin composing the message. If your schedule permits, put your outline or organization chart aside for a day or two and then review it with a fresh eye, looking for opportunities to improve the flow of ideas. When you feel confident that you finally have the structure that will achieve your purpose with the intended audience, you can begin to write.

BEHIND THE SCENES AT GENERAL ELECTRIC

The Making of an Annual Report

A company with publicly traded stock is required by the Securities and Exchange Commission (SEC) and by law to present an audited report of its financial status to its shareholders each year. This annual report enables the company's owners to make informed decisions before voting at the annual meeting. Annual reports are among the most common business messages created.

General Electric's stock is widely held, and each year the company spends more than $1.5 million to print and distribute 1.25 million annual reports. David Warshaw, manager of corporate communications at GE's headquarters in Fairfield, Connecticut, oversees the creation of these reports. It takes five months for one editor, two financial writers, and dozens of people elsewhere in the company to plan, compose, revise, and print the 70-page document. "The shareholder," says Warshaw, "is our primary audience, whether an individual investor with one share or a bank trust department with many thousands. But others read our report as well: job applicants, reporters, securities analysts, accounting teachers, and employees." Al-though legal requirements dictate the financial information to be included—which made up 48 of the 70 pages in a recent year—the format, text, and production quality are up to the individual company.

A small organization (or one in a single industry) can often select a theme for its annual report: quality, for example, or service. But the size and diversity of GE prohibits such an approach. Instead, Warshaw emphasizes the company's strategy as the main idea, both to guide the people working in various divisions as they write the copy and to give unity to the finished report: "Our strategic goals are (1) to be a global player and (2) to run businesses that are number 1 or number 2 in their global markets. The format calls on each of our 14 major businesses to comment on how they fit into that strategy. The financial results prove whether the strategy is working."

A logical order is critical to the success of General Electric's annual report, especially given its length and complexity. "We want recipients to be able to understand the report, so to help them, we organize the sections from the general to the specific. We open with a

THE COMPOSITION PROCESS

As you compose the first draft, don't worry too much about getting everything perfect. Just put down your ideas as quickly as you can. You'll have time to revise and refine the material later. Composition is relatively easy if you've already figured out what to say and in what order, although you may need to pause now and then to find the right word. You may also discover as you go along that you can improve on your outline. Feel free to rearrange, delete, and add ideas, as long as you don't lose sight of your purpose.

If you're writing the draft in longhand, leave space between lines so that you'll have plenty of room to make revisions. If you're using a typewriter, leave wide margins and double-space the text. Probably the best equipment for drafting the message is a word processor, which allows you to make changes very easily. Alternatively, you might try dictating the message, particularly if you're practicing for an oral delivery or if you're trying to create a conversational tone. For details on the equipment available for the composition process and other communication tasks, see Chapter 18.

STYLE AND TONE

In composing the message, vary the style to create a tone that suits the occasion.

Style is the way you use words to achieve a certain tone, or overall impression. You can vary your style—your sentence structure and vocabulary—to sound forceful or passive, personal or impersonal, colorful or colorless. The right

letter from our chairman to all shareholders, which states our strategy and direction. Many recipients turn here first. It's probably the most-read section of the report, so it's written with all readers in mind."

A narrative section comes next. Taking a portfolio approach, each GE business (from appliances and financial services to the National Broadcasting Corporation) reports on its own activity. "That allows 14 large, independent, and diverse businesses to present themselves, their markets, their successes, and finally, their strategies and how these fit into the overall strategy as described in the chairman's opening letter."

Financial details make up the third and final section. "A lot is determined by what SEC regulations require. Using charts, tables, and even narrative, we provide various levels of information. Depending on the readers' level of interest and sophistication, all interested parties can find the detail they need."

Even illustration and design are considered part of the composition. "We decide what ideas we want illustrated by photographs, and the headlines and captions are chosen with the main idea in mind. That way, if folks merely leaf through the report looking at pictures and reading captions, they'll get some idea about the status of the company."

Does Warshaw still enjoy doing the report even after 11 years with GE? "It's a fascinating exercise.

You have a diverse group of people from various locations who work for the same company, and you get them to focus on clearly communicating the company's goals, strategies, and direction. You are exposed to the entire company. You really get to know how a company 'thinks.' " What more could you ask of a well-organized and well-written report?

APPLY YOUR KNOWLEDGE

1. Two weeks before going to print with the annual report, you learn that the board of directors approved shortening your company's name from American Steel and Railroad Corporation to AMX. What impact would this have on the organization and composition of the report?

2. Your company had a good year in 1991: Two new products were launched, market share was increased, and an international distributor was acquired—all leading to record sales and earnings. However, 1992 was a bad year: Design problems caused a major recall of one of your new products, a competitor introduced a product targeted at your leading brand, and three key executives resigned—all of which resulted in slumping sales, little profit, and no dividend to stockholders. List the ways your annual report's organization and composition would differ for the two years.

choice depends on the nature of your message and your relationship with the reader.

Your use of language is one of your credentials, a badge that identifies you as being a member of a particular group. Although your style should be clear, concise, and grammatically correct, it should also conform to the norms of your group. Every organization has its own stylistic conventions, and many occupational groups share a particular vocabulary.

Although style can be refined during the revision phase (see Chapter 5), you will save yourself time and a lot of rewriting if you compose in an appropriate style. Before you even begin writing, focus on the role you're playing, your purpose, and the probable reaction of your audience. All these elements influence the tone of a message.

Think about the relationship you want to establish

The first step toward getting the right tone is to think about your relationship with the audience. Who are you and who are they? Are you friends of long standing with common interests, or are you total strangers? Are you equal in status, experience, and education, or are you clearly unequal? Your answers to these questions will help you define your relationship with the audience so that you can use the right "voice" in your message.

If you're addressing an old friend, you can often take an informal tack. But if you're in the lower echelon of a large organization, you generally have to adopt a respectful tone when communicating with the people above you. Some people in high positions are extremely proud of their status and resent any gesture from a lower-level employee that is even remotely presumptuous. For example, they may not like you to offer your own opinions, and they may resent any implied criticism of their actions or decisions. If you are writing to someone of this type, you have to show a keen appreciation of rank, or your message will be ineffective.

Although various situations require different tones, most business communication should sound businesslike without being stuffy. The tone should suggest that you and your audience are sensible, logical, unemotional people—objective, interested in the facts, rational, competent, and efficient. You are civilized people who share a mutual respect.

To achieve this tone, you must avoid being too familiar. For example, don't mention things about anyone's personal life unless you know the individual very well. Such references are indiscreet and presumptuous. You should also avoid phrases that imply intimacy, such as "just between you and me," "as you and I are well aware," and "I'm sure we both agree." And you should be careful about sounding too folksy or chatty; the audience may interpret this tone as an attempt on your part to seem like an old friend when, in fact, you're not.

Humor is another type of intimacy that may backfire. It's fine to be witty in person with old friends but very difficult to hit just the right note of humor in a written document, particularly if you don't know the reader very well.

You should also avoid obvious flattery. Although most of us respond well to honest praise and proper respect, we are suspicious of anyone who seems too impressed. When someone says, "Only a person of your outstanding intellect and refined tastes can fully appreciate this point," little warning lights flash in our minds. We suspect that we are about to be conned.

We are often quick to take offense when someone starts preaching to us. Few things are more irritating than people who assume that they know it all and that we know nothing. People who feel compelled to give lessons in business are particularly offensive. If for some reason you have to tell your audience something obvious, try to make the information unobtrusive. Place it in the middle of a paragraph, where it will sound like a casual comment as opposed to a major revelation. Alternatively, you might preface an obvious remark with "as you know" or some similar phrase.

Bragging is closely related to preaching, and it is equally offensive. When you praise your own accomplishments or those of your organization, you imply that you are better than your audience. References to the size, profitability, or eminence of your organization may be especially annoying (unless, of course, those in your audience work for the same organization). For example, you are likely to evoke a negative reaction with comments such as "We at McMann's, which is the oldest and most respected firm in the city, have a reputation for integrity that is beyond question."

Perhaps the most important thing you can do to establish a good relationship with your audience is to be yourself. People can spot falseness quickly, and they generally don't like it. If you don't try to be someone you're not, you will sound sincere.

Use the "you" attitude

Once you've thought about the kind of relationship you want to establish, try to project yourself into your audience's shoes. What do they want from you? What are their expectations? How will they feel about what you have to say?

To achieve a warm but businesslike tone
- Don't be too familiar
- Use humor only with great care
- Don't flatter the other person
- Don't preach
- Don't brag
- Be yourself

The "you" attitude is best implemented by expressing your message in terms of the audience's interests and needs.

By asking yourself these questions, you can begin to establish empathy with your audience. You can see the subject through their eyes. Too many business messages have an "I" or "we" attitude, which causes the sender to sound selfish and not interested in the receiver. The message tells what the sender wants; the recipient is expected to go along with it.

If you want to get your message across, you have to adopt the "you" attitude instead and talk in terms of your receiver's wishes, interests, hopes, and preferences. Talk about the other person, and you are talking about the thing that most interests him or her. On the simplest level, you can adopt the "you" attitude by substituting terms that refer to your audience for terms that refer to yourself. In other words, use *you* and *yours* instead of *I, me, mine, we, us,* and *ours*:

INSTEAD OF THIS	USE THIS
To help us process this order, we must ask for another copy of the requisition.	So that your order can be filled promptly, please send another copy of the requisition.
We are pleased to announce our new flight schedule from Atlanta to New York, which is any hour on the hour.	Now you can take a plane from Atlanta to New York any hour on the hour.

Using *you* and *yours* requires finesse. If you overdo it, you are likely to create some rather awkward sentences. You also run the risk of sounding like a high-pressure carnival barker at the county fair. The most effective approach is to balance references to yourself with references to your audience.

On some occasions, you are justified in avoiding the "you" attitude. For instance, when you need to establish blame but want to do so impersonally to minimize the possibility of ill will, you might say "there is a problem" instead of "you caused a problem." Using *you* in a way that might sound dictatorial is also impolite:

Avoid using *you* and *yours*
- To excess
- When assigning blame
- If your organization prefers a more formal style

INSTEAD OF THIS	USE THIS
You should never use that kind of paper in the copy machine.	That type of paper doesn't work very well in the copy machine.
You need to make sure the staff follows instructions.	The staff may need guidance in following instructions.

Keep in mind the attitudes and policies of your organization as well. Some companies have a tradition of avoiding references to *you* and *I* in their memos and formal reports. If you work for a company that expects a formal, impersonal style, confine your use of personal pronouns to informal letters and memos.

In any case, the best way to implement the "you" attitude is to be sincere in thinking about the audience. The "you" attitude is not just a matter of using one pronoun as opposed to another; it is a matter of genuine empathy. You can use *you* 25 times in a single page and still ignore your audience's true concerns. In the final analysis, it's the thought that counts, not the pronoun. One way of touching the right spots in your audience is to find a parallel situation in your own experience. Build your message around this experience, or use what you have learned as a basis for your thoughts.

The word *you* does not always indicate a "you" attitude, and the "you" attitude can be displayed without using the word *you*.

Emphasize the positive

Explain what you can do and what you will do—not what you haven't done, can't do, or won't do.

Another way of showing sensitivity to your audience is to emphasize the positive side of your message. Focus on the silver lining, not the cloud. For example, Drake Beam Morin would focus on what the company can do for potential clients, not on how painful the termination process can be. Most information, even bad news, has at least some redeeming feature. If you can make your audience aware of that feature, you will make your message more acceptable.

INSTEAD OF THIS	USE THIS
It is impossible to repair this vacuum cleaner today.	We can repair your vacuum cleaner by Tuesday.
We apologize for inconveniencing you during our remodeling.	The renovations now under way will enable us to serve you better.

When you are offering criticism or advice, focus on what the person can do to improve.

In the same vein, when you are criticizing or correcting, don't hammer on the other person's mistakes. Avoid referring to failures, problems, or shortcomings. Focus instead on what the person can do to improve:

INSTEAD OF THIS	USE THIS
The problem with this department is a failure to control costs.	The performance of this department can be improved by tightening cost controls.
You filled out the order form wrong. We can't send you the paint until you tell us what color you want.	So that we can process your order properly, please check your color preferences on the enclosed card.

Show your audience how they will benefit from complying with your message.

If you're trying to persuade the audience to buy a product, pay a bill, or perform a service for you, emphasize what's in it for them. Don't focus on why *you* want them to do something. Instead of saying, "Please buy this book so I can make my sales quota," say, "The plot of this novel will keep you in suspense to the last page." Instead of saying, "We need your contribution to the Boys and Girls Club," say, "You can help a child make friends and build self-confidence through your donation to the Boys and Girls Club." An individual who sees the possibility for personal benefit is more likely to respond positively to your appeal.

Avoid words with negative connotations; use meaningful euphemisms instead.

In general, try to state your message without using words that might hurt or offend your audience. Substitute mild terms (euphemisms) for those that have unpleasant connotations. Instead of advertising "cheap" merchandise, announce your bargain prices. Don't talk about "pimples and zits"; refer more delicately to complexion problems. You can be honest without being harsh. Gentle terms won't change the facts, but they will make those facts more acceptable:

POSSIBLY OFFENSIVE	INOFFENSIVE
toilet paper	bathroom tissue
used cars	resale cars
high-calorie food	high-energy food

On the other hand, don't carry euphemisms to extremes. If you're too subtle, people won't know what you're talking about. "Derecruiting" someone to the "mobility pool" instead of telling them they have six weeks to find another job isn't really very helpful. There's a fine line between softening the blow and hiding the facts. Referring to the stock market crash of October 13, 1989, as a "technical correction" may actually be misleading to some, while doing nothing to change the amount of money lost by investors. In the final analysis, people respond better to an honest message delivered with integrity than to a dose of sugar-coated double-talk.

Establish credibility

People are more likely to react positively to your message when they have confidence in you.

Because the success of your message may depend on the audience's perception of you, their belief in your competence and integrity is important. You want people to believe that you know what you're doing and that your word is dependable. The first step in building credibility is to promise only what you can do and then to do what you promise. After that, you can enhance credibility through your writing style.

If you're communicating with someone you know well, your previous interactions influence your credibility. The other person knows from past experience whether you are trustworthy and capable. And if the person is familiar with your company, its reputation may be ample proof of your credibility.

But what if you are complete strangers? Or worse, what if the other person starts off with doubts about you? First and foremost, show an understanding of the other person's situation by calling attention to the things you have in common. For example, if you're communicating with someone who shares your professional background, you might say, "As a fellow engineer (lawyer, doctor, teacher, or whatever), I'm sure you can appreciate this situation." Or you might use technical or professional terms that identify you as a peer.

You can also gain the audience's confidence by explaining your credentials, but you need to be careful that you don't sound pompous. Generally, one or two aspects of your background are all that you need to mention. Possibly your title or the name of your organization will be enough to indicate your abilities.

Your credibility is also enhanced by the quality of the information you provide. If you support your points with evidence that can be confirmed through observation, research, experimentation, or measurement, your audience will recognize that you have the facts, and they will respect you. But exaggerated claims do more harm than good.

You risk losing credibility if you seem to be currying favor with insincere compliments. So support compliments with specific points:

Credited with single-handedly making the junk bond market into the phenomenon of the 1980s, Michael Milken persuaded thousands of institutional investors to put their money into high-risk junk bonds in return for high rates of interest. When the junk bond market collapsed, Milken not only lost his credibility, he destroyed his career and served time in prison.

INSTEAD OF THIS	USE THIS
My deepest heartfelt thanks for the excellent job you did. It's hard these days to find workers like you. You are just fantastic! I can't stress enough how happy you have made us with your outstanding performance.	Thanks for the fantastic job you did filling in for Gladys at the convention with just an hour's notice. Despite the difficult circumstances, you managed to attract several new orders with your demonstration of the new line of coffeemakers. Your dedication and sales ability are truly appreciated.

Doesn't the more restrained praise seem more credible?

The other side of the credibility coin is too much modesty and not enough confidence. Many writing authorities suggest that you avoid such words as *if*, *hope*, and *trust*, which express a lack of confidence on your part:

INSTEAD OF THIS	USE THIS
We hope this recommendation will be helpful.	We're glad to make this recommendation.
If you'd like to order, mail us the reply card.	To order, mail the reply card.
We trust that you'll extend your service contract.	By extending your service contract, you can continue to enjoy top-notch performance from your equipment.

The ultimate key to being believable is to believe in yourself. If you are convinced that your message is sound, you can state your case with authority so that the audience has no doubts. When you have confidence in your own success, you automatically suggest that your audience will respond in the desired way. But if you lack faith in yourself, you're likely to communicate a "maybe this, maybe that" attitude that undermines your credibility.

Be polite

The best tone for business messages is almost always a polite one. When you are courteous to your audience, you show consideration for their needs and feelings by expressing yourself with kindness and tact.

Although you may be tempted now and then to be brutally frank, try to express the facts in a kind and thoughtful manner.

Undoubtedly, you will be frustrated and exasperated by other people many times in your career. When those times occur, you will be tempted to say what you think in blunt terms. To be sure, it's your job to convey the facts precisely and accurately. But venting your emotions will rarely improve the situation and may jeopardize the goodwill of your audience. Instead, be gentle when expressing yourself:

INSTEAD OF THIS	USE THIS
I've seen a lot of dumb ideas in my time, but this takes the cake.	This is an interesting suggestion, but I'm not sure it's practical. Have you considered the following possible problems?
You've been sitting on my order for two weeks now. When can I expect delivery?	As I mentioned in my letter of October 12, we are eager to receive our order as soon as possible. Could you please let us know when to expect delivery.

Use extra tact when writing and when communicating with higher-ups and outsiders.

Of course, some situations require more diplomacy than others. If you know your audience well, you can get away with being informal. However, correspondence with people who outrank you or with those outside your organization generally calls for an added measure of courtesy. And in general, written communication requires more tact than oral communication. When you're speaking, your words are softened by your tone of voice and facial expression. Plus, you can adjust your approach according to the feedback you get. Written communication, on the other hand, is stark and self-contained. If you hurt a person's feelings in writing, you can't soothe them right away. In fact, you may not even know that you've hurt anyone because the lack of feedback prevents you from seeing any reaction.

In addition to avoiding things that give offense, try to find things that might bring pleasure. Remember a co-worker's birthday, send a special note of thanks to a supplier who has done a good job, acknowledge someone's help, or send a clipping to a customer who has expressed interest in a subject. People remember the extra little things that indicate you care about them as individuals. In this impersonal age, the human touch is particularly effective.

Another simple but effective courtesy is to be prompt in your correspondence. If possible, answer your mail within two or three days. Or if you need more time to prepare a reply, write a brief note or call to say that you're working on an answer. Most people are willing to wait if they know how long the wait will be. What annoys them is the suspense.

Project the company's image

Although establishing the right tone for your audience should be your main goal, you must also give some thought to projecting the right image for your company. When you communicate with outsiders, on even the most routine matter, you serve as the spokesperson for your organization. The impression that you make can enhance or damage the reputation of the entire company. Thus your own views and personality must, at least to some extent, be subordinated to the interests and style of the company.

You can save yourself a great deal of time and frustration if you master the company style early in your career. In a typical corporation, 85 percent of the letters, memos, and reports are written by someone other than the higher-level managers who sign them. Most of the time, managers reject first drafts of these documents for stylistic reasons. In fact, the average draft goes through five revisions before it is finally approved.[6]

You might wonder whether all this effort to fine-tune the style of a message is worthwhile. But the fact is, people in business care very much about saying precisely the right thing in precisely the right way. Their willingness to go over the same document five times demonstrates just how important style really is.

CEO John Sculley wants Apple to recapture its image of innovation—an image it earned a decade ago with the Macintosh computer. To be seen as innovative, Apple will have to engineer another important breakthrough product. But a company's image is also projected through its employees. So whenever an employee speaks for the company, says Sculley, personal values must be aligned with company values.

SUMMARY

In a well-organized message, all the information is related to a clear subject and purpose, the ideas are presented in a logical order, and all necessary information is included. Good organization is important because it makes the message more effective and simplifies the communicator's job.

Organizing a message requires grouping ideas and deciding on the order of their presentation. The two basic organizational approaches are direct and indirect. With the direct approach, the main idea comes first; with the indirect approach, the main idea comes later. The indirect approach is best for people who are likely to react with skepticism or hostility to the message, but the direct approach is best in most other cases.

When you communicate, you establish a relationship with the audience. The success of the relationship depends on the tone, or overall impression, you create. Try to be both businesslike and likable; try to look at the subject through the audience's eyes. Emphasize positive ideas. Convey your credibility, and be courteous. Also remember that you represent your organization and must adjust your style to reflect its standards.

ON THE JOB:
Solving a Communication Dilemma at Drake Beam Morin

Drake Beam Morin's success in selling outplacement services rests squarely on its sensitivity to its clients' attitudes and needs. William J. Morin, chairman of the firm, points out that nobody likes to fire people: "Outplacement walks in the door and becomes a conscience-abating ingredient that helps management deal with a very unpleasant activity." Morin's clients want to make the termination process as easy as possible for both the dismissed employees and the company.

Drake Beam Morin satisfies that need. Like other leading outplacement firms, it has traditionally emphasized individual counseling for dismissed senior executives. The typical package includes psychological assessment, career counseling, resume preparation, advice on interview techniques, and access to computerized job listings. Although the outplacement industry focuses on higher-level managers, many firms also offer one- to six-day group programs for middle managers and clerical workers.

In addition to counseling terminated workers, Morin and his staff teach managers how to dismiss people. Most managers responsible for doing the firing are extremely uncomfortable with the role of "bad guy." They need help in handling the actual dismissal process and in coping with their guilt. Through lectures and role-playing exercises, Drake Beam Morin teaches these managers techniques for dealing with the dismissed workers' probable range of reactions. This training enables corporations to handle an extremely difficult situation with compassion, and it reduces the risk of lawsuits.

In addition, outplacement can save a company money by shortening the worker's job search and thus the corporation's severance payment obligations. With 35 offices across the country, Drake Beam Morin has a large network of "graduates" who, with the firm's help, have found responsible positions in major companies. When these executives need new employees, they often contact Drake Beam Morin. The job openings are entered into the firm's computerized job-lead data bank, which lists some 4,000 positions paying salaries of $30,000 and up. These contacts, combined with Drake Beam Morin's other services, enable the dismissed employees to find jobs more quickly than they could on their own. "We save about three months on the job search," says Morin.

A corporation also derives an important public relations benefit when it provides outplacement service for dismissed workers. Morin believes that by showing it cares about people, a company polishes its image and builds internal morale. Generally speaking, the survivors in a corporate layoff are apprehensive. Many of them identify more with their terminated co-workers than with the company. They worry that they might be the next to go if the company does not do well. Often, they are expected to assume additional duties or to take a pay cut until business improves. Under the circumstances, management needs all the help it can get in restoring confidence.

Since its inception in 1967, Drake Beam Morin has communicated the benefits of its services to countless clients and, in the process, has earned its position as the leading firm in the outplacement business. During that same period, it has helped thousands of executives cope with one of business's most difficult situations—the loss of a job.

Your Mission: You are a counselor at Drake Beam Morin. Since one of your responsibilities is to find new business for the firm, you are always on the lookout for opportunities to sell your services. Needless to say, you are interested when an article in the morning paper announces that a local corporation plans to reorganize two of its divisions in a cost-cutting move. The final paragraph of the article suggests that several senior executives will lose their jobs:

> While management would not comment on layoffs and terminations growing out of the announced reorganization, the company is reportedly seeking ways to reduce costs in order to improve bottom-line performance. In two previous reorganizations, the company reduced levels of management, merged departments, and laid off workers for up to six months. "We seek to trim operations in order to better compete in the international marketplace," said incoming president Bob Waters.

Based on the article, you decide to contact the company's vice president of human resources about the possibility of providing outplacement services. You quickly draft a letter to the local company. Here is a copy of your draft. Read it and then select the best response to the questions that follow.

Have you ever been fired? If so, you know how painful the experience can be. Many people never recover. They are pulled into a downward spiral of failure that ends in despair and ruin for both themselves and their families. The people responsible for the termination decision also suffer an emotional burden. As they watch their former colleagues deteriorate, they are plagued by guilt. Their loyalty to the company erodes, and their productivity suffers. Ultimately, they too may lose their jobs.

This painful cycle can be avoided. Although no one can make termination a pleasant experience, a professional outplacement firm such as Drake Beam Morin can mitigate the problems inherent in the process. Using our proven workshop format, we will teach your managers how to terminate their colleagues with compassion and sensitivity. And we will help the dismissed employees regain their confidence and self-respect. With the aid of our trained staff of professional outplacement counselors, the terminated employees will soon find new positions. Many will look back on their dismissal as being the best thing that ever happened to them. Their bitterness and hostility will be defused, and they will be less inclined to bring legal action against you.

If you would like to learn more about how we can assist you as you face the difficult ordeal ahead, please contact me at 555-7765. I will be happy to meet with you in person and discuss our fees, which generally equal approximately 15 percent of the terminated employees' annual salary.

1. What is the purpose of the letter? Is the purpose clear and appropriate?
   a. The purpose is unclear.
   b. The purpose is to obtain an appointment to call on the vice president of human resources. It is clear and appropriate.
   c. The purpose is to obtain a commitment from the vice president of human resources to retain Drake Beam Morin's outplacement services for the terminated executives. This is a clear and appropriate purpose.
   d. The purpose is to introduce the firm and explain its services. This is a clear and appropriate purpose.

2. Does the letter conform to the guidelines for good organization?
   a. No. The letter takes too long to get to the point. The opening question is too much of a gimmick; it establishes an emotional, unprofessional tone and does not provide any useful information. It should

be eliminated. The description of the problem is unnecessary, melodramatic, and vague. The dire picture should be replaced by a more specific reference to the company and its possible need for help in handling the termination process. The letter's main fault is that it leaves out necessary information about the specific benefits of Drake Beam Morin's services. The brief reference to benefits should be expanded into several paragraphs, one that focuses on benefits to terminated employees and one or two that present the benefits to the company. In addition, another paragraph should be added that gives a bit of background on Drake Beam Morin and refers the reader to an enclosed brochure. The final paragraph should request an appointment and mention that the firm will telephone to set a specific time. The reference to fees is premature and should be omitted.
   b. The letter is basically well organized, but some of the ideas are grouped and sequenced in an illogical manner. The opening paragraph should introduce Drake Beam Morin and describe its outplacement package. This should be followed by a reference to the newspaper article and a polite suggestion that the reader's company might need assistance. The third paragraph should provide information on financial arrangements, and the final paragraph should mention an enclosed brochure.
   c. The letter is very well organized. The purpose and subject are clear. All information is related to the subject and purpose. The ideas are grouped and presented in a logical way. All necessary information is included.

3. Does the letter do a good job of motivating the reader to hire Drake Beam Morin?
   a. Yes. By painting a vivid picture of the problem, the letter motivates the reader to hire Drake Beam Morin.
   b. No. By emphasizing the negative aspects of the termination situation, the letter arouses the reader's sense of guilt and, thus, his or her defenses. Instead of emphasizing the problem, the letter should focus on the positive aspects of outplacement counseling.

4. You decide to rewrite the draft. Your first step is to develop an outline. What should you use as the main idea of the letter?
   a. Executives who are terminated after devoting their lives to a company often suffer from severe depression; to avoid causing unnecessary suffering, the company should provide outplacement counseling.
   b. If the company is looking for an outplacement counseling service, Drake Beam Morin is the best choice.

c. The company should retain Drake Beam Morin because both the company and its terminated executives would benefit from the firm's outplacement service.

d. The company should retain Drake Beam Morin to help the company avoid legal action on the part of terminated employees.

5. What basic points can be used to develop the main idea?

   a. Companies that fail to provide outplacement counseling often suffer serious consequences: They inflict lasting pain on decent, competent people; they make their remaining managers feel guilty; they face the prospect of lawsuits; and they weaken the morale of the remaining employees. Therefore, the company should hire an outplacement firm. Drake Beam Morin is the leading outplacement firm. Compared with other outplacement firms, it has more experience, better resources, and a superior staff.

   b. Outplacement counseling involves a variety of services directed toward both the departing employees and the company that must terminate their employment. These services are expensive, but the cost is justified by the benefits. Drake Beam Morin is the finest outplacement firm in the country.

   c. Drake Beam Morin is the country's leading outplacement firm, with over 20 years of experience in outplacement counseling. The firm helps both the departing employees and the managers who must terminate their employment. Employees benefit from counseling in two ways: They adjust more easily to termination, and they find new jobs more quickly. The organization's managers also benefit: They feel less distressed about having to hurt their associates; they handle the termination process more smoothly and therefore minimize the threat of lawsuits; and they improve their image with remaining employees.

6. Which of the following would be the best way to support the claim that Drake Beam Morin's services are of practical value to the terminated employee?

   a. A series of three or four quotes from executives who have been helped by Drake Beam Morin

   b. A list of the services provided, followed by a statement that these services shorten a typical executive's job search by about three months

   c. A graph showing the number of executives that Drake Beam Morin has guided to new jobs over the past 20 years

   d. A description of the results achieved during a recent outplacement counseling assignment for a similar company

7. Which organizational plan should the letter follow?

   a. Indirect. Open with an attention-getting account of a company that botched the termination process and ended up losing several wrongful termination suits. Explain how Drake Beam Morin will train the company's managers to handle the termination process in a manner that will minimize the possibility of legal complications. Discuss the firm's fee structure. Close with a request for an appointment.

   b. Indirect. Briefly mention the potential client's problem. Indicate, in general, how Drake Beam Morin can be of service. Explain how outplacement counseling benefits the terminated employee. Follow this with a paragraph on the benefits the company will derive from providing this service. Provide some background on Drake Beam Morin and refer the reader to an enclosed brochure for further information. Close with a request for an appointment.

   c. Indirect. Describe how the termination process creates emotional problems for both the dismissed employee and the manager responsible for the termination. Explain how outplacement counseling can reduce these problems. Describe Drake Beam Morin and mention the enclosed brochure. Close with a discussion of costs and contract terms.

   d. Direct. Ask for an appointment to discuss the company's problem. Describe Drake Beam Morin and its services. Describe several of the firm's outplacement counseling assignments, choosing examples that are similar to the potential client's situation. Refer the reader to the enclosed brochure. Close by repeating your request for an appointment.

8. What is your relationship to the reader, and what does this imply about the "voice" you should use in the letter?

   a. Because the reader is a potential client, assume a position of deference. Use a passive, subordinate style.

   b. Because you are an expert in outplacement counseling and the reader lacks experience in this area, assume an authoritative position. Use a forceful style.

   c. Because both you and the reader are professional people interested in the welfare of the terminated employees, try to create a friendly, intimate relationship. Use a personal style.

   d. Strive for an objective, businesslike relationship aimed at addressing an emotional situation in a logical, rational manner. Use an impersonal, relatively colorless style.

9. What is the best way to build the reader's confidence in you?
   a. Provide some background about your education, experience, and position in Drake Beam Morin.
   b. Mention a mutual acquaintance in the field of human resources.
   c. Describe Drake Beam Morin's services in objective, concrete terms and rely on the firm's reputation to establish your credibility.
   d. Use bold, assertive language that emphasizes your self-confidence.[7]

QUESTIONS FOR DISCUSSION

1. Some people feel that cushioning bad news is manipulative. What do you think?
2. Do you agree that every message, regardless of its length, can be boiled down to a single main idea? Why or why not?
3. Why is it important to support major points with specific details?
4. What is the difference between the style and the tone of a business message?
5. Explain how you can reconcile these conflicting instructions: (a) "In all your correspondence, be yourself." (b) "In all your correspondence, keep the image of the company in mind."
6. Where does a company's style originate?

DOCUMENTS FOR ANALYSIS

DOCUMENT 4.A

Revise the following outline for an insurance information brochure, putting the information in a more logical sequence with appropriate subordination of ideas and parallel phrasing.

ACCIDENT PROTECTION INSURANCE PLAN
   I. Coverage is only pennies a day
   II. Benefit is $100,000 for accidental death on common carrier
   III. Benefit is $100 a day for hospitalization as a result of motor vehicle or common carrier accident
   IV. Benefit is $20,000 for accidental death in motor vehicle accident
   V. Individual coverage is only $17.85 per quarter; family coverage is just $26.85 per quarter
   VI. No physical exam or health questions
   VII. Convenient payment--billed quarterly
   VIII. Guaranteed acceptance for all applicants
   IX. No individual rate increases
   X. Free, no-obligation examination period
   XI. Cash paid in addition to any other insurance carried
   XII. Covers accidental death when riding as fare-paying passenger on public transportation, including buses, trains, jets, ships, trolleys, subways, or any other common carrier
   XIII. Covers accidental death in motor vehicle accidents occurring while driving or riding in or on automobile, truck, camper, motorhome, or nonmotorized bicycle

DOCUMENT 4.B

Read the following letter; then (1) analyze the strengths or weaknesses of each sentence and (2) revise the letter so that it follows this chapter's guidelines.

I am a new publisher with some really great books to sell. I saw your announcement in Publishers Weekly about the bookseller's show you're having this summer, and I think it's a great idea. Count me in, folks! I would like to get some space to show my books. I thought it would be a neat thing if I could do some airbrushing on T-shirts live to help promote my hot new title, T-Shirt Art. Before I got into publishing, I was an airbrush artist and I could demonstrate my techniques. I have done hundreds of advertising illustrations and have been a sign painter all my life, too, so I will also be promoting my other book, hot off the presses, How to Make Money in the Sign Painting Business.

I will be starting my PR campaign about May 1993 with ads in PW and some art trade papers, so my books should be well known by the time the show comes around in August. In case you would like to use my appearance there as part of your publicity, I have enclosed a biography and photo of myself.

P.S. Please let me know what it costs for booth space as soon as possible so that I can figure out if I can afford to attend. Being a new publisher is mighty expensive!

EXERCISES

1. The associate administrator of Mercy Hospital is preparing to recommend to the board of directors that a new heating system (called cogeneration) should be installed. He has the following information in his files:

   - History of the development of the cogeneration heating process
   - Scientific credentials of the developers of the process
   - Risks assumed in using this process
   - His plan for installing the equipment at Mercy Hospital
   - Stories about its successful use in comparable facilities
   - Specifications of the equipment that would be installed
   - Plans for disposing of the old heating equipment
   - Costs of installing and running the new equipment
   - Advantages and disadvantages of using the new process
   - Detailed ten-year cost projections
   - Estimates of the time needed to phase in the new heating system
   - Alternate systems that the board might wish to consider

   Help this administrator by eliminating from the list those topics that aren't essential; then arrange the other topics so that his report will give the board a clear understanding of the heating system and a balanced, concise justification for using it.

2. Indicate whether the direct or indirect approach would be best in each of the following situations, and briefly explain your reasoning:
   a. A letter asking when next year's automobiles will be put on sale locally
   b. A letter from a recent college graduate requesting a letter of recommendation from a former instructor
   c. A letter turning down a job applicant
   d. An announcement that, because of high air-conditioning costs, the plant temperature will be held at 78 degrees during the summer months

3. If you were trying to persuade someone to take the following actions, how would you organize your argument?
   a. You want your boss to approve your plan for hiring two new people.
   b. You want professional photographers to purchase your cameras.
   c. You want amateur photographers to purchase your cameras.
   d. You want to be hired for a job.

4. Rewrite the memo to Drake Beam Morin's potential client. (See this chapter's On-the-Job simulation.) You may invent any details that would enhance your message.[8]

5. Substitute inoffensive phrases for the following:
   a. you claim that
   b. it is not our policy to
   c. you neglected to
   d. it is our definite policy
   e. in which you assert
   f. we are sorry you are dissatisfied
   g. you failed to enclose
   h. we request that you send us
   i. if we are at fault
   j. apparently you overlooked our terms
   k. we hereby deny your claim
   l. we have been very patient
   m. we are at a loss to understand
   n. you forgot
   o. we will be forced to

6. Revise these sentences so that they are positive rather than negative:
   a. Unfortunately, your order cannot be sent until next week.
   b. To avoid the loss of your credit rating, please remit payment within ten days.
   c. You should have realized that waterbeds will freeze in unheated houses during winter months. Therefore, our guarantee does not cover the valve damage and you must pay the $9.50 valve-replacement fee (plus postage).

■ CHAPTER FIVE

After studying this chapter, you will be able to

- Edit a message for content and organization, style and readability, and mechanics and format
- Identify functional and content words and explain their qualities
- Choose the most correct and most effective words to make your point
- Balance simple, compound, and complex sentences to clarify the relationships among ideas and to make your writing interesting
- Write more effective sentences by using techniques of style
- Describe the elements of a paragraph
- Write and develop paragraphs in a variety of ways

REVISING BUSINESS MESSAGES

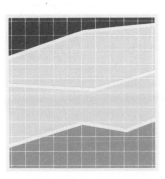

ON THE JOB:
Facing a Communication Dilemma at McDonald's
A Little More Polish on the Golden Arches, Please

If you hanker for a Big Mac, a Coke, and some fries, here's a job for you: being a quality control representative for McDonald's. David Giarla has been one for ten years, and he still loves the smell of Egg McMuffins in the morning. On a typical day, he visits seven or eight McDonald's, samples the food, inspects the kitchen, surveys the storeroom, and chats with the manager and employees. If he likes what he eats and sees, everybody breathes a sigh of relief and goes back to flipping burgers and wiping tables. But if the food, service, or facilities are not up to snuff, watch out. Giarla might file a negative report with head-quarters. And if enough negative reports pile up, McDonald's might cancel the franchisee's license.

Giarla's aim, however, is not to get people into trouble. On the contrary, he wants the store managers to succeed. He believes that by holding them to McDonald's high standards, he can help them build their businesses. When he spots a problem, he always points it out and gives the manager a chance to fix it before he files a negative report. His aim is to offer criticism in a diplomatic and constructive manner, and he usually succeeds.

Next time you're in a McDonald's, put yourself in Giarla's position. What would you tell the manager and employees to help them improve their operation? How would you phrase your suggestions? What words would you choose, and how would you arrange them in sentences and paragraphs?[1]

PRACTICING THE CRAFT OF REVISION

McDonald's

Whether offering criticism or praise, David Giarla understands that once you have completed the first draft of your message, you owe it to yourself and to your audience to review and refine it. In fact, many writing authorities suggest that you plan to go over a document at least three times: once for content and organization, once for style and readability, and once for mechanics and format. The letter in Figure 5.1 has been thoroughly revised, using proofreading marks. To review correction symbols, see Appendix D.

The basic editing principles discussed here apply to both written and oral communication. However, the steps involved in revising a speech or an oral presentation are slightly different, as Chapter 16 explains.

EDIT FOR CONTENT AND ORGANIZATION

Ideally, you should let your draft age a day or two before you begin the editing process; then you can approach the material with a fresh eye. As you get under way, read through the document quickly to evaluate its overall effectiveness. At this point, you are mainly concerned with content, organization, and flow. Compare the draft with your original plan. Have you covered all points in the most logical order? Is there a good balance between the general and the specific? Do the most important ideas receive the most space, and are they placed in the most prominent positions? Have you provided enough support and double-checked the facts? Would the message be more convincing if it were arranged in another sequence? Do you need to add anything?

On the other hand, what can you eliminate? In business, it's particularly important to weed out unnecessary material. Three-fourths of the executives who participated in one survey complained that most written messages are too long.[2] They are most likely to read documents that efficiently say what needs to be said.

In the first phase of editing, spend a few extra moments on the beginning and ending of the message. These sections have the greatest impact on the audience. Be sure that the opening of a letter or memo is relevant, interesting, and geared to the reader's probable reaction. In longer messages, check to see that the first few paragraphs establish the subject, purpose, and organization of the material. Review the conclusion to be sure it summarizes the main idea and leaves the audience with a positive impression.

Michael D. Eisner, chairman and CEO of the Walt Disney Company, appears to be the perfect heir of Walt Disney himself, possessing childlike enthusiasm, charisma, and creativity. But his detail-oriented business sense is apparent too. For Eisner, careful review and revision of budgets, reports, and long-term strategic growth proposals is critical to running a company.

EDIT FOR STYLE AND READABILITY

Once you are satisfied with the content and structure of the message, turn your attention to its style and readability. Ask yourself whether you have achieved the right tone for your audience. Look for opportunities to make the material more interesting through the use of lively words and phrases.

At the same time, be particularly conscious of whether your message is clear and readable. You want the audience to understand you with a minimum of effort. Check your vocabulary and sentence structure to be sure you are relying mainly on familiar terms and simple, direct statements. Ask yourself whether you have effectively highlighted the important information. Are your sentences easy to decipher? Do your paragraphs have clear topic sentences? Are the transitions between ideas obvious?

FIGURE 5.1
Sample Revised Letter

Content and organization: In the first paragraph, stick to the point, the main idea. In the middle, highlight the key advantage of the frequent-guest program, and discuss details in subsequent paragraphs. Eliminate redundancies.

Style and readability: Reword to stress the "you" viewpoint. Clarify the relationship among ideas through placement and combination of phrases. Moderate the excessive enthusiasm, and eliminate words (such as "amenities") that may be unfamiliar.

Mechanics and format: To prevent confusion, spell out the abbreviated phrase "FG." Fix typos, as in "advantage."

November 12, 1993

Miss Louise Wilson
Corporate Travel Department
Brother's Electric Corp.
2300 Wacker Drive
Chicago, IL 60670

Dear Miss Wilson:

Thank you for your interest in the frequent-guest program at the Commerce Hotel. We are delighted to hear that the people at Brother's Electric are thinking about joining. Incidentally, we are planning a special Thanksgiving weekend rate, so keep that in mind in case you happen to be in Chicago for the Holiday.

The enclosed brochure explains the details of the frequent-guest program. As a corporate member, Brother's Electric will be entitled to a 20 percent discount on all rooms and services. Use the enclosed ID card whenever you make reservations with us to obtain your corporate discount. Your executives will receive special courtesy, including free use of the health club. Organizations enrolled in the frequent-guest program also qualify for discounts on convention facilities and banquet rooms. We hope you and your company will take advantage of these facilities the next time you book a convention. If you have any questions, please feel free to call me personally. I will be happy to answer them.

Sincerely,

Mary Cortez
Account Representative

In addition, give some thought to the visual presentation of the message; people have trouble comprehending long, uninterrupted pages of text. By using headings, indented lists, boldface type, and white space, you can provide visual clues to the importance of various ideas and their relationships. These clues will help the reader grasp the message more easily, particularly if it exceeds a page or two.

EDIT FOR MECHANICS AND FORMAT

The final step is to edit the document so that it's letter-perfect. Although such things as grammar, spelling, punctuation, and typographical errors may seem trivial to you, your readers will view your attention to detail as a sign of your professionalism. If you let mechanical errors slip through, people automatically wonder whether you're unreliable in more important ways. You might want to

Credibility is affected by your attention to the details of mechanics and format.

BEHIND THE SCENES AT THE LA JOLLA PLAYHOUSE
Greasepaint, Bright Lights, and Rewrites

On a typical midseason day at the La Jolla Playhouse, while the actors are rehearsing and the directors, composers, and designers are discussing endless set, score, and costume details, Constance Harvey is likely to be holed up in her office at a computer terminal, writing. No, she's not a playwright, but her job is almost as important to the internationally acclaimed regional theater. Harvey is the theater's publicist, and without the material she writes, the Playhouse could easily slip from public view. Harvey writes nearly every word the theater sends to reviewers, reporters, entertainment editors, television journalists, potential donors, and season subscribers. Her challenge is to attract local and national media attention to reach audiences, critics, and theater artists.

Every season is an eclectic mix of plays that might include anything from a period comedy performed by clown Bill Irwin to a musical by British rockers Ray Davies (*80 Days*) or Pete Townshend (*Tommy*)—and Harvey must capture the mood of each production. For example, the press release she wrote for Tennessee Williams's *The Glass Menagerie* de-

manded a quiet feeling, whereas her announcements about the performances of the wacky Flying Karamazov Brothers required a kind of verbal free-fall. In addition, Harvey's copy must be full of information for calendar event editors—names, dates, times, locations, and so forth—and her copy must have appealing, pithy phrases that magazine editors can easily lift and use as two- or three-line descriptions of a play. When successful, her writing stirs interest and has a direct effect on ticket sales, donations, and future productions.

To accomplish all this, Harvey begins with an inflated first draft, which includes everything. Her ultimate objective is simplicity and completeness, but she's not afraid to be abstract and colorful—like her subject matter. The first draft goes to her assistant, who reads it for content. "I have two questions for that person," says Harvey, "Does it make sense, and what have I left out?" As she revises that first draft, Harvey keeps her assistant's comments in mind, but she also tries to anticipate the questions that might be asked by some of the theater critics who make up her

refresh your memory of the details of grammar and usage by reviewing Appendix A.

Also give some attention to the finer points of format. Have you followed accepted conventions and company guidelines for laying out the document on the page? Have you included all the traditional elements that belong in documents of the type you are creating? Have you been consistent in handling margins, page numbers, headings, exhibits, source notes, and other details? To resolve questions about format and layout, see Appendix B.

SELECTING THE RIGHT WORDS

The two key aspects of word choice are
- Correctness
- Effectiveness

As a business communicator, you have two things to worry about in choosing and revising your words: correctness and effectiveness. Correctness is generally the easier of the two qualities to achieve, particularly if you have heard "good" English all your life. Without even thinking about grammar and usage, you will generally know what's correct; the words will sound "right" to you. But sometimes you may stumble over an unusual situation. Editors and grammarians themselves occasionally have questions—and even disputes—about correct usage.[3]

primary audience. They are very important to the Playhouse, and over the years, Harvey has learned their needs and preferences. If her releases don't supply enough background about a play or an artist, or if her facts aren't straight, these critics call and let her know. Harvey also solicits input from the theater's associate artistic director, who gives her feedback on whether or not the press release falls in line with a production's artistic concept.

When she is finally satisfied with her second draft, she is ready to "proof it to death." She looks for errors in grammar and punctuation and reads the words aloud to test the rhythm. "To me, that's a dead giveaway," Harvey explains. "If the rhythm is off, then I don't know what I'm talking about, or I've missed the point. And if I've missed the point, then I'm not going to be able to convey it." She also makes sure she hasn't repeated a word too often. "There are only so many ways you can say *production*, and if I've said it already four or five times in the three preceding lines, it has to go." At the same time, she watches for passive voice. She has a bad habit of burying verbs in sentences, covering up more active and more interesting phrases.

"One of my rules of proofing is that three people have to see it, because I don't trust myself. I'm too familiar with the copy and the content." Nevertheless, embarrassing mistakes do slip by. Early in Harvey's career, no one noticed that the names of the producer and the artistic director were missing from a program's title page—until hours before the presses were scheduled to run. In the ensuing uproar, Harvey phoned the printer, who said it was too late for changes. She insisted, threatening to throw herself on the printing press if he didn't acquiesce. Eventually, he did add the missing names, albeit in the wrong places. Now Harvey keeps a special watch for mistakes in the standard boilerplate copy that everyone takes for granted.

APPLY YOUR KNOWLEDGE

1. To demonstrate that writing can almost always be improved, select an article on any subject from a newspaper or magazine. Use a colored highlighter to mark words you would exchange for more colorful, more precise, or less biased words. List your revisions on a separate sheet. Now rewrite any sentences that could be enlivened by a more active voice. Finally, look for paragraphs that could be shortened or simplified without losing meaning.

2. One of the most frustrating problems business writers face is having their words and work misunderstood. However, the problems that cause misunderstandings can lie with the writer as well as with the reader. List the steps you can take to avoid uttering, "But that's not what I meant!" when readers misinterpret your work.

Vaughn Beals, CEO of Harley-Davidson, turned his company around by revising design, work flow, quality, and service. His close attention to detail improved his product's image, and so it is with communication. When you're striving for high-quality, error-free messages, you do a lot of revising.

The "rules" of grammar are constantly changing to reflect changes in the way people speak. So if you have doubts about what is correct, don't be lazy. Look up the answer and use the proper form of expression. And if you suspect that your ear for correct usage is not particularly good, check the grammar and usage guide in this book or any number of special reference books available in libraries and bookstores. Most authorities agree on the basic conventions.

Just as important as using the correct words is choosing the best words for the job at hand. Word effectiveness is generally more difficult to achieve than correctness, particularly in written communication. Professional writers have to work at their craft, using what you might call tricks of the trade to improve their writing style. In the rest of this chapter, you will learn some of these techniques.

FUNCTIONAL WORDS AND CONTENT WORDS

Words can be divided into two categories: functional and content. Functional words express relationships and have only one unchanging meaning in any given context. They include conjunctions, prepositions, articles, and pronouns. Your main concern with functional words is to use them correctly.

Content words, on the other hand, are multidimensional and, therefore, subject to various interpretations. Nouns, verbs, adjectives, and adverbs are in this category. These are the words that carry the meaning of the sentence. They are the building blocks; the functional words are the mortar. In the following sentence, all the content words are in italics:

> *Some objective observers* of the *cookie market give Nabisco* the *edge* in *quality*, but *Frito-Lay is lauded* for *superior distribution*.

Both functional words and content words are necessary, but your effectiveness as a communicator depends largely on your ability to choose the right content words for your message. So let's take a closer look at two important dimensions for classifying content words.

Connotation and denotation

As you know from reading Chapter 1, content words have both a denotative and a connotative meaning. The denotative meaning is the literal, or dictionary, meaning; the connotative meaning includes all the associations and feelings evoked by the word.

Some words have more connotations than others. If you say that a person has failed to pass the test, you're making a strong statement; you suggest that she or he is inferior, incompetent, second-rate. But if you say that the person has achieved a score of 65 percent, you suggest something else. By replacing the word *failed*, you avoid a heavy load of negative connotations.

In business communication, you should generally use terms that are low in connotative meaning. Words that have relatively few possible interpretations are less likely to be misunderstood. Furthermore, because you are generally trying to deal with things in an objective, rational manner, you should avoid emotion-laden comments.

Abstraction and concreteness

In addition to varying in connotative impact, content words also vary in their level of abstraction. An abstract word expresses a concept, quality, or characteristic instead of standing for a thing you can touch or see. Abstractions are usually broad, encompassing a category of ideas. They are often intellectual, academic, or philosophical. For example, *love, honor, progress, tradition,* and *beauty* are abstractions. Concrete terms, on the other hand, are anchored in the tangible, material world. They stand for something particular: *chair, table, horse, rose, kick, kiss, red, green, two*. These words are direct and vivid, clear and exact.

You might suppose that concrete words are better than abstract words because they are more precise. But imagine trying to talk about business without referring to such concepts as *morale, productivity, profits, motivation,* and *guarantees*. Abstractions are indispensable, but they are also troublesome. They tend to be fuzzy, subject to many interpretations. They also tend to be boring. It isn't always easy to become excited about ideas, especially if they are unrelated to concrete experience. The best way to minimize the problem is to blend abstract terms with concrete ones, the general with the specific. State the concept; then pin it down with details expressed in more concrete terms. Save the abstractions for ideas that cannot be expressed any other way. For example, instead of referring to "a sizable loss," talk about "a loss of

---

Functional words (conjunctions, prepositions, articles, and pronouns) express relationships among content words (nouns, verbs, adjectives, and adverbs).

Content words have both a denotative (dictionary) meaning and a connotative (associative) meaning.

The more abstract a word, the more it is removed from the tangible, objective world of things that can be perceived with the senses.

In business communication, use concrete, specific terms whenever possible; use abstractions only when necessary.

$32 million." Or in David Giarla's case, instead of referring only to McDonald's principles of operation, he should talk about specifics such as fast service, good food, and clean facilities.

WORD CHOICE

Wordsmiths are journalists, public relations specialists, editors, letter and report writers—anyone who earns a living by crafting words. Unlike poets, novelists, or dramatists, wordsmiths do not try for creative effects. They are mainly concerned with being clear, concise, and accurate in their use of language. To reach this goal, they emphasize words that are strong, familiar, and short, and they avoid hiding them under unnecessary extra syllables. When you edit your message, try to think like a wordsmith.

Strong words

Nouns and verbs are the most concrete words in any message, so use them as much as you can. Although adjectives and adverbs obviously have parts to play, use them sparingly. They often call for subjective judgments, and business communication should be objective. Verbs are especially powerful because they carry the action; they tell what's happening in the sentence. The more dynamic and specific the verb, the better.

Dan Rather is managing editor and anchor of *CBS Evening News.* Along with three others, he writes and heavily revises each evening's newscast right up to air time. Rather is noted for his concern over each word he uses.

AVOID WEAK PHRASES	USE STRONG WORDS
wealthy businessperson	tycoon
business prosperity	boom
fall	plummet

Familiar words

You will communicate best with words that are familiar to your readers. But bear in mind that words familiar to one reader could be unfamiliar to another:

AVOID UNFAMILIAR WORDS	USE FAMILIAR WORDS
ascertain	find out, learn
consummate	close, bring about
peruse	read, study

Although familiar words are generally the best choice, beware of terms so common that they have become virtually meaningless. Readers tend to slide right by such clichés as these:

interface	time frame	strategic decision
track record	frame of reference	dialogue
viable	prioritize	scenario

Technical or professional terms should also be handled with care. Used in moderation, they add precision and authority to a message. But many people simply do not understand them, and even a technically sophisticated audience

As senior vice president of technology and president of engineered materials research at Allied-Signal, Mary L. Good has both business savvy and scientific knowledge. She is also highly skilled at translating scientific jargon into plain English, a valuable asset in the business world.

will be lulled to sleep by too many. Let your audience's vocabulary be your guide. If they share a particular jargon, you may enhance your credibility by speaking their language.

Short words

Make an effort to use short words. Because they're more vivid and easier to read, they tend to communicate better than long words.

AVOID LONG WORDS	USE SHORT WORDS
During the preceding year, the company was able to accelerate productive operations.	Last year, the company was able to speed up operations.
The action was predicated on the assumption that the company was operating at a financial deficit.	The action was based on the belief that the company was losing money.

Camouflaged verbs

Watch for these endings in the words you use: *-ion, -tion, -ing, -ment, -ant, -ent, -ence, -ance,* and *-ency*. Most of them change verbs into nouns and adjectives. In effect, the words that result are camouflaged verbs. Get rid of them and strengthen your writing:

AVOID CAMOUFLAGED VERBS	USE VERBS
The manager undertook implementation of the rules.	The manager implemented the rules.
Verification of the shipments occurs weekly.	Shipments are verified weekly.

BIAS-FREE WRITING

Avoid biased language that might offend the audience.

Most of us like to think of ourselves as being sensitive, unbiased, and fair. But being fair and objective isn't enough; you must also *appear* to be fair.[4] The following suggestions will help you avoid embarrassing blunders with language related to gender, race and ethnic group, age, and disability.

Sexist language

For many years, the word *man* was used to denote humanity, describing a human being of either gender and any age. Today, however, *man* is associated more with an adult, male human being. The fact that some of the most commonly used words contain the word *man* creates a problem, but some simple solutions exist:

UNACCEPTABLE	PREFERABLE
mankind	humanity, human beings, human race, people
if a man drove	if a person (or someone or a driver)
man-made	artificial, synthetic, manufactured, constructed

manpower	human power, human energy, workers, work force
businessman	business executive, business manager, businessperson
salesman	sales representative, salesperson, salesclerk
insurance man	insurance agent
foreman	supervisor

Replace words that inaccurately exclude women or men.

Avoid using female-gender words such as *authoress* and *actress; author* and *actor* denote both women and men. Similarly, avoid special designations such as *woman doctor* or *male nurse*. Use the same label for everyone in a particular group. For example, don't refer to a woman as a *chairperson*, then call the man a *chairman*.

The pronoun *he* has also traditionally been used to refer to both males and females. Here are some simple ways to avoid this outdated usage:

UNACCEPTABLE	PREFERABLE
The average worker . . . he	The average worker . . . he or she
The typical professional athlete spends four hours a day practicing his sport.	Most professional athletes spend four hours a day practicing their sport.

Certain roles should not always be identified with a specific gender:

UNACCEPTABLE	PREFERABLE
the consumer . . . she	consumers . . . they
the nurse/teacher . . . she	nurses/teachers . . . they

If you are discussing categories of people such as bosses and office workers, avoid referring to the boss as *he* and the office worker as *she*. Instead, reword sentences so that you can either use *they* or use no pronoun at all. In today's business world, it's appropriate to sometimes use *she* when referring to a boss and *he* when referring to an office worker.

Another way to avoid bias is to make sure you don't always mention men first. Vary the traditional pattern with *women and men, gentlemen and ladies, she and he, her and his.*

Finally, identify women by their own names, not by their role or marital status—unless it is appropriate to the context:

UNACCEPTABLE	PREFERABLE
Phil Donahue and Marlo	Phil Donahue and Marlo Thomas
Phil Donahue and Ms. Thomas	Mr. Donahue and Ms. Thomas

The preferred title for women in business is Ms., unless the individual asks to be addressed as Miss or Mrs. or has some other title, such as Dr.

Racial and ethnic bias

Eliminate references that reinforce racial or ethnic stereotypes.

The guidelines for avoiding racial and ethnic bias are much the same as those for avoiding gender bias. The main rule is to avoid language suggesting that members of a racial or ethnic group have the same stereotypical characteristics:

UNACCEPTABLE	PREFERABLE
disadvantaged black children	children from lower-income families
Jim Wong is an unusually tall Asian.	Jim Wong is tall.

The best solution is to avoid identifying people by race or ethnic origin unless such a label is relevant:

UNACCEPTABLE	PREFERABLE
Mario M. Cuomo, Italian-American governor of New York	Mario M. Cuomo, governor of New York

Age bias

Avoid references to an individual's age or physical limitations.

As with gender, race, and ethnic background, mention the age of a person only when it is relevant:

UNACCEPTABLE	PREFERABLE
Mary Kirazy, 58, has just joined our trust department.	Mary Kirazy has just joined our trust department.

In referring to older people, avoid such stereotyped adjectives as *spry* and *frail*.

Disability bias

There is really no painless label for people with a physical, mental, sensory, or emotional impairment. However, if you must refer to such individuals in terms of their limitations, call them *disabled* instead of *handicapped*, *crippled*, or *retarded*.

UNACCEPTABLE	PREFERABLE
Crippled workers face many barriers on the job.	Disabled workers face many barriers on the job.

Most of all, avoid mentioning disability unless it is pertinent. When it is pertinent, present the whole person, not just the disability, by showing the limitation in an unobtrusive manner:

UNACCEPTABLE	PREFERABLE
An epileptic, Tracy has no trouble doing her job.	Tracy's epilepsy has no effect on her job performance.

The goal is to abandon stereotyped assumptions about what a person can do or will do and to focus on an individual's unique characteristics.

CREATING EFFECTIVE SENTENCES

Although looking at individual words is important, you cannot revise your work effectively until you consider each word in relation to a particular sentence. What can you do to improve *Jill, receptionist, the, smiles,* and *at*? These words don't make much sense until they are combined in a sentence to express a complete thought: "Jill smiles at the receptionist." Then you can begin to explore the possibilities for improvement, looking at how well each word performs its particular function. The nouns and noun equivalents are the topics, or subjects, about which something is being said; the verbs and related words, or predicates, make a statement about the subjects. In a more complicated sentence, adjectives and adverbs modify the statement, and various connectors hold the words together.

Every sentence contains a subject (noun or noun equivalent) and a predicate (verb and related words).

THE THREE TYPES OF SENTENCES

Sentences come in three basic varieties: simple, compound, and complex. A simple sentence has a single subject and a single predicate, although it may be expanded by modifying phrases and by nouns and pronouns serving as objects of the action. Here's a typical example, with the subject underlined once and the predicate verb underlined twice:

Profits have increased in the past year.

A compound sentence expresses two or more independent but related thoughts of equal importance, joined by *and, but,* or *or*. In effect, a compound sentence is a merger of two or more simple sentences (independent clauses) that deal with the same basic idea. For example:

Wage rates have declined by 5 percent, and employee turnover has been high.

To give your writing variety, use the three types of sentences:
- Simple
- Compound
- Complex

The independent clauses in a compound sentence are always separated by a comma or by a semicolon (in which case the conjunction—*and, but, or*—is dropped).

A complex sentence expresses one main thought (the independent clause) and one or more subordinate thoughts (dependent clauses) related to it, often separated by a comma. The subordinate thought, which comes first in the following sentence, could not stand alone:

Although you may question the conclusions, you must admit that the research is thorough.

In constructing a sentence, use the form that best fits the thought you want to express. The structure of the sentence should match the relationship of the ideas. For example, if you have two ideas of equal importance, they should be expressed as two simple sentences or as one compound sentence. But if one of the ideas is less important than the other, it should be placed in a dependent clause to form a complex sentence. This compound sentence uses a conjunction to join two ideas that aren't truly equal:

The chemical products division is the strongest in the company, and its management techniques should be adopted by the other divisions.

In the complex sentence that follows, the first thought has been made subordinate to the second. Notice how much more effective the second idea is when the cause-and-effect relationship has been established:

Because the chemical products division is the strongest in the company, its management techniques should be adopted by the other divisions.

In complex sentences, the placement of the dependent clause should be geared to the relationship between the ideas expressed. If you want to emphasize the idea, put the dependent clause at the end of the sentence (the most emphatic position) or at the beginning (the second most emphatic position). If you want to downplay the idea, bury the dependent clause within the sentence:

Most Emphatic:	The handbags are manufactured in Mexico, *which has lower wage rates than the United States.*
Emphatic:	*Because wage rates are lower there*, the handbags are manufactured in Mexico.
Least Emphatic:	Mexico, *which has lower wage rates*, was selected as the production site for the handbags.

The most effective writing balances all three sentence types. If you use too many simple sentences, you cannot properly express the relationship among ideas. On the other hand, if you use too many long, compound sentences, your writing will sound monotonous. Moreover, an uninterrupted series of complex sentences is hard to follow.

SENTENCE STYLE

Whether a sentence is simple, compound, or complex, it should be grammatically correct, efficient, readable, interesting, and appropriate for the audience. In general, you should strive for straightforward simplicity. For most business audiences, clarity and efficiency take precedence over literary style. The following guidelines will help you achieve these qualities in your own writing.

Keep sentences short

Break long sentences into shorter ones to improve readability.

Long sentences are usually harder to understand than short sentences because they are packed with information that must all be absorbed at once. Most business writing should therefore have an average sentence length of 20 words or fewer. This figure is the average, not a ceiling. To be interesting, your writing should contain both longer and shorter sentences.

Long sentences are especially well suited for grouping or combining ideas, listing points, and summarizing or previewing information. Medium-length sentences (those with about 20 words) are useful for showing the relationships among ideas. And short sentences are tailor-made for emphasizing important information.

Rely on the active voice

Active sentences are generally preferable to passive sentences because they are easier to understand.[5] The subject (the "actor") comes before the verb, and the object of the sentence (the "acted upon") follows it: "John rented the office." When the sentence is passive, the subject follows the verb and the object precedes it: "The office was rented by John." As you can see, the passive verb combines the helping verb *to be* with a form of the verb that is usually similar to the past tense. Use of passive verbs makes sentences longer and de-emphasizes the subject. Active verbs produce shorter, stronger sentences:

AVOID PASSIVE SENTENCES	USE ACTIVE SENTENCES
Sales were increased by 32 percent last month.	Sales increased by 32 percent last month.
The new procedure is thought by the president to be superior.	The president thinks the new procedure is superior.

However, using the passive voice makes sense in some situations. For example, when you want to be diplomatic in pointing out a problem or an error of some kind, you might say, "The shipment was lost" as opposed to "You lost the shipment." In this case, the passive version seems less like an accusation; the emphasis is on the problem of the lost shipment rather than on the person responsible for the loss. Similarly, if you want to point out what's being done without taking or attributing either the credit or the blame, you might say something like "The production line is being analyzed to determine the source of problems." Passive verbs are also useful when you are trying to avoid personal pronouns and create an objective tone. For example, in a formal report, you might say, "Criteria have been established for evaluating capital expenditures."

Eliminate unnecessary words and phrases

Some words and combinations of words are unnecessary, others are repetitious, and some have one-word equivalents. Legalistic language is a frequent offender: "This is to inform you that we have" (*We have* is enough); "for the sum of" (*for*); "in the event that" (*if*); "on the occasion of" (*on*); "prior to the start of" (*before*). Redundancy is a somewhat less serious flaw: "Visible to the eye" (*visible* is enough—nothing can be visible to the ear); "surrounded on all sides" (*surrounded* implies on all sides). Relative pronouns such as *who*, *that*, and *which* frequently cause clutter, and sometimes even articles are excessive (mostly too many *the*'s).

However, well-placed relative pronouns and articles serve an important function by preventing confusion. For example, without *that*, the following sentence is ambiguous:

Confusing:	The project manager told the engineers last week the specifications were changed.
Clear:	The project manager told the engineers last week *that* the specifications were changed.
Clear:	The project manager told the engineers *that* last week the specifications were changed.

Here are some more ways to prune your prose:

POOR	IMPROVED
consensus of opinion	consensus
at this point in time	at this time, now
irregardless	(no such word; use *regardless*)
each and every	(either word but not both)
due to the fact that	because
at an early date	soon (or a specific date)
at the present time	now
in view of the fact that	since, because
until such time as	when
we are of the opinion	we believe
with reference to	about
as a result of	because
for the month of December	for December

Avoid needless repetition.

In general, be on the lookout for the needless repetition of words or ideas. For example, try not to string together a series of sentences that all start with the same word or words, and avoid repeating the same word too often within a given sentence. Take a close look at double modifiers. Do you really need to say *modern, up-to-date equipment*, or would *modern equipment* do the job?

Use infinitives to replace some phrases.

Another way to save words is to use infinitives in place of some phrases. This technique not only shortens your sentences but makes them clearer as well:

POOR	IMPROVED
In order to be a successful writer, you must work hard.	To be a successful writer, you must work hard.
He went to the library for the purpose of studying.	He went to the library to study.
The employer increased salaries so that she could improve morale.	The employer increased salaries to improve morale.

Avoid obsolete and pompous language

Obsolete formal phrases can obscure meaning.

The language of business used to be much more formal than it is today, and a few out-of-date phrases remain from the old days. Perhaps the best way to eliminate them is to ask yourself: "Would I say this if I were talking face-to-face with someone?"

OBSOLETE	UP-TO-DATE
as per your letter	as in your letter (do not mix Latin and English)
hoping to hear from you soon, I remain	(omit)

yours of the 15th	your letter of June 15
awaiting your reply, we are	(omit)
in due course	today, tomorrow (or a specific time or date)
permit me to say that	(permission is not necessary; just say what you wish)
we are in receipt of	we have received
pursuant to	(omit)
in closing, I'd like to say	(omit)
attached herewith is	here is
the undersigned	I; me
kindly advise	please let us know
under separate cover	in another envelope; by parcel post
we wish to inform you	(just say it)
attached please find	enclosed is
it has come to my attention	I have just learned; Ms. Garza has just told me
our Mr. Lydell	Mr. Lydell, our credit manager
please be advised that	(omit)

The use of pompous language suggests that you are a pompous person.

Being a good communicator, McDonald's David Giarla understands that pompous language detracts from a clear message. Like out-of-date phrases, it sounds stiff, puffed up, and roundabout. People are likely to use pompous language when they are trying to impress somebody. In hopes of sounding imposing, they use big words, trite expressions, and overly complicated sentences:

POOR

Upon procurement of additional supplies, I will initiate fulfillment of your order.

IMPROVED

I will fill your order when I receive more supplies.

Moderate your enthusiasm

Business writing shouldn't be gushy.

An occasional adjective or adverb intensifies and emphasizes your meaning, but too many ruin your writing:

POOR

We are extremely pleased to offer you a position on our staff of exceptionally skilled and highly educated employees. The work offers extraordinary challenges and a very large salary.

IMPROVED

We are pleased to offer you a position on our staff of skilled and well-educated employees. The work offers challenges and an attractive salary.

Break up strung-out sentences

In many cases, the parts of a compound sentence should be separated into two sentences.

A strung-out sentence is a series of two or more sentences unwisely connected by *and*—in other words, a compound sentence taken too far. You can often improve your writing style by separating the string into individual sentences.

POOR	IMPROVED
The magazine will be published January 1, and I'd better meet the deadline if I want my article included.	The magazine will be published January 1. I'd better meet the deadline if I want my article included.

Avoid hedging sentences

Don't be afraid to present your opinions without qualification.

Sometimes you have to write *may* or *seems* to avoid stating a judgment as a fact. But when you have too many such hedges, particularly several in a sentence, you aren't really saying anything:

POOR	IMPROVED
I believe that Mr. Johnson's employment record seems to show that he may be capable of handling the position.	Mr. Johnson's employment record shows that he is capable of handling the position.

Watch for indefinite pronoun starters

Avoid starting sentences with *it* and *there*.

If you start a sentence with an indefinite pronoun (an expletive) such as *it* or *there*, odds are that the sentence could be shorter:

POOR	IMPROVED
It would be appreciated if you would sign the lease today.	Please sign the lease today.
There are five employees in this division who were late to work today.	Five employees in this division were late to work today.

Express parallel ideas in parallel form

When you use the same grammatical pattern to express two or more ideas, you show that they are comparable thoughts.

When you have two or more similar (parallel) ideas to express, try to present them in the same grammatical pattern. The repetition of the pattern tells readers that the ideas are comparable, and it adds a nice rhythm to your message. In the following examples, parallel construction makes the sentences more readable:

POOR	IMPROVED
Mr. Simms had been drenched with rain, bombarded with telephone calls, and his boss shouted at him.	Mr. Simms had been drenched with rain, bombarded with telephone calls, and shouted at by his boss.
Ms. Reynolds dictated the letter, and next she signed it and left the office.	Ms. Reynolds dictated the letter, signed it, and left the office.

Parallelism can be achieved through a repetition of words, phrases, clauses, or entire sentences:

Parallel Words:	The letter was approved by Clausen, Whittaker, Merlin, and Carlucci.
Parallel Phrases:	We have beaten the competition in supermarkets, in department stores, and in specialty stores.
Parallel Clauses:	I'd like to discuss the issue after Vicki gives her presentation but before Marvin shows his slides.
Parallel Sentences:	In 1991 we exported 30 percent of our production. In 1992 we exported 50 percent.

Eliminate awkward pointers

Tell readers exactly where you want them to look.

To save words, business writers sometimes direct their readers' attention elsewhere with such expressions as *the above-mentioned, as mentioned above, the aforementioned, the former, the latter,* and *respectively.* These words cause the reader to jump from one point in the message to another, a process that hinders effective communication. A better approach is to be specific in your references, even if you must add a few more words:

| POOR | IMPROVED |
| Typewriter ribbons for legal secretaries and beginning clerks are distributed by the law office and stenographic office, respectively. | Typewriter ribbons for legal secretaries are distributed by the law office; those for beginning clerks are distributed by the stenographic office. |

Correct dangling modifiers

Make sure that modifier phrases are really related to the subject of the sentence.

Sometimes a modifier is not just an adjective or adverb but rather an entire phrase defining a noun or verb. You must be careful to construct your sentences so that this type of modifier refers to something in the main part of the sentence in a way that makes sense. For example:

Walking to the office, a red sports car passed her.

The way this sentence is constructed, it implies that the red sports car has the office and the legs to walk there. The modifier is said to be dangling because it has no real connection to the subject of the sentence—in this case, the sports car. This is what the writer is trying to say:

A red sports car passed her while she was walking to the office.

Flipping the clauses produces another correct sentence:

While she was walking to the office, a red sports car passed her.

Dangling modifiers make sentences confusing and ridiculous:

POOR

Working as fast as possible, the budget soon was ready.

After a three-week slump, we increased sales.

IMPROVED

Working as fast as possible, the committee soon had the budget ready.

After a three-week slump, sales increased.

Passive construction is often the cause of dangling modifiers.

The first example shows one frequent cause of dangling modifiers: passive construction in the independent clause. When the clause is made active instead of passive, the connection with the modifier becomes more obvious.

Avoid long sequences of nouns

Stringing together a series of nouns may save a little space, but it causes confusion.

When nouns are strung together as modifiers, the resulting sentence is hard to read. You can clarify the sentence by putting some of the nouns in a modifying phrase. Although you are adding a few more words, your audience won't have to work as hard to understand the sentence.

POOR

The window sash installation company will give us an estimate on Friday.

IMPROVED

The company that installs window sashes will give us an estimate on Friday.

Keep words together that work together

Subject and predicate should be placed as close together as possible, as should modifiers and the words they modify.

To avoid confusing readers, keep the subject and predicate of a sentence as close together as possible. Otherwise, readers will have to read your sentence twice to figure out who did what:

POOR

A 10 percent decline in market share, which resulted from quality problems and an aggressive sales campaign by Armitage, the market leader in the Northeast, was the major problem in 1992.

IMPROVED

The major problem in 1992 was a 10 percent loss of market share, which resulted from both quality problems and an aggressive sales campaign by Armitage, the market leader in the Northeast.

The same rule applies to other parts of speech. Adjectives, adverbs, and prepositional phrases usually make the most sense when they are placed as close as possible to the words they modify:

POOR

We will deliver the pipe soon that you ordered last Tuesday.

IMPROVED

We will soon deliver the pipe that you ordered last Tuesday.

Emphasize key thoughts

In every message, some ideas are more important than others. You can emphasize these key ideas through your sentence style. One obvious technique is to give important points the most space. When you want to call attention to a thought, use extra words to describe it. Take this sentence, for example:

The chairman of the board called for a vote of the shareholders.

Emphasize parts of a sentence by
- Giving them more space
- Putting them at the beginning or the end of the sentence
- Making them the subject of the sentence

To emphasize the importance of the chairman, you might describe her more fully:

> The chairman of the board, who has considerable experience in corporate takeover battles, called for a vote of the shareholders.

You can increase the emphasis even more by adding a separate, short sentence to augment the first:

> The chairman of the board called for a vote of the shareholders. She has considerable experience in corporate takeover battles.

Another way to emphasize an idea is to place it either at the beginning or at the end of a sentence:

LESS EMPHATIC	MORE EMPHATIC
We are cutting the *price* to stimulate demand.	To stimulate demand, we are cutting the *price*.

You can also call attention to a thought by making it the subject of the sentence. In the following example, the emphasis is on the person:

> *I* can write letters much more quickly using a computer.

In this version, the computer takes center stage:

> The *computer* enables me to write letters much more quickly.

Techniques like this one give you a great deal of control over the way your audience interprets what you have to say.

DEVELOPING COHERENT PARAGRAPHS

Paragraphs are functional units that revolve around a single thought.

A paragraph is a cluster of sentences all related to the same general topic. It is a unit of thought. A series of paragraphs makes up an entire composition. Each paragraph is an important part of the whole, a key link in the train of thought. As you edit a message, think about the paragraphs and their relationship to one another.

ELEMENTS OF THE PARAGRAPH

Most paragraphs consist of a topic sentence, related sentences, and transitional elements.

Although paragraphs vary widely in length and form, the typical paragraph contains three basic elements: a topic sentence, related sentences that develop the topic, and transitional words and phrases.

Topic sentence

Every properly constructed paragraph is unified: It deals with a single topic. The sentence that introduces that topic is called the topic sentence. In informal and creative writing, the topic sentence may be implied rather than stated. But in business writing, the topic sentence is generally explicit and often the first sentence in the paragraph. The topic sentence gives readers a summary of the general idea that will be covered in the rest of the paragraph. Notice in the following examples how the topic sentence introduces the subject and suggests how it will be developed:

> The medical products division has been troubled for many years by public relations problems. (In the rest of the paragraph, readers will learn the details of the problem.)

> Relocating the plant in New York has two main disadvantages. (The disadvantages will be explained in subsequent sentences.)

> To get a refund, you must supply us with some additional information. (The details will be described.)

The topic sentence
- Reveals the subject of the paragraph
- Indicates how it will be developed

Related sentences

The sentences that explain the topic sentence round out the paragraph. These related sentences must all have a bearing on the general subject, and they must provide enough specific details to make the topic clear. For instance:

> The medical products division has been troubled for many years by public relations problems. Since 1989, the leading local newspaper has published 15 articles that portray the division in a negative light. We have been accused of everything from mistreating laboratory animals to polluting the local groundwater. Our facility has been described as a health hazard. Our scientists are referred to as "Frankensteins." And our profits are considered "obscene."

Paragraphs are developed through a series of related sentences that provide details about the topic sentence.

Notice that the developmental sentences are all more specific than the topic sentence. Each one provides another piece of evidence to demonstrate the general truth of the main thought. Notice also that each sentence is clearly related to the general idea being developed, which gives the paragraph its unity. A paragraph is well developed when it contains enough information to make the topic sentence convincing and interesting.

Transitional elements

In addition to being unified and well developed, paragraphs need to be coherent. They need to be arranged in a logical order so that the audience can understand the train of thought. Coherence is achieved through the use of transitions that show the relationship between paragraphs and among sentences within paragraphs. They show how one thought is related to another. You can establish transitions in various ways:

Transitional words and phrases show readers how paragraphs and the ideas within them are related.

- Use connecting words such as *and, but, or, nevertheless, however, in addition,* and *therefore.*

- Echo a word or phrase from a previous paragraph or sentence: "A system should be established for monitoring inventory levels. This system . . ."

- Use a pronoun that refers to a noun used previously: "Ms. Arthur is the leading candidate for the president's position. She has excellent qualifications."

■ Use words that are frequently paired: "The machine has a minimum output of . . . Its maximum output is . . ."

These techniques help readers understand the connections you are trying to make.

FIVE WAYS TO DEVELOP A PARAGRAPH

Five ways to develop paragraphs:
■ Illustration
■ Comparison or contrast
■ Discussion of cause and effect
■ Classification
■ Discussion of problem and solution

Paragraphs can be developed in many ways, five of the more common being illustration, comparison or contrast, discussion of cause and effect, classification, and discussion of problem and solution. Your choice of approach should depend on your subject, the intended audience, and the purpose of the message. Remember also that in actual practice, you will often combine two or more methods of development in a single paragraph. You might begin with illustration, shift to cause and effect, and then shift again to problem and solution.

Before you settle for the first approach that comes to mind, think about the alternatives. Try various methods in your mind before committing yourself on paper. And don't fall into the easy habit of repeating the same old paragraph pattern time after time, or your writing will be boring.

By illustration

When you develop a paragraph by illustration, you give examples that demonstrate the general idea:

> Some of our most popular products are available through local distributors. For example, Everett & Lemmings carries our frozen soups and entrees. The J. B. Green Company carries our complete line of seasonings, as well as the frozen soups. A third major distributor, Wilmont Foods, has just begun to carry our new line of frozen desserts.

By comparison or contrast

Similarities or differences between thoughts often provide a strong basis for paragraph development. Here's an example developed by contrast:

> In previous years, when the company was small, the recruiting function could be handled informally. The need for new employees was limited, and each manager could comfortably screen and hire her or his own staff. Today, however, Gambit Products must undertake a major recruiting effort. Our successful bid on the Owens contract means that we will need to double our labor force over the next six months. To hire that many people without disrupting our ongoing activities, we need to create a separate recruiting group within the personnel department.

By discussion of cause and effect

When you develop a paragraph by cause and effect, you focus on the reasons for something:

> The heavy-duty fabric of your Wanderer tent has probably broken down for one of two reasons: (1) A sharp object punctured the fabric,

and the stress of erecting the tent daily for a week without reinforcing the hole has enlarged it; (2) the tent was folded and stored while still wet, which gradually rotted the fibers.

By classification

Paragraphs developed by classification show how a general idea is broken into specific categories:

> Successful candidates for our supervisor trainee program generally come from one of several groups. The largest group, by far, consists of recent graduates of accredited data-processing programs. The next largest group comes from within our own company because we try to promote promising clerical workers to positions of greater responsibility. Finally, we do occasionally accept candidates with outstanding supervisory experience in related industries.

By discussion of problem and solution

Another way to develop a paragraph is to present a problem and then discuss the solution:

> Selling handmade toys by mail is a challenge because consumers are accustomed to buying heavily advertised toys from major chains. However, if we develop an appealing catalog, we can compete on the basis of product novelty and quality. We can also provide craftsmanship at a competitive price: a rocking horse made from birchwood, with a hand-knit tail and mane; a music box with the child's name painted on the top; a real Indian tepee, made by a Native American.

PARAGRAPH POINTERS

Each paragraph should cover a single idea.

As you edit your paragraphs, check to be sure that they are unified, well developed, and coherent. Be particularly careful to limit each paragraph to one general idea. Your readers expect everything to be related; if you throw in unrelated thoughts, your readers will be puzzled by the unexpected shift. Similarly, when you complete a paragraph, your readers automatically assume that you have finished with a particular idea. If you then continue to discuss that idea in the next paragraph, you upset their expectations.

Short paragraphs are easier to read than long ones.

But some ideas are simply too big to be handled conveniently in one paragraph. Unless you break up the thoughts somehow, you'll end up with a three-page paragraph that's guaranteed to intimidate even the most dedicated reader. What do you do when you want to package a big idea in a short paragraph? The solution is to break the idea into subtopics and treat each subtopic in a separate paragraph, being careful to provide plenty of transitional elements.

There is no such thing as the "right" way to develop a paragraph. The first priority in business writing is to be clear and concise. But you should also try to be interesting, and the key to being interesting is variety. As you edit your message, look for opportunities to use alternative methods of paragraph development, varying your approach to suit the purpose and content of each thought. Also try to vary the structure and length of sentences within paragraphs; this variation will make the message not only more interesting but

To write an interesting document
- Use alternative methods to develop the paragraphs
- Vary the length and structure of sentences
- Mix short and long paragraphs

more readable as well. Another way to add variety and improve readability is to mix short paragraphs with longer ones. You might even use a one-sentence paragraph occasionally for emphasis.

Above all, think about what you're doing and why. Consider your words, your sentences, and your paragraphs. You can almost always improve them if you try. The more you write, the easier revision becomes. When you've mastered the elements of style, you can create whatever impression you want. You can be forthright and sincere, crisp and businesslike, warm and sympathetic. Having control over your writing style gives you the flexibility to respond to many communication situations.

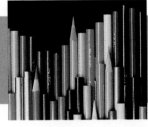

CHECKLIST FOR REVISION

A. Content and Organization
- [ ] **1.** Review your draft against the message plan.
- [ ] **2.** Cover all necessary points in logical order.
- [ ] **3.** Organize the message to respond to the audience's probable reaction.
- [ ] **4.** Provide enough support to make the main idea convincing and interesting.
- [ ] **5.** Eliminate unnecessary material; add useful material.
- [ ] **6.** Be sure the beginning and ending are effective.

B. Style and Readability
- [ ] **1.** Pay attention to word choice.
  - [ ] a. Avoid words with negative connotations.
  - [ ] b. Use concrete words to clarify abstractions and prevent misunderstandings.
  - [ ] c. Rely on nouns, verbs, and specific adjectives and adverbs.
  - [ ] d. Use familiar words, but avoid clichés.
  - [ ] e. Avoid long words.
  - [ ] f. Replace camouflaged verbs.
  - [ ] g. Eliminate terms that suggest bias based on gender, race, religion, age, or disability.
- [ ] **2.** Improve sentence style.
  - [ ] a. Use the sentence structure that best fits the thought.
  - [ ] b. Tailor the sentence style to the audience.
  - [ ] c. Aim for an average sentence length of 20 words.
  - [ ] d. Write mainly in the active voice, but use the passive voice to achieve specific effects.
  - [ ] e. Eliminate unnecessary words and phrases.
  - [ ] f. Avoid obsolete and pompous language.
  - [ ] g. Moderate your enthusiasm.
  - [ ] h. Break up strung-out sentences.
  - [ ] i. Avoid hedging sentences.
  - [ ] j. Watch for indefinite pronoun starters.
  - [ ] k. Express parallel ideas in parallel form.
  - [ ] l. Eliminate awkward pointers.
  - [ ] m. Correct dangling modifiers.
  - [ ] n. Avoid long sequences of nouns.
  - [ ] o. Keep subject and verb close together, and keep adverbs, adjectives, and prepositional phrases close to the words they modify.
  - [ ] p. Emphasize key points through sentence style.
- [ ] **3.** Construct effective paragraphs.
  - [ ] a. Be sure each paragraph contains a topic sentence, related sentences, and transitional elements.
  - [ ] b. Edit for unity, effective development, and coherence.
  - [ ] c. Choose a method of development that suits the subject: illustration, comparison or contrast, cause and effect, classification, problem and solution.
  - [ ] d. Vary the length and structure of sentences within paragraphs.
  - [ ] e. Mix paragraphs of different lengths, but aim for an average of 100 words.

C. Mechanics and Format
- [ ] **1.** Review sentences to be sure they are grammatically correct.
- [ ] **2.** Correct punctuation and capitalization errors.
- [ ] **3.** Look for spelling and typographical errors.
- [ ] **4.** Review the format to be sure it follows accepted conventions.
- [ ] **5.** Apply the format consistently throughout the message.

SUMMARY

Revision is the final step in developing effective business messages. Each message should be edited for content and organization, style and readability, and mechanics and format.

An effective writing style begins with word choice. A meaning may often be expressed in more than one way. In general, however, you should rely on strong words—nouns and verbs—to convey your meaning. Use short, familiar terms. Avoid verbs that have been turned into nouns or adjectives through the addition of suffixes.

The most effective writing also involves a balance of the three types of sentences: simple, compound, and complex. Sentences are more readable when you keep them short and use the active voice. Eliminate unnecessary words and phrases, and avoid obsolete, pompous, or overly enthusiastic language. Try to avoid strung-out sentences, hedging sentences, pronoun starters, awkward pointers, dangling modifiers, and long sequences of nouns. Express parallel ideas in parallel form, and keep words together that work together. Emphasize key thoughts by drawing them out and placing them in prominent positions.

Paragraphs consist of a topic sentence, related sentences, and transitional words and phrases. You can develop paragraphs in many ways: illustration, comparison or contrast, discussion of cause and effect, classification, and presentation of a problem and a solution. For best effect, focus each paragraph on a single idea, and keep each paragraph short.

ON THE JOB:
Solving a Communication Dilemma
at McDonald's

Over the past ten years, David Giarla has learned a great deal about the art of communication. By nature, he is a positive individual, and his communication style reflects that fact. Although his job is to spot problems, you're more likely to hear him use words such as *outstanding, terrific,* and *delicious* rather than *bad, dreadful,* or *unacceptable.* Perhaps that's why the managers and employees on his regular route always greet him with a smile.

Giarla has a list of McDonald's restaurants that he regularly inspects. Every day, he calls on seven or eight of them. If you work in one of Giarla's restaurants, you have a good chance of serving him breakfast, lunch, a snack, or dinner on any given day. You know he's coming, but you don't know when—and that keeps you on your toes.

On a typical visit, Giarla pulls into the parking lot and checks for rubbish. The ideal McDonald's is blindingly clean from the street to the storeroom. He enters the restaurant. Are the lines moving quickly? They'd better be. Are the order takers smiling? You bet. A perky teenager behind the counter recognizes Giarla and asks, "Big Breakfast and a regular Diet Coke?" "Correctomundo," he replies.

He carries his tray to a table. Is it spotless? Yup. He inspects his food. Hmm. The biscuit looks a little small. He

nibbles a hash brown, then heads for the kitchen. "Great hash browns," he says to the person at the deep fryer. "You should get a raise." He pauses a minute to inspect the dates stamped on the hamburger wrappers. Good. They're fresh. So are the cucumbers, cheese, and milk shake mix.

Business is picking up, so Giarla pitches in to help make Egg McMuffins. "These are going to be terrific," he announces. He finds that helping out builds rapport. He tries hard to cultivate goodwill between McDonald's headquarters and the restaurant managers and employees. He does not view himself as "the enemy spy." On the contrary, McDonald's is a team effort, and he is a coach—one of 300 field consultants who spend their days happily checking out the Golden Arches from coast to coast.

When Giarla spots the restaurant manager, he mentions the small-biscuit problem. Could someone be overkneading the dough, he wonders. He recommends that the biscuit maker review the McDonald's videotape that provides instructions for preparing biscuits and other items.

On to the next stop, a recently redecorated McDonald's that positively gleams. Giarla orders another breakfast. Hmm. More biscuit problems. This one slopes a few degrees to one side. He heads for the kitchen. "Outstanding hash browns," he tells the crew. He checks the storeroom. A few cartons look untidy because the lids have not been completely removed—a no-no on the McDonald's list for storeroom procedures. "You'll take care of those boxes, right?" he tells the manager.

The lunch trade is beginning to build, so Giarla offers to work at the drive-through window for a while. "Here's your world-famous Big Mac and delicious soda," he tells the customer. He's delighted when a man drives up and orders a hamburger for his dog. But he frowns when a helper crams too much food in a bag and hands it over. McDonald's does not approve of bag stuffing. The food is apt to get crushed, he explains.

More stops reveal more opportunities for improvement: a ceiling tile is stained and needs to be replaced; a cheeseburger bun is dented—probably because someone wrapped it too tightly; a storeroom is messy; a soft-serve cone is six inches high instead of the recommended three inches. Giarla calls attention to all these problems. You might expect the restaurant managers and employees to resent the criticism, but by and large they welcome his suggestions. Why? Because Giarla knows how to communicate.

Your Mission: You have recently joined McDonald's as a quality control representative. Like David Giarla, you cover seven or eight restaurants a day. Most of the managers are very cooperative, and most of the restaurants maintain very high standards. But there is one exception. Over the past few months, you have pointed out a variety of problems to a particular McDonald's manager. You have been friendly, polite, and constructive in your suggestions, but nothing has been done to correct most of the problems. On your last visit, you warned the manager that you would have to file a negative report with headquarters if you didn't see some improvement immediately. You have decided to put your suggestions in writing and give the manager one week to take action. Here is the first draft of your letter. Using the questions that follow, analyze it according to the material in this chapter.

Please correct the problems listed below. I will visit your facility within the next few days to monitor your progress. If nothing has been done toward rectifying these infractions of McDonald's principles of operation, you will be reported to headquarters for noncooperation and unsatisfactory levels of performance. As you know, I have mentioned these deviations from acceptable practice on previous visits. You have been given ample opportunity to comply with my suggestions. Your failure to comply suggests that you lack the necessary commitment to quality that has long been the hallmark of McDonald's restaurants.

On two occasions, I have ascertained that you are using expired ingredients in preparing hamburgers. On February 14, a package of buns with a freshness date of January 31 was used in your facility. Also, on March 2, you were using cheese that had expired by at least ten days. McDonald's is committed to freshness. All our ingredients are freshness dated. Expired ingredients should be disposed of, not used in the preparation of products for sale to the public. For example, you might contact local charities and offer the expired items to them free of charge, provided, of course, that the ingredients do not pose a health hazard (e.g., sour milk should be thrown out). The Community Resource Center in your area can be reached by calling 555-0909. Although I have warned you before about using old ingredients, the last time I visited your facility, I found expired ingredients in the storeroom.

Your bathrooms should be refurbished and cleaned more frequently. The paper towel dispenser in the men's room was out of towels the last time I was there, and the faucet on the sink dripped. This not only runs up your water bill but also creates a bad impression for the customer. Additionally, your windows need washing. On all my visits, I have noticed fingerprints on the front door. I have never, in fact, seen your door anything but dirty. This, too, creates a negative impression. Similarly, the windows are not as clean as they might be. Also, please mop the floors more often. Nobody wants to eat in a dirty restaurant.

The most serious infraction pertains to the appearance of store personnel. Dirty uniforms are unforgivable. Also, employees, particularly those serving the public, must have clean fingernails and hands. Hair should be neatly combed, and uniforms should be carefully pressed. I realize that your restaurant is located in an economically depressed area, and I am aware that many of your employees are ethnic minorities from impoverished backgrounds and single-parent families. Perhaps you should hold a class in basic cleanliness for these people. It is likely that they have not been taught proper hygiene in their homes.

In addition, please instruct store personnel to empty the trash more frequently. The bins are constantly overflowing, making it difficult for customers to dispose of leftover food and rubbish. This is a problem both indoors and outdoors.

Also bear in mind that all patrons should be served within a few minutes of their arrival at your place of business. Waiting in line is annoying, particularly during the busy lunch hour when people are on tight schedules. Open new lines when you must in order to accommodate the flow of traffic. In addition, instruct the order takers and order fillers to work more rapidly during busy times. Employees should not be standing around chatting with each other while customers wait in line.

As I mentioned above, I will visit your facility within a few days to check on your progress toward meeting McDonald's criteria of operation. If no visible progress has been made, I will have no alternative other than to report you to top management at headquarters. If you have any questions or require clarification on any of these items, please feel free to contact me. I can be reached by calling 555-3549.

1. How would you rate this draft in terms of its content and organization?
   a. Although the style of the letter needs work, the content and organization are basically okay.
   b. The draft is seriously flawed in both content and organization. Extensive editing is required.
   c. The content is fine, but the organization is poor.
   d. The organization is fine, but the content is poor.

2. How would you rate the draft in terms of style and readability?
   a. Acceptable. Although the tone is harsh, this is appropriate, given the circumstances. The style is both clear and readable, and the draft is visually appealing.
   b. Poor. The tone needs to be softened slightly, and the wording needs to be tightened up a bit.
   c. Unacceptable. The tone is too harsh; the style is pompous, wordy, and offensive; and the paragraphs are too long.

3. How would you evaluate the mix of specific and general terms?
   a. The language is much too abstract.
   b. The language is much too specific.
   c. The mix of abstract and specific words is about right.

4. What is the draft's most serious flaw in terms of word choice?
   a. Not enough strong nouns and verbs
   b. Too many unfamiliar terms and big words
   c. Too many camouflaged verbs
   d. No flaws

5. What should be done to eliminate the biased tone of the fourth paragraph?
   a. Omit the last three sentences of the paragraph.
   b. Omit the last three sentences and add something like the following: "Please have your employees review the videotape that deals with McDonald's standards of personal appearance."
   c. Revise the last three sentences along the following lines: "Given the composition of your labor force, you may need to stress the basics of personal hygiene."

6. Assume that you decide to retain the following passage: "McDonald's is committed to freshness. All our ingredients are freshness dated." How would you revise it? Explain your decision.
   a. Leave the passage as it is. The two simple sentences do a good job of expressing the relationship of the ideas.
   b. "Because McDonald's is committed to quality, all our ingredients are freshness dated." A single complex sentence is the best vehicle for expressing the cause-and-effect relationship between McDonald's standards and its use of freshness dating on packages.
   c. "McDonald's is committed to quality, and all our ingredients are freshness dated." A compound sentence best reflects the relationship between the two ideas, which are of equal importance.
   d. "The freshness dates indicate McDonald's commitment to quality. Please observe them." A single simple sentence is the best vehicle for expressing the closely related ideas in the original version. The second sentence is added to make the implied point explicit.

7. Which of the following is the best alternative to this sentence: "If nothing has been done toward rectifying these infractions of McDonald's principles of operation, you will be reported to headquarters for noncooperation and unsatisfactory levels of performance."
   a. "If nothing has been done to correct these infractions, you will be reported to headquarters for noncompliance."
   b. "If you don't shape up immediately, headquarters will hear about it."
   c. "By correcting these problems promptly, you can avoid being reported to headquarters."
   d. "You can preserve your unblemished reputation by acting immediately to bring your facility into compliance with McDonald's principles of operation."

8. Take a look at the third paragraph of the letter. What is its chief flaw?
   a. There is no topic sentence.
   b. The topic sentence is too narrow for the ideas encompassed in the paragraph.
   c. The transition from the previous paragraph is poor.
   d. The paragraph deals with more than one subject.
   e. The topic sentence is not adequately developed with specific details in subsequent sentences.

9. What method of development predominates in the sixth paragraph (which begins, "Also bear in mind . . .")?
   a. None
   b. Cause and effect
   c. Problem/solution
   d. Illustration[6]

QUESTIONS FOR DISCUSSION

1. Which step in the revision process do you think is most important—editing for content and organization, editing for style and readability, or editing for mechanics and format? Explain your answer.
2. Why do business writers tend to use words of low connotative meaning? In what types of business situations might one use words of high connotative value?
3. Some writers argue that trying to avoid stereotyping and bias makes a message sound unnatural and leads to awkward constructions. How would you respond to this criticism?
4. What specific techniques of style could you use to create a formal, objective tone? An informal, personal tone?
5. What technique might you use to develop a paragraph explaining the game of Frisbee? Explain your choice.
6. Why does a good writer develop the ability to express the same idea in several distinct styles?

DOCUMENTS FOR ANALYSIS

Read the following documents; then (1) analyze the strengths or weaknesses of each sentence and (2) revise each document so that it follows this chapter's guidelines.

DOCUMENT 5.A

The move to our new offices will take place over this coming weekend. For everything to run smoothly, everyone will have to clean out their own desk and pack up the contents in boxes that will be provided. You will need to take everything off the walls too, and please pack it along with the boxes.

If you have alot of personal belongings, you should bring them home with you. Likewise with anything valuable. I do not mean to infer that items will be stolen, irregardless it is better to be safe than sorry.

On Monday, we will be unpacking, putting things away, and then get back to work. The least amount of disruption is anticipated by us, if everyone does their part.

We hope there will be no negative affects on production schedules, and current deadlines will be met.

DOCUMENT 5.B

Dear Ms. Giraud:

Enclosed herewith please find the manuscript for your book, Careers in Woolgathering.

After perusing the first two chapters of your 1,500-page manuscript, I was forced to conclude that the subject matter, handicrafts and artwork using wool fibers, is not coincident with the publishing program of Framingham Press, which to this date has issued only works on business endeavors, avoiding all other topics completely.

Although our firm is unable to consider your impressive work at the present time, I have taken the liberty of recording some comments on some of the pages.

I am of the opinion that any feedback that a writer can obtain from those well versed in the publishing realm can only serve to improve the writer's authorial skills.

In view of the fact that your residence is in the Boston area, might I suggest that you secure an appointment with someone of high editorial stature at the Cambridge Heritage Press, which I believe might have something of an interest in works of the nature you have produced.

Wishing you the best of luck in your literary endeavors, I remain

Arthur J. Cogswell
Editor

DOCUMENT 5.C

Directions for delicious air-popped popcorn:
The popper is designed to pop 1/2 cup of popcorn kernels at one time. Never add more than 1/2 cup. A half cup of corn will produce three to four quarts of popcorn. More batches may be made separately after completion of the first batch. Popcorn is popped by hot air. Oil or shortening is not needed for popping corn. Add only popcorn kernels to the popping chamber. Standard grades of popcorn are recommended for use. Premium or gourmet type popping corns may be used. Ingredients such as oil, shorten-

ing, butter, margarine, or salt should never be added to the popping chamber. The popper, with popping chute in position, may be preheated for two minutes before adding the corn. Turn the popper off before adding the corn. Use electricity safely and wisely. Observe safety precautions when using the popper. Do not touch the popper when it is hot. The popper should not be left unattended when it is plugged into an outlet. Do not use the popper if it or its cord has been damaged. Do not use the popper if it is not working properly. Before using the first time, wash the chute and butter/measuring cup in hot soapy water. Use a dishcloth or sponge. Wipe the outside of the popper base. Use a damp cloth. Dry the base. Do not immerse the popper base in water or other liquid. Replace the chute and butter/measuring cup. The popper is ready to use.

EXERCISES

1. Write a concrete phrase for each of these vague phrases:
   a. sometime this spring
   b. a substantial saving
   c. a large number attended
   d. increased efficiency
   e. expanded the work area

2. List words that are stronger than the following:
   a. ran after
   b. seasonal ups and downs
   c. bright
   d. suddenly rises
   e. moves forward

3. As you rewrite these sentences, replace the clichés with fresh, personal expressions:
   a. Being a jack-of-all-trades, Dave worked well in his new selling job.
   b. Moving Leslie into the accounting department, where she was literally a fish out of water, was like putting a square peg into a round hole, if you get my drift.
   c. I knew she was at death's door, but I thought the doctor would pull her through.
   d. Movies aren't really my cup of tea; as far as I am concerned, they can't hold a candle to a good book.
   e. It's a dog-eat-dog world out there in the rat race of the asphalt jungle.
   f. There's been a lot of water under the proverbial bridge since you and I last rubbed elbows and chewed the fat together.

4. Revise the following sentences using shorter, simpler words:
   a. The antiquated calculator is ineffectual for solving sophisticated problems.
   b. It is imperative that the pay increments be terminated before an inordinate deficit is accumulated.
   c. There was unanimity among the executives that Ms. Jackson's idiosyncrasies were cause for a mandatory meeting with the company's personnel director.
   d. The impending liquidation of the company's assets was cause for jubilation among the company's competitors.
   e. The expectations of the president for a stock dividend were accentuated by the preponderance of evidence that the company was in good financial condition.

5. Rewrite each of the following to eliminate bias:
   a. For an Indian, Maggie certainly is outgoing.
   b. He needs a wheelchair, but he doesn't let his handicap affect his job performance.
   c. She's too sensitive; when I criticized her performance, she asked me to explain.
   d. A pilot must have the ability to stay calm under pressure, and then he must be trained to cope with any problem that arises.
   e. "And what would you ladies like us to do about absenteeism?"
   f. David is a teenager and has little experience to draw on when making career decisions.

6. Shorten these sentences by adding more periods:
   a. The next time you write something, check your average sentence length in a 100-word passage; and if your sentences average more than 16 to 20 words, see if you can break up some sentences.
   b. Don't do what the village blacksmith did when he instructed his apprentice as follows: "When I take the shoe out of the fire, I'll lay it on the anvil; and when I nod my head, you hit it with the hammer." The apprentice did just as he was told and now he's the village blacksmith.
   c. Know the flexibility of the written word and its power to convey an idea, and know how to make your words behave so that your readers will understand.
   d. Words mean various things to different people, and a word such as *block* may mean city block, butcher block, engine block, auction block, or several other things.
   e. Mineral classifications will be made by areas, and these areas will show resources that are available

now along with those that will probably become available at some time in the future.

7. Rewrite each sentence so that it is active rather than passive:
   a. The raw data are submitted to the data-processing division by the sales representative each Friday.
   b. High profits are the responsibility of management.
   c. The policies announced in the directive were implemented by the staff.
   d. Our typewriters are serviced by the Santee Company.
   e. The employees were represented by Janet Hogan.

8. Condense these sentences to as few words as possible:
   a. We are of the conviction that writing is important.
   b. In all probability, we're likely to have a price increase.
   c. The price increase exceeded the amount of 5 cents.
   d. We are engaged in the process of building this store.
   e. Our goals include making a determination about that in the near future.
   f. When all is said and done at the conclusion of this experiment, I would like to summarize the final windup.

9. Write up-to-date versions of the following phrases; write *none* if you believe there is no appropriate substitute:
   a. as per your instructions
   b. attached herewith
   c. hold in abeyance
   d. in lieu of
   e. in reply I wish to state
   f. in response to same
   g. kindly note same
   h. please be advised that
   i. pursuant to our agreement
   j. refer back to
   k. take the liberty of
   l. thanking you in advance
   m. this will acknowledge
   n. we wish to advise that
   o. yours of the 11th
   p. we deem it advisable
   q. allow me to express
   r. at all times
   s. according to our records

10. Remove all the unnecessary modifiers from these sentences:
    a. Tremendously high pay increases were given to the extraordinarily skilled and extremely conscientious employees.
    b. The union's proposals were highly inflationary, extremely demanding, and exceptionally bold.

11. Rewrite these sentences so that they no longer contain any hedging:
    a. It would appear that someone apparently entered illegally.
    b. It may be possible that sometime in the near future the situation is likely to improve.

12. Rewrite these sentences to eliminate the indefinite starters:
    a. There are several examples here to show that Elaine can't hold a position very long.
    b. It would be greatly appreciated if every employee would make a generous contribution to Mildred Cook's retirement party.
    c. It has been learned in Washington today from generally reliable sources that an important announcement will be made shortly by the White House.

13. Present the ideas in these sentences in parallel form:
    a. Mr. Hill is expected to lecture three days a week, to counsel two days a week, and must write for publication in his spare time.
    b. The office workers were hired to receive callers, to operate the duplicating equipment, and a variety of duties were handled by them.
    c. All the employees were given instruction in writing letters, using the photocopying machine, and how to keep all of our accounts in alphabetical order.
    d. She knows not only accounting, but she also reads Latin.
    e. My Uncle Bill is young, ambitious, and he is rich.
    f. Both applicants had families, college degrees, and were in their thirties, with considerable accounting experience but few social connections.
    g. This book was exciting, well written, and held my interest.
    h. Don is both a hard worker and he knows bookkeeping.

14. Revise these sentences to delete the awkward pointers:
    a. The vice president in charge of sales and the production manager are responsible for the keys to 34A and 35A, respectively.
    b. The keys to 34A and 35A are in executive hands with the former belonging to the vice president in charge of sales and the latter belonging to the production manager.
    c. The keys to 34A and 35A have been given to the production manager, with the aforementioned keys being gold-embossed.

15. Rewrite these sentences to clarify the dangling modifiers:
    a. Running down the railroad tracks in a cloud of smoke, we watched the countryside glide by.
    b. Lying on the shelf, Ruby saw the seashell.

c. Based on the information, I think we should buy the property.

16. Rewrite the following sentences to eliminate the long strings of nouns:
   a. The focus of the meeting was a discussion of the bank interest rate deregulation issue.
   b. Following the government task force report recommendations, we are revising our job applicant evaluation procedures.
   c. The production department quality assurance program components include employee training, supplier cooperation, and computerized detection equipment.
   d. The supermarket warehouse inventory reduction plan will be implemented next month.
   e. The State University business school graduate placement program is one of the best in the country.

17. Rearrange the following sentences to bring the subjects closer to their verbs:
   a. Trudy, when she first saw the bull pawing the ground, ran.
   b. It was Terri who, according to Ted, who is probably the worst gossip in the office (Tom excepted), mailed the wrong order.
   c. William Oberstreet, in his book *Investment Capital Reconsidered*, writes of the mistakes that bankers through the decades have made.

d. Judy Schimmel, after passing up several sensible investment opportunities, despite the warnings of her friends and family, invested her inheritance in a jojoba plantation.

18. In your capacity as a McDonald's quality control representative (see this chapter's On-the-Job simulation), revise and rewrite the letter to a McDonald's manager.[7]

19. Build a paragraph around each of the following topic sentences:
   a. During its first decade of operations, Perkins Industries almost went bankrupt.
   b. But as the advertising budget increased, so did the sales.

20. Write a paragraph on each of the following topics— one by illustration, one by comparison or contrast, one by discussion of cause and effect, one by classification, and one by discussion of problem and solution:
   a. Types of cameras (or dogs or automobiles) available for sale
   b. Advantages and disadvantages of eating at fast-food restaurants
   c. Finding that first job
   d. Good qualities of my car (or house, apartment, or neighborhood)
   e. How to pop popcorn (or barbecue or cook a steak)

PART THREE

LETTERS, MEMOS, AND OTHER BRIEF MESSAGES

After studying this chapter, you will be able to

- Clearly state the main idea of each direct request you write
- Write letters in a way that indicates you are confident your request will be filled
- Write letters with enough detail for the reader to be able to comply with your request
- Use lists and tables to clarify complicated requests
- Close your letters with a courteous request for specific action

CHAPTER SIX

WRITING DIRECT REQUESTS

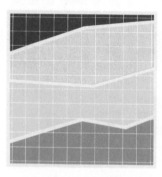

ON THE JOB:
Facing a Communication Dilemma at B. Dalton Bookseller
May the Best Seller Win!

Lots of gloomy news has been written about the sad state of American reading, but the book business has actually boomed in recent years. Through the 1980s, the number of bookstores in this country increased by 78 percent (only fast-food restaurants grew faster). The man leading the charge to sell you books, books, and more books is Leonard Riggio, the head of B. Dalton Bookseller and considered by many to be the most powerful person in the publishing industry.

Riggio got his start as a clerk in a college bookstore and eventually started several college bookstores of his own. His next move was becoming the principal owner of the Barnes & Noble chain, whose Fifth Avenue store in New York City competes for the title of the world's largest bookstore. (The other contender is Foyles, in London.) In 1987 Barnes & Noble purchased B. Dalton; the Barnes & Noble empire is now the largest book retailer in the country, with annual sales around $1.5 billion.

Bookstores fall into three categories. First are independent bookstores, which range from tiny specialty shops to warehouse-size giants carrying hundreds of thousands of books. The second group includes regional chains, such as the Borders chain, based in Ann Arbor, Michigan. Third are the big national chains, including Waldenbooks and third-place Crown. Riggio competes to one degree or another with every category, but in terms of sheer size, the 1,300-store Waldenbooks chain is his primary rival. Waldenbooks (which is owned by K Mart) expanded aggressively in recent years and plans to continue adding such outlets as the Reader's Market boutiques inside K Mart stores.

As you read this chapter, put yourself in Leonard Riggio's shoes. As you try to keep the lead, you must send messages to customers and store managers, requesting both information and action. How can you obtain the information you need to make intelligent decisions? How would you phrase the requests you send to store managers so that they will respond with positive action in the race against Waldenbooks?[1]

ORGANIZING DIRECT REQUESTS

B. Dalton Bookseller

B. Dalton's store managers are certainly interested in helping Leonard Riggio increase book sales, just as book distributors are interested in filling a B. Dalton order. Whenever you can assume that your audience will be interested in what you have to say, or at least willing to cooperate with you, your message should follow the direct, or deductive, plan. You should present the request or the main idea first, follow up with necessary details, and close with a cordial statement of the action you want. This approach works well when your request requires no special tact or persuasion.

Senders of direct requests may be tempted to begin with personal introductions ("I am administrative assistant to the head of a large bookstore chain, and I am interested in expanding our selection of reference books"). But this type of beginning is usually a mistake. The essence of the message, the specific request, is buried and may get lost. A better way to organize a direct request is to state what you want in the first sentence or two and let the explanation follow this initial request.

Even though you expect a favorable response, the tone of your initial request is important. Instead of demanding immediate action ("Send me your catalog #33A"), soften your request with such words and phrases as *please* and *I would appreciate*. An impatient demand for rapid service is not necessary; you can generally assume that the audience will comply with your request once the reason for the request is understood.

> Assume that your reader will comply once he or she understands your purpose.

The middle part of a direct request usually explains the original request ("I would like to order a sample of several of your reference works to determine whether they appeal to our customers"). Such amplifying details help your audience fill your request correctly.

In the last section, clearly state the action you are requesting. You may wish to tell the audience where to send the sought-after information or product, indicate any time limits, or list details of the request that were too complex or numerous to cover in the introductory section. Then close with a brief, cordial note reminding the audience of the importance of the request ("If the sample books sell well, you can expect to receive additional orders from B. Dalton on a monthly basis").

> For direct requests
> - State the request or main idea
> - Give necessary details
> - Close with a cordial request for specific action

Now let's take a closer look at the three main sections of a direct request. Although this discussion focuses on letters and memos, remember that this organizational plan may be appropriate for brief oral messages as well.

DIRECT STATEMENT OF THE REQUEST OR MAIN IDEA

The general rule for the first part of a direct request is to write not only to be understood but also to avoid being misunderstood. If, for example, you request 1990 census figures from a government agency, the person who handles your

When writing direct requests, says former NBC News correspondent and best-selling author Edwin Newman, get directly and clearly to the point by eliminating boastful, complicated vocabulary and words that impress or conceal.

request won't know whether you want a page or two of summary figures or a detailed report running to several thousand pages. Therefore, you should be as specific as possible in the sentence or two that begins your message.

Be aware of the difference between a polite request in question form, which requires no question mark, and a question that is part of a request:

POLITE REQUEST IN QUESTION FORM
Would you please help us determine whether Kate Kingsley is a suitable applicant for a position as landscape designer.

QUESTION THAT IS PART OF A REQUEST
Did Kate Kingsley demonstrate an ability to work smoothly with clients?

Many direct requests include both types of statements, so make sure you distinguish between the polite request, which is your overall reason for writing, and specific questions, which belong in the middle section of your letter or memo.

JUSTIFICATION, EXPLANATION, AND DETAILS

To make the explanation a smooth and logical outgrowth of your opening remarks, you might make the first sentence of your letter's middle section you-oriented by stating a service-to-the-reader benefit. The owner of a Honolulu import company might write to a Southeast Asian supplier: "By keeping me informed about your products, you can help create a new distribution channel for your business. For example, if an American market exists for one of your new specialty items, I can help you reach those customers."

In the middle section
- Call attention to how the reader will benefit from granting your request
- Give details of your request

Another possible approach for the middle section is to ask a series of questions, particularly if your inquiry concerns machinery or complex equipment. You might ask about technical specifications, exact dimensions, and the precise use of the product. The most important question should be asked first. For example, if cost is your main concern, you might begin with a question like "What is the price of your least expensive typewriter?" Then you may want to ask more specific but related questions about, say, the cost of ribbons and maintenance service.

If you are requesting several items or answers, you should number the items and list them in logical order or in descending order of importance. Furthermore, so that your request can be handled quickly, remember (1) to ask only the questions that are central to your main request and (2) to avoid asking for information that you can find on your own, even if the effort takes considerable time.

When you prepare questions
- Ask only questions that relate to your main request
- Don't ask for information you can find yourself
- Make your questions open-ended and objective
- Deal with only one topic in each question

If you are asking many people to reply to the same questions, you should probably word them so that they can be answered yes or no or with some other easily counted response. You may even want to provide respondents with a form or with boxes they can check to indicate their answers. But if you need more than a simple yes or no answer, you must pose an open-ended question. For example, a question like "How fast can you repair typewriters?" is more likely to elicit the information you want than "Can you repair typewriters?" Keep in mind, also, that phrasing questions in a way that hints at the response you want is likely to get you less-than-accurate information. So try to phrase your questions objectively. Finally, deal with only one topic in each question.

If the questions need amplification, keep each question in a separate paragraph.

Other types of information that belong in this section include data about a product (model number, date and place of purchase, condition), your reason for being concerned about a particular matter, and other details about your request. When a reader finishes this section, he or she should understand why the request is important and be persuaded to satisfy it.

COURTEOUS CLOSE WITH REQUEST FOR SPECIFIC ACTION

Close with
- A request for some specific response
- An expression of appreciation
- Information about how you can be reached

Your letter should close with both a request for some specific response, complete with any time limits that apply, and an expression of appreciation or goodwill. Help your reader respond easily by including your phone number, office hours, and other helpful information.

But do not thank the reader "in advance" for cooperating. If the reader's reply warrants a word of thanks, send it after you have received the reply. If you are requesting information for a research project, you might offer to forward a copy of your report in gratitude for the reader's assistance. If you plan to reprint or publish materials that you ask for, indicate that you will get necessary permission. When asking for information about a person, indicate that you will keep responses confidential.

PLACING ORDERS

Because orders are usually processed without objection and refer to a product that the reader knows about, an order is considered one of the simplest types of direct request. When placing an order, you need not excite your reader's interest, just state your needs clearly and directly.

To see what to include in a good order letter, examine any mail-order form supplied by a large firm. It offers complete and concise directions for providing all the information that the company will need to fill an order. After the date, the order form probably starts with "Please send the following" or "Please ship." If you complete the rest of the form and mail it, these statements constitute a legal and binding offer to purchase goods; the supplier's shipment of the goods constitutes an acceptance of the offer and thus completes a legal contract.

Order letters are like good mail-order forms, although they provide more room for explaining special needs.

Order blanks are arranged to document the precise goods you want, describing them by catalog number, quantity, name or trade name, color, size, unit price, and total amount due. This complete identification helps prevent errors in filling the order. When drafting an order letter, you would do well to follow the same format: Present information on the items you want in column form, double-space between the items, and total the price at the end.

Order blanks provide space for you to indicate the address where the goods should be sent. Your letter should also specify the delivery address, especially if it is not the address from which you send your letter. Sometimes the billing and delivery addresses are different. Order blanks may also leave space for you to indicate how the merchandise is to be shipped: by truck, air freight, parcel post, air express, or delivery service. Unless you specify the mode of transportation, the seller chooses.

As executive director of AT&T's new Switching Systems Technology Division of Bell Laboratories, Joseph S. Colson, Jr., is respected not only as a gifted engineer but also as a motivator of people. Known for his effective communication, Colson recommends that written requests spell out exactly the action required.

Like any letter sent with money, your order letter should mention the amount of payment as well as explain how the amount was calculated and, if necessary, to what account it should be charged. Again, the order form provides an excellent model. Most have spaces for showing unit prices, the total amount for each item, the cost of shipping and handling, the total amount of the payment, and the form of payment (check, money order, bank draft, or other means).

Here's an example that follows the order-form format and adds important information:

Please ship by air express to the above address the following ten items, which are shown in your April catalog:

The general request is stated first.

```
3-#256 Men's nylon raincoats; in
    gray; sizes 42 long, 40 regular,
    and 38 regular; @ $19.95          $59.85
2-#5823 Women's plastic raincapes;
    in yellow; sizes medium and small;
    @ $17.50                           35.00
5-#353898 Unisex rain parkas; in red;
    sizes large (1), medium (3), and
    small (1); @ $23.95               119.75
Total sale                           $214.60
Sales tax                              15.02
Air express                            45.73
Amount due                           $275.35
```

All necessary details are provided (in a format similar to an order form).

Because information about such additional charges as tax and shipping was provided in the catalog, the writer calculated the amount to ensure quick processing of the order.

I am enclosing a check for $275.35 to cover all charges.

We need some of your famous rain gear for an upcoming field experiment to be conducted in the rain forest in the state of Washington. So please call us collect at once at (714) 833-9717 if you cannot deliver all ten items to us by May 9.

The closing paragraph sets a time limit and cordially requests a specific procedure if problems arise.

When ordering nonstandard items, include a complete description.

Not every item ordered through the mail is neatly displayed in a catalog or newspaper advertisement. If the goods are somewhat unusual, the problem of identifying them becomes more complex. For instance, the office manager of a small company ordering specially cut lumber for a set of bookcases would need to be more descriptive:

Please deliver the following pieces of cut lumber to the above address this Friday afternoon (August 12). We are having bookshelves built on Saturday to fit into two rather oddly shaped areas of our office.

Be sure to cut the shelves to the following specifications, all from your finest-quality walnut, 3/4 inch thick and 6 inches wide:

5 boards measuring 4 feet 3 inches

6 boards measuring 4 feet 8 inches

4 boards measuring 5 feet

So that I can have a check ready for your delivery person on Friday, please let me know by Thursday the total amount due. My phone number is 548-7907.

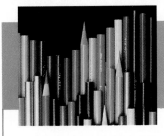

CHECKLIST FOR ORDERS

A. Direct Statement of the Request

☐ **1.** Use wording that indicates an order rather than a request: "Please send me" or "Please ship" instead of "I want" or "I need," which are neither polite nor legally appropriate for a business order.

☐ **2.** Open with a general description of your order that encompasses all the details.

B. Justification, Explanation, and Details

☐ **1.** For complex orders, provide a general explanation of what the requested materials will be used for.

☐ **2.** Provide all specifications: quantity, price (including discounts), size, catalog numbers, product description, shipping instructions (date and place), ar-

rangements for payment (method, time, deposits), and cost totals.

☐ **3.** Use a format that presents information clearly and makes it easy to total amounts.

☐ **4.** Double-check the completeness of your order and the cost totals.

C. Courteous Close with Request for Specific Action

☐ **1.** Include a clear summary of the desired action.

☐ **2.** Suggest a future reader benefit, if possible.

☐ **3.** Close on a cordial note.

☐ **4.** Clearly state any time limits that apply to your order, and explain why they are important.

Notice the added explanation of where and how the boards will be used. In any order for nonstandard items, the additional description will help the recipient identify your needs accurately. In special cases, such as ordering machine parts, you may even choose to make drawings of the parts you need, adding an explanation of their particular use.

When placing orders, be thorough and clear.

A final suggestion about placing orders: Be thorough and clear. If you supply unclear or insufficient information, your reader must make an extra effort to get the missing details. The delays and cross-communications that follow will hold up delivery of the order and may also lead to mistakes in filling it. To make sure your order is filled correctly, retain a copy of your letter. If you haven't received a response in a reasonable time (two weeks, in most cases), write or call to see whether your order has arrived and is being processed.

REQUESTING ROUTINE INFORMATION AND ACTION

In making a routine request, say
- *What you want to know*
- *Why you want to know*
- *Why it is in the reader's interest to help you*

When you need to know about something, to get an opinion from someone, or to suggest a simple action, you usually need only ask. Simple requests say, in essence, this is what I want to know or what I want you to do, why I'm making the request, and why it may be in your interest to help me. Assuming that your reader is able and willing to do what you want, such a straightforward request gets the job done with a minimum of fuss.

Despite their simple organization, routine requests deserve a tactful touch. In many organizations, memos and letters like these are sent to hundreds or even thousands of employees, customers, clients, and shareholders. Thus the potential for creating a positive impression is second only to the risk of causing ill will through ambiguous wording or a discourteous tone. Even when writing a routine request, therefore, you must keep the purpose of your message in mind. That is, you must ask yourself what you want your audience to understand or do as a result of reading the message. As you prepare the request, remember that even the briefest note can create confusion and hard feelings.

REQUESTS TO COMPANY INSIDERS

A request in memo form
- Provides a permanent record
- Saves time and questions
- Tells precisely what is needed

Although requests to fellow employees are often oral and rather casual, some messages are better put in permanent, written form. A clear, thoughtfully written memo saves time and questions and helps readers know precisely what is required. A routine request in memo form follows the standard direct plan. Start with a clear statement of your reason for writing; you can then provide whatever explanation is needed to justify the request and close with a specific account of what you expect, including a deadline, if appropriate. For example, the memo in Figure 6.1 was sent to all employees of a relatively small manufacturing firm.

In the following memo, notice how the writer refers to a previous memo on the same topic and then makes the request for a response from employees:

How do you feel about adopting flextime in your department?

The memo begins with the central question.

Last week you received an explanation of flextime schedules as they could apply to our organization. Now we need your opinion of the proposal.

A little background information orients the reader.

1. Would you want to go on a flextime schedule? Please summarize your reasons.

2. The proposal listed four schedule patterns for employees to choose from. Which pattern now seems best for your department?

3. If your preferred schedule pattern is not available, what other pattern would suit you?

4. Should flextime be mandatory or optional?

5. If flextime is adopted, what problems might arise in your department?

The numbered questions focus responses so that they will be easier to tally.

Please write your answers directly on this sheet and return it to me by Friday. Complete responses will help us formulate the policy that works best for our company.

The memo closes with specific instructions for replying. The courteous tone helps ensure a prompt response.

Craft internal memos just as carefully as letters to outsiders, but adjust the writing style to take shared reference points into account.

Notice that this memo is matter-of-fact and assumes some shared background. This style is appropriate when you are writing about a routine matter to someone in the same company.

FIGURE 6.1
Memo Requesting Routine Action from Company Insiders

MEMO

DATE: April 17, 1993

TO: All employees

FROM: Michael Nardi, Personnel

SUBJECT: Golden Time parties

We are very interested in learning your opinion about award dinners. Please take a few moments to respond to this questionnaire.

Traditionally, employees who have been with the company for 20 years are honored at annual departmental dinners, where their Golden Time pins are awarded.

Recently, however, management has proposed that a company-wide recognition dinner replace these departmental events. Because our firm has only 107 employees, such a dinner could still be a friendly affair. The interdepartmental ties and friendships that many of you share would be part of the celebration. However, our company is proud of the unity within each department, and you may feel that this closeness would be lost in a larger celebration.

Please consider these points and mark your choice below:

_____ VOTE FOR AN ALL-COMPANY PARTY

_____ VOTE FOR DEPARTMENTAL PARTIES

Please feel free to make additional signed or unsigned comments at the bottom of this memo. Return your completed questionnaire by Friday.

The basic request is stated at the beginning.

The next two paragraphs explain the problem that made the inquiry necessary.

The final paragraph requests action and, with a built-in questionnaire, makes a response easy.

REQUESTS TO OTHER BUSINESSES

Many letters to other businesses are requests for information about products; for example, B. Dalton might request a catalog from a reference book distributor. These requests are among the easiest of all letters to write because recipients welcome the opportunity to tell you about their goods and services. In fact, you may need only fill out a coupon or response card and mail it to the correct address. You might find, however, that you'd like to write a brief note requesting further information about something you've seen in an advertisement. One or two sentences would most likely do the job. Companies commonly check on the effectiveness of their advertisements, so they also like to know where you saw or heard them.

When writing a letter in response to an advertisement
- Say where you saw the ad
- Specify what you want
- Provide a clear and complete return address on the letter

If the reader is not expecting your letter, you must supply more detail.

Inquiries that are not prompted by an advertisement usually demand a more detailed letter. If the letter will be welcome, or if the reader won't mind answering it, the direct approach is still appropriate. The following is such a letter:

Would you please supply information and recommendations on the type of refrigerator we might install in two-bedroom apartments.

The overall request is stated at the beginning; phrased politely in question form, it requires no question mark.

Ten refrigerators will be needed for our new apartment building, which is scheduled for completion within four months. Four other buildings now under construction in the same complex will need new appliances later.

The explanation for the request keeps the reader's attention by hinting at the possibility of future business.

Because we're considering your company as the supplier, please answer the following questions:

To avoid burdening the reader with an impossibly broad request, the writer asks a series of specific questions, itemized in a logical sequence.

BEHIND THE SCENES AT THE PHOENIX SYMPHONY
The Art of Making Requests

Making direct requests is a way of life for Gail Warden, director of development for the Phoenix Symphony. Her job is to request donations, in-kind gifts, and grants to keep the symphony in business, competing with about 1,500 orchestras performing in the United States.

At the heart of Warden's efforts are direct-request letters. They are written to wealthy individuals known for their philanthropy, corporations that support community activities, and nonprofit foundations that contribute to the arts. Warden's letters vary in form because she has so many types of potential contributors. But the tone of her requests remains constant throughout: Her letters are personalized as much as possible. "The common wisdom is that you don't write personalized letters to top donors," Warden says, "but I do, and it's effective. They need to hear how much they're appreciated before I ask them for another gift."

One of the most common types of letters Warden writes is to request a donation renewal from symphony sponsors. She opens with what she calls a "feel good" paragraph:

Mr. Williams, you and your company have been generous donors to The Phoenix Symphony for several years. We have been grateful for that support. You know from your personal involvement with the arts how vital contributed income is to our organization's very existence, and so when we say "thank you" it is heartfelt.

She then requests a new pledge: "I'm writing to invite your renewed support and to ask that you please continue for this season with a $1,000 contribution."

Another type of request letter is sent to donors originally solicited by one of the symphony's board members. The opening paragraph includes a reminder of the donor's response to the board member: "You were most generous with your response of a $1,000 contribution." Warden continues with a capsule description of the current successful symphony season, in effect explaining to the donors that their generosity helped make it all possible. Then she asks for a renewal.

A third type of request letter is what Warden calls a "cold renewal"—usually directed to patrons who

1. What size is appropriate for two-bedroom apartments? 14 cubic feet? 16? 18?

2. Do you recommend putting self-defrosting refrigerators in rental units?

3. Do you provide service for the refrigerators you sell? If so, how quickly could you repair them in case of breakdown?

4. What models of apartment-size refrigerators do you carry, and what are their prices?

5. Which of your refrigerators has the best service record?

To avoid receiving useless yes or no answers, the writer asks some open-ended questions.

The refrigerators must be ordered within a month, so we would appreciate receiving your reply by March 26.

The courteous close specifies a time limit.

This letter should bring a prompt and enthusiastic reply because the situation is clearly described, the possibility of current and future business is suggested, and the questions are specific and easy to answer. Additionally, the letter implies confidence in the opinion and assistance of the reader. Because the

haven't been solicited for two or three years because their gifts were for a longer term. Warden begins by reminding donors of their past generosity:

> Last season your corporation completed a very generous three-year pledge to The Phoenix Symphony. We were pleased to recognize your company at the $1,000 Patrons level of giving throughout the three seasons. We hope that you and members of your company have had an opportunity to enjoy some of the wonderful concerts your generosity has helped make possible.

Warden then makes her direct request, only in this case she seeks a financial commitment for another two or three years instead of a specific sum. Because of this approach, she's sure to include a reason: "We would like you to consider another multiyear pledge; your last pledge was extremely helpful to this organization in making short- and long-range plans." Warden then gives a clear example of the type of program the donor's funds support: "Please know that your corporation's contribution not only supports concerts in Symphony Hall, but also enables us to have an extensive educational outreach program."

Warden's foundation requests differ from others because foundations are in the business of making contributions. For example, a "cold" request to a foundation might begin with four paragraphs describing the orchestra and its programs. Only then would a solicita-

tion be made. "Foundations know I'm going to ask them for money," Warden says, "so it doesn't matter as much that the request is in the fifth paragraph."

Another difference is that foundations are asked to sponsor specific programs or events, which would be named for the foundation. Warden gets directly to the point when requesting such donations.

> We have not talked since the fall, and I want to tell you of two new concerts, wonderful opportunities for The Phoenix Symphony's Educational Outreach Program. It is our hope that your foundation will assist in funding these concerts, and with that in mind we respectfully request a grant of $10,000.

APPLY YOUR KNOWLEDGE

1. Write direct requests for donations to your local art museum: (1) a renewal of a $3,000 donation from a regular corporate sponsor; (2) a renewal of a $5,000 gift from a wealthy patron whose husband recently died.

2. Write direct-request letters for donations to your local public broadcasting station: (1) a "cold" request for a multiyear, corporate donation; (2) a request for $100,000 from a foundation to fund an original program on local history.

letter will be sent to a business firm and pertains to a possible sale, the writer did not enclose a stamped, preaddressed envelope.

If you are writing as an individual and are therefore not using letterhead stationery, be sure to write your address on the letter clearly and completely. Many inquiries go unanswered because the address was illegible or was written only on the return envelope, which was tossed away by the recipient.

REQUESTS TO CUSTOMERS AND OTHER OUTSIDERS

Businesses often ask individuals outside the organization to provide information or to take some simple action: attend a meeting, return an information card, endorse a document, confirm an address, or supplement information on an order. Often these messages can be short and simple, but other situations require a more detailed explanation. In such cases, readers may not be willing to respond unless they understand how the request benefits them. Thus more complex letters, with several paragraphs of explanation, are sometimes written. Because the same message must often be sent to many people at the same time, it may be prepared as a form letter and perhaps individualized with a word processor.

The following is an example of a well-planned, detailed form letter:

Requests to customers must often spell out in detail
- What exactly is needed
- How filling the request will benefit them

Under federal tax law, your annuity payments are considered "wages" for income tax withholding purposes. To simplify your record keeping, you may choose to have us withhold taxes from your annuity payments. Or you may choose to receive the full payments and pay estimated taxes yourself.

The opening states the purpose of the letter in simple, reader-oriented terms. Providing details of the law convinces the reader that the request is warranted.

Here's how to decide which option is best for you:

First, estimate your total taxable income this year from all sources: the taxable portion of all annuity payments you receive, dividends, interest, and salary from employment.

An explanation of procedures is another reader-oriented feature of the letter. To make a complex procedure easier to understand, the writer breaks the directions into two clearly defined steps.

Second, estimate your total tax liability for this year by using the income figure you just calculated and your present tax rates. Then subtract your payments of estimated taxes and other amounts withheld for you.

If your calculations show that you will have a tax liability, you may want us to withhold the taxable portion of your pension payments. Simply mark the appropriate box on the enclosed Tax Decision Form, fill in your Social Security number, sign and date the form, and mail it to us.

This paragraph begins to explain the particular action being requested. Again, clear directions are provided to help ensure a response.

If you do not want taxes withheld, mark the "no" box on the form, fill in your Social Security number, sign and date the form, and return it to us.

Providing boxes for the response helps readers comply with the request.

As treasurer for the *Washington Post* Company, Leonade D. Jones manages the company's short-term investments, raises funds for potential acquisitions, manages the company's debt, and oversees $600 million in pension assets. Communication should clarify and expedite, not confuse or waste time, says Jones. So whenever you write to other businesses, state clearly what you want and be specific about time limitations.

Please let us know your decision by November 1 so that we can begin withholding in January. If you need further information about the new requirements, call Larry Bender, our customer service representative, at (919) 744-2063. He is in the office Monday through Friday from 9 a.m. to 5 p.m.

The courteous close motivates action by specifying a person to talk to and a deadline for a reply. The clarity of the language in this letter helps ease the reader's concerns about a complex procedure.

The purpose of routine requests to customers is often to reestablish communication.

Businesses sometimes need to reestablish a relationship with former customers. For example, when unhappy about some purchase or the way they were treated, customers often make no complaint: They simply stay away from the offending business. A letter of inquiry encouraging them to use idle credit accounts offers them an opportunity to register their displeasure and then move on to a good relationship. Additionally, a customer's response to an inquiry may provide the company with insights into ways to improve its products and customer service. Even if they have no complaint, customers still welcome the personal attention. An inquiry to the customer might begin in this way:

When a good charge customer like you has not bought anything from us in six months, we wonder why. Is there some way we can serve you better?

Letters of inquiry sent to someone's home frequently include a stamped, preaddressed envelope to make a reply easier.

Similar inquiry letters are sent from one business to another. For example, the sales representatives of a housewares distributor might send a letter like this to their customers:

Consider enclosing a stamped, preaddressed envelope with routine requests, especially those sent to individuals rather than other businesses.

Because we haven't heard from you in a while, I thought it would be a good idea to touch base. In fact, I'd like to ask a favor.

The opening paragraph states the reason for the letter. The frank request arouses curiosity and encourages a frank response.

Will you take a minute today to give us your honest opinion about our merchandise and service. Just jot your ideas, pro and con, at the bottom of this letter and rush it back in this afternoon's mail. Your response will help us help you.

This request for action is a device for uncovering trouble without actually suggesting that there might be trouble.

So that you'll have a good supply of order forms on hand, I'm enclosing some extra copies. And the enclosed spring bulletin and update on our cooperative advertising program may help you plan your spring promotions.

This paragraph recognizes the possibility that nothing particular is wrong, that the customer just needs a little push.

Remember, Ms. Skovie, you can always count on us when you're in the market for high-style housewares. We have some new merchandise in today's most desirable colors that seems just right for your fashion-conscious customers. Do give us the opportunity to serve your needs soon. That's why we're here.

The actual request for action is left unstated until the end so that it will leave an impression.

CHECKLIST FOR ROUTINE REQUESTS

A. Direct Statement of the Request

- ☐ 1. Phrase the opening to reflect the assumption that the reader will respond to your request favorably.
- ☐ 2. Phrase the opening so clearly and simply that the main idea cannot be misunderstood.
- ☐ 3. Write in a polite, undemanding, personal tone.
- ☐ 4. Preface complex requests with a sentence or two of explanation, possibly a statement of the problem that the response will solve.

B. Justification, Explanation, and Details

- ☐ 1. Justify the request or explain its importance.
- ☐ 2. Explain to the reader the benefit of responding.
- ☐ 3. State desired actions in a positive and supportive, not negative or dictatorial, manner.
- ☐ 4. Itemize parts of a complex request in a numbered series.
- ☐ 5. List specific questions.
  - ☐ a. Don't ask questions that you can answer through your own efforts.
  - ☐ b. Arrange questions logically.
  - ☐ c. Number questions.
  - ☐ d. Word questions carefully to get the types of answers you need: numbers or yes's and no's if you need to tally many replies; more lengthy, detailed answers if you want to elicit more information.
  - ☐ e. Word questions to avoid clues about the answer you prefer so as not to bias the reader's answers.
  - ☐ f. Limit each question to one topic.

C. Courteous Close with Request for Specific Action

- ☐ 1. Courteously request a specific action, and make it as easy as possible to implement, perhaps by enclosing a return envelope or by explaining how you can be reached.
- ☐ 2. Indicate gratitude, perhaps by promising to follow up in a way that will benefit the reader.
- ☐ 3. Clearly state any deadline or time frame, and briefly justify it if it is genuinely important.

WRITING DIRECT REQUESTS FOR CLAIMS AND ADJUSTMENTS

> You are entitled to request an adjustment whenever you receive a product or service that doesn't live up to the supplier's standards.

For most of us, *claim* and *adjustment* are unpleasant words. But most progressive organizations want to know whether you are dissatisfied with their services or merchandise: Satisfied customers bring additional business to the firm; angry or dissatisfied customers do not. In addition, angry customers complain to anyone who will listen, creating poor public relations. If you do have a complaint, it is in your best interest, and in the best interest of the company involved, to bring your claim or request for an adjustment to that organization's attention. When you feel that you are justified in making a claim, communicate at once with someone in the organization who can make the correction. A phone call or visit may solve the problem, but a written claim letter is better because it documents your dissatisfaction.

> Tone is of primary importance; keep your claim businesslike and unemotional.

Your first reaction to a clumsy mistake or defective merchandise is likely to be anger or frustration, but the person reading your letter probably had nothing to do with the problem. Making a courteous, clear, concise explanation of the difficulty will impress the reader much more favorably than an abusive, angry letter. Asking for a fair and reasonable solution will increase your chances of receiving a satisfactory adjustment.

In most cases, and especially in the first letter, you can assume that a fair adjustment will be made. Thus your letter should follow the plan for direct requests. Begin with a straightforward statement of the problem, and follow with a complete, specific explanation of the details. In the middle part of your claim letter, provide any information the adjuster will need to verify your complaint about faulty merchandise or unsatisfactory service. Politely request specific action in your closing, and express the attitude that the business relationship will continue if the problem is solved satisfactorily. Companies usually accept the customer's explanation of what is wrong, but you should be prepared to back up your claim with invoices, sales receipts, canceled checks, dated correspondence, catalog descriptions, and any other relevant documents. Send copies and keep the originals for your files.

If the remedy is obvious, tell your reader exactly what will return her or his company to your good graces—for example, an exchange of merchandise for the right item or a refund if the item is out of stock. If you are uncertain about the precise nature of the trouble, you could ask the company to make an assessment. When you are dissatisfied with a very costly item, you might request that an unbiased third person either estimate the cost of repair or suggest another solution. Be sure to supply your address, your telephone number, and the best time to call so that the company can discuss the situation with you if need be.

A courteous approach is best for any routine request. If you must write a letter that gives vent to your anger, go ahead; but then tear that one up and write a letter that will actually help solve the problem.

Generally, you should suggest specific and fair compensation when asking for an adjustment. However, the following complaint illustrates a case in which the customer does not request a specific adjustment but asks the reader to resolve the problem:

At our October 25 dinner meeting in your restaurant, your rum cake was a big success. You should know, however, that many who attended commented on three areas needing improvement:

1. Serving began half an hour late.

2. The roast beef was cold and tough.

3. The vegetables were cold and overcooked.

What can we do to guarantee that things go better at our next dinner meeting, which is scheduled for December 10?

In the past, we have been quite pleased with the quality of your food and service. Please call me at 372-9200, ext. 271, any time this week to discuss this situation further.

In a letter like this, you must define the problem and express your dissatisfaction in as much detail as possible while conveying a sincere desire to find a fair solution. A courteous tone will allow the reader to save face and still make up for the mistake.

In your claim letter
- Explain the problem and give details
- Provide backup information
- Request specific action

Be prepared to document your claim. Send copies; keep the original documents.

Lorraine C. Scarpa is a corporate communications consultant to a number of companies, including Dun & Bradstreet. Much of Scarpa's career has been spent identifying and serving the information needs of customers worldwide. For any claim or adjustment problem, advises Scarpa, be sure your requests are straightforward and contain complete explanations so that your audience can react effectively.

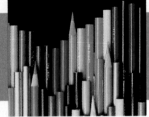

CHECKLIST FOR CLAIMS AND REQUESTS FOR ADJUSTMENT

A. Direct Statement of the Request
☐ 1. Write a claim letter as soon as possible after the problem has been identified.
☐ 2. State the need for reimbursement or correction of the problem.
☐ 3. Maintain a confident, factual, fair, unemotional tone.

B. Justification, Explanation, and Details
☐ 1. To gain the reader's understanding, praise some aspect of the product or the service.
☐ 2. Present facts honestly, clearly, and politely.
☐ 3. Eliminate threats, sarcasm, exaggeration, and hostility.
☐ 4. Specify the problem: product failed to live up to advertised standards, product failed to live up to sales representative's claims, product fell short of company policy, product was defective, customer service was deficient.
☐ 5. Make no accusations against any person or company unless you can back them up with facts.
☐ 6. Use a nonargumentative tone to show your confidence in the reader's fairness.
☐ 7. If necessary, refer to documentation (invoices, canceled checks, confirmation letters, and the like), but mail only photocopies.
☐ 8. Ask the reader to propose fair adjustment, if appropriate.
☐ 9. If appropriate, present your idea of fair settlement, such as credit against your next order, full or partial refund of the purchase price, replacement of the defective merchandise, performance of services as originally contracted, or repair of the defective merchandise.
☐ 10. Do not return the defective merchandise until you have been asked to do so.
☐ 11. Avoid uncertainty or vagueness that might permit the adjusters either to prolong the issue with additional correspondence or to propose a less-than-fair settlement.

C. Courteous Close with Request for Specific Action
☐ 1. Summarize desired action briefly.
☐ 2. Simplify compliance with your request by including your name, address, phone number (including area code, if necessary), and hours of availability.
☐ 3. Note how complying with your request will benefit the reader.

MAKING ROUTINE CREDIT REQUESTS

The first step in requesting credit is to get an application form.

If your credit rating is sound, your application for business credit may be as direct as any other type of simple request. B. Dalton might request credit from a book distributor, just as other companies might approach a local bank, retail store, wholesaler, manufacturer, or national credit card company. But no matter who is requesting credit or who is approached, the information needed is the same. You might phone the company for a credit application or write a letter as simple as this:

We would like to open a credit account with your company. Please send an application blank and let us know what references you will need.

The second step is to supply the necessary information.

Before you get a credit account, you will have to supply such information as the name of your company, the length of time you've been in business, the name of your bank, and the addresses of businesses where you have existing accounts. Businesses trying to establish credit are also expected to furnish a financial statement and possibly a balance sheet. In general, the lender wants proof that your income is stable and that you can repay the loan. You might put this information in your original letter, but it will probably be requested again on the standard credit application form.

A request to buy on credit is sometimes included with a company's first-time order for goods. In these cases, the customer often sends copies of the latest financial statement along with the order letter. If a company's credit standing is good, it may ask with confidence for the order to be accepted on a credit basis. Because the main idea in this situation is to get permission to buy on credit, the letter should open with that request. Figure 6.2 is an example of the way an order may be combined with a request for credit. Notice that the request for credit is supported by documentation of financial ability. In addition, the writer has encouraged a favorable response by adopting a confident tone and mentioning the probability of future business.

Order letters are often combined with a request for credit.

A request for credit should
- Be supported by documentation
- Adopt a confident tone
- Hint at future business

FIGURE 6.2
Letter Making a Routine Credit Request

The main idea is tied in with a statement implying a reader benefit.

The background details of the business are necessary if credit is to be granted.

The possibility of continuing orders is another reason for the reader to grant credit.

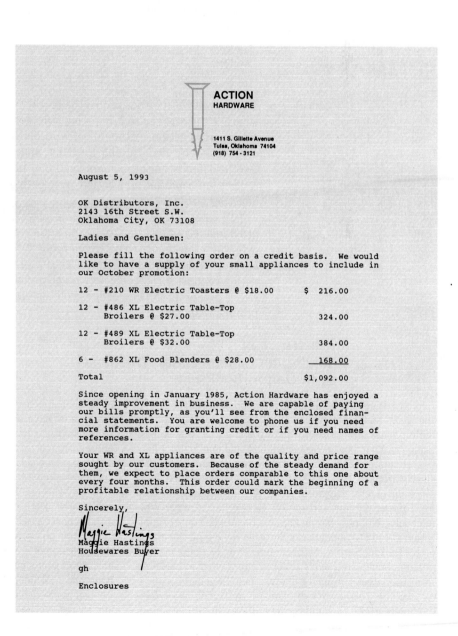

ACTION
HARDWARE

1411 S. Gillette Avenue
Tulsa, Oklahoma 74104
(918) 754 - 3121

August 5, 1993

OK Distributors, Inc.
2143 16th Street S.W.
Oklahoma City, OK 73108

Ladies and Gentlemen:

Please fill the following order on a credit basis. We would like to have a supply of your small appliances to include in our October promotion:

12 - #210 WR Electric Toasters @ $18.00	$ 216.00
12 - #486 XL Electric Table-Top Broilers @ $27.00	324.00
12 - #489 XL Electric Table-Top Broilers @ $32.00	384.00
6 - #862 XL Food Blenders @ $28.00	168.00
Total	$1,092.00

Since opening in January 1985, Action Hardware has enjoyed a steady improvement in business. We are capable of paying our bills promptly, as you'll see from the enclosed financial statements. You are welcome to phone us if you need more information for granting credit or if you need names of references.

Your WR and XL appliances are of the quality and price range sought by our customers. Because of the steady demand for them, we expect to place orders comparable to this one about every four months. This order could mark the beginning of a profitable relationship between our companies.

Sincerely,

Maggie Hastings
Maggie Hastings
Housewares Buyer

gh

Enclosures

INQUIRING ABOUT PEOPLE

The need to inquire about people arises often in business. For example, some companies ask applicants to supply references before awarding credit, contracts, jobs, promotions, scholarships, and so on. If you are applying for a job and your potential employer asks for references, you may want to write a letter to a close personal or professional associate, asking her or him for a letter of recommendation. Or if you are an employer considering whether or not to hire an applicant, you may want to write directly to the person that the applicant named as a reference. Whatever the situation, just remember that the approach to writing letters of inquiry about people is similar to the requests already discussed; that is, such inquiries include a direct statement of the request (or main idea); a justification of the request (explanation of the situation with details); and a courteous close that includes a request for specific action.

SUMMARY

The purpose of a direct request is to gain a specific response from the reader, whether the answer to a question, the delivery of goods or services, or some other sort of action. Although a favorable response is assumed, you can ensure cooperation by maintaining a cordial and you-oriented tone. Direct requests are used for a variety of applications, including placing orders, requesting routine information and action, requesting claims and adjustments, and requesting credit.

To ease the reader's task, you should begin with the request and then provide any justification and explanatory details that will help the reader execute the request correctly. If you request several items or pose several secondary questions, number them for clarity. The letter can then close courteously with a request for specific action and an indication of any deadline. By emphasizing a benefit to the reader, you also increase chances for a favorable and prompt response.

ON THE JOB:
Solving a Communication Dilemma
at B. Dalton Bookseller

Leonard Riggio is holding on to his position at the top of the U.S. bookselling market through a combination of building new bookstores, buying some existing stores, using creative marketing techniques, and employing effective communication. In any business top managers must clearly request the kinds of information they need from store managers. Riggio is using that information to help his company grow and evolve in the battle with Waldenbooks. Not only has he kept his Barnes & Noble organization ahead of Waldenbooks, he is also changing the image of B. Dalton from a lowbrow purveyor of mass-market popular books to a more diverse supplier of everything from the latest thriller to obscure new fiction.

In the 1980s both B. Dalton and archrival Waldenbooks grew by building new stores in the shopping malls that appeared all over the United States. The two chains now have about 2,500 of the roughly 10,000 bookstores in the country. But as one observer put it, the United States is "malled out," and construction of new malls has slowed to a crawl. So Riggio and his Waldenbooks counterpart, Charles Comello, now chase growth primarily through buying smaller chains and building non-mall stores. Both companies, for instance, have ventured into "superstores," very large operations with 100,000 or more titles on the shelf (compared with 15,000 to 25,000 in the typical mall store). And both have purchased smaller, upscale chains such as Scribner's Books (B. Dalton) and Brentano's (Waldenbooks).

Riggio is also working hard to increase sales in existing stores. A key technique, first introduced by Waldenbooks and quickly imitated by B. Dalton, is the frequent-purchase plan. In these programs, customers join for a small fee and then get discounts on every purchase. Just like the frequent-flyer programs offered by airlines, the "frequent-reader" programs stimulate more sales from existing customers.

However, not all Riggio's efforts are aimed solely at making more money. A lifelong lover of books who says that a bookstore should be a "marketplace of ideas," Riggio is working hard to expose the book-buying public to a wider variety of literary works. B. Dalton's "Discovery" program, for instance, highlights books by both new and unknown writers. The program can increase sales of a book tenfold by bringing it to the attention of customers browsing through the store.

Of course, Charles Comello isn't sitting still while Riggio does all this. He plans to establish the Reader's Market boutiques in 1,200 K Mart locations, making it essentially another national chain. He is also cutting back on nonbook products, such as jewelry and T-shirts, in order to put more books in the stores. And like Riggio, Comello is working hard to communicate more effectively with customers. For instance, Waldenbooks can check the preferences of readers in its frequent-purchase programs and let them know about new offerings in subject areas they've enjoyed before. Fans of mystery novels get the word on new mysteries, computer users hear about new computer books, and so on.

As Riggio tries to outhustle and outsmart Comello, he must also keep a close eye on Borders, Crown, and other chains that are growing rapidly, as well as on the large independents, many of which have grown much stronger in recent years. But in a country whose population seems to have a never-ending appetite for new books, Riggio's attention to customers and his talent for selling books should keep him in the leader's spot for a long time to come.

Your Mission: You have recently taken a job as Leonard Riggio's administrative assistant. He relies heavily on you to draft his correspondence to B. Dalton store managers and outside contacts. Using the principles outlined in this chapter for writing direct requests, handle each of the following letters to the best of your ability.

1. Riggio has asked you to contact the store managers and get their impressions of whether the "Discovery" program is affecting sales. Which of the following is the best way to open the letter requesting this information?

   a. I have recently joined Mr. Riggio's staff as his administrative assistant. He has asked me to write to you to obtain your input on the effectiveness of the "Discovery" program. Please reply to the following questions within five working days. [List of questions follows.]

   b. Please tell us what you think of the "Discovery" program. Mr. Riggio is trying to evaluate its impact on our business. Within the next few days, can you take a few moments to jot down your thoughts on its effectiveness. Specifically, Mr. Riggio would like to know . . . [List of questions follows.]

   c. By April 15, please submit written answers to the following questions on the "Discovery" program. [List of questions follows.]

   d. Is the "Discovery" program working? You be the judge. We're polling all the B. Dalton store managers for their reaction to the program. Cast your vote today. Is it thumbs up or thumbs down on "Discovery"?

2. Which of the following is the best choice for the middle section of the letter?

   a. Specifically, has business increased in your store since the campaign began six weeks ago? If so, what is the percentage increase in dollar sales over the previous six weeks? Over the comparable period last year? Have sales of the specific books you've featured increased dramatically during the past six weeks? Have customers mentioned the program? If so, have their comments been positive or negative? Has employee morale been affected by the program? How?

   b. By replying to the following questions, you will help us decide whether to continue with the program as is, revise it, or drop it entirely:

      1. Has business increased in your store since the program began six weeks ago? If so, what is the percentage increase in dollar sales over the previous six weeks? Over the comparable period last year?

      2. Have sales of the specific books you've promoted increased noticeably during the past six weeks? Please quantify.

      3. Have customers mentioned the program? If so, have their comments been positive or negative? Give some typical examples.

      4. Has employee morale been affected by the program? How?

   c. By circling the response that most accurately reflects your store's experience, please answer the following questions regarding the "Discovery" program:

      1. Since the program began six weeks ago, sales have
         a. increased
         b. decreased
         c. remained about the same

      2. Sales of the specific books you've promoted have
         a. increased
         b. decreased
         c. remained about the same

3. Customers (have/have not) mentioned the program. Their comments have been primarily (positive/negative).
4. Employee morale (has/has not) been affected by the campaign.

3. For a courteous close with a request for specific action, which of the following paragraphs is the best?
   a. Thank you for your cooperation. Please submit your reply in writing by April 15.
   b. Mr. Riggio is meeting with his senior staff on April 17 to discuss the program. He would like to have your reaction to the program in writing by April 15 so that he can present your views during that meeting. If you have any questions, please contact me at 697-2886.
   c. You may contact me at 697-2886 if you have any questions or require additional information about this survey. Mr. Riggio requires your written response by April 15 so that he can discuss your views on the campaign with his senior staff on April 17.
   d. Thank you for your input. As the frontline troops in our campaign to outsell Waldenbooks, you are in the best position to evaluate the results of the "Discovery" program. We're doing our best here at corporate headquarters to support you, but we need your feedback on our efforts. Please submit your written evaluation of the program by April 15 so that Mr. Riggio can use the results as ammunition in his meeting with senior staff on April 17.

4. Mr. Riggio has decided to order 795 large cutout cardboard displays of Mickey Mouse to promote a new line of children's books featuring the famous cartoon character. He has identified the item he needs in a catalog that features promotional materials licensed by the Walt Disney Company. Which of the following letters should you send to the vendor?
   a. Please send 795 large cardboard cutouts of Mickey Mouse (item #90067-C in the April catalog) to the above address by parcel post. We need the shipment by April 25. I am enclosing a check for $4,397.50 to cover the order (795 @ $5.00), tax ($397.50), and shipping ($25).
   b. This may seem like a "Mickey Mouse" request, but we need 795 cardboard cutouts of the famous rodent by April 25. Item #90067-C in your April catalog looks like it should do the trick. Please send the shipment to the above address. I am enclosing a check for $4,397.50.

   Contact me immediately if Mickey is not available. We are counting on him to help us launch a new children's book at our stores on May 1.
   c. We need some free-standing cardboard cutouts of Mickey Mouse to promote a new children's

book that will go on sale in our B. Dalton stores throughout the country on May 1. Item #90067-C shown in the upper left corner of page 56 of your April catalog appears to be well suited for our purpose. Please send 795 of these cutouts to me at our corporate headquarters, at the above address, by parcel post.

I am enclosing a check for $4,397 to cover all costs:

795 #90067-C @ $5.00 each	$3,975.00
Sales tax	397.50
Shipping and handling	25.00
Total sale	$4,397.50

Our May 1 book launch depends on our receiving the shipment by April 25, so please call me collect at 697-2886 if you cannot deliver all 795 cutouts by then.

5. B. Dalton has received its shipment of 795 Mickey Mouse cardboard cutouts but has discovered that 50 of the displays are bent and cannot be used in promoting the new line of children's books. You have been asked to prepare a fax letter requesting an adjustment. Select the best version.
   a. On March 25, we ordered 795 cardboard cutouts of Mickey Mouse (item #90067-C in your April catalog). When the shipment arrived last week, we discovered that 50 of the cutouts were bent. Whether the damage occurred during shipping or at your place of business, I do not know. However, I do know that we cannot use the cutouts in their present form. If you can replace them before April 25, please do so. We are withholding payment until the matter is straightened out.
   b. Fifty of the Mickey Mouse cardboard cutouts that we ordered from your firm on March 25 arrived in poor condition. Can you replace them before April 25? If so, we would still like to use them in our May 1 book promotion.

   I am enclosing a copy of the invoice for your convenience. As you can see, our original order was for 795 cutouts (catalog item #90067-C), priced at $5.00 each. Our bill for the total order is $4,397.50. We will send payment in full when we receive the 50 undamaged cutouts. If replacements are not available by April 25, we will send you a check for the 745 good cutouts, which we plan to use in any case. Including tax and handling costs, the adjusted total would be $4,139.50.

   Would you like us to return the damaged items? Perhaps they can be salvaged for another purpose.

Please call me at 697-2886 any time this week to discuss the situation. We are eager to receive the replacement cutouts so that all 795 B. Dalton bookstores can benefit from the Mickey Mouse display during our nationwide book promotion scheduled for May 1.

c. Please call me immediately at 697-2886 to discuss a problem with the Mickey Mouse cutouts that we ordered from you. Fifty of them are bent and cannot be used in our nationwide book promotion scheduled for May 1.

Time is running short, I know, but we would really like you to replace the 50 damaged cutouts if you can do so in time for our promotion. If that is not possible, we will adjust our payment to reflect a sale of 745 cutouts as opposed to 795.

Thanks for your cooperation. The good cutouts are really cute, and we expect they will do wonders for our book sales.

6. B. Dalton has decided to expand its selection of reference books. One of Dalton's buyers has identified a publisher, McFarland & Company, that issues some 70 general and technical reference books a year. The buyer has drafted a letter placing an initial order for several of these books on a credit basis. Critique the following letter:

As you are undoubtedly aware, B. Dalton is one of the largest and most profitable booksell-ing chains in the country, with 795 retail outlets located throughout the nation. Our reputation with publishers is excellent.

We are currently expanding the reference sections in some of our larger bookstores. Accordingly, we would like to order a sample of several of your reference works to determine whether they appeal to our customers. Specifically, please send us the following books in the quantities indicated below:

Title	Copies	Cost
Inside the Copyright Laws	75 @ $12.50	$937.50
Legal Terms and Phrases	55 @ $ 3.00	165.00
Reptiles of South America	40 @ $ 8.50	340.00

If these books sell well, you can expect to receive additional orders from B. Dalton on a regular (monthly) basis. Please ship the books promptly. We will pay within 60 days of receiving the shipment.

a. The letter is fine the way it is—businesslike and efficient.
b. Tone of the letter is condescending, but contents are well organized.
c. Tone is appropriate, but organization is poor.
d. Tone and organization can be improved.[2]

QUESTIONS FOR DISCUSSION

1. What does a writer who plans to use the direct approach assume about the reader?
2. What precautions should be taken when writing secondary questions in a direct request?
3. What element of an order letter makes it a legally binding contract?
4. What types of request letters might businesses write to regular customers?
5. Why are you doing a business a favor when you speak up about defective products or poor service?
6. If you are writing to a firm to request an adjustment, to whom should you address your letter? Why?

DOCUMENTS FOR ANALYSIS

Read the following letters; then (1) analyze the strengths or weaknesses of each sentence and (2) revise each letter so that it follows this chapter's guidelines.

DOCUMENT 6.A

Your ads in a recent local newspaper have caught my attention. I'd appreciate it greatly if you could send me accurate answers to these questions:

1. What information can you provide about the stainless steel ElectroPerk coffee pot? Does it work OK?
2. Can it be repaired when it breaks, and are repairs covered by a warranty or store policy? Or will I have to pay for repairs on faulty merchandise?
3. What is the price range on the machine?

4. Does it come with attachments? Do attachments cost extra? Is the machine hard to use?

Let me know the answers to these questions as soon as possible, please. When evaluating equipment for my company, I am considering several other models.

DOCUMENT 6.B

I'm writing to inquire about your recent order for a custom wedding suit. You forgot to mention what color you want and also failed to include your measurements. I'd like to clear up this confusion quickly so that we will be able to provide you with the suit before the wedding. When, exactly, is the happy day?

I know you must be busy getting ready for the wedding, but if you can spare the time, you might want to stop by in person to pick out your suit because we do offer an incredibly wide selection of fine wedding attire. At that time, you could also select an appropriate tie and shirt. I would also suggest that you choose clothing for your best man and ushers, assuming that you are having a large wedding. We can provide the best in both custom and rental formal attire for your entire wedding party, regardless of how large or small it is. Incidentally, you should also bring your fiancé along to coordinate the men's clothing with the bridesmaids' dresses. You know how picky women are about clothes.

If you can't come by in person, you should send me a letter stating your measurements and indicating your color and style preferences, or call me at 633-4296. After we receive this information, we will need at least two weeks to complete the suit. Thank you for your cooperation in this matter.

CASES

PLACING ORDERS

1. More mellow music: Memo ordering CDs for the Wherehouse
This has been the busiest month you can remember since you started working for a Wherehouse Records outlet. For the second time, your boss asks you to contact the Wherehouse's West Coast distribution headquarters in Long Beach, California, to let them know that you're out of certain titles and to pass on some special orders.

"Maybe it's the weather, but tell them we're selling New Age CDs like crazy, so they'd better increase our shipments," she explains as she gives you the list. "I think Music Design in Milwaukee distributes all these titles—you might mention that in your memo. I wonder if this stuff is selling as quickly on the East Coast? Ask them to send 15 of each title, except for the special orders. Some guy came in here looking for all this weird stuff; he said he's researching brain-response patterns to chants and environmental sounds. No, on second thought, better get a few extra of the nature sounds; we've sold a lot of those lately, too. Ask for five each. Here—" she reaches for a Music Design wholesale catalog and hands it to you. "Give them the item numbers and prices. If we make their job easier, we'll get our order sooner. I don't want to lose any more customers because we don't have what they want."

You stop scribbling notes when she leaves the back room and glance at the list. It definitely shows a pattern.

Your task: Write a memo requesting a special supplement to your regular shipment from Wherehouse headquarters in Long Beach. Mention that Music Design's fall catalog carries all the compact discs on your list and that you have included their order numbers for easy reference. The special-order CDs are Gyuto Monks, "Tibetan Tantric Choir," W50-172, $11.49 wholesale, $18.98 list; "Gregorian Chants of Hungary," Vol. 3, Q1-103, $11.49 wholesale, $18.98 list; Gyume Monks, "Tantric Harmonics," SR-103, $11.49 wholesale, $18.98 list; Lamas & Monks of the Four Great Orders, "Tibetan Ritual Music," L6-102, $10.98 wholesale, $17.98 list. Order five CDs each of Atmosphere Collection/Brazilian Rainforest, "Jungle Journey/Evening Echoes," RY-134, $6.59 wholesale, $10.98 list; Earth Sounds, "Cedar Creek," P9-105, $9.69 wholesale, $15.98 list; Earth Sounds, "Ebb and Flow," P9-103, $9.69 wholesale, $15.98 list; and Atmosphere Collection/A Week in Hawaii, "Midnight Rainshower," RY-121, $6.59 wholesale, $10.98 list. The CDs you've run out of are Eric Tingstad/Nancy Rumbel, "In the Garden," N1-259, $9.98 wholesale, $15.98 list; David Lanz, "Skyline Firedance" (double CD), N1-244, $10.79 wholesale, $17.98 list; David Arkenstone, "In the Wake of the Wind," N1-256, $9.98 wholesale, $15.98 list; and "The Narada Wilderness Collection," N1-233, $9.98 wholesale, $15.98 list.[3]

2. A better gas cap: Letter ordering a sample from Beverly Hills Motoring
When you visited the auto show last weekend, you spent a little time scouting out all the new gadgets offered on the sidelines: sunglass holders, car covers, biodegradable cleaners, even a special bib for people who eat while they drive.

You were thinking of your auto parts store, Auto Excellence—nothing fancy, just a one-of-a-kind neighborhood retail operation that caters mostly to the guys stationed at a nearby Army base. They like the usual products, the familiar brands, but every once in a while you'll spot something at one of these shows that catches your interest—and theirs.

Last year, it was an on-board tracking device to thwart car thefts. The theft-recovery device sent out a signal that police could follow, and it was packaged with a noisy exterior alarm to deter the "amateurs" and joyriders. The gadget was popular but a little pricey at $795 installed. This year you were looking for something less expensive.

After watching demonstration after demonstration at the convention, you found something that interested you: the EZ-Flo Gas Cap. Made of black plastic with a spring-loaded flap in the middle, the cap never has to be removed. The fuel hose nozzle pushes back the center flap, and when the gas is pumped and the nozzle removed, the flap claps back into place. No more gas caps left at the pump; no more greasy, smelly hands from screwing on old-fashioned caps.

There was such a crowd around the booth that you couldn't get near Andy Cohen, the owner of Beverly Hills Motoring Accessories, who was demonstrating the new gas cap. You learned his name and his list price ($19.95, just what you were looking for) from the brochure you managed to pick up. Now you'd like to test the gas cap before ordering a hundred of them to sell at your store.

Your task: Write a letter to Andy Cohen at Beverly Hills Motoring Accessories (200 S. Robertson Blvd., Beverly Hills, CA 90211) ordering one EZ-Flo Gas Cap for $19.95, plus 7.25% sales tax and $4 shipping and handling. Use the letter as an opportunity to establish a good working relationship by explaining your plans to sell the gas cap at your retail store if it proves satisfactory. Inquire about the wholesale price.[4]

3. Real fatigues: Complex order for Banana Republic

Ever since you saw *Indiana Jones and the Temple of Doom*, you've been intrigued with Banana Republic Travel & Safari Clothing Company. So becoming an assistant buyer has been a dream come true. Mel and Patricia Ziegler, the free-spirited husband-and-wife team who founded the firm, spend about half their time traveling to remote places looking for clothes that will appeal to weekend adventurers. You help handle the paperwork associated with their buying trips.

On a recent trip to Germany, the Zieglers arranged to buy some authentic NATO (North Atlantic Treaty Organization) fatigues, first worn by Western armies in Korea and later by NATO troops on maneuvers in the North Atlantic. The fatigues are a brownish-green blend of wool flannel and nylon. They feature thigh pockets with an outside compartment for writing tools, flashlight, or knife; ribbon ties to secure keys, canteen, or ice axe; and suspender buttons. NATO is asking a price of $9 per pair.

The Zieglers originally ordered 9,000 pairs: 1,500 each in sizes 30, 32, 34, 36, 38, and 40. Within each size category, the Zieglers stipulated that the pants should be divided into three lengths: 500 short, 500 medium, and 500 long. After thinking over the order, however, the Zieglers have decided to request 500 additional medium-length pants in sizes 32, 34, and 36, a total of 1,500 pairs. At the same time, they have decided to decrease their order for size 30 pants in the long length from 500 to 250 and to decrease their order for size 40 short pants from 500 to 250.

Your task: Write to Lt. Colonel Karl Westheim at NATO headquarters, clarifying the change in the order. The address is 1110 Wollenstrasse, Brussels, Belgium. Be sure to specify that the merchandise should be shipped to you within two weeks, care of Banana Republic Travel & Safari Clothing Company, P.O. Box 7737, San Francisco, CA 94120. The Zieglers have already paid a deposit of $1,800. The balance will be paid by check within 30 days of receiving the merchandise.[5]

REQUESTING ROUTINE INFORMATION AND ACTION

4. Leonard Riggio checks on progress: Letter requesting information from B. Dalton's store managers

In order to compete with Waldenbooks and offer more attractive purchase arrangements for his customers, Leonard Riggio recently instituted a frequent-purchase program for customers at his B. Dalton bookstore chain (see this chapter's On-the-Job simulation). He wants to make sure that customers understand the program and that it isn't causing any problems for store personnel. He envisions some potential hang-ups, such as checkout delays if customers expect to get a higher discount than they are actually eligible for. Although he's fairly sure that the program has been well designed and clearly communicated to customers, he wants to be sure.

Your task: Write a letter to store managers to see whether any of them have encountered problems with the program and whether customers seem confused by it.[6]

5. Who has the weakest knees? Memo requesting information from within the Hospital Corporation of America

Your boss has been put in charge of planning new sports medicine facilities for the giant Hospital Corporation of America (HCA), which is based in Nashville, Tennessee. "Top management is really excited about this idea," he tells you. "They want us to come up with a plan for adding new sports medicine facilities throughout the country. The big question is, What should we add in which locations?"

"Well," you say, "I suppose that depends on population density to a great extent. But it also depends on how many people engage in which sports in various regions. And we need to know what injuries they sustain. Are there more sprained ankles per capita in Los Angeles than there are in New York City, for example?"

Your task: Seeing that you have a good grasp of the issues involved, your boss tells you to write a memo asking the marketing and industry research department for help in analyzing regional patterns in sports injuries. It should be addressed to David Young, who's the assistant vice president. Suggest the specific types of information you need, such as the numbers of various sports-related injuries currently being handled at existing HCA hospitals and the types of sports activities common to some well-defined regions. Your boss wants to receive this information within three weeks.[7]

6. The sweet smell of success: Letter requesting information about the impact of fragrance on performance
As a management consultant with Arthur D. Little, you specialize in helping manufacturers optimize their factory operations. In the course of your work, you have discovered that little things can make a big difference. For example, in one plant, you boosted productivity by simply changing the intensity of the light bulbs.

Given your experience with such factors, you are always on the lookout for information about the effects of seemingly inconsequential details. Naturally, you were intrigued when you ran across an article in *The New York Times* on the behavioral impact of fragrances. From the standpoint of your manufacturing clients, a couple of points in the article were particularly interesting:

1. Research conducted at Catholic University reveals that people doing mundane tasks are more alert when they receive occasional whiffs of peppermint and lily of the valley.
2. The fifth-largest construction company in Japan, the Shimizu Corporation, has patented a system for delivering fragrances to large buildings through their ventilation apparatus. Shimizu's tests indicate that the system can have a dramatic impact on productivity among certain types of workers. Errors among key-punch operators declined 50 percent after they were exposed to a lemon scent and almost 80 percent after whiffs of lavender.

Needless to say, you would like to know more about these developments. You have decided to write to Fragrance Research Fund, Limited, a group that was mentioned in the article as being at the forefront in this area.

Your task: Draft a letter to Annette Green, vice president and administrator of Fragrance Research Fund, Limited, and ask for information on the impact of fragrances on factory workers doing repetitive jobs. One of your objectives is to learn more about the study at Catholic University and the work being done in Japan. In general, however, you want to get an overview of all the research pertaining to the impact of fragrances on job performance.[8]

7. Cycling and recycling: Letter from Trek USA requesting information on recycled papers
Competition is hot in the bicycle business, where tapping into the mood of your buyers means everything. At Trek USA in Waterloo, Wisconsin, your latest catalog is slick and sassy, demonstrating your company's focus on the latest, lightest, strongest materials and on your riders' love of biking off-road, in competition, and down a city block—but in style. The coated paper stock is sleek and shiny, the four-color photographs taken at action angles show lean, mean bicycling machines poised on a rocky mountain face, in the hands of seasoned racers, and even being ferried across a rushing stream. Yes, it's a catalog any marketing director would be proud of, and you are. Then someone handed you Schwinn's latest.

The Schwinn catalog, released the same month as your own, is oversized and rough-textured. The cover shows a drawing of planet Earth with "Handle with Care—Help keep the earth a great place to ride" wrapped around it in white letters. Inside, the emphasis is on people and the environment. Short featurettes accompanying the bicycle photos and specs describe people working to preserve the environment, to persuade cities to add more bike trails, and to teach fitness through cycling. The back cover? A big green box with the familiar triangular recycling emblem, stating that the recycled paper is more than a public relations gimmick; it's a serious effort the Chicago company practices at all levels, going so far as to eschew plastic bubbles to pack its bicycles in recycled cardboard. The green blurb ends with this clincher: "Bikes and bike riding preserve our environment . . . the only energy needed is you!"

Your heart sinks for a moment. They're right, you realize. Sure, your bikes appeal to the racing instinct in both professionals and amateurs. Your company built its strength on popular, high-quality mountain bikes. But who are most of your buyers in the United States *this* year? Could Schwinn be right? Is your appeal outdated—tuned to the 80s instead of the 90s? Not to be outdone or defeated, you start imagining a new campaign, one that can easily outstretch Schwinn's (you sincerely believe in your product's superiority). But maybe there's something to this recycling business. You noticed that another competitor's catalog, Specialized Bicycles and Accessories, was also printed on recycled paper, although their pitch was more subtle. Didn't you just spot an advertisement in *The Wall Street Journal* for a recycled paper company? Better get on it right away . . .

Your task: As marketing director for Trek USA, write a letter to the paper company whose advertisement you've relocated: Champion International Corporation, One Champion Plaza, Stamford, CT 06921. Address your letter to Alice Bryce, as the ad suggests, and request more information about the company's "complete line of recycled alternatives," particularly its Kromekote 2000 Recycled for your posters, and its Benefit Text, Cover, and Writing papers for your catalogs and brochures. Ask for paper samples, and inquire about recycled cardboard packing materials.[9]

8. Please tell me: Request for information about a product

You're a consumer, and you've probably seen hundreds of products that you'd like to buy (if not, look at the advertisements in your favorite magazine for ideas). Choose a big-ticket item that is rather complicated, such as a stereo system or vacation in the Caribbean.

Your task: You surely have some questions about the features of your chosen product or about its price, guarantees, local availability, and so on. Write to the company or organization offering it, and ask four questions that are important to you. Be sure to include enough background information so that the reader can answer your questions satisfactorily.

If requested to do so by your instructor, mail a copy of your letter (after your instructor has had an opportunity to review it) to the company or organization. After a few weeks, you and your classmates may wish to compare responses and to answer this question: How well do companies or organizations respond to unsolicited inquiries?

9. On second thought, don't express it: Request for cooperation in cutting the cost of express mail

Overnight mail delivery can be a real boon when you're facing a tight deadline, but all those express packages do add up. At Turner Broadcasting System, for example, the bill for overnight delivery was running around $1,000,000 a year. That number seemed a little high to William Ghegan, the corporate controller, so he decided to take a hard look at the situation.

What he saw was not a pretty sight. People were sending all sorts of things by express mail, regardless of whether rapid delivery was essential. Many employees were sloppy about noting what type of service they wanted, so the couriers automatically gave the packages highest priority. As a consequence, letters that could have been delivered in two days for $3 were delivered overnight for $8.50. Furthermore, nobody was making any effort to consolidate shipments to and from Turner's various offices around the world. This meant that the company often sent several individual packages to the same place on the same day and paid for three or four deliveries instead of one. To top it all off, the couriers frequently made billing errors that inflated delivery costs by as much as 20 percent.

Needless to say, Ghegan decided to do something. His solution was to require that all express mail be funneled through a central coordinator in each office who would ensure that priority handling was justified. This person would also fill out the forms correctly, consolidate shipments, and check for billing errors.

Your task: As an assistant to William Ghegan, you have been asked to draft a memo to Turner employees asking for their cooperation in handling express mail. Outline the actions you would like them to take.[10]

WRITING DIRECT REQUESTS FOR CLAIMS AND ADJUSTMENTS

10. Spoiled in Argentina: Claim from California peach growers

When President Carlos Menem of Argentina took office in 1989, he vowed to try a new tactic to stimulate his nation's productivity. Previous leadership had kept import tariffs high to support local industry; unfortunately, although the local factories responded by producing a wider range of goods, their products were both expensive and of poor quality. So Menem and his economy minister, Domingo Cavallo, decided that competition from foreign producers would stimulate Argentine business to provide better products at competitive prices. To the delight of Argentine shoppers, the import tariffs were lowered and goods began pouring in from all over the world: calculators and copy machines, scissors and automobiles, bicycles, toothpicks—and peaches.

When Menem's new policies took effect, California peach growers responded eagerly to the opening of the new market. Individual growers banded into the California Peach Growers Association to ship their fruit to Edcadassa, the Argentine firm that oversees all imported goods while they await customs clearance at Ezeiza International Airport.

As supervisor of the Argentine project for the growers association, you were extremely pleased with the success of the first few shipments; everything had gone smoothly. Then word came back from angry Argentine buyers that the fresh, firm California peaches they had expected arrived at their stores ready for the garbage bin. They refused to pay for the rotten fruit, and your growers lost $50,000.

You made inquiries and discovered that Edcadassa was overwhelmed by the level of imported goods flowing into Argentina (an average of 150 tons a day, compared with 60 tons two years before). Your peach shipment was lost in the confusion, and by the time it was cleared through customs, three weeks late, the peaches were already rotten. Since you'd shipped the fruit when it was at the perfect stage to make the journey, await the normal customs delay, and ripen gently in the supermarkets of Buenos Aires, you believe the responsibility for the shipment's destruction rests with Edcadassa.

Your task: Write a letter to Edcadassa (Columbia 4300, 1425 Buenos Aires, Argentina) requesting full compensation for the ruined peaches.[11]

11. Missing makeup: Memo requesting fulfillment of an incomplete order at M.A.C. Greenwich Village
When Canadian makeup artist Frank Toskan started M.A.C. (Make-Up Art Cosmetics) in his kitchen in 1985, he probably never dreamed how many of his lipsticks you'd be selling at his Greenwich Village store a decade later. But selling them you are, and you're also selling plenty of mascara, blush, professional makeup brushes, and even the T-shirts the company has become famous for: "Cruelty-Free Beauty" (a plea against animal testing) and "Make Up, Make Out, Play Safe" (proceeds of which go to the Design Industries Foundation for AIDS).

Toskan was looking for professional-quality products to use himself when he began. Now his customers love the company's social conscience (for every six used cases returned for recycling, they get a free lipstick) and its status among models and celebrities (Paula Abdul and Gloria Estefan certainly helped the bottom line). But mostly they love the M.A.C. products, which come in 400 fashion colors. When some of those colors aren't in stock, they get angry.

Sure enough, your last shipment from M.A.C. headquarters in Canada was missing two of your best sellers: Russian Red and Chili Matte lipsticks. You specifically ordered three cases of each, but they were neither in the box nor listed on the packing list. You've been making promises to regulars all week, "Any day now . . ." You know the company is having trouble keeping up with orders because it's been getting so much media coverage, because its specialty stores are springing up across the United States, and because more department stores are carrying the popular cosmetics. But you decide that's no excuse—your customers come first.

Your task: As assistant manager, write a memo to M.A.C. Canada (233 Carleton St., Toronto, Ontario M5A 2L2, Canada) explaining that your last order, dated March 2 and received April 17, was short the two items mentioned. Ask that they be shipped to the M.A.C. store in Greenwich Village immediately, via priority mail.[12]

MAKING ROUTINE CREDIT REQUESTS
12. Quick sales: Letter requesting credit to purchase portable cash registers for Saks Fifth Avenue
At the National Retail Federation's business and equipment exposition in New York, you found a new device that could really impress Saks Fifth Avenue's biggest spenders: a portable cash register. Manufactured by Telxon Corporation in Akron, Ohio, the hand-held registers operate with the same 16-bit computer chip that Nintendo uses for its video games. A magnetic strip reader authorizes and records credit card purchases, sending the information to the store's main computer through radio signals. The tiny register even has a bar-code scanner to read prices, a small display screen, and a printer to produce a receipt. The only drawback is that the register can't handle cash sales, but most of the business in the range you're thinking of is conducted with credit cards anyway.

What impresses you most about the portable register is the opportunity to have one of your salespeople following the customer from department to department, ready and able to ring up purchases without forcing your elite buyer to stand in separate checkout lines in formal wear, lingerie, sportswear—or any department, for that matter. At Saks, such speedy, personalized service rates very high.

As a regional buyer, you've persuaded the company to give the new technology a try at your Manhattan store. You've been authorized to buy six of the hand-held machines at $3,000 each; if they're as popular with customers as you think they'll be, Saks will use the portable registers as part of a personalized shopping service available at all your stores. You may end up ordering several dozen of them.

Your task: Write to Telxon Corporation (91 Springside Dr., Akron, OH 44313) ordering the six portable cash registers on a credit basis. Mention Saks Fifth Avenue's reputation and long history in the retail business, which should eliminate the need for enclosing a financial statement—particularly since your interest in the new technology will undoubtedly cause a flutter among Telxon's top marketing executives. Expect them to call on you very soon.[13]

After studying this chapter, you will be able to

- Choose when to write a routine, good-news, or goodwill message
- Adjust the basic pattern to fit the type of letter or memo you are writing
- Add resale and sales promotion material when appropriate
- Encourage your reader to take any desired action
- Avoid the pitfalls when writing credit approvals and recommendation letters
- Use the correct form for such specialized messages as instructions and press releases
- Adopt the proper tone in writing goodwill letters

CHAPTER SEVEN

WRITING ROUTINE, GOOD-NEWS, AND GOODWILL MESSAGES

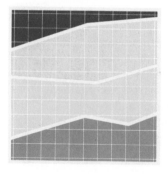

ON THE JOB:
Facing a Communication Dilemma at Campbell Soup Company
Food Giant Tries to Light a Fire under Its Sales

Zoe Coulson knows that staying on top of consumer demands and competitive pressures is a nonstop job. In her role as vice president of consumer affairs at Campbell Soup, Coulson plays a key role in making sure the company knows what consumers are thinking and what they want. Coulson must also keep customers happy by responding to questions and complaints, which requires strong writing skills and a good way with people. These tasks can be tough anywhere, but they're a special challenge in a company that's been struggling as much as Campbell Soup has been.

It's hard to imagine how a company whose products are found in virtually every U.S. kitchen, that has two-thirds of the U.S. soup market and major shares of other food markets both here and abroad, and that has a history of high-quality products stretching back nearly to the Civil War, could find itself in such unpleasant straits. But that was the situation facing Campbell in the late 1980s. Failed new products, ill-advised diversification, a controversial proposal to merge with Quaker Oats, and a bitter feud among the family members who control the company's stock left the New Jersey giant reeling. Even though revenues increased from under $3 billion to more than $6 billion through the 1980s, the company's profits on those sales dropped from $130 million to a mere $4 million.

And the internal struggles and problems weren't all that the company had to worry about. Consumer tastes were changing. Campbell's reliance on concentrated soups sold in uniform mixtures nationwide was less and less in line with regionalized tastes and a growing interest in convenience.

As the firm's in-house consumer advocate, Coulson is an important link between the public and the research kitchens. Her job is to find out what people are hungry for and then lobby the company to deliver—a role that constantly tests her communication skills. If you were Zoe Coulson, how would you communicate with the public to answer their inquiries and complaints? How would you plan and write positive business messages?[1]

PLANNING POSITIVE MESSAGES

Campbell Soup Company

Whether letters written for Zoe Coulson or memos prepared for your own business, most business communication consists of routine, good-news, and goodwill messages, so you'll probably get a lot of practice composing them. A clear understanding of how such messages are organized will allow you to write excellent ones quickly. Whether written or oral, they follow a simple formula: clear statement of the main idea, necessary details, courteous close. Because the main idea comes right at the beginning, this type of message is said to follow the direct plan.

CLEAR STATEMENT OF THE MAIN IDEA

Almost all business communication has two basic purposes: (1) to convey information and (2) to produce in the audience a favorable (or at least accepting) attitude or response. When you begin a message with a statement of your purpose, you are preparing your audience for the explanation that follows. The opening must be clear and concise. The following introductory statements make the same point; however, one is cluttered with unnecessary information that buries the purpose, whereas the other is brief and to the point:

INSTEAD OF THIS	WRITE THIS
I am pleased to inform you that after deliberating the matter carefully, our personnel committee has recommended you for appointment as a staff accountant.	You've been selected to join our firm as a staff accountant, beginning March 20.

The best way to write a clear opening is to have a clear idea of what you want to say. Before you put one word on paper, ask yourself this: What is the single most important message I have for the audience?

NECESSARY DETAILS

The middle part is typically the longest section of a routine, good-news, or goodwill message. Your reason for communicating can usually be expressed in

Russian president Boris Yeltsin is working to bring his own country into the world economy and also to strengthen the alliance among the republics that formed the Commonwealth of Independent States. Yeltsin believes positive messages must be based on both fact and performance if they are to create a lasting impact, generate support, and gain press coverage.

a sentence or two, but you'll need more space or time to explain your point completely so that the audience won't be left with confusion or lingering doubt. The task of providing necessary details is easiest when you are responding to a series of questions. You can simply answer them in order, possibly in a numbered sequence.

In addition to providing details in the middle section, you must maintain the supportive tone established at the beginning. This tone is easy to continue when your letter is purely good news. For example, consider this letter:

As we discussed, your major responsibilities as staff accountant in the internal accounting division will be to monitor our accounts receivable program. For this position, we're happy to offer you $2,750 monthly. You'll immediately be eligible for our health and pension plans as well as reduced membership fees at the Fitness and Racquet Club on Chestnut Avenue, near our office. Knowing how much you like to play squash, I'd also like to invite you to sign up right away for our Accountants' Squash Tournament, which begins next month.

When a routine message must convey mildly disappointing information, put the negative answer into as favorable a context as possible. Take a look at the following example:

INSTEAD OF THIS	WRITE THIS
No, we no longer carry the Sportsgirl line of sweaters.	The new Olympic line has replaced the Sportsgirl sweaters that you asked about. Olympic features a wider range of colors and sizes and more contemporary styling.

A bluntly negative explanation should be replaced with a more complete description that emphasizes how the audience could benefit from the change. Be careful, though. You can use negative information in this type of message only if you're reasonably sure the audience will respond positively to your message. Otherwise, use the indirect approach, which is described more thoroughly in Chapter 8.

COURTEOUS CLOSE

Make sure each audience member understands what to do next and how that action will benefit her or him.

Your message is most likely to succeed if your readers are left with the feeling that you have their personal welfare in mind. In addition, if follow-up action is required, you should clearly state who will do what next. The following closing statement not only highlights a benefit to the audience, it also clearly summarizes the desired procedure: "Mail us your order this week so that you can be wearing your Shetland coat by the first of October."

WRITING POSITIVE REPLIES

Many memos and business letters are written in response to an order, an inquiry, or a request. If the answer is yes or is straightforward information, the direct plan is appropriate.

Jane Wolchonok is the director of service quality for the northeast division of Citibank's Consumer Banking Group. She and her nine-member executive communications department handle the most serious and complicated service problems arising in the 230 regional branches in the New York metropolitan area. What usually happens is this: A Citibank customer has a problem and is dissatisfied with the outcome or the lack of an outcome. So the customer complains to a Citibank senior manager. The complaint winds up in Wolchonok's department. Wolchonok not only oversees the resolution of such problems but also sets service quality priorities for the division. In addition, it is her responsibility to monitor the execution of various service programs.

"I would not call our correspondence routine," Wolchonok points out very quickly. "Certainly the customer doesn't consider it routine. Anytime you deal with a person's money, there is heightened tension. Our responses to customer complaints must be prompt and correct, and they must address each customer's specific problem, which means our letters are anything but routine."

The events causing the problems aren't routine, either. Nor are they usually the customer's fault. "For example, one customer made a $20,000 payment to reduce a credit line, but his account was credited with only $200. We investigated, found he was correct, and restored the missing $19,800—with interest. We not only wrote a letter telling the customer we corrected the problem, but we also sent along a small gift. Given the size of the error, we wanted to emphasize the fact that we really regretted what had happened." On another occasion, a man's deposits were unaccounted for on three separate occasions over a six-month period. "First," says Wolchonok, "mislaying a deposit is a rare occurrence. Second, each lost deposit was in the same amount. It turned out that when the customer was depositing his paycheck, he was writing his branch number in the space intended for his account number.

ACKNOWLEDGING ORDERS

Acknowledgment letters play a role in building goodwill.

One of the simplest letters to write is one confirming that a customer's order has been received and is being filled. An order acknowledgment is unnecessary if the products are being shipped or the services are provided immediately. But acknowledgments of large orders, first orders from a customer, and orders that cannot be filled right away are appropriate. To foster goodwill, the wise business communicator sends a letter personalized with the customer's name and specific product information, even though stock paragraphs may be used.

In accordance with the direct plan, the first paragraph of an acknowledgment letter is a statement of "good news." The customer has placed an order and looks forward to receiving the merchandise; all you have to say is that the order is being processed and that the merchandise is on its way.

The middle section should demonstrate the professionalism of the firm through a clear, accurate summary of the transaction: when the delivery may be expected; the cost of the merchandise, shipping, and taxes; and an explanation of problems that might have arisen. If you have recently established a new credit account for this customer, you should summarize your credit terms.

Resale: information about the company or product that confirms the customer's good judgment in making the transaction

Letters of this type frequently do a bit of selling in the middle or closing section as well. Resale information bolsters the customer's confidence by pointing out the good points of the product or the company and the way those good points will benefit the customer. Sales promotion—the discussion of something you offer that the customer may not be aware of, may not have thought of buying, or hasn't yet purchased—takes advantage of the customer's obvious

Some processors caught it, but others didn't. When we didn't, the funds were misallocated."

Although there may be similarities in the situations Wolchonok deals with, she does not use form letters. "Of course, we've developed some paragraphs we've come to rely on from time to time. But we customize every response to the spirit in which the customer has contacted us. We begin with a welcoming and orienting comment. In the case of the missing credit line payment, we might begin, 'Thank you for your letter to our chairman letting us know about our error with your line of credit.' That reminds them of what we're writing about. In addition, I feel that taking responsibility for the error in the opening statement builds a bond between the customer and the bank. We then go on to spell out the action we've taken, explaining why we've done things that way." Wolchonok also insists on a courteous close that points out that Citibank does not consider the customer's recent experience an acceptable level of service: "We made it clear to the fellow with the missing deposits, for example, that we held our own people accountable for catching his error."

Wolchonok's department creates approximately 6,000 letters a year, 90 percent of which deal with problem situations. "Of those," Wolchonok estimates, "90 percent are favorably disposed of. That is, we re-

solve the situation to the customer's satisfaction. Our goal is nothing less than to restore the confidence of the customer in the bank." Thus Wolchonok and her people make the unusual routine. "We know we've done our job right when a customer writes to thank us and to say that, based on his experience, he'd recommend Citibank to anyone." That's as good as goodwill gets in business today.

APPLY YOUR KNOWLEDGE

1. What strategy would you employ if Wolchonok asked you to respond to an inquiry from a large depositor demanding to know why you closed a branch in her neighborhood? Outline the key points of your letter, and write the opening paragraph in the Citibank model.

2. The editor of a foreign-language newspaper (serving a close-knit community where there are two busy branches) has written to Citibank's board members, pressing them to advertise in his publication. He states that he has a great deal of influence in the community and implies that he will use it against the bank if his request is not honored. What approach would you take in responding? Outline the key points of your letter, and write the opening paragraph.

Sales promotion: information about goods or services that may supplement the customer's purchase

interest in your products. Sending along brochures or order blanks makes an additional purchase easier. To be effective, both resale and sales promotion material should demonstrate the "you" attitude. Emphasize benefits to the customer rather than benefits to the company.

Despite its business purpose, an order acknowledgment should end on a warm, personal note and with a look toward future dealings. The following letter was designed to leave the customer satisfied with the handling of the order and prepared to do more business with the writer's firm:

In a little over two weeks, you'll receive your Span-a-Vision videocassette recorder. Be watching for the United Parcel Service delivery van.

The main message is stated clearly right at the start.

Because you live in Massachusetts, you're exempt from the Illinois sales tax. So I'm enclosing a check for $26.15, the amount of the sales tax that you included in your payment.

The middle section conveys specific details about the order.

Mr. Harmon, you're going to enjoy your new videocassette recorder day after day. It's quite versatile. And to make it even more so, you might want to add a remote-control device. Wired and wireless models compatible with

The customer's name is mentioned, as in a personal conversation, to increase the feeling of friendliness.

your new videocassette recorder are pictured in the enclosed brochure. Thanks to these state-of-the-art electronic controllers, you can run a videotape on fast forward, rewind the tape, and search quickly for specific portions of the tape--all without budging from your most comfortable chair! Many users have come to think of their remote-control devices as a "must have." Let me urge you to order yours now, during our limited-time 10%-off sale.

When your new videocassette recorder arrives, spend a few minutes with the user's manual that accompanies it. It should answer all your questions about how to operate your recorder. If it doesn't, just pick up your phone and call toll-free 1-800-441-6446 between 9 a.m. and 6 p.m. weekdays (Central Standard Time). One of our expert staff members will be happy to help you.

Resale and sales promotion build on the customer's goodwill toward the product and the company.

In closing, the writer offers friendly, accessible help.

REPLYING TO REQUESTS FOR INFORMATION AND ACTION

Any request is important to the person making it, whether inside or outside the organization. That person's opinion of your company and its products, your department, and you yourself will be influenced by how promptly, graciously, and thoroughly the request is handled. As vice president of consumer affairs, Zoe Coulson needs to be sensitive to the tone of her letters.

When written on letterhead stationery, a reply legally commits the company to any promised action.

Admittedly, complying with a request is not always easy. The information may not be immediately at hand, and decisions to take some action must often be made at a higher level. Furthermore, because a letter written on letterhead stationery is legally binding, you must often plan your response carefully.

Fortunately, however, many requests are similar. For example, a human resources department gets a lot of inquiries about job openings. Companies usually develop form responses to handle repetitive queries like these. Although form responses are often criticized as being cold and impersonal, much time and thought may go into wording them, and computers permit personalization and paragraph reorganization. Thus a computerized form letter prepared with care may actually be more personal and sincere than a quickly dictated, hastily typed "personal" reply.

When a potential sale is involved

Prospective customers often request an annual report, catalog, brochure, swatch of material, or other type of sample or information to help them make a decision about a product encountered through advertising. A polite and helpful response may prompt them to buy. When the customer has not requested the information and is not looking forward to a response, you must use persuasive techniques like those described in Chapter 9. But in a "solicited" sales letter, which the customer is anticipating, you may use the direct plan.

Three main goals when a potential sale is involved:
- *Respond to the immediate request*
- *Encourage a sale*
- *Convey a good impression of you and your firm*

When answering requests involving a potential sale, you have three main goals: (1) to respond to the inquiry or answer all the questions, (2) to encourage the future sale, and (3) to leave your reader with a good impression of you and your firm. The following letter succeeds in meeting these three objectives:

Here's the copy of "Brightening Your Bathroom" that you recently requested.

A clear, conversational statement of the main point is all that's required to start.

As beautiful as the full-color photographs are, you really need to inspect Brite-Tiles in person. Only then can you fully appreciate the sparkling beauty of their designer colors and patterns and the quality of their fabrication. Baywood Hardware, 313 Front Street in Clear Lake, is the nearest outlet carrying Brite-Tiles. While you're there, ask the salesperson to explain how easy it is to install Brite-Tiles with our chemically compatible cements and grouts.

Key information—the address of the local store that carries the merchandise—is presented immediately, along with resale and sales promotion.

From antique Victorian to sleek contemporary, Brite-Tiles will help you achieve just the look you want. Spend a few moments now with the handy chart, "The Right Pattern for Your Decor," on page 5 of the enclosed booklet. Then you'll know which patterns to look for when you visit Baywood Hardware.

A reference to a specific page further emphasizes the benefits of the product. This suggestion also encourages the reader to take one more step toward an actual purchase.

Mrs. Lyle, if you have any questions before or during installation, please phone our toll-free Service Hotline: 1-800-459-3678. You'll get easy-to-follow answers every time.

The personal close confidently points toward the possible sale.

When no sale is involved

Two goals when no sale is involved:
- Respond to the request
- Leave a favorable impression of your company or foster good working relationships

Some requests from outsiders and most requests from fellow employees are not opportunities to sell a product. In replies to those requests, you have two goals: (1) to answer all the questions honestly and completely and (2) to leave a favorable impression that prepares the way for future business or smooths working relationships. The following is a well-written response to a request from an outsider that does not involve an immediate sale:

Thanks for writing to ask us about the warranty on your Micro-9 computer. Here are the answers to your questions, in the order you asked them:

A brief statement introduces the purpose of the letter.

1. All needed repairs to your computer are covered by the warranty, with the exception of damage caused by abuse, such as dents on the external frame, sheared wiring, or shorting from water penetration. If the cause of damage is in dispute, you may appeal your claim to our independent consumer panel. We will accept their decision.
2. When repair is needed, we'll be happy to pick up your computer and return it repaired for a total delivery charge of only $40. Whenever possible, pickups are made on a next-day basis--and always within two working days of your call.

Specific questions are answered clearly and fully, in the order asked, and with consideration for the reader's needs.

3. Yes, you can buy a one-year computer service policy any time before the expiration of your 12-month warranty. You can renew this policy indefinitely.

Making sure you're 100-percent satisfied is always our goal, Ms. Worthington. Whenever you have more questions, just let me know. And be sure to let me know how you like your new Micro-9 computer.

A warm, personalized, appreciative close encourages goodwill.

When writing to a fellow employee, you can assume a shared background and goals.

A similar approach is appropriate for responding to requests from fellow employees, although memo format should be used instead of letter format. The memo in Figure 7.1 is a reply written to an employee. Notice that the tone of the memo, while still respectful, is a bit less formal than the tone in the previous letter.

FIGURE 7.1
Memo Replying to a Routine Request

The good news is announced without any fanfare, and the specific actions are enumerated for easy reference.

The problem's cause and eventual solution are explained to demonstrate awareness and goodwill.

An appreciative, personal, cooperative close confirms the desire to foster good working relationships.

MEMO

DATE: May 9, 1993

TO: Mark Gundy

FROM: Bill Apodaca B.A.

SUBJECT: Temporary Measures to Alleviate Parking Problems

Today we have taken action that should relieve the situation you alerted me to in your memo:

1. We have asked the security department to post new signs at the entrances to the plant warning that our parking facilities are private. They have also been instructed to work with city police to ticket any nonemployee vehicles that block our driveways.

2. Until the problem is completely solved, plant workers have been given a "grace period" extending their clock-in time by five minutes so they can find a parking space.

Apparently, this problem arose because city streets in the surrounding neighborhood are being resurfaced. According to the city traffic department, this work should be completed by the end of next week. Until then, we'll do our best to be good neighbors despite the inconvenience.

Thanks for making me aware of the seriousness of the parking problem. If you have any other suggestions for improvements, please let me know. I plan to stay posted on this matter until parking is once more convenient for you and our other employees.

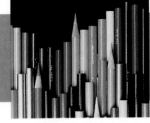

CHECKLIST FOR POSITIVE REPLIES

A. Initial Statement of the Good News or Main Idea

☐ **1.** Respond promptly to the request.

☐ **2.** Indicate in your first sentence that you are shipping the customer's order or fulfilling the reader's request.

☐ **3.** Avoid such trite and obvious statements as "I am pleased to," "We have received," "This is in response to," or "Enclosed please find."

☐ **4.** If you are acknowledging an order, summarize the transaction.

    ☐ a. Describe the merchandise in general terms.

    ☐ b. Express appreciation for the order and the payment, if it has arrived.

    ☐ c. Welcome a new customer aboard.

☐ **5.** Convey an upbeat, courteous, you-oriented tone.

B. Middle, Informational Section

☐ **1.** Imply or express interest in the request.

☐ **2.** If possible, answer all questions and requests, preferably in the order posed.

    ☐ a. Adapt replies to the reader's needs.

    ☐ b. Indicate what you have done and will do.

    ☐ c. Include any necessary details or interpretations that the reader may need to understand your answers.

☐ **3.** Provide all the important details about orders.

    ☐ a. Provide any necessary educational information about the product.

    ☐ b. Provide details of the shipment, including the approximate arrival time.

    ☐ c. Clear up any questions of charges (shipping costs, insurance, credit charges, or discounts for quick payment).

☐ **4.** Use sales opportunities when appropriate.

    ☐ a. Enclose a brochure that provides routine information and specifications, if possible, pointing out its main value and the specific pages of potential interest to the reader.

    ☐ b. Call the customer's attention to related products with sales promotion material.

    ☐ c. Introduce price only after mentioning benefits, but make price and the method of payment clear.

    ☐ d. Send a credit application to new customers and cash customers, if desirable.

☐ **5.** If you cannot comply with part of the request, perhaps because the information is unavailable or confidential, tell the reader why this is so, and offer other assistance.

☐ **6.** Embed negative statements in positive contexts, or balance them with positive alternatives.

C. Warm, Courteous Close

☐ **1.** Avoid clichés ("Please feel free to").

☐ **2.** Direct a request to the reader ("Please let us know whether this procedure does not have the effect you're seeking"), or specify the action you want the reader to take, if appropriate.

    ☐ a. Make the reader's action easy.

    ☐ b. Refer to the reader benefit of fulfilling your request.

    ☐ c. Stimulate the reader to act promptly.

☐ **3.** Use resale material in acknowledging orders to remind the reader of benefits to be derived from this order.

☐ **4.** Offer additional service, but avoid suggestions of your answer's being inadequate, such as "I trust that," "I hope," or other doubtful statements.

☐ **5.** Express goodwill or take an optimistic look into the future, if appropriate.

RESPONDING FAVORABLY TO CLAIMS AND ADJUSTMENT REQUESTS

In general, it pays to give customers the benefit of the doubt.

As anyone in business knows, customers sometimes return merchandise to a company, complain about its services, ask to be compensated, and the like. The most sensible reaction is to assume that the customer's account of the transaction is an honest statement of what happened—unless the same customer repeatedly submits dubious claims, a customer is patently dishonest (returning a dress that has obviously been worn, claiming it's the wrong size), or the dollar amount in dispute is very large. Very few people go to the trouble of requesting an adjustment unless they actually have a problem.

The usual human response to a complaint is to say, "It wasn't my fault!" But Campbell's Zoe Coulson must take a different stance, as must any business person who receives requests for claims or adjustments. Even when the company's terms of adjustment are generous, a grudging tone can actually increase the customer's dissatisfaction.

> An ungracious adjustment may increase customer dissatisfaction.

To protect your company's image and to regain the customer's goodwill, refer to your company's errors carefully. Don't blame an individual or a specific department, and avoid such lame excuses as "Nobody's perfect" or "Mistakes will happen." You shouldn't promise that problems will never happen again; such guarantees are unrealistic and often beyond your control. But if you explain your company's efforts to do a good job, you imply that the error was an unusual incident.

Imagine that customers who complain to a food company receive the following form letter, which is customized through word processing and is individually signed:

Your letter about the Golden Harvest canned fruit you recently purchased has been forwarded to our vice president of operations for review. We're pleased you took the time to write. Your satisfaction is important to us.

Since 1906, Golden Harvest has been packaging fine food products. Our workers and inspectors monitor quality carefully, using the most up-to-date technology, but we want to do an even better job. Your letter will help us do just that.

The next time you shop, use the enclosed half-price coupon to pick up a gift-boxed set of Golden Harvest Holiday Spices. This coupon, which will be honored wherever our fine specialty foods are sold, is our way of thanking you for your interest in our products.

> You may send form letters in response to claims, but word them carefully so that they are appropriate in a variety of circumstances.

Notice the following points about this letter:

- A form letter like this, which is sent to people with various types of requests or complaints, cannot start with a clear good-news statement because various customers are seeking various types of good news.

- The letter starts instead with what might be called a "good attitude" statement; it is you-oriented to put the customer at ease.

- At no time does this letter suggest that the customer was mistaken in questioning the quality of the product; on the other hand, the writer does not admit to any defect in the product.

- The middle, explanatory section nicely combines the old and the new: Golden Harvest has been doing business for over 80 years, but its equipment is thoroughly modern. This explanation of the company's quality controls may restore the reader's confidence in the product.

- The letter closes with some resale and sales promotion made personal by the use of *you* and *your*.

A letter written as a personal answer to a unique claim situation would start with a clear statement of the good news: the settling of the claim according to the customer's request. Look at this letter:

In just a few days you'll receive a new factory-tested electronic metric scale to replace the one you returned. Thanks, Dr. Clark, for giving us the opportunity to back up our claim of total buyer satisfaction.

Our goal for the past 104 years has been to provide precise and reliable measuring devices that meet the most exacting standards. Throughout our manufacturing process, every scale must meet stringent factory tests for accuracy and durability. Technicians in our test laboratories have been alerted to your experience, however, so that we can maintain the high ratings we have been given by all major professional journals.

We appreciate your interest in our products, Dr. Clark. Please continue telling us how we may supply your needs for dependable measuring devices.

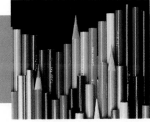

CHECKLIST FOR FAVORABLE RESPONSES TO CLAIMS AND ADJUSTMENT REQUESTS

A. Initial Statement of the Good News or Main Idea
☐ **1.** State immediately your willingness to honor the reader's claim.
☐ **2.** Accept your reader's account as entirely accurate unless good business reasons demand another interpretation of some points.
☐ **3.** Adopt a tone of consideration and courtesy; avoid being defensive, recriminatory, or condescending.
☐ **4.** Thank the reader for taking the time to write.

B. Middle, Informational Section
☐ **1.** Minimize or, if possible, omit any disagreements with your reader's interpretation of events.
☐ **2.** Maintain a supportive tone through such phrases as "Thank you for," "May we ask," "Please let us know," and "We are glad to work with you."
☐ **3.** Apologize only under extreme circumstances; then do so crisply and without an overly apologetic tone.
☐ **4.** Admit your firm's faults carefully.
  ☐ a. Avoid blaming any particular person or office.
  ☐ b. Avoid implying general company inefficiency.

☐ c. Avoid blaming probability ("Mistakes will happen").
☐ d. Avoid unrealistic promises about the future.
☐ e. Remind the reader of your firm's quality controls.
☐ **5.** Handle carefully the customer's role in producing the problem.
  ☐ a. If appropriate, honor the claim in full but without negative comment.
  ☐ b. If appropriate, provide an objective, nonvindictive, impersonal explanation.

C. Warm, Courteous Close
☐ **1.** Clarify any necessary actions that your reader must take.
☐ **2.** Remind the reader of how you have honored the claim.
☐ **3.** Avoid negative information.
☐ **4.** Encourage the customer to look favorably on your company and the product in question (resale).
☐ **5.** Encourage the customer to continue buying other goods from you (sales promotion), but avoid seeming greedy.

HANDLING ROUTINE CREDIT REQUESTS

Today, much of our economy runs on credit. Consumers often carry a wallet full of credit cards, and businesses of all sizes operate more smoothly because firms can pay for their purchases over time. Since credit is so common, most credit requests are routine, as are credit approvals and credit references.

APPROVING CREDIT

State credit terms factually and in terms of the benefits of having credit.

Letters approving credit are, of course, good-news letters and the first step in what may be a decades-long business relationship. Thus the opening of a letter granting credit may start out with the main idea. In the middle section of the letter, you must include a reasonably full statement of the credit arrangements: the upper limit of the account, dates that bills are sent, possible arrangements for partial monthly payments, discounts for prompt payments, interest charges for unpaid balances, and due dates of payments. The terms should be stated positively and objectively, not negatively or in an authoritarian manner:

INSTEAD OF THIS	WRITE THIS
Your credit balance cannot exceed $5,000.	With our standard credit account, you can order up to $5,000 worth of fine merchandise.
We expect your payment within 30 days of receipt of our statement.	Payment is due 30 days after you receive our statement.

Because the letter approving credit is considered a legal document, the wording should be checked for accuracy, completeness, and clarity.

The final section of the letter should provide resale information and sales promotion highlighting the benefits of buying from you. The following letter was written both to approve credit and to bring in customers:

As president of Colonial Mortgage Company in Montgomery, Alabama, R. J. Wynn understands that credit is affected by economic and legislative changes, both on the national and on the international level. But credit also depends on clarity, so Wynn advises that every credit transaction be meticulously handled and spelled out in the clearest terms.

Welcome aboard! Here's your new Ship-to-Shore credit card, which will make shopping at Conrad's even easier than before. Now you can make credit purchases up to a total of $1,000.

The good-news opening gets right to the point.

With a Ship-to-Shore card in your wallet, you can enjoy storewide shopping. Or if you prefer, phone in orders to 834-2230 for delivery within two days. A statement mailed on the tenth of each month will list all credit purchases made within the period and the amount due. When you pay the entire balance by the due date, no interest is charged. Otherwise, you may pay as little as 10 percent of the balance or $20, whichever is greater. A monthly interest charge of 1-1/2 percent of the outstanding balance will be added to your next statement.

An objective statement of the terms constitutes a legal contract. Positive, you-oriented wording avoids an authoritarian tone.

Do visit Conrad's today. You'll find that every department is overflowing with up-to-the-minute merchandise for your whole family. From gourmet foods to casual clothing to appliances for land and sea, this is your one-stop shopping center. And remember our free delivery service. Even if you're berthed in the city docks, we'll deliver your purchases right to your door.

The courteous close provides resale for the store and sales promotion, noting a range of customer benefits.

PROVIDING CREDIT REFERENCES

When responding to an inquiry about someone's credit worthiness
- *Make sure the request is legitimate*
- *Limit yourself to factual statements*

The great majority of credit applications are checked electronically: Computer terminals at many stores connect directly with data banks maintained by national credit-reporting agencies. Generally, the data are fed to the inquiring business without recommendation. At times, however, one businessperson will request a credit rating directly from another. If you are answering an inquiry about someone's credit worthiness, your first responsibility is to make sure the

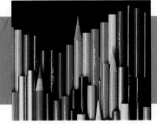

CHECKLIST FOR CREDIT APPROVALS

A. Initial Statement of the Good News or Main Idea

☐ **1.** Cheerfully tell the reader that he or she now has approved credit with your firm.

☐ **2.** Tell the reader, with brief resale, that he or she will soon enjoy the use of any goods ordered with the request; specify the date and method of shipment and other purchase details.

☐ **3.** Establish a tone of mutual warmth and trust.

B. Middle, Informational Section

☐ **1.** Explain the conditions under which credit was granted.

☐ **2.** Include or attach a full explanation of your firm's credit policies and expectations of payment.

☐ **3.** Stress the advantages of prompt payment in a way that assumes your reader will take advantage of them ("When you pay your account in full within ten days . . .").

☐ **4.** Include legally required disclosure statements.

☐ **5.** Inform or remind the reader of the general benefits of doing business with your firm (resale).

☐ a. Tell the consumer about benefits your firm offers, such as free parking, mail and phone shopping, personalized shopping services, your home decorating bureau, bridal consultants, restaurants, child care, gift wrapping, free deliveries, and special discounts or purchase privileges.

☐ b. If the customer is a retailer or wholesaler, tell about benefits your firm offers, such as nearby warehouses, factory representatives, quantity discounts, free window or counter displays, national advertising support, ads for local newspapers and other media, repair services, manuals, factory guarantees, prompt and speedy deliveries, toll-free phone number, and research department.

☐ **6.** Inform or remind the reader of a special sale, discount, or promotion (sales promotion).

☐ **7.** Avoid exaggerations or flamboyant language that might make this section of your letter read like an advertisement.

C. Warm, Courteous Close

☐ **1.** Summarize the reasons your reader will enjoy doing business with your firm.

☐ **2.** Use the "you" attitude and avoid clichés.

☐ **3.** Invite the reader to a special sale or the like, or provide resale information to motivate him or her to use the new account.

inquiry is legitimate. You're being asked to provide confidential information, which should not be made available unless it is requested by a stable business. As you write a credit reference, remember that the decision to approve is not yours but must be made by the company that has been asked to extend credit. Therefore, no matter how strong your opinion of the applicant may be, limit yourself to factual statements. If you don't, you may end up in court.

CONVEYING POSITIVE INFORMATION ABOUT PEOPLE

Professors, supervisors, and managers are often asked to write letters recommending students or employees for jobs, and almost anyone may be asked to recommend acquaintances for awards, membership in organizations, and other honors. Such letters may take the direct approach when the recommendation is generally positive. Employers use the same type of organizational plan when telling job applicants the good news: They got the job.

RECOMMENDATION LETTERS

It is important that letters of recommendation contain all the relevant details:

- The full name of the candidate
- The job or benefit that the candidate is seeking
- Whether the writer is answering a request or taking the initiative
- The nature of the relationship between the writer and the candidate
- Facts relevant to the position or benefit sought
- The writer's overall evaluation of the candidate's suitability for the job or benefit sought

A recommendation letter that will be held confidential may give a balanced view of the candidate.

Recommendation letters are usually mailed directly to the person or committee who requested them and are not shown to the candidate. A writer who has been assured of confidentiality can be more candid and present the important negatives along with the positives.

Oddly enough, the most difficult recommendation letters to write are those for truly outstanding candidates. A reader will have trouble believing uninterrupted praise for someone's talents and accomplishments. Thus good writers often illustrate the general points they are making with a specific example or two that point up the candidate's abilities, and they discuss the candidate's abilities in relation to the "competition."

A serious shortcoming should not be ignored, but beware of being libelous:
- Include only relevant, factual information
- Avoid value judgments
- Balance criticisms with favorable points

Most candidates are not perfect, however, and the danger in writing a critical letter is that you might engage in libel—that is, make a false and malicious written statement that injures the candidate's reputation. In the past five years, some 8,000 suits have been filed by workers charging former employers with slander or libel. Over a seven-year period in California, employees won 72 percent of libel and related cases against employers, with an average award of $582,000. Thus most employers have established a policy of not providing recommendation letters. At most, they will supply basic employment information about a past worker, such as position held, dates of employment, and final rate of pay.

Those employers who do still write letters of recommendation tend to stick to positive statements about the employee. But one problem with this approach is that the person who is hired on the basis of glowing recommendations may be unsuited to the new job. Also, such recommendations may make the letter writer vulnerable to lawsuit on the basis of negligence—that is, failure to provide essential information that could have significant bearing on job performance. Some companies consider it unethical to omit negative information from a recommendation if that information is truthful and relevant.

So if you do choose to write a letter, be aware of the legal ramifications and keep in mind that your wording could one day be scrutinized in court. Make sure the information you provide is accurate. State what is known and pertinent. Stick to the facts. Avoid volunteering information that is not related to the person's work performance, and refrain from using abusive language. As long as you reply honestly and in good faith, you are within the law.[2]

You can best protect yourself by sticking to the facts and placing your criticism in the context of a generally favorable recommendation, as in the following example:

I am pleased to support Jim Esposito's application for membership in the West Bay Umpires' Association.	The candidate's full name and the main point are clearly stated.
For the past two years, Jim and I have officiated at both high school and college baseball games. Working closely with him, I have found that he is a good umpire. Not only is he alert on the field, but he makes his calls quickly and sticks by them. Even though Jim has changed his calls because of managers' complaints more often than most of our league's other umpires have, he is highly respected by both managers and players. I've really enjoyed working games with him.	The duration and nature of the relationship are specified to give weight to the evaluation. A possible weakness related to the position is embedded in the discussion of good qualities without resort to overly negative terms.
We need more umpires like Jim Esposito in the Association! I would be happy to elaborate on his skills if you call me at home any evening (231-0977).	A supportive, personal summary of the writer's evaluation provides a good close. The phone number and invitation to discuss the candidacy further constitute another helpful touch.

In this letter, the writer avoids the risk of libel by supporting his statements with facts and by steering clear of vague, critical judgments.

You can also avoid trouble by asking yourself the following questions before mailing a recommendation letter:

- Does the person receiving this frank, personal information have a legitimate right to the information?

- Does all the information I have presented relate directly to the job or other benefit being sought?

- Have I put the candidate's case as strongly as I honestly can?

- Have I avoided overstating the candidate's abilities or otherwise misleading the reader?

If you can answer yes to all four questions, you may confidently mail off the letter and turn to your next project.

GOOD NEWS ABOUT EMPLOYMENT

Finding suitable job applicants and then selecting the right person is a task fraught with hard choices and considerable anxiety. In contrast, writing a letter to the successful applicant is a pleasure. Most of the time such a letter is eagerly awaited, so the direct approach serves quite well:

After interviewing a number of qualified applicants for the position of executive secretary to Cynthia Hargrove, our vice president of marketing, we have selected you. Welcome to Southwest Specialties!

We would like you to report for work on July 24 so that the person who currently has the job can spend a week showing you around. You will be paid a monthly salary of $1,500 and will receive the standard benefits package described during the interview process.

Please plan to arrive at 8:30 a.m. on the 24th; ask for me at the reception desk. We will spend an hour or so filling out the necessary forms and going over company employment policies. Then I will introduce you to the people in the marketing department--and your new career with Southwest Specialties will be under way!

Notice that this letter takes a friendly, welcoming tone and that it explains the necessary details: job title, starting date, salary, and benefits. The last paragraph, with its explanation of the first day's routine, helps allay the bewilderment and uncertainty that might afflict the new employee.

A letter telling someone that she or he got the job is a legal document, so make sure all statements are accurate.

Although letters like these are pleasant to write, you should be aware that, legally, a letter to a successful applicant constitutes a job offer. You and your company may be held to any promises you make. Thus attorneys sometimes recommend stating salary as a monthly amount and keeping the timing of performance evaluations and raises vague; you want to avoid implying that the employee will be kept on, no matter what, for a whole year or until the next evaluation.[3]

WRITING DIRECTIVES AND INSTRUCTIONS

Directives tell employees what to do; instructions tell readers how to do something.

Directives are memos that tell employees *what* to do. Instructions, which tell people inside and outside the company *how* to do something, may take the form of memos, letters, or even booklets. Both are considered routine messages because readers are assumed to be willing to comply.

The goal in writing directives and instructions is to make the point so obvious and the steps so self-explanatory that readers will not have to ask for additional help. Internal directives and instructions are especially important; faulty directives and bungled instructions are expensive and inefficient. The following directive explains exactly what employees should do:

Please send me employee vacation schedules for the third quarter, July through September, no later than June 16.

The deadline for submitting the schedules has been pushed back by two weeks, thanks to our new computerized personnel system. The new deadline should give your line workers more time to firm up their vacation plans.

Use the attached form, which has also been simplified, for reporting third-quarter vacation schedules.

Notice that this directive is brief and to the point. Drawn-out explanations are unnecessary because readers are expected simply to follow through on a well-established procedure. Yet it also covers all the bases, answering these questions: Who? What? When? Where? Why? How?

Instructions (see Figure 7.2) need to answer the same questions, but they differ from directives in the amount of explanation they provide. For example,

FIGURE 7.2
Instructions for Writing Instructions

HOW TO WRITE INSTRUCTIONS

When you need to explain in writing how to do something, a set of instructions is your best choice. By enumerating the steps, you make it easy for readers to perform the process in the correct sequence. Your goal is to provide a clear, self-sufficient explanation so that readers can perform the task independently.

Equipment Needed: Writing materials

Preparing to Write Useful Instructions
1. Perform the task yourself, or ask experts to demonstrate it or describe it to you in detail.
2. Analyze prospective readers' familiarity with the process so that you can write instructions at their level of understanding.

Making Your Instructions Clear
1. Include four elements as needed: an introduction, a list of equipment and materials, a description of the steps involved in the process, and a conclusion.
2. Explain in the opening why the process is important and how it relates to a larger purpose.
3. Divide the process into short, simple steps, presented in order of occurrence.
4. Present the steps in a numbered list, or present them in paragraph format, making plentiful use of words indicating time or sequence, such as first and then.
5. If the process involves more than ten steps, divide them into groups or stages identified with headings.
6. Phrase each step as a command ("Do this" instead of "You should do this"); use active verbs ("Look for these signs" instead of "Be alert for these signs"); use precise, specific terms ("three" instead of "several").
7. When appropriate, indicate how readers may tell whether a step has been performed correctly and how one step may influence another. Supply warnings when performing a step incorrectly could result in damage or injury, but limit the number of warnings so that readers do not underestimate their importance.
8. Include diagrams of complicated devices, and refer to them in the appropriate steps.
9. Summarize the importance of the process and the expected results in the conclusion.

Testing Your Instructions
1. Review the instructions to be sure they are clear and complete. Also judge whether you have provided too much detail.
2. Ask someone else to read the instructions and tell you whether they make sense and are easy to follow.

Zoe Coulson might write a simple three-sentence directive to employees to tell them of a change in the policies regarding employee scholarships; however, a detailed set of instructions would be more appropriate when explaining the procedure for applying for a scholarship. Figure 7.2 is a set of instructions for writing instructions. The key with instructions is to take nothing for granted. Assuming that readers know nothing about the process you're describing is better than risking confusion and possible harm by overlooking some basic information.

CONVEYING GOOD NEWS ABOUT PRODUCTS AND OPERATIONS

As vice president of brand marketing for all beauty products, gifts, and jewelry at Avon Products, Joyce Roché is responsible for the introduction of over 500 new products each year. Well aware of the power of the media, Roché urges you to communicate a clear product message by including information your readers will be interested in.

It's good business to spread the word about such positive developments as the opening of new facilities, the appointment of a new executive, the introduction of new products or customer services, and the sponsorship of community events. For example, imagine that So-Good Foods has successfully introduced a new line of vegetable chips (carrot, turnip, and yam chips, not the same old potato chips) to the stores it serves. To maintain its position on supermarket shelves, So-Good decides to offer a new discount program to stores that buy large quantities of its vegetable chips. It supplements the personal visits of its sales force with a good-news letter describing the new program to existing customers. The letter begins by trumpeting the news, fills in the details of the discount program in the middle, and closes with a bit of resale information and a confident prediction of a profitable business relationship.

When the audience for a good-news message is large and scattered, however, it is usually easier to communicate through publications, television, or radio. If McDonald's were to begin selling pizza, for example, the burger giant would probably want to let the media spread the word. In fact, McDonald's is test-marketing pizza in Indiana.[4] What better way to get reactions from across the country than to publicize the testing.

Press releases are the specialized documents that convey news to the media. They are written to match the style of the medium they are intended for. Press releases should be typewritten on plain $8\frac{1}{2}$-by-11-inch paper or on special letterhead—not on regular letterhead—and should be double-spaced for print media, triple-spaced for electronic media. Clean photocopies may be sent by first-class mail to radio and television news directors and to editors of magazines and weekly newspapers. But individually typed, hand-delivered copies are more impressive to city editors of the daily newspapers. These decision makers expect to see a format like the one shown in Figure 7.3.

Notice that the content of the press release in the figure follows the customary pattern for a good-news letter; however, it avoids explicit references to any reader. Instead, it displays the "you" attitude by presenting information presumed to be of interest to readers. Furthermore, because no honest editor will run a press release that sounds like an advertisement, the "plug" for the company's products has been relegated to the final section.

WRITING GOODWILL MESSAGES

Business is not all business. To a great extent, it's an opportunity to forge personal relationships. You can enhance your relationships with customers and

FIGURE 7.3
Press Release Format

Noted at the top is the name, affiliation, address, and phone number of the person who wrote the release and who can provide more information.

Most news is released immediately.

Provide your own suggestion for a title, or leave two inches here so that the editor can insert a headline.

This release for a newspaper starts with a dateline and a summary (who, what, when, where, why) of the rest of the story.

Put a release on one page if you can, but indicate carryover to a second page like this.

Head the second page like this, with a short title and the page number.

Do not split a paragraph; start the new page with a new paragraph. The "plug" is in the last paragraph.

Indicate the end of the release like this.

News Release

Time Inc.
Rockefeller Center
New York, NY 10020
212 586 1212

Contact:

For Immediate Release

Louis J. Slovinsky
Director, Corporate Public Affairs
(212) 841-3911

Time Inc.

A NEW LOGO FOR TIME INC.

NEW YORK, MARCH 13, 1985--Time Inc., the information and entertainment company, is introducing a new corporate logotype this week. It appears for the first time on the cover of Time Inc.'s 1984 Annual Report, now being distributed to the company's shareholders.

The new logotype, modeled on the classic Baskerville letterform, was designed by Walter Lefmann, who retired last year as _Time_ magazine's promotion art director.

--more--

Time Inc. Logo   2-2-2-2

In announcing the new logo to the Time Inc. staff, J. Richard Munro, president and chief executive officer, said: "A key element in the way a company is perceived is its use of graphics. To establish a strong, consistent identity for Time Inc., we have designed this new logo. It will set a standard that is consistent with our goal of being a top-quality company in every respect."

# # #

---

other businesspeople by sending friendly, unexpected notes with no direct business purpose. Some examples would be congratulations, thanks, condolences, and greetings. Goodwill messages like these have a positive effect on business because people prefer to deal with those who are warm, human, and not interested strictly in money.

One way to come across as sincere is to avoid exaggeration. What do you think a reader's reaction would be to these two sentences?

We were overjoyed to learn of your promotion.

Congratulations on your promotion.

Most likely, the reader would not quite believe that anyone (except perhaps a relative or very close friend) would be "overjoyed." But the reader will accept

Hal Riney's creativity has produced memorable TV advertising for Saturn, Perrier, and Swanson. Riney is president of Hal Riney and Partners in San Francisco, and he thinks too few people take goodwill seriously. Preferring scenes that are tender and sympathetic rather than loud and aggressive, he believes in spending the time it takes to build goodwill.

the writer's simple congratulations, a human, understandable intention. To demonstrate your sincerity, back up any compliments with specific points.

INSTEAD OF THIS	WRITE THIS
Words cannot express my appreciation for the great job you did. Thanks. No one could have done it better. You're terrific! You've made the whole firm sit up and take notice, and we are ecstatic to have you working here.	Thanks for taking charge of the meeting in my absence. You did an excellent job. With just an hour's notice, you managed to pull the legal and public relations departments together so that we could present a united front in the negotiations. Your dedication and your communication abilities have been noted and are truly appreciated.

Notice also the difference in the words used in these two examples. The reader would probably feel that the more restrained praise was the more sincere. Similarly, although offering help in a goodwill message is fine, be sure to promise only what you can and will provide. Avoid giving even the impression of an offer of help where none is intended.

Although goodwill messages have little to do with business transactions, they might include some sales information if you have the opportunity to be of particular service or want to remind the reader of your company's product. But any sales message should be subdued and secondary to the helpful, thoughtful message. In the following example, the dealer succeeds in seeming more interested in the relationship with the reader than in a possible sale:

Congratulations on reeling in the big one at the Grainger County fishing contest! The second we saw the newspaper picture of you holding that beauty in one hand and our Fish-Pro collapsible rod in the other, we felt button-popping proud.

Now that you're a local fishing expert, Lou, you might want to check out our other Fish-Pro equipment. At least come by sometime and let us shake your hand. Maybe we can talk you into telling us about your big catch.

Only the slightest hint of a sales pitch should ever appear in a goodwill message.

The reader of this letter will not feel a great deal of pressure to buy but will feel that the dealer took special notice of his accomplishments. If you add a sales pitch, make sure that it takes a back seat to your goodwill message. Honesty and sincerity must come across above all else.

CONGRATULATIONS

Taking note of significant events in someone's personal life helps cement the business relationship.

One prime opportunity for sending congratulations is news of a significant business achievement—for example, being promoted or attaining an important civic position. Notice that the sample congratulatory note in Figure 7.4 moves swiftly into the subject of the letter, the good news. It gives reasons for expecting success and avoids such extravagances as "Only you can do the job!"

FIGURE 7.4
Letter Congratulating a Business Acquaintance

The point of writing comes first.

The reason for congratulating the reader is expressed early and concisely.

Additional detail fleshes out the letter and clarifies the writer's purpose.

The letter ends with a personalized expression of confidence.

TWA
11495 NATURAL BRIDGE BRIDGETON (ST. LOUIS), MISSOURI, U.S.A. 63044

November 8, 1993

Mr. Lawrence Andrews, General Manager
St. Louis Landscape Design, Inc.
7600 Regents Road
St. Louis, MO 63155

Dear Mr. Andrews:

   Congratulations! We noted in this morning's news
that your firm has been chosen by the Lambert-St. Louis
International Airport to redesign the landscaping at
the airport.

   We are delighted to learn that you have been awarded
the contract. By beautifying the airport, you will help
establish a pleasant atmosphere for our passengers and for
our employees.

   Judging by your award-winning work along the water-
front, we are indeed fortunate that your firm is handling
the project. We are confident that you will make the
entrance to the airport more beautiful and convenient.

                          Cordially,

                          Jessica Rogers
                          Jessica Rogers
                          Director, Airport Relations

nb

TRANS WORLD AIRLINES, INC.

Highlights in people's personal lives—weddings and births, graduations, success in nonbusiness competitions—are another reason for sending congratulations. You may congratulate business acquaintances on their achievements or on their spouse's or children's achievements. You may also take note of personal events, even if you don't know the reader well. However, if you are already friendly with the reader, you can get away with using a very personal tone.

Some alert companies develop a mailing list of potential customers by assigning an employee to clip newspaper announcements of births, engagements, weddings, and graduations. They then introduce themselves by sending out a form letter that might read like this:

Congratulations!

We thought you might like this extra copy of your picture and wedding announcement from the <u>Evening Herald</u>. It's a pleasure to send it to you. Please accept our good wishes for your happiness.

In this case, the company's letterhead and address is enough of a sales pitch. This simple letter has a natural, friendly tone, even though the sender has never met the recipient.

LETTERS OF APPRECIATION

A letter of appreciation documents a person's contributions.

An important quality for managers to have is the ability to see employees (and other business associates) as individuals and to recognize their contributions. People often value praise more highly than monetary rewards, and a letter of appreciation may also become an important part of an employee's personnel file:

Thanks a million for programming the computer for the fulfillment department. I suppose only those of us close to this task can really appreciate the size and complexity of the job you did in such a short time. Even during a time when your own work load is usually heavy, you managed to develop a series of programs that will significantly improve our ability to handle the work of our department.

Always remember, Kathy, your time and talents are truly appreciated. We view your accomplishment as outstanding!

cc: Personnel Department

With its references to specific qualities and deeds, this note may provide support for future pay increases and promotions.

Anyone who does you or your organization a special favor should receive written thanks.

Suppliers also like to know that you value some exceptional product or the service you received. Long-term support deserves recognition too. Your praise doesn't just make the supplier feel good; it also encourages further excellence. Notice how the brief message that follows expresses gratitude and reveals the happy result:

Thank you for the quick service.

You got me that power pack in time for the 8 a.m. flight, and the customer was in service by noon!

Thanks again, especially to Brian McKee in your customer service department, for making us both look good.

When you write a letter of appreciation to a supplier, try to mention specifically the person or people you want to praise. Your expression of goodwill might net the employee some future benefit. In any case, your letter also honors the company that the individual represents.

Guest speakers at meetings should also be thanked, even if they have been paid an honorarium or their travel expenses—and surely if they have not.

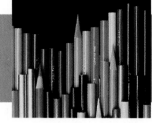

CHECKLIST FOR GOODWILL MESSAGES

A. Planning Goodwill Messages

☐ **1.** Choose the appropriate type of goodwill message for your purpose.

☐ a. Offer congratulations to make the reader feel noticed.

☐ b. Express praise or thanks to show your appreciation for good performance.

☐ c. Offer condolences to show appreciation for the deceased or the person suffering a loss.

☐ d. Send greetings to put a positive business image before the reader.

☐ **2.** Be prompt in sending out goodwill messages so that they lose none of their impact.

☐ **3.** Because a written message can be savored more than once, send a written goodwill message rather than a telephone message, but keep in mind that a telephone message is better than none at all.

B. Format

☐ **1.** Use the format most appropriate to the occasion.

☐ a. Use letter format for condolences and for any other goodwill message sent to outsiders or mailed to an employee's home.

☐ b. Use memo format for any goodwill messages sent through interoffice mail, except for condolences.

☐ c. Use a preprinted greeting card for condolences (with a brief handwritten message added) or for seasonal greetings.

☐ **2.** Handwrite condolences; otherwise, type the goodwill message.

☐ **3.** Use special stationery, if available.

☐ **4.** For added impact, present congratulations in a folder with a clipping or photo commemorating the special event.

C. Opening

☐ **1.** State the most important idea first to focus the reader's attention.

☐ **2.** Incorporate a friendly statement that builds goodwill, right at the beginning.

☐ **3.** Focus on the good qualities of the person or situation.

D. Middle

☐ **1.** Even in a short message, provide sufficient details to justify the opening statement.

☐ **2.** Express personalized details in sincere, not gushy, language.

☐ **3.** Be warm but concise.

☐ **4.** Make the reader, not the writer, the focus of all comments.

E. Close

☐ **1.** Use a positive or forward-looking statement.

☐ **2.** Restate the important idea, when appropriate.

Letters of appreciation are also appropriate for acknowledging donations to campaigns or causes. They should usually include a few details about the success of the campaign or about how the donation is being used.

SUMMARY

Positive replies, favorable responses to claims and requests for adjustment, responses to routine credit requests, positive information about people, directives and instructions, good news about products and operations, and goodwill messages—these make up much of the daily correspondence in business. Their purpose is to convey a message that readers will either welcome or accept without question. Some of these messages also encourage readers to take a specific action.

Routine, good-news, and goodwill letters follow a straightforward pattern: first, a clear statement of the news or main point; then, the necessary explanatory details; and finally, a warm and courteous close. Some include resale information or sales promotion, which are complimentary references to the writer's company and its products. Most are rather short and depend heavily on the "you" attitude. A sincere and courteous tone highlights the positive image that such messages seek to convey and helps maintain a warm business relationship.

ON THE JOB:
Solving a Communication Dilemma at Campbell Soup Company

You would have to search far and wide to find a person more qualified for her job than Zoe Coulson, Campbell Soup's vice president for consumer affairs. In addition to her many years of experience dealing with consumers, she is a recognized expert in package design, she is the author of the *Good Housekeeping Illustrated Cookbook*, and she counts among her credits past roles as advertising specialist, food editor, member of the board of directors of the Food and Drug Law Institute, and director of the Good Housekeeping Institute. In short, she knows consumers and the food business inside and out, and she knows how to communicate.

Few companies need Coulson's expertise more than Campbell Soup does. During the 1980s, Campbell tried to compensate for two decades of sluggish product innovation by introducing hundreds of new products and branching out into new product areas and new markets. Some of these efforts produced winners, but many products were rushed to market without adequate input from consumers. These expensive flops and the aggressive diversification plans put a big strain on the company's finances and were partly responsible for the former CEO's resignation.

In the last few years, however, the company has begun to refocus on its core businesses (such as soups, frozen foods, and baked goods) and has begun to pay a lot more attention to consumer tastes and trends. To better meet the diverse needs of consumers across the United States, Campbell divided its U.S. organization into 22 units, each focused on a particular region. Now, for instance, consumers in the Southwest can enjoy a spicier blend of Campbell's nacho cheese soup/sauce than consumers elsewhere in the country. Another restructuring effort in Europe was designed to bring costs under control and to better coordinate marketing of various Campbell brands. Not surprisingly, Zoe Coulson plays a major role in Campbell's efforts to better meet the needs of its millions of customers worldwide, whether she's responding to dissatisfied customers or answering simple requests for information.

Campbell's efforts have begun to bear fruit. Its profit margin has increased nearly 50 percent in just the last five years, also due in part to aggressive cost-cutting measures. Annual sales, while not as vigorous as the company would hope for, crossed the $6 billion mark in 1990 and continue to climb steadily, if somewhat slowly.

When fine-tuning its product line over the next few years, Campbell will get plenty of input from Zoe Coulson. Two of her major concerns, for instance, have been reducing the salt and fat content of Campbell's soups and improving product labeling. As Campbell moves into the next century, Coulson will be communicating with consumers and employees to make sure the giant food producer keeps sales and profits cooking.

Your Mission: You have joined Campbell's consumer marketing staff. As an assistant to Zoe Coulson, you are responsible for handling correspondence with both consumers and Campbell employees. Your objective is to improve the flow of communication between the public and the company so that Campbell can respond quickly and knowledgeably to changing consumer needs. Choose the *best* alternatives for responding to the situations described below:

1. Coulson has received a letter from a Mrs. Felton who, although pleased that Campbell has introduced Special Request reduced-sodium soup, would like to see more flavors added to the low-salt line. Which is the best opening paragraph for your reply?
   a. The Campbell Soup Company was founded at the turn of the century by a chemist named J. T. Dorrance, who invented condensed soup and sold it in a 10-ounce can for a dime. He was a conservative man and a stickler for quality. His only son, Jack Dorrance, followed his father into the business and had a similar management philosophy. As chairman of the company, he used to wander down to pinch

the tomatoes and taste the carrots from time to time, just to make sure that the folks in the factory were maintaining high standards. Only 12 days before he died at the age of 70 in April 1989, Jack Dorrance was at the Campbell test kitchen in Camden, New Jersey, sampling new soups. He was especially interested in the low-salt line and would be pleased to know that it appeals to you.

b. Thank you for your enthusiastic letter about Campbell's Special Request soups. We are delighted that you enjoy the flavors currently available, and we are working hard to add new varieties to the line.

c. Good news! Our world-renowned staff of food technologists is busy in the test kitchen at this very moment, experimenting with additional low-sodium recipes for Special Request soups. Hang on to your bowl, Mrs. Felton, more flavors are on the way!

2. Which of the following versions is preferable for the middle section of the letter to Mrs. Felton?

a. You can expect to see several exciting new Special Request soups on your supermarket shelf within the next year. Before the new flavors make their debut, however, they must undergo further testing in our kitchens and in selected markets across the country. We want to be sure our soups satisfy consumer expectations.

While you're waiting for the new flavors of Special Request, you might like to try some of Campbell's other products designed especially for people like you who are concerned about health and nutrition. I'm enclosing coupons that entitle you to sample both Pepperidge Farm Five-Star Fibre bread and Le Menu Light Style frozen dinners "on the house." We hope you enjoy them.

b. We are sorry that the number of Special Request flavors is limited at this time. Because of the complexities of testing flavors both in the Campbell kitchens and in test markets around the country, we are a bit behind schedule in releasing new varieties. But several new flavors should be available by the end of the year, if all goes according to plan.

In the meantime, please accept these coupons; they can be redeemed for two other fine Campbell products designed for the health-conscious consumer.

c. Additional flavors of Special Request reduced-sodium soups are currently in formulation. They will arrive on supermarket shelves soon. In the meantime, why not enjoy some of Campbell's other fine products designed for

the health-conscious consumer? The enclosed coupons will allow you to sample Le Menu Light Style frozen dinners and Pepperidge Farm Five-Star Fibre bread at our expense.

3. Which of the following paragraphs is the best conclusion for the letter to Mrs. Felton?

a. No conclusion is necessary.

b. We are gratified that Special Request soups appear regularly on your dinner table. It's nice to know that someone appreciates our efforts to provide the public with nutritious products.

c. Again, thank you for taking the time to write. Comments from people like you help us keep our product-development efforts on track. Please let us know how you like the new flavors of Special Request soup.

4. Campbell has just received its first order from Fiesta Marts, a grocery chain based in Houston that caters to the Hispanic population. Typically, orders are processed by another department within the company, but in this case, you have been asked to reply because your department is involved in researching the Hispanic market. You would like to let Fiesta's managers know that you offer a special line of soups designed for Hispanic tastes and that you will sponsor an in-store promotion to introduce these soups to Fiesta's customers and to analyze their reaction. Additionally, you want to explain that filling Fiesta's order will take an extra day or two because the order calls for cans labeled in Spanish. Here is the draft of your reply. Read it and decide what, if anything, needs to be changed:

Thank you very much for your recent order for 20 cases of Campbell's Soup in assorted flavors. We welcome you as a new client.

Our traditional soups have a universal appeal, but given your demographic orientation, you might also like to try our Casera line, which is specifically formulated to appeal to Hispanic tastes. Our salespeople would be happy to arrange a special in-store promotion so that your customers can sample several Casera soups. We have found that promotions of this type are an excellent way to get people to try a new product. Additionally, we learn quite a bit from the customers' reactions to the product. A Campbell representative will call on you shortly to discuss details.

Your order for the 20 cases of traditional Campbell's Soup should arrive in approximately seven days. Generally, we can deliver within three to five days, but at the moment our inventory of soup with Spanish labels is low because we just filled a very large order for the Argentine government.

Once again, thank you for your order. We look forward to a long and happy business relationship with Fiesta markets.

a. The letter is fine the way it is.
b. The third paragraph should be combined with the first paragraph and should express the main idea: The order will be delivered within seven days. The second paragraph should be edited to improve clarity and style. The final paragraph is adequate as is.
c. The letter should begin with the second paragraph, which expresses the main point: Campbell offers a special line of soups formulated for Hispanic tastes, and the company would like to provide an in-store promotion to introduce these soups to Fiesta's customers. The first and third paragraphs should be combined and should become the second paragraph. The final paragraph is okay.

5. Campbell has received a letter from the American Heart Association asking for information on the fat and sodium content of Campbell's products. Your department has developed a brochure that provides the necessary data, and you plan to send it to the association. Which of the following cover letters should you send along with the brochure?
a. Please consult the enclosed brochure for the answers to your questions regarding the composition of Campbell's products. The brochure provides detailed information on the sodium and fat content of all Campbell's products, which include such well-known brands as V-8, Pepperidge Farm, Swanson's, Mrs. Paul's, and Le Menu, as well as Campbell's Soups.
b. Thanks for your interest in Campbell's products. We are concerned about nutrition and health issues and are trying to reduce the salts and fats in our products. At the same time, we are striving to retain the taste that consumers have come to expect from Campbell. In general, we feel very good about the nutritional value of our products and think that after you read the enclosed brochure, you will too.
c. Thank you for your interest in Campbell's Soup. The enclosed brochure provides the information you requested about the fat and sodium content of our products. Over the past ten years, we have introduced a number of reduced-sodium and low-fat products designed specifically for consumers on restricted diets. Additionally, we have reformulated many of our regular products to reduce the salt and fat content. We have also revised our product labels so that information on sodium and fat content is readily apparent to health-conscious consumers. If you have any questions about any of our

products, please contact our consumer information specialists at 1-800-227-9876.

6. Campbell has received a letter from a disgruntled consumer, Mr. Max Edwards, who was disappointed with his last can of Golden Classic beef soup with potatoes and mushrooms. It appears that the can contained an abundance of potatoes, little beef, and few mushrooms. You have been asked to reply to Mr. Edwards. Which of the following drafts is best?
a. We are extremely sorry that you did not like your last can of Golden Classic beef soup with potatoes and mushrooms. Although we do our very best to ensure that all our products are of the highest quality, occasionally our quality-control department slips up and a can of soup comes out a bit short on one ingredient or another. Apparently you happened to buy just such a can--one with relatively few mushrooms, not much beef, and too many potatoes. The odds against that ever happening to you again are probably a million to one. And to prove it, here's a coupon that entitles you to a free can of Golden Classic soup. You may pick any flavor you like, but why not give the beef with potatoes and mushrooms another try? We bet it will meet your standards this time around.
b. You are right, Mr. Edwards, to expect the highest quality from Campbell's Golden Classic soups. And you are right to complain when your expectations are not met. Our goal is to provide the best, and when we fall short of that goal, we want to know about it so that we can correct the problem.

And that is exactly what we have done. In response to your complaint, our quality-control department is reexamining its testing procedures to ensure that all future cans of Golden Classic soup have an even blend of ingredients. Why not see for yourself by taking the enclosed coupon to your supermarket and redeeming it for a free can of Golden Classic soup? If you choose beef with potatoes and mushrooms, you can count on getting plenty of beef and mushrooms this time.
c. Campbell's Golden Classic soups are a premium product at a premium price. Our quality-control procedures for this line have been carefully devised to ensure that every can of soup has a uniform distribution of ingredients. As you can imagine, your complaint came as quite a surprise to us, given the care that we take with our products. We suspect that the uneven distribution of ingredients was just a fluke, but our quality-control depart-

ment is looking into the matter to ensure that the alleged problem does not recur.

We would like you to give our Golden Classic soup another try. We are confident that you will be satisfied, so we are enclosing a coupon that entitles you to a free can. If you are not completely happy with it, please call me at 1-800-227-9876.

7. Zoe Coulson was recently named one of corporate America's 100 most promising women executives by a nationwide business magazine. As her administrative assistant, you have been asked to draft a press release to the local newspapers announcing the good news. Here is your first draft. How can it be improved?

For many years, the Campbell Soup Company has been a leader in equal employment opportunities for women and minorities. Campbell is proud of its reputation for nurturing outstanding female and minority employees. Given the company's commitment to affirmative action, it is gratifying to announce that Ms. Zoe Coulson, Campbell Soup Company's vice president of consumer affairs, has been selected one of corporate America's 100 top women executives.

Ms. Coulson has been with Campbell since 1981. Before joining Campbell, she was the director of the Good Housekeeping Institute. She holds an M.B.A. degree from the Harvard Business School.

In her capacity as Campbell's in-house consumer advocate, Ms. Coulson has been instrumental in reducing the sodium and fat content of Campbell's products. She has also worked to ensure that all product labels are clear and "user friendly."

a. Omit the initial portion of the press release, down to the section that reads, "Ms. Zoe Coulson, Campbell Soup Company's vice president of consumer affairs, has been selected one of corporate America's 100 top women executives." Move the third paragraph up so that it follows this sentence and becomes part of the first paragraph. Complete the press release with the second paragraph, which describes Coulson's previous experience.
b. Add several paragraphs that describe Campbell's products.
c. Rework the press release so that it is more of a personality profile of Zoe Coulson. Add information about her personal life, her hobbies, her management style, and her career progress. Include several direct quotes from Ms. Coulson to illustrate her reaction to the honor.[5]

QUESTIONS FOR DISCUSSION

1. How should negative information be conveyed in a routine or good-news message? A goodwill message?
2. Why should anyone bother to write letters acknowledging orders?
3. Which is better for replying to requests for information and action—a form letter or a personal reply? Why?
4. How can selling information be incorporated in a routine or good-news message? A goodwill message?
5. How can you avoid engaging in libel when writing a letter of recommendation about someone who has limitations?
6. Why should directives and instructions be phrased as commands?

DOCUMENTS FOR ANALYSIS

Read the following letters; then (1) analyze the strengths or weaknesses of each sentence and (2) revise each letter so that it follows this chapter's guidelines.

DOCUMENT 7.A
After receiving your shipment of returned books, we checked our records to see why we had sent them to you in the first place. Our records show that you were late in returning your card indicating that you did not want the selections. As you know, we will automatically send you the month's new books unless you specifically ask not to receive them by our clearly stated deadline. This policy enables us to see that our subscribers have access to the newest books as soon as possible.

However, you are in luck. Because we value your membership in the Read-a-Lot Club, we are crediting your account for $29.18--the full price of the books that you returned!

In the future, please try to return your reply card more promptly so that you won't face the inconvenience of returning the books. In any case, we want to express our thanks for your long-term patronage of the Read-a-Lot Club. We think you will want next month's selection, which is a murder mystery by John D. MacDonald.

DOCUMENT 7.B

Please accept our apologies for the delay in repairing your video game, which is being shipped under separate cover.

Let me explain what happened: Four Star Games, the manufacturer of your video game system, had expanded their production facilities to capitalize on the boom in video game sales that occurred in the early 1980s. When the market for such games declined, the firm was unable to meet the payments on their bank loans. The firm went bankrupt early this year, and we bought their assets. We also acquired their liabilities, which included all repairs under warranty.

Your broken game was just one of many that fell in our lap, so to speak. As you can imagine, it took us a while to sort out what was happening--hence the delay in repairing your video game.

In the future, we will be handling any further re-

pairs covered by warranties through a new dealer network, created through the combination of Four Star's best dealers and our own existing dealers. If you have any further problems with the game, please contact one of these dealers for repairs.

Thanks for your patience in this matter. Again, we apologize for the delay. Incidentally, I am enclosing a brochure showing some of our exciting new products.

DOCUMENT 7.C

I was really glad to hear that you were promoted to vice president of research and development at ChemCo. I know that you have wanted that job for years, and I can imagine how happy you must be now that you have finally achieved your goal. But before you break out the champagne, take a hard look at what you're getting into.

As you know, I received an important promotion myself last year. And let me tell you, it's not all a bed of roses up here in the executive suite. I've been working 12 and 15 hours a day since I became general manager of the Wingate plant; my wife and children hardly recognize me anymore, and my former friends in the company act like they're afraid of me. As they say, it's lonely at the top. If you find yourself wishing you could undo it all, give me a call. Maybe we can run away and join the circus together.

CASES

WRITING POSITIVE REPLIES

1. Thank you, Japan: Letter from Xerox acknowledging an order
No one believed Xerox could do it, but it has: Not only has it regained some of the low-cost copy machine market lost to Japanese manufacturers in the early 1970s (when Xerox's copier patents expired), but it is now selling its copy machines to Japanese companies.

Xerox's success is the result of a slow rebuilding process, in which the company took great pains to increase its market share by dramatically improving the quality of its products. In a process Xerox calls "competitive bench-marking," company executives visited and studied the methods of firms known for excellence in certain areas of manufacturing or distribution, such as L. L. Bean and Toyota. To develop Xerox Model 5100, the copier that has begun to crack the Japanese market, Xerox engineers spent over four years in research and development, inviting engineers from the company's Japanese joint-venture partner, Fuji

Xerox Company, to participate in the process. Chief Engineer Daniel W. Cholish and other executives traveled to Japan to meet with potential customers. After surmounting the barriers of language and culture, Xerox officials learned that Japanese companies need copiers that can reproduce *kanji* (fine, handwritten Japanese characters) on the lightweight and oversize papers frequently used in Japan. And the instructions, of course, must be printed in Japanese.

So far, it looks as if all of Xerox's efforts are paying off. In 1989 the company won the Malcom Baldrige National Quality Award. And in Japan the Xerox 5100 is selling well among companies like Tokyu Corporation (nucleus of a huge, multinational conglomerate) and Tokyo Electric Power Company (which provides a third of Japan's total electric power). In fact, as a communication specialist at company headquarters in Stamford, Connecticut, you've been asked to develop an appropriate letter of acknowledgment that can be forwarded overseas to each new Japanese customer.

Your task: Write the form letter that acknowledges an order for the new Xerox 5100. The letter will be reproduced with individual company names. Be sure to use this opportunity to reinforce your sales message.[6]

2. Naturally soothing: Letter describing the contents of The Body Shop By Mail's stress kit

When Anita Roddick founded The Body Shop in 1976, in Brighton, England, she offered a few simple cosmetics featuring natural ingredients, limited packaging, and no seductive advertising (although the enterprising Roddick, who needed to feed her family, frankly admits that she sprinkled strawberry oil on the sidewalk in front of that first Body Shop to entice new customers). Over the years Roddick's simple philosophy evolved into the motto "Profits with Principles," and The Body Shop thrived. Annual sales of Roddick's "naturally based hair- and skin-care preparations" are approaching $400 million from over 700 shops in 40 countries.

Despite her extraordinary financial success, Roddick's principles are holding firm. The Body Shop has always opposed any use of animals in testing cosmetics and, with posters and T-shirts, has set in motion an active campaign that others in the industry have since copied. Employees are encouraged to spend some portion of their company-paid time working as volunteers for community groups. The company has set up "Trade Not Aid" programs in both First and Third World countries, urged its customers to get out and vote, and worked to help orphans, political prisoners, and rain forest inhabitants. Long before it was fashionable, The Body Shop used price discounts to encourage customers to bring back their plastic bottles for refills of White Musk lotion or Kiwi lip balm. Initially that was because Roddick couldn't afford to invest in new containers; now everything that can possibly be recycled is reused.

"Quite simply, we want to work with our customers to make the world a better place to be," Roddick explains. Every shop carries racks of leaflets and pamphlets—not only on skin and hair care but also on the current issues that have attracted the company's concern.

Recently, the company began offering everything from Banana Shampoo to Dewberry Fruit Soap through a mail-order catalog, *The Body Shop By Mail*. Since customers can't sniff and dab and sample, they often send letters asking for more information about the items they've seen in the unusual catalog (which features almost as many calls to action as cosmetics). In the three months you've been working at the catalog's headquarters in Cedar Hills, New Jersey, you've already answered about 16 such letters. Now there's another one on your desk.

Suzanne Timmons in Warrensburg, Missouri, wants to know more about the contents of your "Stress Kit" and whether or not it would be suitable as a gift for her boyfriend. The kit includes a 4.2-ounce bottle of rich pink Peppermint Foot Lotion, a 0.4-ounce jar of refreshing Elderflower Under Eye Gel (to wake up tired eyes), a 4.2-ounce bottle of unscented Body Massage Oil, and a 100 percent cotton washcloth, all tucked into a clear, heavy plastic drawstring bag. All three products are popular with both men and women. Peppermint Foot Lotion, for example, was developed for runners in the London Marathon as a remedy for tired feet and is now a best seller around the world. The products are "naturally based" but also contain synthetic ingredients to prevent contamination.

Your task: Write to Suzanne Timmons at 1255 Butcher Road, Warrensburg, Missouri 64093, and answer her questions. Include copies of the appropriate pages from The Body Shop's Product Information Manual, which all shops display and which lists the ingredients of the products contained in the stress kit. Be sure to let her know that her purchases will also support The Body Shop's humanitarian efforts worldwide.[7]

3. Calming fear at Eli Lilly: Reply to a woman whose grandmother took DES—a "wonder drug" disaster

When it first became available in 1947, DES (diethylstilbestrol) was hailed as a miracle drug. Thousands of pregnant women in the midst of the postwar baby boom eagerly ingested the new synthetic hormone. They had been told by their doctors that it would prevent premature labor, and even "build bigger and stronger babies." Then tragedy struck.

By 1971 the drug was definitely linked to clear cell adenocarcinoma, and its use was restricted by the U.S. Food and Drug Administration. The rare form of cancer was turning up, not in the women who took the drug, but in their daughters. At the time this tragic link was discovered, your employer, Eli Lilly, produced 75 percent of the country's supply of DES.

For nine years before its release, Eli Lilly tested the new drug extensively. Independent researchers concluded that it would save babies who might not otherwise have been carried to term, with no harm to the mother or the unborn child. Not until years later did officials at your company learn with the rest of the world that 1 out of every 1,000 DES daughters would develop clear cell cancer. Many of these daughters have sued the companies that produced the DES their mothers took (one damage award alone cost your company $12.2 million).

Although no scientific evidence so far has indicated that DES is passed down genetically to *third* generations, public concern is growing. Dr. Ruthann Giusti of the National Cancer Institute has issued a statement that, despite the lack of proof for genetic linkage, there is an *indirect* link between the drug and third-generation babies, who may suffer serious handicaps caused at birth by their mothers' cervical and uterine abnormalities, possibly caused by the DES their own mothers ingested. (This statistical conclusion has not yet been confirmed by clinical research.)

On your desk is a letter from Kimberly Horton, whose grandmother took DES. Her mother had a hysterectomy at 29 as a result of cervical cancer, then had a benign lump removed from her breast, and later lost both ovaries and fallopian tubes when an ovarian cyst ruptured. She never suffered from the clear cell adenocarcinoma attributed to DES. Kimberly, now 25, says she has already had one miscarriage and doctors tell her that she, too, suffers from reproductive abnormalities. Her letter is a poignant, fearful plea: "Please tell me everything you know about the effects of DES on third-generation women. Will I suffer from cancer like my mother because my grandmother took the drug your company produced? Although my mother did not have miscarriages, I understand other DES daughters have—is this why I lost my baby?"

Your task: As a company spokesperson, you've been asked to write a reassuring response to Kimberly (Box 116, Williamstown, MA 01267). At hand is a previous company statement, cold and factual: "The third-generation claims now being asserted by a few plaintiffs' attorneys allege injuries resulting from premature births and do not involve claims of genetic damage or defect due to DES exposure." Kimberly mentioned in her letter that she was not born prematurely.[8]

RESPONDING FAVORABLY TO CLAIMS AND ADJUSTMENT REQUESTS

4. The short-sighted promotion: Letter from Residence Inn to deal with objections to an ad

As manager of marketing communications for Residence Inn, Joe Okon wanted his advertising to differentiate the chain from the competing suite-type hotels cropping up across America. He thought about using a photo of the hotel chain's rooms but rejected that idea as being too similar to everybody else's ads. Instead, he decided to go with something a little bit whimsical—a picture of twelve pairs of men's undershorts: ten to show the average stay at a Residence Inn, and two to show the average stay at most other hotels.

In many respects, the ad was a big success. During the campaign, calls to the reservation center increased by 150 percent over the preceding year. However, there was one small problem: The ad offended many female business travelers. Thirty of them took the time to complain about the "tasteless, sexist" ads. Sarah Carlston, a publicist, was typical of the women who wrote. She said: "You'd think they could have picked

better symbols. I wonder what they would have used if they were trying to reach women—bras or panties?"

Your task: Write a letter to Ms. Carlston apologizing for the ad. Feel free to offer her a reasonable inducement to give Residence Inn another chance.[9]

HANDLING ROUTINE CREDIT REQUESTS

5. Silicon Valley Bank chips in: Letter granting a line of credit to a start-up company

As a credit officer at Silicon Valley Bank, you've talked to plenty of entrepreneurs—American, French, Hungarian, and Iranian. But these days the typical loan customers sitting across your desk are from China, Taiwan, or Hong Kong. They came to the United States to earn their degrees, staying to work as top engineers for some of the largest high-tech electronics firms in Northern California's Silicon Valley. But the former engineers tell you that they were frustrated because, despite their contributions to these companies, they were passed over for promotions into management. Quite a few believe that a subtle bias is working against them, a misconception that Asians are good technicians but bad managers. They point to statistics gathered at one well-known company indicating that 26 percent of its engineers and 20 percent of its professional workers are Asian, but only 12 percent of its managers come from the Far East. The apparent bias is a mistake, they say, and they're going to prove why.

Increasing numbers of Silicon Valley's best engineers are taking their ambitions and their creativity and leaving those "safe" but stagnant jobs to establish themselves at the top of the ladder. Whether in partnership with other Asians or on their own, they're securing investment capital from both overseas and domestic sources to start companies that manufacture everything from data storage disks to pen-based computers. These Asian-owned U.S. companies are challenging foreign-dominated markets (such as those for computer monitors), and more than a dozen are already publicly traded. Meanwhile, the new owners are developing important business links with the Far East while providing jobs for Silicon Valley. All the new executives, of course, hope to follow the pattern set by Chinese immigrant An Wang, whose Wang Laboratories in Lowell, Massachusetts, logged $2.1 billion in revenues last year.

Silicon Valley Bank views this development in the local economy as a healthy situation for everyone. That's why you are going to approve an unsecured $50,000 line of credit for Knights Technology, a company that manufactures computer chip testing equipment, to help it balance operating expenses against cash flow. Founded by Dr. Shao-Hung (Gerry) Liu and several Taiwanese partners, Knights Technology appears to have done quite well for its first three years in business, based on your analysis of the financial statements and background submitted by Dr. Liu. Since Silicon Valley Bank built its own foundation on the entrepreneurial spirit of people like Dr. Liu, you're happy to count his company among your customers.

Your task: Write a letter to Dr. Shao-Hung Liu, president, Knights Technology, Inc. (3506 Bassett St., Santa Clara, CA 95054), granting his request for the $50,000 line of credit. Your letter will formally welcome the company as a new customer; all the appropriate loan documentation will be signed and exchanged at a meeting in your office, which you suggest for Thursday, April 23.[10]

CONVEYING POSITIVE INFORMATION ABOUT PEOPLE

6. On a course for Harvard: Reply to a request for a recommendation letter
After working for several years for Zoe Coulson in Campbell Soup Company's department of consumer affairs (see this chapter's On-the-Job simulation), one of your co-workers, Angela Cavanaugh, has decided to apply for admission to the Harvard Business School's M.B.A. program. She has asked Coulson, a Harvard graduate, to write a letter of recommendation for her. Here are the facts about Angela Cavanaugh:

1. She has an undergraduate degree in journalism from the University of Iowa, where she was an honors student.
2. She joined Campbell directly after graduating and has worked for the firm for the past five years.
3. Her primary responsibility has been to answer letters from consumers; she has done an outstanding job.
4. Her most noteworthy achievement has been to analyze a year's worth of incoming mail, categorize the letters by type and frequency, and create a series of standardized replies. The department now uses Cavanaugh's form letters to handle approximately 75 percent of its mail.
5. Although Cavanaugh has outstanding work habits and is an excellent writer, she lacks confidence as a speaker. Her reluctance to present her ideas orally has prevented her from advancing more rapidly at Campbell. This could be a problem for her at Harvard Business School, where skill in classroom discussion influences a student's chances of success.

Your task: Because you have worked closely with Cavanaugh, Zoe Coulson has asked you to draft the letter, which Coulson will sign.[11]

7. Bon voyage! Letter offering a position as overseas sales representative for International Discount Telecommunications
When Howard Jonas sent his hotel-brochures sales staff to Israel to open a new office for his publishing business, the youthful entrepreneur nearly suffered heart failure. He expected each sales representative's phone bill to triple to about $1,000 a month as he or she kept in touch with customers in the United States. But the bills he received were closer to $8,000!

Although the competition among AT&T, US Sprint, and MCI has lowered long-distance rates in the United States, most countries have a state-owned phone monopoly. So even though it costs only about $5 to call Italy from the United States, a comparable call from Italy to the United States runs around $18. Thus Jonas set out to devise a way for people located overseas to use U.S. phone lines for their international calls.

At first he hired a secretary to answer calls from his overseas employees and to call them back after patching in a conference call with their stateside customers. But a friend suggested that Jonas could accomplish the same result with a computerized automatic telephone dialer (about $50) and a few other gadgets. Driven by sheer necessity, Jonas set to work with his computer-wise friend and, within a few months, an innovative business service was born: International Discount Telecommunications.

For $250 a month, the service offers overseas customers two phone lines and a black box. The customer calls the company, lets the phone ring once, and hangs up. The equipment in the black box is programmed to call back with the second line connected to a U.S.-based long-distance carrier. Then with that dial tone, the customer can call anywhere in the world, saving about 75 percent of what the call would have cost using the state-owned phone system. The service is also considerably cheaper than the international dialing packages offered directly by U.S. carriers to customers traveling abroad.

Now Jonas's challenge is to sell his service to companies and individuals throughout the world. Although a patent is pending for the black box, it's only a matter of time before his competitors duplicate it. Another problem is that some customers are afraid of offending the telephone monopoly in the country where they do business and losing their regular service as a result. What Jonas needs are some top-notch sales reps to convince the telecommunications managers at these companies that the savings are worth the risk. He's hired you as personnel director for International Discount Telecommunications, headquartered in the Bronx, New York. Your top priority is to recruit the best sales staff you can find.

One of those individuals is Jorge Banuelos, who has worked both in the United States and in Europe as an overseas sales representative for office equipment. You like him personally, and his qualifications are excellent, as was his sales record.

Your task: Write to Jorge Banuelos (12 Fifth Avenue, Apt. C, New York, NY 10010), and offer him the job, which will require plenty of overseas travel.[12]

WRITING DIRECTIVES AND INSTRUCTIONS

8. Wrinkle-free service: Memo directing Nordstrom employees to stress customer service

Another great story has reached corporate headquarters in Seattle. It seems that a clerk in the menswear department of a Nordstrom store learned that a customer was buying a new dress shirt to wear to an important business meeting that afternoon. The clerk dashed into the back room and gave the shirt a good pressing to get the wrinkles out. The customer was so astonished by the good service that he wrote the store manager a note of appreciation. And the clerk received a $200 gift certificate in recognition of his efforts.

You're pleased to see additional proof that Nordstrom's emphasis on service is paying off. In the competitive world of retailing, your company is growing more rapidly than most department store chains, and your sales per square foot are twice the industry average. Furthermore, morale among your employees is high. Knowing that they are the company's chief competitive asset makes the clerks feel important. The company does everything it can to reinforce this feeling.

Your task: Draft a directive that your boss, the head of personnel, can send to store managers. The message isn't new, but it bears repeating: They are to encourage clerks to take initiative in serving customers, just as the menswear clerk did. And they are authorized to use Nordstrom gift certificates, within the constraints of their overall budget, to reward employees who best exemplify the company's philosophy.[13]

CONVEYING GOOD NEWS ABOUT PRODUCTS AND OPERATIONS

9. Crayola classics: Memo announcing new washable crayons and the reissue of eight old favorites

Change doesn't come easy to Binney & Smith, the Pennsylvania manufacturer of Crayola brand crayons. It's not that the company moves slowly, or lacks ideas; your product just happens to be one the public carries close to its childlike heart. You should know; you're a manager in the marketing department.

Take, for instance, the company's decision to retire eight dowdy old colors for snappy new neons designed to have a greater appeal for today's kids. Who wouldn't want to color with wild strawberry, vivid tangerine, teal blue, royal purple, jungle green, fuchsia, dandelion, and cerulean?

Moms, that's who. And Dads. By the hundreds, they deluged Binney & Smith with letters of protest. They formed groups with names like RUMPS (Raw Umber and Maize Preservation Society) and CRAYON (Committee to Reestablish All Your Old Norms). Three hundred letters a week finally had an impact; your bosses relented—but only for a little while. "Kids love the eight new colors, but Moms like the old eight we replaced," explained company president Richard Gurin.

Everyone knows who buys the crayons in the house, so for now Gurin has decided they're both right. The old favorites will reappear for a limited time in two special packages. A limited-edition Collector's Colors box will contain the classic eight: blue gray, green blue, lemon yellow, maize, orange red, orange yellow, raw umber, and violet blue. For the serious collector, a commemorative tin facsimile of the original 1903 Crayola package will hold a box of 64 crayons, including the new neons, and the small box of old favorites, for a suggested retail price of $6.99.

But Binney & Smith hasn't given up on innovation. You've been working on the marketing campaign for a breakthrough that Moms are sure to love (and you hope kids will, too): washable crayons. They'll come in preschooler large and "So Big" sizes. Instead of having a wax base, the parent-friendly crayons are made of water-soluble compounds like those used in cosmetics. A test team of grown-ups has scrawled them over all kinds of painted and papered wall surfaces, and every bit of this toddler-style art has proved scrubbable with soap and water—for up to two months. Who says you can't improve on an old favorite? (The washable crayons will be issued in the original 1903 Crayola colors: red, green, yellow, orange, blue, black, brown, and violet.)

Your task: As head of your department, write a memo to all Binney & Smith employees announcing these new product marketing plans.[14]

WRITING GOODWILL MESSAGES

10. Good work: Congratulations to Digital's new mail-order PC department

Digital Equipment Corporation built its reputation on large computer systems, but the Massachusetts company has attempted several times to dip into the lucrative ($27 billion) personal computer market. Digital's first attempt in the early 1980s was an embarrassing failure that cost the manufacturer an estimated $1 billion. Now the new U.S. desktop unit of Digital is ready to give it another try—this time going head-to-head with mail-order PC giants Dell Computer and Gateway 2000 to win a share of the $1.5 billion mail-order market.

In an internal memo, Dennis Schneider, director of marketing for the new division, outlined the mail-order campaign. To begin, Digital officially released its new mail-order catalog, slashing PC prices by 50 percent to beat the competition. The desktop machines are manufactured by Tandy, Intel, and Olivetti but "co-engineered" by Digital. During the next year, Schneider will spend over $20 million on advertising to promote Digital's ability to configure each personal computer system to meet customers' specifications and to ship the machines within 48 hours. The company will also offer on-site installation, a 30-day money-back guarantee, and an on-site one-year warranty from its 10,000-member service organization. No other mail-order PC vendor has the capability of matching Digital's service network, and that's what the new division is banking on.

The announcement of the new venture was a real coup for Schneider and his team. They face some pretty stiff competition, and there's a chance they could fail. But this time it seems that Digital might just have a profitable edge. As marketing director for mainframe systems, you were the one who hired Schneider, and you've been watching his career over the years. Now seems like a good time to extend congratulations for his recent achievements and to wish him well.

Your task: Write a congratulatory memo to Dennis Schneider, Director of Marketing, U.S. Desktop Division.[15]

11. The crosscut compromise: Letter thanking Stanley distributors for their support

When a company expands into international markets, all sorts of unforeseen problems crop up. Consider the dilemma facing the Stanley Works, for example. When the old-line Yankee firm decided to sell its crosscut saws in Europe, it discovered that the French and English don't see eye to eye on saw teeth and saw handles. The English favor wooden handles and hard teeth, but the French like their saws to have plastic handles and soft teeth that can be resharpened periodically. Because

making separate saws for the two markets is an expensive proposition, Stanley hopes to convince customers from both cultures to buy the same model. But as Allan Bing has discovered, selling the French and the English on a common solution to the crosscut saw problem is no easy trick.

Bing, a French-speaking Englishman who is a marketing manager for Stanley, has taken on the task of reconciling the opposing French and English tastes. After crisscrossing the channel for the umpteenth time in search of a solution, Bing finally settled on a design that he thinks may please both markets: a plastic-handled saw with hard teeth. He is now hard at work convincing customers to give the compromise a try. Thanks to the help of Stanley's distributors who are pushing the saw's benefits, Bing is optimistic that both the French and the English will snap it up. The British are beginning to view the plastic handle as an improvement, and the French are impressed with the speedy cutting attainable with the hard-toothed blade.

Your task: Bing believes that the distributors will be pleased to know how much Stanley appreciates their efforts to promote the new design. He has suggested that Stanley's top European marketing executive write a form letter thanking the distributors for their efforts. You have been asked to draft the letter.[16]

CHAPTER EIGHT

After studying this chapter, you will be able to

- Choose appropriately between the indirect and direct approach
- Maintain the proper tone from the beginning of your message
- Present bad news in such a way that a reader will accept it as reasonable and understandable
- Write closings that motivate the reader to take constructive action
- Compose bad-news messages that will leave the reader willing to continue a business relationship with your firm

WRITING BAD-NEWS MESSAGES

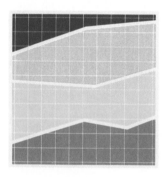

ON THE JOB:
Facing a Communication Dilemma at Creative Associates
Working for "Peanuts"

When he was a little boy growing up during the 1920s in St. Paul, Minnesota, "Sparky" Schulz loved to read the comic strips. His deepest ambition was to become a cartoonist. After serving in the Army in World War II, he worked as an art instructor for a correspondence school and sent stacks of comic strips to magazines and syndicates. In 1950, he got lucky. United Feature Syndicate picked up Charles Schulz's *Peanuts*—and Lucy, Charlie Brown, Linus, Snoopy, and the rest of the gang became part of the American culture. Today, the Peanuts characters appear in 2,100 newspapers around the world, as well as on toys, greeting cards, lunch pails, music boxes, toothbrushes, T-shirts, cookie jars, paper cups, refrigerator magnets . . .

Unlike many other cartoonists, who employ assistants to fill in backgrounds and do the lettering on their comic strips, Charles Schulz personally creates each installment of *Peanuts*. He also draws for the thousands of licensed products that represent the Peanuts gang. Nothing bears the "Peanuts stamp" without Schulz's personal approval. He is determined to protect the strip from being cheapened by association with second-rate merchandise.

Of course, thousands of applicants would like to become Peanuts vendors, so just responding to all those people is a full-time job. And dozens of other requests must be dealt with on a daily basis. If you were a member of Schulz's business organization, Creative Associates, how would you say no to people in a way that maintains goodwill?[1]

EASING THE PAIN OF BAD-NEWS MESSAGES

A Charles Schulz *Peanuts* cartoon

To cushion bad-news messages, use
- Appropriate tone
- The "you" attitude
- Positive words
- The most appropriate arrangement

Even if you're not as famous as Charles Schulz, it is important for you to realize that some people interpret being rejected as a personal failure; being turned down for a job or for credit, or even being rejected in less sensitive areas, usually complicates people's lives. Admittedly, business decisions should not be made solely to avoid hurting someone's feelings, but mixing bad news with consideration for the other person's needs helps the audience understand that your unfavorable decision is based on a business judgment, not on a personal one.

When the time comes to compose a bad-news message, you must address two basic questions. The first is, What tone will best contribute to the message's effectiveness? For example, on October 17, 1989, San Francisco was shaken to its roots by a major earthquake, and Lloyds of London predicted early that property losses would exceed $1 billion.[2] As an insurance adjuster, what tone would you have used to tell homeowners that they would be receiving only a fraction of what they expected from their claim? In bad-news messages of any kind, you must try to adopt a tone that supports three specific goals:

- You want your audience to understand that your bad-news message represents a firm decision.

- You want your audience to understand that under the circumstances, your decision is fair and reasonable.

- You want your audience to remain well disposed toward your business and, possibly, toward you.

With the right tone, you can make an unwelcome point while preserving the audience's ego. One key is to make liberal use of the "you" attitude. For example, point out how your decision might actually further the audience's goals, even though it first causes disappointment. You can also convey concern by looking for the best in your audience. Even if the person is at fault, assume that he or she is interested in being fair. And you can ease the pain by using positive instead of negative words.

The second question is, What arrangement of the main idea and supporting data will most completely ease the audience's disappointment? The answer is found by choosing between the two basic strategies described in Chapter 4: (1) the indirect plan, in which you present supporting data first and then the main idea; or (2) the direct plan, in which you present the main idea first and then the supporting data.

INDIRECT PLAN

The indirect plan is actually a familiar approach. You've probably used it many times, saying something in a roundabout way to avoid upsetting another person. So you can see how beginning a business message with a blunt no might keep someone from reading or listening to your reasons. The point of using the indirect plan is to ease the audience into the part of your message that demonstrates you are fair-minded or eager to do business on some other terms.

The indirect plan consists of four parts: (1) a buffer; (2) reasons supporting the negative decision; (3) a clear, diplomatic statement of the negative decision;

and (4) a helpful, friendly, positive close. By presenting the reasons for your decision before the bad news itself, you gradually prepare the audience for disappointment. In most cases, this approach is more appropriate than an abrupt statement of the bad news.

Buffer

Buffer: neutral lead-in to bad news

The first step in using the indirect plan is to put the audience in an accepting mood by making a neutral, noncontroversial statement closely related to the point of the message. For example, in a memo telling another supervisor that you can't spare anyone from your customer service staff for a temporary assignment to the order fulfillment department, you might begin with a sentence like this: "Customer service, I'm sure you agree, is one of our major concerns at National Investments. And this department shares your goal of processing orders quickly and efficiently." If possible, base the buffer on statements made by the person you are responding to. The danger in using an unrelated buffer is that you will seem to be "beating around the bush," thus appearing unethical and losing your audience's respect.

Also avoid giving the impression in the buffer that good news will follow. Building up the audience at the beginning only makes the subsequent letdown even more painful. Imagine your reaction if you were to get a letter with this opening from Schulz's Creative Associates: "Your resume indicates that you would be well suited as a vendor for our Peanuts characters." Now compare that opening with this: "Your resume shows very clearly why you are interested in becoming a vendor for our Peanuts characters." The second opening, which emphasizes the applicant's favorable interpretation of her or his qualifications rather than the company's evaluation, is less misleading but still positive.

Here are some other things to avoid when writing a buffer:

For more than a decade, Johnson & Johnson's yearly profit gains have averaged over 19 percent. Nevertheless, CEO Ralph S. Larsen faces fiercely competitive markets and the need to cut costs. To succeed in today's market, says Larsen, you have to be tough-minded. When communicating bad news, don't cloud the issues. Show that you understand your audience's needs, but don't undermine your message with apologies.

- *Avoid saying no.* An audience who encounters the unpleasant news right at the beginning will react negatively to the rest of the message, no matter how reasonable and well phrased it is.

- *Avoid using a know-it-all tone.* Do not use phrases such as "You should be aware that." The audience will expect your lecture to lead to a negative response and will therefore become resistant to the rest of your message.

- *Avoid wordy and irrelevant phrases.* Do not use phrases such as "We have received your letter," "This letter is in reply to your request," and "We are writing in response to your request." You make better use of the space by referring directly to the subject of the letter.

- *Avoid apologizing.* An apology weakens your explanation of the unfavorable decision.

- *Avoid writing a buffer that is too long.* Briefly identify something that both you and the audience care about and agree on; then proceed in a businesslike way.

Table 8.1 shows some ways you could tactfully open a bad-news message.

After you have composed a buffer, evaluate it by asking yourself four questions: Is it pleasant? Is it relevant? Is it neutral, saying neither yes nor no?

Does it provide for a smooth transition to the reasons that follow? If you can answer yes to all four, you may proceed confidently to the next section of your message.

Reasons

If you've done a good job composing the buffer, the reasons will follow naturally. Cover the more positive points first; then move to the less positive ones. Provide enough detail for the audience to understand your reasons. But be concise; a long, roundabout explanation may make the audience impatient.

Present reasons to show that your decision is justifiable and fair.

It is important to explain *why* you have reached your decision before you say *what* that decision is. If you present your reasons effectively, they will help convince the audience that your decision is justified, fair, and logical. However, someone who realizes you are saying no before he or she understands why may either quit paying attention altogether or be set to rebut the reasons when they're finally given.

Focus on how the audience might benefit from your negative message.

Tactful business communicators highlight the benefits to the audience instead of focusing on the company. For example, when saying no to a credit request, show how your decision will keep the person from becoming financially overextended. Facts and figures are often helpful in convincing the audience that you are acting in her or his best interests. Experienced business communicators do not try to cushion bad news by hiding behind company policy. A statement like "Company policy forbids our hiring anyone for this posi-

TABLE 8.1 Types of Buffers

BUFFER	EXAMPLE
Agreement: Find a point on which you and the reader share similar views.	We both know how hard it is to make a profit in this industry.
Appreciation: Express sincere thanks for receiving something.	Your check for $127.17 arrived yesterday. Thank you.
Cooperation: Convey your willingness to help in any way you realistically can.	Employee Services is here to smooth the way for those who work to achieve the company's goals.
Fairness: Assure the reader that you've closely examined and carefully considered the problem, or mention an appropriate action that has already been taken.	For the past week, we have carefully monitored those using the photocopying machine to see whether we can detect any pattern of use that might explain its frequent breakdowns.
Good news: Start with the part of your message that is favorable.	A replacement knob for your range is on its way, shipped February 10 via UPS.
Praise: Find an attribute or an achievement to compliment.	Your resume shows an admirable breadth of experience, which should serve you well as you progress in your career.
Resale: Favorably discuss the product or company related to the subject of the letter.	With their heavy-duty, full-suspension hardware and fine veneers, the desks and file cabinets in our Montclair line have become a hit with many value-conscious professionals.
Understanding: Demonstrate that you understand the reader's goals and needs.	So that you can more easily find the typewriter with the features you need, we are enclosing a brochure that describes all the Olsen typewriters currently available.

tion who does not have two years' management experience" seems to imply that you have not considered the person on her or his own merits. Skillful communicators refrain from apologizing, which is appropriate only if someone in your company has made a severe mistake or done something terribly wrong. If no one in the company is at fault, an apology gives the wrong impression.

The tone of your language does a great deal to make your audience receptive to the bad news that follows. Avoid negative, counterproductive words such as these:

broken	dissatisfied	regret
cannot understand	error	shocked
damage	fault	unfortunately
delay	inconvenience	wrong

Also, protect the audience's pride by using language that conveys respect; do not adopt an accusing tone. Use third-person, impersonal, passive language to explain the audience's mistakes in an inoffensive way. For example, say, "The appliance won't work after being immersed in water" instead of "You shouldn't have immersed the appliance in water." In this case, the "you" attitude is better observed by avoiding the word *you*.

Sometimes the "you" attitude is best observed by avoiding the word you.

If you had to turn down a management trainee applicant, your tactfully worded letter might give these reasons for the decision not to hire:

Because these management trainee positions are quite challenging, our human relations department has researched the qualifications needed to succeed in them. The findings show that the two most important qualifications are a bachelor's degree in business administration and two years' supervisory experience.

Well-written reasons are
- *Detailed*
- *Tactful*
- *Individualized*
- *Unapologetic*
- *Positive*

This paragraph does a good job of stating the reasons for the refusal:

- It provides enough detail to make the reason for the refusal logically acceptable.

- It implies that the applicant is better off avoiding a program in which she or he would probably fail, given the background of the other management trainees.

- It does not make the case solely on company policy. A relevant policy exists, but it is presented as logical rather than rigid.

- It offers no apology for the decision.

- It avoids negative personal expressions ("You do not meet our requirements").

Sometimes detailed reasons should not be provided.

Although specific reasons help the audience accept bad news, they cannot always be given. For example, don't include them when they involve confidential, excessively complicated, or purely negative information, or when they benefit only you or your firm (enhancing company profits, for instance). Instead, move directly to the next section.

Jane Bryant Quinn is a financial columnist for *Newsweek*. She points out that companies can paint an overall positive picture and then use phrases such as "subject to," "except for," and "despite the" to moderate the impact of bad news.

When writing a bad-news message, avoid negative wording and personal language.

The bad news

So that the audience is psychologically prepared, the bad news should be the logical outcome of the reasons that come before it. Even so, the audience may still react emotionally if the message is handled carelessly. Here are some methods for de-emphasizing bad news:

- Minimize the space or time devoted to it.

- Subordinate it in a complex or compound sentence ("My department is already shorthanded, so I'll need all my staff for at least the next two months").

- Embed it in the middle of a paragraph.

Two other techniques are especially useful for saying no as clearly and as painlessly as possible. First, using a conditional (*if* or *when*) statement implies that the audience could possibly have received or might someday receive a favorable answer: "When you have more managerial experience, you are welcome to reapply." A statement like this could motivate the applicant to improve his or her qualifications. The other technique is to tell the audience what you did do, can do, or will do rather than what you did not do, cannot do, or won't do. Rather than saying, "Our company is unable to serve you, so please call your nearest dealer," say, "Our company sells exclusively through retailers, and the one nearest you that carries our merchandise is . . ." Here's the same principle applied in a letter rejecting a job applicant: "The five positions currently open have been staffed with people whose qualifications match those uncovered in our research." A statement like this need not be followed by the explicit news that you will not be hiring the reader. By focusing on the positive and only implying the bad news, you soften the blow.

However, it would not be ethical to overemphasize the positive. If an implied message might leave doubt, state your decision in direct terms. Just be sure to avoid blunt statements that are likely to cause pain and anger. The following phrases are particularly likely to offend:

I must refuse	we must reject
I am unable to	we cannot allow
you must understand	much as I would like to
we must deny	we must turn down
we cannot afford to	

Instead, use impersonal, positive language so that you don't undermine the audience's feelings of self-worth. Your goal is for the audience not only to accept your unfavorable decision but also to pay attention to the end of your message.

Positive close

After giving the bad news, your job is to end the message on a more pleasant note. You might propose an attainable solution to the audience's problem. For example, when one supervisor requests to borrow customer service staff temporarily, the customer service supervisor might refuse by saying, "The human resources department has offered to bring in temporary workers when I need them, and I'm sure they would consider doing the same for you." In a message to a current or potential customer, an off-the-subject ending that includes re-sale information or sales promotion is also appropriate. If you've asked the audience to decide between alternatives or to take some action, make sure she or he knows what to do, when to do it, and how to do it with ease.

Whatever type of close you choose, observe these don'ts:

An upbeat, positive close
- Builds goodwill
- Offers a suggestion for action
- Provides a look toward the future

- Don't refer to or repeat the bad news.

- Don't apologize for the decision or reveal any doubt that the reasons will be accepted ("I trust our decision is satisfactory").

- Don't urge additional communication ("If you have further questions, please write") unless you're really willing to discuss your decision further.

- Don't anticipate problems ("Should you have further problems, please let us know").

- Don't include clichés that are insincere in view of the bad news ("If we can be of any help, please contact us").

- Don't reveal any doubt that you will keep the person as a customer ("We hope you will continue to do business with us").

BEHIND THE SCENES AT AMERICA WEST AIRLINES
Navigating Bad News

How do you tell 14,000 employees that their company has just filed for reorganization in federal bankruptcy court—especially after many of them already saw it in the morning paper or on television? This was the task facing Daphne Dicino, senior director of corporate communications at America West Airlines.

Months of negotiations between the Phoenix-based airline and its creditors suddenly collapsed, and the airline had to file for reorganization under Chapter 11 of the U.S. Bankruptcy Code. Unfortunately for Dicino, America West was legally obligated to notify the public immediately even before employees, many of whom learned about the filing from the press instead of from their own company.

"That was unfortunate and, I suspect, terrifying for our employees," says Dicino. "Initially, the employees didn't believe it. They couldn't believe it was happening. They were filled with fear and anxiety about their jobs and were under a lot of pressure from the press and the public." Because practically every employee had daily contact with the public—and, there-fore, was exposed to the press—how they represented the airline was important. So it was crucial for top management to effectively explain the bad news to employees. If the communication was mishandled, employee morale would decline, possibly affecting customer service and, ultimately, revenues—which were more necessary than ever. However, if the bad news was related properly, employees would pull together through rough times to help save the airline.

The communication process began when chairman Edward Beauvais, president Michael Conway, and Dicino spent hours that first night writing a letter to employees. Dicino purposely decided to use an indirect approach. The top management team needed to break the bad news in a manner that would explain the situation forthrightly while encouraging employee morale. Using a direct approach was considered too risky.

Dicino's letter to employees opened with a factual buffer intended to present a neutral message. The letter explained that the 14 largest U.S. airlines, not just America West, had lost money for three consecutive

As senior vice president of human resources for Metropolitan Life Insurance, Catherine Rein supports the direct method for bad news when you want to maintain a position of strength. Cutting a program can bother those responsible for it, explains Rein, but well-made decisions must prevail.

In the case of the applicant for the management trainee position, you could observe these rules by writing a close like this:

> Many companies seek other qualifications in management trainees, so I urge you to continue your job search. You'll certainly find an opening in which your skills and aspirations match the job requirements exactly.

Keep in mind that the close is what the audience will remember you by. Try to make the memory a positive one.

DIRECT PLAN

A bad-news message organized on the direct plan would start with a clear statement of the bad news, proceed to the reasons for the decision, and end with a courteous close. Stating the bad news at the beginning has two potential advantages: (1) It makes a shorter message possible, and (2) the audience needs less time to reach the main idea of the message, the bad news itself.

Although the indirect approach is preferable in bad-news messages, you may sometimes want to move right to the point. For example, memos are often organized so that the bad news comes before the reasons. In fact, some managers expect all internal correspondence to be brief and direct, regardless of whether the message is positive or negative. Even so, remember that a tactful

quarters—$5 billion in total. The industrywide slump was the result of two side effects of the Persian Gulf war: Fuel prices were shooting up and people were flying less because they feared terrorism. The drain on cash reserves at America West forced the airline into the reorganization filing.

With the reasons for the bad news presented, the letter went on to explain that reorganization "did not mean that America West had failed or was going out of business." The letter stressed the importance of the airline's employees, and it emphasized a "business-as-usual" approach. The letter made it clear that employees would be paid as usual and that all benefits were safe. Employees were told about the necessity for pulling together, and the letter ended with a message of reassurance: "This is without question an extremely difficult decision for all of us. However, we will ultimately be viewed as survivors." A question-and-answer communication was attached, addressing questions that customers would most likely ask of employees so that employees would be prepared.

In addition to the initial letter, Dicino realized that continued open communication with employees would be necessary to keep morale high. Employees' questions, management's answers, updates of reorganization proceedings, and legal definitions and explanations were communicated companywide through the in-house monthly magazine, *AWARE*; through newsletters; and through in-depth executive reports.

Dicino's goal was to do more than merely inform; she had to maintain employees' self-esteem in the face of incredible pressures. One message was stressed through all the communication vehicles: The airline's reorganization filing was no one's fault. "The key was to display our confidence in the employees," Dicino says. "So we sent a clear message that the product itself had been proven successful, particularly because the employees had done their jobs so well." Indeed, as the company worked to secure new financing and emerge from the protection of bankruptcy court, employees worked to maintain customer loyalty, and the number of passengers actually increased.

APPLY YOUR KNOWLEDGE

1. How would you write a letter explaining to employees the following decisions: (a) To cut costs throughout the airline, salaries will be frozen by 10 percent. (Top managers have already cut their salaries.) (b) To cut costs, service to six cities (including New York City) will be discontinued.

2. Should the indirect approach be used every time bad news has to be given to employees? Can employee morale be maintained using the direct approach?

tone, a focus on reasons, and a courteous close will help your audience accept negative messages more easily.

Routine bad-news messages to other companies also commonly follow the direct plan, especially if they relay decisions that have little or no personal impact. Moreover, you will sometimes know from prior experience whether someone prefers the bad news first in any message. The direct plan is also appropriate when you want to present an image of firmness and strength; for example, the last message in a collection series (sent just before the matter is turned over to an attorney) usually gets right to the point.

Use the direct plan when
- Your boss prefers that internal messages come right to the point
- The message has little personal impact
- You want to make your point emphatically

CONVEYING BAD NEWS ABOUT ORDERS

For several reasons, businesses must sometimes convey bad news concerning orders. In writing to a would-be customer, you have three basic goals:

- To work toward an eventual sale along the lines of the original order
- To keep instructions or additional information as clear as possible
- To maintain an optimistic, confident tone so that your reader won't lose interest

BACK ORDERS

Use the indirect plan when telling a customer that you cannot immediately ship the entire order.

When you must back order for a customer, you have one of two types of bad news to convey: (1) You are able to send only part of the order, or (2) you are able to send none of the order. When sending only part of the order, you actually have both good news and bad news. In such situations, the indirect plan works very well. The buffer should contain the good news that part of the order is en route, along with a resale reminder of the product's attractiveness. After the buffer come the reasons for the delay of the remainder of the shipment. A strong close should encourage a favorable attitude toward the total transaction. For a customer whose order for a lawn mower and its companion grass catcher can be only partly filled, your letter might read like the one in Figure 8.1.

Had you been unable to send the customer any portion of this order, you would still have used the indirect approach. However, because you would have had no good news to give, your buffer would only have confirmed the sale, and the explanation section would have stated your reason for not filling the order promptly.

SUBSTITUTIONS

Use the indirect plan to notify a customer that you must send a substitute, especially when the replacement is more expensive than the original item.

Once in a while, a customer will request something that you no longer sell or that is no longer produced. If you are sure the customer will approve a substitute product, you may go ahead and send it. But when in doubt, first send a letter that "sells" the substitute product and gives the customer simple directions for ordering it. In either case, be careful to avoid calling the second product a *substitute*; the term carries a negative connotation and detracts from your sales information. Instead, say that you now stock the second product exclusively.

FIGURE 8.1
Letter Advising of a Back Order

The Greenery
4550 Cedar Street, Omaha, NE 68106 (402) 555 - 2471

April 4, 1993

Mr. and Mrs. Eric Larsen
411 Fourth Street
Blue Springs, NE 68318

Dear Mr. and Mrs. Larsen:

Your lawn mower is being shipped to you today. The 22-inch Kleen-Kut mower with the vacuum grass catcher will not only give you a clean, beautifully manicured lawn but will also give you one free of brown rot, the disease that afflicts lawns when cuttings are not removed.

So far this spring, almost every customer who has purchased a Kleen-Kut lawn mower has also taken advantage of the special savings on the vacuum grass catcher. Because such demand was not anticipated, our supply of grass catchers is temporarily depleted.

When we realized that we were running out of this popular product, we phoned the manufacturer to order additional vacuum grass catchers. This shipment is now on its way, and we should have it within one week. On the day the grass catchers reach us, we will send yours by parcel service. Within two weeks, you can be enjoying the convenience of your grass catcher.

Other Kleen-Kut products that will help you maintain your lawn and flower beds are shown in the enclosed catalog. Note that during our spring promotion, the prices of some products have been reduced by as much as 50 percent. At those savings, your yard could be the envy of the entire neighborhood.

Sincerely,

Art Brill

Arthur Brill
Manager

br

Enclosure

The buffer conveys the good news and confirms the wisdom of the customer's choice.

The reason for the bad news shows that the grass catcher is popular and therefore a good choice.

The bad news itself is implied by telling the reader what is being done, not what cannot be done.

The positive close includes sales promotion material.

As you can imagine, the challenge is greater when the substitute is more expensive than the original item. You must show that the more costly item can do much more than the one originally ordered so that additional charges seem justified to the customer. Say a customer has ordered a drill that is no longer manufactured. Because of problems with the old model, the motor has been upgraded. As a result, the price has increased from $24.95 to $31.95. You must send a letter convincing the customer to buy the more expensive drill:

The people at Alpha-Omega, manufacturer of the Mini-Max drill you ordered, are committed to your satisfaction with every product they make.

The buffer includes resale information on the manufacturer.

For this reason, we conduct extensive testing. Results for the 1/4-inch Mini-Max with the 1/8-horsepower motor show that although it can drill through two inches of wood or a quarter inch of metal, thicker materials put a severe strain on the motor. We know that household jobs come in all sizes and shapes, so we now make a more powerful 1/4-inch drill with a 3/8-horsepower motor. The new Mini-Max can cut through materials twice as thick as those the former model could handle.

The reasons for the bad news are explained in terms of the customer's needs.

Even with its superior capabilities, the new Mini-Max costs only about 30 percent more. Using this improved model, you'll know that even heavy-duty household drilling will cause no overheating.

The bad news is stated positively. The writer emphasizes the product the firm carries rather than the one it does not.

You can be using your new heavy-duty drill by this time next week if you just check the YES box on the enclosed form, tuck the form into the postage-paid envelope with $7.00, and mail it today. Your new, worry-free Mini-Max will be on its way to you at once.

The close, which asks the reader to authorize shipment of the substitute item, makes action easy and reinforces the benefits described earlier.

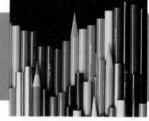

CHECKLIST FOR BAD NEWS ABOUT ORDERS

A. Overall Strategy
☐ 1. Use the indirect plan in most cases.
☐ 2. Use the direct plan when the situation is routine (between employees of the same company), when the reader is not emotionally involved in the message, or when you know that the reader would prefer the bad news first.

B. Buffer
☐ 1. Express appreciation for the specific order.
☐ 2. Extend a welcome to a new customer.
☐ 3. Avoid flashy, attention-getting devices or phrasing.
☐ 4. Avoid negative words (*won't, can't, unable to*).
☐ 5. Avoid expressions of pleasure in receiving the order.
☐ 6. Use resale information on the ordered merchandise to build the customer's confidence in her or his choice (except for unfillable orders).

C. Reasons
☐ 1. Emphasize what the firm is doing rather than what it isn't doing, what it has rather than what it lacks.

☐ 2. Avoid apologies.
☐ 3. Avoid expressions of sorrow or regret.
☐ 4. Thoroughly explain the problem with unclear orders.
  ☐ a. Stress your desire to send exactly what the customer wants.
  ☐ b. Include details (such as styles and colors available) that will enable the customer to specify the merchandise desired.
  ☐ c. Provide photographs, sketches, catalog numbers, and other aids for ordering properly.
  ☐ d. Avoid negative personal expressions, such as "You forgot" and "You neglected to."
☐ 5. Handle back orders carefully.
  ☐ a. Specify shipping dates.
  ☐ b. Avoid negative phrases, such as "cannot send" or "out of stock."
  ☐ c. Explain why the item is out of stock by using terms such as "high popularity" or "exceptional demand" in order to stimulate the customer's desire for the item.
  ☐ d. Reinforce the customer's confidence with resale (for consumers: personal attention, credit, repair

UNFILLABLE ORDERS

Use the indirect plan to say that you cannot fill an order at all.

Occasionally you will not be able to fill an order either in part or with a substitute. In this case, your job is to say no and still be as helpful as possible. One good way to maintain the customer's confidence in you and your company is to mention another source from which the requested product might be obtained, as in the following letter from an upholsterer:

Your couch and chair are truly exquisite antiques. And the upholstery fabric you've selected will enhance their beauty even more.

The buffer is appreciation for the customer's good taste, highlighting a point on which both writer and reader agree.

Antiques demand special care when being upholstered because of their dry, delicate wood and intricate curves and pleats. I know how important it is to you that someone spend all the time needed to do a painstaking job. Because I have several unusually heavy commitments, May 15 is the earliest I can start work on your couch and chair and give them the special attention they need. If my shop were clear of this other work, I could easily promise you a two-week delivery date.

The reasons and the bad news itself are intertwined in one paragraph. By emphasizing the care that the writer believes this project deserves, she "resells" the reader on her services.

services, free delivery, special discounts, telephone shopping, and other services; for dealers: free counter and window displays, advertising materials, sales manuals, factory guarantees, and nearby warehousing).
   - ☐ e. Refer to sales promotion material, if desirable.
- ☐ **6.** Explain substitutions in detail.
   - ☐ a. Introduce the benefits of the substitute before relating the bad news that the ordered item is unavailable.
   - ☐ b. Avoid the word *substitute* because of its negative connotation.
   - ☐ c. Describe enough reader benefits to justify any higher price.
- ☐ **7.** Explain why orders can't be filled.
   - ☐ a. Explain in positive terms the way you market your products (for example, through authorized dealers who may provide benefits such as personal service, faster delivery, shipping at little or no cost, credit, adjustment and repair services, and the opportunity to see goods before buying).
   - ☐ b. Name alternate sources, with addresses, telephone numbers, and positive statements about them.
   - ☐ c. Stress the benefits to the customer of dealing with other sources.

- ☐ **8.** Thoroughly explain the problem with nonconforming orders.
   - ☐ a. Stress your desire to send exactly what the customer wants.
   - ☐ b. Explain the reasons for requiring a deposit or minimum order.
- ☐ **9.** Avoid hiding behind company policy.

D. The Bad News
- ☐ **1.** State the bad news as positively as possible.
- ☐ **2.** State the bad news clearly, and when possible, do so by implication.
- ☐ **3.** Stress the reader benefit of the decision.

E. Positive, Friendly, Helpful Close
- ☐ **1.** Remind the reader of how his or her needs are being met, if appropriate.
- ☐ **2.** Explain the desired reader action as clearly and simply as possible.
- ☐ **3.** Use resale information to clinch the sale, especially for replies about unclear orders, back orders, and nonconforming orders.
- ☐ **4.** Make reader action as easy as possible.
- ☐ **5.** Adopt a tone that shows you remain in control of the situation and will continue to give customers' orders personal attention.

I know that you want the job done very soon, so let me recommend Peter Aarons of A & J Upholstery. I talked with him just this morning, and he assured me that he can complete work on your furniture within two weeks. You'll find his expertise and prices comparable to mine. To discuss the details, phone Peter at 257-2543.

The suggestion of an alternative, which is technically part of the bad-news section, rates a paragraph of its own.

Thank you, Mrs. Nasseri, for making me your first choice for this important job. The next time you call, you should receive my usual prompt, on-time service. Please let me know whenever I can help.

The main point of this close is to convince the customer to come back under other circumstances.

COMMUNICATING NEGATIVE ANSWERS AND INFORMATION

Use the direct plan when your negative answer or information will have little personal impact; use the indirect plan in more sensitive situations.

The businessperson who tries to say yes to everyone will probably not win many promotions or stay in business for long. Occasionally, your response to inquiries must simply be no. Imagine Charles Schulz's schedule if he were to say yes to everyone asking him to give a speech. It is a mark of your skill as a communicator to be able to say no clearly yet not cut yourself off from future dealings with the other person.

Depending on your relationship with the reader, you could use either the direct plan or the indirect plan in these situations. If the reader is unlikely to be deeply disappointed, use the direct plan. Otherwise, use a buffer that expresses appreciation for being thought of, assures the reader of your attention to the request, compliments the reader, or indicates your understanding of the reader's needs. Continue with the reasons for the bad news and the bad news itself, couched in terms that show how the reader's problem can be solved and what you can do to help. Then close with a statement of interest, encouragement, or goodwill. You can demonstrate your sincerity and minimize the reader's hostility or disappointment by promptly fulfilling any promises you make.

DENYING COOPERATION WITH ROUTINE REQUESTS

Consider the direct or indirect plan to tell someone you cannot do what has been requested.

When people ask you for information or want you to do something and you cannot honor the request, you may answer with either the direct plan or the indirect plan. Let's assume that you have asked Blodgett Corporation to participate in a research project concerning sales promotion. However, Blodgett has a policy against disseminating any information about projected sales figures. How would you react to the following answer?

This letter is to inform you that Blodgett Corporation has no interest in taking part in your Sales Management Techniques research project.

In fact, our company has a policy that prohibits dissemination of any projected sales figures.

Thank you for your interest in our organization. If we can help you in any other way, please let us know.

Meredith Fernstrom is senior vice president for public responsibility at American Express Company. Known as responsive and flexible, Fernstrom has still had to present her share of bad-news messages because some requests must simply be refused. However, Fernstrom believes that tact and careful wording can help readers accept bad news.

This letter would offend most readers, for several reasons:

- The direct plan is used, even though the reader is outside the company and may be emotionally involved in the response.

- The words "This letter is to inform you" are stodgy and condescending.

- The tone of the first paragraph is unnecessarily negative and abrupt.

- The phrase "has no interest in taking part" implies that the research is unimportant.

- The writer hides behind a company policy that the reader may find questionable.

- Clichés in the final paragraph undercut any personal, friendly impact that the letter might have had.

- The offer to help is an unpleasant irony, given the writer's unwillingness to do so in this instance.

Wording, tone, and format conspire to make a letter either offensive or acceptable. Notice how the letter that follows conveys the same negative message but without sounding offensive:

Your upcoming research project sounds fascinating. Thanks for thinking of Blodgett Corporation as a possible contributor.	The buffer is supportive and appreciative.
Each year, we receive a number of requests for help in various studies. Although we would like to assist everyone who asks, we've had to set up guidelines for deciding which requests we can honor. Many competitors and shareholders would like to get an advance look at some of the figures that researchers request. That's why our sales and earnings projections must be kept within corporate headquarters until they are publicly announced through press releases.	Without falling back on references to company policy, the reason for the policy is fully explained. The bad news is implied, not stated explicitly.
Ms. Dalle, we would like to help you in another way. If you can use sales and earnings data from a previous period, which are shown in the enclosed annual report, please do. Best of luck with your study.	The close is friendly, positive, and helpful.

DECLINING REQUESTS FOR FAVORS

Consider the direct or indirect plan to turn down a request for a favor.

The plan to use when saying no to a requested favor depends on your relationship with the reader. For example, suppose that the president of the local Chamber of Commerce asks you to speak at a luncheon five weeks away; however, you are scheduled for a business trip at that time. If you do not know the president well, you would probably use the indirect plan:

The chamber of commerce has accomplished many worthwhile projects, and I've always	The buffer recaps the request and demonstrates respect.

admired the local organization. Thank you for asking me to speak at your luncheon meeting next month.

As you know, I'm a sales representative for Midland Grain Cooperative, and I do quite a bit of traveling. In fact, I'm scheduled to be in Dubuque on the day you asked me to speak.

The reason for declining implies the bad news itself.

Can you suggest an alternative date? Any Thursday during April would be fine for me. The opportunity to speak to your members would be most rewarding.

The close suggests an alternative plan.

If you were writing a similar letter to a close friend instead of an acquaintance or a stranger, you could use the direct plan:

Dave, I won't be able to speak at the chamber of commerce luncheon next month. As you know, I'm on the road about half the time, and the middle of next month puts me in Dubuque.

But I'm not always on the road! Keep me in mind; I'll be in town every Thursday during April. With you at the helm, the chamber of commerce is finally making a difference here. I'll be glad to contribute what I can to a good meeting.

This letter gets right to the point but still uses some blow-softening techniques: It compliments the person and organization making the request and looks toward future opportunities for cooperation.

REFUSING ADJUSTMENT OF CLAIMS AND COMPLAINTS

Use the indirect plan in most cases of refusing to make an adjustment.

In almost every instance, a customer who requests an adjustment is emotionally involved; therefore, the indirect plan is generally used for a reply. Your job as a writer is to avoid accepting responsibility for the unfortunate situation and yet avoid blaming or accusing the customer. To steer clear of these pitfalls, remember that the tone of your letter is extremely important. Keep in mind that a tactful and courteous letter can build goodwill while denying the claim.

Let's say that you work for a sportswear company. A customer who bought one of your swimsuits a month and a half ago has returned it to you because a seam has split. In a pleasant letter, she asks for a refund of the purchase price. Your negative response might read like this:

I agree. You have every right to expect high quality and a comfortable, lasting fit in the Fun 'n' Sun swimsuit you selected.

The buffer covers a point that both reader and writer agree on.

Because sunshine and chlorine rapidly destroy the fabric of any swimsuit, few manufacturers are willing to take responsibility for wear-related problems. But we believe the customer comes first. That's why a tag is attached to every Fun 'n' Sun swimsuit explaining our

The reason puts the company's policy in a favorable light. The bad news, stated indirectly, tactfully puts some of the responsibility on the customer's shoulders.

guarantee. We're always happy to refund every penny if the customer returns a suit within 30 days of purchase for reasons other than a change in taste or fit.

But we do want to help. So that you can continue enjoying your swimsuit, we've reinforced the inside seams with flexible cloth tape. They should now hold through many, many wearings. Inspect it carefully.

A positive alternative action should help soothe the customer.

Also inspect the new Hampton House catalog I'm enclosing. You'll find a full line of quality fashions, including a delightful variety of festive swim coverups. You'll also find an entry form for our big $2,000 Designer Wardrobe Giveaway. Fill it in and rush it back today. You could be the lucky winner!

The close blends sales promotion with acknowledgment of the customer's interests.

You may be tempted to respond to a particularly outrageous claim by calling the person responsible a crook, a swindler, or an incompetent. Resist! If

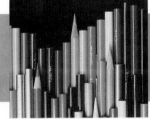

CHECKLIST FOR REFUSALS TO MAKE ADJUSTMENTS

A. Buffer
☐ **1.** Use a topic of mutual agreement or a neutral topic to start, but keep to the subject of the letter.
☐ **2.** Indicate your full understanding of the nature of the complaint.
☐ **3.** Avoid all areas of disagreement.
☐ **4.** Avoid any hint of your final decision.
☐ **5.** Keep the buffer brief and to the point.
☐ **6.** Maintain a confident, positive, supportive tone.

B. Reasons
☐ **1.** Provide an accurate, factual account of the transaction.
☐ **2.** Offer enough detail to show the logic of your position.
☐ **3.** Emphasize the ways the product should have been handled (or the contract followed) rather than the reader's negligence.
☐ **4.** Word the explanation so that the reader can anticipate the refusal.
☐ **5.** Avoid relying on unexplained company policy.
☐ **6.** Avoid accusing or preaching ("You should have").
☐ **7.** Do not blame or scold the reader.
☐ **8.** Do not make the reader appear or feel stupid.

☐ **9.** Inject a brief resale note after the explanation, if desirable.

C. The Bad News
☐ **1.** Make the refusal clear by tactful wording, or possibly by implying it.
☐ **2.** Avoid any hint that your decision is less than final.
☐ **3.** Avoid words such as *reject* and *claim*.
☐ **4.** If desirable, make a counterproposal for a compromise settlement or partial adjustment in a willing (not begrudging) tone, in a spirit of honest cooperation, and without making it sound like a penalty.
☐ **5.** Include a resale note for the company or product.
☐ **6.** Emphasize a desire for a good relationship in the future.
☐ **7.** Extend an offer to replace the product or provide a replacement part at the regular price.

D. Positive, Friendly, Helpful Close
☐ **1.** Eliminate any reference to your refusal.
☐ **2.** Avoid any apology.
☐ **3.** Eliminate words suggesting uncertainty (*hope, trust*).
☐ **4.** Refer to enclosed sales material.
☐ **5.** Make any suggested action easy to comply with.

you don't, you could be sued for defamation (a false statement that tends to damage someone's character or reputation). To avoid libelous letters, follow these guidelines:

- Avoid using any kind of abusive language or terms that could be considered defamatory, such as *quack*, *shyster*, *cheat*, *blackmailer*, *thief*, *racketeer*, *bankrupt*, *liar*, *drug addict*, *Communist*, and *deadbeat*.
- In all your messages, provide accurate information and stick to the facts.
- Never let anger or malice motivate your messages.
- Consult your company's legal department or an attorney whenever you think a message might have legal consequences.
- Always communicate honestly, and make sure that what you are saying is what you believe to be true.

When refusing to make an adjustment
- Demonstrate understanding of the complaint
- Explain your refusal
- Suggest alternative action

Demonstrate that you understand and have considered the complaint. Then, even if the claim is unreasonable, you must rationally explain why you are refusing the request. (But don't apologize or rely on company policy.) The letter should end on a respectful and action-oriented note.

REFUSING TO EXTEND CREDIT

Use the indirect plan when turning down a credit applicant.

Credit is refused for a variety of reasons, all involving sensitive personal or legal considerations. When denying credit to the applicant with a proven record of delinquent payments or to the applicant with an unstable background, you would probably be justified in offering little hope for future credit approval. However, you could be more encouraging to other types of applicants. You most certainly would like their current cash business, and you may want their future credit business. The following letter refuses credit for the present but points to the possibility of credit being extended in the future:

Your request for a charge account at Talton's Clothiers tells us something important: You enjoy the rewards of owning a smart, up-to-the-minute wardrobe.

The buffer expresses understanding and offers some subtle resale on the company.

Year after year, value-minded customers like you return to Talton's because of our low prices. How do we do it? We buy our entire inventory of fine men's clothing on a cash basis so that we can get manufacturers' discounts and avoid interest charges. You benefit because we can offer you superb quality at some of the lowest prices in the clothing industry.

The reasons for the refusal are explained in some detail.

So that we can continue to deal with suppliers on a cash basis and to offer you low prices, customer credit applications are approved only when the applicant makes at least $20,000 yearly and has lived in the area for one year or more. As soon as you meet these criteria, we will be glad to reconsider your application.

The actual refusal is stated in positive terms, and the criteria are stated explicitly.

In the meantime, Mr. O'Neill, I want to show you how much we value your business. Enclosed is a certificate that entitles you to a 10 percent discount on any purchase from our Stagg Shoppe. Also, be sure to take advantage of our big storewide sale on August 25 and 26. You'll find some tremendous bargains!

The letter closes gracefully with some sales promotion.

Notice how this writer has taken pains to make the reader feel welcome and realize that his business is appreciated.

Denials of business credit, as opposed to denials of individual credit, are less personally sensitive but more financially significant. Businesses have failed because major suppliers have suspended credit at inconvenient times.

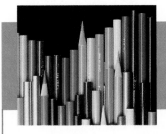

CHECKLIST FOR CREDIT REFUSALS

A. Buffer
☐ **1.** Introduce a topic that is relevant and that both you and the reader can agree with.
☐ **2.** Eliminate apologies and negative-sounding words.
☐ **3.** Phrase the buffer to avoid misleading the reader.
☐ **4.** Limit the length of the buffer.
☐ **5.** Express appreciation for the credit request.
☐ **6.** Introduce resale information.

B. Reasons
☐ **1.** Check the lead-in from the buffer for smoothness.
☐ **2.** Make a transition from the favorable to the unfavorable message.
☐ **3.** Make a transition from the general to the specific.
☐ **4.** Avoid a condescending lecture about how credit is earned.
☐ **5.** Avoid relying on unexplained company policy.
☐ **6.** Stress the benefits of not being overextended.
☐ **7.** If future approval is realistic, encourage a later credit application.
☐ **8.** Phrase reasons in terms of experience with others.
☐ **9.** Present reasons for the refusal carefully.
  ☐ a. Clearly state the reasons only if the reader will accept them.
  ☐ b. Explain your general credit criteria.
  ☐ c. Refer to a credit reporting agency you have used.
  ☐ d. Use "insufficient information" as a reason only if this is the case.
  ☐ e. To avoid the risk of legal action, omit reasons entirely for extraordinarily sensitive or combative readers or when evidence is unusually negative or involves behavioral flaws.
☐ **10.** Remind the reader of the benefits of cash purchases.

C. The Bad News
☐ **1.** Make the refusal clear to the reader.
☐ **2.** Offer only honest encouragement about considering the credit application at a later date.
☐ **3.** Avoid negative words such as "must decline" or "not able."
☐ **4.** Suggest positive alternatives such as cash and layaway purchases.
☐ **5.** Handle refusals of business credit somewhat differently.
  ☐ a. Recommend cash purchases for small, frequent orders.
  ☐ b. Describe cash discounts (include figures).
  ☐ c. Suggest a reduction of inventory so that the business can strengthen its credit rating.
  ☐ d. Offer promotional and marketing aid.
  ☐ e. Suggest a later review of the credit application, if future approval is realistic.

D. Positive, Friendly, Helpful Close
☐ **1.** Avoid business clichés, apologies, and words of regret.
☐ **2.** Suggest actions the reader might take.
☐ **3.** Encourage the reader to look toward the future, when the application may be approved.
☐ **4.** Include sales promotion material only if the customer would not be offended.

In a letter denying credit to a business
- Be more factual and less personal than in a letter to an individual
- Suggest ways to continue doing business

When refusing to grant business credit, explain your reasons as factually and impersonally as possible (perhaps the firm's latest financial statements don't meet your criteria or its credit rating has fallen below an acceptable minimum). Also explain clearly the steps that must be taken to restore credit. Emphasize the benefits of continued dealings on a cash basis until the firm's credit worthiness has been established or restored. You might also offer discounts for cash purchases or assistance in cooperative merchandising to reduce the firm's inventory and increase cash flow. Third-party loans are another possibility you might suggest.

Be aware that credit is a legally sensitive subject.

With any candidate, companies that deny credit must exercise good judgment in order to avoid legal action. A faulty decision may unfairly damage a person's reputation, which may in turn provoke a lawsuit and other bad publicity for the company. Handling credit denials over the phone instead of in writing is no guarantee of avoiding trouble; companies that orally refuse credit should still proceed with caution.

SUMMARY

The purpose of a bad-news message is to convey unfavorable information without alienating the audience. To accomplish both goals, you must first consider the audience's point of view; if possible, explain how the bad news can work to the audience's advantage. You can convey tact and concern by assuming that the audience is basically honest and wants to be fair.

Bad-news messages can be based on either the indirect or the direct plan, depending on the circumstances. The indirect plan begins with a buffer and moves to the reasons; it then states the bad news and closes courteously, perhaps suggesting other options for the audience. The direct plan, which is used mainly for sending bad news that will have little emotional impact on the audience, begins with a clear statement of the bad news, moves to the reasons, and then provides a courteous close.

ON THE JOB:
Solving a Communication Dilemma
at Creative Associates

When he first started drawing his comic strip, licensing was the last thing on Charles Schulz's mind. His primary goal was—and still is—to do a good job on the daily strip. As he says, "I just wanted to draw something that was really good and was different." On the other hand, he realized that cartooning was a business and that he could make a lot of money—not an unattractive prospect.

The licensing of *Peanuts* began modestly in 1952 with the publication of the first paperback collection of reprinted strips. New books followed every year—over 100 have been published so far. Snoopy dolls appeared; then in 1960, Hallmark applied for a license to create a line of Peanuts greeting cards. CBS produced the first Peanuts TV special in 1965. The Peanuts characters recently turned 40, and over the years, literally thousands of licensed products have come along.

Schulz prefers not to divulge his income from licensing, but as his financial manager, Ron Nelson, points out, "This is obviously a big business." Informed sources estimate that the annual retail sales of Peanuts products run about $1 billion. Licensees pay a royalty that ranges from 5 to 10 percent of the wholesale price of the merchandise. The royalty is split 50-50 between Schulz and United Feature Syndicate. Given his reputation, Schulz could probably cut a better deal with United Feature, but he isn't greedy. "There's plenty of money to go around for everybody," he says.

What Schulz really cares about is control. His original contract with United Feature gave the syndicate power over all licensing agreements. And for a while, that worked well. United Feature understood Schulz's strong feelings about *Peanuts* and deferred to his judgment.

However, as the popularity of *Peanuts* grew, it became more difficult for Schulz to respond to all the licensing requests. United Feature took on more of the decision making, and often, their decisions upset Schulz.

He became "terribly unhappy" with this state of affairs. Finally, about ten years ago, he negotiated a new contract with United Feature that gave him veto power over every licensed product. By this time, Schulz had set up an organization known as Creative Associates to handle his business affairs, which were becoming increasingly complicated. With the new contract in effect, the burden of responding to licensing requests fell to the six-person staff of Creative Associates.

They all work along with Schulz (who still goes by the nickname "Sparky") in a modest stone-and-wood building at the end of Snoopy Lane in Santa Rosa, California. They get lots and lots of letters—fan letters, invitations, requests for information and contributions, and inquiries about licenses. The staff of Creative Associates answers them all, and often, the answer must be no.

Your Mission: You work for Creative Associates. Your job is to respond to requests of all sorts—requests for information, for licensing arrangements, for donations, for personal appearances by Mr. Schulz, for employment, for advice from Lucy . . . Handle the assignments outlined below to the best of your ability:

1. You have received a letter from the American Association of Retired Persons (AARP) asking Mr. Schulz to give a speech on creativity in older people at the association's annual convention. Schulz does not feel that he can spare the time to prepare a speech or attend the convention. In addition to doing his usual work on the daily comic strip, he is preparing a TV special, which is due to be completed at about the same time as the AARP convention. He has asked you to decline the invitation. Which of the following paragraphs is the best choice for the first paragraph of your reply?
   a. I'm very sorry, but I will be unable to appear at your convention. Much as I respect AARP, my work load is such that I cannot spare the time to prepare a speech or attend the convention.
   b. Creativity in older people is an intriguing topic for the keynote speech at the AARP annual convention. I'm flattered that you are interested in my views on the subject and appreciate your invitation to appear as guest speaker.
   c. I am deeply honored by your kind invitation to appear as guest speaker at the American Association of Retired Persons' annual convention in Atlantic City. Addressing your group--an admirable organization, which I personally support--would be a privilege.

2. Which version is best for presenting Schulz's reasons for declining the AARP invitation?
   a. Much as I would like to oblige you, I'm sorry to say that I must decline your invitation for a couple of reasons. For one thing, I'm overburdened with work. And also, I haven't been feeling too well the last few years.
   b. Since my heart surgery in 1981, I have made it a policy to limit my speaking engagements to one or two appearances per year. I find that if I allow myself to say yes to too many things, my energy level sinks and my work suffers. Accordingly, I must decline your kind invitation.
   c. I believe that creativity can be cultivated at any age and that it enriches our lives immeasurably, regardless of whether we are 7 or 70. But, as I approach retirement age myself, I recognize that my creative energy depends increasingly on my physical condition. If I take on too many projects, my work suffers. Currently, I have about all I can handle doing the daily comic strip and preparing for a TV special to be aired on April 25.

3. Which version is best for the closing of Schulz's reply to AARP?
   a. Again, thank you for thinking of me. I'm sorry that I cannot help you out on this occasion. Perhaps I can speak to your group next year.
   b. Are you planning to pursue the topic of creativity by holding informal workshops on the subject during your convention? If so, I have some videotapes on how to draw cartoons that I would be happy to lend you. They might provide an interesting supplement for a seminar. Please contact me at (707) 435-0192 if you would like more information about the tapes.
   c. If you cannot find another keynote speaker or if you run into a cancellation at the last minute, give me a call. There's always a chance that I might complete the script for the TV special early. If that happens, perhaps I could squeeze in an appearance at the AARP convention.

4. You have received a letter from Mr. Vernon McGurr who wants to know why his local paper, the *Marble City Courier*, does not carry *Peanuts* every day instead of just on Sunday. You can't help him because you have no idea what motivates the editor of the *Courier*. Which of the following replies is the best?
   a. Thank you for your enthusiastic support of Peanuts. I'm delighted that you would like to read about Lucy, Charlie, Snoopy, Linus, and all the other characters on a daily basis. Fans like you make producing the strip more fun.

The actual marketing of <u>Peanuts</u> is handled by United Feature Syndicate, which offers the strip to newspapers on either a daily or a Sunday basis. Ms. Sarah Gillespie, United Feature's director of cartoon art, might be able to answer your question regarding the <u>Marble City Courier</u>'s account. You can write to her at:

United Feature Syndicate
200 Park Ave.
New York, NY 10166

However, the most direct course would be to write to the newspaper itself. Why not ask the local editor to carry <u>Peanuts</u> every day? Better yet, ask your friends to write too. If enough loyal fans demand the strip on a daily basis, the editor might just decide to accommodate you. And that would make me and the Peanuts gang very happy. Good luck!

b. I wish I could tell you why the <u>Marble City Courier</u> carries <u>Peanuts</u> only on <u>Sunday</u>, but I'm afraid I don't have the answer. I just draw the strip; the marketing is handled by:

Ms. Sarah Gillespie
Director of Cartoon Art
United Feature Syndicate
200 Park Avenue
New York, NY 10166

She might be able to answer your question. A more direct approach, however, would be to contact the editor of the <u>Marble City Courier</u>. He or she would be in the best position to explain the paper's decision.

Thanks for your support.

c. I wish I could tell you why the <u>Marble City Courier</u> carries <u>Peanuts</u> only on <u>Sunday</u>, but I'm afraid I don't have the answer. I suggest you contact the editor of the paper. He or she would be in the best position to explain the decision.

Thanks for your support.

5. Mr. Schulz is working on the drawings and script for a new Charlie Brown TV special, but he is behind schedule. He had planned to submit the first half of the material to CBS on February 15, but he now estimates that it will not be ready until the end of the month. He is late because he decided to change a portion of the story line that wasn't working out. He thinks the new version will be much better. Although Schulz knows that the slippage is inconvenient for CBS, he thinks the damage can be controlled. He expects to catch up with the schedule and complete the entire script on March 15, as planned. The second

half of the material should go very quickly now that he's on the right track. Which of the following letters should Schulz send to CBS?

a. I've just had a fresh idea about how to handle the conflict between Charlie Brown and Lucy in "The Fourth of July" TV special. As usual, Lucy will set Charlie up for a fall, and as usual, he will succumb. But this time, I have a special twist that should please all Charlie's supporters. I'm reworking some of the early drawings to accommodate the changes, and I'm making good progress. You can expect to see the first half of the material by February 28. When you read the script, I think you'll agree that the revisions are worth the extra trouble.

Now that I'm on the right track, the work should move along quickly. I plan to deliver the second half of the material on March 15, as we originally planned. This promises to be our best Charlie Brown special ever.

b. I've been having second thoughts about the plot for the Charlie Brown TV special. As we originally sketched out the script, the conflict between Lucy and Charlie Brown was too predictable. The problem has been gnawing at me for the past few weeks, but last night I finally had a breakthrough. I've come up with a fresh plot twist that should please all Charlie's supporters.

Unfortunately, though, I'm going to have to redo quite a few of the drawings to accommodate the new plot line. I think I can finish the revisions in a couple of weeks. You can expect to receive the first half of the material by February 28, which is two weeks later than we originally planned.

I know the delay will hold up the animation crew, and I apologize for the inconvenience. But I do think the changes are worth waiting for, and I'm sure you'll agree when you see the results.

Although I hate to make any promises, I'm reasonably confident that I can complete the entire project by March 15, the original due date. Now that I'm on the right track, the rest of the work should proceed quite quickly.

c. I've got some good news and some bad news. First the good news. I've just had a terrific new idea for freshening up the plot of our Charlie Brown TV special.

Now the bad news: It will take me an extra two weeks to redo some of the early drawings. That means you will not be able to begin animating the first half of the script on February 15 as we originally planned. I think you'd better reschedule the animation crew for the 28th.

If it's any consolation, I think I can make up the lost time on the second half of the script. Now that I'm on the right track, the rest of the work should move faster than the Cannonball Express. I plan to submit the final installment by March 15, right on time.

6. Creative Associates has received a letter from Pet Products, a manufacturer of specialty items for dogs and cats. The firm's product line includes food bowls, grooming equipment, leashes, chew toys, and pet beds. The president, Gerald Adams, would like to add doghouses to the list. He envisions a white house with a red roof, just like Snoopy's, and he wants to top it off with a three-dimensional Snoopy roof ornament. He is writing to ask whether he can license Snoopy's image for this purpose. Mr. Schulz agrees that the doghouse is a cute idea, but he has some doubts about Pet Products. In checking on the firm's financial condition, he has discovered that Pet Products is deeply in debt and has failed to keep up the payments on its bank loans. Under the circumstances, Schulz prefers to say no, at least for the time being. He has asked you to draft a letter to that effect. Which of the following versions is the best?
   a. Thank you for your interest in licensing Snoopy for your doghouse. The design sounds very appealing.

      We have developed several guidelines to help us evaluate the many licensing applications that we receive. Our number-one priority is product quality. We want the Peanuts characters to be associated with only the best merchandise. On this score, Pet Products appears to make the grade.

      We are also concerned with market potential. Because we limit the number of licenses we sign, we like to be certain that the ones we select will give us "the most bang for our buck." On this score, we have some doubts about the Pet Products proposal. We feel that the market for doghouses is too small to provide significant sales and profit potential.

      Another important criterion is the financial position of the licensee. We prefer to do business with firms that are operating on a sound financial footing. Unfortunately, Pet Products does not appear to be in this position at the moment.

      Adding it all up, we have decided to turn down your application for a license at this time. We

      would be willing to reconsider your proposal at a future time, provided that you get your finances in order.
   b. We've screened thousands of licensing applications over the years, but yours is the first for a doghouse. Your design is both original and appealing, and Snoopy would be flattered that you value his image.

      Mr. Schulz likes to provide personal input on all the products that bear the Peanuts stamp. Since his time for working with licensees is limited, he accepts only a small percentage of the licensing applications that he receives. One of the things he takes into account is the financial strength of the potential licensee. After running a routine credit check on you with TRW Credit Services, he has decided to defer a decision on your licensing application until your financial position improves. Launching the Snoopy doghouse might be difficult given your current capital constraints.

      We wish you the best of luck with your business and hope that you will contact us again when you are in a better position to add new products to your line.
   c. What a cute idea! We've seen proposals for just about everything, but you're the first to think of a Snoopy doghouse. We can just picture the famous pooch perched on the red roof.

      As you might expect, Mr. Schulz limits the number of licensing proposals he accepts. His first concern is to ensure that the Peanuts gang is associated with only the very finest merchandise--a criterion that Pet Products clearly meets. His second priority is to earn a significant profit. In this regard, he looks at such factors as market size and the financial resources of the licensee, preferring to do business with firms having a strong capital base.

      We believe that the Snoopy doghouse could be a successful product, once your financial position improves. We look forward to hearing from you at a later date.

7. You have received a letter from Alice Amstahl, an avid *Peanuts* fan who wants Charlie Brown to wise up. She complains that Lucy always gets the best of Charlie and that it just isn't fair. She insists that it is high time Charlie won a round, and she wants Mr. Schulz to do something about it. "Please," she concludes her letter, "won't you let Charlie triumph over Lucy once in a while?" Schulz is touched by Amstahl's concern, but he feels that Charlie's innocence is essential to his character. Which of the fol-

lowing replies is the best way to handle the complaint?

a. Thank you for sticking up for Charlie Brown. He would be touched to know that you are rooting for him.

I'll grant that Charlie is certainly due for a victory over Lucy, but given his character, I don't see how he can ever win. His gullibility is an essential part of his personality. Without his innocence, he would lose much of his appeal. We all root for Charlie because he is the perpetual underdog, the nice guy who finishes last.

I sincerely appreciate your interest in Peanuts. Hearing from fans like you makes creating the strip more fun. Thanks again for your letter.

b. I wish I could grant your request, Ms. Amstahl, but I'm afraid Charlie Brown is doomed to perpetual gullibility. If he ever got the best of Lucy, I'll bet you wouldn't like him nearly as well as you do now. Charlie's innocence is the key to his appeal. His fans love him because he is the perpetual underdog.

I appreciate your letter, though. It's fun to hear from fans. Please keep on reading the strip and rooting for Charlie. Heaven knows, he needs the support.

c. Thank you for taking the time to express your views on the conflict between Charlie Brown and Lucy. I enjoy receiving feedback from the public regarding my characters.

Despite the importance of pleasing the audience, an artist must be true to his own voice. The act of creation is inherently a solitary activity involving independent effort. As I see Charlie Brown, he is the perpetual innocent, the gullible soul who lives his life in a trusting manner, regardless of how many times his trust is betrayed. He is, I think, an admirable and winsome character, largely because of his innocence.

Again, thank you for your comments. I'm sorry that I cannot change Charlie to suit you, but I hope that you will understand my decision and continue to enjoy the strip.[3]

QUESTIONS FOR DISCUSSION

1. What is the single chief purpose behind all bad-news messages?
2. How do you decide whether to use the direct or the indirect approach in bad-news messages?
3. What are the qualities of a good buffer?
4. If you were writing a bad-news letter to someone you no longer wished to do business with, would you still close on a helpful, friendly, positive note? Explain.
5. What is the overriding goal in conveying bad news about an order?
6. How should you justify refusing credit to an applicant who is a credit risk?

DOCUMENTS FOR ANALYSIS

Read the following documents; then (1) analyze the strengths or weaknesses of each sentence and (2) revise each document so that it follows this chapter's guidelines.

DOCUMENT 8.A

We have included with this letter a list of videotapes, films, slides, and other material that you may wish to order on the subjects of business mathematics and economics. Also included is a price list for these materials plus some other books you may wish to order.

Per your request, we are sorry to tell you that we cannot ship to you free examination copies of the books you requested as a result of reading a review in the Business Education Journal. The books, Business Mathematics Made Easy by Chester Sims and Economics Made Easy by Joanna Wesson, are well written in spite of being about a subject most people find difficult. The cost of printing and publishing these supplementary textbooks is getting higher every year, so I'm sure you can understand the reason for our not complying with your request for free examination copies.

We must request prompt payment for these books. The cost is $5.95 each plus $1.00 per book for postage and handling. These books would make good additions to your college's bookstore, even if you don't require them in your classes; they are helpful supplements to the primary textbooks your students are probably using now. Your students could use the extra help, we're sure. Let us know whether you decide to buy these books or not; because the price is going up, let us know soon.

DOCUMENT 8.B

<u>MEMO</u>

Yes, in the past we always did provide free setup for parties using our Grand Ballroom. We have found, however, that parties vary greatly in size. Table settings also vary depending on the menu being served.

Therefore, tell everyone in your department that the Banquet Department will no longer provide free setup.

When working with customers to plan their events, please add a $1.00 setup charge for each person in the party. That fee will cover arrangement of tables and chairs, table draping and place setting, bar setup, and setup of microphone and podium, if needed. This policy takes effect immediately for any events for which contracts have not already been signed. If any customers have a problem with the new policy, please have them call me.

DOCUMENT 8.C

We'd like to express our thanks for your letter of about six weeks ago. However, we regret to inform you that your claim for an adjustment on the Model XL dictation unit has been denied. Careful inspection by our engineering staff confirmed our original supposition that the unit has been damaged by improper treatment, either by user or by carrier.

Are you aware of the possibility that the Model XL dictation unit could have been dropped or abused by your employees? If this has not happened, you may file a claim against the carrier. It is more than likely that the unit was damaged in transit; according to you, the unit has never worked properly, and we are clearly not at fault.

Our charges for repairing the unit will be $50 to cover labor costs; the parts will be replaced at no charge under the terms of our 90-day warranty.

Please remit payment to us promptly.

We hope to see your representative at our sale, which will be held soon; pertinent facts appear in the promotional literature that is enclosed.

CASES

CONVEYING BAD NEWS ABOUT ORDERS

1. Something fishy: Letter attempting to clarify an order for neckties from Ralph Marlin

Nothing lasts for long in the fashion business—except Ralph Marlin's fish ties. Launched as a venture between two old high school buddies who thought of it while sitting in a bar one Saturday night, Ralph Marlin ties have become quite a phenomenon in the fickle fashion retailing industry. They've been steady sellers since the mid-1980s.

The first ties produced by the Wisconsin company did indeed resemble dead fish. No one can really account for their popularity—except that wearers aren't likely to encounter anyone else wearing the same tie on the same day. Unlike some notorious gift ties, a spiffy cobalt and yellow "Designer Tuna," complete with a golden gaff hook tie clasp, leaves no doubt in the mind of the recipient that he's the brunt of someone's joke—and if he's a good sport, he'll wear the tie to work and share the fun.

In fact, so many people have gotten into the spirit of fun that company founder Mark Abramoff (his buddy put up the first $50,000) patented the fish tie design and has expanded the line to include boxer shorts, T-shirts, and watches. The company also sells ties depicting assorted animals from armadillos to zebras, including the ever-popular pig tie, and other ties depict action sports, golfing scenes (golf balls and poised golf clubs), Harley-Davidson symbols ("Chrome Pipe," "Power Connection," and the like), and even Butteries (bow ties resembling six butterfly species). For the man of more refined taste, Ralph Marlin offers a series of "Artwear" ties (slices of famous paintings), as well as ties covered with famous faces (from Marilyn Monroe to Buckwheat). All Ralph Marlin ties are processed in a unique method that permanently transfers the artwork into the fibers of the satin polyester fabric without altering their silky finish.

Department stores may not carry all 30 fish tie species (ever see a red-hot lobster tie?), so Ralph Marlin now offers its full line through mail order. But as a clerk in the catalog department, which promises to ship within 24 hours, you've encountered a problem. The styles have proliferated so quickly that not every item pictured was given an identifying name before the catalog went to press. You are trying to fill an order that arrived in handwritten form: "Please send me the following Mai Tai Tropicals: one of the bright blue and orange ones on the left, two of the parrots, and an orchid." You can guess from the picture which of the dozen Mai Tais is meant by the "bright blue and orange" and the "orchid." But there are two versions of parrots offered on the same page, a tie with blue and yellow parrots on a bright red background and a cummerbund with red and blue parrots on a blue background. And on a previous page titled "Featured Creatures," the catalog offers a tie called "Parrots," which has larger birds and looks less like a Hawaiian shirt. The customer also requested a money bow tie, but didn't specify whether he wanted the bill depicted in 100 American dollars, Deutsch marks, Swedish kronen, Dutch gilders, British pounds, or French francs.

Your task: Write to John Perryman (2927 W. Hildegard Avenue, Faribault, Minnesota 55021) to clarify his order.[4]

2. Green and gone: Letter explaining that orders for Rubbermaid's litterless lunch kit will be late

It sounded like a good idea—an insulated lunch box with plastic containers inside to hold a sandwich, a drink, and a side dish—but no one in your department (sales) knew for certain how consumers would respond to kids' lunch pails costing more, taking up more space, and worst of all, having no Teenage Mutant Ninja Turtles on the outside. Rubbermaid's new Sidekick cooler, in bright turquoise or violet with lime-green trim, did have an edge, though. For all those environmentally sensitive youngsters who had been hounding their parents to do more to save the planet, this lunch bucket was ecologically sound. No more plastic sandwich wrap; no more juice boxes to clutter landfills.

In fact, it was that youthful ecological concern that prompted one of your biggest buyers, Canadian Tire Corporation, to suggest the idea for Sidekick. The retail chain wanted a litter-free lunch box to sell in its leisure products departments in time to hit the back-to-school market. Rubbermaid, already at work on a similar idea, quickly agreed. Fortunately, your company's engineers are accustomed to speedy product-development cycles. They lost no time adapting a design used for larger coolers, with high-density polyethylene liners for insulation. They chose three of your most popular Servin' Savers to fit into a four-quart model and settled on the youthful color scheme with a splashy red "Rubbermaid" logo. Within months, Sidekick was ready to ship.

You were a little nervous about the $10 price tag necessary to recoup development costs, but retailers liked the higher margin potential (the traditional cartoon-character boxes sell for $5 to $7).

Still, there was no way to predict the phenomenal success of the "green" lunch box. Kids love it. And apparently their parents are willing to pay more for it, because you've been swamped with orders from retailers who can't keep Sidekick in stock. Neither can you. The demand caught Rubbermaid by surprise, and

you've just been informed that all orders will be delayed by four weeks while production speeds up. The good news from marketing is that the company will be adding six new versions of Sidekick, featuring new colors and different food containers. One slightly larger model will be targeted for lunch-packing adults. It will include a reusable ice pack to keep foods cool.

Your task: As assistant sales manager, you've been asked to draft a form letter to send to retailers in the United States and Canada, advising them of the shipping delay. Be sure to ease the bad news with mention of the new products on the way.[5]

3. Please don't scream: Letter from Haagen-Dazs explaining a flavor switch

Apparently the British have never had much taste for ice cream; per capita consumption has been one-third the amount gobbled in the United States. Traditionally, Britons have been content with low-quality brands, some without so much as a spot of real cream. Now U.S.-produced Haagen-Dazs has introduced the British to the joys of superpremium ice cream—costly, but fit for a queen's palate. When it opened, the Haagen-Dazs shop in London's Leicester Square quickly broke worldwide ice cream sales records. The store scooped out $2.5 million worth of rich chocolate, vanilla, or strawberry to over a million people in the first year.

The success of the superrich ice cream in England came about when Britain's Grand Metropolitan bought Pillsbury, the producer of Haagen-Dazs. The new owners hoped to find a market hungry for super-premium ice cream both in Europe and in Asia. And they were right. Despite a cost often double the price of local brands, Haagen-Dazs hit the spot with consumers. In just two years, European sales reached $30 million, and a joint venture with Suntory in Japan logged $120 million. The sales figures just keep rising.

Until a new Haagen-Dazs factory in Arras, France, can be completed, the U.S. plant has been scrambling to produce enough ice cream for the European, Asian, and U.S. markets combined. This isn't always easy—as you know; you're an overseas sales supervisor based in the Bronx, New York, where the brand originated. Right now you've got a situation on your hands that could lead to some screaming in London if you don't handle it carefully.

Europa Foods convenience stores in London have been selling so much Haagen-Dazs that the brand now accounts for over 20 percent of the chain's ice cream sales. Although that makes everyone happy, their success has put an additional strain on the shipping schedule. Europa's next shipment won't have any of the popular mocha chip they're expecting. Until production can be stepped up, coffee flavor will be substituted for all mocha chip orders.

Your task: You've been asked to communicate the substitution plans to Colleen Downey, the head of Europa

Foods' purchasing department. Write to Ms. Downey at Europa Foods, Ltd., 8 Bedford Square, London WCIB 3 RA, England.[6]

4. Toys Aplenty: Letter to straighten out a problem order
This letter arrived in today's mail from Bill Breen, Manager, Toys Aplenty, 454 Cass Road, Brockton, MA 02401:

Please send the following as soon as possible:

1 doz	Puffees (Styrofoam filled), blue	#12231 A
1 doz	Clarence the Clown, 2-foot size	#12775
6	Smiley Face bed-side lamps	
	2 lemon	#12998 C
	2 avocado	#12998 D
	2 plum	#12998 F
1 doz	Freddy Frogs, green	#12466 B
3 doz	I-See-Me mirrored dinner plates	#12423
6 doz	Baby Walkers (with attached Talkers)	#12969
4 gross	Polka Dot diaper sets	#12128
3 doz	Popeye bubble pipes	#12903

According to my calculations, this order qualifies for a 5 percent volume discount.

For several years, Toys Aplenty has had an open account with your company, Happy Day Toys, and it generally pays promptly. Its orders are subject to your usual terms: 5 percent discount on orders over $500, with the smaller orders at 2/10, net 30 (which means a 2 percent discount for paying within 10 days and the total due within 30 days in any case). The customer is charged for shipping.

You have Smiley Face bedside lamps in lemon and plum, but no avocado lamps will be available for ten days. The order number given for the Freddy Frogs is for the yellow model, not green as specified in the order. You no longer carry Popeye bubble pipes. You do not stock the Baby Walkers; they are sent to customers directly from the factory in Peoria, Illinois. The other items present no problem. But if you pull the Popeye bubble pipes from this order, the reduced total no longer qualifies for the 5 percent quantity discount. When you call Mr. Breen to explain matters, you learn that he will be out of town for ten days. The clerk who takes your call advises you to send a letter to the store so that Mr. Breen can see the status of the order when he returns. With the information in hand, he can then call you with instructions regarding his order.

Your task: Write to Mr. Breen to explain the situation.

COMMUNICATING NEGATIVE ANSWERS AND INFORMATION

5. Sparky isn't talking: Letter refusing information
Creative Associates (see this chapter's On-the-Job simulation) has received a letter from a journalist asking how much money Charles Schulz earns each year from writing the *Peanuts* comic strip and licensing the characters. Schulz prefers not to divulge this information.

Your task: Schulz has asked you to draft a reply. Prepare the draft.[7]

6. The baby bottle boycott: Letter from Yale New Haven Hospital canceling a purchase agreement
As one of the buyers for Yale New Haven Hospital in New Haven, Connecticut, you have routinely purchased large quantities of Enfamil baby formula from Bristol-Myers for use in the obstetrics and pediatrics wards. This morning, though, the hospital's assistant administrator drops by your office to report on a recent staff meeting. Evidently, a number of the doctors who attended the meeting were upset over Bristol-Myers's decision to advertise a new infant formula directly to the public.

"You should have heard the talk going around the table," the administrator says. "Dr. J. was really mad. He swore he'd never recommend another Bristol-Myers product to his patients. He thinks the company has no business advertising directly to parents. As far as he's concerned, doctors should advise mothers on the proper nutritional program for their children."

"Hmm," you reply. "One of the trade journals had an article about Bristol-Myers's new formula just the other day. Apparently, it's a pretty good product. They're making it, and the Gerber company is selling it. In fact, it's called Gerber Baby Formula. I suspect that Gerber is calling the shots on the advertising program. If you want my opinion, Bristol-Myers is getting a bum rap."

"Well, that may be," the administrator replies, "but the upshot of the staff meeting was—stop buying Enfamil and let Bristol-Myers know what we think of their advertising campaign."

"So, who's going to tell Bristol-Myers the good news?" you ask.

The administrator smiles a crocodile smile and points his finger at you.

Your task: Write to Bristol-Myers. Cancel your most recent order for Enfamil and explain the hospital's decision.[8]

7. Save the wave: Refusal to remove a large sign from Julian Surf & Sport
Ever since she bolted it to the front of her tiny sporting goods store, Marcia Hegranes has heard more than an earful of controversy

over the bright blue, 14-foot, carved wooden wave cascading its message around the shop's door: "Surf's Up in Julian." Apparently, the old California mining community wasn't ready for the blond grandmother's business style. The town is buzzing with people who think that the wave clashes with Julian's rustic image as a mountain tourist stop famous for its history and its fresh apple pie. Even though Hegranes's 300-square-foot shop is tucked into the base of an old depression-era water tower, they say the sign is too contemporary; the wave must go. Before long, Hegranes heard these demands echoed from city and county officials.

Last summer Marcia Hegranes hired you to help out because the shop had become so popular. Grandmother or not, she has a great rapport with local teenagers. Many of them are transplants from the surf-conscious coastal zone, having moved to Julian when their parents sought out the slow-paced, woodsy atmosphere that makes the town so popular with tourists. But the kids feel stuck, living a mile above sea level and an hour's drive from their beloved Pacific waves. For them, the irreverent wave is a symbol—just like the half-eaten apple core on the shop's window with its defiant proclamation, "Dedicated to the Hard-Core."

Speaking for the city, Julian Architectural Review Board member Richard Zerbe says that the sign disrupts the historical character of Julian, which is modeled after area photographs dating from 1870 to 1930. He explains that the board has issued carefully developed architectural guidelines for the Julian Historical District, which encompasses the town's commercial area. As chief of zoning code enforcement for San Diego County, Sue Gray believes the wave sign is simply too big. Furthermore, Hegranes failed to go through the proper permit process for signage, so Gray has notified Hegranes that she must remove the wave within two months.

Together, you and Hegranes have decided to fight for the wave—mostly for the kids who love its spirited message. After all, the sculpted wave is more than a sign; it's a work of art. On that basis, you think you might be able to persuade officials to let it stand. You've received dozens of letters of support: "As mother and father of a teenager, we wholeheartedly support Hegranes's shop, the wave artwork, and her kindnesses to young people. The kids are watching," wrote one couple. "Why does every store have to look the same?" asked another supporter. "If all the buildings here were really historically accurate, we'd all be doing business under sheets of corrugated tin."

Your task: Write a letter stating the intention of Julian Surf & Sport to keep the wave in place as a sculptural work of art. Provide ample reasoning to back up your position. Address the letter to Sue Gray, chief of San Diego zoning code enforcement (1222 First Ave., San Diego, CA 92101). You can send a copy to the Julian Architectural Review Board (1836 Main, Julian, CA 92036).[9]

8. Sorry, Dad: Memo denying a First Boston employee's request for paternity leave It's becoming a touchy subject, but so far nothing has been done about formalizing First Boston Corporation's policy with regard to paid child-care leave—which used to be known as maternity leave. Company executives have decided for now to operate on a case-by-case basis, considering each employee's circumstances and making a decision based on that individual's job duties, performance, and other intangible factors (such as an executive's gut feeling about the situation).

As a manager in the information systems division, you have received a request from one of the men under your supervision for three months' paid leave commencing with the birth of his second child, due in about six weeks. Jon Golding cites in his favor the recent paid maternity leave granted to a female supervisor under similar circumstances. "Surely First Boston is required by law to administer this benefit equally among both men and women," his memo concludes. You're not sure about that, since you've never received such a request from a man, so you ask the vice president of human resources. She informs you that First Boston has no such policy of equal treatment. In fact, men who request either paid or unpaid paternity leave are routinely denied.

All your subsequent efforts to convince upper management that Mr. Golding's request has merit are unsuccessful. You learn that First Boston may eventually develop a more equitable policy (especially if Congress passes the family-leave bill now under consideration, which would mandate unpaid leave for both men and women). But such a change won't occur in time for the birth of Mr. Golding's second child.

Your task: Write a tactful memo to Jon Golding refusing his request for paternity leave.[10]

REFUSING ADJUSTMENT OF CLAIMS AND COMPLAINTS

9. That's showbiz: Form letter from Columbia Pictures denying refunds Marketing a new film not only is expensive (the typical marketing budget averages $12 million) but also requires keen insight, good intuition, and plenty of research. In other words, no one in the film industry really has a solid formula for success. Although a movie trailer (also known as a coming attraction or preview) costs between $75,000 and $500,000 to produce, film studios depend heavily on them. They can make or break a film, and it's not unusual for a studio to screen three or four versions for test audiences before deciding which trailer sends the right message.

When Columbia Pictures executive Paula Silver set out to promote *The Prince of Tides*, she tested a number of trailers. They all featured shots of the love relationship between the characters portrayed by director-star Barbra Streisand and actor Nick Nolte. Silver found that the more the trailer revealed of the sophisticated plot, the more test audiences wanted to see the romantic film. So the preview Columbia released to movie theaters gave away a good portion of the story, with a voice-over that could easily have come from a screenwriter's one-line summary: "Behind all the joy and all the tears lie the memories that haunt us and the truth that sets us free." The film not only reaped high praise from critics (garnering several Academy Award nominations), it found an enthusiastic audience that extended its success for weeks through positive word of mouth.

Unfortunately, Columbia also received quite a few complaints about the tell-all trailer. Many of those who wrote of their disappointment over the story giveaway also asked for refunds—so many, in fact, that Silver has decided to develop a form letter for replying to such complaints. Since the tell-all technique worked so beautifully for *The Prince of Tides*, she just might want to use it again.

Your task: Silver has asked you to develop the form letter. Explain that it is inappropriate for Columbia to refund movie admissions collected by theater operators, who function independently of the studio. As a thank you to those who wrote to share their views, each letter will include a $3.50 discount coupon redeemable at screenings of any Columbia Pictures film.[11]

10. Of course they're ugly: Letter from boutique refusing claim over "unsightly" Doc Martens
At the trendy Na-Na boutique in Santa Monica where you work as a manager, you've sold so many pairs of "Doc Martens"—the clunky, street-combat boots made by Dr. Marten—that your buyer can barely keep them in stock. Even your employees wear them because they're easy on the feet. Like Birkenstock and Mephisto, Dr. Marten makes footwear that caters to comfort first and fashion—not at all.

Ugly as they are, you can't remember receiving a single customer complaint about the comfy boots, that is, until you opened your mail today and found this letter from Susan Stone of Ventura:

Several months ago, I purchased a pair of burgundy Doc Martens with black laces after one of your salespeople convinced me that they're the most comfortable boots around. I like the way they look cool with both short and long skirts and with jeans, and besides, everyone is wearing them. But a week ago I got a job as a waitress at the Eggshell Café. After two days of eight-hour shifts, I figured

I'd wear my Doc Martens and save what was left of my feet. I got fired. I argued with the manager, pointing out that she lets the girls wear whatever they want—miniskirts or leather pants or tank tops—but she said, "You're out of here." Why? Customer complaints about my "unsightly footwear."

I was misled by your salesperson, who told me that Doc Martens can be worn anywhere in L.A. I believed him—but he was wrong. I think I'm entitled to a full refund of the $116 I paid for the boots, plus $1,200 compensation (a month's wages and tips) for losing my job over them.

First of all, the writer says she bought the boots "several months ago," so a full refund is out of the question, even if she had returned the boots with the letter (which she did not). Second, you're not so sure it was the boots that caused her to be fired, since waitress dress codes in Los Angeles are liberal. It could be that the manager used the boots as an excuse to fire an employee who simply wasn't capable—particularly one who had been on the job for only two days. (It's unfortunate, but you know that some managers have difficulty telling fired employees the whole truth.) Since Ms. Stone makes no mention of receiving a second chance to improve her wardrobe choice, which is how you'd handle a potentially good employee, you're convinced that she was actually fired for reasons other than her Doc Martens. In any case, the claim for job-loss compensation seems extreme for a shoe retailer, and you're not about to pay it. The boutique's owner agrees.

Your task: Write a letter to Susan Stone (235 W. Alameda, #42, Ventura, CA 93001) refusing her refund request and her claim for job-loss compensation. As a goodwill gesture, invite her to visit the store for a 20 percent discount on any of the other popular footwear the boutique sells.[12]

11. Many happy returns: Letter from Cliffs Notes refusing a claim in a complicated transaction
Like most publishers, Cliffs Notes, Inc., of Lincoln, Nebraska, gives full credit to any bookstore that returns unsold copies of its publications, provided that they are received in salable condition within six months of their original shipment to the bookstore. The bookstore pays postage. However, even though most large publishers have return rates of 30 to 50 percent, only about 6 percent of Cliffs Notes's 222 titles are returned. Nevertheless, today's mail includes the following large return from the University of Wyoming Bookstore, Laramie, WY 82071:

21 copies, *MacBeth*
6 copies, *The Scarlet Letter*

12 copies, *Crime and Punishment*
5 copies, *Hamlet*

All Cliffs Notes titles sell for a retail (list) price of $3.50, and the bookstores get a 40 percent discount off that.

The cover letter from the University of Wyoming Bookstore indicates that 23 copies of *MacBeth* have been sent, but you count only 21. Although the carton has sustained some damage, nothing appears to have spilled out. Five of the booklets are so worn that they cannot be resold. One copy of *Crime and Punishment* is water-stained and cannot be resold. One copy of *The Scarlet Letter* was damaged in shipping because of a combination of careless packing and rough handling in transit. The shipment also includes four copies of *A Tale of Two Cities*, published by Monarch Notes, one of Cliffs Notes's competitors. Obviously, the company does not owe the bookstore anything for these booklets.

As a customer service representative for Cliffs Notes, you have decided to return the four copies of *A Tale of Two Cities* to the university bookstore, to return the unsalable copies to them with an explanation, to charge them $2.20 for postage, and to tell them that they shipped you only 21 copies (not 23 copies) of *MacBeth*.

Your task: Figure out where things stand and write a letter explaining your decision.[13]

REFUSING TO EXTEND CREDIT
12. Pat the Painter: Letter refusing credit to a new business
Patricia Whitman is a young woman of boundless ambition. Doing business as Pat the Painter (1427 Queen Street East, Sault Sainte Marie, Ontario P6A 5P2), she proposes to blanket the area with fliers promoting her painting and carpentry business. She tells you that she has scaffold builders, scrapers, paint mixers, and commission salespeople in place and that paint and equipment will be delivered to work sites by college students before and after their classes. She also tells you that her start-up capital is small and her start-up expenses high. She wants to purchase paint, brushes, solvents, and ladders from your firm, Hobson's Builders Supply, and she wants the payments to begin in 60 days.

You admire Pat's energy and ambition, but you are less enthusiastic about the success of her venture. You certainly want to supply her business needs but prefer to deal on a cash basis, at least for now.

Your task: Write Pat a letter, turning down her request for credit.

13. No more advances: Memo outlining Banc One policy against IRS refund loans
A few years ago, Banc One in Columbus, Ohio, joined a number of banking institutions in offering its customers "IRS Refund Loans." The consumer loans provided an opportunity for customers to borrow against their income tax refunds early in the year—arranging as part of the loan agreement to have the Internal Revenue Service send their refunds directly to the bank to pay off the loan. The refund loans seemed like a good move for the bank; they brought in new customers, they were extremely low risk (who could be more dependable than the IRS?), and they were a good promotional tool among existing customers, reinforcing the bank's image as a service organization. No one at Banc One foresaw the glitch that ultimately fouled up a "perfect" idea.

The catch was that customers had to first file an electronic tax return, making use of newly implemented IRS technology. Once the computerized return was filed, the IRS responded with immediate confirmation of any refund due the taxpayer. The bank then made its loan based on the IRS-verified amount, which would later be repaid directly to the bank. It seemed an airtight, foolproof system—until a programming error at the IRS started creating problems, affecting not just one or two returns, but filings from all over the country.

The first year the problem emerged, the IRS was forced to apologize for errors that added up to $3 million in mistakenly confirmed refunds. Banc One lost some money on uncollected loans, but not much. The second year, IRS errors during one 17-day period, between January 10 and January 27, totaled nearly $40 million, so Banc One cashed out of the IRS refund loan business. Too risky, bank executives decided. If the IRS confirmed a refund that wasn't forthcoming, the bank could be left with an unsecured balance due that the customer might not be able to pay. Collection costs alone could cause the once-secure loans to become highly unprofitable for the bank.

Although news reports have quoted IRS officials stating that the computer glitch has been corrected, Banc One executives remain firm in their decision to suspend the refund loan program. The only exceptions will be made under special circumstances involving long-term customers with exemplary credit records and with whom the bank has had prior lending experience, so even if the IRS should err in confirming the refund amount, the bank could feel confident that the customer would be able to repay the loan. The bank's advertisements no longer promote the refund loans, but bank officers are expected to receive numerous requests from customers wanting to borrow against their tax refunds during the first few months of next year.

Your task: As communications director, you have been asked to write a form letter that tactfully explains the new policy to customers inquiring about IRS refund loans. Convey the text of this form letter in a memo to all branch managers, suggesting that it can be reproduced on their own letterhead for issuing to customers.[14]

CHAPTER NINE

WRITING PERSUASIVE MESSAGES

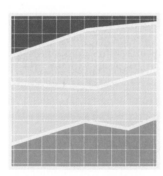

ON THE JOB:
Facing a Communication Dilemma at Lawrence County Hospital
Rx for an Ailing Hospital

A stay at the Lawrence County Hospital used to be something of a status symbol for the 3,000 residents of Moulton, Alabama. When the facility was built in 1954, most of the local women delivered their babies at home. Checking into the hospital's maternity ward for a week was a real vacation. Older folks liked the facility too. Quite a few of them signed in for a complete physical every year on the theory that an ounce of prevention is worth a pound of cure. While there, they were apt to run into friends having minor surgery, most of whom checked in two or three days early to get ready for their operations and stayed several days afterward to avoid complications. You practically needed a reservation a month in advance to get a room.

Today, though, 80 of the 99 beds are empty. Some wards are used so rarely that the hall lights aren't even turned on. The maternity wing is gone—the victim of high insurance rates. The specialists have all been dismissed from the medical staff, and the hospital's chief administrator, Ronald Sparkman, is looking for still more ways to cut costs. He recently eliminated the free cafeteria meals for hospital employees, and he thinks maybe the ambulance service will be the next to go.

Lawrence County Hospital's problems began in 1983 when Congress passed legislation to curb Medicare costs—a move that dramatically altered the economics of running a hospital. The new rules discourage doctors from hospitalizing patients and also discourage hospitals from keeping patients any longer than necessary. The inevitable outcome has been a decrease in both the number and length of hospital stays.

The fewer patients a hospital has, the harder it is to make a profit. Regardless of whether Lawrence County has 99 patients or 19, it still has to pay its utility bills, run its laboratories, equip its operating rooms, and pay its nurses, doctors, technicians, and administrators. With 99 patients paying bills, covering these costs is not too difficult; but with only 19 patients, breaking even is a real trick.

In order to run in the black, Ronald Sparkman has two options: cutting costs and increasing the occupancy rate. He has already cut almost every conceivable cost. If he cuts any more, the hospital will have little left to offer, and occupancy rates will decline even more. Sparkman's best bet at this point is to attract more patients. If you were in charge, how would you convince patients to use Lawrence County Hospital? What sort of persuasive message would you send? In what form?[1]

PREPARING TO WRITE A PERSUASIVE MESSAGE

Lawrence County Hospital

Ronald Sparkman understands that persuasion is much more than simply asking somebody to do something. In formal terms, it's the process of changing people's attitudes or influencing their actions, either immediately or at some time in the future. Because persuasive messages aim to influence an audience that is inclined to resist, they depend heavily on strategic planning. Before you begin to write a persuasive message, ask yourself what you are writing about, what audience you are writing to, and what you want to happen as a result.

APPEALING TO THE AUDIENCE

Convincing an uninterested or wary audience is a difficult job requiring much insight. Fortunately, a great deal of research has been conducted to determine how a communicator can overcome people's resistance to a message and motivate them to change their actions or beliefs.

Needs and appeals

People are motivated by needs.

What makes people think or act as they do? Needs. People have many needs, of course, but some researchers believe that certain needs have priority and that the most basic needs (such as safety and security) must be met before a person will seek to fulfill higher-level needs (such as esteem and status). Imagine that you supervise someone who consistently arrives late for work. Once you have analyzed the need motivating him to arrive late, you can craft an appeal, a "hook" that will make him interested in your message about changing his behavior.

Advertising researchers have come up with long lists of appeals that make people take notice. But because their needs differ, people respond to any given message in different ways. Not everyone is interested in economy, for instance, or fair play; as a matter of fact, some people's innermost needs make appeals to status and greed much more effective. Because of these individual differences, you must analyze your audience and then construct a message that appeals to their needs.

Emotion and logic

Emotional reactions may result when an audience's needs are overlooked.

When people's needs are not being met, they are likely to respond emotionally. For example, a person who lacks a feeling of self-worth is likely to be sensitive to the tone of respect in a message. To yield the best results, a collection letter to such a person must take care to avoid any hint that the person is considered dishonorable. The danger is that the person will become upset and not pay attention to the message. Not even the best-crafted, most reasonable message will persuade someone who is emotionally unable to accept it.

In some cases, emotional issues are a pitfall for persuasive messages; in many other cases, however, persuasive messages make use of the emotion surrounding certain words. *Freedom*, for instance, brings forth strong feelings, as do such words as *success*, *prestige*, *credit record*, *savings*, *free*, *value*, and *comfort*. The use of such words puts the audience in a certain frame of mind and helps them accept the message.

Although thinking of oneself as rational is as strong a need as any other, emotion and logic work together in a rather strange way: People need to have reasons for an attitude they've already embraced in their hearts. To take advantage of this need, you should be sure to use both emotional appeals and logical proof when you write persuasive messages, as in the following excerpt:

Mary Kay Ash, founder of Mary Kay Cosmetics, uses every imaginable form of communication (from handwritten memos to training manuals, videocassettes, and gala award shows) to motivate and manage the 100,000 sales people in her company.

The streets of Calcutta swarm with orphaned, homeless children. To you and me, a few cents for milk and bread seems so little. But to them, a supper like this would be a feast. Think how good you'd feel to know you're helping feed the children of Calcutta and other burdened cities around the world. Your monthly pledge of $5, $10, or more is all it takes to put food in the mouth of a starving child.

The scene described in this letter tugs at the heartstrings; the implication that $5 is relatively little to someone in this country and a fortune to a hungry, homeless orphan provides a logical reason for contributing.

Credibility

Enhance your credibility by supplying evidence that is objective and specific.

Without credibility, your skillful use of needs, appeals, emotion, and logic may seem to be nothing more than manipulation. It is especially important for a skeptical or hostile audience to believe that you know what you are talking about and that you are not trying to mislead anyone.

One of the best ways to gain credibility is to support your message with facts. Testimonials, documents, guarantees, statistics, research results, and the like, all provide seemingly objective evidence for what you have to say and thus make your message more credible. The more specific and relevant your proof, the better. Naming your sources helps too, especially if they are respected by your audience.

Express personal qualities that enhance credibility through your approach and writing style.

A number of personal qualities will enhance your own credibility. If you can demonstrate the following characteristics, your audience will more readily believe what you say:

- *Enthusiasm.* Infectious excitement about the subject of the message

- *Objectivity.* Understanding of and willingness to acknowledge all sides of an issue

- *Sincerity.* Honesty, genuineness, good faith, and truthfulness

- *Expertise*. Knowledge of the subject area in the message (or even of some other area)

- *Good intentions*. Willingness to keep the audience's best interests at heart

- *Trustworthiness*. Honesty and dependability

- *Similarity*. Beliefs, attitudes, and background like those of the audience

If you want the audience to "buy" your message, let them know that you have or are associated with someone who has these qualities.

Semantics

In his attempts to regain market share from the Japanese, Black & Decker's CEO Nolan Archibald used persuasive messages to transform an entire corporate culture, recapture customers with his vision, and recruit the talent he needed. To persuade others to adopt your point of view, says Archibald, present your case as though you were on the other side and needed to be convinced yourself.

Abstractions are most persuasive when combined with details.

How do you let an audience know that you are, for example, enthusiastic or trustworthy? An outright claim that you have these qualities is sure to raise suspicion. Word choice, however, can do much of the job for you.

The words you choose for your message say much more than their dictionary definition. For instance, *useful, beneficial,* and *advantageous* may be considered synonyms. Yet these three words cannot be used interchangeably and still convey the same meaning:

> She suggested a *useful* compromise. (The compromise allowed the parties to get to work.)

> She suggested a *beneficial* compromise. (The compromise not only resolved the conflict but also had a positive effect, perhaps for both parties.)

> She suggested an *advantageous* compromise. (The compromise benefited her or her company more than it benefited the other party.)

Another way that semantics can affect persuasive messages is in the variety of meanings that people attribute to certain words. Because abstractions refer to things that people cannot experience with their senses, they are subject to interpretation. Thus they can be used to enhance the emotional content of a persuasive message. For example, you may be able to sell more flags by appealing to people's patriotism (which may be interpreted in many ways) than by describing the color and size of the flags. Ronald Sparkman may have better luck collecting an overdue hospital bill by mentioning honesty and fair play than by repeating the sum owed and the date it was due. But you must include both the abstraction and the details for your message to have the effect you want; the very fact that you are using abstract words creates room for misinterpretation.

ORGANIZING THE MESSAGE

The AIDA plan:
- Attention
- Interest
- Desire
- Action

Once you have laid a foundation, you may begin to build your message. Persuasion requires the indirect approach, often a specialized one called the AIDA (attention, interest, desire, action) plan.

Your goal in the attention phase is to convince the audience right at the beginning that you have something useful or interesting to say. The audience wants to know "What's in this message for me?" Try to tell them without making extravagant claims or threats and without bringing up irrelevant points. For example:

Begin every persuasive message with an attention-getting statement that is
- Personalized
- You-oriented
- Not extravagant
- Relevant

You've mentioned several times in the past two weeks that constructing an employee schedule has become increasingly difficult. Let me share an idea that could substantially reduce the time you spend making and revising schedules.

In the interest phase, you explain how your message relates to the audience. Continuing the theme that you started with, you paint a more detailed picture with words. Your goal is to get the audience thinking, "This is an interesting idea; maybe it is a possibility for solving my problems."

In the interest section
- Continue the opening theme in greater detail
- Relate benefits specifically to the attention-getter

Inc. magazine ran an article in the July 2 issue about a scheduling concept called flextime. It gives employees leeway to schedule their own work, within certain guidelines. Two companies profiled in the article were having problems (as we have been) with late arrivals, long lunches, early departures, and too many "sick days." They found it nearly impossible to set up a schedule that everyone would adhere to. But once these companies instituted flextime, their problems practically disappeared.

Notice how this section ties together the factual description and the benefits of instituting the program. Notice also that the benefits relate specifically to the attention-getter that precedes this paragraph. Even though the flextime system might help improve employee morale, that benefit is secondary to the main interest of the intended audience (to reduce the frustration of devising useless schedules) and is therefore not mentioned.

The desire section of a persuasive message is used to back up claims and thereby increase your audience's willingness to take the action that you will suggest in the next section. The point is to get the audience to think, "I really need this." Whatever you use to prove your claim, make sure the evidence is directly relevant to your point. For example:

In the desire section
- Provide relevant evidence to prove your claim
- Draw attention to any enclosures

One of the people interviewed in the article, the head of manufacturing for a $10 million company, said: "I seemed to be spending all my time making schedules and then tearing them up. Now I let my employees figure out their own schedules. I have more time to oversee the work that's being done and to track the quality of the products we ship." This company had a flextime program in full operation within three months of deciding to start it. Attached is a copy of an article about the factors to consider before going to flextime and the three steps involved in instituting it.

Notice how this example draws attention to the evidence and suggests the lessons that may be drawn from it.

All persuasive messages end with a section that urges specific action. But the so-called action ending should be more than a statement like "Institute this program as soon as possible" or "Send me a refund." In fact, it offers a good opportunity for one last reminder of the main benefit the audience will realize from taking the action you want. For example:

End by
- Describing precisely what you would like to happen
- Restating how the audience will benefit by acting as you wish
- Making action easy

Let's meet early next week (Monday, 3 p.m.?) to see how we might implement a flextime schedule. With a little bit of extra effort now, you could soon be concentrating on something more important than scheduling.

The secret of the final section is to make action easy. In sales letters, for example, you might ask the audience to fill out an enclosed order form and use a preaddressed, postpaid envelope for reply.

WRITING PERSUASIVE REQUESTS FOR ACTION

Many persuasive messages are written to solicit funds, favors, information, or cooperation. In an organization, for example, persuasive techniques are often required to get someone to change policies or procedures, to spend money on new equipment and services, to promote a person, or to protect turf.[2] Persuasive letters to outsiders might solicit donations or ask for some other type of help.

This type of message is one of the most difficult persuasive tasks you could undertake. For one thing, people are busy, and doing something new takes time without offering a guaranteed reward in return. Second, there are plenty of competing requests. In fact, the public relations departments of many large corporations receive so many requests for donations to worthy causes that they must sometimes resort to lotteries to decide which to support.

Why do people respond to requests for action on an issue that is more important to you than to them? If you're lucky, they may believe in the project or the cause you're writing about. Even so, you must persuade them that your request will give them some benefit, perhaps an intangible benefit down the road or a chance to make a meaningful contribution. Also, especially in the case of requests for professional favors or information, people may believe that they are obliged to "pay their dues" by helping others.

When making a persuasive request, therefore, take special care to highlight direct and indirect benefits. Direct benefits might include a reduced work load for the supervisor who institutes flextime or a premium for someone who responds to a survey. Indirect benefits might include better employee morale or the prestige of giving free workshops to small businesses.

The attention-getting device at the beginning of a persuasive request for action usually serves to show the reader that you know something about his or her concerns and that you have some reason for making such a request. In this type of persuasive message, more than in most others, a flattering comment about the reader is acceptable, especially if it is sincere. For example, if Ronald Sparkman wrote to local businesspeople asking them to serve on Lawrence County Hospital's advisory board, his complimenting them on their business success would suggest they are able to contribute to the hospital's future. The body of the letter or memo covers what you know about the problem you are trying to solve with the reader's help: the facts and figures, the benefits of helping, and your experience in attacking the problem. The goal is to give you and your request credibility, to make the reader believe that helping you will indeed help solve a significant problem. Once you have demonstrated that your message is relevant to your reader, you can request some specific action. Take a look at the request in Figure 9.1. Be aware, however, that a persuasive memo is somewhat more subdued than a letter to an outsider might be.

The most important thing to remember when you prepare a persuasive request for action is to keep your request within bounds. Nothing is so distressing as a request so general, all-encompassing, or inconsiderate that it seems impossible to grant, no matter how worthy the cause. And don't doom your request to failure by asking your reader to do all your work for you: to

Three problems with requests for action:
- They frequently offer nothing tangible in return
- They take time that could be used for something else
- There are so many competing requests

A former teacher, Lane Nemeth founded Discovery Toys, a company that markets educational toys through home demonstration parties. Whether you're wooing investors, negotiating a loan, or ordering inventory, advises Nemeth, let your readers know you understand their concerns.

FIGURE 9.1
Memo Requesting Action

A provocative statement and remarkable statistics help get the reader's attention.

By detailing the nature and dimensions of the problem, the writer gives the request credibility.

The suggested solution is specific enough to appear workable.

The final paragraph tells the reader exactly what must be done and reinforces the main reason for doing it.

MEMO

TO: Elaine Tyson   DATE: August 10, 1993

FROM: Bob Binks   SUBJECT: Order Processing

We may not be getting our money's worth from the three new data-entry clerks we hired six months ago, although the clerks aren't really to blame. Take a look at these figures, which Sarah and I have compiled over the past month:

--About 18 percent of customer orders lack some piece of information, such as a ZIP code, needed to process and ship the merchandise efficiently.

--In six cases that we know about (because customers called to complain), orders never showed up in the computer records and were therefore never processed, although we did find the paperwork.

When the new order-processing system was installed two years ago, we selected computers with plenty of capacity. In fact, even at present growth rates, they should be adequate for another two or three years.

The software is another matter. Although it was the best available at the time, new software on the market is much more "goof-proof." With audible prompts to remind operators when necessary information is missing and with a simplified "save" function, OrderMaster II could solve our data-entry problems and upgrade customer service at the same time. OrderMaster II can easily be customized to suit our operations. And note this fact particularly: The total cost is less than we have spent in the past month to have someone resolve order-processing problems.

The requisition form we need to obtain OrderMaster II (complete except for your signature) is attached. The software manufacturer assures me that we can have it within a week; a field representative will come out for a day or two to set it up and show the data-entry clerks how to use it.

Do you have any questions about this program? If so, call me at ext. 157. Otherwise, please sign the requisition form and send it back to me right away. The sooner we order the program, the sooner we can solve some serious problems with order processing.

Make only reasonable requests.

provide information that you were too lazy to seek, to spend time saving you from embarrassment or inconvenience, or to provide total financial support for a cause that nobody else is supporting.

WRITING SALES LETTERS

By and large, sales letters are written by specialized and highly skilled professionals. The letters come in a variety of sizes, with brochures or without. They can be one-of-a-kind messages from a single individual to another, or they can be mass mailings from one company to thousands of consumers. The common denominator is their attempt to motivate people to spend money or to patronize an organization.

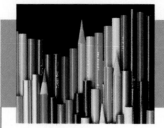

CHECKLIST FOR PERSUASIVE REQUESTS FOR ACTION

A. Attention
☐ **1.** Demonstrate that you understand the audience's concerns.
☐ **2.** Introduce a direct or indirect benefit that can be developed as a central selling point.
☐ **3.** Craft statements so that they don't sound like high-pressure sales tactics or bribes.
☐ **4.** Use an effective opening: comment or assertion that the audience will agree with, compliment (if sincere), frank admission that you need the audience's help, problem that is the basis of your request, one or two rhetorical questions, or statement(s) of what is being done (has been done) to solve a problem.

B. Interest and Desire
☐ **1.** Early in the body of the message, introduce the reason you are writing.
  ☐ a. Mention the main audience benefit before the actual request.
  ☐ b. Thoroughly explain your reason for asking the favor.
☐ **2.** Include all necessary descriptions: physical characteristics and value of the project.
☐ **3.** Include all facts and figures necessary to convince the audience that his or her contribution will be enjoyable, easy, important, and of personal benefit (as much as is true and possible).
  ☐ a. In a request for cooperation, explain the problem, facts, suggestions, other participants' roles, and the audience's part.
  ☐ b. In a request for a donation, explain the problem, past and current attempts to remedy it, future plans, your organization's involvement, and projected costs, along with suggestions about how the audience can help.
  ☐ c. Describe the possible direct benefits.
  ☐ d. Describe the possible indirect benefits.
☐ **4.** Anticipate and answer possible objections.
  ☐ a. Ignore objections if they are unimportant or might not occur to the audience or if you can focus on positive facts instead.
  ☐ b. Discuss objections (usually) about half or two-thirds of the way through the body of the letter or memo.
  ☐ c. Acknowledge objections calmly; then overcome them by focusing on more important and more positive factors.
  ☐ d. Turn objections into an advantage by looking at them from another viewpoint or by explaining the facts of the situation more clearly.
  ☐ e. Overcome objections to providing restricted material by giving assurance that you will handle it in whatever limited way is specified.
☐ **5.** Introduce any enclosures after you have finished the key message, with an emphasis on what to do with them or what information they offer.

C. Action
☐ **1.** Confidently ask for the audience's cooperation.
☐ **2.** Make the desired action clear and easy.
☐ **3.** Stress the positive results of action.
☐ **4.** Include the due date for a response (if necessary), and tie it in with audience benefits (if possible): adequate time for ordering supplies, prominent billing on the program, and so forth.
☐ **5.** Replace negative or tentative statements ("If you can donate anything") with positive, confident statements ("To make your contribution, just return . . .").
☐ **6.** As a last audience-benefit plug, tie in the last sentence with an appeal or a statement featured in the opening paragraph (if appropriate).

Some aspects of sales letters can lead to serious legal problems, but being aware of the laws and how they change will help you avoid such difficulties. For example, the Quaker Oats Company currently sells a cereal called Oat Bran, which claims to reduce cholesterol. However, the Food and Drug Administration is drafting a regulation that would prohibit such claims without sound scientific support.[3] So when writers at Quaker Oats compose sales letters—to grocers, for example—they have to know what is and what is not acceptable.

Sales letters are considered contracts under the laws of many states, so avoid even implying offers or promises you can't deliver. Also, making a false statement in a sales letter is fraud, so avoid misrepresenting the price, quality, or performance capability of a product, and avoid using testimonials made by persons misrepresented as being experts.

Using a person's name, photograph, or other identity in a sales letter without permission constitutes invasion of privacy. Legal problems can also result from publicizing a person's private life, past-due debts, medical records, or x-rays. Knowing the laws that govern sales letters is an important step in writing them.

However, merely avoiding what is illegal may not always be enough. To maintain the highest standards of business ethics, you must make every attempt to persuade without manipulating. For example, you want to choose words that won't be misinterpreted. When de-emphasizing negatives, you want to be sure you don't distort the truth. You want to show consideration for the audience by adopting the "you" attitude with honest concern for the needs and interests of your current and potential customers.

> Be aware of the potential legal problems associated with sales letters.

PREWRITING

The three steps involved in planning a sales letter are similar to those involved in planning any persuasive message: (1) Determine the main idea (in sales letters, it revolves around a selling point and related benefits), (2) define the audience, and (3) plan the approach and format.

Determining selling points and benefits

Selling points are the most attractive features of a product; consumer benefits are the particular advantages that buyers will realize from those features. For example, one selling point of a personal computer might be its numeric keypad; the consumer benefit of this selling point is that the user doesn't need a separate calculator or the skill to type numbers on the regular keyboard.

Obviously, you cannot write about either selling points or benefits without a thorough understanding of your subject. Therefore, the first step in writing any sales letter is to take a good look at the product. Ask yourself (or someone else, if necessary) everything that you think a potential buyer might want to know about it.

Once you have a complete file on the product, you must think of how its features can help potential buyers. The product benefits that you focus on should be relatively few, and you should determine which are most appealing so that you can direct your audience's attention to them. Ultimately, you will want to single out one benefit, which will become the hallmark of your campaign.

Sandra Gordon is vice president of communications for the National Easter Seal Society, a nonprofit agency. More than a million people receive Easter Seal services each year, which requires both money and volunteers. Gordon advises that letters soliciting donations, whether of time or of funds, must give donors reasons to respond—benefits besides helping those who receive services.

Defining the audience

You must start with a general idea of your audience in order to define benefits. However, you can, and should, learn a great deal more about them. For example, a bakery's pool of potential customers includes grocery stores, convenience markets, delicatessens, and so on, each with its own special needs. Bread retailers may also be divided on the basis of geographic location; rye bread, for instance, may sell much better in large cities and on the East Coast than in rural areas. Such considerations as the specific location of the retailer and the characteristics of the people who shop there would also be of interest.

> The most persuasive sales letters are written to appeal to a specific audience.

Marketers seek to define consumers in terms of
- Demographics: age, gender, occupation, income, and education
- Psychographics: personality, attitudes, and lifestyle

When analyzing an audience of individual consumers, marketers refer to demographics and psychographics. *Demographic surveys* determine the age, gender, occupation, income, education, and other quantifiable characteristics of people who buy products. *Psychographic surveys* determine the psychological characteristics of potential buyers, their personality, attitudes, and lifestyle. Psychographics are less easily determined, but they provide valuable insights into the preferences of potential customers.

After collecting data about your audience, you should try to form a mental image of the typical buyer for the product you wish to sell. The point of this exercise is to help you formulate an idea of the central concerns of potential buyers. Then you can check the selling points and benefits you have already come up with against your audience's actual characteristics.

Planning the format and approach

Once you know what you need to say and what audience you want to say it to, you have to decide how you're going to say it. Will you send just a letter? Or will you include brochures, samples, response cards, and the like? Will the letter be printed with an additional color or with special symbols or logos? How many pages will it run? You'll also need to decide whether to rely on a single hard-hitting mailing or to conduct a multistage campaign (with several mailings and some sort of telephone or in-person follow-up).

The more difficult the selling job, the more elaborate the direct-mail package.

All these decisions depend on the audience you are trying to reach—their characteristics, their likely acceptance or rejection of your message—and what you are trying to get your audience to do. Generally speaking, expensive items and hard-to-accept propositions call for a more elaborate campaign than low-cost products and simple actions.

PREPARING THE COPY

A number of tried-and-true attention-getting devices are used in sales letters for a wide variety of products.

Sales letters are prepared according to the AIDA plan used for any persuasive message—that is, they start with an attention-getting device, move to whet the reader's interest and desire, and end with a specific call to action. Special techniques give them added impact. Figure 9.2 is a typical example employing some of these techniques.

Getting attention

Take a look at these attention-getting devices commonly used in sales letters:

- *A piece of genuine news.* "In the past 60 days, auto manufacturers' inventories have shrunk by 12 percent."

- *A personal appeal to the reader's emotions and values.* "The only thing worse than paying taxes is paying taxes when you don't have to."

- *The most attractive feature plus the associated benefit.* "New control device ends problems with employee pilferage!"

- *An intriguing number.* "Here are three great secrets of the world's most loved entertainers."

- *A sample of the product.* "Here's your free sample of the new Romalite packing sheet."

FIGURE 9.2
Letter Selling a Product

A single selling point, the service center's specialized cold-weather servicing, is emphasized.

Benefits of the major feature have both a logical appeal (higher trade-in value) and an emotional appeal (family safety).

The emphasis on quality prepares the reader to pay more for these services.

The reader's intelligence and desire to save time and money are the basis of this appeal.

The special time-limited offer should induce quick action.

AUTO CARE CENTRE
MOWBRY'S
1401 Smith Street
Winnipeg, Manitoba
R3C 1J8

October 3, 1993

Dear Friend:

Before you know it, the thermometer is going to be stuck on "Brrr." Yes, Old Man Winter is on his way, bringing some tough times for your automobile. So don't wait for signs of trouble. Come in and give your auto the cold-weather servicing it needs, right now!

By having your automobile winterized now, you'll not only protect its trade-in value but also enjoy that great feeling of security every time you and your family back out of the driveway. You'll know your auto is going to get you where you have to go.

To make sure your whole family is protected, our expert service facilities are ready and waiting. Factory-trained mechanics, up-to-the-minute equipment, the latest tools, genuine parts--all are ready to make sure your automobile performs at its best.

Do make a point to drive in during the next day or two. Let us give your auto a complete inspection, from fender to fender. Then you'll know what's needed to make sure it runs right, even on the coldest days. Remember, a checkup now can easily save you much time and hundreds of dollars later, when the really cold weather arrives.

Drive in today or tomorrow . . . Hand the enclosed card of introduction to one of our attendants for a 10 percent discount, which is good for the next ten days. The attendant will see that you get special, personal attention.

Don't put off your auto's winter checkup. It pays in every way to act now and beat the cold!

Sincerely,

Glen Mowbry

Glen Mowbry
Manager

- *A concrete illustration with story appeal.* "In 1982 Earl Colbert set out to find a better way to process credit applications. After ten years of trial and error, he finally developed a procedure so simple but so thorough that he was cited for service to the industry by the American Creditors Association."

- *A specific trait shared by the audience.* "Busy executives need another complicated 'time-saving' device like they need a hole in the head!"

- *A provocative question.* "Are you tired of watching inflation eat away at your hard-earned profits?"

- *A challenge.* "Don't waste another day wondering how you're going to become the success you've always wanted to be!"

■ *A solution to a problem.* "Tired of feeling that icy Arctic air rush through the cracks around your windows? Stay warm and save energy with StormSeal Weatherstripping."

> Choose an attention-getter that encourages the reader to read more.

A look at your own mail will show you how many products these few techniques can be applied to, but not all attention-getting devices are equally effective. The best is the one that makes the audience read the rest of the letter. Look closely at the three examples below. Which seems most interesting to you?

How would you like straight A's this semester?

Get straight A's this semester!

Now you can get straight A's this semester with . . .

If you're like most people, you'll find the first option the most enticing. The question invites your response—and, by no mistake, a positive response designed to encourage you to read on. The second option is fairly interesting too, but its commanding tone may make you wary of the claim. The third option is acceptable, but it certainly conveys no sense of excitement, and its quick introduction of the product may lead you to a snap decision against reading further.

Sales letters prepared by professionals also use a variety of formats to get your attention, including personalized salutations, special sizes or styles of type, underlining, color, indentions, and so on. But whatever special techniques are used, the best attention-getter for a sales letter is a hook that gets the reader thinking about the needs your product might be able to help fill.

Emphasizing the central selling point

> To determine your product's central selling point, ask
> ■ What does the competition offer?
> ■ What is special about my product?
> ■ What are potential buyers really looking for?

Let's say that your company's alarm device is relatively inexpensive, durable, and tamperproof. Although these are all attractive features, you would be wise to focus on only one. To determine the central selling point, ask what the competition has to offer, what most distinguishes your product, and what most concerns potential buyers. The answers to these three questions will help you select the single point around which to build your sales message. Make this point a feature of your letter, in the heading or within the first paragraph, and make it stand out through typography, design, or high-impact writing.

Highlighting benefits

> Selling points + "you" attitude = benefits.

The exercise you go through to determine the central selling point will help you define the benefits to potential buyers. For example, perhaps your company's alarm device has been built mainly to overcome the inadequacies of the competition in resisting tampering by would-be burglars. The benefits of this feature, your central selling point, are that burglars will not be able to break in so easily and that burglaries will therefore be reduced. You'll want to make this point repeatedly, in both words and pictures (if possible), near the beginning and the end of your letter. You might get attention by using a news item to stress this benefit: "Burglaries of businesses in our county have increased 7.7 percent over the past year; police department officials cite burglars' increasing sophistication and familiarity with conventional alarm devices." Or: "Worried about the reliability of your current alarm system in repelling today's sophisticated burglars?"

In the rest of the letter, you should continue to stress this theme, of course, but you should also weave in references to other benefits. For example: "You can get this worry-free protection for much less than you might think." Or: "The same technology that makes it difficult for burglars to crack your alarm system makes the device durable, even where it must be exposed to the elements." Remember, sales letters reflect the "you" attitude through references to benefits, so always try to phrase the selling points in terms of what such features will do for potential customers.

Using action terms

Active words give force to any business message and are especially important in sales letters. Compare the following:

INSTEAD OF THIS	USE THIS
The NuForm desk chair is designed to support your lower back and relieve pressure on your legs.	The NuForm desk chair supports your lower back and relieves pressure on your legs.

The second version says the same thing in fewer words and puts more emphasis on what the chair does for the user ("supports") than on the intentions of the design team ("is designed to support").

In general, you should use colorful verbs and adjectives that convey a dynamic image. Be careful, however, not to overdo it: "Your factory floors will sparkle like diamonds" is hard to believe and may prevent your audience from believing the rest of your message.

> To give force to a message
> - Use action terms
> - Use colorful verbs and adjectives

Talking about price

The price that customers will pay for a product depends on the prices of similar products, the general state of the economy, and the psychology of the buyer. Price is therefore a complicated issue and often a sensitive one.

Whether the price of your product is highlighted or downplayed, your entire letter should prepare the reader for it. Such words as *luxurious* and *economical* provide unmistakable clues about how your price compares with that of competitors and help the reader accept the price when you finally state it. If your price is relatively high, you should definitely stress features and benefits that justify it. If the price is low, you may wish to compare the features of your product with those of the competition, either directly or indirectly. In either case, if the price you eventually mention is a surprise to the reader, you've made a mistake that will be hard to overcome.

Here's an example of a sales letter offering a product at a bargain price:

> You can prepare readers for your product's price by subtle choice and arrangement of words.

All the Features of Name-Brand Pantyhose at Half the Price!

Why pay for fancy packaging or that little tag with a famous name on it when you can enjoy cotton lining, reinforced toes, and matchless durability for only $1.99?

Notice in this example that the price falls right at the end of the paragraph, where it stands out. In addition, the price issue is featured in a bold headline. This technique may even be used as the opening of a letter if the price is the most important feature and the audience for the letter is value conscious.

> If the price is an attractive feature, emphasize it by displaying it prominently.

To de-emphasize price
- Bury actual figures in the middle of a paragraph near the end
- Mention benefits and favorable money matters before the actual price
- Break a quantity price into units
- Compare the price with the cost of some other product or activity

If price is not a major selling point, you can handle it in several ways. For instance, you could leave out the price altogether or mention it only in an accompanying brochure. Or you could de-emphasize the price by putting the actual figures in the middle of a paragraph close to the end of your sales letter, well after you've presented the benefits and selling points. The same paragraph might include a discussion of related topics such as credit terms, special offers, and volume discounts. Mentioning favorable money matters before the actual price also reduces its impact.

Only 100 prints of this exclusive, limited-edition lithograph will be created. On June 1, they will be made available to the general public. But you can reserve one now for only $350, the special advance-reservation price. Simply rush the enclosed reservation card back today so that your order is in before the June 1 publication date.

Emphasis on the rarity of the edition signals value and thus prepares the reader for the big-ticket price that follows. Buried in the middle of a sentence, the actual price is tied in with another reminder of the exclusivity of the offer.

The pros use two other techniques for minimizing price. One is to break a quantity price into units. For example, instead of saying that a case of wine costs $60, you might say that each bottle costs $5. The other is to compare your product's price with the cost of some other product or activity: "The daily cost of owning your own spa is less than you'd pay for a health club membership." Your aim should be to make the cost seem as small and affordable as possible, thereby eliminating price as a possible objection.

Supporting your claims

You can't assume that people will believe what you say about your product just because it's in writing. You will have to prove your claims, especially if your product is complicated, expensive, or representative of some unusual approach.

Types of support for product claims:
- Samples
- Brochures
- Examples
- Testimonials
- Statistics
- Guarantees

Support for your claims may take several forms. Samples and brochures, often with photographs, are enclosures in the sales package but should also be referred to in the letter. In addition, the letter should describe (or highlight typographically) examples of how the product has benefited others, should include testimonials (actual quotations) from satisfied customers, or should cite statistics from scientific studies of the product's performance. Guarantees of exchange or return privileges, which may also be woven into the letter or set off in a special way, indicate that you have faith in the product and are willing to back it up.

It's almost impossible to provide too much support. A highly regarded direct-mail writer recommends that you anticipate "every question that the recipient is likely to want answered. . . . You must put yourself in the role of the reader. You must ask, and answer, all of the 'what-ifs.' "[4]

Motivating action

The overriding purpose of a sales letter is to get the reader to do something. Many consumer products sold through the mail simply ask for a check—in other words, an immediate decision to buy. On the other hand, big-ticket and more complex items frequently ask for just a small step toward the final buying decision, such as sending for more information or authorizing a call by a sales representative.

Try to persuade readers to take action, whatever it is, right away. You need to convince them that they must act now, perhaps to guarantee a specific delivery date. If there's no particular reason to act quickly, many sales letters offer discounts for orders placed by a certain date or prizes or special offers to, say, the first 500 people to respond. Others suggest that purchases be charged to a credit card or be paid off over time. Still others offer a free trial, an unconditional guarantee, or a no-strings request card for information, all in an effort to overcome the reader's natural inertia.

> Aim to get the reader to act as soon as possible.

CHOOSING THE FORMAT AND MAILING LIST

Sales letters often do not stand alone. Instead, they are part of a package of materials and, much more, part of a campaign to market a product or idea.

Direct-mail packages

> Direct-mail packages traditionally have five elements, all coordinated to reinforce the central selling point.

In the United States, 61.9 billion pieces of direct mail promoting some product or organization were sent in one year, and each piece included a persuasive sales letter.[5] Traditionally, a direct-mail package has five elements: (1) outer envelope telegraphing a sales message, (2) multipage sales letter, (3) brochure (usually in color), (4) order blank, and (5) postage-paid return envelope. A postage-paid order card sometimes takes the place of the order blank and return envelope. And sometimes other elements are included, such as samples or small gifts, catalogs, invitations, coupons, plastic "credit cards," and a short folded note "for those who have decided not to buy at this time." All these pieces should emphasize the same theme and be written in the same style and tone. Of course, the information in all elements should be consistent, although it should not merely repeat the same message.

An alternative to the traditional package is a self-mailer, a single piece of cleverly folded paper that both conveys a message to the reader and carries the order back to the original sender. Another format is the simulated telegram or invitation, which may entice recipients into reading the message.

Very often, personalized letters are more effective than those addressed to, say, "Occupant" or "Office Manager." However, people have become accustomed to personalization, and it is expensive. So before using it, determine whether the cost is justified by test-mailing letters with and without personalized messages.

> In sales letters, use visual emphasis to keep the reader's attention.

Advertising professionals seem to agree that a longer letter is more effective than a short one because it provides plenty of room for the specific information that will convince a reader to accept your message. Don't avoid long messages simply because they're long. A well-written four-page letter can keep a reader's attention better than one short page of boring copy.[6] However, because very few recipients have the patience to read all of a long letter, attention-getting devices such as underlining, indenting, and colored type are used to help them find the points of greatest interest. Enclosures give necessary details about the product too.

Mailing lists

Direct mail is especially useful for organizations trying to reach special groups of people. For example, perhaps you are trying to market expensive exercise

Direct mail is an effective means of reaching a specialized audience.

A key to direct-mail success is to choose the right kind of mailing list.

equipment. Although exercise and fitness have become important to large segments of the public, television and magazine advertising is very expensive and scatters the message to many people who may not be interested in exercise or who may not be willing to spend much money for it. The secret is to find the people who would definitely be interested in hearing about your product.

Fortunately, you can rent, buy, or create a mailing list that focuses on people who buy certain products, subscribe to certain magazines, belong to certain organizations, and so on. Three types of direct-mail lists exist:

- *House lists* are compiled from the rolls of previous customers and even those who have inquired about the company's product. This is often the best type of list because the people on it tend to be receptive to the company (assuming it has cultivated their goodwill).

- *Compiled lists* are taken from easily obtained sources of data, such as automobile registration lists or the telephone book. Compiled lists provide many names, but they are often too general to target interested parties. For example, selling exercise equipment by mailing promotional

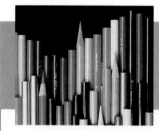

CHECKLIST FOR SALES LETTERS

A. Planning the Direct-Mail Package
☐ **1.** Determine the specific purpose of the mailing.
☐ **2.** Define selling points and consumer benefits.
☐ **3.** Analyze the audience, using demographic and psychographic information if available.
☐ **4.** Plan the approach and format.
  ☐ a. Determine the appeal, remembering that the most potent appeals relate to making money, saving money, saving time, or avoiding effort.
  ☐ b. Write a sales letter that is long enough to present all necessary information.
  ☐ c. Use short paragraphs, underlining, handwritten notes, bullets, color, and so on, to make the letter visually appealing.
  ☐ d. Include several enclosures to improve response.
  ☐ e. Enclose or offer a free sample to demonstrate your product.
  ☐ f. Telegraph your main appeal on the envelope.
☐ **5.** Pretest every element of your package.

B. Attention
☐ **1.** Design a positive opening that awakens in the reader a favorable association with the product.
☐ **2.** Promise a benefit to the reader.
☐ **3.** Write an opening that is appropriate, fresh, honest,

interesting, specific, and relevant to the central selling point.
☐ **4.** Keep the first paragraph short, preferably two to five lines, sometimes only one.
☐ **5.** Design an attention-getting opening that uses any of the following techniques: significant fact about the product, solution to a problem, special offer or gift, testimonial, stimulation of the senses or emotions, reference to current events, action picture, startling fact, agreeable assertion, comparison, event or fact in the reader's life, problem the reader may face, or quotation.

C. Interest
☐ **1.** State information clearly, vividly, and persuasively, and relate it to the reader's concerns.
☐ **2.** Develop the central selling point.
☐ **3.** Feature the product in two ways: physical description and consumer benefits.
  ☐ a. Interweave benefits with a physical description, or place benefits first.
  ☐ b. Describe the objective details of the product: size, shape, color, scent, sound, texture, and so on.

literature to every name in the telephone book would not be cost-effective; however, literature about tax-preparation services might well be sent to every name in the phone book.

■ *Mail-response lists* are like house lists, except that they come from other companies. Usually, direct competitors do not trade mail-response lists; however, list brokers often accumulate competitors' lists and make them available temporarily or for a certain number of mailings. Mail-response lists are valuable because they contain the names of people who have responded to direct mail in the past.

Direct Mail List Rates & Data, published by Standard Rate and Data Service, tells who has lists for rent or sale. Columbia Record & Tape Club (Columbia House), for example, has 1,135,745 active members and rents their names for $60 per thousand. Its list can be subdivided by listening preference (country and western, jazz, and so forth), by ZIP code, by state, or by any one of a host of other factors.

c. Through psychological appeals, present the sensation, satisfaction, or pleasure your reader will gain, translating the product or service into the fulfillment of needs and desires.
☐ d. Blend cold facts with warm feelings.

D. Desire
☐ **1.** Enlist one or more appeals to support the central selling point.
☐ a. Provide one paragraph of desire-creating material in a one-page letter with descriptive brochure; provide several paragraphs if the letter itself is two or more pages long, with or without an enclosed brochure.
☐ b. Emphasize reader use and benefits.
☐ c. If the product is valued mainly because of its appearance, describe its physical details.
☐ d. If the product is machinery or technical equipment, describe its sturdiness of construction, fine crafting, and other technical details in terms that help readers visualize themselves using it.
☐ e. Include technical sketches and meaningful pictures, charts, and graphs, if necessary.
☐ **2.** Anticipate and answer the reader's questions and objections.
☐ **3.** Use an appropriate form of proof.
☐ a. Include facts about users' experience with the product, including verifiable reports and statistics from users.
☐ b. Provide names (with permission only) of other satisfied buyers and users.

☐ c. Present unexaggerated testimonials from persons or firms that are users of the product and whose judgment the reader respects.
☐ d. Provide the results of performance tests by recognized experts, testing laboratories, or authoritative agencies.
☐ e. Offer a free trial.
☐ f. Offer a guarantee.
☐ g. Refer to samples if they are included.
☐ **4.** Note enclosures in conjunction with a selling point.

E. Action
☐ **1.** State clearly the action you desire.
☐ **2.** Provide specific details on how to order or specific information on how to contact your place of business.
☐ **3.** Make action easy through the use of a mail-back reply card, preaddressed envelope, phone number, or promise of a follow-up call or visit.
☐ **4.** Offer a special inducement to act: time limit, special price for a limited time, premium for acting before a certain date, free gift for buying, free trial, no obligation to buy but more information or a suggested demonstration, easy payments with no money down, or credit card.
☐ **5.** Supply a final consumer-benefit plug.
☐ **6.** Include a postscript conveying an important sales point (if desired for emphasis).

BEHIND THE SCENES WITH JOHN KEIL

The Case of The Rat's Guillotine

John M. Keil has over 20 years in advertising. His work includes creating ads for Toyota, Life Savers, and L'eggs, as well as doing the TV voice of McGruff, the (Take a Bite Out of) Crime Dog. He approaches every persuasive challenge with six questions: (1) What is my single most important objective? (2) Who is my audience? (3) What reaction do I want from my message (what do I want my audience to do)? (4) What is the principle thought I wish the audience to be left with? (5) What is there about the message that will help the audience believe the principle thought (what is the "because" statement)? (6) What's happening in the marketplace (what perceptions do people have) that might influence my ability to persuade people to my objective? Consider Keil's approach as he develops a persuasive presentation for a common household product:

The product: a new high-quality spring-type rat trap. It has a long-lasting oak base, a strong steel spring, a "wicket," and an exclusive release mechanism that can be put on "safety" until the trap is baited and then put in a ready position with the tip of a pencil. Its advantages are that it will last longer than the average rat trap because of its quality materials, it is extremely efficient and thus [humane] because of the strong spring, and it is less accident prone because of the safety feature. Disadvantage: It costs more than other rat traps. We also know that rats congregate in urban areas and along waterfronts, are not partial to cold weather, and have insatiable appetites.

Now let's go through Keil's persuasion strategy point for point:

1. *The objective.* We could hope that our audience would buy our rat trap rather than using poison. Or we could hope that they would pay more money for ours because it's more efficient and lasts longer than other spring-type traps, or that they would buy ours because of the safety features. These are all laudable objectives, but if we use all of them, we will be forced into a three-headed message. Let's narrow our choices.

PREPARING COLLECTION MESSAGES

People have many reasons for not paying bills; give debtors the benefit of the doubt as long as reasonably possible.

The causes of overdue accounts are as varied as the individuals and companies they represent. Once in a while, the bill may truly be lost in the mail or misfiled. In the case of Lawrence County Hospital, some patients may simply be unable to afford the medical treatment they must have—which would make any collection message sensitive and difficult. A few people mistakenly borrow more than they can possibly repay. Some have an unforeseen difficulty that makes timely repayment a problem. Still others are irresponsible about paying bills, dissatisfied with their purchase, or temporarily negligent. But luckily for the writers of collection letters, most individuals and businesses value their good name and credit rating and respond quickly to reminders and inquiries.

THE COLLECTION CONTEXT

Your dual goal in sending collection messages:
- Collect what is owed
- Maintain goodwill

The purpose of the collection process is to maintain goodwill while collecting what is owed. Three factors should influence decisions about how to achieve these twin goals:

- The creditor's attitude, based on the amount of money owed, the time elapsed, and the nature of the credit agreement

People who use poison are people who want nothing to do with baiting and setting traps. They are not our audience. By saying, "Use our trap rather than poison," we are heading in the wrong direction.

Efficiency? Research tells us that most people believe there's very little difference in the efficiency of rat traps. One or two seconds gained by our product is not important. Long-lasting? Who likes to think of needing rat traps that last a lifetime?

That leaves us the safety feature. Ask people what they don't like about rat traps. Odds are that 9 out of 10 will say: "I hate to set them. I'm scared stiff one is going to go off and de-finger me." And so our persuasive objective might read: "We want our audience to buy our rat trap rather than the competition's because of the safety feature."

2. *The audience.* This includes apartment house owners and managers, food store owners, restaurant owners and managers, and people who live near or on waterfronts. Our audience statement might read: "The message is directed to all people who are particularly susceptible to rodent problems."

3. *The reaction.* As stated in the objective, we want our audience to buy our rat trap.

4. *The core idea.* We've arrived at it through our deduction. The safety feature becomes the one outstanding difference between our product and the competition's. And so, "The principal thought that we'd like to leave with our audience is that our rat trap is safer to use than any other."

5. *The "because" section.* Here, we prove our point: "It's safer to use than any other because it has an exclusive release mechanism that can be put on 'safety' while you set it and bait it."

6. *Influences and perceptions.* What influences might affect the persuasive message? We know rats don't like cold weather. That means their presence in houses, stores, and so on, will increase as cold weather arrives. This is the type of circumstance that might influence our ability to persuade people that our objective is correct.

APPLY YOUR KNOWLEDGE

1. Select a memorable direct-mail package you've received recently. Does the letter reflect Keil's six-point prescription for persuasive presentations? Comment on each question the letter does and does not address.

2. How would the presence or absence of visuals influence your comments on the direct-mail package just discussed? What sort of visual aids would be useful for each of Keil's six questions?

- The debtor's attitude, based on feelings of self-esteem and values regarding financial responsibility

- The debtor's ability to solve the problem and withstand external and internal pressures

Credit is a sensitive issue. Ironically, the more the customer agrees with the justice of your claim, the more likely he or she is to react defensively. The true "deadbeat" expects to be dunned and has little reaction to requests for payment, but a conscientious customer is embarrassed about such a slip. In such an emotional state, the customer may (consciously or unconsciously) blame you for the problem, procrastinate, avoid the situation altogether, or react aggressively. Your job is to neutralize those feelings by accentuating the positive: the benefits of complying with your request for payment.

Here are a few examples of positive appeals:

Positive appeals are usually more effective than negative ones.

- *Sense of pride.* "A good credit rating is something to be proud of. It isn't acquired overnight. Send in your payment today, and your credit standing with us will remain unblemished."

- *Need to belong.* "We want you back in the fold. Send us your payment today, and we will continue uninterrupted service."

- *Sense of fair play.* "We special-ordered your tools when you needed them. You know you can depend on us. We also depend on you to send in your payment today."

- *Need to follow rules.* "We supplied you with the products you required. You agreed to pay for them. Please send your payment in the return envelope."

- *Recognition of mutual effort.* "If you're having budget problems, why not let us help? After all, our business is to help people meet their financial needs. Please let us know the reason for the delay so that we can suggest a solution to the problem."

- *Need for closure.* "You agreed to make your payments according to the schedule we worked out together. If you send us your check today, the matter will be settled and your credit protected."

If positive appeals fail, you may need to point out the actions legally available to you.

If positive appeals fail, you may have to consider a negative appeal, which stresses the unpleasant consequences of not acting rather than the benefits of acting. Remembering that persuasion is the opposite of force, continue to use a polite and businesslike tone, and point out some of the actions legally available to you:

- Reporting the delinquent customer to a central credit agency

- Repossessing the purchased item

- Demanding the surrender of collateral put up to secure the loan

- Turning the account over to a collection agency

- Engaging the services of a lawyer and taking the matter to court

Indirect negative consequences such as embarrassment and inconvenience are also associated with these actions.

It is important to be aware of the laws governing collection messages. The Fair Debt Collection Practices Act of 1978 outlines a number of collection procedures. You may not, for example,

- Falsely imply that a lawsuit has been or will be filed

- Contact the debtor's employer or relatives about the debt

- Communicate to other persons that the person is in debt

- Harass the debtor

- Use abusive or obscene language

- Threaten violence

The law also delineates when you may contact a debtor, how many times you may call, and what information you must provide to the debtor. Persons who believe that this law has been violated may sue for damages. But that doesn't mean you can't be tough in collection letters, as long as what you state is true and lawful. Don't forget that your real aim is to persuade the customer to make the payment. Thus your best approach is to try to maintain the customer's goodwill so that the two of you can cooperate to solve the problem.

THE COLLECTION SERIES

In a well-managed company, past-due accounts are flagged early (often by computer), and simple reminders (often form letters) are sent out immediately. As the past-due period lengthens, a series of collection letters reflecting the increasing seriousness of the problem is sent to the customer at predetermined intervals.

The typical collection series includes a notification, a reminder, an inquiry, an urgent notice, and an ultimatum. Usually, only the first step or two is required for a simple oversight or temporary problem on the part of a debtor who normally pays bills; the latter steps are usually reserved for those who deliberately refuse to accept responsibility for a debt. At these later stages, the customer's past credit and buying history, the amount of money owed, and the customer's overall credit rating determine the content and style of collection messages.

Steps in the collection series:
- Notification
- Reminder
- Inquiry
- Urgent notice
- Ultimatum

Notification

The standardized notification is a sign of trust.

Most creditors send bills to customers on a regular schedule, depending on the terms of the credit agreement. Typically, this standard notification is a form letter or statement (often computerized) clearly stating the amount due, the date due, the penalties for late payment, and the total amount remaining to be paid. The standardized form, far from being an insult to the recipient, indicates the creditor's trust that all will go according to plan.

Reminder

The reminder notice, which still assumes only a minor problem, may be a standardized form or an informal message.

If the payment has not been received within a few days after the due date, most creditors send out a reminder. Again, a standardized letter is reassuring. A reminder notice should be written under the assumption that some minor problem has delayed payment—in other words, that the customer has every intention of paying and needs only to be reminded. The tone should not be too serious:

As of October 1, we still hadn't received your September payment of $197.26. Has the payment been overlooked? Please check your records.

Using a different strategy, some companies send out a copy of the unpaid bill at this stage, with a handwritten note or preprinted stamp or sticker indicating that payment has not yet been received.

Inquiry

The inquiry
- Assumes that something unusual is preventing payment
- Is personalized
- Avoids any suggestion of customer dissatisfaction

As frustrating as it may be to send out a reminder and still get no response, the creditor cannot yet assume that the customer plans to ignore the debt, especially if the customer has paid bills promptly in the past. Thus the inquiry message must avoid accusations. However, the time has passed for assuming that the delay is merely an oversight; instead, you may now assume that some unusual circumstance is preventing payment:

Because you're a valued customer who's been conscientious about paying bills on time, Ms. Jablonski, I'm wondering why we haven't received your September payment of $197.26. Is there a problem we should know about?

Please send us your payment right away, or phone me at 555-4495 to discuss your situation. We want to help you fulfill your obligations.

Notice that this letter uses a name. Personalization at this stage is appropriate because you are asking the customer to work out an individualized solution. Notice also that the letter avoids any suggestion that the customer might be dissatisfied with the purchase. Instead, it emphasizes the reader's obligation to communicate about the problem and the creditor's willingness to discuss it. The inclusion of the writer's name and a phone number is very helpful in motivating a response at this stage.

Urgent notice

This stage represents a significant escalation. The purpose here is to convey your desire to collect the overdue payment immediately and your willingness to get serious, although you want to avoid any overt threats. To communicate a

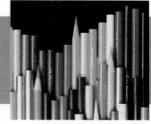

CHECKLIST FOR COLLECTION MESSAGES

A. Effective Collections

1. Reflect in your message the fact that you are communicating with a person, not with an account number.
2. Employ a tactful, courteous "you" attitude, coupled with firmness and patience.
3. Assume that the customer honestly wants to pay as agreed.
4. Balance your two main goals—collecting the money and retaining the customer's goodwill—because too much emphasis on one reduces the chance of achieving the other.
5. Keep communication between collector and debtor open.
6. Focus on only one appeal in each letter.
   a. Use positive appeals—cooperation, fair play, and pride—if possible.
   b. Use negative appeals—self-interest and fear—after positive appeals have failed.
7. Avoid giving the debtor any reason for not paying you ("Your company has had a lot of problems this year, but . . .").
8. Take the debtor's past behavior into account when deciding on the timing of collection messages.
   a. Allow generous time intervals for a customer with a good credit record.
   b. Shorten intervals for a customer who has earned the reputation of being slow.
9. Regardless of the stage in the collection procedure, clarify the amount due and the account number.
10. Include an easy-action postpaid envelope for every stage.

B. Collection Stages

1. At every stage, make it easy for the debtor to respond.
   a. Clarify the account number and the amount due.
   b. Include an easy-action postpaid envelope.
2. Send out an initial notification.
   a. Provide details on how much is owed, when it's due, where it should be sent, and what happens if it isn't paid on time.
   b. Use a standard, impersonal format to avoid implying that anything is out of the ordinary.
3. In the reminder stage, provide a routine, direct request to jog the customer's memory.
   a. Present the main question or subject first, then explain (when necessary), and follow up with a request for action.
   b. Assume the payment is delinquent because of customer oversight.

An urgent notice
- Might be signed by a top company official
- Might indicate the negative consequences of noncompliance
- Should leave an opening for payment without loss of face

sense of urgency, you may need to resort to a letter signed by a top official in the company or to a negative appeal. However, an urgent notice should still leave an opening for the debtor to make a payment without losing face:

I was very surprised this morning when your file reached my desk with a big tag marked OVERDUE. Usually I receive customer files only when a serious problem has cropped up.

An attention-getter focuses on the unusual circumstances leading to this letter.

Opening your file, I found the following facts: Your order for five cases of Panza serving trays was shipped six months ago. Yet we still haven't received the $232.70 due. You're in business too, Mr. Rosen, so you must realize that this debt needs to be paid at once. If you had a customer this far behind, you'd be equally concerned.

The recipient is reminded of the order. Personalization and an attempt to emphasize common ground may motivate the reader to respond.

☐ c. Subordinate sales material or humorous gimmicks to the main goal: collecting the debt.

☐ d. Include a duplicate copy of the original bill, perhaps stamped "Reminder" or "Past Due," with a short note (usually a form) specifying the amount, due date, late charge, and account number.

☐ **4.** In the inquiry stage, provide a personalized message with an inside address and a salutation with the customer's name.

  ☐ a. Assume that something unusual has happened and that for some reason unknown to you the customer cannot or does not want to pay.

  ☐ b. Employ a positive tone.

  ☐ c. Avoid suggesting that reader dissatisfaction with your goods or services might be responsible for the late payment.

  ☐ d. Demonstrate a genuine willingness to help.

  ☐ e. Attract attention in the first paragraph with a reader-benefit theme: something pleasant, interesting, or important to the reader.

  ☐ f. Include in the body of the letter facts, figures, or reasons why the customer will benefit by doing as requested.

  ☐ g. Leave the reader with alternatives that allow her or him to recover from the transaction with dignity intact.

  ☐ h. Provide for easy action.

☐ **5.** In an urgent notice, convey the seriousness of the situation.

  ☐ a. Assume that the customer must pay.

  ☐ b. Phrase the letter to retain the customer's goodwill and future business (although probably for cash), if possible.

☐ c. Employ the strongest appeal—fear—by mentioning the unfortunate consequences of collection enforcement.

☐ d. Tell the customer that you would prefer not to take this drastic action, but (because of obligations to credit reporting agencies and company procedures) you must do so unless the debtor pays or explains.

☐ e. Tell the customer that by not paying, she or he is likely to lose credit privileges, goods or services not paid for, additional money or property, reputation, and self-respect.

☐ f. Employ urgent language.

☐ g. Insist on immediate payment, and set a date by which you must receive it.

☐ h. To protect yourself from legal problems, state facts correctly, make no malicious or defamatory accusations, and send messages in sealed envelopes addressed to the debtor personally.

☐ i. Offset the negativity of an appeal to fear with at least one positive appeal, to give the debtor a chance to avoid the drastic action and extra costs.

☐ j. Arrange for the letter to be signed by a higher executive, such as a vice president or even the president (if desirable).

☐ **6.** In an ultimatum, you may resort to a bad-news message.

  ☐ a. Make the action request firm, and be definite about the amount to be sent and the place to which it should be sent.

  ☐ b. Be polite, businesslike, and impersonal.

  ☐ c. Put into effect any actions you have stated you will take.

Please see that a check for $232.70 is mailed to us at once. Or if you need to work out an alternate plan for payment, call me now at (712) 693-7300.

Sincerely,

Artis Knight
Vice President

The preferred action is spelled out; an option is also suggested in case of serious trouble.

The signature of a ranking official lends weight to the message.

A well-written urgent notice has a good chance of persuading customers who still view themselves as responsible and trustworthy. At this stage, a telephone call backing up your written message may also get a promise to pay. However, the irresponsible debtor is unlikely to be swayed by anything less than an ultimatum.

Ultimatum

An ultimatum
- Should state the exact consequences of nonpayment
- Must avoid any hint of defamation or harassment
- Need not take a personal, helpful tone

Some people's finances are in such disorder that you won't get their attention until this stage. But do not send an ultimatum unless you intend to back it up and are well supported by company policy. Even then, maintain a polite, businesslike manner and avoid defaming or harassing the debtor.

By setting down on paper the precise consequences of not paying the bill, you can encourage debtors to reevaluate their priorities. You are no longer interested in hearing why it has taken them so long to respond; you are interested in putting your claim at the top of their list. The tone of the ultimatum need not be so personal or individualized as the inquiry or urgent notice. At this stage, you are in a position of justified authority and should no longer be willing to return to an earlier stage of communication and negotiation. For example:

On September 2, 1992, we shipped a standard assortment of consumer publications to City News (invoice number CN3-0014). Your application for credit was approved because of the references you supplied.

Under our usual terms, we sent a statement for $757.93, due October 3. Although we were concerned when we didn't receive payment by that date, we assumed there was some oversight. After all, you had a history of paying debts promptly.

Over the past three months, we've tried repeatedly to get you to send a check for $757.93. So far, we have had only your oral agreement to pay. Ms. Park in our credit department phoned you, as you'll recall. At that time, you assured her a check would be mailed to us at once.

No longer can we accept such assurances. If we don't receive payment in full within the next five days, we will have to turn your account over to a collection agency.

To save embarrassment and a black mark on your permanent credit record, do mail your check today.

This letter outlines the steps that have already been taken, implying that the drastic action to come is the logical follow-up. Although earlier collection messages were based on persuasion, this one is essentially a bad-news letter.

If a letter like this doesn't yield results, the only remaining remedy is actually to begin legal collection procedures. As a final courtesy, you may wish to send the debtor a notice of the action you are about to take. By maintaining until the bitter end your respect for the customer, you may still salvage some goodwill.

SUMMARY

The purpose of a persuasive message is to influence attitudes and actions. Persuasive techniques are especially important for an audience that may not completely agree with you or gain any direct benefits from doing as you ask.

You can motivate an audience to do as you wish by using the AIDA plan for organizing persuasive messages: attention, interest, desire, action. The benefits of complying with your request should be stressed.

Persuasive messages are used in many business contexts, including requests for action. In preparing a sales letter, highlight a major feature and related benefit of the product that's being promoted; in the close, make a response easy. Debt-collection letters also follow the AIDA plan.

ON THE JOB:
Solving a Communication Dilemma at Lawrence County Hospital

Given current pressures to contain health-care costs, most hospitals are facing some financial problems, but Lawrence County Hospital faces more than most. Its patients are mostly older people, and poor ones at that. Sixty percent of them are Medicare recipients, and since 1983, earning a profit on Medicare patients has been difficult.

Congress revised Medicare's "blank check" reimbursement policy, limiting payments to a set amount for specific ailments, or diagnosis-related groups (DRGs). Under the new rules, if a patient is hospitalized for pneumonia, for example, Medicare pays $1,441. The hospital makes a profit if the treatment costs less, but it loses money if the treatment exceeds the DRG rate. The new rules motivate the hospital to shorten the length of the patient's stay. As one Lawrence County doctor pointed out, "Death has become the most cost-effective treatment. If a person dies in 13 hours, [the hospital] gets paid the same as if they'd stayed 13 weeks." A patient who exceeds the usual stay for a particular ailment can send a hospital's profits into a tailspin, particularly at a facility with relatively few patients, like Lawrence County.

The problem is compounded by the red tape that surrounds Medicare's reimbursement system. When the paperwork on a patient is submitted to Medicare for payment, the government may reject the bill if it disagrees with the doctor's decision to hospitalize the patient, even though the hospital has already provided treatment. Moreover, if the diagnosis changes from a minor to a major condition during the patient's stay, the hospital is stuck with the original diagnosis. At Lawrence County Hospital, unpaid Medicare bills are largely to blame for last year's $500,000 loss.

But Medicare isn't the hospital's only problem; high insurance rates have also hurt. The cost of malpractice insurance for the obstetrics unit forced the hospital to stop delivering babies a few years ago. That decision prompted young families to turn to larger hospitals in Birmingham or Huntsville for obstetrics care. And once people start using a bigger hospital, it is difficult to win them back to a place like Lawrence County.

As potential patients turn elsewhere, the hospital becomes increasingly vulnerable. The young people with private health insurance go to the bigger hospitals, and Lawrence County is left with the old and the uninsured, who simply do not have the money to pay their hospital bills. Rather than turn away the sick, Lawrence County treats them for nothing. Roughly 15 percent of its outstanding bills are uncollectible. The situation forces Ronald Sparkman to cut costs wherever he can. But the more he cuts, the less appealing the hospital becomes and the fewer paying patients it attracts.

Your Mission: In your new job as Ronald Sparkman's administrative assistant, you are responsible for handling most of the hospital's correspondence. You find that you spend much of your time trying to persuade people to do things: pay their bills, use the hospital, join the staff, and accept cuts in services. In the following situations, choose the *best* communication alternatives:

1. Sparkman is trying to improve the hospital's stature in Moulton by creating an advisory board of 25 local business and professional people who would meet every month to guide the hospital's community relations efforts. By convincing influential people to serve on the board, he hopes to build support for the hospital. He thinks that if the town's leading citizens are working to improve the hospital, they will be more inclined to use the facility themselves and to influence their friends and employees to do the same. He also believes that the board will be an excellent source of fresh ideas. He has asked you to draft a form letter inviting people to serve on the board. The letter should be worded so that it can be modified slightly for each recipient. Which of the following versions is preferable for the attention-getter?

   a. Lawrence County Hospital is recruiting leading citizens to serve on a special advisory board that will guide the hospital's community relations activities. We would like you to join the board.

   b. Can you spare a few hours a month to serve your community? If so, we would like you to join a special advisory board that will help Lawrence County Hospital respond to the town's health-care needs.

   c. Through your involvement with _____ (insert a reference to the person's business or civic activities), you have shown how one dedicated person can make a difference to an organization. Quite frankly, Lawrence County Hospital needs people like you to advise the organization on its future. We are facing an economic crisis. If we hope to survive, we must be willing to change. But how? In what direction? How can we refocus our institution to best meet the community's needs within the limits of our financial resources?

   d. Fact: Of the 5,700 acute-care hospitals now operating in America, 700 will be out of business by 1995.

      Fact: Lawrence County Hospital lost $500,000 last year.

      Fact: We need your help.

2. Which version is preferable for the interest and desire section?

   a. By recruiting a group of 25 civic leaders to serve on an advisory board, the hospital hopes to obtain guidance in reshaping its services to meet the needs of the community. Your knowledge of our town, coupled with your experience as (a banker, a lawyer, an accountant, whatever), would be invaluable to our efforts.

   The board's first task will be to help the hospital decide on its basic identity: what services we should provide and what we should concede to larger hospitals in Birmingham and Huntsville. After resolving this issue, the board will advise us on how to present our unique areas of competence to the public.

   Serving on the board should not pose too much of a burden on your time. You would be expected to attend a meeting once a month, beginning this July, and to spend approximately two or three hours a week on subcommittee activities. In return, you would have the satisfaction of helping us rebuild our reputation and regain a solid financial position.

   b. We hope to form the advisory board by June 25th and to hold our first meeting during the week of July 1 to 7. The board's initial job will be to assess the needs of the community and to evaluate the services offered by competing hospitals in Birmingham and Huntsville. Once that is accomplished, the board will advise the hospital on how to rebuild its reputation with doctors and potential patients.

   c. Lawrence County Hospital believes that it can best solve its financial problems by redefining its mission and focusing on a narrower range of activities. Instead of trying to be all things to all people, we will try to do a few things well and leave other activities to the larger hospitals in Birmingham and Huntsville. The advisory board's first task will be to help us identify the services that would be most useful to Moulton's population. Once that has been accomplished, the board will help us communicate our expertise to the public.

   Your knowledge of the community and your experience in business would be a big help to us. If you agree to serve on the board, you will be expected to attend an evening meeting once a month, starting in July, and to devote a few hours a week to subcommittee activities.

3. Which of the following versions is the best action section for the letter?

   a. If you would be interested in joining the board, please contact me at 465-0334 before June 25. I believe you would find that serving will be a rewarding and worthwhile experience. I will be happy to answer any questions you might have regarding the board or your role on it.

   b. We plan to limit the board to 25 members. By contacting me prior to June 25, you can be sure of being included in this group of Moulton's civic leaders. Bill Phillips, our Mayor, and Russ Leonard, President of the First National Bank of Moulton, have both agreed to join. Please let me know your decision as soon as possible.

c. If you have any questions about the advisory board, please feel free to contact me at 465-0334. I would be happy to discuss the board's mission and responsibilities with you in more detail. You might also want to talk with Bill Phillips and Russ Leonard, both of whom have agreed to serve. Incidentally, please give my regards to (name of spouse). Let's try to get together for dinner soon.

d. Your participation on the board will make a real difference to the hospital and the town of Moulton. If you have any questions about serving, please contact me at 465-0334. I'd be happy to discuss the details with you. The hospital hopes to finalize the composition of the board by June 25th.

4. Although Lawrence County Hospital has closed its maternity wing, Sparkman is reluctant to say good-bye to the young mothers. He would like to woo them back to the hospital after their babies are born, and with that in mind, he has decided to offer a couple of inexpensive classes aimed at young parents. He figures that if he can get them to come to the hospital for medical education, he will have a good chance of winning back their business from larger hospitals. He has developed a mailing list of all the families in Moulton with young children. He wants you to draft a form letter inviting these parents to participate in the classes. Which version is the best?

a. Last year, over 5,000 children in the United States were killed in accidents: traffic accidents, falls, fires, drownings, chokings, bullet wounds, and poisonings. Many of these children would be alive today if their parents had known how to administer first aid and cardiopulmonary resuscitation.

Don't wait until it is too late to learn the life-saving techniques that may save your children from an accidental death. Come to Lawrence County Hospital and learn how to handle common childhood emergencies. During the month of June, we are offering two inexpensive courses for concerned parents. In the first class, dealing with childhood emergencies, you will learn what to do in case of poisoning, electrical injury, burning, and drowning. You will also learn about car-seat safety, child proofing your home, toy and crib safety, and accident prevention. This six-hour course will be held in the cafeteria on June 4 and 11, from 7:00 p.m. to 10:00 p.m. The cost is $20.00 per family.

The second class, infant and child CPR, is designed to provide new parents with the skills to respond to a choking, respiratory, or car-

diac emergency. It will be offered on June 17 from 7:00 p.m. to 10:00 p.m. for a fee of $15.00 per family.

To sign up for the classes, call 465-0334 by May 29.

b. What would you do if your baby suddenly stopped breathing? If your two-year-old swallowed those old pills you've been meaning to throw out? If your five-year-old fell out of that tree he insists on climbing?

If you aren't sure you know how to handle these and other childhood accidents, check out the classes at Lawrence County Hospital:

1. Dealing with childhood emergencies. Learn what to do in case of poisoning, electrical injury, burning, and drowning. Learn about car-seat safety, child proofing your home, toy and crib safety, and accident prevention. This six-hour course is offered at the hospital on June 4 and 11, 7:00-10:00 p.m. FEE: $20.00 per family.

2. Infant and child CPR. This three-hour class is designed to provide new parents with the skills to respond to a choking, respiratory, or cardiac emergency. Hands-on practice in CPR is included. Offered on June 17, 7:00-10:00 p.m. FEE: $15.00 per family.

To reserve a spot in either class, call Ronald Sparkman at 465-0334 before May 29. Enrollment is limited to the first 15 families that sign up. You'll be glad you learned what to do BEFORE the accident happens.

c. During the month of June, Lawrence County Hospital is offering two classes for parents of young children:

1. Dealing with childhood emergencies. Learn what to do in case of poisoning, electrical injury, burning, and drowning. Learn about car-seat safety, child proofing your home, toy and crib safety, and accident prevention. This six-hour course is offered at the hospital on June 4 and 11, 7:00-10:00 p.m. FEE: $20.00 per family.

2. Infant and child CPR. This three-hour class is designed to provide new parents with the skills to respond to a choking, respiratory, or cardiac emergency. Hands-on practice in CPR follows. FEE: $15.00 per family.

To reserve a spot in either class, please contact Ron Sparkman at 465-0334 before May 29. Enrollment is limited to the first 15 families that sign up.

5. The administrators of the Medicare program have refused to pay the hospital for treating a patient who

came in for a hip replacement but ended up also having a malignant tumor removed. Sparkman wants you to explain the situation to Medicare and ask them to reconsider their decision. Which version is best?

a. I'm writing to ask why you paid us only $8,187 for Charles Johnson's hip replacement when his total bill came to $23,879 and included not only the hip replacement but also emergency surgery to remove a malignant tumor of the colon. (See enclosed copy of bill.) We would like you to pay the difference of $15,692.

If Johnson had come in on two separate occasions, once for his hip and once for his colon surgery, you would have paid for both operations, and the total bill would have exceeded $23,879. We actually saved money on his treatment by performing both operations during a single hospital stay. We also did our best to treat Mr. Johnson properly. He did not know he had a colon tumor when he checked in, and neither did we. The tumor came to light when Johnson began to bleed heavily following hip replacement surgery. In trying to find out why, we discovered the colon tumor. The prudent treatment was to operate immediately.

Now, we could have dismissed Johnson from the hospital for 24 hours, readmitted him for colon surgery, and billed you separately for each operation--and you would have paid for both procedures. But Johnson might be dead by now if we had done that.

Your decision to withhold payment for the colon surgery is clearly unfair and illogical, and we expect you to correct the mistake. Please send us a check for $15,692.

b. By and large, the Medicare program does an excellent job of ensuring that older people with limited incomes have access to quality health care. But there are a few administrative Catch-22s in the program that create serious financial problems for health-care providers like Lawrence County Hospital.

We faced a difficult decision on March 27 when we discovered that Mr. Charles Johnson, who had checked in for hip replacement surgery, was also suffering from cancer of the colon. We knew that Johnson needed immediate surgery to remove the tumor, but we also knew that Medicare might decline to pay for the operation because Johnson was not originally admitted to the hospital for that procedure. If we had released Johnson from the hospital for 24 hours and readmitted him under a new diagnosis, we would have been assured of being reimbursed for his treatment. But that 24 hours was critical to Mr. Johnson. We opted to do the surgery immediately--regardless of the financial risk to the hospital--because his life depended on it. What would you have done?

Mr. Johnson's total bill for both operations was $23,879, as the enclosed copy of his record indicates. You reimbursed us for $8,187, the cost of the hip replacement. We would like you to send us a check for $15,692 to cover the colon surgery as well. The total bill is actually less than it would have been had we submitted two separate DRG claims.

c. We have received your payment of $8,187 for the hip replacement operation performed on Mr. Charles Johnson on March 27th of this year. However, we have not received payment for the removal of a malignant tumor in Mr. Johnson's colon performed on the same day.

We wondered whether this was an oversight on your part or the result of an intentional decision. Although Mr. Johnson was originally admitted for a hip replacement, we felt compelled to operate immediately when we discovered a malignant tumor in his colon. Releasing him and then readmitting him in order to comply with an arbitrary provision of the Medicare program would have exposed us to a charge of malpractice. More important, it would have jeopardized Mr. Johnson's life.

Given the circumstances, we are certain you will agree that the hospital acted prudently and deserves to be paid for removing Mr. Johnson's tumor. We look forward to receiving your check for $15,692 to cover the cancer surgery.[7]

QUESTIONS FOR DISCUSSION

1. How can a business writer attain credibility?
2. Why is it sometimes necessary to use persuasive techniques in memos?
3. What sorts of attention-getting devices used in sales letters might be appropriate in memos and other types of persuasive letters?
4. How should the issue of price be handled in a sales letter?
5. Why is it important to write collection letters that maintain goodwill while collecting what is owed?
6. What are some positive appeals that writers of collection letters employ?

DOCUMENTS FOR ANALYSIS

Read the following documents; then (1) analyze the strengths or weaknesses of each sentence and (2) revise each document so that it follows this chapter's guidelines.

DOCUMENT 9.A

We have developed a revolutionary new fertilizer that can easily be applied to lawns to keep them green and weed-free during the summer months with a minimum of effort. For just pennies, our trained experts will make weekly applications (in liquid form) of our fantastic fertilizer that kills weeds and strengthens the fibers of the roots. It works in both shady and sunny areas and works particularly well in your climate zone!

Green-Gro works in any kind of climate and should not harm pets or birds. All you have to do is water your lawn and keep the grass cut; we will do all the rest to ensure that you have a green lawn for the entire season! We look forward to having your business, and we trust that you'll want to purchase many of our other excellent lawn products.

Please fill out the enclosed coupon and avail yourself of the "early-bird discount" of 25 percent off the prices we regularly charge.

DOCUMENT 9.B

Find a direct-mail package that contains a letter. Bring the package to class, along with answers to the following questions:

1. Who is the intended audience?
2. What are the demographic and psychographic characteristics of the intended audience?
3. What is the purpose of the direct-mail package? Has it been designed to obtain a sales lead, make a mail-order sale, obtain a charitable contribution, or do something else?
4. What kind of letter is included? Is it fully printed, printed with computer fill-in, or fully computer typed? Is the letter personalized? If so, how many times?
5. Did the writer use the AIDA plan? If not, explain how the letter is organized.
6. What needs are being appealed to?
7. What emotional appeals and logical arguments are given in the letter?
8. How many and what kinds of enclosures (supporting pieces such as brochures and order cards) are used?
9. What has been done to encourage you to open the envelope?
10. Is the message in the letter and on the supporting pieces believable? Would the letter sell the product to you?
11. What selling points and consumer benefits are offered?
12. Is an unusual format used? Are eye-catching graphics used?

CASES

WRITING PERSUASIVE REQUESTS FOR ACTION

1. Shape up: Letter offering wellness incentives for Johnson & Johnson employees Something has to be done. Health-care costs are soaring so rapidly that if not halted, they're going to put a lot of companies out of business. Good employees need and want decent health-care benefits—but how long can corporations meet the demands of insurance premiums' rising into the stratosphere?

In addition, as a human resources specialist at Johnson & Johnson, you've identified another costly problem related to employee health. Every time a worker calls in sick or comes to the office feeling lousy and unable to perform well, productivity slides and the company loses money. Not just a little money— thousands of dollars each year.

To put a lid on the high cost of employee illness, Johnson & Johnson has decided to try a new concept that's gaining popularity among businesses. Instead of building another gymnasium or adding more low-cholesterol foods to the cafeteria menu (earlier tactics that haven't paid off so well), Johnson & Johnson will depend on its "Live for Life" wellness campaign, offering incentives for achieving and maintaining good health. Even if the program ends up costing the company several hundred dollars per employee, your calculations indicate that it could save millions of dollars per year through reduced absenteeism and lowered health claims.

The "Live for Life" program targets several major contributors to poor health and accidents: smoking, drinking, lack of exercise, stress, high blood pressure and high cholesterol, weight gain, and not using automobile seat belts. Instead of rewarding results (which can be temporary), the company will reward the process, thus encouraging employees to develop new habits that should keep them healthier, happier, and more productive over the long term.

For example, every employee who exercises an average of four hours per week for a month will earn 30 "Live for Life" dollars—play money exchangeable for merchandise like sweatshirts, sweatsocks, or health club memberships. A blood-pressure or cholesterol check is worth 5 "Live for Life" dollars, and a talk with the children about drug and alcohol abuse is worth 10. Always wearing a seat belt when driving or riding in a car brings a reward of 25 "Live for Life" dollars. And for all nonsmokers, Johnson & Johnson will reduce employees' health insurance co-payment rates by 5 percent.

To implement the reward system, the company plans to accept all claims employees make about their wellness efforts. As work and family director Melvin Benjamin explained to the human resources staff, "To lie about health, they have to think about health, and that may prod them to do something about it."

Your task: Write a letter introducing "Live for Life" and persuading workers and their families to participate in the new wellness campaign.[8]

2. Chrysler cries foul: Letter demanding the halt of a television ad campaign by Volvo

They've done it again; this time the aggressive advertising agency working for your competitor, Swedish automaker AB Volvo, has put what appears to be a demolished Chrysler minivan in a television ad hawking the superior safety of Volvo's station wagons. The commercial has already appeared in 12 major U.S. markets. Unconscionable, you fume, and everyone up and down the corridors of Chrysler's corporate headquarters is echoing your response.

Last year, Volvo embarrassed itself in an ad campaign that showed an oversize exhibition truck apparently unable to wreck a Volvo automobile. But it was soon revealed that the car's roof had been secretly reinforced (and its competitor's weakened) by a well-meaning individual or individuals before the commercial was filmed. Although the parties responsible were never disclosed, the Swedish automaker publicly apologized, pulled the ad, and fired the agency that handled the campaign. You'd love to see them eat crow once again.

In the offending spots, American consumers are urged to steer clear of minivans (for which Chrysler holds 51 percent of the U.S. market). An announcer intones statistics from a report released by the Insurance Institute for Highway Safety, "The study found that minivans as a group had an occupant death rate twice as high as the car with the lowest death rate, the Volvo 240 wagon." On screen appear two startling images: a family test-driving a minivan resembling General Motors' Astro, and an accident scene with a wrecked minivan resembling those produced by Chrysler.

What the ad doesn't say is that the IIHS study was based on 1984 through 1988 model minivans. During those years, the Insurance Institute discovered that minivan accidents led to 1 death per 10,000 accidents. Half as many deaths resulted from accidents involving the Volvo 240 station wagon. But current models of Chrysler minivans are now equipped with airbags on the driver's side, and as the study indicated, the airbags should considerably improve the minivan's safety record.

Thomas McAlear, Chrysler's marketing director, thinks Volvo is desperate to change its image after the earlier advertising fiasco (during which Volvo dropped its slogan, "A car you can believe in," for the new "Drive Safely" campaign). McAlear has released a statement to the media describing Volvo's ads as "a low blow" that is "deceptive and misleading."

Your task: You've been asked by McAlear to write a letter to Volvo executives in Sweden (Volvo AB SWE, 5-405 08, Gothenburg, Sweden) and to Volvo's advertising agency, Messner Vetere Berger Carey Schmetterer (375 Hudson St., 8th floor, New York, NY 10014), urging that the commercials be taken off the air. Cite the age of the statistics used and the unfairness of the ad's audiovisual implication that a Chrysler minivan caused a death.[9]

3. We hate it: Letter demanding removal of Health Club Television from New York's Vertical Club

When you finally shelled out for a membership at the Vertical Club, the priciest gym in Manhattan, the only thought on your mind was its testimony to your financial success—and the chance that you might bump into Brooke Shields one day. Now you're staring at something you never dreamed could happen to such a classy place.

Across from your Stairmaster, an evil glow disrupts your rhythm with its relentless flicker. Obnoxious voices hawking yogurt and soap are booming from the ugly box, with a few brief interludes in which well-known sports celebrities are interviewed by unknown reporters. Yes—it's a television screen, right here in your upscale, color-coordinated, sweat-smelling environs, blaring out the Health Club Television Network (HCTN). And it has no knobs, no remote control, no way for you or any of your fellow exercisers to shut the darn thing off. You'd heard these things were coming to doctor's waiting rooms and to supermarket checkout lines, and now it's here in your exclusive health club.

Everyone at the Vertical Club is complaining about the 24-hour channel. To smooth things over, management tried circulating a polite memo advising all members that the installation of the television sets (two in each room) was a test-run for the new satellite service. According to the memo, HCTN claims that 80 percent of consumers love the idea of being able to watch TV while they exercise, and the sets were free, installed by HCTN as a "bonus" for Vertical Club members. The memo made no mention of the fact that 30 percent of the channel's programming consists of commercials, sold to advertisers at a high rate because viewers are virtually captive. Rather than calming the rumbling in the locker room, the memo made members angrier. You and the rest of the Thursday afternoon regulars had no trouble gathering 400 signatures on a petition demanding that the sets be removed.

Members plan to send a cover letter echoing the petition's demands to top management at Bally's Health & Tennis Corporation, which owns the Vertical Club. A copy of both petition and letter will also go to executives at the Health Club Television Network. And every advertiser spotted on the channel will receive a copy of the petition, with a special letter informing them that club members are boycotting their products. In addition, your group of regulars hopes to catch the media's interest with a press release headed, "Vertical Club Members Held Captive." (Fortunately, the whole campaign is being funded by the Vertical Club's wealthy membership; your efforts won't stop until the television screens are history. It has become a matter of high principle among you.)

Your task: Impressed by your offhand remark that the Vertical Club was becoming "a commercial police state," your fellow regulars have decided you're the right person to formulate the letter to Bally's Health & Tennis Corporation, demanding removal of the TV sets. The address is 7755 Center Avenue, Huntington Beach, CA 92647.[10]

4. Thanks-A-Bunch: Plea for continued funding of a rehabilitation flower shop

At Thanks-A-Bunch flower shop in Chula Vista, California, former psychiatric patients can learn the skills—and regain the confidence—to reenter the workaday world. In a little over a dozen years, more than 400 people have successfully "graduated" from the innovative program. Once day-treatment patients suffering from hallucinations, these individuals are now functioning normally, thanks to the right psychotropic drugs rectifying certain chemical imbalances. But functioning normally and rejoining society are sometimes two different matters. That's where Thanks-A-Bunch can help.

At the flower shop, the former patients become trainees, handling all the tasks necessary to operate the retail business. They assemble flowers, truck them to delivery sites, and handle cash sales. The trainees earn minimum wages—but the chance to work in a "safe environment" (where no one pushes too hard or demands too much) is priceless. "They won't get fired if they screw up," explains program director Nina Garcia.

Because of your background in floral design, Garcia recently hired you to help teach new trainees how to dethorn and wrap flower stems and how to arrange the blossoms in both simple and elaborate styles. You love to work with flowers, but you also like people, and the new job is a perfect combination for you.

Thanks-A-Bunch was founded by a private, nonprofit organization, Kinesis South, as a practical method for solving a common problem. The company helps rehabilitate patients and conducts family education programs on mental health. Individuals who are able to overcome their illness must still conquer their own fears, and the fears of future employers, that they might not be able to handle a regular job again. Working at Thanks-A-Bunch gives them an opportunity to prove themselves. For all 400 of the program's success stories, Thanks-A-Bunch was the stepping-stone to the regular jobs they now hold. Their lives are no longer subsidized by others, and they feel good about their contributions to society.

Unfortunately, the nonprofit rehabilitation program may soon succumb to cuts in its funding. Support from local businesses, who buy most of the shop's flower arrangements, isn't enough to pay for the costly program, so the shop depends on additional funding from San Diego County Mental Health Services (CMHS). But now, even though Thanks-A-Bunch has been used as a model for developing other rehabilitation centers throughout the county (breakfast cafés, furniture stores, ceramics shops, bakeries, and so on), the flower shop is being threatened by county budget cuts. Garcia has received news that Thanks-A-Bunch may be targeted for elimination as the county board of supervisors weighs alternatives for stretching dwindling government funds.

Your task: Garcia, who spotted the business communication course you listed on your resume, has asked you to write a strong letter to Collins Munns, regional director for San Diego County Mental Health Services. Munns's recommendations will affect the final budget decision of the county board of supervisors, so you must persuade him that Thanks-A-Bunch deserves to survive the impending budget cuts. Write to him at San Diego County Mental Health Services, 1700 Pacific Highway, San Diego, CA 92186.[11]

5. Tax lift-off: Letter from Learjet lobbying for removal of luxury tax

Back in the 1970s, working for a manufacturer of small airplanes was a fairly stable career. Sales of small planes, for both business and private use, had climbed steadily since the end of World War II, reaching a peak in 1978 when United States manufacturers shipped 17,000 airplanes over a 12-month period. But a lingering recession, rising product liability costs, and two unfriendly tax laws have contributed to the general aviation industry's steady decline. Several well-known manufacturers of business jets, small commuter planes, and personal aircraft are disappearing, whether through bankruptcy (Piper), sale (Cessna), or relocation to another country (Cyrus Eaton Group International).

Your employer, Learjet, has managed to stay in business, but president Brian E. Barents, who also serves as chairman of the General Aviation Manufacturers Association trade group, points to the most recent year's dismal statistics. Industrywide, only 1,021 small airplanes were produced. "That's how you reduce employment in the general aviation manufacturing sector by half," he complains.

But Barents isn't the type to stand aside and let the world slip from Learjet's grasp. Two things can be done to improve the economic climate for small aircraft, says Barents to a gathering of anxious executives, and they are both spelled T-A-X R-E-F-O-R-M. Restoring the investment tax credit (eliminated in 1986) would give businesses a tax break for their investments in capital goods and equipment (including new business jets), and then it wouldn't take much to restimulate interest in general aviation, claims Barents. He also points out that the 10 percent "luxury tax" imposed during the Bush administration has been penalizing owners of private planes who fly them mostly for personal use or pleasure (the rule is "less than 80 percent for business"). When the luxury tax law came into effect in 1990, says Barents, sales of small airplanes plummeted immediately, whereas tax revenues showed no measurable increase.

One executive in the gathering suggests that an alternative reform might be the Bush administration's proposal to stimulate spending by providing an accelerated depreciation option for business investments, in lieu of reintroducing the investment tax credit.

Barents responds that even that much would help. The group decides that for general aviation to survive, the government must approve some sort of tax reform favorable to the industry. Otherwise, more companies like Cyrus Eaton may move their operations out of the United States.

Your task: As chief of corporate communications, you've been designated to write Learjet's official letter to congressional representatives urging adoption of new tax legislation more favorable to the general aviation industry.[12]

6. The real "Doc Hollywood" stands up: Letter from Dr. James Hotz urging a new practitioner to lower fees
Down in the swampy, piney regions of southern Georgia, there's a revolution going on. Folks who could never before afford a doctor's care are finding relief from a network of practitioners who have decided that helping people is more important than making $180,000 a year. "When all is said and done, I think

that [helping people] may be a lot more valuable to the psyche," explains Dr. Neil Shulman, a professor at Atlanta's Emory University who has persuaded quite a few young graduates to practice in doctor-deficient rural communities.

One of Shulman's converts, Dr. James Hotz, experienced such an unusual transformation that the professor wrote a book about him, which became a film (*Doc Hollywood*) starring Michael J. Fox. Shulman had persuaded the cardiologist-to-be to spend two years in urban Athens, Georgia, before going off to earn his fortune. While en route, Hotz and his wife were literally hijacked by car and driven 200 miles south to rural Leesburg. The townspeople were desperate for a doctor; like many small towns in the area, Leesburg hadn't had one for over a decade. The entire community turned out to cajole Hotz into staying with a home-cooked chicken dinner. He stayed.

Eventually, Hotz brought in eight other doctors and set up a revolutionary system for providing low-cost (sometimes free) health care for indigent patients: Doctors in three counties agree to keep their fees about 25 percent lower than normal, and Phoebe-Putney Memorial Hospital in Albany treats patients whether they can pay or not (all of Hotz's doctors serve on the board). The founder of Coca-Cola, who owns a nearby plantation, built a $1 million medical clinic for Hotz. And most specialists have agreed to perform for free such costly procedures as bypass surgery or cancer therapy for patients who can't afford them.

To help defray the cost of free services, Hotz applies for federal grant monies from the Community Health Center Program. He gets $250,000 worth of free drugs through special programs set up by drug companies. But most important to area residents is the fact that doctors are actually available—for both rich and poor.

You met Dr. Hotz recently while visiting relatives in nearby Putney. When he heard you were a business student, the good doctor immediately put you to work (he's a genius at marshaling support for his style of people-friendly medicine, you discovered). It seems a new doctor has moved into the Albany area and is charging fees better suited to big-city practices. The newcomer, Dr. Albert Reed, hasn't yet discovered that doctors in Hotz's loose network won't be referring patients to him, and worse, the only hospital in the area (Phoebe-Putney) won't let him work there unless he adopts the team spirit that has made health care in southern Georgia affordable for one and all.

Your task: Dr. Hotz wants you to compose a letter to Dr. Reed (25 Franklin Road, Newton, GA 31770), explaining the situation and persuading him to cooperate. There are no rules or formal requirements, just a verbal agreement that binds practitioners who agree never to turn away a person who needs medical care.[13]

7. Welcome to capitalism: Memo persuading General Electric's Hungarian managers to think "quality" When General Electric purchased a controlling share of Tungsram in Budapest, Hungary, the U.S. manufacturer bought a piece of lighting history. At the dawning of the twentieth century, Tungsram pioneered the use of tungsten filaments in incandescent light bulbs. But the ensuing years of political oppression (first the Nazis, then the Stalinists) drove away Tungsram's best scientists. Under the dronelike conditions imposed to meet quotas set by the Communist central government, the factory fell into disrepair. But Tungsram somehow managed to hold a 7 percent share of the European lighting market (about $300 million annually), so when Communist rule was overthrown in the late 1980s, GE stepped in.

The U.S. manufacturer immediately set out to revive Tungsram, beginning with $50 million in capital improvements. One by one, GE addressed the Hungarian company's problems, from an assembly line that broke one of every four light bulbs to a finance department that used pencils instead of computers. But GE may have underestimated the effect of 40 years of communism on the factory's 18,000 employees. *Profit* had become an evil word to them.

As executive vice president of GE Lighting in Cleveland, you've just received a fax from David Gadra, one of your managers sent to establish Tungsram's first information systems department. Gadra is introducing 500 new computer terminals and a retraining program for Tungsram employees. But he writes that he's having trouble teaching Hungarian managers to think like capitalists.

For instance, when asked to brainstorm about a problem, the managers are terrific at relating the details of what went wrong, including a thorough analysis of the current situation. But they never speak up with proposed solutions, since under the Communist system, creative thinking and initiative were discouraged. He's also having trouble explaining the need for producing quality products. Hungarian workers are accustomed to standing in line for hours for the basic necessities of life, and they are grateful to find goods of any quality.

Gadra is asking you for a memo of support and encouragement from GE's U.S. division to present at an upcoming "Business Made Easy" seminar. He thinks such a memo might spark additional enthusiasm for quality-mindedness among the Hungarians, who are eager to adapt to capitalism but thoroughly baffled by the way GE conducts business. His seminar will encourage employees "to win, not just to exist" and to feel free to express their ideas and opinions, even if they aren't complimentary. He'll discuss the concepts of reward for effort, quality, innovation, and enthusiasm, with personal and corporate pride as a major benefit and with profit as the ultimate goal. Gadra wants to make it clear to workers that the company's strength will mean future pay raises, and possibly new jobs for family and community. But one of his greatest challenges will be to overcome the Hungarians' skepticism, another carryover from years of false promises.

Your task: Write a persuasive memo reinforcing the points Gadra mentions and emphasizing the need for quality. Address your remarks to all Tungsram employees.[14]

8. Hospital cuts: Memo asking department heads to cut their budgets In his ongoing war against costs (see this chapter's On-the-Job simulation), chief administrator Ronald Sparkman has identified yet another opportunity for trimming expenses at Lawrence County Hospital. He has decided to ask all department heads to cut their budgets by 3 percent in the coming year. He feels that 3 percent is a modest sum and quite achievable, but he knows that his request will meet with resistance.

Your task: Sparkman wants you to draft a memo asking for reductions of 3 percent in each department head's annual plan.[15]

WRITING SALES LETTERS
9. The eye of the beholder: Sales letter from Anne Droid Security Systems The minute you saw Anne, you were intrigued. Like most mannequins, she's a classic beauty, but she's much smarter than the average. That unusual twinkle in her eye is a hidden camera through which she surveys the customers. Her delicate nose conceals a tiny microphone that picks up and records the conversations of potential shoplifters. All that Anne sees and hears is either videotaped or projected on a monitor in another room where it can be viewed privately.

You first met Anne through a friend—a dress-shop owner—who was trying her out for F. Jerry Gutierrez, her creator. "She's terrific," you said. "I'll bet she's selling like hotcakes."

"Not yet," your friend replied. "Jerry is just getting his company started, and he doesn't have much experience in marketing. What he really needs is somebody like you to help him out."

As a free-lance marketing and advertising consultant, you are always on the lookout for new clients, so you gave Jerry a call. He retained you on the spot to develop a marketing campaign for Anne Droid, his surveillance mannequin. One of your first steps was to attend a trade show featuring security systems aimed at retailers. While you were there demonstrating how Anne works, you took down the names and addresses of approximately 500 people who stopped by your booth, most of whom are security managers with major retail chains. Now you want to follow up by writing to those people to set up appointments with them.

Your task: Write a form letter to the security managers. They have all seen Anne in action, but given the number of booths at the trade show, you will want to refresh their memory about her features.[16]

10. Virgin Lightships: Sales letter introducing lighted blimp billboards from England

Every time a Virgin Lightship flies over a major city, switchboards all over town light up with calls from people who think they've spotted a slow-moving UFO. That's just fine with you. As a sales rep in charge of leasing the lighted blimps to advertisers, you're constantly telling prospects, "When a lighted billboard flies—people notice."

Virgin Lightships was started by British entrepreneur Richard Branson, also founder of Virgin Records and Virgin Atlantic Airways. At first, Branson wanted only to use a blimp to promote his airline, but the old military design was too expensive to build (Sea World's cost $6 million) and too costly to operate (most airships lease—with 25 crew members—for about $350,000 per month). Then Branson stumbled across the work of James Thiele. The Oregon engineer was creating a new kind of blimp. Reducing the old military airship's size from 200 to 130 feet, he designed it to work with a standard aviation engine. Then he relocated the cables that hold the gondola (where pilot and passengers are stationed) from the inside to the outside of the airship. With the cables out of the way, Thiele was able to insert a separate bladder for holding the helium that makes the ship lighter than air—and this left room for the two 1,000-watt stadium lights that make Thiele's ships glow in the dark like giant fireflies.

Since the helium is held separately, the outside sheath of a Thiele airship can be removed so that one advertiser's name can be easily replaced with another. Thiele's ships are assembled in 5 days instead of 30, need only a 12-member support crew, and cost about $1.4 million. Best of all—they're visible day and night. Branson bought two.

The British entrepreneur outfitted one of his new ships with a "Fly Virgin" logo, for Virgin Atlantic Airways, and flew it in Boston day and night for two weeks, along with a complementary mix of print, radio, and television ads. At the same time, he conducted a traditional advertising campaign, without the airship, in Los Angeles. An independent research company found that brand awareness in Los Angeles was 8 percent after a three-month campaign. But in Boston, it was a whopping 30 percent after only two weeks.

Thus Virgin Lightship was born. Branson's ships are leased for $200,000 per month. Considering that it can cost up to $300,000 for a single 30-second television commercial, Virgin Lightship advertising seems worthy of serious consideration. Branson now owns three Lightships, available for a two- or three-month

minimum lease (with an option for interchangeable messages using the replaceable sheath).

You're in charge of finding advertisers to lease the ships, but you've encountered some resistance among potential clients. First, whenever you mention *blimp*, everyone thinks back to the tragic crash in 1937 of the Hindenberg dirigible, loaded with passengers and exploding in midair. You're constantly explaining that, although helium was used during that time, it was hard to come by, and at the last minute, the Hindenberg was inflated with highly explosive hydrogen gas—as were many of the turn-of-the-century zeppelins that met similar fates. But unlike hydrogen gas, helium is perfectly safe. Second, you've been encountering what your industry calls the "giggle factor"—people simply have trouble thinking of bulging blimps as efficient and effective.

Your task: Write a form sales letter introducing new prospects to the benefits of advertising with a Virgin Lightship.[17]

11. PC pianists: Letter announcing the Miracle Piano Teaching System from Software Toolworks

Imagine a piano teacher who is firm, but infinitely patient. Think of an instructor with enough sense of fun to set up a "shooting gallery" in which your knowledge of the correct notes was tested by how well you could "shoot" little ducks placed on a musical staff where the notes should be. Yes, it sounds like a video arcade, but actually the shooting gallery is being displayed on the monitor of your desktop PC. It's a learning game called the Miracle Piano Teaching System, your company's latest creation.

You've been instructed to play with the new piano-teaching program by your boss, the sales manager at Software Toolworks. "The best way for you to learn the system's selling features is through firsthand experience," she grinned. So now your crowded desktop features the usual PC components plus a brand new 49-key electronic piano keyboard. The full-size piano keys are velocity-sensitive, meaning that the faster you press them, the louder they sound. (That took a little getting used to.) But this $479.95 software/hardware teaching system was designed to offer the equivalent of six months to a year of traditional piano lessons, with the advantage of allowing the student—child or adult—to advance at an individual pace. If it works for you, with your tin ear, it can work for anyone. And according to Joe West at San Francisco's Computers and Music store, customers have been begging for something like it for years.

The Miracle system includes keyboard, software, and cable (to connect it to your computer). If you wished, you could play the keyboard without the computer since it has a built-in stereo amplifier, two speakers, a headphone jack, and even a sustain foot pedal (an external amplifier is optional). The software lets you choose between the "classroom," where lessons are introduced; the "practice room," where the program gives you feedback about missed keys or poor timing and makes you repeat unsatisfactory lessons; and the "performance studio," where you play along with a background orchestra. When you're ready, you can select the "recording studio," which lets you save performances on a disk. When you get tired, you can tune in to prerecorded songs on the "jukebox," or slip into the "arcade" for a variety of amusing learning games.

By the end of the first chapter, you're playing "Ode to Joy" (with one hand, anyway). But you realize with a sigh that you'll probably never make it through all 40 chapters—1,000 lessons—before the boss decides you should get back to work.

Your task: Now that you've warmed up your fingers, use them to write a form letter to music retailers, introducing the IBM-compatible Miracle Piano Teaching System. Mention that versions for Macintosh, Nintendo, Super Nintendo, and Commodore Amiga will be available soon. The Nintendo version will be a little simpler and cost $100 less.[18]

12. Here's looking at you: Letter promoting AT&T's Videophone 2500

At $1,500 a pop, no one knows yet whether consumers will go for AT&T's newest attempt to produce a mass-market "picture phone." In the early 1960s, the telecommunications giant tried to fulfill the futuristic dream of people communicating like they do on the starship *Enterprise*—appearing on screens so that they can talk to one another "face to face." The company spent $500 million to develop the first consumer videophone, expecting to sell tens of thousands of them, but only a few hundred ever sold.

This is a particularly touchy issue for you, since you work for the marketing department of AT&T Communications Products. The new telephone, the AT&T Videophone 2500, is no bigger than a standard multiline telephone—the kind you see sitting on a business desk—and is priced at about one-twentieth the cost of the equipment sold to huge corporations for video teleconferencing. The teleconferencing equipment transmits pictures comparable in quality to ordinary color television, but it sells for up to $25,000 and can cost almost that much to operate for a single conference. Even slower versions, which transmit fewer than the standard 30-frames-a-second format, require special phone lines at a minimum rate of $25 per hour. The Videophone 2500, however, is the result of a painstaking engineering effort to squeeze and crunch the transmitted information into 10 frames a second, a format that can be transmitted over an ordinary copper telephone line. A consumer who buys the unit can take it home and plug it into a standard telephone jack. What is lost in quality is made up in savings: Because the videophone uses the same lines used by voice-only phones, it costs the same to operate.

Okay, so why shouldn't everyone rush out to buy one, fascinated as they certainly will be by this technological achievement? Perhaps they'll have trouble accepting the image of Mom on the palm-size screen, moving her lips in slow motion like some kind of underwater ghost. Or maybe they won't like the idea of callers looking in on them. Someone in your department circulated an editorial written by a Southern California professor who claims that people in his lectures rarely respond positively to the idea; in fact, he writes, a majority say they'd actually pay *not* to have such a phone installed in their homes if they ever became standard.

The Videophone 2500 will soon be available in AT&T Phone Center stores, department stores, and other retail outlets. They'll also be available for short-term rental at less than $30 a day. But your job is to find a way to get the picture phones installed in airports, hotel lobbies, and other public places where people can try them out and get used to the idea of talking and seeing at the same time.

Your task: You've decided to begin with several large hotel chains. Develop a form letter that will persuade general managers to meet with you to discuss the benefits of installing AT&T videophones in their lobbies.[19]

PREPARING COLLECTION MESSAGES

13. Gentle persuasion: Typical collection call from Mid-Continent Agencies

As a new employee with Mid-Continent Agencies, you are trying to get the hang of the collection business. The firm's president, Les Kirschbaum, has outlined Mid-Continent's standard procedures for collecting on overdue accounts, which are turned over to the agency. The first step is to call the indebted company on the phone and explore the situation. Kirschbaum explains, "You always try to talk to the person in charge of authorizing the payment of bills. That's generally the president if the company is relatively small, or the controller if it's a larger business. Don't bother to talk to lower-level people. They'll pass the buck."

To teach you how to handle these calls, Kirschbaum suggests that you do some role-playing. He'll take the part of the debtor and you play the bill collector. Your mission is to talk the debtor into paying something on the overdue account.

Before you begin the training session, Kirschbaum explains that most of the accounts are at least 90 days in arrears by the time they are turned over to Mid-Continent for collection. By this time, the company that is owed the money has generally tried all the obvious collection ploys, to no avail. Many of the debtors are honest businesspeople caught in a tight spot, but some are scam artists.

Your task: Plan three possible responses for replying to the debtor in the following training exercise:

You: "Good afternoon, Mr. Jones. This is (your name) with Mid-Continent Agencies. I'm calling about your bill to TNT Enterprises. You owe TNT $85,000 for decorating services that they provided last March. You're 90 days late with your payment, Mr. Jones, and TNT has turned the bill over to us for collection. When can we expect payment?"

Debtor: "I never got an invoice from TNT, and I don't remember what I owe them, but I'm sure it isn't $85,000. They did crummy work anyway. The carpet they installed is already worn. It's a piece of junk, and I don't plan to pay anything for it. If they want it back, they can come rip it out. They'd be doing me a favor. As for the rest of the bill, I doubt it amounts to more than $5,000 or $6,000."

How do you respond to Mr. Jones?[20]

14. The weeping willow follow-up: Middle-stage collection letter Many tree surgeons require cash payment immediately on completion of their work, but Cutter Tree Care has a different policy. Most of its work is done in the affluent communities of Austin, Texas, where people generally pay their bills. Furthermore, Cutter finds it most convenient to schedule work when the property owners may not be at home.

Bills are sent immediately after completion of the work, and three-fourths of the customers pay within 14 days. If payment has not been received by that time, a friendly reminder is sent, a brief note printed on letterhead with a picture of a sadly weeping willow tree on the bottom. If payment is not received within an additional 30 days, a final notice is sent, threatening legal action (which is taken) if the full amount due is not remitted within 14 days. Legal action has been taken in fewer than 4 percent of the cases, but given the expense and ill will, you have convinced Charlie Cutter that this figure is too high.

"Charlie," you say, "I think we'd get better results if we sent a middle-stage collection letter after the friendly reminder letter and before the final threat of legal action. We might not have to go to court so often if we could get people to agree to play fair."

The puzzled look on Charlie's face backs up his words: "Sorry. I'm not sure I know what you're talking about. Maybe you could write some kind of a model letter to show me what you mean."

Your task: Draft a form letter to be sent to nonpaying customers of Cutter Tree Care 30 days after the friendly reminder has been sent. The main thrust of the letter should be an appeal to fair play, but introduce other types of appeals if they seem helpful.

15. "Have no money": Last-ditch attempt to collect overdue bills When you signed on as part-time receptionist for David Cortez, D.D.S., bill collecting became one of your assignments. Dr. Cortez refers all accounts more than 120 days past due to Medical Collectors, Inc., which keeps a commission of 50 percent of the first $100 it collects and 35 percent of any amount over $100. But the difficulty in collecting on accounts that old means that Dr. Cortez receives few checks from Medical Collectors.

You suggest to Dr. Cortez that a different approach might be more successful: seeking small monthly payments from those patients who are unable to settle their bills in full. "OK, you try it out," he answers, and he hands you the card he was about to send to Medical Collectors. Mr. Harris (1010 Shadrack Street, Houston, TX 77013) had a root canal done four months ago, for which Dr. Cortez billed him $450. Mr. Harris has simply returned the last bill with this scrawled note: "Have no money. Honest. Sorry. Sincerely, Billy."

Your task: Prepare for Dr. Cortez's signature a letter to Mr. Harris that will produce good results.

16. The stained couch: Final collection letter You stand politely at Dawn D'Arcy's front door, trying to reason with her through the screen. So far, you aren't having much luck. "You know why you won't repossess that couch?" she says. "The condition it's in, that's why. You should see what's been spilled on it—and all the cigarette burns. I owe $750 on the darn thing, but you couldn't get $100 for it."

You press on bravely: "You know, you still owe the full $750 whether we take back the couch or not."

"I can't pay what I don't have. You can't squeeze blood out of a whatchamacallit, you know what I mean?"

"OK, so give me something to keep your account open. Let's say $50."

"Go home."

You try again: "How about $1? I don't want to turn your account over to a lawyer. Give me something, and we leave the lawyers off the case for a while."

"Go home. And take the couch with you if you want to. It's garbage. Just get off my property."

So much for the threat of repossession. You make a mental note to start repossession proceedings more promptly next time, but for the moment what Ms. D'Arcy says is true. Back at the store, you decide that you have gone as far as you can with Ms. D'Arcy. Appeals to fair play, pride, and loss of credit standing haven't brought in a single payment, and you are convinced that repossession would be a waste of time.

Your task: Write one last letter to Dawn D'Arcy (1599 S. Kingston, Aurora, CO 80012), indicating that if she does not make a substantial payment on her account, you will turn it over to an attorney for full collection. Provide specific details. Sign as credit manager of Van Ness Furnishings.

PART FOUR

REPORTS AND PROPOSALS

■CHAPTER TEN

After studying this chapter, you will be able to

- Identify the qualities of good business reports and proposals
- Choose the proper format and length for your report
- Decide when to use direct versus indirect order
- Organize informational and analytical reports
- Establish an appropriate degree of formality in a report
- Use headings, lists, transitions, openings, and summaries to guide readers through the report

WRITING SHORT REPORTS

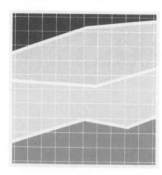

ON THE JOB:
Facing a Communication Dilemma at Motown Records
Hot on the Comeback Trail

In its glory days, Motown Records consistently topped the charts with its unique blend of pop and soul. The firm's founder, Berry Gordy, Jr., had a surefire instinct for spotting talent: Diana Ross and the Supremes, Stevie Wonder, Marvin Gaye, Smokey Robinson and the Miracles, the Jackson Five, the Temptations, Gladys Knight and the Pips, the Spinners, and the Four Tops.

In the 1980s, though, Motown lost its magic touch. Gordy diversified and began spending more time on television and movie projects. Many of his top artists defected to other labels that could afford to pay more and that could provide stronger marketing and distribution support. Motown had no new stars to replace them. The firm missed out completely on rap and hip-hop. By the late 1980s, golden oldies accounted for over half of Motown's sales, and annual revenues had dropped from nearly $100 million to $20 million.

But after a change of ownership and management in 1988, Motown is solidly back on track. Gordy sold Motown to a partnership that includes Boston Ventures and MCA. The new owners brought in Jheryl Busby, the former head of MCA's black-music division, to serve as Motown's chief executive. He has an impressive track record, both at MCA and in previous jobs with other recording companies.

Busby got off to a fast start, luring Diana Ross back into the fold and signing such fast-rising new stars as Boyz II Men, Another Bad Creation, Johnny Gill, Shanice Wilson, and The Boys. Boyz II Men's *Cooleyhighharmony* has been a huge hit, establishing itself as the top selling rhythm-and-blues album of all time. But Busby hardly has a clear path to nonstop success.

Other record labels are working feverishly to capitalize on the resurgent popularity of black music. And a dispute among Motown's owners over distribution and marketing promises to keep Busby busy in court.

In short, Busby has his work cut out for him. Monitoring and controlling the Motown operation, developing new talent, making a host of decisions—all Busby's activities require accurate information. In order to keep Motown charging past the competition, Busby must receive and prepare good reports. But what makes one report better than another?[1]

WHAT MAKES A GOOD BUSINESS REPORT?

Motown Records

Business reports are like bridges spanning time and space. Organizations such as Motown use them to provide a formal, verifiable link among people, places, and times. Some reports are needed for internal communication; others are vehicles for corresponding with outsiders. Some are required as a permanent record; others are needed to solve an immediate problem or to answer a passing question. Many move upward through the chain of command to help managers monitor the various units in the organization; some move downward to explain management decisions to lower-level employees responsible for day-to-day operations.

Reports are essentially a management tool. Even the most capable managers must often rely on other people to observe events or collect information for them. Managers are often too far away to oversee everything themselves, and they don't have enough time. In addition, they often lack the specialized background required to research and evaluate certain subjects. Thus reports are usually for management or on its behalf.

You may be surprised at the variety of documents that qualify as reports. The word *report* covers everything from preprinted forms to brief, informal letters and memos to formal three-volume manuscripts. Some reports are even delivered orally, as Chapter 16 explains. But in general, when businesspeople speak of reports, they are thinking of written, factual accounts that objectively communicate information about some aspect of the business.

Make business reports as concise as possible.

The goal in developing a report is to make the information as clear and convenient as possible. Because time is precious, you tell the readers what they need to know—no more, no less—and you present the information in a way that is geared to their needs. Although reports vary widely in purpose and often in the audience they're written for, all good reports have at least three things in common: (1) The information is accurate, (2) the content shows the writer's good judgment, and (3) the format, style, and organization respond to the reader's needs.

ACCURACY

To ensure accuracy
- **Check the facts**
- **Reduce distortion**

The first thing a business report writer must learn is how to tell the truth. If Jheryl Busby received information that was inaccurate or incomplete, any decisions he made based on it would be bad ones. As a result, Motown would suffer and so would Busby's reputation. Unfortunately, telling the truth is not always a simple matter. We all see reality a little differently and describe it in a unique way. The following guidelines will help limit the distortions introduced by differences in perception:

- *Describe facts or events in concrete terms.* It's better to say, "Sales have increased from $400,000 to $435,000 in the past two months" rather than "Sales have skyrocketed." Indicate quantities whenever you can. Be specific.

- *Report all the relevant facts.* Regardless of whether these facts will support your theories or please your readers, they should be included. Omitting the details that undermine your position might be convenient, but it isn't accurate. Readers will be misled if you hesitate to be the bearer of bad news and leave out unpleasant information.

- *Put the facts in perspective.* If you tell readers, "The value of the stock has doubled in three weeks," you are giving only a partial picture. They will have a much clearer understanding if you say, "The value of the stock has doubled in three weeks, rising from $2 to $4 per share on the rumor of a potential merger." Taken out of context, even the most concrete facts can be misleading.

- *Give plenty of evidence for your conclusions.* You can't expect readers to fully understand your conclusions unless you offer substantial supporting evidence. Statements like "We have to reorganize the sales force or we're bound to lose market share" may or may not be true. Readers have no way of knowing unless you provide enough data to support your claim.

- *Present only valid evidence and supportable conclusions.* You will, of course, check your facts and figures and obtain your information from reliable sources. In addition, try to avoid drawing hasty or ill-founded conclusions from your data. Just because one sales representative reports that customers are dissatisfied with your product doesn't mean that all customers are dissatisfied. You are likely to distort the truth when you generalize from too small a sample. In addition, you should not assume that a preceding event is the cause of what follows. The fact that sales declined right after you switched advertising agencies doesn't necessarily mean that the new agency is to blame. Other factors, such as the general state of the economy, may be responsible. When you offer a conclusion, be certain that you have ample evidence to support it, and avoid drawing conclusions in areas where you have limited experience or an inadequate professional background.

- *Keep your personal biases in check.* Even if you have strong feelings about the subject of your report, try to keep those feelings from influencing your choice of words. Here's an example of emotionally charged language taken from a relocation study: "Locating a plant in Kraymore is a terrible idea. The people there are mostly students, they'd rather play than work, and they don't have the ability to operate our machines." Language like this not only offends but also obscures the facts and provokes emotional responses.

GOOD JUDGMENT

Do not include anything in a report that might jeopardize you or your organization.

Some things simply don't belong in a report, whether or not they are true. You can do both yourself and your employer a great deal of harm by being indiscreet. Of course, you should not abandon good business ethics by covering up wrongdoing. But you should be prepared to back up in a court of law whatever

you write. Business documents are frequently used as evidence in legal proceedings.

You should also be aware that managers have distinct preferences when it comes to reports. They particularly dislike personal gripes, criticism, alibis, attempts to blame someone else, incomplete or sugarcoated data, unsolicited opinions, and attempts to bypass the manager through distribution of the document. On the other hand, they like five things:

- Getting the main idea at the beginning of the report
- Seeing the facts
- Receiving the whole story
- Reading language they can understand
- Learning something that will make their jobs easier [2]

It's fair to say that all readers, not just managers, will appreciate your attention to these five points.

Regardless of what type of report you are preparing, try to keep the likes and dislikes of your readers in mind. As you make decisions about the content, the needs of your audience should be your main concern, and you should exercise your best judgment in trying to meet those needs.

RESPONSIVE FORMAT, STYLE, AND ORGANIZATION

Before you write, you have to decide whether to use letter, memo, or manuscript format (see Appendix B for details); whether to group the ideas one way or another; and whether to employ a formal or an informal style. All these decisions revolve around the reader's needs. In thinking about these issues, ask yourself the following questions and tailor the report accordingly:

- *Who initiated the report? Voluntary* reports, prepared on your own initiative, require more detail and support than *authorized* reports, which are prepared at the request of another person. In writing a voluntary report, you need to give more background on the subject and explain your purpose more carefully.

- *What subject does the report cover?* The subject of a business report affects its vocabulary and format. For example, an audit report (one that verifies an accountant's inspection of a firm's financial records) must contain a lot of numbers, often in the form of tables. A report from the corporate legal department about the company's patents would contain many legal terms. When both writer and reader are familiar with the subject and share the same background, the writer does not need to define terms or explain basic concepts.

- *When is the report prepared? Routine* reports submitted on a repeat basis (daily, weekly, monthly, quarterly, annually) require less introductory and transitional material than do *special*, nonrecurring reports that deal with unique situations. Routine reports are often prepared on preprinted forms, which the writer simply fills in, or they are organized in some standard way.

Keep "politics" out of your reports; provide a clear, direct accounting of the facts.

Select a format, a style, and an organization that reflect the reader's needs.

In making decisions about the format, style, and organization of a report, consider its
- *Origin*
- *Subject*
- *Timing*
- *Distribution*
- *Purpose*
- *Probable reception*

Before writing complicated decisions, Supreme Court Justice Sandra Day O'Connor devotes considerable time to organizing her thoughts and developing a logical order for her arguments and opinions. She maintains that time spent in planning is never wasted.

- *Where is the report being sent? Internal* reports, prepared for use within the organization, are generally less formal than *external* reports, which are sent to people in other organizations. Many internal reports, especially those under ten pages, are written in memo format. External reports, on the other hand, may be in letter format if they are no longer than five pages, or they may be in manuscript format if they exceed five pages.

- *Why is the report being prepared? Informational* reports focus on facts; *analytical* reports include analysis, interpretation, conclusions, and recommendations. Informational reports are usually organized around subtopics; analytical reports are generally organized to highlight conclusions, recommendations, or reasons.

- *How receptive is the reader?* When the reader is likely to agree with the content of the report, the material is presented in *direct order*, starting with the main idea (key findings, conclusions, recommendations). If the reader may have reservations about the report, the material is presented in *indirect order*, starting with the details and leading to the main idea.

As you can see from this list and from Table 10.1, the origin, subject, timing, distribution, purpose, and probable reception of a report all have a substantial impact on its format, style, and organization.

PLANNING SHORT REPORTS

When planning short reports, your audience, purpose, and subject matter must be considered. Each of these three elements influences the format and length of your report, as well as its basic structure.

DECIDING ON FORMAT AND LENGTH

Decisions about the format and length of your memo or report may be made for you by the person who requests the document. If you are preparing a periodic status report, for example, you will probably follow a standard pattern that enables the reader to quickly compare results from one reporting period to the next. Generally speaking, the more routine the report, the less flexibility you have in deciding on format and length.

When you do have some leeway about these issues, your decisions should be based on your readers' needs. Your goal should be to tell them what they need to know in a format that is easy for them to use. In selecting a format for your report, you have four options:

- *Preprinted form.* Basically for "fill in the blank" reports. Most are relatively short (five or fewer pages) and deal with routine information, often mainly numerical. Use this format when it is requested by the person authorizing the report.

- *Letter.* For reports of five or fewer pages that are directed to outsiders. These reports include all the normal parts of a letter, but they may also have headings, footnotes, tables, and figures.

You may present a report in one of four formats.

TABLE 10.1 FACTORS AFFECTING REPORT FORMAT, STYLE, AND ORGANIZATION

FACTOR	POSSIBILITIES	IMPLICATIONS FOR FORMAT, STYLE, AND ORGANIZATION
WHO originates it?	Voluntary reports prepared on the writer's own initiative	Require plenty of introductory information to explain purpose of report
	Authorized reports prepared at the request of another person	Require less introductory material than voluntary reports; should be organized to respond to the reader's request
WHAT subject does it cover?	Sales reports, compensation policies, affirmative action plans, engineering proposals, research studies, progress reports	Presentation dictated by characteristics of subject (for example, detailed statistical information summarized in tabular format)
WHEN is it prepared?	Routine, recurring reports prepared on daily, weekly, monthly, quarterly, or annual basis	Require standard format that facilitates comparisons from one period to next; need relatively little background and transitional information
	Special, nonrecurring reports prepared in response to unique situations	Do not need standardization; require plenty of background and transitional information
WHERE is it sent?	Internal reports prepared for use within the organization	Can be relatively informal; written in memo or manuscript format
	External reports sent to people outside the organization	Should be relatively formal in tone; written in letter or manuscript format
WHY is it prepared?	Informational reports providing facts	Organized around subtopics
	Analytical reports providing analysis, interpretation, conclusions, and often recommendations	Organized around conclusions/recommendations or logical arguments
HOW will it be received?	Receptive readers	Arranged in direct order
	Skeptical or hostile readers	Arranged in indirect order

- *Memo.* The most common format for short (fewer than ten pages), informal reports distributed within an organization. Memos have headings at the top: "Date," "To," "From," and "Subject." In addition, like longer reports, they often have internal headings and sometimes visual aids. Memos exceeding ten pages are sometimes referred to as memo reports to distinguish them from their shorter cousins. They, too, begin with the standard memo headings. The checklist at the end of this chapter provides guidelines for preparing memo reports and other short, informal reports.

- *Manuscript.* For reports (from a few pages to several hundred pages) that require a formal approach. As their length increases, reports in manuscript format require more elements both before the text of the report (prefatory parts) and after the text (supplementary parts). Chapter

12 explains these elements and includes additional instructions and a checklist for preparing formal reports.

Length depends on
- Subject
- Purpose
- Your relationship with the readers

The length of your report obviously depends on your subject and purpose, but it is also affected by your relationship with the readers. If they are relative strangers, if they are skeptical or hostile, or if the material is nonroutine or controversial, you generally have to explain your points in greater detail. Thus you end up with a longer document. You can afford to be brief if you are on familiar terms with your readers, if they are likely to agree with you, or if the information is routine or uncomplicated. Generally speaking, short reports are more common in business than long ones, and you will probably write many more 5-page memos than 250-page formal reports.

ESTABLISHING A BASIC STRUCTURE

In addition to deciding on format and length, you have to decide on the basic structure of your report. This problem involves three issues:

- What information should you include? Should you cover all the facts at your disposal or eliminate some of the data?

BEHIND THE SCENES AT THE SAN DIEGO ZOO
Even Tapirs Leave a Paper Trail

When zoo curator Rick Barongi flew to Panama to rescue six wild Baird's tapirs, he probably wasn't thinking about the report he'd have to write at the end of his adventure. Left to starve at the ranch of deposed dictator Manuel Noriega, the long-nosed mammals (distant relatives of horses and rhinos) were in the care of people who regard these endangered animals as creatures to be hunted for food in the tropical forests of Panama.

Barongi made four trips to Noriega's government-seized estate, and for the last trip, he organized an international team of zoo experts to accompany him. They saved five of the tapirs, and they helped educate local officials about the special care that is needed by such endangered animals to live in captivity.

After braving touchy politics, hair-raising traffic, and tropical heat (not to mention the razor-sharp canine teeth of unhappy, 300-pound tapirs), Barongi returned home to his regular job as children's zoo director at the San Diego Zoo, and he promptly turned out

an eight-page activity report of "The Panama Tapir Project." Writing reports is as much a part of Barongi's working life as making sure the baby monkeys that live in the nursery beneath his office are diapered and fed properly by their keepers. As director of the children's zoo, he's responsible for a million-dollar budget, a staff of 20 keepers, and a collection of domestic and exotic animals larger than many entire zoos. To manage both people and animals successfully, Barongi writes a lot of memo and letter reports.

Barongi explains that he doesn't *always* have to justify his acquisitions when obtaining new animals for the children's zoo; managing the animal collection is part of his curatorial tasks. But he usually sends a memo report to all departments affected by the animals' arrival.

For example, when he acquired a colony of naked mole rats, "a very bizarre rodent from Africa," Barongi's superiors were concerned about the cost of building the rodents' new exhibit/home. So Barongi's first memo report about these animals was written to jus-

Choice of structure involves three decisions:
- What to say?
- Direct or indirect order?
- Topical or logical organization?

- What psychological approach is best with your particular readers? Should you use direct order, which leads off with the main idea (a summary of key findings, conclusions, recommendations)? Or should you use indirect order, which lays out the facts and gradually builds to the main idea?

- What method of subdivision will make your material both clear and convincing? Should you use a topical organization based on order of importance, sequence, chronology, location, spatial relationships, or categories? Or should you organize your ideas around logical arguments?

Key points to cover

Your report should answer the audience's key questions.

If Jheryl Busby asked you to write a report on Motown's current status, what ideas would you include? In deciding on the content of your report, the first step is to put yourself in the audience's position. What major questions do you think your audience has about the subject? Your objective is to answer all those questions in the order that makes the most sense.

In most situations, your audience has one main question of greatest importance: "Why are we losing money?" "Is this a good investment?" "What will our sales and profits be over the next six months?" "What is the progress to date on the work assigned?" Whether it's one of these or another, the main question must be defined as precisely as possible before you can begin to formulate your

tify that cost. Later, he organized information about the rats in a direct format for subsequent short reports to the zoo's veterinary hospital (reserving space for the mole rats' month-long quarantine) and to the public relations and photography departments (initiating publicity about the new residents). Barongi says he strives to keep such reports "really short—I don't want to be redundant." If people are interested, they'll call him for more background information.

But some of Barongi's reports require more thoroughness. His dream is to revamp and expand the children's section of San Diego's huge zoo, making it an interactive, state-of-the-art conservation learning experience that will be set in a simulated rain forest. Barongi is currently preparing a justification report to persuade the zoo's board of directors to raise funds for the project. He wants this preliminary report to be "short, colorful, and eye-catching," but he also wants to include enough supporting data to make the project seem feasible, exciting, and essential to the zoo's future.

The short report will draw on months of brainstorming by a zoo task force, set up by Barongi to plan a "children's zoo for the twenty-first century." It will be about ten pages, with watercolor illustrations to convey a feeling of the lush, tropical setting that Barongi and his colleagues envision. To save every-

one's time, he will use the direct approach, opening with a plan for the zoo that will serve as an interactive learning center "not just for children, but for all age groups."

He may cite a single statistic in the opening section of his report—perhaps a survey by the World Wildlife Fund showing that preserving the environment is the number one concern of high school students. At this early planning stage, says Barongi, "I don't want to get too specific. I want these colorful images to explode in the minds of board members as they read the report, so it will have short descriptions with a few colorful illustrations."

APPLY YOUR KNOWLEDGE

1. If you were proposing a major renovation of a museum or a zoo exhibit area, would you use a direct approach or an indirect approach? Why? What topics or categories would you use to subdivide your report?

2. How would Barongi's proposal for the new children's zoo differ if the idea had actually originated with the board of directors? Explain why it's important that this distinction be clear in the report writer's mind.

answer. Defining the main question may seem to require the skills of a mind reader, but nine times out of ten, the main question is simply the reason you have been asked to write the report. Once you've defined the main question, you can sketch a general answer, based on the information available. Your answer, like the question, should be broad.

The next step is to determine what additional questions your audience is likely to ask based on your answer to the main question. Your answers to these questions will raise additional questions. As the chain of questions and answers is forged, the points multiply and become increasingly specific, as Figure 10.1 illustrates. When you've identified and answered all your audience's probable questions, you have defined the content of your report or presentation. The process is akin to outlining.

The question-and-answer chain clarifies the main idea of the report (your answer to the main question) and establishes the flow of ideas from the general to the specific. All effective reports and presentations are constructed in this way, with a mix of broad concepts and specific details. When the mix is right, the message works: Members of the audience grasp both the general meaning and the practical implications of the ideas. They get the gist of the message and can relate the broad concepts to the everyday world of objects and actions. The general ideas sum up and give direction to the message; the specific ideas clarify and illustrate the meaning.

Business communication tends to be concerned with the details: facts, figures, and hard data. Routine, recurring messages are especially heavy on details; analytical, problem-solving messages are heavier on generalizations. In either case, the trick is to draw conclusions and generalizations out of all the information and relate them to your audience's needs. For every piece of information that you are tempted to include, ask why the audience needs it and how it relates to the main question.

> Pursue the chain of questions and answers from the general to the specific.

FIGURE 10.1
A Typical Question-and-Answer Chain

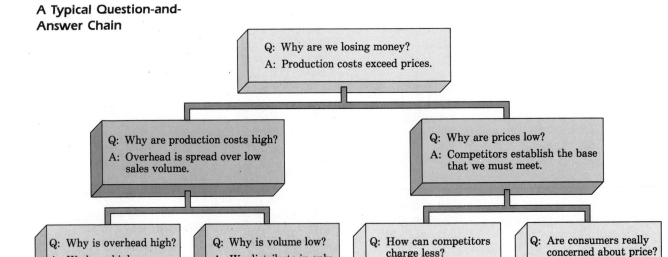

Direct versus indirect order

The direct approach, which gives readers the main idea first, saves time and makes the report easier to understand.

Audience attitude is the basis for decisions about organization. When the audience is considered either receptive or open-minded, you should use the direct approach: Emphasize your key findings, conclusions, and recommendations. This approach, which is most common for business reports, enables readers to get the main idea of the report at the outset, which saves time and makes the rest of the report easier to follow. For those who have questions or want more information, later parts of the report provide complete findings and supporting details. In addition to being more convenient for readers, the direct approach generally produces a more forceful report. You sound sure of yourself when you state your conclusions confidently at the outset instead of beating around the bush.

The indirect approach, which withholds the main idea until later in the report, helps overcome resistance.

However, confidence may sometimes be misconstrued as arrogance. If you are a junior member of a status-conscious organization or if your audience is skeptical or hostile, you may want to use indirect order. With this approach, you introduce the complete findings and supporting details before the conclusions and recommendations, which come last. The indirect approach gives you a chance to prove your points and gradually overcome your audience's reservations. By deferring the conclusions and recommendations, you imply that you have weighed the evidence objectively without prejudging the facts. You also imply that you are subordinating your judgment to that of the audience, whose members are capable of drawing their own conclusions when they have access to all the facts.

Although the indirect approach has its advantages, there is always the possibility that report readers will be in a hurry to get to "the answer," flipping immediately to the recommendations and defeating your purpose. For this reason, length should enter into your decision on whether to use direct or indirect order. Generally speaking, the longer the message, the less effective an indirect approach is likely to be. Furthermore, an indirect argument is harder to follow than a direct argument.

Because both the direct and indirect approaches have merit, business people often combine them. They reveal their conclusions and recommendations as they go along, rather than putting them either first or last. For example, Figure 10.2 contrasts the introductions from two reports with the same general outline (see page 256). In the direct version, the writer makes a series of statements summarizing the conclusion reached in relation to each main topic on the outline. In the indirect version, the writer simply introduces the same topics (in the same order) without drawing any conclusions about them. The conclusions appear within the body of the report instead. So, is the report that uses this second introduction direct or indirect? Real reports are often just as hard to classify.

Division of ideas

Regardless of whether you use the direct or indirect approach, you must still deal with the question of how your ideas will be subdivided and developed. For example, let's say you are writing a controversial report recommending that your company revise its policy on who reports to whom. You know that some of your readers will object to your ideas, so you decide to use indirect order. But how do you develop your argument?

FIGURE 10.2 Direct Approach Versus Indirect Approach in an Introduction

THE DIRECT APPROACH	THE INDIRECT APPROACH
Since the company's founding 25 years ago, we have provided regular repair service for all our electric appliances. This service has been an important selling point as well as a source of pride for our employees. However, we are paying a high price for our image. Last year, we lost $500,000 on our repair business.	Since the company's founding 25 years ago, we have provided repair service for all our electric appliances. This service has been an important selling point as well as a source of pride with our employees. However, the repair business itself has consistently lost money.
Because of your concern over these losses, you have asked me to study the pros and cons of discontinuing our repair service. With the help of John Hudson and Susan Lefkowitz, I have studied the issue for the past two weeks and have come to the conclusion that we have been embracing an expensive, impractical tradition.	Because of your concern over these losses, you have asked me to study the pros and cons of discontinuing our repair business. With the help of John Hudson and Susan Lefkowitz, I have studied the issue for the past two weeks. The following pages present our findings for your review. Three basic questions are addressed:
By withdrawing from the electric appliance repair business, we can substantially improve our financial performance without damaging our reputation with customers. This conclusion is based on three basic points that are covered in the following pages: --It is highly unlikely that we will ever be able to make a profit in the repair business. --Service is no longer an important selling point with customers. --Closing down the service operation will create few internal problems.	--What is the extent of our losses, and what can we do to turn the business around? --Would withdrawal hurt our sales of electric appliances? --What would be the internal repercussions of closing down the repair business?

ORGANIZING SHORT REPORTS

In the following sections, you'll see how people in a variety of situations develop arguments. The key is to decide first whether the purpose of the report is to provide chiefly information or analysis. From there, you can choose an organizational plan that suits your topic and goals.

ORGANIZING INFORMATIONAL MEMOS AND REPORTS

The purpose of informational reports is to explain.

Informational reports have one basic purpose: to explain something in straightforward terms. Informational reports, which have hundreds of uses in business, include reports for monitoring and controlling operations, statements of policies and procedures, reports on the organization's compliance with government requirements, personal activity reports, and reports documenting client work.

Make clarity your main objective in informational reports.

In writing informational reports, you usually don't have to worry too much about reader reaction. Because readers will presumably respond unemotionally to your material, you can present it in the most direct fashion possible. What you do need to worry about with informational reports is reader comprehension. The information must be presented logically and accurately so that readers will understand exactly what you mean and be able to use the information in a practical way.

Even as successful as they've been with such movies as *Flashdance, Beverly Hills Cop,* and *Top Gun,* Hollywood producers Don Simpson and Jerry Bruckheimer are emphatic about keeping costs in line. Their spending decisions are based on expense reports they receive daily. In such reports, insist Simpson and Bruckheimer, the information must be both accessible and accurate.

Periodic reports are recurring reports that keep managers informed about departments reporting to them.

Most periodic reports follow a set sequence.

Periodic reports must expose any problems that exist.

In structuring an informational report, you can let the nature of whatever you're describing serve as the point of departure. For example, if you're reporting on the company's sales, you might present results for the country as a whole and then for each of the various geographic regions. If you're describing a machine, each component can correspond to a part of your report. If you're describing an event, you can approach the discussion chronologically, and if you're explaining how to do something, you can describe the steps in the process.

Some informational reports, especially those to government regulators and those prepared on preprinted forms, are organized according to instructions supplied by the person requesting the information. In addition, many proposals conform to an outline specified in the request for proposal issued by the client: statement of the problem, background, scope of work, limitations, sources and methods, work schedule, qualifications of personnel, facilities, anticipated costs, expected results.

Informational reports take many forms, but the two examples that follow, a brief periodic report and a personal activity report on a conference, will give you an idea of the typical organization and tone.

A periodic report

A periodic report is an internal report that describes what has happened in a department or division during a particular period. The purpose of these recurring documents, which are sometimes called status reports, is to provide a picture of how things are going so that managers will be up-to-date and can take corrective action if necessary.

Periodic reports are usually written in memo format and do not need much of an introduction; a subject line on the memo is adequate. They should follow the same general format and organization from period to period. Most are organized in this sequence:

- *Overview of routine responsibilities.* A brief description of activities related to each of the writer's normal responsibilities. In some cases, the overview focuses on statistical or financial results; in other cases, it is written in paragraph form.

- *Discussion of special projects.* A description of any new or special projects that have been undertaken during the reporting period.

- *Plans for the coming period.* A schedule of activities planned for the next reporting period.

- *Analysis of problems.* Although often included in the overview of routine or special activities, problem analysis is sometimes put in a separate section to call attention to areas that may require high-level intervention.

The important thing to remember in writing periodic reports is to be honest about problems as well as accomplishments. In fact, the bad news is probably more important than the good news; problems require action, whereas good news often does not.

The periodic report in Figure 10.3 was prepared by Liz Rockwell, director of campus recruiting for the Minneapolis office of an accounting firm. Liz has this to say about her report: "Campus recruiting is a big deal for our firm because we hire most of our staff right out of college. Between January and

**FIGURE 10.3
Sample Periodic
Report**

MEMO

DATE: February 16, 1993
TO: Joyce Roberts, V.P., Personnel
FROM: Liz Rockwell, Director, Campus Recruiting *LR*
SUBJECT: Recruiting activities, February 1-15

ACTIVITIES COMPLETED

We've been working on three campuses February 1-15:

--University of Wisconsin. Jud Morgan and I had dinner with five good candidates identified by Professor Neiburgh. I have invited three of them to visit our offices and am awaiting their replies.

--University of Minnesota. We interviewed 54 undergraduate business/accounting majors during regular campus interviews on the 7th and 8th. Joe Damon and Linda Sawyer handled the candidates who had been invited to sign up in advance, and I handled the rest. We have reviewed the evaluations and are sending invitations to 10 students to come in for additional interviews at our office.

--Northwestern University. The resume book from Northwestern arrived on the 3rd, and we are now prescreening the graduating business majors. We expect to invite about 25 candidates to sign up for campus interviews, which will be held on March 3.

ACTIVITIES SCHEDULED

Recruiting activities scheduled for the next two weeks are indicated below:

Date	Activity	Responsibility
Feb. 18-19	University of Michigan, undergraduate business majors: 1st-round interviews	Rockwell, Lipp, Pritsky, Lloyd
Feb. 21	University of Chicago: 1st-round interviews	Taylor
Feb. 28	University of Iowa, undergraduate business majors: 1st-round interviews	Rockwell, Damon

PROBLEMS

Some of the staff are already complaining about the burden of interviewing so many candidates. In addition to screening resumes, contacting former professors, and helping with campus interviews, the staff will be talking with approximately 40 people here in our offices between now and April 14. Since each of the 40 will be seen by three staff members, we'll actually have to schedule 120 office interviews.

The scheduling problem is compounded by the fact that many of our people travel extensively. On any given day, only about 60 percent of them are in the office. Moreover, some interviewers are better than others, and I am reluctant to use those who lack confidence or ability in this area.

April, we visit eight or ten campuses and screen about 500 candidates in an effort to hire roughly 20 people. During the recruiting season, I prepare a memo twice a month to let my boss know where we stand. The rest of the year, I submit my report on a monthly basis."

A personal activity report

A personal activity report calls for an individual's description of what occurred during a conference, convention, or trip, for example. It is intended to inform management of any important information or decisions that emerged.

Personal activity reports are ordinarily written in memo format. Because they are nonrecurring documents, they require more of an introduction than a periodic report does. They are often organized chronologically, but some are organized around topics that reflect the reader's interests.

Personal activity reports, often in the form of brief memos, describe the facts and decisions that emerge during conventions, trips, and business meetings.

Figure 10.4 gives an example of a personal activity report organized by topic. It is a conference report prepared by Chris Bowers, who is on the staff of a large housing-development company. Says Chris, "My boss sent me to the Manufactured Housing Convention to find out whether we might be able to use factory-built houses to reduce our development costs. Because I knew my boss was mainly interested in learning about different kinds of factory-built housing, I went to the seminars that covered the four main types. When I wrote my conference report, I devoted a section to each one."

ORGANIZING ANALYTICAL REPORTS

The purpose of an analytical report is to convince the reader that the conclusions and recommendations developed in the text are valid

Analytical reports differ from informational reports in their purpose and, thus, in their organization. Informational reports are mainly intended to educate readers. Analytical reports are designed to persuade readers to accept certain conclusions or recommendations; they include justification reports, research reports, client proposals, and troubleshooting reports. In informational reports, the information alone is the focus of attention. In analytical reports, the

FIGURE 10.4
Sample Personal Activity Report

MEMO

DATE: October 23, 1993
TO: Gary Boone
FROM: Chris Bowers   *C.B.*
SUBJECT: Manufactured Housing Convention

My trip to the Manufactured Housing Convention, held October 16-20 in Miami, was extremely interesting. One clear point was made repeatedly by many speakers: Factory-built homes have the potential to transform the housing industry. By 1997, 37 percent of all new homes will be manufactured away from the development site, freeing the developer to concentrate on site acquisition, preparation, and marketing. The four main types of manufactured housing discussed at the convention are described below.

MOBILE HOMES

Design improvements and price advantages are both swelling demand for mobile homes. The new models are spacious and attractive--hard to distinguish from conventional site-built homes. In fact, most so-called mobile homes are never relocated once they are in place at their first site. With proper landscaping, they create an impression that is far better than the unattractive trailer camps of the 1940s. The attached brochures will give you an idea of how some of the new models look.

Sales of new mobile homes are growing at an annual rate of 6 percent and will reach 500,000 units per year by 1997. Currently, almost 50 percent of all new single-family homes priced at less than $80,000 are mobile homes. Buyers range from first-time homeowners to middle-income retirees.

MODULAR HOUSING

The main difference between modular and mobile homes is that modular homes must be trucked to their site, whereas mobile homes can be towed on their own chassis. Sales of new modular homes are increasing by 7 percent per year and should total 120,000 units by 1997.

PANELIZED HOUSING

Panelized housing is assembled at the development site from large factory-built components, such as walls, floors, and roofs. The developer has the option of using the components in various configurations. Shipments are increasing at an annual rate of 8 percent and will reach 175,000 units by 1997.

PRECUT HOUSING

People who want to build their own homes or act as their own general contractor can now buy precut but unassembled components packaged in kit form. This market has traditionally been dominated by mail-order firms featuring log cabins, geodesic domes, and A-frames, but a few manufacturers are currently trying to gear their packages to the development market. Sales are beginning to pick up. Shipments are growing by 6 percent annually and will reach 42,000 units by 1997.

Liz Claiborne attributes the success of her clothing designs to the reports prepared by her marketing department: reports that analyze sales figures, define women's roles and issues, identify trends, and communicate recommendations that can be translated into fashions. When writing such analytical reports, it is important to use the facts in a convincing way.

information plays a supporting role. The facts are a means to an end rather than an end in themselves.

Analytical reports are generally written to respond to special circumstances. They go by various names, but no matter what you call them, they all have one thing in common: They are designed to guide the reader toward a decision. Suppose you wanted to convince Jheryl Busby that new artists should get more money from Motown; you would write an analytical report.

Regardless of which type of analytical report you are writing, you must organize your ideas so that they will convince readers of the soundness of your thinking. Your choice of a specific approach should be based on your estimate of the readers' probable reactions: direct if you think they are likely to agree with you, indirect if you think they will resist your message. If you use the direct approach, you can base the structure of the report on your conclusions and recommendations, using them as the main points of your outline. If you employ an indirect approach, your organization should reflect the thinking process that will lead readers to your conclusions.

A justification report

When the reader is concerned about what action to take, use recommendations as the main points.

Justification reports are internal proposals used to persuade top management to approve an investment or a project. The justification report shown in Figure 10.5 provides a good example of the direct approach. It was written by Raymond Verdugo, director of manufacturing engineering at a paper-products company in New Jersey. Verdugo was asked by top management to suggest ways to increase the company's production of facial tissue without making a heavy investment. Says Raymond: "I must have looked at a dozen different ways we could increase our output. When I wrote up the results, I thought about discussing all the options I'd evaluated, but then it occurred to me that management wasn't really interested in the ideas that wouldn't work. So I just talked about the two things we could do to increase capacity."

Notice in Figure 10.5 how Verdugo uses recommendations to organize his discussion. This structure is extremely efficient because it focuses the reader's attention on what needs to be done. You can use a similar approach when you are asked to analyze a problem or an opportunity and draw conclusions, rather than provide recommendations. In such situations, the main headings of the report correspond to your conclusions instead of to your recommendations.

A new business proposal to an outside client

Proposals for obtaining new business typically define a problem and describe the proposed solution.

Proposals to outside clients are attempts to get products, plans, or projects accepted by outside businesses or government clients. The letter in Figure 10.6 also takes a relatively direct approach, but instead of being organized around conclusions or recommendations, it is organized around the statement of a problem and its solution (see pages 262–263). This is a very common approach in proposals. The proposal was prepared by Lia Chung, who works for the Communication Skills Institute, an organization that trains business people to write and speak more effectively.

This particular proposal was submitted to Arnold Hastings, the director of training and development for a rapidly growing management consulting firm that advises small to mid-size companies on organizational issues. In writing the proposal, Chung was relatively sure of a positive response. As she says:

FIGURE 10.5
Sample Justification Report

MEMO

DATE: August 4, 1993

TO: Marshall Boswell, Plant Manager

FROM: Raymond Verdugo, Manufacturing Engineering RV

SUBJECT: Expansion of facial tissue production capacity

The steady increase in facial tissue sales is making it more difficult to keep our inventory levels where they should be for efficient distribution. Our back-order situation has become worse in recent months, and the marketing department is complaining about it. The new plant won't be ready until next March, so we can't expect any relief for at least ten months.

I've studied the product flow on our three facial tissue lines, and I believe we can increase capacity 22 percent by taking two short-term measures that do not require a significant investment:

1. Speed up cut-off machine on #1 line to eliminate bottleneck.
2. Eliminate the green, pine-scented tissue product.

SPEED UP #1 CUT-OFF MACHINE

The bottleneck on #1 line is the old Evans cut-off machine. This unit runs at a speed of only 200 packs per minute. The rest of the #1 line can handle 300 packs per minute, as can line #2.

I propose to speed up the Evans machine by installing a 20-horsepower motor to replace the old 15-horsepower motor, by thickening the transfer bolts, and by replacing two cams. Stress analysis shows that the machine can then safely be run at 300 packs per minute. This change will give us 50 percent more output on line #1 at a cost of roughly $6,500 and one day's lost production.

ELIMINATE GREEN, PINE-SCENTED TISSUE

Eliminating the green, pine-scented tissue is a sensitive subject. I'm aware of your running battle with marketing on this, but I'd like to urge you to try once again to get them to kill this product. When we run it on line #3, we can operate at only 120 packs per minute because the tissue is weakened by the dye and pine perfume. The other colored tissues run on line #3 are capable of 200 packs per minute.

The green pine product constitutes only 4 percent of total tissue sales and, by marketing's own data, sells well only in Maine and northern Minnesota. I have to believe that those customers would buy one of our other colors if we pulled the green pine off the market. If you can swing this, I estimate that we can get another 9 percent out of line #3.

SUMMARY

I recommend the following steps:

1. Speed up #1 line cut-off machine; capital cost = $6,500; output increases from 200 to 300 packs/minute.
2. Eliminate green pine product on #3 line; cost = zero; output increases from 120 to 200 packs/minute.

"This particular proposal was pretty short because I knew that the prospective client would be receptive. We had already discussed the need for such a program and I had outlined our qualifications. The proposal was basically a follow-up to that conversation. However, some of the proposals I write are considerably longer and contain more background on why a program is needed, what the alternatives are, and why a particular choice is best.

"Regardless of their length, all of my proposals have one thing in common: They offer to solve a problem for a specific price. Every time I write one, I follow the same basic formula: (1) Here's the problem, (2) here's the solution, and (3) here's what it will cost."

FIGURE 10.6
Sample New Business Proposal to an Outside Client

OMMUNICATION
SKILLS INSTITUTE

515 Hammond Way, Dallas, TX 75260
(214) 627-1683

May 25, 1993

Mr. Arnold Hastings
Director of Training and Development
The Atlanta Consulting Group
1123 Peachtree Plaza
Atlanta, GA 30304

Dear Mr. Hastings:

As you requested at our meeting last week, I have prepared this written proposal outlining how the Communication Skills Institute can help the Atlanta Consulting Group (ACG) meet its training needs.

THE PROBLEM: UNEVEN SKILLS IN HANDLING
CLIENT RELATIONSHIPS

In the past year ACG has hired 12 new consultants, boosting the firm's total professional staff to 40 people. The new staff members all have excellent qualifications to advise ACG's clients in general business matters. However, some of the new people have relatively little experience in handling client relationships, a skill that is important to their success.

THE SOLUTION: COMMUNICATION SKILLS INSTITUTE
COURSE IN EFFECTIVE SPEAKING AND HUMAN RELATIONS

To help the 12 new members of the ACG professional staff develop their human relations skills, you would like to offer a training program in communication and leadership. Rather than "reinvent the wheel" with an in-house training program, you would like to hire an organization with a proven track record in management education. The Communication Skills Institute is a recognized leader in this field.

Over the past 70 years, literally millions of people have improved their human relations skills by attending Communication Skills Institute training programs. Our courses are offered throughout the United States and in 60 foreign countries.

The Communication Skills Method

Participants are encouraged to learn by doing. Instead of listening to dry lectures, students present reports and talks, engage in friendly competitions, and practice problem-solving

Continued on next page

A troubleshooting report

Whenever a problem exists, someone must investigate it and propose a solution. A troubleshooting report is a decision-oriented document prepared for submission to top management. When you want your readers to concentrate on *why* your ideas make sense, your best bet is to let your logical arguments provide the structure for your report. The main points in your outline correspond to the reasons that underlie your conclusions and recommendations. You support each of these reasons with the evidence you have collected during your analysis.

Gary Johansen, executive assistant to the president of a diversified company, was asked to prepare a report analyzing the performance of the restaurant division. He was also asked to recommend what to do with it: continue the current course, sell off the chain, or remodel existing facilities and build new restaurants.

By using reasons as the main divisions in your outline, you can gradually build a case for your conclusions and recommendations.

FIGURE 10.6
Continued

and decision-making techniques. Applying the lessons in class reinforces the learning process and gives students constructive feedback from instructors.

Anticipated Results of the Program

The Communication Skills course in effective speaking and human relations is ideally suited to the needs of your consulting staff. This course is designed to enhance communication skills and help people develop their leadership potential. Your consultants will be taught how to get better results from meetings and how to gain the cooperation of clients. During the course, the participants will study and practice various techniques to improve their business and personal relationships. They will learn how to handle responsibility, work under pressure, and motivate themselves and others. At the conclusion of the program, they will be more confident and effective in their work.

Instructor's Qualifications

Communication Skills instructors are carefully chosen and well trained. Each is a successful professional with experience directly related to the course. To ensure that the courses are uniform in quality, all instructors undergo a rigorous training program and use the same proven methods and course materials. Your course would be taught by Melissa Steinberg, who has been a Communication Skills instructor for five years. She has a master's degree in psychology from New York University.

Course Scheduling and Costs

The Communication Skills course in effective speaking and human relations consists of 14 sessions, which last approximately 3-1/2 hours each. Classes will be held at your offices on Monday mornings from 9:00 to 11:30 for 14 consecutive weeks. The cost for 12 students will be $9,000.

CONCLUSION

If you have any questions about the course, I would be happy to answer them. You can reach me at my office during working hours by calling (555) 555-8976. I look forward to working with you on this interesting assignment.

Sincerely,

Lia Chung

Ms. Lia Chung
Director

But Gary had a problem: "I knew that whatever I recommended would alienate somebody. My difficulties were compounded by the nature of the problem. I could have made a good case for any of the three options. But as an objective, neutral, and unbiased observer, I gradually came to a conclusion of my own: that we should sell some of the restaurants and use the proceeds to offset the cost of remodeling the remaining locations and adding new outlets. In writing my report, I decided that my strategy would be to build a case for this course of action by gradually presenting the various reasons that had emerged from my analysis of the options."

Figure 10.7 is a copy of Gary's report (see pages 264–266). Notice that the introduction does not reveal his position. Instead of summarizing his recommendations, he begins by discussing the report's purpose and scope, the background of the study, and his methods of research. In the body, he presents the facts in an objective tone, without revealing his own point of view. He saves his recommendations for the fourth section, where he finally adds up all the reasons.

**FIGURE 10.7
Sample
Troubleshooting
Report**

MEMO

DATE: March 27, 1993
TO: Alton Sanders, President
FROM: Gary Johansen, Executive Assistant to the President
SUBJECT: Possibilities for the Restaurant Division in 1999

INTRODUCTION

This report was authorized by President Alton Sanders on January 11, 1993. Its purpose is to analyze the performance of our restaurant division and to recommend a course of action. The analysis does not include institutional food-service operations.

The first Gateway restaurant was opened over 25 years ago in Falls Church, Virginia. Initially, the chain consisted of moderately priced cafeteria-style restaurants located in the suburbs of Washington, D.C. Encouraged by the success of these operations, Gateway management gradually expanded the chain into surrounding states, moving first into the Middle Atlantic and New England areas, then into the Southeast. As the chain grew, the cafeteria format was modified. Although some sites still feature a self-serve buffet, most of the restaurants now provide table service and a complete breakfast, lunch, and dinner menu.

Historically, the restaurant division has been one of Gateway's strongest operations, providing approximately 20 percent of the corporation's sales and 26 percent of its profits for much of the past decade. However, in the past two years, the restaurant division's sales and profits have fallen below expectations. In an attempt to determine why, management has decided to take a closer look at the division's recent performance in light of trends in the restaurant industry as a whole. These issues are examined in the following sections. A final section analyzes the alternatives available to management and presents recommendations for the future.

In preparing this report, the study team analyzed internal data and reviewed published information pertaining to the restaurant industry. The team also analyzed demographic data furnished by the business development agencies of the 21 states in which Gateway restaurants are located. In addition, the team has interviewed over 50 restaurant owners and managers, politicians, civic leaders, and real estate professionals and has surveyed some 1,500 Gateway restaurant patrons.

RECENT PERFORMANCE OF THE RESTAURANT DIVISION

By historical standards, the restaurant division shows signs of slowing down. Instead of growing at the customary rate of 8 to 10 percent each year, the division's sales and profits have edged up by only 3 percent for the past two years (Figure 1).* Despite this leveling off, restaurant operations still account for approximately 25 percent of the corporation's business (Figure 2). Restaurant division sales in the most recent fiscal year totaled $44 million, and profits were $3.9 million.

A closer look at the division's financial results suggests that two internal factors are involved in the restaurant division's relatively slow growth:

--In years past, the growth in sales and profits was fueled by the addition of new restaurants to the chain. However, in the past two years, only three new restaurants have been opened. This record is less than half the average annual rate of openings throughout the 1970s and most of the 1980s (Figure 3).

--Performance has been uneven. Sales have declined in the Middle Atlantic and New England states, where facilities are aging, but sales have increased in the Southeast, where most of the newer restaurants are located (Figure 4).

* To conserve space, the figures are not included with this sample report.   *Continued on next page*

Organizing an analytical report around a list of reasons that collectively support your main conclusions or recommendations is a natural approach to take. Many problems are solved this way, and readers tend to accept the gradual accumulation of evidence, even though they may question one or two points.

However, not every problem or reporting situation can be handled with this organizational plan. Some analytical reports are organized to highlight the pros and cons of a decision; others might be structured to compare two or more alternatives against a set of criteria. The best organizational approach in any given situation depends on the nature of the facts at your disposal. Essentially,

**FIGURE 10.7
Continued**

-2-

These facts suggest that the leveling off in the restaurant division's growth is at least partially attributable to a lack of investment in the chain's facilities rather than to a fundamental
weakness in the chain itself. In fact, a survey of Gateway patrons underscores the restaurants'
continued popularity. Offering moderate prices in a pleasant, family-oriented environment still
has broad appeal. (See Appendix A.)

TRENDS IN THE RESTAURANT INDUSTRY

Although Gateway's restaurant division appears to be fundamentally sound, the flattening of
its growth curve reflects a slowdown in the restaurant industry as a whole. The rate of sales
growth for full-service restaurants has fallen from 5 percent in the early 1980s to roughly 1.1
percent today (Figure 5).[1]

Many analysts contend that this slowing growth reflects a subtle shift in consumer behavior.
In the 1970s and 1980s, as more women joined the work force, eating out became increasingly
common, and restaurants sprang up to satisfy demand. In the past few years, however, the
number of meals eaten in restaurants seems to have reached a plateau. Many people would rather
pop a "gourmet" frozen dinner into the microwave and watch a movie on the VCR than pay restaurant prices.

Whatever the reasons, the leveling out of demand has left too many restaurants vying for too
few patrons, a situation that spells trouble for many participants in the industry. Typically,
when an industry has excess capacity, a shakeout period occurs; weaker companies fail and only
the strong survive. Once the shakeout ends, the survivors generally enjoy a period of higher
sales and profits.

If the restaurant industry follows the usual pattern, the small, independent restaurants will
be most likely to fail. Larger chains can be expected to weather the shakeout because of their superior financial strength. Ultimately, the survivors will be the restaurants with the best locations and the most appealing combinations of food, price, atmosphere, and service.[2]

If a shakeout does occur, our restaurant division should be in a strong position, particularly
in the Southeast. The division's facilities in this region are relatively new, and they are located
in rapidly growing, affluent suburbs (Figure 6). Furthermore, Gateway patrons in the Southeast
are particularly loyal, typically dining at a Gateway restaurant at least twice a month (Appendix
A).

ANALYSIS OF ALTERNATIVES

Management is considering three alternatives for the restaurant division:
--Continue to operate the existing restaurants, but minimize the capital reinvested in the
  business.
--Sell off the chain.
--Upgrade the chain by remodeling older facilities and adding new sites.

The first alternative is certainly viable. Although sales and profits have leveled off, the restaurant division is still a major source of earnings. One could argue that by maintaining the status quo, Gateway can generate approximately $4 million per year in cash to reinvest in other
businesses with higher growth potential. On the other hand, without additional investment the
restaurant division is likely to experience a further erosion as its aging facilities become less and
less appealing to patrons.

1. Steve Whitelaw, "Trends in the Restaurant Industry," speech delivered at the 1991 Western
Restaurant Convention and Exposition, Los Angeles, California.
2. Conrad Hammond, "Recipes for Success in Restaurant Management," Restaurant News, December 1992, 24.

Continued on next page

you choose a structure that matches the reasoning process you used to solve
the problem. The objective is to focus your reader's attention on the rationale
for your conclusions and recommendations.

MAKING REPORTS AND PROPOSALS READABLE

When the time comes to write your report, you face the challenge of finding the
most effective way to communicate your message to an audience. Decisions
about formality and structure affect the way your message will be received and
understood by readers.

FIGURE 10.7
Continued

-3-

The alternative of selling off the division is somewhat more appealing from a financial stand-point. Instead of gradually pulling cash out of the restaurant operation until the business deteriorates, Gateway could sell its holdings immediately while the business is still performing well. The restaurant operation has a market value of approximately $40 million, a sum that would go a long way toward funding management's diversification program. But selling the operation would mean the loss of about a quarter of our sales and profits. Unless management can immediately acquire a business of similar size, this loss would have a severe impact.

The third alternative is to expand and upgrade the restaurant operation in an effort to restore its historical growth pattern. According to division management, such a program would require an investment of approximately $22 million over the next three years for remodeling 20 of the older restaurants and adding 9 new sites (Figure 7). This expansion could result in a 10 percent annual growth in sales and a 12 percent annual growth in profits over the next five years (Figure 8).

The key stumbling block to this alternative is the required allocation of $22 million in invest-ment capital. In the company's most recent strategic plan, management committed itself to a program of diversification into new, higher-growth businesses. The lion's share of the firm's investment funds is being channeled into new areas, leaving very little for shoring up existing operations.

One possible solution would be to sell off several of the restaurant division's existing sites, then use the money to refurbish other locations and add new restaurants to the chain. Discus-sions with real estate professionals suggest that a number of Gateway's older restaurants are located on land that has appreciated greatly in value. Many of these sites were purchased in the early 1970s, when land values were considerably lower than they are today. These same sites tend to be Gateway's oldest, least attractive restaurants, where sales have slipped most dramati-cally. As Figure 9 illustrates, by selling off 7 of the chain's 80 restaurants, Gateway could raise approximately $12.6 million, which is over half the amount required to fund the remodeling and expansion program. The remaining $9.4 million could be obtained by reinvesting the division's annual earnings for three years. Although selling the 7 sites would initially reduce the division's sales and earnings, over a five-year period the loss would be more than offset by gains from new and remodeled locations (Figure 10).

SUMMARY

The restaurant division appears to be fundamentally sound. The fall-off in its sales and earn-ings growth is due largely to a reduction in the cash being reinvested in the business. Although the restaurant industry as a whole is maturing, strong chains like Gateway can expect to achieve continued growth in sales and profits as weaker operations fall by the wayside. By selling off some of its older, less appealing sites and using the cash to refurbish and expand the chain, the restaurant division can resume its historic growth pattern and continue to play a major role in the corporation.

CHOOSING THE PROPER DEGREE OF FORMALITY

Write informal reports in a personal style, using the pronouns "I" and "you."

The issue of formality is closely related to considerations of format, length, and organization. If you know your readers reasonably well and if your memo or report is likely to meet with their approval, you can generally adopt an infor-mal tone. In other words, you can speak to readers in the first person, refer-ring to yourself as "I" and to your readers as "you." This informal, personal approach is often used in brief memo or letter reports, although there are many exceptions.

Being formal means putting your readers at a distance and establishing an objective, businesslike relationship.

Longer reports dealing with controversial or complex information are traditionally handled in a more formal vein, particularly if the audience is a group of outsiders. You achieve this formal tone by using the impersonal style, eliminating all references to "you" and "I" (including "we," "us," and "our"). Borrowed from journalism, the style stresses the reporter's objectivity. However, avoiding personal pronouns may lead to overuse of such phrases as "there is" and "it is," which are not only dull but also wordy.

Even so, formality is more than a matter of personal pronouns; it is a question of your relationship with your audience. When you write in a formal style, you impose a certain distance between you and your readers. You remain businesslike, unemotional, and objective. You use no jokes, no similes or metaphors, and very few colorful adjectives or adverbs. You eliminate your own subjective opinions and perceptions and retain only the objective facts.

The formal style does not guarantee objectivity, however. In determining the fairness of a report, the selection of facts is far more important than the way they are phrased. If you omit crucial evidence, you are not being objective, even though you are using an impersonal style. In addition, you can easily destroy objectivity by exaggerating and by using overblown language: "The catastrophic collapse in sales, precipitated by cutthroat pricing on the part of predatory and unscrupulous rivals, has jeopardized the very survival of the once-soaring hot-air balloon division." This sentence has no personal references, but its objectivity is highly questionable.

Although the impersonal style has disadvantages, you should use it if your readers expect it.

Despite these limitations, the impersonal style is a well-entrenched tradition. Many readers are uncomfortable with informality in a report. They associate the personal tone with sloppy thinking, lack of objectivity, and excessive familiarity. You can often tell what tone is appropriate for your readers by looking at other reports of a similar type in your company. If all the other reports on file are impersonal, you should probably adopt the same tone yourself, unless you are confident that your readers prefer a more personal style. Most organizations, for whatever reasons, expect an unobtrusive, impersonal writing style for business reports.

For an example of the short but formal report, take another look at Figure 10.7. Because Johansen was dealing with an important and controversial issue, he wanted to give his report a formal tone. To achieve this effect, he used the third person and a manuscript format rather than a memo format. Although the text is only three pages long, the report also has several figures (not shown here), which add to the formality. The final copy includes a cover page and a table of contents that lists the figures as well as the major headings.

DEVELOPING STRUCTURAL CLUES

As you begin to write, remember that readers have no concept of how the various pieces of your report relate to one another. Because you have done the work and outlined the report, you have a sense of its wholeness, and you can see how each page fits into the overall structure. But readers see the report one page at a time. Your job, as you begin to write, is to give readers a preview or road map of the report's structure so that they can see how the parts of your argument relate to one another.

In a short report, readers are in little danger of getting lost. But as the length of a report increases, so do the opportunities for readers to become confused and to lose track of the relationship among ideas. If you want readers to understand and accept your message, you must prevent this confusion. Four tools are particularly useful for giving readers a sense of the overall structure of your document and for keeping them on track as they read: the opening, headings and lists, smooth transitions, and the ending.

The opening

A good opening must do at least three things:

- Introduce the subject of the report
- Indicate why the subject is important
- Give readers a preview of the main ideas and the order in which they will be covered

In the opening, tell readers what to expect and orient them toward your organizational plan.

If you fail to provide readers with these clues to the structure of your report, they will read aimlessly and miss important points, much like drivers trying to find their way through a strange city without a map.

If your audience is skeptical, the opening should downplay the controversial aspects of your message while providing the necessary framework for understanding your report. Here's a good example of an indirect opening, taken from the introduction of a controversial memo on why a new line of luggage has failed to sell well. The writer's ultimate goal is to recommend a shift in marketing strategy.

In the two years since its introduction, the Venturer line has failed to achieve the sales volume that we expected. The disappointing performance of this product line is a drain on the company's total earnings. The purpose of this report is to review the luggage-buying habits of consumers in all markets where the Venturer line is sold so that we can determine where to put our marketing emphasis.

This paragraph quickly introduces the subject of the document (disappointing sales), tells why the problem is important (drain on earnings), and indicates the main points to be addressed in the body of the report (review of markets where the Venturer line is sold), without revealing what the conclusions and recommendations will be.

Headings and lists

Use headings to give readers the gist of your report.

Headings are useful markers for clarifying the framework of a report. They visually indicate shifts from one idea to the next, and when both subheadings and headings are used, they help readers see the relationship between subordinate and main ideas. In addition, busy readers can quickly understand the gist of a document simply by scanning the headings.

Phrase all same-level headings within a section in parallel terms.

Headings within a given section that are of the same level of importance should be phrased in parallel form. In other words, if one heading begins with a verb, all same-level headings in that section should begin with verbs. If one is a noun phrase, all should be noun phrases. Putting comparable ideas in similar terms tells readers that the ideas are related. The only exception might be such descriptive headings as "Introduction" at the beginning of a report and "Conclusions" and "Recommendations" at the end. Many companies specify a

**FIGURE 10.8
Heading Formats
for Reports**

TITLE

The title is centered at the top of the page, underlined, and typed in capital letters. When the title runs to more than one line, the lines should usually be double-spaced and arranged as an inverted pyramid (longer line on the top).

FIRST-LEVEL HEADING

A first-level heading should indicate what the following section is about, perhaps by describing the subdivisions. All first-level headings should be grammatically parallel, with the possible exception of such headings as "Introduction," "Conclusions," and "Recommendations." Some text should appear between every two headings, regardless of their levels.

Second-Level Heading

Like first-level headings, second-level headings should indicate what the following material is about. All second-level headings within a section should be grammatically parallel. Never use only one second-level heading under a first-level heading. (The same is true for every other level of heading.)

Third-Level Heading

A third-level heading should be worded to reflect the content of the material that follows. All third-level headings beneath a second-level heading should be grammatically parallel.

Fourth-Level Heading. Like all the other levels of heading, fourth-level headings should reflect the subject that will be developed. All fourth-level headings within a subsection should be parallel.

Fifth-level headings are generally the lowest level of heading used. However, you can indicate further breakdowns in your ideas by using a list:

1. The first item in a list. You may indent the entire item in block format to set it off visually. Numbers are optional.
2. The second item in a list. All lists should have at least two items. An introductory phrase or sentence may be underlined for emphasis, as shown here.

format for headings. If yours does, use that format. Otherwise, you can use the scheme shown in Figure 10.8.

Setting off important ideas in a list provides an additional structural clue. Lists can show the sequence of ideas or visually heighten their impact. Like headings, list items should be phrased in parallel form.

> Use lists to set off important ideas and to show sequence.

Transitions

Such phrases as "to continue the analysis," "on the other hand," and "an additional concept" are another type of structural clue. Transitions like these tie

Use transitions consisting of a single word, a few words, or a whole paragraph to provide additional structural clues.

ideas together and keep readers moving along the right track. Here is a list of some words and phrases frequently used to provide continuity between parts of sentences and paragraphs:

Additional detail	moreover, furthermore, in addition, besides, first, second, third, finally
Causal relationship	therefore, because, accordingly, thus, consequently, hence, as a result, so
Comparison	similarly, here again, likewise, in comparison, still
Contrast	yet, conversely, whereas, nevertheless, on the other hand, however, but, nonetheless
Condition	though, if
Illustration	for example, in particular, in this case, for instance
Time sequence	formerly, after, when, meanwhile, sometimes
Intensification	indeed, in fact, in any event
Summary	in brief, in short, to sum up
Repetition	that is, in other words, as has been stated

As director of the Red Cross's risk management division, Gregory L. Daniels gets reports generated by a computerized information system. However, it is his own communication style—his ability to articulate difficult concepts to a diverse audience—that has led to his success. One key to clarity, says Gregory, is to strengthen the connections among your ideas by using good transitions.

Although transitional words and phrases are useful, they are not sufficient, in themselves, to overcome poor organization. Your goal is to put your ideas in a strong framework and then to use transitions to link them together even more strongly.

In longer reports, transitions that link major sections or chapters are often complete paragraphs that serve as mini-introductions to the next section or as summaries of the ideas presented in the section just ending. Here's an example:

Given the nature of this problem, the alternatives are limited. As the following section indicates, we can stop making the product, improve it, or continue with the current model. Each of these alternatives has advantages and disadvantages. The following section discusses pros and cons of each of the three alternatives.

The ending

Re-emphasize your main ideas in the ending.

Research shows that the final section of a report leaves a strong and lasting impression, so use the ending to emphasize the main thrust of your message. In a memo or report written in direct order, you may want to remind readers once again of your key points, conclusions, or recommendations. If your report is written in indirect order, you should end (except in short memos) with a summary of key points. In analytical reports, you should end with conclusions and recommendations as well as key points. In general, the ending ties up all the pieces and reminds readers how those pieces fit together. It provides a final opportunity to emphasize the wholeness of your message.

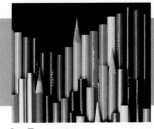

CHECKLIST FOR SHORT, INFORMAL REPORTS

A. Format

☐ 1. For brief external reports, use letter format, including a title or a subject line after the reader's address that clearly states the subject of the document.

☐ 2. For brief internal reports, use memo or manuscript format.

☐ 3. Present all short, informal reports properly.
- ☐ a. Single-space the text.
- ☐ b. Double-space between paragraphs.
- ☐ c. Use headings where helpful, but try not to use more than three levels of headings.
- ☐ d. Call attention to significant information by setting it off visually with lists or indention.
- ☐ e. Include visual aids to emphasize and clarify the text.

B. Opening

☐ 1. For short, routine memos, use the subject line of the memo form and the first sentence or two of the text as the introduction.

☐ 2. For all other short reports, cover these topics in the introduction: purpose, scope, background, restrictions in conducting the study, sources of information and methods of research, and organization of the report.

☐ 3. If using direct order, place conclusions and recommendations in the opening.

C. Body (Findings and Supporting Details)

☐ 1. Use direct order for informational reports to receptive readers, developing ideas around subtopics (for example, chronologically, geographically, categorically).

☐ 2. Use direct order for analytical reports to receptive readers, developing points around conclusions or recommendations.

☐ 3. Use indirect order for analytical reports to skeptical or hostile readers, developing points around logical arguments.

☐ 4. Use an appropriate writing style.
- ☐ a. Use an informal style ("I" and "you") for letter and memo reports, unless company custom calls for the impersonal third person.
- ☐ b. Use an impersonal style for more formal short reports in manuscript format.

☐ 5. Maintain a consistent time frame by writing in either the present or the past tense, using other tenses only to indicate prior or future events.

☐ 6. Give each paragraph a topic sentence.

☐ 7. Link paragraphs by using transitional words and phrases.

☐ 8. Strive for readability by using short sentences, concrete words, and terminology that is appropriate for your readers.

☐ 9. Be accurate, thorough, and impartial in presenting the material.

☐ 10. Avoid including irrelevant and unnecessary details.

☐ 11. Include documentation for all material quoted or paraphrased from secondary sources, using a consistent format.

D. Ending

☐ 1. In informational reports, summarize major findings at the end, if you wish.

☐ 2. Summarize points in the same order in which they appear in the text.

☐ 3. In analytical reports using indirect order, list conclusions and recommendations at the end.

☐ 4. Be certain that conclusions and recommendations follow logically from facts presented in the text.

☐ 5. Consider using a list format for emphasis.

☐ 6. Avoid introducing new material in the summary, conclusions, or recommendations.

SUMMARY

Preparing the final draft of a report involves decisions on length, format, and organization. Short, informal reports often take the form of memos or letters; longer, more formal reports are presented in manuscript form.

When readers are receptive or open-minded, you may present your ideas in direct order, with the main point first. When readers are hostile or skeptical, use indirect order, presenting key findings, conclusions, and recommendations last. Informational reports are organized around subtopics. Analytical reports are organized around conclusions or recommendations or around a logical argument.

The task of organizing a report is not complete until you decide on the proper degree of formality and develop such structural clues as the opening, headings, lists, transitions, and ending.

ON THE JOB:
Solving a Communication Dilemma
at Motown Records

In attempting to keep the reinvigorated Motown at the forefront of popular music, Jheryl Busby has a number of things going for him. For starters, the music business is booming. Moreover, Motown itself has plenty of residual strength, including several superstars, a well-known brand name, a valuable library of old hits, and plenty of financial backing from MCA and Boston Ventures. The firm also has a strong leader in Busby, who is, as insiders say, "one of the top executives in the business, with an ability to make things happen."

Growth in the music business as a whole should give Motown a real boost. After slumping in the 1980s, sales of recorded music are growing every year in the United States and worldwide. Listeners around the world buy over $20 billion worth of LPs, cassettes, and compact discs (CDs) every year. The advent of the Sony Walkman and its imitators fueled the demand from people who listen to music as they jog, walk, run, and otherwise exercise. Cassettes account for the greatest percentage of all album-length music sold in the United States, although CD sales continue to gain momentum.

With the advent of CD players, the mix of buyers of recorded music has shifted. Traditionally, the pop music industry has been geared toward teenagers. But older buyers have started buying CDs too, so record stores are finding that over half of their sales are now made to adults. Many of these buyers are replacing their old LPs with re-releases in CD format—a trend that is especially beneficial for Motown, with its extensive library of old favorites.

But there's more to the revival in the music business than golden oldies. Listeners have plenty of new sounds to entice them, from rap and hip-hop to New Age to grunge rock. In almost every segment of the business, talented new performers are capturing attention.

Busby is committed to turning Motown's young performers into major forces in contemporary music. Summing up his philosophy, he says he views his mission as "developing artists' careers rather than selling records." He believes that artists have to develop an image, identify a target market, and promote themselves consistently and aggressively. In Busby's estimation, Motown's number one challenge is to find and cultivate new musical artists. His goal is to be tops in all forms of black music, from pop and soul to rap, gospel, and jazz. At the same time,

though, he does not plan to ignore the general market. The Motown label has always transcended racial barriers, and Busby aims to keep it that way.

Busby also has plans for the Motown brand name. A name that famous has to be good for more than just music, so why not license it for a line of clothing, for example. Busby has been approached for everything from a Motown theme park to special Motown Edition automobiles. As he says, "There are endless opportunities." And business reports will continue to play a key role in the successful management of Motown.

Your Mission: You have recently joined Motown as Jheryl Busby's administrative assistant. Your job is to help him with a variety of special projects. During an average week, he might ask you to handle three or four assignments and then report back to him in writing. In the following situations, choose the *best* communication alternatives from among those listed:

1. Busby has asked you to do some research on trends in the retailing of recorded music. He is specifically interested in the growth of large retailing chains like Tower Music and Wherehouse. He wants to know what problems and opportunities might be created for Motown by the growing dominance of these chains. Which approach, direct or indirect, should you use in writing your report on this subject? Choose between the two introductions shown below.

a. Recognizing that major changes are occurring in recorded music retailing, Motown management has decided to investigate how these changes will affect the company's distribution and marketing operations. Specifically, management wants to review two issues:

   1. Who are the key players in the industry, and what are their business strategies?
   2. How can Motown best utilize the various distribution channels for recorded music?

   The following pages present the results of a two-week study of these questions.

b. Major changes are occurring in recorded music retailing. Large specialized chains like Tower

Music, Musicland, and Wherehouse are gaining market share at the expense of smaller, independent retailers. Furthermore, large mass merchandisers like Wal-Mart, K mart, and Target are competing for the music-buyer's dollar. Many small shops will undoubtedly fail during the current shakeout; others will survive by carving out special niches that the larger chains and mass merchandisers cannot fill.

The growing dominance of the specialized chains and mass merchandisers is generally a favorable development for Motown because these stores can be serviced more efficiently than the small independent retailers. However, independents will continue to play an important role in Motown's distribution network, given the nature of our product line and the demographics of our customers. These conclusions are examined in detail in the following pages.

2. Motown's majority owner, Boston Ventures, has asked Busby to provide a brief overview of several major competitors in the recorded music business: A&M, Atlantic, BMG, Capitol, Elektra, Geffen, MCA, and Sony. This information will be handed out to the investors at a meeting in Boston. Some of these people know very little about the music business. Busby has asked you to write a brief informational memo on the subject, and he wants you to cover the following points for each label: (1) its biggest-selling artists in the last year, (2) its most promising rising star, and (3) the names of key managers and producers. You have very little time to prepare, but you'll just have to go with whatever facts you can find. Which of the following versions is preferable?

   a. The eight companies in question, A&M, Atlantic, BMG, Capitol, Elektra, Geffen, MCA, and Sony, have been a mixed bag, performance-wise, in the last year. Big sellers include Sting, Amy Grant, Extreme, and Bryan Adams (A&M); Skid Row, AC/DC, and Genesis (Atlantic); Whitney Houston and Alan Jackson (BMG); Garth Brooks, Hammer, and Bonnie Raitt (Capitol); Metallica, Natalie Cole, and Motley Crue (Elektra); Aerosmith, Guns N' Roses, and Nirvana (Geffen); Guy, Ralph Tresvant, Heavy D, and Jodeci (MCA); and Mariah Carey, C+C Music Factory, Michael Bolton, Public Enemy, Harry Connick, Jr., Luther Vandross, Ozzy Osbourne, and Michael Jackson (Sony).

   Here is each label's most promising rising star: A&M--Soundgarden; Atlantic--no one in

particular shows great promise to break out of the pack in the next year; BMG--Stacy Earl; Capitol--Blind Melon; Elektra--Ephraim Lewis; Geffen--Teenage Fan Club; MCA--Lyle Lovett; Sony--Pearl Jam.

Finally, here are some of the leading figures behind the artists at each label: A&M--Al Cafaro; Atlantic--Sylvia Rhone and Danny Goldberg; BMG--Joe Galante; Capitol--Hale Milgrim; Elektra--Bob Krasnow; Geffen--John Kalodner, Tom Zutaut, and Gary Gersh; MCA--Al Teller; Sony--Donny Ienner.

   b. Here are the biggest sellers, the most-promising new artists, and the names of key executives or producers at eight of our competitors (the names of other labels owned by the same company are shown in parentheses):

   A&M: Sting, Amy Grant, Extreme, and Bryan Adams did very well in the last year. Soundgarden looks promising. The top executive is Al Cafaro.

   Atlantic (EastWest/Atco): Atlantic had an off year; Skid Row, AC/DC, and Genesis were the biggest sellers, but they didn't match Atlantic's output in recent years. We've been unable to identify any strong newcomers. Sylvia Rhone is CEO of EastWest/Atco; we don't have data on the current executive staff at parent Atlantic, other than knowing that Danny Goldberg will be joining the executive ranks.

   BMG (Arista, RCA, Jive Records): The BMG family is "floundering" in the words of one observer. The best they've done is with Whitney Houston, KLF, and country stars Alan Jackson and Clint Black. The most promising is Stacy Earl. Joe Galante is chief executive.

   Capitol: Country superstar Garth Brooks has two smash albums for Capitol, and albums from Hammer and Bonnie Raitt are doing well also. The best hope for next year is Blind Melon. Capitol's top executive is Hale Milgrim.

   Elektra: Elektra's best performers are Metallica, Natalie Cole, and Motley Crue. Ephraim Lewis promises to be tomorrow's rising star. Bob Krasnow heads Elektra.

   Geffen (DGC): Geffen continues to score big with three rock groups: Aerosmith, Guns N' Roses, and Nirvana. Geffen's top newcomer is Teenage Fan Club. Three important executives are John Kalodner, Tom Zutaut, and Gary Gersh.

   MCA: MCA's black-music division continues to be hot, with hit albums from Guy, Ralph Tresvant, Heavy D, and Jodeci. Lyle Lovett should break out of his cult following and move into the popular mainstream this year. Al Teller is a key executive.

Sony (Columbia, Epic): Sony's labels have had some big successes recently: Mariah Carey, C+C Music Factory, Michael Bolton, Public Enemy, Harry Connick, Jr., Luther Vandross, Ozzy Osbourne, and Michael Jackson. Pearl Jam looks like a winner in the near future. Donny Ienner is a top producer at Columbia.

c. Here's the lowdown on the poor hapless souls that Motown will continue to mow down in the next year:

A&M: Sting, Amy Grant, Extreme, and Bryan Adams are hot. Soundgarden looks promising. The head honcho at A&M is named Al Cafaro.

Atlantic (EastWest/Atco): Atlantic had a dog of a year; Skid Row, AC/DC, and Genesis were the biggest sellers, but they didn't match Atlantic's output in recent years. We don't think Atlantic has any newcomers with much promise. Sylvia Rhone is CEO of EastWest/Atco; we don't have data on the current executive staff at parent Atlantic, other than knowing that Danny Goldberg will be joining the executive ranks.

BMG (Arista, RCA, Jive Records): The BMG family is "floundering," in the words of one observer. The best they've done is with Whitney Houston, KLF, and country yokels Alan Jackson and Clint Black. The most promising is Stacy Earl. Joe Galante is chief executive.

Capitol: Country boy Garth Brooks has two smashes, and albums from Hammer and Bonnie Raitt are cookin' also. The best hope for next year is Blind Melon (who names these groups, anyway?). Capitol's top cat is Hale Milgrim.

Elektra: Elektra's best performers are Metallica, Natalie Cole, and Motley Crue (an odd mix, huh?). Ephraim Lewis promises to be tomorrow's rising star. Bob Krasnow heads Elektra.

Geffen (DGC): Geffen continues to score big with three monster groups: Aerosmith, Guns N' Roses, and Nirvana. Geffen's top newcomer is Teenage Fan Club. Three top executives are John Kalodner, Tom Zutaut, and Gary Gersh.

MCA: MCA's black-music division continues to be hot, with hit albums from Guy, Ralph Tresvant, Heavy D, and Jodeci. Lyle Lovett should break out of his cult following and move into the popular mainstream this year. Al Teller is a key executive.

Sony (Columbia, Epic): Sony's labels have had some big successes recently: Mariah Carey, C+C Music Factory, Michael Bolton, Public Enemy, Harry Connick, Jr., Luther Vandross, Ozzy Osbourne, and Michael Jackson. Pearl Jam should join these heavy hitters in the near future. Donny Ienner is a top producer at Columbia.

3. Jheryl Busby wants to promote the Motown label by creating a TV special on the company's history. He has talked with the head of MCA's television group about cooperating on the project. The MCA executive is excited about the concept and has asked Busby to send him "something in writing." Busby has asked you to draft the proposal, which should be no more than ten pages long. Which of the following outlines should you use?

a. First version

    I. An overview of Motown's history
       A. How company was founded
       B. Major groups and their top songs
       C. Sale of Motown to MCA/Boston Ventures
    II. The Motown TV special
       A. Performers to be included
       B. Sequence of musical numbers
       C. Staging and production arrangements
       D. Costs
       E. Production schedule
    III. Pros and cons of producing a Motown TV special

b. Second version

    I. Introduction: Purpose and overview of the Motown TV special
       A. Program content
       B. Anticipated benefits
       C. Estimated cost (general)
    II. Description of the program
       A. Format, theme, and staging
       B. Sequence of performers and musical numbers
       C. Production schedule
       D. Support requirements
          1. Facilities
          2. Equipment
          3. Personnel
    III. Detailed cost estimates
    IV. Next steps
    V. Summary

c. Third version

Who: Motown and MCA television group
What: Motown TV special
When: October 13
Where: Los Angeles or Detroit?
Why: To promote Motown label
How: Overview of schedule, facilities, personnel, and costs

d. Fourth version
  I. Introduction: The rationale for producing a TV special celebrating Motown's history and contributions to popular music
     A. Program would make money
     B. Program would boost sales of Motown label
     C. Program would boost morale of Motown's performers and help company attract new musical acts
     D. Program would honor great names in history of black music
  II. Program description
     A. Master of ceremonies, nonmusical guests
     B. Musical performers and sequence of songs
     C. Staging of numbers
     D. Location of show
  III. Production plan
     A. Organization of project
     B. Timing and sequence of steps
     C. Facilities
     D. Personnel
  IV. Detailed cost estimate
  V. Summary of costs and benefits

4. Busby has asked you to give some thought to the problem of attracting new musical talent. You have talked with a number of aspiring musical groups to get some idea of what they're looking for in a recording company. During these conversations, you have discovered that the main problem facing most new groups is money. You believe that Motown would have a tremendous advantage over other recording companies if it could offer new groups a more attractive financial package. As a relatively junior person at Motown, you are a little apprehensive about suggesting your idea. You don't want to seem presumptuous, but on the other hand, you think you are really on to something. You have decided to raise the issue with Busby. Which of the following approaches is preferable?

a. You recently asked me to give some thought to how Motown might attract new musical talent. I decided to sound out a number of aspiring groups to get a feel for what they're looking for in a recording company. Over the past three weeks, I have discussed this subject with 25 promising acts. Interestingly enough, all of them agree on one point: The thing they want and need the most is more financial support.

The Stapleheads are typical of the groups I talked with; they told more or less the same story as everyone else, and I must say, it's a discouraging tale. The Stapleheads started their group seven years ago when they were in high school in Chicago. For several years, they worked in local clubs and were well received by audiences and critics. In 1986, EMI offered them a five-record contract. They signed--then they took a look at the fine print. Under the terms of their contract, they must reimburse EMI for all the expenses associated with cutting the albums. Furthermore, their royalties are low--$1 per disk--and the royalties don't kick in until after 150,000 records are sold.

The Stapleheads' first album, Hallowed Halls, cost $65,000 to make. Although it was critically acclaimed, it sold only 80,000 copies, not enough to kick in the royalties. The group decided to spend a bit more producing their second album, hoping that the investment would pay off. They hired a big-name producer and also cut a video, which was aired on MTV, spending a total of $120,000. Again, they got rave reviews and few sales. Their third album, which was just released, cost them another $120,000 to produce. The group will have to sell 400,000 records just to pay the recording costs.

The Stapleheads are trying to build their reputation by going on tour. But touring is expensive too. EMI fronts the expenses, but again, the Stapleheads must reimburse the company. The group earns $1,000 a night playing in clubs, but their income is more than offset by their touring costs, which average $1,500 a day, including food, lodging, and transportation.

With one thing and another, the Stapleheads currently owe EMI $500,000. They have almost no hope of getting out of the hole. They don't own cars, they live with their parents, and they think a hamburger is a real extravagance. Theirs is not an easy life, but they plan to stick it out as long as they can. They believe in their music.

A person has to wonder whether there isn't a better way to go about this business. If Motown could offer these young groups a better financial deal, the company would have an enormous advantage in attracting talent.

b. In response to your request, I have investigated ways in which Motown could increase its ability to attract new musical groups. In conducting this investigation, I have talked with some 25 aspiring musical groups over a three-week period. The groups were all quite consistent in their comments regarding recording companies.

A typical group spends approximately ten years building its reputation. During that period, the group generally covers its expenses by "borrowing" from its recording company.

The recording company puts up the money for recording an album, which may cost anywhere from $60,000 to $150,000. The musical group is expected to pay the company back from the proceeds of the album. Once the production costs are recovered, the group starts to earn a royalty. For new groups, royalties are generally quite low--$1 per album is typical. Often, the albums do not sell well enough to cover production costs, so the group ends up owing the recording company money. Most recording company contracts cover several albums. After recording three or four albums, a group may owe the company as much as $500,000 in recording costs.

Recording companies also put up money to cover a group's touring costs, which average approximately $1,500 per night for a four-person rock band. Here again, the group generally loses money because most new bands receive only about $1,000 per night for performing.

If a group ultimately succeeds, the recording company gets its investment money back and makes a great deal besides. If not, the contract is generally canceled, and the group's debt is wiped off the recording company's books.

Recording companies lose money on many of the groups they finance, and they expect to. The companies are hardly guilty of rapacious deal-making. On the contrary, without their support, only independently wealthy musicians could ever become rock stars. However, looking at the situation from the standpoint of the new musical groups, it often appears that the recording companies are the villains.

The thing that most aspiring groups want more than anything else is a better financial deal. If Motown could figure out some way to give it to them without losing money in the process, it would have a tremendous competitive advantage in attracting new talent.

c. Instead of sending a memo, arrange a conference with Busby, the Stapleheads, yourself, and one or two of Motown's other artists to present the issues firsthand.[3]

QUESTIONS FOR DISCUSSION

1. If a report is pushing strongly toward a specific recommendation, should the writer include information that might support a different recommendation? Why or why not?
2. What would you do if your boss asked you to alter or destroy a report that might be used as evidence in legal proceedings?
3. How do you explain the fact that so many kinds of documents qualify as reports? What makes them all reports?
4. What are the advantages and disadvantages of the direct and the indirect approaches?
5. Why do some companies require an impersonal tone in their reports? What are the advantages and disadvantages of such a tone?
6. How can a writer help readers understand the structure of a report?

EXERCISES

1. List three entry-level positions for which you will be qualified after graduation; then list the types of reports that you might be responsible for preparing in each position.
2. Interview several people working in a career that you might like to enter. Ask them about the types of written reports they receive and prepare. How do these reports tie into the decision-making process?

Who reads the reports they prepare? Summarize your findings in writing to your instructor, and be prepared to discuss them with the class.
3. Motown's Jheryl Busby (see this chapter's On-the-Job simulation) has asked you to write a memo on the background and current status of Johnny Gill, one of Motown's top recording stars. The following is the first draft of your memo; how can you improve it?

Contents in Brief

CONTENTS

PART TWO: THE WRITING PROCESS

Chapter Three:

Planning Business Messages   46

Chapter Four:

Organizing and Composing Business Messages   67

Chapter Seven:

Writing Routine, Good-News, and Goodwill Messages 147

Chapter Eight:

Writing Bad-News Messages 180

PART FOUR: REPORTS AND PROPOSALS

Chapter Twelve:

Writing Long Reports 304

PART FIVE: EMPLOYMENT MESSAGES

Chapter Thirteen:

Writing Resumes and Application Letters 354

PART SEVEN: SPECIAL TYPES OF BUSINESS COMMUNICATION

Chapter Seventeen:

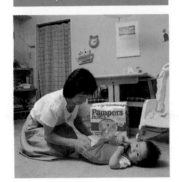

Intercultural Business Communication 452

Chapter Eighteen:

Business Communication Technology 471

CHECKLISTS

Preface

Excellence in Business Communication, Second Edition, provides an exciting and dynamic new way of bringing the real world into the classroom. This is the first textbook that offers business communication experience through real-world simulations featuring actual companies. These simulations provide a unique opportunity for students to apply concepts to real events and to sharpen their business communication problem-solving skills.

Students are introduced to a cross section of real people—men and women who work for some of America's most fascinating companies and who, on a typical day, encounter a variety of communication problems. In each chapter, students are asked to help these businesspeople find solutions to their communication problems. Moreover, students find it easy to relate to the highly visible companies featured, including such well-respected giants as McDonald's, Mattel, Coca-Cola, B. Dalton, and Ben & Jerry's, to name just a few.

Excellence in Business Communication is the next step in the evolution of business communication textbooks. Of course, this text covers all the basic principles and presents them in a traditional sequence. But its real-life simulations, involving writing style, and eye-opening graphics all bring the subject to life, capturing the essence of business communication as no other text has done before. We believe this book will instill in students both respect for the field of business communication and confidence that the subject can be understood and mastered.

The textbook itself is the centerpiece of a comprehensive teaching and learning package that targets a single goal: to demonstrate how business communication works in the real world, thus helping students understand the concepts behind effective communication while developing and refining their own abilities.

Features Link Concepts to the Real World

Excellence in Business Communication, Second Edition, paints a vivid picture of the world of business communication. It offers an overview of the wide range of communication skills that are used by businesspeople to present ideas clearly and persuasively. It also gives specific examples of the communication techniques that have led to sound decision making and effective teamwork. In addition, its insights into the way organizations operate help clarify student career interests by identifying the skills needed for a lifetime of career success.

Because it encourages students to view themselves as part of an actual organization when completing assignments, *Excellence in Business Communication* is the next best thing to on-the-job training. It shows how standard approaches to routine assignments can help business professionals complete work quickly and efficiently. But it also stresses that every situation is different and advises students to think for themselves.

On-the-Job Simulations The opportunity to learn by doing is what sets this textbook apart from others. Not only do students learn from other people's successes and failures, they also make "on the job" decisions about communication problems. To understand our commitment to this concept, glance at the table of contents. You'll also see that this textbook was written with the cooperation of many small and large businesses, including General Motors, Campbell Soup, Lawrence County Hospital, Motown Records, and Metropolitan Life.

Each chapter opens with an exclusive concept, On the Job: Facing a Communication Dilemma. This slice-of-life vignette summarizes a communication problem being faced by an actual company. The solution to the dilemma is found in the concepts presented in the chapter, and the dilemma reappears from time to time throughout the chapter to dramatize the connection between the principles discussed and life on the job.

But we don't stop there. Each chapter ends with another exclusive feature, On the Job: Solving a Communication Dilemma. These simulations are factually based on real companies, and they expand on the chapter-opening dilemma. Students are asked to solve the dilemma by applying the principles discussed in the text, by making decisions about the communication process, and by selecting the best alternatives from the choices offered. Not only do these simulations give students the opportunity to practice real-world decision making, they also tie the textual information to real-life examples, providing a concrete basis for analyzing the chapter principles.

Finally, the dilemma is dealt with in one of the exercises or cases so that each On-the-Job simulation spans the entire chapter. This feature provides a dimension of reality unmatched by other textbooks in the field.

Behind the Scenes Special Features Boxed and carefully placed within each chapter, Behind-the-Scenes sidebars extend the chapter material by focusing on real people, real products, and real companies. We personally interviewed accomplished business communicators at actual companies to provide insights into the business world that cannot be found in other textbooks. Eighteen Behind-the-Scenes special features bring even more of the world of business into the classroom. Examples include

- Behind the Scenes at America West: Navigating Bad News

- Behind the Scenes at Federal Express: When It Absolutely, Positively, Has to Be Perfect

- Behind the Scenes at IBM: Secrets to Winning an Interview

The discussion questions at the end of each of these special features give students numerous opportunities to analyze business communication principles and practices.

Gallery of Business Communication Professionals Another unique feature of this text is the inclusion of full-color photographs with incisive captions that focus on 72 highly successful communication professionals from business, industry, government, and the media. Among the individuals featured are Paul Fireman (Reebok), John Sculley (Apple), Michael Eisner (Disney), Dan Rather (CBS News), and Sandra Day O'Connor (U.S. Supreme Court).

Strategically placed in the margins throughout each chapter, these captions with accompanying photographs expand the amount of insight to be gained from this book. Each caption relates specifically to the text and gives a communication expert's views about a particular aspect of business communication, adding a new dimension to student learning.

Example after Example of Letters, Memos, and Reports Throughout *Excellence in Business Communication*, Second Edition, you'll find numerous up-to-date sample documents, many collected in our

consulting work. These superb business examples provide students with benchmarks for achievement.

The chapters on letters and memos contain outstanding examples from numerous types of organizations and from people working in a variety of functional areas. Many of these documents are fully formatted, and some are presented on the letterheads of such well-known companies as TWA, JC Penney, Kentucky Fried Chicken, General Mills, and Mattel Toys. Accompanying sentence-by-sentence analyses help students see precisely how to apply the principles discussed in the text. Poor and improved examples illustrate common errors and effective techniques for correcting them.

The report-writing chapters give numerous examples too. And the last chapter of the report unit illustrates the step-by-step development of a long report, which appears in its entirety to show how all the parts fit together.

Focus on Ethics throughout the Book Business communication is more than speaking persuasively and writing clearly. It is also how you listen, respond, and interact with others. Everything you say, whether verbal or nonverbal, communicates something about your values and ethics. Thus students should be given the means to anticipate and analyze the ethical dilemmas they will face on the job. Moreover, the adherence to high ethical standards takes on new importance in this age of wavering business behavior. Ethical questions addressed in this book include

- How far should you go in emphasizing the positive in business messages?

- How should you handle negative information in recommendation letters?

- Where do you draw the line between persuasion and manipulation when writing sales letters?

- How do you construct visual aids in a form that will convey a company's point of view without misleading the audience?

Excellent Coverage of Today's Most Important Topics According to several surveys, recent graduates are not prepared to handle the full range of communication assignments that come across their desks. *Excellence in Business Communication* addresses that problem in two ways: (1) by emphasizing basic principles that can be applied to many diverse situations and (2) by including coverage of such important topics as organizational communication, the writing process, listening, nonverbal communication, and intercultural business communication.

The boundaries of business communication are always expanding. So in addition to covering all the traditional subjects, *Excellence in Business Communication*, Second Edition, examines many current topics. For example, because technology is so advanced and so important in today's business world, we have provided an up-to-date chapter on office technology. The book also contains an unparalleled discussion of employment-related topics, including indispensable techniques for getting a job in our service-oriented economy. In addition, the text covers these current issues:

- What the *Valdez* oil spill taught companies about handling crisis communication (Chapter 2)

- How the stock market crash of October 13, 1989, has been "euphemized" out of existence (Chapter 4)

- How McDonald's pizza test-marketing exemplifies the effective use of press releases (Chapter 7)

- What the 1989 San Francisco earthquake taught companies about communicating bad news (Chapter 8)

- How oat bran in cereals demonstrates the importance of tracking changes in federal law when writing sales letters (Chapter 9)

- What effects changes such as the reunification of Germany and the collapse of the Soviet Union are having on international business communication (Chapter 17)

- How office technology has affected the Chinese movement toward democracy since the Tiananmen Square massacre (Chapter 18)

Tools That Help Develop Skills and Enhance Comprehension

Having an accurate picture of how businesspeople communicate is important, but students need more if they are to develop usable skills. That's why, in *Excellence in Business Communication*, Second Edition, we've included a number of helpful learning tools.

Lively, Conversational Writing Style   Read a few pages of this textbook; then read a few pages of an-

other textbook. We think you'll immediately notice the difference.

The lucid writing style in *Excellence in Business Communication* makes the material pleasing to read and easy to comprehend. It stimulates interest and promotes learning. The writing style also exemplifies the principles presented in this book. In addition, we have carefully monitored the reading level of *Excellence in Business Communication* to make sure it's neither too simple nor too difficult.

Checklists   To help students organize their thinking when they begin a communication project, make decisions as they write, and check their own work, we've included numerous checklists throughout the book. Appearing as close as possible to the related discussion, the checklists are reminders, not "recipes." They provide useful guidelines for writing, without limiting creativity. Students will find them handy when they're on the job and need to refresh their memory about effective communication techniques.

Documents for Analysis   In this textbook we have provided a selection of documents that students can critique and revise—24 documents in 9 chapters. Documents include letters and memos, a letter of application, and a resume. This hands-on experience in analyzing and improving sample documents will help students revise their own.

Exercises and Cases   A wealth of exercises and cases, many of them memo-writing tasks, provide assignments like those that students will most often face at work. The exercises and cases deal with all types and sizes of organizations, domestic and international. And we have written them for a variety of majors: management, marketing, accounting, finance, information systems, office administration, and many others. With such variety to choose from, students will have ample opportunity to test their problem-solving skills.

Excellence in Business Communication, Second Edition, includes numerous cases featuring real companies. Examples include

- Green and gone: Letters explaining that orders for Rubbermaid's litterless lunch kit will be late

- Satisfaction guaranteed: Letter from L. L. Bean granting a claim

- On second thought—don't express it: Memo requesting cooperation in cutting the cost of overnight mail delivery at Turner Broadcasting System

- Naturally soothing: Letter describing the contents of the Body Shop By Mail's stress kit

- Crayola classics: Memo announcing new washable crayons and the reissue of eight old favorites

These cases are yet another tool for demonstrating the role of communication in the real business world.

Learning Objectives Each chapter begins with a concise list of goals that students are expected to achieve by reading the chapter and completing the simulations, exercises, and cases. These objectives are meant to guide the learning process, motivate students to master the material, and aid them in measuring their success.

Margin Notes Short summary statements that highlight key points and reinforce learning appear in the margins of *Excellence in Business Communication*, Second Edition. They are no substitute for reading the chapters but are useful for quickly getting the gist of a section, rapidly reviewing a chapter, and locating areas of greatest concern.

Chapter Summaries Each chapter ends with a concise overview. We have included the summaries to help students understand and remember the relationships among key concepts.

End-of-Chapter Discussion Questions Questions for Discussion are designed to get students thinking about the concepts introduced in each chapter. The questions may also prompt students to stretch their learning beyond the chapter content. Not only will students find them useful in studying for examinations, but the instructor may also draw on them to promote classroom discussion of issues that have no easy answers.

Appendixes *Excellence in Business Communication*, Second Edition, contains four appendixes:

1. FUNDAMENTALS OF GRAMMAR AND USAGE. A primer in brief, Appendix A presents the basic tools of language. The format is concise and easy to read, presenting material on grammar, punctuation, mechanics, and vocabulary.

2. FORMAT AND LAYOUT OF BUSINESS DOCUMENTS. Appendix B discusses formatting for all types of documents in one convenient place. Topics include appearance and formatting of letters, envelopes, memos, time-saving messages, reports, and meeting documents.

3. DOCUMENTATION OF REPORT SOURCES. Appendix C presents information on conducting secondary research and gives basic guidelines for handling reference citations, bibliographies, and source notes.

4. CORRECTION SYMBOLS. Appendix D provides convenient symbols for students to use when revising documents.

Color Art and Strong Visual Program To enliven the book and heighten student interest, *Excellence in Business Communication* is the first text in this market to be printed in full color throughout. We believe you'll agree that the book has been attractively printed and that the dramatic use of color gives it exceptional visual appeal. Also, in each chapter, students learn from a rich selection of carefully crafted illustrations—graphs, charts, tables, and photographs—that demonstrate important concepts.

Book Design The state-of-the-art design is based on extensive research and invites students to delve into the content. It also makes reading easier, reinforces learning, and increases comprehension. For example, the special features do not interfere with the flow of text material, a vital factor in maintaining attention and concentration. The design of this book, like much communication, has the simple objective of gaining interest and making a point.

A Teaching/Learning Package That Meets Real Needs

The instructional package for this textbook is specially designed to simplify the task of teaching and learning. The instructor may choose to use the following supplements.

Instructor's Resource Manual This comprehensive paperback book is an instructor's toolkit. Among the many things it provides are a wealth of supplementary tidbits of information for enriching lectures, a section about collaborative writing, suggested solutions to exercises, suggested solutions and fully formatted letters for *every* case in the letter-writing chapters, and a grammar pretest and posttest.

An audiovisual guide is also included in the manual. It lists hundreds of videotapes and films that can be used to supplement your course. Each entry is fully described and keyed to the textbook.

The *Instructor's Resource Manual* also has an answer key to selected exercises in the *Study Guide*.

Video Exercises   Now you can add an exciting new dimension to your course with seven professionally produced videos, one for each part of the text. Developed by the authors specifically for this book, these business communication video exercises are easy to use and are closely integrated with the content of the text to help students successfully apply important concepts and principles.

For the instructor, *Video Exercise Teaching Notes* include teaching objectives, a list of the concepts covered in the video, discussion questions, and suggested answers to the discussion questions and video exercises.

Test Bank   This manual is organized by text chapters and includes a mix of multiple-choice, true-false, and fill-in questions for each chapter, approximately 1,500 objective items in all, carefully written and reviewed to provide a fair, structured program of evaluation.

You can also get the complete test bank on computer disk, or you can get even more flexibility with McGraw-Hill's phone-in customized test service.

Testing Services   Two major programs are available:

1. COMPUTERIZED TEST BANK FOR *EXCELLENCE IN BUSINESS COMMUNICATION*, SECOND EDITION. A powerful microcomputer program allows the instructor to create customized tests using the questions from the test bank, self-prepared items, or a combination. This versatile program incorporates a broad range of test-making capabilities, including question editing and scrambling to create alternative versions of a test. This program is available for both MacIntosh and IBM computers.

2. CUSTOMIZED TEST SERVICE. Through its Customized Test Service, McGraw-Hill will supply adopters of *Excellence in Business Communication*, Second Edition, with custom-made tests of items selected from the test bank. The test questions can be renumbered in any order. Instructors will receive an original test, ready for reproduction, and a separate answer key. Tests can be ordered by mail or by phone, using a toll-free number.

Acetate Transparency Program   A set of 100 large-type transparency acetates, available to adopters on request, helps bring concepts alive in the classroom and provides a starting point for discussing communication techniques. All transparencies are keyed to the *Instructor's Resource Manual*, and many contrast poor and improved solutions to cases featured in the textbook.

Film/Video Library   McGraw-Hill will arrange free rentals of numerous films and videos from the University of Illinois Media Library. To guide you in selecting these materials, an extensive list keyed to the parts of the book is included in the *Instructor's Resource Manual* along with details about how to order them.

Report Card: Classroom Management Software   This software makes compiling students' grades accurate and easy and is available for both IBM PC/PC-XT and Apple II.

Business Communication Update Newsletter   Issued four times a year and filled with stimulating ideas, this newsletter is written exclusively for instructors of business communication. The newsletter provides interesting materials that can be used in class, and it offers practical ideas about teaching methodology.

Study Guide   This paperback book contains a wealth of material reinforcing the information presented in the textbook. Students who are interested in maximizing their learning will appreciate its fill-in-the-blank chapter outlines, self-scoring quizzes on chapter contents, skill-building exercises, supplementary readings, and vocabulary and spelling exercises. In addition, to help students brush up on their English skills, the study guide includes an extensive review of grammar, punctuation, and mechanics interspersed with reinforcement exercises.

Computer Software for Students   The instructor may also choose to use our interactive software, *Activities in Business Communication*. Three modules—dealing with job-search strategies, vocabulary development, and writing style—contain innovative learning activities. All the modules are interactive learning tools, so students are continually reinforced by word and sound. Also available is the McGraw-Hill College Version of WordPerfect for the IBM PC and compatibles. It assists composition on a word processor and permits inserting, deleting, or moving text; correcting; automatic formatting; and storing material. For additional information on software, videos, and other ancillary materials, please contact your McGraw-Hill sales representative.

Personal Acknowledgments

Excellence in Business Communication is the result of the concerted efforts of a number of people. A heartfelt thanks to our many friends, acquaintances, and business associates who agreed to be interviewed so that we could bring the real world into the classroom.

Our thanks to Terry Anderson, whose outstanding communication skills and organizational ability assured this project's clarity and completeness.

We are grateful to Jackie Estrada for her expert assistance and sound advice; to Bonnie Blake, Purdue University, for her remarkable talents and valuable contributions; to Lecia Archer for her unique insights and perspectives; to Lianne Stevens for her tenacity and inventiveness; and to Marie Painter for her diligence and specialized skills in word processing.

We also feel it is important to acknowledge and thank the Association for Business Communication, an organization whose meetings and publications provide a valuable forum for the exchange of ideas and for professional growth.

The insightful comments and helpful suggestions of the individuals who reviewed the manuscript for this book were invaluable as was the feedback from adopters. Thanks to Anita S. Bednar, Central State University; Donna Cox, Monroe Community College; Sauny Dills, California Polytechnic State University—San Luis Obispo; Charlene A. Gierkey, Northwestern Michigan College; Sue Granger, Jacksonville State University; Bradley S. Hayden, Western Michigan University; Michael Hignite, Southwest Missouri State; Cynthia Hofacker, University of Wisconsin–Eau Claire; Louise C. Holcomb, Gainesville College; Larry Honl, University of Wisconsin–Eau Claire; Kenneth Hunsaker, Utah State University; Robert O. Joy, Central Michigan University; Paul Killorin, Portland Community College; Al Lucero, East Tennessee State University; Rachel Mather, Adelphi University; Betty Mealor, Abraham Baldwin College; Mary Miller, Ashland University; Richard Profozich, Prince George's Community College; Brian Railsback, Western Carolina University; John Rehfuss, California State University—Sacramento; Joan C. Roderick, Southwest Texas State University; Jean Anna Sellers, Fort Hays State University; Carla L. Sloan, Liberty University; Michael Thompson, Brigham Young University; Betsy Vardaman, Baylor University; Billy Walters, Troy State University; George Walters, Emporia State University; F. Stanford Wayne, Southwest Missouri State; Robert Wheatley, Troy State University; Rosemary B. Wilson, Washtenaw Community College; and Beverly C. Wise, SUNY–Morrisville.

We also want to extend our warmest appreciation to the very devoted professionals at McGraw-Hill. They include June Smith, Bonnie Binkert, Seib Adams, Dan Loch, Lee Medoff, Safra Nimrod, Dundee Holt, and the outstanding McGraw-Hill sales representatives. Finally, we thank editor Bob Greiner for his dedication and expertise, and we are grateful to copyeditor Alice Jaggard and designer Jack Ehn for their superb work.

John V. Thill
Courtland L. Bovée

PART ONE

FOUNDATIONS OF BUSINESS COMMUNICATION

After studying this chapter, you will be able to

- Explain how nonverbal and verbal communication convey meaning
- Describe the process of communication
- Explain how misunderstandings can arise during the communication process
- Describe the special difficulties of business communication
- Explain how to overcome common communication barriers

UNDERSTANDING BUSINESS COMMUNICATION

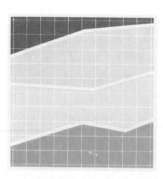

ON THE JOB:
Facing a Communication Dilemma at Ben & Jerry's Homemade
Serving Up Ice Cream and a Strong Social Message

Every company communicates with customers, employees, and various other groups. But for Ben & Jerry's Homemade, of Waterbury, Vermont, communication has a special importance. The company makes more than premium ice cream; it makes an unusual effort to operate as a force for social change. This mission presents Ben & Jerry's with some unusual communication challenges.

Co-founders Ben Cohen and Jerry Greenfield wanted to start an ice cream parlor and then sell it once the business got going. But something always forced them to keep at it—a new competitor or the need to replace or fix equipment. Almost in spite of itself, Ben & Jerry's grew beyond its founders' expectations. But Cohen and Greenfield didn't want to run a conventional company. The pair aren't satisfied with a narrow pursuit of profit. They want their company not only to contribute to society but also to help save the rain forests, encourage conservation, help family farmers, and so on.

However, this plan involves several communication challenges. Perhaps the most important is keeping the founders' vision alive as the company grows bigger and bigger. Back when the operation involved only Cohen, Greenfield, and a handful of employees, communicating with employees regarding the company's social goals was a fairly easy task. But with more employees, more suppliers, customers spread across the nation, and even stockholders (once the company went public and began selling stock to investors), communication has become a big challenge indeed. Just one example: Cohen and Greenfield worry that some of the managers they've hired have lost touch with the original message and are more interested in racking up profits than in helping society.

How can Cohen and Greenfield use communication to keep their vision alive in the minds of customers, employees, and investors? What is the process of communication, and how can the managers at Ben & Jerry's use it to keep the company true to the founders' vision? How can misunderstandings arise in business communication, and how can Ben & Jerry's avoid them?[1]

THE BASIC FORMS OF COMMUNICATION

Ben & Jerry's Homemade

As Cohen and Greenfield are well aware, effective communicators have many tools at their disposal when they want to get across a message. Whether writing or speaking, they know how to put together the words that will convey their meaning. They reinforce their words with gestures and actions. They look you in the eye, listen to what you have to say, and think about your feelings and needs. At the same time, they study your reactions, picking up the nuances of your response by watching your face and body, listening to your tone of voice, and evaluating your words. They absorb information just as efficiently as they transmit it, relying on both nonverbal and verbal cues.

NONVERBAL COMMUNICATION

The most basic form of communication is nonverbal. Anthropologists theorize that long before human beings used words to talk things over, our ancestors communicated with one another by using their bodies. They gritted their teeth to show anger; they smiled and touched one another to indicate affection. Although we have come a long way since those primitive times, we still use nonverbal cues to express superiority, dependence, dislike, respect, love, and other feelings.[2]

Nonverbal communication differs from verbal communication in fundamental ways. For one thing, it is less structured, which makes it more difficult to study. A person cannot pick up a book on nonverbal language and master the vocabulary of gestures, expressions, and inflections that are common in our culture. We don't really know how people learn nonverbal behavior. No one teaches a baby to cry or smile, yet these forms of self-expression are almost universal. Other types of nonverbal communication, such as the meaning of colors and certain gestures, vary from culture to culture.

Nonverbal communication also differs from verbal communication in terms of intent and spontaneity. We generally plan our words. When we say "please open the door," we have a conscious purpose. We think about the message, if only for a moment. But when we communicate nonverbally, we often do so unconsciously. We don't mean to raise an eyebrow or blush. Those actions come naturally. Without our consent, our emotions are written all over our faces.

Nonverbal communication has few rules and often occurs unconsciously.

Why nonverbal communication is important

Although nonverbal communication is often unplanned, it has more impact than verbal communication. Nonverbal cues are especially important in conveying feelings, accounting for 93 percent of the emotional meaning that is exchanged in any interaction.[3]

One advantage of nonverbal communication is its reliability. Most people can deceive us much more easily with their words than they can with their bodies. Words are relatively easy to control; body language, facial expressions, and vocal characteristics are not. By paying attention to these nonverbal cues, we can detect deception or affirm a speaker's honesty. Not surprisingly, we have more faith in nonverbal cues than we do in verbal messages. If a person says one thing but transmits a conflicting message nonverbally, we almost invariably believe the nonverbal signal.[4] To a great degree, then, an individual's credibility as a communicator depends on nonverbal messages.

Nonverbal communication is important for another reason as well: It can be efficient from both the sender's and the receiver's standpoint. You can transmit a nonverbal message without even thinking about it, and your audience can register the meaning unconsciously. By the same token, when you have a conscious purpose, you can often achieve it more economically with a gesture than you can with words. A wave of the hand, a pat on the back, a wink—all are streamlined expressions of thought.

> *Nonverbal communication is more reliable and more efficient than verbal communication.*

The functions of nonverbal communication

Although nonverbal communication can stand alone, it frequently works with speech. Our words carry part of the message, and nonverbal signals carry the rest. Together, the two modes of expression make a powerful team, augmenting, reinforcing, and clarifying each other.

Experts in nonverbal communication suggest that it has six specific functions:

> *People use nonverbal signals to support and clarify verbal communication.*

- To provide information, either consciously or unconsciously

- To regulate the flow of conversation

- To express emotion

- To qualify, complement, contradict, or expand verbal messages

- To control or influence others

- To facilitate specific tasks, such as teaching a person to swing a golf club[5]

Nonverbal communication plays a role in business too. For one thing, it helps establish credibility and leadership potential. If you can learn to manage the impression you create with your body language, facial characteristics, voice, and appearance, you can do a great deal to communicate that you are competent, trustworthy, and dynamic. For example, Ben Cohen and Jerry Greenfield have developed an informal style that puts people at ease and sets the tone for the kind of business they want to run.

> *By controlling the nonverbal messages you send, you can project the image you desire.*

Furthermore, if you can learn to read other people's nonverbal messages, you will be able to interpret their underlying attitudes and intentions more accurately. When dealing with co-workers, customers, and clients, watch carefully for small signs that reveal how the conversation is going. If you aren't having the effect you want, check your words; then, if your words are all right, try to be aware of the nonverbal meanings you are transmitting. At the same time, stay tuned to the nonverbal signals that the other person is sending.

> *By watching for nonverbal cues, you can get a more accurate picture of others.*

VERBAL COMMUNICATION

Although you can express many things nonverbally, there are limits to what you can communicate without the help of language. If you want to discuss past events, ideas, or abstractions, you need words—symbols that stand for thoughts—arranged in meaningful patterns. In the English language, we have a growing pool of words—currently about 750,000, although most of us recognize only about 20,000 of them.[6] To create a thought with these words, we arrange them according to the rules of grammar, putting the various parts of speech in the proper sequence.

We then transmit the message in spoken or written form, hoping that someone will hear or read what we have to say. Figure 1.1 shows how much time business people devote to the various types of verbal communication. They use speaking and writing to send messages; they use listening and reading to receive them.

> Language is composed of words and grammar.

Speaking and writing

When it comes to sending business messages, speaking is more common than writing. Giving instructions, conducting interviews, working in small groups, attending meetings, and making speeches are all important activities, and you'll learn more about them in Chapters 15 and 16. Even though writing may be less common, it is important too. When you want to send a complex message of lasting significance, you will probably want to put it in writing. Thus Chapters 6 through 12 deal with writing letters, memos, and reports.

Listening and reading

Although this book focuses on writing and speaking, it's important to remember that effective communication is a two-way street. People in business spend more time obtaining information than transmitting it, so to do their jobs effectively, they need good listening and reading skills. Unfortunately, most of us are not very good listeners. Immediately after hearing a ten-minute speech, we typically remember only half of what was said. A few days later, we've forgotten three-quarters of the message.[7] To some extent, our listening problems stem from our education, or lack of it. We spend years learning to express our ideas, but few of us ever take a course in listening.

Similarly, our reading skills often leave a good deal to be desired. Recent studies indicate that approximately 38 percent of the adults in the United

> Effective business communication depends on skill in receiving messages as well as on skill in sending them.

FIGURE 1.1
Forms of Business Communication

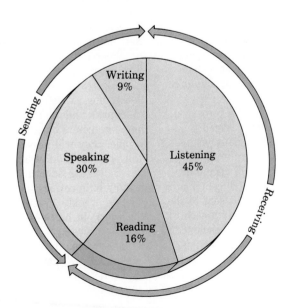

States have trouble reading the help-wanted ads in the newspaper, 14 percent cannot fill out a check properly, 26 percent can't figure out the deductions listed on their paychecks, and 20 percent are functionally illiterate.[8] Even those who do read may not know how to read effectively. They have trouble extracting the important points from a document, so they cannot make the most of the information presented.

As a college student, you are probably better at listening and reading than are many other people, partly because you get so much practice. On the basis of your own experience as a student, you no doubt realize that your listening and reading efficiency varies tremendously, depending on how you approach the task. Obtaining and remembering information takes a special effort.

Although listening and reading obviously differ, both require a similar approach. The first step is to register the information, which means that you must tune out distractions and focus your attention. You must then interpret and evaluate the information, respond in some fashion, and file away the data for future reference.

The most important part of this process is interpretation and evaluation, which is no easy matter. While absorbing the material, you must decide what is important and what isn't. One approach is to look for the main ideas and the most important supporting details, rather than trying to remember everything you read or hear. If you can discern the structure of the material, you can also understand the relationships among the ideas.

If you're listening as opposed to reading, you have the advantage of being able to ask questions and interact with the speaker. Instead of just gathering

> To absorb information, you must concentrate, evaluate, and retain what you read or hear.

BEHIND THE SCENES AT FEDERAL EXPRESS
When It Absolutely, Positively Has to Be Perfect

As senior manager of Federal Express's LBE (Latrobe, Pennsylvania) Station, Jon Sutton helps bring to life an automated system that picks up and delivers over 1 million priority packages every day. Air express delivery is big business—with revenues exceeding $10 billion annually. Federal Express has become the runaway leader in handling such freight by combining state-of-the-art technology with clear and effective interpersonal communication.

When you dial toll-free to a Federal Express call center to start your package on its way, someone answers you within three rings, despite a daily volume of 250,000 calls. The customer service representative places your pickup order in the COSMOS computer system and sends it on-line to the dispatch center at a station near you. From there, the order is sent to the courier over DADS, a mobile unit linked with each Federal Express van, and your package is scheduled for pickup. When the courier arrives, he or she runs an on-line scanner over your package's number, letting

COSMOS know where it is. Then every step of delivery is tracked as the package travels through the system: to the sending station, the airplane, the airport sorting hub, the receiving station, the delivering courier, and finally the recipient.

People make this hi-tech system work. Sutton uses a variety of communication skills to help his 52-member team meet both management's and customers' demanding expectations: 100-percent perfection. "The company's philosophy, People-Service-Profits, is the key," he points out. "If you take good care of your people, they will provide good service, which in turn will provide Federal Express with a profit."

To take good care of his people, Sutton relies heavily on meetings: face-to-face meetings with individuals, weekly 15-minute work-group meetings to get the word out on things that affect the couriers or customer service agents, and informal monthly meetings with the work groups to bring out issues on a more human scale. "That's the time to tell it like it is," says

information, you can cooperate in solving problems. This interactive process requires additional listening skills, which are discussed in Chapter 17.

THE PROCESS OF COMMUNICATION

Whether you are speaking, writing, listening, or reading, communication is more than a single act. It is a chain of events that can be broken into five phases:

> The communication process consists of five phases linking sender and receiver.

1. The sender has an idea.

2. The idea becomes a message.

3. The message is transmitted.

4. The receiver gets the message.

5. The receiver reacts and sends feedback to the sender.

Then the process is repeated until both parties have finished expressing themselves. Communication is effective only when each step is successful.

THE SENDER HAS AN IDEA

The world constantly bombards us with information: sights, sounds, scents, and so on. Our minds filter this stream of sensation and organize it into a

---

Sutton. "You don't like the way I part my hair? You want to know why something is done the way it is? You can suggest a change in a van's route to improve our efficiency? Speak up!" Sutton understands that people are often reluctant to bring up problems, so he prompts discussions by starting with something like, "I overheard someone say . . ."

Nonverbal techniques play an equally important role. "Watching is very important to me," says Sutton. A person's facial expression or behavior lets Sutton know how things are going. And he shows his own feelings: "Just a subtle look, a glance, or a hint of action can often get my point across without having to say anything."

About written communication, Sutton says he usually writes only memos and then only when "procedures change or when I want to praise someone or something, update people, remind them of something, or clarify a point." He doesn't want any misunderstandings when it affects his team's work.

To succeed as a manager, Sutton advises, you first have to know how to listen: "Always, always listen. And I mean listen to everything, both verbally and nonverbally." Beyond that, he recommends that you should be willing to talk about anything: "You have to be able to discuss matters openly to get to the bottom of a problem and get it resolved." Such an approach

will help you run a pressure operation flawlessly. At Federal Express, this approach is expected to work 100 percent of the time.

APPLY YOUR KNOWLEDGE

1. How should Jon Sutton handle these problems: (a) There are areas in certain courier routes where communications via the DADS computer unit are cut off. (b) A new courier picks up the package at one office in a building on his route, but he unknowingly misses the pickup at two other offices in the same building. (c) A seasoned courier leaves a small package in the back of his van when he returns to the station, clocks out, and goes home. Which communication techniques are most appropriate to use in each situation?

2. In the past three months you've become disappointed in the pace and outcome of your monthly open-forum meetings. No one speaks up, and no suggestions are made; people just eye each other nervously, seeming anxious to get it over with and get back to work. What would you do to encourage greater participation? What specific communication techniques would you use? Include at least two strategies each of oral, written, and nonverbal communication.

All ideas are simplifications and abstractions of reality, filtered through the individual mind.

mental map that represents our perception of reality. In no case is the map in a person's mind the same as the world itself, and no two maps are exactly alike. As you view the world, your mind absorbs your experiences in a unique and personal way. For example, if you and a friend go out for a pizza, each of you will mentally grasp different things. One of you may notice the coolness of the air-conditioning as you enter the restaurant; the other may notice the aroma of pizza or the music from the sound system.

Because your perceptions are unique, the ideas that you want to express are different from other people's. Even when two people have experienced the same event, their mental images of that event will not be identical. As a communicator, you filter out the details that seem unimportant and focus your attention on the most relevant and general, a process known as abstracting.

You also make assumptions and draw conclusions, even though you cannot directly verify those assumptions. You assume, for example, that the music in the pizza parlor comes from a sound system, although you cannot see it as you enter the door. Often your inferences are correct, but sometimes they are not. Thus, in the process of conceiving an idea, you leave out many things and assume many others. This means that the idea in your mind is a simplification of the real world, so whenever you send a message, you inevitably distort reality.

THE IDEA BECOMES A MESSAGE

In a process not completely understood, the idea in your mind is transformed into words; you decide such issues as the message's length, organization, tone, and style. You can express an idea in an almost infinite number of ways, but something makes you choose one approach over another. For example, you may decide to say, "The man was driving a car," rather than, "The old geezer was poking along in a beat-up green 1982 Ford." Your choice of words depends on your subject, your purpose, your audience, and your personal style or mood.

Any given idea may be expressed in many ways, depending on your
- Subject
- Purpose
- Audience
- Personal style or mood
- Cultural background

To some extent, your choice of words also depends on your cultural background. If you are a government bureaucrat, you might say, "Expedited adjustment assistance may be ineffective in helping the industry cope with current problems of severe inventory overhang, low prices, and financial losses." That sort of language is considered appropriate in some bureaucracies. On the other hand, if you're a straightforward manager, you might say, "Even a swift government bailout won't save us from going broke." When you choose your words, you signal that you are a member of a particular club and that you know the code.

The nature of your code—your language and vocabulary—imposes its own limits on your message. For example, Eskimos are unable to express the difference between a car and a motorcycle. They use the same word for both. But their language has at least 30 separate terms for snow. Similarly, the language of a lawyer differs from that of an accountant or a doctor, and the difference in their vocabularies affects their ability to recognize and express ideas.

THE MESSAGE IS TRANSMITTED

The third step in the communication process is physical transmission of the message from sender to receiver. The channel may be nonverbal or verbal,

Now in his mid-20s, Johnny Gill's voice has been making music for nearly two decades. His first group was called by the name "Johnny Gill and the Wings of Faith." As you probably guessed from the name, it was a gospel group.

Gill is now one of the popular music's top recording stars. He has also been successful singing duets with former schoolmate--and former Atlan-

tic Records star--Stacy Lattisaw, now another of Motown's current greats.

Before becoming a solo star, Johnny replaced Bobby Brown (who has gone on to a great solo career as well) in the group New Edition. He was a solo and duet act with Atlantic Records prior to that.[4]

CASES

1. That's class: Personal report on class activities
You may have experienced a peculiar or particularly interesting discussion in class and had trouble telling friends why it was so notable. Here's your chance to practice.

Your task: Prepare a memo, addressed to a friend, about the discussion in one of your classes. Use made-up names to identify the instructor and students. Try to show how ideas took shape and what conclusions resulted from this discussion.

2. "Would you carry it?" Sales proposal recommending a product to a retail outlet
Select a product you are familiar with, and imagine that you are the manufacturer trying to get a local retail outlet to carry it.

Your task: Write a sales proposal in letter format to the owner (or manager) of the store, proposing that the item be stocked. Making up some reasonable figures, tell what the item costs, what it can be sold for, and what services your company provides (return of unsold items, free replacement of unsatisfactory items, necessary repairs, and the like).

3. Who's best? Report comparing job candidates
Imagine that you're the interviewer for a company you have selected. You have just interviewed three people for the position of personnel management trainee.

Your task: Write a report in memo format to Mona Martin, director of personnel. In it, you must describe the three candidates (use three friends) and recommend them, in rank order, for the position. Consider at least the following areas for comparison: education, experience, and personal attributes.

4. Taste test: Report on the results of consumer research
Here's your chance to check the advertising claims of soft-drink manufacturers. Blindfold four or five friends (one at a time), and ask them to taste several competing soft drinks.

Your task: After you have conducted the test, write a memo that summarizes your findings. Could your friends tell the difference between the soft drinks? If so,

how did they describe the difference? Did they seem to prefer one of the brands? Did the order in which they tested the drinks seem to have any bearing on the results? You might also address the problem of whether soft drinks without sugar or caffeine taste as good to your friends as drinks containing these ingredients.

5. Mansfield Center or Cat Spring? Report comparing potential plant locations
Current plant capabilities are inadequate for manufacturing Victory Valves' new line of gate valves, globe valves, check valves, ball valves, and butterfly valves. The company is seeking a new location removed from the strains of rapid urbanization and union pressures but still close to potential markets. Two locations have been proposed: Mansfield Center, Connecticut, and Cat Spring, Texas. Fellow members of the site-selection committee (you're in charge) submitted the following raw data about these two locations:

- *Mansfield Center, Connecticut.* An attractive town of about 5,000 near the Mansfield Hollow Reservoir, with rivers and forested recreation areas. Good schools, with moderately expensive housing available. Tax rates generally low and subject to negotiation; the town might forgive taxes during a three- to five-year start-up period. Adequate rail and road transportation available. Located within 50 miles of markets in Hartford, Providence, Springfield, Worcester, and New Haven. Energy costs ranging from average to high, and rising. Experienced factory workers available. Steel must be brought in by rail, probably from Pennsylvania or the Chicago-Gary area. Moderate climate. The University of Connecticut, at nearby Storrs, might provide research facilities and assistance, as well as a supply of seasonal workers. In this heavily industrialized area, valves are in constant demand, but the presence of nearby competitors would force heavy price competition.
- *Cat Spring, Texas.* A tiny, dry town about 50 miles from the Gulf of Mexico; conveniently located on the Houston–Fort Worth rail line. Real estate prices low and taxes minuscule. Adequate labor available from the Houston and Dallas–Fort Worth areas, but housing would have to be built to accommodate the

influx of workers. Local schools presently inadequate for any increase from workers' families but could presumably be expanded. Steel from Europe arrives at the port of Houston and could be delivered economically by rail to Cat Spring. The climate is hot and dry nine months of the year, making air conditioning of the plant necessary. Markets in Houston, Waco, Fort Worth, Dallas, and Austin are all about 200 miles away. The need for our type of valves appears to be growing as industrialization increases in southern Texas. Electricity and water are expensive, although recent developments in solar power appear to be reducing the costs of air-conditioning.

Your task: Write a memo in which you recommend one of the two locations and justify your recommendation. The report has been requested by Ron Wasserman, chief executive officer of Victory Valves, Inc.

6. On the books: Report on improving the campus bookstore
Imagine that you are a consultant hired to improve the profits of your campus bookstore.

Your task: Visit the bookstore and look critically at its operations. Then draft a memo offering recommendations to the bookstore manager that would make the bookstore more profitable, perhaps suggesting products that the store should carry, hours that the store should remain open, or added services that the store should make available to students. Be sure to support your recommendations.

7. With an eye toward change: Report on converting a building to a new use
The company you work for, Video Vendors, Inc., has just bought an abandoned fast-food restaurant with the intention of converting it to an outlet for renting and selling videotapes and video equipment. You are a planning specialist with Video Vendors, and it's your job to outline the architectural changes that will be necessary for successful remodeling.

Your task: Visit any fast-food restaurant in your area and draw a diagram that shows its current use of indoor and outdoor space. Next, determine the architectural changes that will be necessary to convert the building into a video outlet, the major fixtures that must be removed, and the major items that must be purchased. Present your findings in a memo to Angelica Smythe, vice president of planning for Video Vendors, Inc. Include a diagram showing the proposed layout of the video outlet.

8. Prospects for growth: Report on a small firm
Choose a small independent business in your area, and assume that the owners have hired you to help them approach a local bank for financial help with their expansion. The bank will require a complete financial statement and a brief narrative description of the business, covering such topics as the length of time it has been operating, its chief product lines and services, the size of its market area, its usual mix of customers, and the general prospects for growth in its neighborhood.

Your task: Draft the report that you will submit to the bank for your client. Several paragraphs of objective writing will be sufficient, and no financial figures are necessary because they will appear in accompanying financial statements. Remember that your job is to describe the business, not to recommend that the bank lend money to it.

■ CHAPTER ELEVEN

After studying this chapter, you will be able to

- Define the problem to be solved by studying and outlining the issues to be analyzed
- Prepare a work plan for conducting the investigation, planning the necessary steps, estimating their timing, and deciding on the sources of information required
- Organize the research phase of the investigation, including the identification of secondary and primary sources of data
- Draw sound conclusions and develop practical recommendations
- Develop a final outline and visual aid plan for the report

PLANNING LONG REPORTS

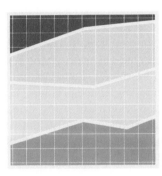

ON THE JOB:
Facing a Communication Dilemma at Harley-Davidson

Getting Harley Back on the Road

When the Japanese began selling heavyweight motorcycles in the United States in the early 1970s, Harley-Davidson remained calm. The Milwaukee company controlled 99.7 percent of the market and saw no reason to panic. After all, if your customers love your product so much that they tattoo your logo on their chests, can't you count on their loyalty?

But the company was mistaken. The Harley was no longer the superb machine it once was. It leaked oil, vibrated like a jackhammer, and broke down frequently. Harley's older customers patiently pulled apart their motorcycles and rebuilt them correctly, but younger riders were not so forgiving. They increasingly chose the trouble-free, smooth-riding imports, and Harley's market share eventually tumbled to 23 percent.

Although Harley's new chairman, Vaughn Beals, had never ridden a motorcycle, he recognized a company with a serious problem. If Harley couldn't make its existing line of bikes correctly, how was it going to introduce competitive new models? At the heart of Harley's difficulties were its outmoded manufacturing systems, which dated from Harley's days as a small, family-owned firm. When Harley tried to increase production to meet the import threat, those systems collapsed.

Beals knew that things had to change. But like any good manager, he knew that wholesale change couldn't take place without the careful research and analysis that would answer countless questions about issues ranging from factory design to inventory control to customer service. If you were in charge of writing reports on these issues, how would you go about planning them? What steps would you take to define each problem, do the research, and analyze the data necessary for such reports?[1]

DEFINING THE PROBLEM

Harley-Davidson

The first step in writing a report is to narrow the focus of your investigation.

Whether you're employed by Harley-Davidson or by another business, you usually have some work to do before you begin to write a report. Even if you're preparing a strictly informational report that does nothing more than transmit facts, you must still gather those facts and arrange them in a convenient format. However, your first step is to write a statement of the problem. You must decide what information you need to complete your report. Let's say you've been asked to study the extent of drug and alcohol abuse by assembly-line workers in your company's main plant. All you've been asked to do is to make a factual report on what is happening.

Before conducting your investigation, you have to decide on a few boundaries for your report. For example, are you going to study the source and distribution of drugs and alcohol in the plant, or are you going to disregard the question of where these substances come from? What time period are you going to cover? This month? The past 12 months? The past five years? Your answers to these and similar questions establish the extent of your investigation and, ultimately, the content of your report.

If you're writing an analytical document that interprets facts and draws conclusions about them, you generally shape your investigation by the way you define the problem to be solved. For example, say that you've been asked to analyze the alcohol and drug abuse problem, not just report the facts. Do you try to determine why workers are using drugs and alcohol at the plant and recommend ways to keep them from turning to these substances? Or do you try to determine the impact of drug and alcohol abuse on productivity and product quality, recommending measures to make up for their effects? In other words, exactly what is the problem to be solved? The way you define the problem establishes the framework for your investigation.

ASKING THE RIGHT QUESTIONS

Often, the problem is defined for you by the person who authorizes the report. When this is the case, talk about the objectives of the report before you begin your investigation to ensure that you understand exactly what is required. Find out specifically

- What needs to be determined
- Why the issue is important
- Who is involved in the situation
- Where the trouble is located
- When it started
- How the situation originated

Ted Koppel is anchor of ABC's *Nightline*. He points out that you don't have to become an expert on every subject you undertake, but he urges you to learn enough about the subject you are investigating to pose intelligent questions.

Not all these questions apply in every situation, but asking them helps you clarify the boundaries of your investigation.

DEVELOPING THE STATEMENT OF PURPOSE

Once you've asked some preliminary questions, you should develop a clear written statement of the purpose of your report. Then double-check this state-

Prepare a written statement of your purpose; then review it with the person who authorized the study.

ment with the person who authorized the study. When the authorizer sees the purpose written in black and white, she or he may decide to redirect the study toward other areas.

For example, say you've been asked to evaluate four candidates for the job of personnel director and recommend one to your boss. You might state your purpose in one of three ways:

A study's purpose may be stated in one of three ways.

- *Use an infinitive.* "The purpose of this report is to determine which of four job candidates is best qualified to be personnel director."

- *Use a question.* "This report answers the question, Which of four candidates is best qualified to be personnel director?"

- *Use a declarative statement.* "The best qualified of four job candidates will be selected to serve as personnel director."

Regardless of which form you choose for your statement of purpose, be sure to make the goal of the investigation clear so that you won't be sidetracked into irrelevant issues.

OUTLINING ISSUES FOR ANALYSIS

The second step in report writing is to outline the issues you plan to study.

Once you have defined the problem and established the purpose of the study, you are ready to begin your investigation. To organize the research effort, you need to break the problem into a series of specific questions. This process is sometimes called factoring. Chances are, you already use this approach subconsciously when facing problem. When your car won't start, what do you do? You look at the various possibilities—the battery, the gas, the ignition system—checking one thing at a time until you find the cause. Subdividing the problem like this helps you cover every important aspect.

The process of outlining the issues for analysis enables you to solve a problem methodically, just as outlining a report enables you to write in a systematic way. However, the way you outline an investigation may be different from the way you outline the resulting report; solving the problem is one thing, but "selling" the solution is another.

DEVELOPING A LOGICAL STRUCTURE

Informational and analytical studies are factored differently.

Because any subject can be factored in many ways, your job is to choose the most logical method, the one that makes the most sense. Start by looking carefully at the purpose of your study. Informational assignments are structured differently from analytical assignments.

Be aware, however, that many assignments require both information and analysis. You must therefore be able to discern the overall purpose of the study. If your general goal is to provide background information that someone else will interpret, then an informational outline is appropriate overall, even though subsections of the study may require some analysis to emphasize important facts. If the purpose of your study is to scrutinize the data and generate your own conclusions and recommendations, then you should use an analytical outline overall, even though your opinions must obviously be based on facts. You may use a variety of structural schemes in problem solving, as long as you avoid errors in logic.

Informational assignments

Studies that lead to factual reports with very little analysis or interpretation are generally factored on the basis of subtopics dealing with specific subjects. These subtopics can be arranged in various ways:

Studies that emphasize the discovery and reporting of facts may be factored by subtopic.

- *In order of importance.* Let's say you're reviewing five product lines. You might organize your study in order of sales for each product line, beginning with the line that produces the most revenue and proceeding to the one that produces the least revenue.

- *Sequentially.* If you're studying a process, present your information step by step—1, 2, 3, and so on.

- *Chronologically.* When investigating a chain of events, organize the study according to what happened in January, what happened in February, and so on.

- *Spatially.* If you're studying a physical object, study it left to right, top to bottom, or outside to inside.

- *Geographically.* If location is important, factor your study geographically.

- *Categorically.* If you're asked to review several distinct aspects of a subject, look at one category at a time, such as sales, profit, cost, or investment.

These methods of subdivision are commonly used in the preparation of monitor/control reports, policies and procedures, compliance reports, and interim progress reports.

Analytical assignments

Studies that focus on problem solving may be factored on the basis of hypotheses; those that focus on the evaluation of alternatives may be factored on relative merits.

Studies that result in reports containing analyses, conclusions, and recommendations are generally categorized by a problem-solving method. Hypotheses and relative merits are the two most common structural approaches of this type. When the problem is to discover causes, predict results, or find a solution to a problem, one natural way to proceed is to formulate hypothetical explanations. Let's say your problem is to determine why your company is having trouble hiring secretaries. You would factor this problem by speculating about the reasons; then you would collect information to confirm or disprove each reason. Your outline of the major issues might look something like this:

Why are we having trouble hiring secretaries?
I. Salaries are too low.
   A. What do we pay our secretaries?
   B. What do comparable companies pay their secretaries?
   C. How important is pay in influencing secretaries' job choices?
II. Our location is poor.
   A. Are we accessible by public transportation and major roads?
   B. Is the area physically attractive?
   C. Are housing costs affordable?
   D. Is crime a problem?
III. The supply of secretaries is diminishing.
   A. How many secretaries were available five years ago as opposed to now?
   B. What was the demand for secretaries five years ago as opposed to now?

When the problem is to evaluate how well various alternatives meet your criteria, the natural way to subdivide your analysis is to focus on the criteria. For example, if the problem is to decide where new Harley-Davidson dealerships should be located, you might factor the investigation along the following lines:

Where should we build a new store?
I. Construction costs
   A. Location A
   B. Location B
   C. Location C
II. Labor availability
   A. Location A
   B. Location B
   C. Location C
III. Transportation facilities
   A. Location A
   B. Location B
   C. Location C

Another way of using relative merits is to identify the alternatives first and then analyze how well each alternative meets your criteria.

FOLLOWING THE RULES OF DIVISION

Dividing something physical, like a pie, is much easier than dividing something intangible, like an idea. How do you know that the pieces of an idea are cut in the right size, shape, and number? Over the centuries, scholars have developed a concise set of rules for dividing an idea into components:

Follow the rules of division to ensure that your study will be organized in a logical, systematic way.

- *Choose a significant, useful basis or guiding principle for the division.* For example, you could subdivide production problems into two groups: problems that arise when the machines are turned off and problems that occur when the machines are turned on. However, this basis for breaking down the subject would not be of much use to anyone. A better choice might be dividing the subject into problems caused by human error versus problems caused by machine failure.

- *When subdividing a whole into its parts, restrict yourself to one basis at a time.* If you switch from one basis to another, you get a mixed classification, which can confuse your analysis. Let's say you're subdividing your study of the market for toothpaste according to sales of fluoride versus nonfluoride brands. You would upset the investigation by adding another category to your analysis (say, sales of toothpaste in Alabama). If you are dealing with a long, complex subject, you will no doubt have to use several bases of division before you complete your work, but the shift from one basis to another must be made at a logical point, that is, after you have completed your study of a particular issue. For example, after you have looked at sales of fluoride versus nonfluoride toothpaste, you might then want to look at toothpaste sales by geographic location or socioeconomic group.

- *Make certain that each group is separate and distinct.* The groups must be mutually exclusive, or you will end up talking about the same item under two or more headings. Subdividing a population into males, females, and teenagers wouldn't make any sense, because the categories overlap.

- *Be thorough when listing all the components of a whole.* For example, it would be misleading to subdivide an engine into parts without mentioning the pistons. An important part of the whole would be missing, and the resulting picture of the engine would be wrong.

If you follow these rules, your investigation will be logical, systematic, and complete.

PREPARING A PRELIMINARY OUTLINE

Organize your study by preparing a detailed preliminary outline.

As you go through the factoring process, you may want to use an outline format to represent your ideas (see Figure 11.1). But, you may ask, if a few notes on a piece of paper are enough to guide you, why should you bother with a more formal outline? Perhaps you shouldn't for a short, informal report in memo form. But a preliminary outline does give you a convenient frame of reference for your investigation. And a detailed outline is definitely worth the effort under these circumstances:

- When you are one of several people working on an assignment
- When your investigation will be extensive and will involve many sources and many types of data

FIGURE 11.1
Two Common Outline Formats

ALPHANUMERIC	DECIMAL
I. ________	1.0 ________
A. ________	1.1 ________
B. ________	1.2 ________
1. ________	1.21 ________
2. ________	1.22 ________
a. ________	1.221 ________
b. ________	1.222 ________
3. ________	1.23 ________
C. ________	1.3 ________
II. ________	2.0 ________
A. ________	2.1 ________
1. ________	2.11 ________
a. ________	2.111 ________
b. ________	2.112 ________
2. ________	2.12 ________
3. ________	2.13 ________
B. ________	2.2 ________

TABLE 11.1 Types of Outline Captions

DESCRIPTIVE (TOPICAL) OUTLINE	INFORMATIVE (TALKING) OUTLINE	
	QUESTION FORM	SUMMARY FORM

I. Industry characteristics
  A. Annual sales
  B. Profitability
  C. Growth rate
    1. Sales
    2. Profit
	I. What is the nature of the industry?
	  A. What are the annual sales?
	  B. Is the industry profitable?
	  C. What is the pattern of growth?
	    1. Sales growth?
	    2. Profit growth?
		I. Flour milling is mature industry.
		  A. Market is large.
		  B. Profit margins are narrow.
		  C. Growth is modest.
		    1. Sales growth averages less than 3 percent a year.
		    2. Growth in profits is flat.

■ When you know from past experience that the person who requested the study will revise the assignment during the course of your investigation (and you want to keep track of the changes)

Two widely used systems of outlining, the alphanumeric system and the decimal system, are illustrated in Figure 11.1. Both are perfectly acceptable, but some companies traditionally favor one method over the other. You usually write the captions at each level of your outline in the same grammatical form. In other words, if item I uses a verb, then items II, III, and IV should also use verbs. This parallel construction enables readers to see that the ideas are related, of similar importance, and on the same level of generality. It makes the outline a more useful tool for establishing the table of contents and headings in your final report, and it is considered the correct format by most of the people who might review your outline.

Use the same grammatical form for each group of items in your outline.

When writing the outline, you must also choose between descriptive (topical) and informative (talking) captions. Descriptive captions label the subject that will be discussed, whereas informative captions (in either question or summary form) suggest more about the meaning of the issues (see Table 11.1). Although outlines with informative captions take a little longer to write, they are generally more useful in guiding your work, especially if written in terms of the questions you plan to answer during the study. In addition, they have the advantage of being easier for others to review. If other people are going to comment on your outline, they may not have a very clear idea of what you mean by the descriptive heading "Advertising." But they will get the main idea if you use the informative heading "Cuts in ad budget may explain sales decline."

Informative outlines are generally more helpful than descriptive outlines.

Remember that, at this point, you are only developing a preliminary outline to guide your investigation. Later on, when you have completed your research and are preparing a final outline or a table of contents for the report, you may want to switch from a working outline to an outline that summarizes your findings.

PREPARING THE WORK PLAN

The third step in report writing is the work plan.

Once you have defined the problem and outlined the issues for analysis, you are ready to establish a work plan based on your preliminary outline. If you are preparing this plan for yourself, it can be relatively informal: a simple list of

As senior vice president of marketing and corporate communications at Federal Express, Carole Presley determines the resources needed to solve a problem and gets everybody working together. To coordinate the efforts of nine departments, says Presley, a detailed work plan is mandatory.

the steps you plan to take, an estimate of their sequence and timing, and a list of the sources of information you plan to use. If you're conducting a lengthy, formal study, however, the work plan should be quite detailed because it will guide the performance of many tasks over a span of time. Moreover, most proposals require a detailed work plan, which becomes the basis for a contract if the proposal is accepted. A formal work plan might include the following items (especially the first two):

- Statement of the problem

- Statement of the purpose and scope of your investigation

- Discussion of the sequence of tasks to be accomplished (indicating sources of information, required experiments or observations, and any restrictions on time, money, or available data)

- Description of the end products that will result from the investigation (such as reports, plans, operating improvements, or tangible products)

- Review of project assignments, schedules, and resource requirements (indicating who will be responsible for what, when tasks will be completed, and how much the investigation will cost)

Some work plans also include a tentative outline of the report. Figure 11.2 is an example of a work plan for a study of whether to launch a company newsletter.

DOING THE RESEARCH

The fourth step in report writing is to do the research by consulting primary (first-hand) and secondary (secondhand) sources.

The value of your report depends on the quality of the information it's based on. So when the time comes to gather information, your first concern is to get organized. If you're working alone on a project, getting organized may mean nothing more than setting up a file and checking out a few books and periodicals from the nearest library. But if you are part of a team, you have to work out your assignments and coordinate activities. Your work plan will be a big help during this research effort.

The work plan should contain a list of the primary and secondary sources you will consult. As the name implies, primary sources provide firsthand information; secondary sources are secondhand reports. Most business problems call for a mix of both secondary and primary sources. You are likely to find, however, that much of what you need to know has never been collected. For example, you probably wouldn't locate much information on what Harley-Davidson dealerships should look like. This reliance on primary sources is one of the main differences between business reports and school reports.

REVIEWING SECONDARY SOURCES

Do secondary research by locating information that has already been collected, usually in the form of books, periodicals, and reports.

Even though you may plan to rely heavily on primary sources, you are wise to begin your study with a thorough review of the information that has already been collected. By searching the literature, you are protected against the embarrassment of failing to report something that is common knowledge. You are also saved the trouble of conducting a study of something that has already been done. Once you gain a feel for the structure of the subject, you can decide what additional research will be required.

FIGURE 11.2
Sample Work Plan for a
Formal Study

Statement of the Problem
The rapid growth of our company over the past five years has reduced the sense of community among our staff. People no longer feel like part of an intimate organization where they matter as individuals.

Purpose and Scope of Work
The purpose of this study is to determine whether a company newsletter would help rebuild employee identification with the organization. The study will evaluate the impact of newsletters in other companies and attempt to identify features that might be desirable in our own newsletter. Such variables as length, frequency of distribution, types of articles, and graphic design will be considered. Costs will be estimated for several approaches. In addition, the study will analyze the personnel and procedures required to produce a newsletter.

Sources and Methods of Data Collection
Sample newsletters will be collected from 50 companies similar to ours in size, growth rate, and types of employees. The editors will be asked to comment on the impact of their publications on employee morale. Our own employees will be surveyed to determine their interest in a newsletter and their preferences for specific features. Production procedures and costs will be analyzed through conversations with newsletter editors and possible printers.

Preliminary Outline
    I. Do newsletters affect morale?
      A. Do people read them?
      B. How do employees benefit?
      C. How does the company benefit?

    II. What are the features of good newsletters?
      A. How long are they?
      B. What do they contain?
      C. How often are they published?
      D. How are they designed?

    III. How should a newsletter be produced?
      A. Should it be written, edited, and printed internally?
      B. Should it be written internally and printed outside?
      C. Should it be totally produced outside?

    IV. What would a newsletter cost?
      A. What would the personnel costs be?
      B. What would the materials costs be?
      C. What would outside services cost?

    V. Should we publish a company newsletter?

    VI. If so, what approach should we take?

Work Plan

Collect and analyze newsletters	Sept. 1-14
Interview editors by phone	Sept. 16-20
Survey employees	Sept. 14-28
Develop sample newsletter	Sept. 28-Oct. 5
Develop cost estimates	Oct. 7-10
Prepare report	Oct. 10-24
Submit final report	Oct. 25

When conducting a thorough search for secondary business sources, recommends best-selling novelist James Michener, consult the card catalog, the *Business Periodicals Index*, and the reference librarian in addition to simply browsing in the stacks.

Depending on your subject, you may find useful information in general reference works, popular publications, and government documents. In addition, each field of business has a handful of specialized references that are considered indispensable. You will quickly come to know these sources once you've joined a particular industry. And don't overlook internal sources. Often, the most useful references are company reports and memos. Also check company brochures, newsletters, and annual reports to shareholders.

If you are working for a large organization with a company library, you may have direct access to a professional librarian who can help you identify and obtain other useful materials. If not, look for the nearest public or university library, and ask the librarians there for help. Reference librarians are trained to know where to find just about everything, and many of them are pleased to help people pursue obscure information.

When it comes to choosing your references, be selective. Avoid dated or biased material. If possible, check on the author's qualifications and the reputation of the publisher.

The amount of library research you do depends on the subject you're studying and the purpose of your investigation. In most cases, when you find yourself reading essentially the same things over and over again, move out of the library and on to the next phase of your work. Remember that in business, time is money. Your objective is to be as accurate and as thorough as possible, but within a reasonable length of time.

Regardless of the amount of research you do, retain complete and accurate notes on the sources of all the material you collect, using one of the systems explained in Appendix C, "Documentation of Report Sources." Documenting your sources through footnotes, endnotes, or some similar system lends credibility to your report.

COLLECTING PRIMARY DATA

Do primary research by collecting basic information yourself.

When the information you need is not available from secondary sources, you have to collect and interpret the data yourself by doing primary research. You must go out into the real world to gather information through your own efforts. The four main ways to collect primary data are to examine documents, observe things, survey people, and conduct experiments.

Documents

Documentary evidence and historical records are sources of primary data.

In business, a great deal of information is filed away for future reference. Your own company's files may provide you with accurate, factual historical records that you cannot obtain any other way. Business documents that qualify as primary data include sales reports prepared by field representatives, balance sheets, income statements, policy statements, correspondence with customers and suppliers, contracts, and log books. Many government and legal documents are primary sources as well, because they represent a decision made by those present at some official proceeding.

A single document may be both a secondary source and a primary source. For example, in citing summaries of financial and operations data from an annual report, you are using it as a secondary source. But that same report would be considered a primary source if you were analyzing its design features or comparing it with annual reports from other years or other companies.

Observations

Observation applies your five senses and your judgment to the investigation.

Informal observations are a rather common source of primary data in business. All you have to do is use your five senses, especially your eyes and ears, to gather information. Many reports, for instance, are based on the writer's visiting a facility to observe operations.

More objective information can be gathered through formal observations, which give observers a structure for noting what they see, thus minimizing opportunities for interpretation. For example, if you were trying to find out how teenagers react to various video arcade games, you might send researchers to a number of arcades to observe what goes on. Your results would be more useful if your observers were armed with a specific list of things to watch for. That way, you could compare the results from arcade to arcade and reach relatively objective conclusions.

In general, observation is a useful technique when you are studying objects, physical activities, processes, the environment, or human behavior. It does, however, have one major drawback: The value of the observation depends on the reliability of the observer. Many people have a tendency to see what they want to see or to interpret events in light of their own experience. But if the observer is trustworthy and has proper instructions, observation can provide valuable insights that would be difficult to obtain with other methods.

Surveys

Often the best way to obtain answers to your questions is to ask people who have relevant experience and opinions. Such surveys include everything from a single interview to the distribution of thousands of questionnaires.

A common way to conduct primary research is to interview well-qualified experts.

When you need specialized information that hasn't been recorded anywhere, you may want to conduct a personal interview with an expert, which is the simplest form of survey. Many experts come from the ranks of your own organization: people from other departments who have specialized knowledge, your predecessor in the job, and "old-timers" who've seen it all. On occasion, you may also want to talk with outsiders who have some special expertise. Doing an interview may seem an easy way to get information, but you must prepare carefully. You don't want to waste anyone's time, and you want your efforts to be productive.

A formal survey is a way of finding out what a crosssection of people think about something.

Although they have the same purpose, interviews are quite different from formal, large-scale surveys in which a sample population answers a series of carefully tested questions. A formal survey requires a number of important decisions:

- Should you use face-to-face interviews, phone calls, or printed questionnaires?

Two important research criteria:
- Reliability—when the same results would be obtained if the research were repeated
- Validity—when research measures what it is intended to measure

- How many individuals should you contact to get results that are *reliable* (that is, reproducible if the same study were repeated), and who should those people be (what sample is an accurate reflection of the population)?

- What specific questions should you ask in order to get a *valid* picture (a true reflection of the group's feelings on the subject)?

Your answers to these questions have a profound effect on the results of your survey.

Having seen rival preelection polls that come up with conflicting projections of who's going to win, you may wonder whether it makes sense to rely on survey results at all. The answer is yes, as long as you understand the nature of surveys. For one thing, surveys reveal only what people think about something at a specific moment. For another, pollsters ask various people different questions in different ways and, not surprisingly, get different answers. Just because surveys produce varying results does not mean that they are a poor form of research. But conducting a reliable, valid survey is not easy to do. Generally speaking, it helps to have the advice of a specialist.

One of the most critical elements of a survey is the questionnaire. To develop one, begin by making a list of the points you are trying to determine. Then break these points into specific questions, choosing an appropriate type of question for each point (see Figure 11.3 for some variations). The following guidelines will help you produce valid results:

Developing an effective questionnaire requires care and skill.

FIGURE 11.3
Types of Survey Questions

OPEN-ENDED	How would you describe the flavor of this ice cream?
EITHER–OR	Do you think this ice cream is too rich? _____ Yes _____ No
MULTIPLE CHOICE	Which description best fits the taste of this ice cream? (Choose only one.) a. Delicious b. Too fruity c. Too sweet d. Bland e. Too intensely flavored f. Stale
SCALE	Please make an X on the scale to indicate how you perceive the texture of this ice cream. ←————————————————————→ Too light Light Creamy Too creamy
CHECKLIST	Which flavors of ice cream have you had in the past 12 months? (Check all that apply.) _____ Vanilla _____ Chocolate _____ Strawberry _____ Chocolate chip _____ Coffee
RANKING	Rank these flavors in order of your preference, from 1 (most preferred) to 5 (least preferred): _____ Vanilla _____ Cherry _____ Maple nut _____ Chocolate ripple _____ Coconut
FILL IN THE BLANK	In the past month, how many times did you buy ice cream in the supermarket? _____ In the past month, how many times did you buy ice cream in ice cream shops? _____

- Provide clear instructions so that respondents know exactly how to fill out the questionnaire.

- Keep the questionnaire short and easy to answer. People are more likely to respond if they can complete the questionnaire within 10 or 15 minutes, so ask only those questions relevant to your research, and don't ask questions that require too much work on the respondent's part. People aren't willing to dig up the answers to questions like "What was your monthly rate of water consumption in 1991?"

- Formulate questions that provide easily tabulated or analyzed answers. Numbers and facts are easier to deal with than opinions are. Nevertheless, you may be able to elicit countable opinions with multiple-choice questions, or you might group open-ended opinions into a limited number of categories.

- Avoid questions that lead to a particular answer; they bias your survey. For example, Harley-Davidson would gain little useful information by asking customers, "Would you prefer that we offer our motorcycles in more colors?" The question obviously calls for a yes answer. A less biased question would be, "What color motorcycle do you prefer?"

- Ask only one thing at a time. When you pose a compound question like "Do you read books and magazines regularly?" you don't allow for the respondent who reads one but not the other.

- Avoid questions having vague or abstract words. Instead of asking, "Are you frequently troubled by colds?" ask, "How many colds did you have in the past 12 months?"

- Pretest the questionnaire on a sample group to identify questions that are subject to misinterpretation.

- Include a few questions that rephrase earlier questions, as a cross check on the validity of the responses.

If you are mailing your questionnaire, as opposed to administering it in person, include a persuasive cover letter that explains why you are conducting the research. Try to convince the person that her or his response is important to you. If possible, offer to share the results with the respondent. Include a preaddressed envelope with prepaid postage so that the respondent won't have to find an envelope or pay the postage to return the questionnaire to you. However, remember that even under the best of circumstances, you may not get more than a 10 to 20 percent response.

Steve Jobs co-founded Apple Computer and is now deeply involved with his latest project, the NeXT machine. Jobs sees an added dimension to researching customers' wants: technology. He cautions that customers are unable to foresee what technology can do, so in addition to asking customers what they want, it's important to acquaint them with what's possible.

Experiments

Although some general business questions justify the need for experiments, their use is far more common in technical fields. That's because an experiment requires extensive manipulation of the factors involved, which is often expensive and may even be unethical when people are one of the factors involved. Nevertheless, experiments do have their place. For example, if you want to find out whether a change in lighting levels increases the productivity of the pattern cutters in your dressmaking business, the most objective approach is to conduct an experiment using two groups of cutters: one working under existing conditions and the other working under the new lighting.

The aim in conducting an experiment is to keep all variables the same except for the one you are testing.

When conducting an experiment, you have to be careful to control those factors (called variables) you are *not* testing. For the results to be valid in the lighting experiment, the only difference in the environments of the two groups should be the lighting, and there should be no differences between the groups themselves. Otherwise, discrepancies in productivity could be attributed to such factors as age differences or experience on the job. It's even possible that introducing any change into the pattern cutters' environment, whether it be lighting or something else entirely, might be enough to increase productivity.

ANALYZING DATA

The fifth step in report writing is to analyze your results by calculating statistics, drawing reasonable conclusions, and if appropriate, developing a set of recommendations.

Once you've completed your research, you have to analyze your findings. The analytical process is essentially a search for relationships among the facts and bits of evidence you've compiled. By looking at the data from various viewpoints, you attempt to detect patterns that will enable you to answer the questions outlined in your work plan. Your mind begins to fit pieces together and to form tentative conclusions. As your analysis proceeds, you either verify or reject these conclusions because your mind is constantly filtering, sorting, and combining ideas.

CALCULATING STATISTICS

Much of the information you compile during the research phase will be in numerical form. Assuming that it has been collected carefully, this factual data is precise, measurable, and objective—and therefore credible. However, statistical information in its raw state is of little practical value. It must be manipulated so that you and your readers can interpret its significance.

Averages

The same set of data can be used to produce three kinds of averages: mean, median, and mode.

One useful way of looking at data is to find the average, which is one number that represents a group of numbers. Consider the data presented in Figure 11.4, the sales booked by a group of nine salespeople over one week. To analyze this information, you could calculate the average. But which average? Depending on how you plan to use the data, you would choose the mean, the median, or the mode.

The most commonly used average is the mean, or the sum of all the items in the group divided by the number of items in the group. The mean is useful when you want to compare one item or individual with the group. In the example, the mean is $7,000. If you were the sales manager, you might well be interested in knowing that Wimper's sales were average; that Wilson, Green, and Carrick had below-average sales; and that Keeble, Kemble, O'Toole, Mannix, and Caruso were above average. One problem with using the mean, however, is that it can give you a false picture if one of the numbers is extreme. Let's say that Caruso's sales for the week were $27,000. The mean would then be $9,000, and eight of the nine salespeople would be "below average."

The median is the "middle of the road" average.[2] In a numerical ranking like the one shown in Figure 11.4, the median is the number right in the middle of the list: $7,500. The median is useful when one (or a few) of the numbers is extreme. For example, even if Caruso's sales were $27,000, the median would still be $7,500.

FIGURE 11.4
Three Types of Averages: Mean, Median, and Mode

SALES-PERSON	SALES	
Wilson	$ 3,000	
Green	5,000	
Carrick	6,000	
Wimper	7,000	Mean
Keeble	7,500	Median
Kemble	8,500	
O'Toole	8,500	Mode
Mannix	8,500	
Caruso	9,000	
Total	$63,000	

FIGURE 11.4
Three Types of Averages: Mean, Median, and Mode

The mode is the "fashionable" average, the pattern followed most often, the case you're most likely to come across.[3] It's the best average for answering a question like "What is the usual amount?" For example, if you wanted to know what level of sales was most common, you would answer with the mode, which is $8,500. Like the median, the mode is not affected by extreme values. It's much easier to find than the median, however, when you have a large number of items or individuals.

While you're analyzing averages, you should also consider the range, or the spread, of a series of numbers. The fact that, in the example, sales per person ranged from $3,000 to $9,000 may raise the question of why there is such a wide gap between Wilson's and Caruso's performances. A range tells you the context in which the averages were calculated and demonstrates what values are possible.

Trends

Trend analysis involves an examination of data over time so that patterns and relationships can be detected.

If you were overseeing the work of Wilson, Caruso, and the rest, you might be tempted to make some important personnel decisions on the basis of the week's sales figures. But you would be a lot smarter to compare them with sales figures from other weeks, looking for a pattern in the performance of salespeople over time. You could begin to see which salespeople were consistently above average and which were consistently below. You could also see whether sales for the group as a whole were increasing, declining, or remaining steady and whether there were any seasonal fluctuations in the sales pattern. This type of analysis, known as trend analysis, is common in business. By looking at data over a period of time, you can detect patterns and relationships that will help you answer important questions.

Correlations

A correlation is a statistical relationship between two or more variables.

Once you have identified a trend, you should look for the cause. Let's say that Caruso consistently produces the most sales. You would undoubtedly be curious about the secret of her success. Does she call on her customers more often? Is she a more persuasive person? Does she have larger accounts or a bigger sales territory? Is she simply more experienced than the others?

To answer these questions, you could look for a consistent relationship between each person's sales and other variables, such as average account size or years of selling experience. For example, if salespeople with the largest accounts consistently produced higher sales, you might assume that these two factors were correlated, or related in a predictable way. And you might conclude that Caruso's success was due, at least in part, to the average size of her accounts. However, your conclusion might be wrong. Correlations are useful evidence, but they do not prove a cause-and-effect relationship. Caruso's success might well be the result of several other factors. To know for sure, you would have to collect more evidence.

DRAWING CONCLUSIONS

Conclusions may be based on a combination of facts, value judgments, and assumptions.

Regardless of how much evidence you amass, at some point in every analysis you move beyond hard facts, which can be objectively measured and verified. When you reach that point, you begin to formulate conclusions, interpretations of what the facts mean. You then step into the realm of assumptions and value judgments that have been formed by your own experience. Nothing is inherently wrong with assumptions and value judgments; very few decisions are made on the basis of facts alone. But you must understand the extent to which conclusions may be based on subjective factors.

Imagine that, as sales manager, you have gathered these facts:

- Sales in New England are three times as high as sales in the Southeast.

- The two regions are roughly equal in the size and number of potential accounts.

- Both regions have the same number and type of salespeople, who have all been trained in the same selling techniques.

- In the past three years, six of the eight salespeople in the Southeast have requested a transfer.

- Sales in the Southeast have declined by 5 percent over the past three years.

- The current manager of the Southeast region has been there for three years.

With additional investigation, using scientific research and statistical analysis, you might come up with an objective, indisputable conclusion about the cause of these facts.

In the fast-paced world of business, however, you are far more likely to seek a quicker, more subjective conclusion. Again, there is nothing inherently wrong with this type of decision making; in fact, skill at making subjective decisions is often highly valued. But you should be aware of the possible pitfalls.

Your own personal values may affect your thought process. For example, you may believe that the difference in sales between the two regions is unacceptable; another person, with different values, might be willing to accept the discrepancy. In analyzing the facts, you might assume that something within your control is responsible for the disparity, even though it's possible that some unknown characteristics of buyers or competing products are responsible. Nevertheless, to the extent that your value judgments and assumptions correspond to the facts, you can draw a sound conclusion.

In this case, after applying a subjective thought process to objective evidence, you may well conclude that the current manager of the Southeast region is associated with the sales problem. You are probably right, although you might want more evidence to confirm your hunch before you recommend any action.

But what if you don't have enough hard facts to go on? Or what if the facts are inconclusive or inconsistent? In either case, subjectivity becomes more of a factor. For example, a decision to hire one candidate rather than another is largely a matter of personal judgment. In situations of this type, testing your logic is particularly important. Try to be as objective as possible; be aware of possible biases that aren't justified by the circumstances. Diminish subjectivity by establishing criteria and measuring each candidate against the same standards.

If you're working as part of a team, you have the benefit of being able to discuss your conclusions with co-workers, so values and assumptions come into focus. But don't expect everyone to agree all the time. Some business decisions

Check the logic that underlies your conclusions.

The best conclusion is often the one that gains the most support.

are fuzzy; the "right" answers are not always clear. Often the best bet is to accept the consensus position rather than fight for a conclusion that others will not accept and therefore will not implement with enthusiasm. Then, once the decision has been made, stick with it unless conditions change significantly.

DEVELOPING RECOMMENDATIONS

Conclusions are opinions or interpretations; recommendations are suggestions for action.

Concluding that the sales manager of the Southeast region is somehow associated with low sales is one thing. Deciding what to do about it and then recommending a solution is something else. Recommendations are inappropriate in a report when you are not expected to supply them, so be sure you know the difference between conclusions and recommendations. A conclusion is an opinion or interpretation of what the facts mean; a recommendation suggests what ought to be done about the facts. Here's an example of the difference:

CONCLUSION

I conclude that, on the basis of its track record and current price, this company is an attractive buy.

RECOMMENDATION

I recommend that we write a letter to the president offering to buy the company at a 10 percent premium over the market value of its stock.

When you have been asked to take the final step and translate your conclusions into recommendations, be sure to make the relationship between them clear.

You might also want to test the soundness of your recommendations against the following criteria:

- The recommendations should offer real advantages to the organization.
- The recommendations should be financially and politically feasible.
- Specific plans should be developed for dealing with roadblocks that might impede implementation of the recommendations.
- The risks associated with the recommendations should be acceptable.
- The picture of what should happen next (of who should do what) must be clear.

Good recommendations are
- Practical
- Acceptable to readers
- Explained in enough detail so that readers can take action

Consider whether your recommendations are practical and acceptable to your readers; they are the people who have to make the recommendations work. You must also be certain that you have adequately described the steps that come next. Don't leave your readers scratching their heads and saying, "This all sounds good, but what do I do on Monday morning?"

OUTLINING THE REPORT AND PLANNING THE VISUAL AIDS

Once you have completed your research and analysis, you can prepare the final outline of the report. Sometimes you can use the preliminary outline that guided your research as a final blueprint for the report. More often, however, you have to rework it to take into account your purpose, your audience's proba-

The final outline of the report should be geared to your purpose and the audience's probable reaction.

ble reactions, and the things you learned during your study. As you'll recall from the previous chapter, informational reports are generally organized around topics suggested by the information itself, such as steps in a process, divisions of a company, or results in various geographical areas. Analytical reports, on the other hand, are organized around conclusions or recommendations if the audience is receptive, and around problem-solving approaches if the audience is skeptical or hostile. The placement of conclusions and recommendations depends on the audience's probable response. Put them up front if you expect a positive reaction, toward the end if you anticipate resistance.

The final outline should be phrased so that the points on the outline can serve as the headings that appear in the report. Bear in mind that the phrasing of the headings will affect the tone of the report. If you want a hard-hitting, direct tone, use informative phrasing. If you prefer an objective, indirect tone, use descriptive phrasing. Be sure to use parallel construction in wording the points on the outline.

Visual aid: illustration in tabular, graphic, schematic, or pictorial form

Once you have an outline in mind, you can begin to identify which points can be, and should be, illustrated with visual aids—tables, graphs, schematic drawings, or photographs. Ask yourself whether there is some way to visually dramatize the key elements of your message. You might approach the problem as though you were writing a picture book or making a movie. Think of each

BEHIND THE SCENES AT GANNETT COMPANY
Getting the Scoop on a Media Giant

Sheila J. Gibbons is director of public affairs for Gannett Company, the nation's largest newspaper publisher. Gannett owns 118 newspapers, including *USA Today*, as well as 10 television stations and 16 radio stations. In the course of a year, Gibbons's department compiles and publishes a half dozen in-depth reports for higher management.

"We're working on one right now," says Gibbons, "that's to be a 'white paper' analyzing media coverage of Gannett. Management wants a 'big-picture' assessment of how the outside world looks at us. The various newspapers, electronic media, and magazines are all being reviewed—everything that has appeared about us in the last 12 months."

In planning the report, Gibbons is considering issues such as (1) how Gannett is perceived by the public and (2) how those perceptions are affected by Gannett's being both a large corporation and a media company. Says Gibbons: "First, we don't know a lot about the public perception of Gannett. Many see us as *USA Today*, so if you mention *USA Today* and Gannett, people connect them. But if you mention Gannett

alone, they don't necessarily connect it with *USA Today*. We want to know what implications this has for Gannett. Second, attitudes about large corporations tend to shift back and forth between positive and negative, and people tend to vary how much or how little they trust the media. Because our company is both large and media-concerned, we are curious about how all these factors affect public perceptions of Gannett."

"So far, we're only in the information-gathering stage," points out Gibbons, who has taken an unusual approach to the research for this report. "I've given part of that assignment to our college intern. She is reviewing data, looking for themes and a consistency of views. She is not 'of Gannett,' so she won't be biased by our philosophy and corporate culture. Another staff member is looking into the impact of image campaigns that have been launched by other large corporations."

Whenever she works with college interns or with new staff members, Gibbons asks them first to review files and old reports and to take note of the various forms such communication has taken in the past.

main point on your outline as a separate scene. Your job is to think of a "picture," a chart or graph, that will communicate that point to the audience.

Then take your analysis a step further. Undoubtedly, some of the supporting items on your outline involve the presentation of detailed facts and figures. This sort of information may be confusing and tedious when presented in paragraph form. Often the best approach is to display this information in a table, which arrays the data in a convenient format. You might want to use flow charts, drawings, or photographs to clarify physical relationships or procedures.

Use visual aids to simplify, clarify, and emphasize important information.

When planning the illustrations for your report or presentation, aim to achieve a reasonable balance between the verbal and the visual. The ideal blend depends on the nature of the subject. Some topics are more graphic than others and require more visual aids. But remember that illustrating every point dilutes the effectiveness of all your visual aids. In a written report, particularly, too many visuals can be a problem. If readers are told in every paragraph or two to consult a table or chart, they are likely to lose the thread of the argument you are trying to make. Furthermore, readers tend to assume that the amount of space allocated to a topic indicates its relative importance. If you use visual aids to illustrate a minor point, you may be sending a misleading message about its significance.

"That's the best way to learn how the company communicates," says Gibbons. In other words, get to know your subject through background reading.

The shape of the final report is beginning to emerge. Gibbons says she'll "use a cover to make it stand out from routine paperwork, followed by a title page and an executive summary written as an inverted pyramid. In all, there will be about ten pages of text, normal for our long reports. Any illustrations will go in the appendix. I'll probably not do a bibliography for this particular report. First, we're looking at everything that's been written or said about us in a one-year period, so any bibliography will be extensive. Second, the intended audience will be looking for a short assessment of an important issue. My job is to simplify the complexities. The language will be kept simple to encourage readership, and the report will be concise and tightly written to benefit the time-pressured executives who will receive it. One other thing: there will be no typos."

This report, like others Gibbons prepares, will go to her boss, the vice president of public affairs and government relations, and from there to selected Gannett executives. Although this particular report will be unusual, Gibbons expects all members of the management committee to read it and give her a response.

"All our reports are analytical reports. Each has a portion that leads to recommendations for further action." Small-group conferences (usually four or five people) meet to hash over the findings and recommendations, and Gibbons gets feedback from them. "In this case, there will no doubt be a lot of discussion," Gibbons speculates. "The conference will address whether there is anything we should do to improve the way others see us, report on us, and so forth." The result may well be additional projects for Gibbons's department during the coming year.

APPLY YOUR KNOWLEDGE

1. Sheila Gibbons points out that one of the biggest worries for anyone doing long reports is that the report may not see the "light of day." List the circumstances that might lead to a long report's being tabled before it can be read. If you are responsible for the preparation of such a report, what could you do to prevent the circumstances you have listed?

2. If you were the intern Sheila Gibbons assigned to research how other media report on Gannett, how would you define the scope of your task? How many examples of each of the media—press, electronic media, magazines—would you include? For instance, among television stations, would you cover only the major networks? All nationally available cable channels? Or some combination of these? How would you decide the combination? Answer similar questions for the press and magazines. Would you recommend that Gibbons report the findings by media group? By broad theme? By issues uncovered? Why?

SUMMARY

Effective business reports begin with a clear definition of the problem to be investigated. Once the problem has been defined, you can determine what information will be required to solve it and develop a plan for obtaining that information.

During the research phase, you should review such secondary sources as books, periodicals, and reports. You may also conduct primary research to obtain information that is not available from existing sources. This research may involve examining documents, conducting surveys, making firsthand observations, or doing experiments.

When you have completed your research and analyzed the data, you are ready to develop conclusions and recommendations. Be certain that your suggestions are both logical and practical.

Before you begin to write, prepare a final outline of the report, taking into account your purpose and the audience's probable reaction. Plan to use visual aids to simplify, clarify, and emphasize important information.

ON THE JOB:
Solving a Communication Dilemma at Harley-Davidson

In order to get Harley-Davidson back on track, Vaughn Beals had to collect and analyze mountains of information, much of it in the form of reports. A major source of trouble was the company's bloated, disorganized inventory. Parts at Harley's assembly plant in York, Pennsylvania, were made in large batches for long production runs, stored until needed, and then loaded onto the 3.5-mile conveyor that clattered endlessly around the plant. In Harley's cavernous inventory storage area, employees sometimes took hours to find the right parts; then when the parts were found, they were often rusty or damaged. Even though Harley spent $25 million a year to maintain its inventory, over half its motorcycles came off the assembly line missing parts.

Harley's production machinery could not be easily switched from production of one bike model to production of another, so the company had to produce large numbers of a single model at a time. When a piece of machinery broke down, hundreds of parts piled up behind it. And to make matters worse, Harley plants were labyrinths of poorly organized work stations. In the 72 days it took to build each bike frame, Harley workers had to cart components and partly assembled bikes all over the plant. All of this inefficiency increased costs and manufacturing time, and it increased the possibility of lower-quality products slipping through cracks in the system.

When Beals introduced the Cafe Racer, a new model meant to signal Harley's return to quality, he established an ad hoc team to inspect the first 100 bikes off the assembly line and present him with reports about any defects. The news was terrible. The group uncovered $100,000 worth of problems, or an average of $1,000 per bike. Real-

izing how many mistakes had been going out the door, Beals expanded his inspection teams to cover all Harley models, and the quality of cycles leaving the factory improved. But Beals realized that the Quality Audit Program was an expensive, time-consuming Band-Aid that identified defects only after they were made.

After analyzing information on Honda's manufacturing processes, Beals set his staff to work installing a new system of inventory management. Known as just-in-time (JIT), the new system has propelled some of the world's leading manufacturers to success. Among other things, JIT lowers the number of parts and supplies held in waiting, which allowed Harley to funnel more money into research to improve product quality and to speed up the manufacturing process.

JIT forced Harley to change everything from its purchasing practices to the layout of its factories. Harley forged cooperative relationships with a select group of suppliers who could deliver high-quality parts on time, which allowed the company to both cut costs and increase quality. Because Harley now uses fewer suppliers, it can place larger orders that qualify for bulk discounts. Also, with a smaller number of suppliers, Harley's design and production teams can work more closely with suppliers to ensure the quality of parts and supplies.

By redesigning its production machinery and creating more standardized parts for multiple bike models, Harley can now build individual models in smaller batches, which allow product upgrades more frequently and which boost quality by limiting defects to fewer parts.

These changes (along with a hefty, temporary tariff on imported heavyweights) helped Harley roar back into the motorcycle business. Harley's share of the U.S. heavy-weight market is up to 60 percent, well ahead of second-place Honda's 19 percent. It has beaten back competition from Japanese firms, while demonstrating that it's possible for a U.S. firm to be a low-cost, high-quality producer. Beals clearly showed that careful collection and analysis of key business data can help any company get back on the road to success.

Your Mission: Since 1986, Harley-Davidson's sales have nearly doubled, and its earnings have grown at an annual rate of 57 percent. But Richard Teerlink, who replaced Vaughn Beals as CEO, doesn't want the company to grow complacent and forget how intense the competition is today. He is particularly interested in continuing to improve customer service at Harley dealerships around the world. As his executive assistant, you've been asked to plan a report that will outline ways to increase customer satisfaction by improving customer service. You'll need to conduct the necessary research, analyze the findings, and present your recommendations.

1. Which of the following represents the most appropriate statement of purpose for this study?
   a. The purpose of this study is to identify any customer service problems in Harley-Davidson's worldwide dealer network.
   b. This study answers the following question: "What improvements in customer service can our dealers make in order to increase overall customer satisfaction?"
   c. This study identifies those dealers in the worldwide network who are most responsible for poor customer satisfaction.
   d. This study identifies steps that dealers should take to change customer service practices.
2. You have tentatively identified the following factors for analysis:
   I. To improve customer service, we need to hire more salespeople
      A. Compute competitors' employee-to-sales ratio
      B. Compute our employee-to-sales ratio
   II. To improve customer service, we need to hire better salespeople
      A. Assess skill level of competitors' salespeople
      B. Assess skill level of our salespeople
   III. To improve customer service, we need to re-train our salespeople
      A. Review competitors' training programs
      B. Review our training programs
   IV. To improve customer service, we need to compensate and motivate our people differently
      A. Assess competitors' compensation levels and motivational techniques

   B. Assess our compensation levels and motivational techniques
   Should you proceed with the investigation based on this preliminary outline, or should you consider other approaches to factoring the problem?
   a. Proceed with this outline.
   b. Do not proceed. Factor the problem by asking customers how they perceive Harley's current customer service efforts. In addition, ask dealers what they think they should be doing differently.
   c. Do not proceed. Factor the problem by considering what successful car dealers do in terms of customer service.
   d. Do not proceed. Factor the problem by considering what the rest of the company, aside from the dealers, could be doing to improve customer service.

3. Which of the following work plans is the best option for guiding your study of ways to improve customer service?
   a. Version one:
      Statement of Problem: As part of Harley-Davidson's continuing efforts to offer the most attractive heavyweight motorcycles in the world, Richard Teerlink wants to improve customer service at the dealer level. The challenge here is to identify service improvements that are meaningful and valuable to the customer without being too expensive or time consuming.

      Purpose and Scope of Work: The purpose of this study is to identify ways to increase customer satisfaction by improving customer service at our dealerships worldwide. A four-member study team, composed of the vice president of marketing and three dealers, has been appointed to prepare a written service-improvement plan. To accomplish this objective, this study will survey customers to learn what changes they'd like to see in terms of customer service. The team will analyze these potential improvements in terms of cost and time requirements and then design new service procedures that dealers can use to better satisfy customers.

      Sources and Methods of Data Collection and Analysis: The study team will assess current dealer efforts by (1) querying dealership employees regarding their customer service, (2) observing employees in action dealing with customers, (3) surveying current Harley owners regarding their purchase experiences, and (4) surveying visitors to dealerships who decide not to purchase Harleys (by intercepting a sample of these people as they leave the dealerships). The team will also visit competitive dealerships to determine firsthand how they treat customers, and the team will mail questionnaires to a sample of registered motorcycle owners and classify the results by brand name. Once all these data have been collected, the team will analyze them to determine where buyers and potential buyers consider customer service to be lacking. Finally, the team will design procedures to meet their expectations.

Schedule:

Query dealer employees	Jan 10 - Jan 20
Observe employees in action	Jan 21 - Jan 30
Survey current Harley owners	Jan 15 - Feb 15
Survey nonbuyers at dealerships	Jan 20 - Jan 30
Visit competitive dealerships	Jan 31 - Feb 15
Conduct mail survey of registered owners	Jan 15 - Feb 15
Analyze data	Feb 15 - Mar 1
Draft new procedures	Mar 2 - Mar 15
Prepare final report	Mar 16 - Mar 25
Present to management/ dealer committee	Mar 28

b. Version two:

Statement of Problem: Harley's dealerships need to get on the ball in terms of customer service, and we need to tell them what to do in order to fix their customer service shortcomings.

Purpose and Scope of Work: This report will address how we plan to solve the problem. We'll design new customer service procedures and prepare a written report that dealers can learn from.

Sources and Methods of Data Collection: We plan to employ the usual methods of collecting data, including direct observation and surveys.

Schedule:

Collect data	Jan 10 - Feb 15
Analyze data	Feb 15 - Mar 1
Draft new procedures	Mar 2 - Mar 15
Prepare final report	Mar 16 - Mar 25
Present to management/ dealer committee	Mar 28

c. Version three:

Task 1--Query dealer employees: We will interview a sampling of dealership employees to find out what steps they take to ensure customer satisfaction. Dates: Jan 10 - Jan 20

Task 2--Observe employees in action: We will observe a sampling of dealership employees as they work with potential buyers and current owners, in order to learn firsthand what steps employees typically take. Dates: Jan 21 - Jan 30

Task 3--Survey current Harley owners: Using a sample of names from Harley's database of current owners, we'll ask owners how they felt about the purchase process when they bought their bikes and how they feel they've been treated since then. We'll also ask them to suggest steps we could take to improve service. Dates: Jan 15 - Feb 15

Task 4--Survey nonbuyers at dealerships: While we are observing dealership employees, we will also approach people who visit dealerships but leave without making a purchase. In the parking lot, we'll go through a quick survey, asking them what they think about Harley's customer service policies and practices and whether these had any bearing on their decisions not to purchase a Harley. Dates: Jan 20 - Jan 30

Task 5--Visit competitive dealerships: Under the guise of shoppers looking for new motorcycles, we will visit a selection of competitive dealerships to discover how they treat customers and whether they offer any special services that Harley doesn't. Dates: Jan 31 - Feb 15

Task 6--Conduct mail survey of registered owners: Using vehicle registration files from several states around the country, we will survey a sampling of motorcycle owners (of all brands). We will then sort the answers by brand of bike owned to see which dealers are offering which services. Dates: Jan 15 - Feb 15

Task 7--Analyze data: Once we've collected all these data, we'll analyze them to identify (1) services that customers would like to see Harley dealers offer, (2) services offered by competitors that aren't offered by Harley dealers, and (3) services currently offered by Harley dealers that may not be all that important to customers. Dates: Feb 15 - Mar 1

Task 8--Draft new procedures: From the data we've analyzed, we'll select new services that should be considered by Harley dealers. We'll also assess the time and money burdens that these services are likely to present, so that dealers can see whether each new service will yield a positive return on investment. Dates: Mar 2 - Mar 15

Task 9--Prepare final report: This is essentially

a documentation task, during which we'll describe our work, make our recommendations, and prepare a formal report. Dates: Mar 16 - Mar 25

Task 10--Present to management/dealer committee: We'll summarize our findings and recommendations and make the full report available to dealers at the quarterly meeting. Date: Mar 28

4. You are working on the questionnaire to send to current Harley-Davidson owners. One of the questions concerns the amount of information that the salesperson shared with the customer. You want to make sure that customers get all the information they need to make a good decision, but you don't want them to get overloaded with technical details. Which of the following questions would do the best job of gathering this bit of information?
   a. Were you overloaded with technical information when you spoke with a Harley-Davidson salesperson?
      _____ Yes
      _____ No
   b. Did you receive enough information to make a smart purchase decision?
      _____ Yes
      _____ No
   c. When you purchased a Harley, did the salesperson give you too little information, too much

information, or just the right amount?
      _____ Too little
      _____ Too much
      _____ Just the right amount
   d. Which of the following best describes how you felt about the amount of information you were given at the Harley dealership when you purchased your bike?
      _____ I think I did not receive enough information.
      _____ I am convinced that I did not receive enough information.
      _____ I didn't need any information from the salesperson; I knew what I wanted.
      _____ I think I received too much information.
      _____ I am convinced that I received too much information.

5. Assume that your survey results indicate that BMW motorcycle dealers rank highest in terms of customers' satisfaction with the treatment they received while buying motorcycles. Which of the following conclusions can you safely draw from this piece of data?
   a. Harley needs to improve its customer service.
   b. BMW sells the most motorcycles in the regions of the country covered by the survey.
   c. Because BMW is not one of the world's leading motorcycle manufacturers, customer service is not very important.
   d. None of the above.[4]

QUESTIONS FOR DISCUSSION

1. Why are informational assignments factored differently from analytical assignments?
2. Why is the outline for a study likely to differ from the outline used for the report on that study?
3. If you were in charge of a study, would you instruct your assistants to restrict their research, or would you prefer that they exhaust all possible sources of information? Explain your answer.

4. What are the advantages and disadvantages of primary research using documents, observations, surveys, and experiments?
5. After an exhaustive study of an important problem, what would you do if you came to a conclusion that you knew your company's management would reject?
6. What is the difference between conclusions and recommendations?

EXERCISES

1. State the purpose of a report written to address each question below. Then factor the problem and indicate whether subtopics, hypotheses, or relative merits are the basis for the outline.
   a. Which of two careers would be best for you?
   b. What should be considered when renting an apartment?
   c. How should you go about starting a small business?

   d. How should convenience stores protect themselves against robberies?
   e. What computer printer would be the best for you to buy?
2. The following statements of purpose indicate how problems have been factored. Critique each breakdown for violations of the rules of division.
   a. This report will analyze the pros and cons of advertising our hardware store in each of the major

local media: radio, newspapers, and yellow pages.

b. This report will analyze the major market segments in the Pacific Northwest for our line of raincoats: teenagers, yuppies, baby boomers, affluent over-50s, and senior citizens.

c. This report focuses on the six main categories of products carried in our chain of music stores: keyboards, stringed instruments, beginning band instruments, professional band instruments, sheet music, and accessories.

d. This report analyzes inventory methods, distribution channels, point-of-purchase advertising, and product pricing for our line of suntan lotions, hand creams, and beauty soaps.

3. As a member of the planning staff at Harley-Davidson, research the literature to obtain information on customer service in the industry (see this chapter's On-the-Job simulation). In addition to looking under customer service in general, you might want to look for articles about Harley's major competitors, such as Kawasaki, Honda, BMW, Suzuki, and Yamaha. Read the articles and draw your own conclusions about how to provide outstanding customer service. Report these conclusions in a brief memo (five pages or fewer) addressed to Richard Teerlink. Be sure to support your conclusions with specific information obtained during your research.[5]

4. Your four-person accounting business specializes in going directly to clients' places of business. Your clients appreciate this personal attention, and you benefit from the availability of material on the premises, material your clients might not remember to bring to your central office. Your policy has been for each accountant to log business mileage and then to be reimbursed 25 cents per mile. But accountants with large cars complain that they should be receiving more than the fixed rate. They argue that the large cars aid the company's image but that 25 cents per mile is inadequate reimbursement. "Do you want us all to show up in old Chevettes?" they ask.

   Thus you are considering leasing or purchasing four company cars. Before deciding, however, you want to compare the cost of the three options: (a) maintaining the present system (possibly with some minor adjustments), (b) leasing four cars, or (c) purchasing four cars. If you provide the cars, accountants will use them only for company business and for commuting to work.

   Factor the problem in the form of an outline. To begin, list eight or ten factual questions that must be answered before you can seriously address the problem.

5. For one of the cases at the end of Chapter 12, draft a tentative work plan that includes the following:
   a. Statement of the problem
   b. Statement of the purpose

c. Factors of the problem (in the form of an outline)
d. Tasks to be accomplished, indicating general sources of information and any experiments or observations required
e. Schedule that indicates when various tasks will be completed

6. The baking business is highly competitive, but you are succeeding with the small Philadelphia bakery turned over to you by your father. You produce an attractive line of sweet cookies, the type that children point to in the supermarket and that their mothers buy because of the low price. Your secret is to employ people who are certified "economically disadvantaged" and who have been unemployed for over two years. The federal government gives you tax credits for these workers, and you have found that they are very conscientious.

   In a trade journal, you read about a small, fully operational bakery outside Trenton, New Jersey. It is for immediate sale at a modest price (because of the owner's failing health). One of your workers has been with you for six years and understands your system; she could manage this bakery if you bought it. What you don't know is whether there is any demand for your product in Trenton or what the extent of the local competition is.

   You are also concerned about the bakery itself: its size, the age and condition of its equipment, and its location. Given your fairly modest budget for activities outside the normal sweep of your business, what types of primary research might you conduct to examine the feasibility of extending operations into Trenton? What specific questions would you like answered?

7. You have parlayed promises ("You'll get 3 percent of the gross"), a little luck, your contagious faith, and a lot of goodwill into an almost-completed motion picture, the story of a group of unknown musicians finding work and making a reputation in a difficult world. You have captured vibrant vignettes, both painful and happy, along with considerable footage of successful and less successful gigs. The work is almost done. Some of your friends leave the first complete screening saying that the 132-minute movie is simply too long; others (including you) can't imagine any more editing cuts. You decide to test the movie on a regular audience, members of which will be asked to complete a questionnaire that may or may not lead to additional editing. You obtain permission from a local theater manager to show your film at 4:30 and 8:15, straddling his scheduled presentation. Design a questionnaire that can solicit valid answers.

8. Select a business problem that interests you, and explain how you would conduct an experiment to solve it. Assume that you have sufficient time and money to conduct the experiment properly. Carefully define the problem, and describe the exact procedures you would use.
9. Prepare a list of ten questions about a current political issue or a class of consumer products. Then interview five randomly chosen people over the telephone. To obtain the five interviews, you will probably need to make more than twice that number of calls. Tabulate your results, and write a one- or two-page summary of your findings.
10. Visit a supermarket or fast-food outlet during a busy time in its operation, and observe customers passing through one cash register for half an hour. You are interested in the gender and approximate age of the customers, the size and composition of the groups they're in, and the size of their purchases. Before your investigation, you need to prepare a sheet that will help you collect data systematically; afterward, draft a brief narrative and a statistical report of your findings for your instructor. You should be able to answer these three questions: Do men or women make larger purchases? Does the age of the customer help predict the size of the purchase? How many purchases can this check-out counter handle in 30 minutes?

WRITING LONG REPORTS

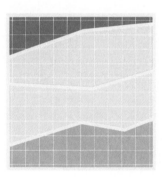

ON THE JOB:
Facing a Communication Dilemma at Penn State
What's the Score?

Common sense would tell you that a good football team is an asset to any college town, but it takes more than common sense to figure out exactly how much a team is worth in dollars and cents. Take the Nittany Lions of The Pennsylvania State University, for example—a good strong team with a solid record of wins. Under the direction of head football coach Joe Paterno, the Lions consistently pack the college stadium with fans for Saturday afternoon home games.

How much do you suppose those fans contribute to the economy of State College, Pennsylvania, every time there's a game? Would you believe $500,000? $1 million? $2 million? $3 million? More? Rodney A. Erickson, director of Penn State's Center for Regional Business Analysis, decided to find out. He wanted to document just exactly how important the Nittany Lions are to local businesses.

If you were reporting on the subject, how would you approach the task? Would the report be a formal one? Would you include a table of contents? An executive summary? A letter of transmittal? Just what sort of components are included in formal reports?[1]

THE REPORT PROCESS

As Rodney Erickson knows, planning formal reports and proposals, conducting the necessary research, organizing the ideas, and drafting the text are demanding and time-consuming tasks. But don't assume that the process ends there. When you are writing a formal document, one important task remains: producing a polished final version.

Penn State

How the final version is actually produced depends on the nature of the organization. If you work for an organization that produces many reports and proposals, the preparation process is likely to involve the interaction of a number of people. You and other members of a study team may subdivide the writing job, an arrangement sometimes called collaborative writing. Working from a jointly developed outline, each of you may draft a section of the text and then delegate final preparation of the report or proposal to the company editor, the secretarial staff, and the art department. If this is the case, you won't be involved in the finer points of formatting, like setting up a title page or positioning page numbers properly. The support staff will handle these tasks, using the approved company format. Your role will be to review their work and be sure it reflects the proper professionalism. On the other hand, if you work for a small business with a limited staff, you may compose and type the entire report yourself, handling everything from outline to final version.

Personal computers can automatically handle many of the mechanical aspects of report preparation.

The equipment available also has a bearing on the production process. If you draft the report on a personal computer, using a word-processing program and perhaps a computer graphics package, you can easily incorporate editorial changes and reviewer comments. In addition, you can let the computer handle such mechanical chores as setting margins, adding footnotes, numbering pages, and checking your spelling. Some software programs even edit your draft for readability. Without a computer, the preparation process may take longer. If you don't have access to a sophisticated electronic typewriter either, you may have to retype the entire document in order to make changes, and each page must be formatted separately.

Be sure to schedule enough time to turn out a document that looks professional.

Regardless of precisely how the final product is produced, you should allocate enough time for a thorough job. Be realistic about what you expect from the support staff. Secretaries can type only about eight pages an hour; editors may spend 10 to 15 minutes on a single page; graphic artists may spend an hour or more preparing just one chart. And every person who reviews the draft of the report will take as much time as possible and will recommend changes that are time consuming to incorporate.

In terms of your own part in the process, remember that you don't have to start writing on page one. A person with a strong visual sense might begin by developing the visual aids. Someone who thinks in broad, general terms might start with the introduction. Someone else might prefer to write the main analytical sections first. If you are writing as part of a team, you will be forced to work on sections taken out of context and out of sequence. Although this practice may be disconcerting, it is often necessary in business, and it seems to work, provided one person takes responsibility for assembling all the pieces, developing transitions, and editing the whole report to ensure consistency.

When you've completed a major report and sent it to the readers, you will naturally expect a positive response, and quite often you'll get one. But in the real world, you won't always get the response you want. For instance, you may get half-hearted praise or no action on your conclusions and recommendations. Or worse, you may get some serious criticism. Try to learn from these experiences; don't consider them a personal insult. Constructive criticism will prepare you for the next time.

Sometimes you won't get any response at all, which is frustrating. If you haven't heard from your readers within a week or two, you might want to ask politely whether the report arrived. In hopes of stimulating a response, you could also offer to answer their questions or provide them with additional information.

COMPONENTS OF A FORMAL REPORT

A formal report conveys the impression that the subject is important.

When Penn State's Rodney Erickson assembles the final version of his report on the economic impact of college football, he will include many components not usually found in informal reports. Formal reports differ from informal ones in both format and tone. Manuscript format and an impersonal tone convey an impression of professionalism. But a formal report can be either short (fewer than ten pages) or long (ten pages or more). It can be informational or analytical, direct or indirect. In many cases, a formal report is directed to readers outside the organization, but it may also be written for insiders. What sets it apart from other reports is its polish.

The longer the report (and the more information in it), the greater the number of components it usually contains; complex information is easier to digest when presented in smaller pieces. Notice that the components listed in Figure 12.1 fall into three categories, depending on where they are found in a report: prefatory parts, text of the report, and supplementary parts. The parts included in a report depend on the type of report you are writing, the requirements of your audience, the organization you are working for, and the length of your report. For instance, the prefatory parts of a short report usually include only a title page, a letter of transmittal combined with a synopsis, and a table of contents; usually no supplementary parts are included. (In very short formal reports, the table of contents and letter of transmittal are omitted too.) Long reports often include all the components listed in Figure 12.1. Later in this chapter, a sample formal report illustrates how the parts fit together.

The three basic divisions of a formal report:
- Prefatory parts
- Text
- Supplementary parts

PREFATORY PARTS

Prefatory parts may be written after the text has been completed.

Although the prefatory parts are placed before the text of the report, you may not want to write them until after you have written the text. Many of these parts—such as the table of contents, list of illustrations, and synopsis—are easier to prepare after the text is complete because they directly reflect the contents. Other parts can be prepared at almost any time.

Cover

Many companies have standard covers for reports, made of heavy paper and imprinted with the company's name and logo. Report titles are either printed on these covers or attached with gummed labels. If a company does not have

FIGURE 12.1
Parts of a Formal Report

Prefatory Parts	Text of the Report	Supplementary Parts
Cover	Introduction	Appendixes
Title fly	Body	Bibliography
Title page	Summary	Index
Letter of authorization	Conclusions	
Letter of acceptance	Recommendations	
Letter of transmittal	Notes	
Table of contents		
List of illustrations		
Synopsis or executive summary		

standard covers, you can usually find something suitable in a good stationery store. Look for a cover that can be labeled with the title of the report, the writer's name (optional), and the submission date (also optional).

Think carefully about the title before you put it on the cover. A business report is not a mystery story, so give your readers all the information they need: the who, what, when, where, why, and how of the subject. At the same time, try to be reasonably concise. You don't want to intimidate your audience with a title that is too long, awkward, or unwieldy. One approach is to use a subtitle: "Opportunities for Improving Market Share in the Athletic Shoe Department: Customer Attitudes Toward Marshall's Athletic Footwear, December 1993." You can reduce the length of your title by eliminating phrases like "A report of," "A study of," or "A survey of."

Put a title on the cover that is informative but not too long.

Title fly and title page

The title fly is a plain sheet of paper with only the title of the report on it. You don't really need one, but it adds a touch of formality to a report. The title page includes four blocks of information, as shown in the sample report later in this chapter: (1) the title of the report; (2) the name, title, and address of the person, group, or organization that authorized the report (which is usually the intended audience); (3) the name, title, and address of the person, group, or organization that prepared the report; and (4) the date on which the report was submitted. The title page can serve as the cover if the report is relatively short and is intended solely for internal use.

The title page usually includes four blocks of information.

Letters of authorization and acceptance

If you received written authorization to prepare the report or proposal, you may want to include that letter or memo (or a copy of the request for proposal) in your report. There may be times when you'll want to include your letter (or memo) of acceptance as well. These documents are useful "for the record."

The authorization document normally follows the direct-request plan described in Chapter 6. It typically specifies the problem, scope, time and money limitations, special instructions, and due date. The reply is the letter or memo of acceptance, which acknowledges the assignment to conduct the study and to prepare the report. Following the good-news plan, the acceptance confirms time and money limitations and other pertinent details. This document is rarely included in a report.

A letter of authorization usually follows the direct-request plan.

Use the good-news plan for a letter of acceptance.

Letter of transmittal

The letter (or memo) of transmittal conveys the report to the readers. It says what you'd say if you were handing the report directly to the person who authorized it. Thus the writing style is less formal than that of the rest of the report: The letter could use personal pronouns and conversational language.

Generally, the transmittal letter appears right before the table of contents. But if your report is quite formal, with wide distribution, you may want to include the letter of transmittal only in selected copies, making certain comments to a specific audience. Say you're recommending that two departments be merged, which will displace one of the department heads. In your report, you might not want to recommend either person for the remaining position, especially if both department heads will receive a copy of it. Rather, you might want to discuss the issue privately in a letter of transmittal to top management.

Use a less formal style for the letter of transmittal than for the report itself.

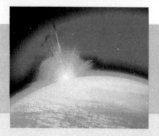

BEHIND THE SCENES AT THE ROCKY MOUNTAIN INSTITUTE
Energy Efficiency: Getting the Word to the World

The Rocky Mountain Institute (RMI) has plans to save the world's resources. Its primary tool? Words. The nonprofit environmental think tank expends most of its own energy convincing governments, corporations, utilities, architects, and anyone else who will listen that "it's cheaper to save energy than to waste it." To get this message to the world, RMI's 40 researchers produce thousands of pages of written reports each year for some 200 clients in over 32 countries. Many of these reports are highly technical, but the institute's founders, Amory and Hunter Lovins, like to present them in witty, straightforward language that anyone can understand. They've even invented words when necessary—like *negawatt*, a measure of electricity *saved*.

Amory, a child prodigy who became a Harvard and Oxford scholar, built his reputation as an energy wizard in the mid-1970s when his book, *Soft Energy Paths*, correctly predicted that economic growth could be accompanied by lowered energy consumption. Hunter, RMI's president and executive director, is an attorney-turned-activist who rides rodeo and dirt bikes

in her spare time. For years the married couple traveled the world as energy efficiency consultants, but in 1982 they settled in Snowmass, Colorado, in a state-of-the-art, environmentally sound building that serves as home and office for RMI's research team.

The institute's programs are in five areas: energy efficiency, water usage, economic renewal of rural areas, sustainable agriculture, and global security through more efficient resource usage and distribution. "What we do concerns policy," Hunter explains. "We do very little hardware testing, invention, or fiddling around." Instead, staffers may use the telephone to contact officials who have successfully implemented efficiency programs. The researchers ask what worked and what didn't, how much it cost, what roadblocks were overcome, and where to obtain any equipment that was used. This information may be combined with hardware evaluations, supply sources, and implementation recommendations in reports as long as 600 pages; Hunter calls them "tomes as big as a Manhattan phone book." Other reports are smaller and friendlier and wind up in the hands of consumers (such as the popu-

The most famous long report was written by Federal Express founder Frederick Smith. It detailed the then-revolutionary idea of air express delivery and persuaded investors to fund him. Smith believes that your reports reflect on you. If the report looks good, you look good. Messy reports may not even get read.

In terms of organization, the letter of transmittal should follow the routine and good-news plans described in Chapter 7. Begin with the main idea, officially conveying the report to the readers and summarizing its purpose. Typically, such a letter begins with a statement like "Here is the report you asked me to prepare on . . ." The rest includes information about the scope of the report, the methods used to complete the study, and the limitations that became apparent. In the middle section of the letter, you may also highlight important points or sections of the report, make comments on side issues, give suggestions for follow-up studies, and transmit any information that will help readers better understand and use the report. If the report does not have a synopsis, you can use the letter of transmittal to summarize the major findings, conclusions, and recommendations. You may also wish to acknowledge help given by others. The concluding paragraph of the transmittal letter should be a note of thanks for having been given the report assignment, an expression of willingness to discuss the report, and an offer to assist with future projects.

Table of contents

The table of contents indicates in outline form the coverage, sequence, and relative importance of the information in the report. In fact, the headings used

lar softcover, *Practical Home Energy Savings*). But most begin as commissions from clients like PG&E, General Motors, and the World Bank.

Hunter admits that organizing such lengthy reports can be challenging. She must often rewrite early drafts to make sure readers can follow the flow of what she calls "the argument." When the U.S. Environmental Protection Agency (EPA) commissioned a 100-page report from RMI to serve as a manual for local water utilities, "they were interested in what water efficiency measures existed and how to implement them," says Hunter. But the first draft, written by a junior staff member, wandered a bit, so Hunter reshaped it. "I try in the introduction to set up a structure of argument that is sign-posted along the way. For example, I'll say, 'In almost every instance it will be more cost-effective for you to save water than to try to bring in new supplies, and this is true because of the following six reasons.' Then I have six subheads or chapters, depending on the amount of material; I try to prove the argument at each step along the way; and then I sum it all up." For the EPA report, Hunter stressed RMI's recommendations throughout the body, then briefly reinforced them in a "Final Note."

But organization wasn't the only problem. Hunter recalls that "the gal who originally commissioned the report was a Carter appointee," but by the time the Bush administration was in office, RMI staffers had revised the document six times to suit new reviewers.

Some of their comments were helpful, Hunter remembers, "but one guy scrawled in big red letters all the way across the page, 'Where's the beef?' That wasn't very useful. On the other hand, he was a senior guy at EPA, so we had to figure out what he meant by that. That took a lot of phone calls."

More than a year and plenty of headaches later, the "Water Efficiency" report was accepted and printed. It's rich with case studies, and it includes a table of contents, a formal introduction, brief overviews introducing each section, 172 footnotes, 7 appendixes, 9 figures, and 5 tables. There's no bibliography or index, but an appendix lists over a hundred names and addresses of water efficiency contacts. Because the institute retained the right to distribute the booklet, "Water Efficiency" has now become part of RMI's save-the-world toolbox.

APPLY YOUR KNOWLEDGE

1. Hunter Lovins says that executive summaries often omit important information executives need. What steps would you take to avoid this problem?

2. Amory Lovins has written a ground-breaking treatise proving that plutonium waste from nuclear power reactors can be used to develop nuclear weapons. How would you arrange this material for a report to be distributed among government policymakers in countries that might fund nuclear power programs in developing nations?

The table of contents outlines the text and lists prefatory and supplementary parts.

Be sure the headings in the table of contents match up perfectly with the headings in the text.

in the text of the report are the basis for the table of contents. However, depending on the length and complexity of the report, the contents page may show only the top two or three levels of headings, sometimes only first-level headings. Excluding some levels of headings may frustrate readers who want to know where to find every subject you cover, but simplification of the table of contents also helps readers focus on the major points.

The table of contents should be prepared after the other parts of the report have been typed so that the beginning page numbers for each heading can be shown. The headings should be worded exactly as they are in the text of the report.

Also listed on the contents page are the prefatory parts (only those that follow the contents page) and the supplementary parts. If you have four or fewer visual aids, you may wish to list them in the table of contents too; if you have more than four visual aids, you should list them separately in a list of illustrations.

List of illustrations

For simplicity's sake, some reports refer to all visual aids as illustrations or exhibits. In other reports, as in the sample report in this chapter, tables are labeled separately from all other types of visual aids, which are called figures.

Put the list of illustrations on a separate page if it won't all fit on one page with the table of contents; start the list of figures and the list of tables on separate pages if they won't both fit on one page.

Regardless of the system used to label visual aids, the list of illustrations gives their titles and page numbers.

If there is enough space on a single page, type the list of illustrations directly beneath the table of contents. Otherwise, type it on a separate page following the contents page. When tables and figures are numbered separately, they should also be listed separately. Both lists can be typed on the same page if they fit; otherwise, start each list on a separate page.

Synopsis or executive summary

Provide an overview of the report in a synopsis or an executive summary.

A synopsis is a brief overview (one page or less) of a report's most important points and is designed to give readers a quick preview of the contents. It is particularly likely to be included in long informational reports dealing with technical, professional, or academic subjects. Because it is a concise representation of the whole report, it may be distributed separately to a wide audience; interested readers can then opt to order a copy of the entire report.

An informative synopsis summarizes the main ideas; a descriptive synopsis states what the report is about.

The phrasing of a synopsis can be either informative or descriptive, depending on whether the report is in direct or indirect order. An informative synopsis presents the main points of the report in the order in which they appear in the text. A descriptive synopsis simply tells what the report is about and is only moderately more detailed than the table of contents; the actual findings of the report are omitted. Here are examples of statements from each type:

Informative Synopsis:	Sales of super-premium ice cream make up 11 percent of the total ice cream market.
Descriptive Synopsis:	This report contains information about super-premium ice cream and its share of the market.

Use a descriptive synopsis for a skeptical or hostile audience, an informative synopsis for most other situations.

The way you handle a synopsis should reflect the approach you use in the text. If you're using an indirect approach in your report, you are better off with a descriptive synopsis. An informative synopsis, with its focus on conclusions and key points, may be too confrontational if you have a skeptical audience. You don't want to spoil the effect by providing a controversial beginning.

Many business report writers prefer to include an executive summary instead of a synopsis. A synopsis is essentially a prose table of contents that outlines the main points of the report; an executive summary is a fully developed "mini" version of the report itself, intended for readers who lack the time or motivation to study the complete text. As a consequence, an executive summary is more comprehensive than a synopsis, generally about 10 percent of the document length.

Put enough information in an executive summary so that an executive can make a decision without reading the entire report.

Unlike a synopsis, an executive summary may contain headings, well-developed transitions, and visual aids. It should be organized in the same way as the report, using a direct or indirect approach, depending on the audience's receptivity. In analytical reports, enough evidence should be provided in the executive summary to make a convincing case for the conclusions and recommendations. After reading the summary, the executive should know the essentials and be in a position to make a decision. Later, when time permits, he or she may read certain parts of the report to obtain additional detail.

Many reports do not require either a synopsis or an executive summary. Generally speaking, length is the determining factor. Most reports of fewer than 10 pages either omit one or combine it with the letter of transmittal. But if your report is over 30 pages long, you should probably include either a synopsis or an executive summary as a convenience for readers. Which to provide depends on the traditions of your organization.

TEXT OF THE REPORT

Chapters 10 and 11 tell you a good deal about how to write the text of a report. But apart from deciding on the fundamental issues of content and organization, you must also make decisions about the design and layout of the report. You can use a variety of techniques to present your material effectively. Many organizations have format guidelines that make your decisions easier, but the goal should always be to focus the readers' attention on major points and on the flow of ideas.

Headings are the most powerful format tool available to you. Each heading should give clues to the material that follows. By skimming along from heading to heading, readers should be able to pick up the structure or outline of your report. This process is easier if the headings are phrased and typed in a consistent way. To highlight the headings, you can use typographical distinctions such as all capital letters, initial capitals, underlining, italics, and boldface print. But be sure that you use these signals consistently so that the hierarchy among the headings is visually apparent. You can also emphasize the headings by allowing extra white space between them and the text. In fact, in longer reports, you should call attention to the major breaks in thought by beginning each main section or chapter on a separate page. In shorter reports, the sections or chapters may run continuously, with only first-level headings separating the major divisions.

Visual aids are also useful tools for calling attention to key points and helping readers grasp the flow of ideas. By depicting important information visually, you capture the attention of readers who are leafing through the report. Eye-catching graphics dramatize the high points of the message, and informative captions explain their meaning.

It is also a good idea to preview key points at the beginning of each major section or chapter and to sum them up at the end. In other words, readers benefit when you

1. Tell them what you're going to tell them

2. Tell them

3. Tell them what you told them

When accomplished without being overly redundant, this strategy keeps readers positioned and reinforces the substance of your message.

Introduction

The introduction of a report serves a number of important functions:

- It puts the report in a broader context, tying it to a problem or an assignment.

- It tells readers the report's purpose.

- It lets readers know what to expect in terms of the report's contents and organization.

- It establishes the tone of the report and the writer's relationship with the readers.

Aids to understanding in the text of a report:
- Headings
- Visual aids
- Preview and summary statements

Debi Coleman is head of worldwide manufacturing for Apple Computer. She oversees the modernization of plants and manufacturing processes, and many of her decisions are based on reports. If the reports are well researched, accurate, and clear, says Coleman, then the risks involved in decision making are reduced, resulting in better decisions.

An introduction has a number of functions and covers a wide variety of topics.

The length of the introduction depends on the length of the report. If you're writing a relatively brief report, the introduction may be only a paragraph or two and may not be labeled with a heading of any kind. But the introduction to a major formal report may extend to several pages and should be identified as a separate section by the first-level heading "Introduction."

Here's a list of topics that are generally covered in an introduction:

- *Authorization.* When, how, and by whom the report was authorized; who wrote it; and when it was submitted. This material is especially important when no letter of transmittal is included.

- *Problem/purpose.* The reason for the report's existence and what is to be accomplished as a result of the report's being written.

- *Scope.* What is and what isn't going to be covered in the report. The scope indicates the report's size and complexity.

- *Background.* The historic conditions or factors that have led up to the report. This section should enable readers to understand how the problem developed and what has been done about it so far.

- *Sources and methods.* The secondary sources used and the surveys, experiments, and observations carried out. This section tells readers what sources were used, how the sample was selected, how the questionnaire was constructed (a sample questionnaire and cover letter should be included in the appendix), what follow-up procedures were used, and the like. It should provide enough detail to give readers confidence in the work and to convince them that the sources and methods were satisfactory.

- *Definitions.* A brief introductory statement leading into a column of terms used in the report and their definitions. The terms may be unfamiliar but essential to understanding the report (such as *duopsony*: "a market situation in which two rival buyers determine the demand for a product"), or the terms may be familiar expressions used in a specific way (such as *business education* used exclusively to mean "the education of business teachers"). Terms may be defined in other places as well: in the body, as the terms are used; in explanatory footnotes; or in a glossary, an alphabetical listing of terms placed at the end of the report.

- *Limitations.* Factors affecting the quality of the report, such as a budget too small to do all the work that should have been done, an inadequate amount of time to do all the research desired, the unreliability or unavailability of data, or the social or environmental conditions beyond your control. This is the place to mention doubts about any aspect of the report. Although candor may lead readers to question the results, it will also enable them to assess the results more accurately and will help maintain the integrity of the report. However, limitations are no excuse for conducting a poor study or writing a bad report.

- *Report organization.* The organization of the report (what topics are covered and when), along with a rationale for following this plan. This section is a road map that helps readers understand what comes next and why.

Some of these items may be combined in the introduction; some may not be included at all. Make your decision about what to include by figuring out what kind of information will help your readers understand and accept the report.

In preparing the introduction, give some thought to its relationship to the prefatory parts of the report. In longer reports, you may have a letter of transmittal, a synopsis or an executive summary, and an introduction, all of which cover essentially the same ground. To avoid redundancy, you may need to juggle the various sections. If the letter of transmittal and synopsis are fairly detailed, for example, you might want the introduction to be relatively brief. However, remember that some people may barely glance at the prefatory parts; thus the introduction should be detailed enough to provide an adequate preview of the report. If you need to repeat information that has already been covered in one of the prefatory parts, simply use different wording in the introduction.

Body

The body of the report follows the introduction. It consists of the major sections or chapters (with various levels of headings) that present, analyze, and interpret the material gathered as part of your investigation. These chapters contain the "proof," the detailed information necessary to support your conclusions and recommendations.

One of the decisions you have to make when writing the body of your report is how much detail to include. Your decision should depend on the nature of your information, the purpose of the report, and the preferences of your readers. Some situations call for detailed coverage; others lend themselves to shorter treatment. However, you should generally provide only enough detail in the body to support your conclusions and recommendations; if needed, put additional detail in tables, charts, and appendixes.

Summary, conclusions, and recommendations

The final section of text in a report tells readers "what you told them." In a short report, this final wrap-up may be only a paragraph or two. But a long report generally has separate sections labeled "Summary," "Conclusions," and "Recommendations." Here's how the three differ:

- *Summary.* The key findings of your report, paraphrased from the body and stated or listed in the order in which they appear in the body.

- *Conclusions.* The writer's analysis of what the findings mean. These are the answers to the questions that led to the report.

- *Recommendations.* Opinions, based on reason and logic, about the course of action that should be taken. These should come directly from and be supported by the findings and conclusions.

If the report is organized in direct order, the summary, conclusions, and recommendations are presented before the body and are reviewed only briefly at the end. If the report is organized in indirect order, they are presented for the first time at the end and are covered there in detail.

Some report writers combine the conclusions and recommendations under one heading. Whether you combine them or not, if you have several conclusions and recommendations, you may want to number and list them. An appropriate lead-in sentence for the list of conclusions is, "The findings of this study lead to the following conclusions." A statement that could be used for the list of recommendations is, "Based on the conclusions of this study, the following

John Akers is CEO of IBM and is often called on to make decisions based on reports. But if a report makes a recommendation and lacks the detail to support it, the recommendation is useless. Likewise, a recommendation buried in too much detail may be too difficult to uncover. Akers advises balancing the amount of detail to complement the subject and its complexity.

Summaries, conclusions, and recommendations serve different purposes.

recommendations are made." No new findings should be presented in either the conclusions or the recommendations section.

In reports that are intended to lead to action, the recommendations section is particularly important because it spells out exactly what should happen next. It brings all the action items together in one place and gives the details about who should do what, when, where, and how. Readers may agree with everything you say in your report but still fail to take any action if you are vague about what should happen next. Readers must understand what is expected of them and must have some appreciation of the difficulties that are likely to arise. A timetable and specific assignments are helpful because concrete plans have a way of commanding action.

In action-oriented reports, put all the recommendations in a separate section and spell out precisely what should happen next.

Notes

In writing the text of the report, you will have to decide how to acknowledge your sources. You have an ethical and legal obligation to give other people credit for their work. When you use someone else's research, it is unfair, and also illegal, to pass it off as your own. At the same time, acknowledging your sources enhances the credibility of your report. By citing references in the text, you demonstrate that you have thoroughly researched the topic.

Give credit where credit is due.

Citing sources is desirable, but you want to do it in a way that doesn't make your report read like an academic treatise, dragging along from footnote to footnote. The source references should be handled as conveniently and as inconspicuously as possible (see Appendix C for some alternatives). One approach, especially for internal reports, is simply to mention a source in the text:

According to Dr. Lewis Morgan of Northwestern Hospital, hip replacement operations account for 7 percent of all surgery performed on women ages 65 and over.

If your report will be distributed to outsiders, however, you should include additional information on where you obtained the data.

VISUAL AIDS

In his report about the impact of college football on the local economy, Erickson can complement his text by including tables, bar charts, pie charts, organization charts, maps, or other visual aids. When illustrating the text of any report, you face the problem of choosing the specific form that best suits your message. Moreover, good business ethics demand you choose a form of visual aid that will not mislead your audience.

Tables

When you have to present detailed, specific information, choose a table. Tables are ideal when the audience needs all the facts and the information would be either difficult or tedious to handle in the main text.

Use tables to help your audience understand detailed information.

Most tables contain the same standard parts, which are illustrated in Figure 12.2. What makes a table a table is the grid that allows you to find the point where two factors intersect. Every table must therefore include vertical columns and horizontal lines, with useful headings along the top and side. Tables that are projected on a screen for use in oral presentations should be limited to

FIGURE 12.2
Parts of a Table

Stub Head	Multicolumn Head		Single-Column Head*	Single-Column Head
	Subhead	Subhead		
Line head	XXX	XXX	XX	XX
Line head				
Subhead	XX	XXX	XX	XX
Subhead	XX	XXX	X	XX
Totals	XXX	XXX	XX	XX

TABLE 1   Title

Source: (in the same format as a text footnote; see Appendix C)
* (for explanation of elements in the table; a superscript number or small letter may be used instead of an asterisk or other symbol)

three column heads and six line heads; tables presented on paper may include from one or two heads to a dozen or more. If the table has too many columns to fit comfortably between the margins of the page, turn the paper horizontally and insert it in the report with the top toward the binding.

Although formal tables set apart from the text are necessary for complex information, some data can be presented more simply within the text. The table becomes, in essence, a part of the paragraph, typed in tabular format. These "text tables" are usually introduced with a sentence that leads directly into the tabulated information. Here's an example:

> Tabular information can be introduced within the text without a formal title.

The farm population has declined steadily since 1960, but the average size of a farm has increased:

Year	Farm Population (in millions)	Average Farm Size (in acres)
1960	15.6	297
1970	9.7	374
1980	6.0	429
1990	5.2	435

The flow of people away from farming seems likely to continue, but many experts believe that farm size will stabilize at around current acreages.

In setting up a numerical table, be sure to identify the units in which amounts are given: dollars, percentages, price per ton, or whatever. All items in a column should be expressed in the same units.

Line and surface charts

Line charts illustrate trends over time or plot the interaction of two variables; they are common in business reports. In charts showing trends, the vertical axis is used to show amount, and the horizontal axis shows time or quantity being measured. Ordinarily, both scales begin at zero and proceed in equal increments. However, if the data are plotted far above zero, the vertical axis can be broken to show that some of the increments have been left out.

A simple line chart may be arranged in many ways. One of the most common is to plot several lines on the same chart for comparative purposes, as

> Use line charts
> - To indicate changes over time
> - To plot the interaction of two variables

shown in Figure 12.3. If at all possible, use no more than three lines on any given chart, particularly if the lines cross.

Surface charts are a form of line chart with a cumulative effect; all the lines add up to the top line, which represents the total (see Figure 12.4). This form of chart is useful when you want to illustrate changes in the composition of something over time. When preparing this type of chart, put the most important segment against the baseline, and limit the number of strata to four or five.

A surface chart is a kind of line chart showing cumulative effect.

Bar charts

Bar charts are almost as common in business reports as line charts, and in some ways they are more versatile. As Figure 12.5 illustrates, they are particularly valuable when you want to

Bar charts are useful in many situations and take a variety of forms.

- Compare the size of several items at one time

- Show changes in one item over time

- Indicate the composition of several items over time

- Show the relative size of components of a whole

The opportunities for being creative with bar charts are almost infinite. You can align the bars either vertically or horizontally and double the bars for comparisons. You can even use bar charts to show both positive and negative quantities.

Pie charts

Although they are somewhat less versatile than either line or bar charts, pie charts are nevertheless a valuable item in your inventory of visual aids. Nothing is better for showing the composition of a whole than a pie chart. (See Figure B in the Report Writer's Notebook on visual aids.)

Use pie charts to show the relative sizes of the parts of a whole.

FIGURE 12.3
Line Chart Plotting Three Lines

Figure 1 **Big Cars Lose Market Share, Little Cars Gain**

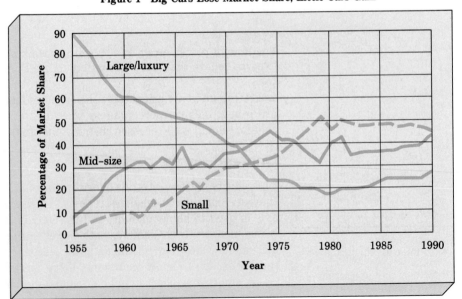

Source: Data from U.S. Department of Commerce.

FIGURE 12.4
Surface Chart

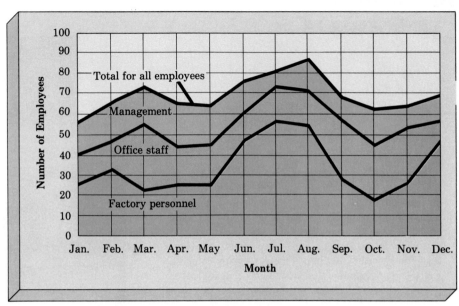

Figure 1   Average Daily Employee Absences

FIGURE 12.5
The Versatile Bar Chart

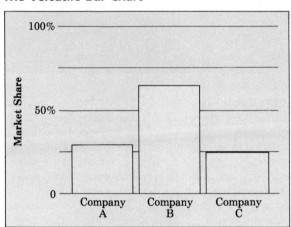

Figure 1
Company B Dominates the Market
at This Time (August 1, 1993)

Figure 1
Company B Has Steadily Gained Market
Share Over Time

Figure 1
Company B Has Captured Most of the Growth in the
Total Market Over the Past Four Years

Figure 1
Advertising and Promotion
Represent 10 Percent of
Company B's Expenses

Report Writer's Notebook
Creating Colorful Visual Aids with Computers

As computers become increasingly common in the workplace, more people are learning to use graphics software to create visual aids. But computer-generated visual aids may be ineffective if the computer's capabilities, especially color, aren't handled well.

Color helps make a point more effectively than black and white. But there's more to using color in visual aids than simply picking colors that appeal to you. To choose an effective color scheme, ask yourself these questions:

- *What colors will best convey the effect I want?* As a general rule, bright, solid colors are more pleasing to the eye and easier to distinguish than pastel, patterned colors. Yellow, blue, and green are usually good choices, but there are many other possibilities. Just keep in mind that too many colors may overwhelm the message. Use color as an accent, bright color for emphasis, and darker or lighter colors for background information.
- *Are these colors appropriate for my message, purpose, and audience?* Liking red is not enough of a reason for using it in all your graphic designs. It's too "hot" for some people and conveys the wrong message in some instances. For example, using red to show profits in an annual report might confuse readers, because they are likely to associate it with "red ink," or losses. Be aware that people in other cultures also make associations with some colors.
- *Can I improve the effect by changing any of the colors?* When you have the opportunity to use more than one color, choose those that contrast. Colors without contrast blend together and obscure the message.

In this notebook, you'll see some examples of color visual aids generated with various types of computer equipment. The captions accompanying the examples will help you duplicate their effect.

FIGURE A
Computer with Graphic Capabilities
To create your own visual aids with a computer, you'll need hardware and software that are capable of producing them. Your hardware will limit your software choices and determine the form and quality of the visual aids you're able to produce. At a minimum, you'll need a microcomputer with ample memory and graphics capability, a monitor (preferably color), an input device (keyboard, joystick, or special stylus), and an output device (printer, plotter, or film recorder). The graphics software you choose must be compatible with the hardware. Some software is designed to create only a particular form of output: hard copy, 35-mm slides, or overhead transparencies. Other software is specialized according to the types of visual aids it produces: graphs, diagrams, word charts, maps.

FIGURE B
Pie Chart with Color Overlay

Many of the most popular integrated software packages for microcomputers, including several spreadsheet and database management programs, have a built-in graphics capability that enables you to convert words and numbers into graphic output. Creating visual aids is a simple matter of selecting choices from a menu and responding to prompts that appear on the screen. Here's a typical sequence of events for constructing a chart:

1. Give the chart a title, and indicate the categories of information that you wish to portray.
2. Enter the numerical values for each point or segment on the chart, either by using the keyboard or by instructing the computer to take the data from an existing file.
3. Select the kind of chart you want to create: pie, bar, or line chart.
4. Identify the range of data that will be portrayed (that is, the highest and lowest values you want on the chart).
5. Label the scales (the horizontal and vertical axes) or segments.
6. Choose colors, if you have a color output device.
7. Print the graph.

The visual aid shown here was created with a very common combination of hardware and software: a microcomputer, integrated software, and a black-and-white dot matrix printer. Color was added by superimposing pieces of colored transfer film (available at most office supply stores). This type of visual aid is suitable for relatively informal communication.

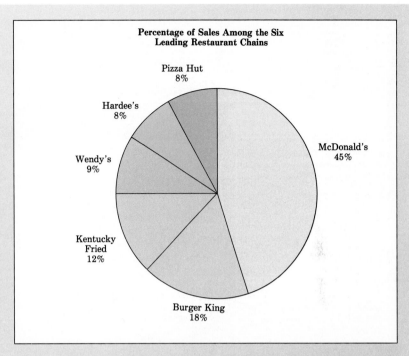

Percentage of Sales Among the Six Leading Restaurant Chains

Pizza Hut 8%
Hardee's 8%
Wendy's 9%
Kentucky Fried 12%
Burger King 18%
McDonald's 45%

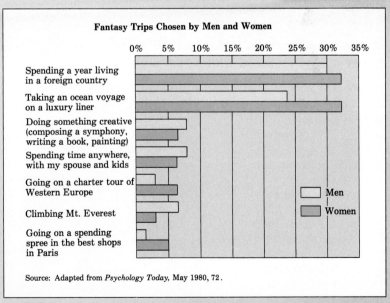

Fantasy Trips Chosen by Men and Women

Spending a year living in a foreign country
Taking an ocean voyage on a luxury liner
Doing something creative (composing a symphony, writing a book, painting)
Spending time anywhere, with my spouse and kids
Going on a charter tour of Western Europe
Climbing Mt. Everest
Going on a spending spree in the best shops in Paris

Men
Women

Source: Adapted from *Psychology Today*, May 1980, 72.

FIGURE C
Bar Chart Produced on Color Printer

More professional-looking visual aids require the use of specialized graphics software and output devices. This chart was created with a presentation-quality software program and printed out on a color printer that produces either paper copies or overhead transparencies. Because of its precise lines and dense colors, this type of visual aid is suitable for more formal communication.

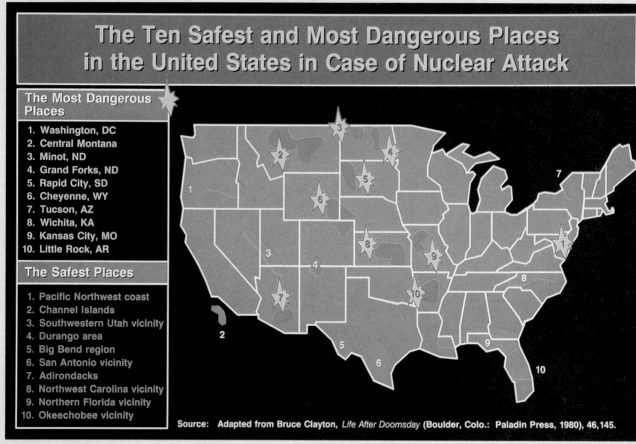

The Ten Safest and Most Dangerous Places in the United States in Case of Nuclear Attack

The Most Dangerous Places

1. Washington, DC
2. Central Montana
3. Minot, ND
4. Grand Forks, ND
5. Rapid City, SD
6. Cheyenne, WY
7. Tucson, AZ
8. Wichita, KA
9. Kansas City, MO
10. Little Rock, AR

The Safest Places

1. Pacific Northwest coast
2. Channel Islands
3. Southwestern Utah vicinity
4. Durango area
5. Big Bend region
6. San Antonio vicinity
7. Adirondacks
8. Northwest Carolina vicinity
9. Northern Florida vicinity
10. Okeechobee vicinity

Source: Adapted from Bruce Clayton, *Life After Doomsday* (Boulder, Colo.: Paladin Press, 1980), 46,145.

FIGURE D Map Produced with a Film Recorder

FIGURE E
Line Chart Using Special Graphics

Mastery of top-of-the-line graphics packages requires dedication, because neither the hardware nor the software is simple. But the end result is superb. The examples in Figures D and E were originally produced in the form of 35-mm slides, using a film recorder (which can also produce overhead transparencies). Few companies find it worthwhile to buy equipment this specialized, but independent computer services are now available to serve those who need top-quality visual aids.

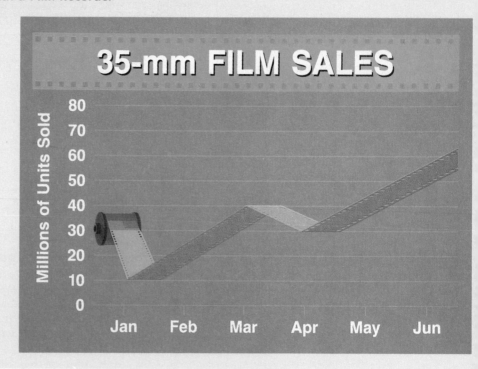

FIGURE F
Memo with Embedded Bar Chart

One of the newer developments in computer graphics is the ability to combine text and graphics on the same page. Many simple hardware and software packages are capable of producing documents like this one. More sophisticated packages can produce complex layouts, with a column of text and a visual aid set side by side on the page.

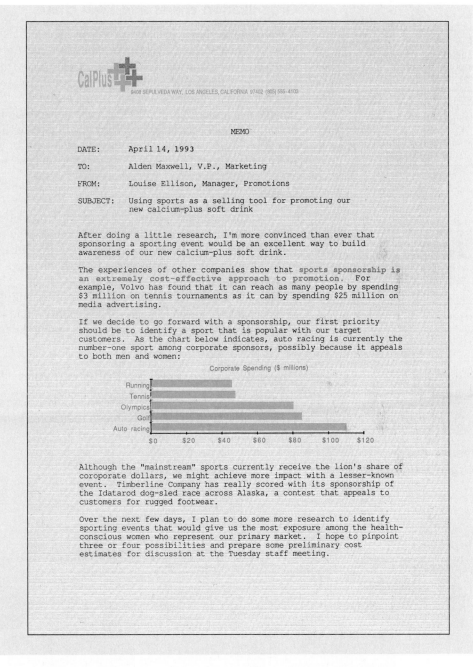

When composing pie charts, try to limit the number of slices in the pie to no more than seven. Otherwise, the chart looks cluttered and is difficult to label. If necessary, lump the smallest pieces together in a "miscellaneous" category. Ideally, the largest or most important slice of the pie, the segment you want to emphasize, is placed at the 12 o'clock position; the rest are arranged clockwise either in order of size or in some other logical progression. You might want to shade the segment that is of the greatest interest to your readers or use color to distinguish the various pieces. In any case, be sure to label all the segments and to indicate their value in either percentages or units of measure so that your readers will be able to judge the value of the wedges. The segments must add up to 100 percent.

Organization charts and flow charts

Use organization charts to depict the interrelationships among the parts of an organization.

If you need to show physical or conceptual relationships rather than numerical ones, you might want to use an organization chart or a flow chart. Organization charts, as the name implies, are used to illustrate the positions, units, or functions of an organization and the way they interrelate. An organization's normal communication channels are almost impossible to describe without a chart like the one in Figure 12.6. Flow charts are indispensable in illustrating processes, procedures, and relationships. They can illustrate the entire sequence of activities from start to finish. The various elements in the process may be represented by pictorial symbols or geometric shapes, as in Figure 12.7.

Use flow charts
- To show a series of steps from beginning to end
- To show relationships

Maps

Use maps
- To represent statistics by geographic area
- To show locational relationships

For certain applications, maps are ideal. One of the most common uses is to show concentrations of something by geographic area (see Figure D in the Report Writer's Notebook on visual aids). In your own reports, you might use maps to show regional differences in such variables as your company's sales of a product. Or you might indicate proposed plant sites and their proximity to sources of supply or key markets. Most office supply stores carry blank maps of this country, various regions of the country, and areas of the world. You can illustrate these maps to suit your needs, using dots, shading, labels, numbers, and symbols.

Drawings, diagrams, and photographs

Business reports occasionally use drawings, diagrams, and photographs, although these tend to be less common than some of the other visual aids. Drawings and diagrams are most often used in technical reports to show how some-

FIGURE 12.6
Organization Chart

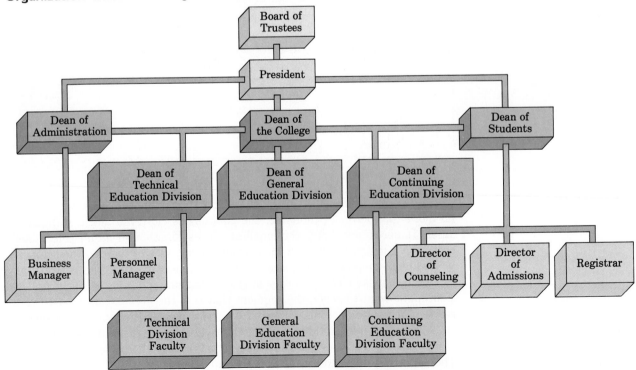

Figure 1   Administration of Atlantic College

FIGURE 12.7
Flow Chart

Figure 1   Flow of Clients Through Health Center

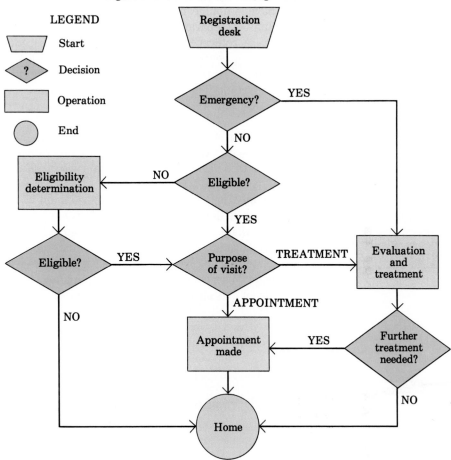

FIGURE 12.8
Diagram

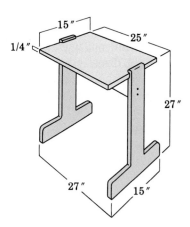

thing looks or operates. Figure 12.8, for example, is taken from a report describing furniture for use with computers. Although this diagram was professionally prepared, even a hand-drawn sketch is better than words alone for giving your audience a clear idea of how an item looks or how it can be used. In industries such as engineering and architecture, computer-aided design systems are capable of producing detailed diagrams and drawings. In addition, a variety of widely available programs for use on microcomputers provide a file of symbols and pictures of various types that can be used (sparingly) to add a decorative touch to reports and presentations.

Photographs have always been popular in business documents such as catalogs and annual reports, where their visual appeal is used to capture the interest of readers. As the technology for reproducing photographs improves and becomes less expensive, even analytical business reports for internal use are beginning to have more photographs in them. Nothing can demonstrate the exact appearance of a new facility, a piece of property or equipment, or a new product the way a photograph can.

Incorporation of visual aids in the text

Every visual aid you use should be clearly referred to by number in the text of your report. Some report writers refer to all visual aids as exhibits and number them consecutively throughout the report; many others number tables and figures separately (everything that isn't a table is regarded as a figure). In a very long report with numbered chapters (as in this book), visual aids may have a double number, consisting of the chapter number and an individual number separated by a period or a hyphen.

A reference to a visual aid should precede the piece itself so that readers are not confronted with visual aids whose significance they can't yet understand. The reference should make readers understand why the table or chart is important. The following selection from a report on the market for motorcycles shows how the connection can be made:

> Figure 1 shows the financial history of the motorcycle division over the past five years, with sales broken into four categories. Total sales were steady over this period, but the mix of sales by category changed dramatically.

In-text references tell readers why the illustration is important.

Ideally, it is best to place each visual aid right beside or right after the paragraph it illustrates so that readers can consult both the explanation and the visual aid at the same time (see Figure F in the Report Writer's Notebook on visual aids). But unless your company has a specialized desktop publishing system, you'll have trouble creating layouts with artwork and text on the same page. With conventional office equipment, the most practical approach is to put visual aids on separate pages and mesh them with the text after the report has been typed.

Put a visual aid as close as possible to its in-text reference to help readers understand the illustration's relevance.

But this solution raises the question of where you should put the pages with the visual aids. Some writers prefer to cluster them at the end of the report, either as a separate section or as an appendix. Others group them at the end of each chapter. Still others prefer to place them as close as possible to the paragraphs they refer to. Although a case can be made for each approach, the best one is generally to place the pages of visual aids right after the pages containing references to them. This arrangement encourages readers to look at the visual aids when you want them to, in the context you have prepared.

SUPPLEMENTARY PARTS

The supplementary parts come after the text of the report and include the appendix(es), bibliography, and index. They are more common in long reports than in short ones.

An appendix contains materials related to the report but not included in the text because they are too lengthy, too bulky, or not directly relevant. Sample questionnaires and cover letters, sample forms, computer printouts, and statistical formulas are frequently included in appendixes; a glossary of terms may be either an appendix or a separate supplementary part; and as mentioned, visual aids may be included in an appendix, particularly if they are tangential to the report.

Include in an appendix those materials that are
- Bulky or lengthy
- Not directly relevant to the text

Each type of material deserves a separate appendix. Identify the appendixes by labeling them, for example, "Appendix A: Questionnaire," "Appendix B: Computer Printout of Raw Data," and the like. All appendixes should be mentioned in the text and listed in the table of contents.

List your secondary sources in the bibliography.

A bibliography is a list of sources consulted in preparing the report. The way a bibliography should be constructed is shown in the sample report that follows and in Appendix C.

An index lists names, places, and subjects alphabetically with the page numbers of where each item occurs in the report, as in the index for this book. An index is rarely included in unpublished reports.

The report presented in the following pages was prepared by Andy O'Toole, an analyst in the cost accounting department of TriTech Industries, a medium-size company headquartered in San Francisco. TriTech's main product is optical character recognition equipment, which is used by the U.S. Postal Service for sorting mail. Andy's job is to help analyze the company's costs. He has this to say about the background of his report:

"For the past three or four years, TriTech has been on a roll. Our A-12 optical character reader was a real breakthrough, and the post office grabbed up as many as we could make. Our sales and profits kept climbing, and morale was fantastic. Everybody seemed to think that the good times would last forever. Unfortunately, everybody was wrong. When the Postal Service announced that they were 'postponing' all new equipment purchases because of cuts in their budget, we woke up to the fact that we are essentially a one-product company with one customer. At that point, management started scrambling around looking for ways to cut costs until we can diversify our business a bit.

"The vice president of administration, Jean Alexander, asked me to help identify cost-cutting opportunities in the travel and entertainment area. On the basis of her personal observations, she felt that TriTech was overly generous in its travel policies and that we might be able to save a significant amount by controlling these costs more carefully. My investigation confirmed her suspicion.

"I was reasonably confident that my report would be well received. I've worked with Ms. Alexander before and know what she likes: plenty of facts, clearly stated conclusions, and specific recommendations for what should be done next. I also knew that my report would be passed on to other TriTech executives, so I wanted to create a good impression. I wanted the report to be accurate and thorough, visually appealing, readable, and appropriate in tone."

In writing the analytical report that follows, Andy used an organization based on conclusions and recommendations, presented in direct order. The first two sections of the report correspond to Andy's two main conclusions: that TriTech's travel and entertainment costs are too high and that cuts are essential. The third section presents recommendations for achieving better control over travel and entertainment expenses. As you review the report, notice both the mechanical aspects and the way Andy presents his ideas.

Capitalize the title; use uppercase and lowercase letters for all other lines.

Follow the title with the name, title, and organization of the recipient.

Balance the white space between the items on the page.

When centering the lines horizontally on the title page, allow an extra ½-inch margin on the left side if it's a left-bound report.

For future reference, include the report's publication date.

REDUCING TRITECH'S TRAVEL AND ENTERTAINMENT COSTS

Prepared for
Jean Alexander, Vice President of Administration
TriTech Industries

Prepared by
Andrew O'Toole, Director
Cost Accounting Services
TriTech Industries

May 15, 1993

The "how to" tone of this title is appropriate for an action-oriented report that emphasizes recommendations. A more neutral title, such as "An Analysis of TriTech's Travel and Entertainment Costs," would be more suitable for an informational report.

Use memo format for transmitting internal reports, letter format for transmitting external reports.

Present the main conclusion or recommendation right away if you expect a positive response.

Use an informal, conversational style for the letter or memo of transmittal.

Acknowledge any help that you have received.

Close with thanks, an offer to discuss results, and an offer to assist with future projects, if appropriate.

<u>MEMORANDUM</u>

DATE: May 15, 1993

TO: Jean Alexander, Vice President of Administration

FROM: Andrew O'Toole, Director of Cost Accounting Services   *A.O.*

SUBJECT: Reducing TriTech's Travel and Entertainment Costs

Here is the report you requested April 30 on TriTech's travel and entertainment costs.

Your suspicion was right. We are spending far too much on business travel. Our unwritten policy has been "anything goes." We have no real control over T&E expenses. Although this offhanded approach may have been understandable when TriTech's profits were high, we can no longer afford the luxury of "going first class."

The solutions to the problem are obvious: We need to put someone in charge of travel and entertainment; we need a clear statement of policy; we need an effective control system; and we need to retain a business-oriented travel service that can optimize our travel arrangements. Perhaps more important, we need to change our attitude. Instead of viewing business travel as a free vacation, we need to act as though we were paying the bills ourselves.

Getting people to economize is not going to be easy. In the course of researching this issue, I've found that our employees are deeply attached to their first-class travel privileges. I almost think they would prefer a cut in pay to a loss in travel status. We'll need a lot of top management involvement to sell people on the need for moderation. One thing is clear: People will be very bitter if we create a two-class system in which top executives get special privileges while the rest of the employees make the sacrifices.

I'm grateful to Mary Lehman and Connie McIllvain for their help in rounding up and sorting through five years' worth of expense reports. Their efforts were truly Herculean.

Thanks for giving me the opportunity to work on this assignment. It's been a real education. If you have any questions about the report, please give me a call.

ghc

In this report, Andy decided to write a brief memo of transmittal and include a separate executive summary. Short reports (fewer than ten pages) often combine the synopsis or executive summary with the memo or letter of transmittal.

Word the headings exactly as they appear in the text.

Extend spaced periods (leaders) from the end of the heading to the page number. (For spaced periods, strike the space bar and the period alternately.) Align the periods under one another.

Type only the page numbers where sections begin; align the last digits of the page numbers.

Because figures and tables were numbered separately in the text, they are listed separately here. If all were labeled as exhibits, a single list would have been appropriate.

Number the contents pages with lowercase roman numerals centered 1 inch from the bottom.

CONTENTS

LIST OF ILLUSTRATIONS

iii

Andy included only first- and second-level headings in his table of contents, even though the report contains third-level headings. He prefers a shorter table of contents that focuses attention on the main divisions of thought. To save space, he also chose to list illustrations on the same page. Notice the informative titles, which are appropriate for a report to a receptive audience.

Begin by stating the purpose of the report.

Present the points in the executive summary in the same order as they appear in the report; use subheadings that summarize the content of the main sections of the report without repeating those that appear in the text.

Type the synopsis or executive summary in the same manner as the text of the report. Single-space if the report is single-spaced, and use the same format in both the executive summary and the text for margins, paragraph indentions, and headings.

EXECUTIVE SUMMARY

This report analyzes TriTech's travel and entertainment costs and presents recommendations for reducing those costs.

T&E Costs Are Too High

Travel and entertainment (T&E) is a large and growing expense category for TriTech Industries. The company currently spends about $10 million per year on business travel, and costs are increasing by 7 percent annually. Company employees make some 5,000 trips each year, at an average cost per trip of $2,000. Air fares are the biggest expense, followed by hotels, meals, and rental cars.

The nature of TriTech's business does require extensive travel, but the company's costs appear to be excessive. Every year, TriTech spends twice as much on T&E for each professional employee as its main competitors do. Although the location of the company's facilities may partly explain this discrepancy, the main reason for TriTech's high costs is the firm's philosophy and management style. TriTech encourages employees to go first class and pays relatively little attention to travel costs.

Cuts Are Essential

Although TriTech has traditionally been casual about travel and entertainment expenses, management now recognizes the need to gain more control over this element of costs. The company is currently entering a period of declining profits, prompting management to look for every opportunity to reduce spending. At the same time, rising air fares are making travel and entertainment expenses more important to the bottom line.

TriTech Can Save $4 Million per Year

Fortunately, TriTech has a number of excellent opportunities for reducing its travel and entertainment costs. Savings of up to $4 million per year should be achievable, judging by the experience of other companies. The first priority should be to hire a director of travel and entertainment to assume overall responsibility for T&E spending. This individual should establish a written travel and entertainment policy and create a budgeting and cost control system. The director should also retain a nationwide travel agency to handle our reservations.

iv

Andy decided to include an executive summary because his report was aimed at a mixed audience. He knew that some readers would be interested in the details of his report and some would prefer to focus on the big picture. The executive summary was aimed at the latter group. Andy wanted to give these readers enough information to make a decision without burdening them with the task of reading the entire report.

The hard-hitting tone of this executive summary is appropriate for a receptive audience. A more neutral approach would be better for hostile or skeptical readers.

Number the pages of the executive summary with lowercase roman numerals centered about 1 inch from the bottom of the page.

At the same time, TriTech should make employees aware of the need for moderation in travel and entertainment spending. People should be encouraged to forgo any unnecessary travel and to economize on airline tickets, hotels, meals, rental cars, and other expenses.

In addition to economizing on an individual basis, TriTech should look for ways to reduce costs by negotiating preferential rates with travel providers. Once retained, a travel agency should be able to accomplish this.

These changes, although necessary, are likely to hurt morale, at least in the short term. Management will need to make a determined effort to explain the rationale for reduced spending. By exercising moderation in their own travel arrangements, TriTech executives can set a good example and help make the changes more acceptable to other employees.

v

This executive summary is written in an impersonal style, which adds to the formality of the report. Although the impersonal style is commonly used for a synopsis or an executive summary, some writers prefer a more personal approach. Generally speaking, you should gear your choice of style to your relationship with the readers. Andy chose the formal approach because several members of his audience were considerably higher up in the organization. He did not want to sound too familiar. In addition, he wanted the executive summary and the text to be compatible, and his company prefers the impersonal style for formal reports.

Center the title of the report on the first page of the text, 1 inch (1½ inches if top-bound) from the top of the page.

Begin the introduction by establishing the need for action.

Single-space the report to create a formal, finished look; double-space if your readers prefer it or if your report is a preliminary document.

Mentioning sources and methods increases the credibility of a report and gives readers a complete picture of the study's background.

Use the arabic numeral 1 for the first page of the report; center the number about 1 inch from the bottom of the page.

REDUCING TRITECH'S TRAVEL AND ENTERTAINMENT COSTS

INTRODUCTION

TriTech Industries has traditionally encouraged a significant amount of business travel, in the belief that it is an effective way of conducting operations. To compensate employees for the stress and inconvenience of frequent trips, management has authorized generous travel and entertainment allowances. This philosophy has undoubtedly been good for morale, but the company has paid a price. Last year, TriTech spent $10 million on T&E, $5 million more than it spent on research and development.

This year, the cost of travel and entertainment will have a bigger impact on profits, owing to changes in airline fares. The timing of these changes is unfortunate, because the company anticipates that profits will be relatively weak for a variety of other reasons. In light of these profit pressures, Ms. Jean Alexander, Vice President of Administration, has asked the accounting department to take a closer look at the T&E budget.

Purpose, Scope, and Limitations

The purpose of this report is to analyze the travel and entertainment budget, evaluate the impact of recent changes in air fares, and suggest ways to tighten management's control over travel and entertainment expenses.

Although the report outlines a number of steps that could reduce TriTech's expenses, the precise financial impact of these measures is difficult to project. The estimates presented in the report provide a "best guess" view of what TriTech can expect to save. But until the company actually implements these steps, there is no way of knowing how much the travel and entertainment budget can be reduced.

Sources and Methods

In preparing this report, the accounting department analyzed internal expense reports for the past five years to determine how much TriTech spends on travel and entertainment. These figures were then compared with statistics on similar companies in the electronic equipment industry, obtained through industry association data, annual reports, and magazine articles. In addition, the accounting department screened magazine and newspaper articles to determine how other companies are coping with the high cost of business travel.

1

In a brief introduction like this one, some writers would omit the subheadings within the introduction and rely on topic sentences and on transitional words and phrases to indicate that they are discussing such subjects as the purpose, scope, and limitations of the study. Andy decided to use headings because they help readers scan the document.

Using arabic numerals, number the second and succeeding pages of the text in the upper right-hand corner where the top and right-hand margins meet.

2

Report Organization

This report reviews the size and composition of TriTech's travel and entertainment expenses, analyzes trends in air fare pricing, and recommends steps for reducing the travel and entertainment budget.

THE HIGH COST OF TRAVEL AND ENTERTAINMENT

Although many companies view travel and entertainment (T&E) as an "incidental" cost of doing business, the dollars add up. Last year, U.S. industry paid an estimated $90 billion for travel and entertainment.[1] At TriTech Industries, the bill for air fares, hotels, rental cars, restaurants, and entertainment totaled $10 million. The company's travel and entertainment budget has increased by 12 percent per year for the past five years. By industry standards, TriTech's budget is on the high side, largely because management has a generous policy on travel benefits.

$10 Million per Year
Spent on Travel and Entertainment

TriTech Industries' annual budget for travel and entertainment is only 8 percent of sales. Because this is a relatively small expense category compared with such things as salaries and commissions, it is tempting to dismiss travel and entertainment costs as insignificant. However, T&E is TriTech's third largest controllable expense, directly behind salaries and data processing.[2]

Last year, TriTech personnel made about 5,000 trips, at an average cost per trip of $2,000. The typical trip involved a round-trip flight of 3,000 miles, meals and hotel accommodations for three days, and a rental car. Roughly 80 percent of the trips were made by 20 percent of the staff. Top management and sales personnel were the most frequent travelers, averaging 18 trips per year.

Figure 1 illustrates how the travel and entertainment budget is spent. The largest categories are air fares and lodging, which together account for $7 out of every $10 that

Placement of visual aids titles should be consistent throughout a report. This sample report, however, shows all options for placement: above, below, or beside the visual aid.

Figure 1
Air Fares and Lodging Account
for Over Two-Thirds of TriTech's
Travel and Entertainment Budget

Notice how Andy opened the first main section of the body. He began with a topic sentence that introduced an important fact about the subject of the section. Then he oriented the reader to the three major points developed in the section. He put his data in perspective by comparing growth in travel and entertainment expenses to growth in sales. After all, if sales were also increasing by 12 percent a year, an increase of 12 percent in travel and entertainment expenses might be acceptable.

Introduce visual aids before they appear, and indicate what readers should notice about the data.

Number the visual aids consecutively, and refer to them in the text by their numbers. If your report is a book-length document, you may number the visual aids by chapter: Figure 4-2, for example, would be the second figure in the fourth chapter.

3

employees spend on travel and entertainment. This spending has been relatively steady for the past five years and is consistent with the distribution of expenses experienced by other companies.

Although the composition of the travel and entertainment budget has been consistent, its size has not. As Figure 2 shows, expenditures for travel and entertainment have increased by about 12 percent per year for the past five years, roughly twice the rate of the company's growth in sales. This rate of growth makes travel and entertainment TriTech's fastest-growing expense item.

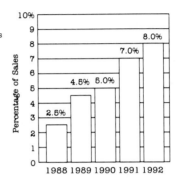

Figure 2
Travel and Entertainment
Expenses Have Increased as
a Percentage of Sales

TriTech's Budget Exceeds Competitors'

There are many reasons why TriTech has a high travel and entertainment budget. TriTech's main customer is the U.S. Postal Service. The company's mode of selling requires frequent face-to-face contact with the customer, yet corporate headquarters is located on the West Coast, some 2,600 miles from Washington, D.C. Furthermore, TriTech's manufacturing operations are widely scattered; facilities are located in San Francisco, Detroit, Boston, and Dallas. To coordinate these operations, corporate management and division personnel must make frequent trips to and from company headquarters.

Although much of TriTech's travel budget is justified, the company spends considerably more on travel and entertainment than its competitors do, as Figure 3 indicates. Data supplied by the International Association of Electronics indicates that the typical company in our industry spends approximately $1,900 per month per professional employee on travel and entertainment.[3] TriTech's per capita travel costs for professional employees are running $4,000 per month.

Andy originally drew this bar chart as a line chart, showing both sales and T&E expenses in absolute dollars. However, the comparison was difficult to interpret because sales were so much greater than T&E expenses. The vertical axis stretched from 0 to $125 million. Switching to a bar chart, expressed in percentage terms, made the main idea much easier to grasp.

Place the visual aid as close as possible to the point it illustrates.

Give each visual aid a title that clearly indicates what it is about.

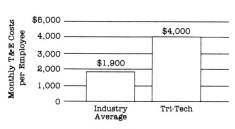

4

Figure 3
TriTech Spends Over Twice the Industry Average
on Travel and Entertainment
Source: International Association of Electronics, 1992.

Spending Has Been Encouraged

Although a variety of factors may contribute to this differential, TriTech's relatively high travel and entertainment budget is at least partially attributable to the company's philosophy and management style. Because many employees do not enjoy business travel, management has tried to make the trips more pleasant by authorizing first-class air fare, luxury hotel accommodations, and full-size rental cars. The sales staff is encouraged to entertain clients at restaurants and to invite them to cultural and sporting events.

The cost of these privileges is easy to overlook, given the weakness of TriTech's system for keeping track of travel and entertainment expenses. The monthly financial records provided to management do not contain a separate category for travel and entertainment; the information is buried under Cost of Goods Sold and under Selling, General, and Administrative Expenses. Each department head is given authority to approve any expense report, regardless of how large it may be. Receipts are not required for expenditures of less than $100. Individuals are allowed to make their own travel arrangements. No one is charged with the responsibility for controlling the company's total spending on travel and entertainment.

GROWING IMPACT ON THE BOTTOM LINE

During the past three years, TriTech has enjoyed healthy profits; as a result, there has been relatively little pressure to push for tighter controls over all aspects of the business. However, the situation is changing. Management is projecting flat to declining profits for the next two years, a situation that has prompted the company to search for ways to cut costs. At the same time, rising air fares have increased the impact of travel and entertainment expenses on the company's financial results.

The chart on this page is very simple, but it creates an effective visual comparison. Andy included just enough data to make his point.

Informative headings focus readers' attention on the main points of the report. Thus they are most appropriate when the report is in direct order and is aimed at a receptive audience. Descriptive headings are more effective when a report is in indirect order and the readers are less receptive.

Documenting the facts adds weight to Andy's argument.

5

Lower Profits Underscore Need for Change

The next two years promise to be difficult for TriTech Industries. After several years of steady increases in spending, the U.S. Postal Service is tightening procurement policies for automated mail-handling equipment. Funding for TriTech's main product, the A-12 optical character reader, has been canceled. As a consequence, sales are expected to decline by 15 percent. Although TriTech is negotiating several promising research and development contracts with nongovernment clients, management does not foresee any major procurements for the next two to three years.

At the same time, TriTech is facing cost increases on several fronts. The new production facility now under construction in Salt Lake City, Utah, is behind schedule and over budget. Labor contracts with union workers in Boston and Dallas expire within the next six months, and management anticipates that significant salary and benefits concessions may be necessary to avoid strikes. Moverover, marketing and advertising costs are expected to increase as TriTech attempts to strengthen these activities to better cope with competitive pressures. Given the expected decline in revenues and increase in costs, management projects that profits will fall by 12 percent in the coming fiscal year.

Air Fares Are Rising

Over the next 8 to 12 months, rising air fares can be expected to inflate TriTech's travel and entertainment costs. The recent round of mergers in the airline industry has reduced competition among carriers, thereby reducing the companies' incentives to cut ticket prices. Ninety-four percent of all air traffic in the United States is controlled by just eight airlines, up from 80 percent in 1978 when the airline industry was decontrolled.[4] The decline in competition is expected to lead to higher air fares, particularly for business travelers. According to industry analysts, the airline price wars that followed deregulation are a thing of the past. Any future fare reductions will be aimed at narrow market segments, such as families taking summer vacations. Meanwhile, business travelers who pay full fare will face price increases of up to 15 percent on some routes.[5]

Several factors apart from the reduction in competition are pushing fares up. Perhaps the most significant factor is the increasing sophistication of the airlines' pricing strategies. For example, airlines used to discount unfilled seats in the moments before flights departed, on the theory that low-fare passengers were better than none at all. Now, though, travelers who arrive at the gate just before departure are likely to pay full fare. The reason: Airlines discovered that most late arrivals were so desperate to get on the plane they would willingly pay almost any price.[6]

The tendency toward increasing fares also reflects the airlines' increasing costs. Higher fuel costs are probably the most important short-term factor, but labor costs are also beginning to rise, as are landing fees, passenger meals, advertising expenses, and debt service costs. Furthermore, the airlines are committed to buying some $95 billion worth of new equipment within the next several years.[7]

Because air fares represent TriTech's biggest T&E expense, Andy included a subsection that deals with the possible impact of trends in the airline industry. Air fares are rising, so it is especially important to gain more control over employees' air travel arrangements.

Pointing out both the benefits and risks of taking action
gives recommendations an
objective flavor.

The indented list format calls
attention to important points
and adds visual interest. You
can also use visual aids,
headings, and direct quotations to break up large, solid
blocks of print.

6

Given the fact that air fares account for 45 percent of TriTech's T&E budget, the
trend toward higher ticket prices will have serious consequences on the company's
expenses unless management takes action to control these costs.

METHODS FOR REDUCING
TRAVEL AND ENTERTAINMENT COSTS

By implementing a number of reforms, management can expect to reduce TriTech's
travel and entertainment budget by as much as 40 percent. However, these measures
are likely to be unpopular with employees. To gain acceptance for the changes, management will need to sell employees on the need for moderation in travel and entertainment allowances.

Three Ways to Trim Expenses

By researching what other companies are doing to curb travel and entertainment
expenses, the accounting department has identified three prominent opportunities that
should enable TriTech to save about $4 million annually in travel-related costs.

Institute Tighter Spending Controls

A single individual should be appointed to spearhead the effort to gain control of the
travel and entertainment budget. The individual should be familiar with the travel industry and should be well versed in both accounting and data processing. He or she
should report to the vice president of administration and should be given the title of
director of travel and entertainment. The director's first priorities should be to establish a written travel and entertainment policy and to implement a system for controlling travel and entertainment costs.

TriTech currently has no written policy on travel and entertainment, despite the
fact that 73 percent of all firms have such policies.[8] Creating a policy would clarify
management's position and serve as a vehicle for communicating the need for moderation. At a minimum, the policy should include the following provisions:

* All travel and entertainment should be strictly related to business and should be
  approved in advance.

* Instead of going first class, employees should make a reasonable effort to economize on air fares, hotels, rental cars, and meals.

Andy created a forceful tone by using action verbs in the third-level subheadings of this section. This approach is appropriate to the nature of the study and
the attitude of the audience. However, in a status-conscious organization, the
imperative verbs might sound a bit too presumptuous coming from a junior
member of the staff.

When including recommendations in a report, specify the steps required to implement them.

7

The travel and entertainment policy should apply equally to employees at all levels in the organization. No special benefits should be allowed for top executives.

To implement the new policy, TriTech will need to create a system for controlling travel and entertainment expenses. Each department should prepare an annual T&E budget as part of its operating plan. These budgets should be presented in detail so management can evaluate how travel and entertainment dollars will be spent and recommend appropriate cuts.

To help management monitor performance relative to these budgets, the director of travel should prepare monthly financial statements showing actual travel and entertainment expenditures by department. The system for capturing this information should be computerized and should be capable of identifying individuals who consistently exceed approved spending levels. The recommended average should range between $1,500 and $2,500 per month for each professional employee, depending on the individual's role in the company. Because they make frequent trips, sales and top management personnel can be expected to have relatively high travel expenses.

The director of travel should also be responsible for retaining a business-oriented travel service that will schedule all employee business trips and look for the best travel deals, particularly in air fares. In addition to centralizing TriTech's reservation and ticketing activities, the agency will negotiate reduced group rates with hotels and rental car agencies. The agency selected should have offices nationwide so all TriTech facilities can channel their reservations through the same company. By consolidating its travel planning in this way, TriTech can increase its control over costs and achieve economies of scale.

Reduce Unnecessary Travel and Entertainment

One of the easiest ways to reduce expenses is to reduce the amount of traveling and entertaining that occurs. An analysis of last year's expenditures suggests that as much as 30 percent of TriTech's travel and entertainment is discretionary. For example, the professional staff spent $1.7 million attending seminars and conferences last year. Although some of these gatherings are undoubtedly beneficial, the company could save money by sending fewer representatives to each function and by eliminating some of the less valuable seminars.

By the same token, TriTech could economize on trips between headquarters and divisions by reducing the frequency of such visits and by sending fewer people on each trip. Although there is often no substitute for face-to-face meetings, management could try to resolve more internal issues through telephone contacts and written communication.

Andy decided to single-space his report to give it a "published" appearance. Double-spacing makes the text of a long report somewhat easier to read and provides more space for readers to write comments.

8

TriTech can also reduce spending by urging employees to economize. For example, instead of flying first class, employees can fly tourist class or take advantage of discount fares. Instead of taking clients to dinner, TriTech personnel can hold breakfast meetings, which tend to be less costly. Rather than ordering a $20 bottle of wine, employees can select a less expensive bottle or dispense with alcohol entirely. People can book rooms at moderately priced hotels and drive smaller rental cars. In general, employees should be urged to spend the company's money as though it were their own.

Obtain Lowest Rates for Travel Providers

Apart from urging individual employees to economize, TriTech can also save money by searching for the lowest available air fares, hotel rates, and rental car fees. Currently, few TriTech employees have the time or specialized knowledge to seek out travel bargains. When they need to travel, they make the most convenient and most comfortable arrangements. However, if TriTech contracts with a professional travel service, the company will have access to professionals who can be more efficient in obtaining the lower rates from travel providers.

Judging by the experience of other companies, TriTech may be able to trim as much as 30 to 40 percent from the travel budget by looking for bargains in air fares and negotiating group rates with hotels and rental car companies.[9] For example, by guaranteeing to provide selected hotels with a certain amount of business, Weston Computer was able to achieve a 20 percent reduction in its hotel expenses. Now, instead of choosing between 40 or 50 hotels in a city like Chicago, Weston employees stay at one of the 6 or 7 hotels where the company has negotiated a corporate rate.[10] TriTech should be able to achieve similar economies by analyzing its travel patterns, identifying frequently visited locations, and selecting a few hotels that are willing to reduce rates in exchange for guaranteed business. By the same token, the company should be able to save up to 40 percent on rental car charges by negotiating a corporate rate.

The possibilities for economizing are promising, but it's worth noting that making the best arrangements is a complicated undertaking, requiring many trade-offs. The airlines currently offer 4 million air fares, and on any given day, as many as 1 million of them might change in some way.[11] In booking a particular reservation, the travel agent might have to choose between 20 or 25 options with varying prices and provisions. The best fares might not always be the lowest. For example, indirect flights are often less expensive than direct flights, but they take longer and may end up costing more in lost work time. By the same token, the cheapest tickets may have to be booked 30 days in advance, often an impossibility in business travel. Similarly, discount tickets may be nonrefundable, which is a real negative if the trip has to be canceled at the last minute. TriTech is currently not equipped to make these and other trade-offs. However, by employing a business-oriented travel service, the company will have access to computerized systems that can optimize its choices.

The use of an example adds credibility and makes the discussion more interesting.

Pointing up the difficulties demonstrates that you have considered all the angles and builds readers' confidence in your judgment.

Notice how Andy made the transition from section to section. The first sentence under the heading on this page refers to the subject of the previous paragraph and signals a shift in thought.

The use of informative titles for illustrations is consistent with the way headings are handled and is appropriate for a report to a receptive audience. The use of complete sentences helps readers focus immediately on the point of the illustrations.

Even though estimated savings may be difficult to project, including dollar figures helps management envision the impact of your suggestions.

9

The Impact of Reforms

By implementing tighter controls, reducing unnecessary expenses, and negotiating more favorable rates, TriTech Industries should be able to reduce its travel and entertainment budget significantly. As Table 1 illustrates, the combined savings should be in the neighborhood of $4 million, although the precise figures are somewhat difficult to project. Reductions in air fares and hotel accommodations are the most important source of savings, accounting for about $2.3 million.

Table 1
TriTech Can Trim Travel and Entertainment Costs
by an Estimated $4 Million per Year

Source of Savings	Amount Saved
More efficient scheduling and selection of airline reservations	$1,400,000
Preferred rates on hotels	900,000
Fewer trips to conferences	700,000
Reduction in interdivisional travel	425,000
Reduced rates on rental cars	375,000
More economical choices by individuals	200,000
TOTAL SAVINGS	$4,000,000

Source: Accounting department estimates based on internal data and experience of other companies.

To achieve the economies outlined in the table, TriTech will incur expenses associated with hiring a director of travel and implementing a travel and entertainment cost control system. These costs are projected at $60,000: $55,000 per year and salary and benefits for the new employee and a one-time expense of $5,000 associated with the cost-control system. The cost of retaining a full-service travel agency will be negligible, because agencies receive a commission from travel providers rather than a fee from clients.

The measures required to achieve these savings are likely to be unpopular with employees. TriTech personnel are accustomed to generous travel and entertainment allowances, and they are likely to resent having these privileges curtailed. To alleviate their disappointment, management should make a determined effort to explain why the changes are necessary. The director of corporate communication should be asked to develop a multifaceted campaign that will communicate the importance of curtailing travel and entertainment costs. In addition, management should set a positive example by adhering strictly to the new policies. To maintain morale, the limitations should apply equally to employees at all levels in the organization.

The table on this page puts Andy's recommendations in perspective. Notice how he called attention in the text to the most important sources of savings and also spelled out the costs required to achieve these results.

Use a descriptive heading for the last section of the text. In informational reports, this section is generally called "Summary"; in analytical reports, it is called "Conclusions" or "Conclusions and Recommendations."

Emphasize the recommendations by presenting them in list format, if possible.

Do not introduce new facts in this section of the text.

10

CONCLUSIONS AND RECOMMENDATIONS

TriTech Industries is currently spending $10 million per year on travel and entertainment. Although much of this spending is justified, the company's costs appear to be high relative to competitors', mainly because TriTech has been generous with its travel benefits.

TriTech's liberal approach to travel and entertainment was understandable during years of high profitability; however, the company is facing the prospect of declining profits for the next several years. Management is therefore motivated to cut costs in all areas of the business. Reducing T&E spending is particularly important, because the impact of these costs on the bottom line will increase as a result of fare increases in the airline industry.

TriTech should be able to reduce travel and entertainment costs by about 40 percent by taking three important steps:

1. Institute tighter spending controls. Management should hire a director of travel and entertainment who will assume overall responsibility for T&E activities. Within the next six months, this individual should develop a written travel policy, insititute a T&E budgeting and cost-control system, and retain a professional, business oriented travel agency that will optimize arrangements with travel providers.

2. Reduce unnecessary travel and entertainment. TriTech should encourage employees to economize on travel and entertainment spending. Management can accomplish this by authorizing fewer trips and by urging employees to be more conservative in their spending.

3. Obtain lowest rates from travel providers. TriTech should also focus on obtaining the best rates on airline tickets, hotel rooms, and rental cars. By channeling all arrangements through a professional travel agency, the company can optimize its choices and gain clout in negotiating preferred rates.

Because these measures may be unpopular with employees, management should make a concerted effort to explain the importance of reducing travel costs. The director of corporate communication should be given responsibility for developing a plan to communicate the need for employee cooperation.

Because Andy organized his report around conclusions and recommendations, readers have already been introduced to them. Thus he summarizes his conclusions in the first two paragraphs, presenting them in the same order in which they were presented in the text. A simple list is enough to remind readers of the three main recommendations. In a longer report, he might have divided the section into subsections, labeled "Conclusions" and "Recommendations," to distinguish between the two. If the report had been organized around logical arguments, this would have been readers' first exposure to the conclusions and recommendations, and Andy would have needed to develop them more fully.

To simplify the typing process, most writers prefer to place all source notes together at the end of the text. (See Appendix C for details on handling documentation.)

NOTES   11

1. Sharon Vargas, "How Companies Cut Travel Costs," Administration Today, February 1993, 12.

2. Damon W. Dayton, "What to Do When the Sky Is Not the Limit," Management Accounting, June 1992, 33.

3. Analysis of Costs in the Electronics Industry (Washington, D.C.: International Association of Electronics, 1989), 23.

4. Kenneth Labich, "Should Airlines Be Reregulated?" Fortune, 19 June 1989, 82.

5. Kenneth Sodomon, "Airline Decontrol and the High Price of Flying," The Bulletin of Public Policy, 20 July 1992, 1.

6. Labich, "Should Airlines Be Reregulated?" 90.

7. Martha M. Hamilton, "Nation's Air Fares Ready for Takeoff," Washington Post, 7 May 1989, H4.

8. Vargas, "How Companies Cut Travel Costs," 13.

9. Interview with Jarad Dettwiler, "Saving a Bundle on Travel Costs," The Prudent Administrator, 22 April 1991, 87.

10. Milton D. Gallanos, Dylan Betts, and Lawton Crawford, "Corporate T&E Expenditures: A Plan for Regaining Control," Journal of Managerial Accounting, October 1991, 139-145.

11. William Stockton, "When Eight Carriers Call the Shots," The New York Times, 20 November 1988, sec. 3, 6.

BIBLIOGRAPHY

Analysis of Costs in the Electronics Industry. Washington, D.C.: International Association of Electronics, 1989.

Dayton, Damon W. "What to Do When the Sky Is Not the Limit." Management Accounting, June 1992, 33-36.

Gallanos, Milton D., Dylan Betts, and Lawton Crawford. "Corporate T&E Expenditures: A Plan for Regaining Control." Journal of Managerial Accounting, October 1991, 139-145.

Hamilton, Martha M. "Nation's Air Fares Ready for Takeoff." Washington Post, 7 May 1989, H1, H4.

Labich, Kenneth. "Should Airlines Be Reregulated?" Fortune, 19 June 1989, 82-90.

"Saving a Bundle on Travel Costs." The Prudent Administrator, 22 April 1991, 87-88.

Sodomon, Kenneth. "Airline Decontrol and the High Price of Flying." The Bulletin of Public Policy, 20 July 1992, 1-4.

Stockton, William. "When Eight Carriers Call the Shots." The New York Times, 20 November 1988, sec. 3, 1, 6.

Vargas, Sharon. "How Companies Cut Travel Costs." Administration Today, February 1993, 12-13.

List references alphabetically by the author's last name or, when the author is unknown, by the title of the reference. See Appendix C for additional details on preparing bibliographies.

Andy's bibliography is a reading list of sources cited in the notes. Some report writers use the bibliography to list additional sources.

COMPONENTS OF A FORMAL PROPOSAL

As mentioned in Chapter 10, certain analytical reports are called proposals, including bids to perform work under a contract and pleas for financial support from outsiders. Such bids and pleas are nearly always formal. The goal is to impress the potential client or supporter with your professionalism, and the goal is best achieved through a structured and deliberate approach.

Formal proposals contain many of the same components as other formal reports. The difference lies mostly in the text, although a few of the prefatory parts are also different. With the exception of an occasional appendix, most proposals have few supplementary parts.

PREFATORY PARTS

The cover, title fly, title page, table of contents, and list of illustrations are handled just as they are in other formal reports. But some prefatory parts are quite different:

Use a copy of the request for proposal in place of the letter of authorization.

- *Copy of the RFP.* Instead of having a letter of authorization, a formal proposal may have a copy of the request for proposal (RFP) issued by the client to whom the proposal is being submitted. If the RFP includes detailed specifications, it may be too long to bind into the proposal; in that case, you may want to include only the introductory portion of the RFP. Or you can omit the RFP and simply refer to it in your letter of transmittal.

Use the good-news pattern for the letter of transmittal if the proposal is solicited; use the persuasive plan if the proposal is unsolicited.

- *Letter of transmittal.* The way you handle the letter of transmittal depends on whether the proposal is solicited or unsolicited. If the proposal is solicited, the transmittal letter should follow the pattern for good-news messages, highlighting those aspects of your proposal that may give you a competitive advantage. If the proposal is unsolicited, the transmittal letter takes on added importance; in fact, it may be all the client reads. The letter must persuade the reader that you have something worthwhile to offer, something that justifies the time required to read the entire proposal. The transmittal letter for an unsolicited proposal should therefore follow the pattern for persuasive messages (see Chapter 9).

Most proposals do not require a synopsis or an executive summary.

- *Synopsis or executive summary.* Although you may include a synopsis or an executive summary for your reader's convenience if your proposal is quite long, these components are somewhat less useful in a formal proposal than they are in other formal reports. If your proposal is unsolicited, your transmittal letter will already have whet the reader's appetite, making a synopsis or an executive summary pointless. It may also be pointless if your proposal is solicited, because the reader is already committed to studying the text to find out how you propose to satisfy the terms of a contract. The introduction to a solicited proposal provides an adequate preview of the contents.

TEXT OF THE PROPOSAL

The text of a proposal performs two essential functions: It persuades the client to award you a contract (or financial support), and it spells out the terms of

A proposal is both a selling tool and a contractual commitment.

Follow the instructions presented in the RFP.

that contract (or what will be done with the funds). The trick is to sell the client on your ideas without making promises that will haunt you later. If the proposal is unsolicited, you have some latitude in arranging the text. The organization of a solicited proposal, on the other hand, is governed by the request for proposal. Most RFPs spell out precisely what you should cover and in what order so that all bids will be similar in form. This uniformity enables the client to evaluate the competing proposals in a systematic way. In fact, in many organizations, a team of evaluators splits up the proposals so that each member can look at a different section. For example, an engineer might review the technical portions of all the proposals submitted, and an accountant might review the cost estimates.

Introduction

In the introduction, establish the need for action and summarize the key benefits of your proposal.

The introduction orients readers to the rest of the proposal. It should identify your organization and your purpose as well as outline the remainder of the text. If the proposal is solicited, the introduction should refer to the RFP; if not, it should mention any factors that led you to submit the bid.

For example, you might refer to previous conversations you've had with the client or mention mutual acquaintances. Subheadings for contract proposals often include the following:

■ *Background or statement of the problem.* A brief review of the client's situation, worded to establish the need for action.

■ *Overview of approach.* A short summary that highlights your key selling points and their related benefits, showing how your proposal will solve the client's problem. The subhead for this section might also be "Preliminary Analysis" or some other heading that will identify this section as a summary of your solution to the problem.

■ *Scope.* A statement of the boundaries of the study, what you will and will not do. This brief section might also be labeled "Delimitations."

■ *Report organization.* A short overview that orients the reader to the remainder of the proposal and calls attention to the major divisions of thought.

Body

The heart of the proposal is the body, which generally has the same purpose as the body of other reports. In a proposal, however, the body must cover some specific types of information:

As chairman of the board for Computer Associates International, Charles B. Wang must often make fast decisions on proposals. A clear purpose stated concisely saves time and promotes understanding, advises Wang, and that allows your reader to make the right decision.

■ *Proposed approach.* Might also be titled "Technical Proposal," "Research Design," "Issues for Analysis," or "Work Statement." Regardless of the heading, this section is a description of what you have to offer: your concept, product, or service. For example, if you are proposing to develop a new airplane, you might describe your preliminary design, using drawings or calculations to demonstrate the soundness of your solution. To persuade the client that your proposal has merit, focus on the strengths of your product in relation to the client's needs. Point out any advantages that you have over your competitors. For example, you might describe how the unique wing design of your plane provides superior fuel economy, a particularly important feature specified in the client's request for proposal.

■ *Work plan.* Describes how you will accomplish the work that must be done (necessary unless you are proposing to provide a standard, off-the-shelf item). For each phase of the work plan, you describe the steps you will take, their timing, the methods or resources you will use, and the person or persons who will be responsible. Indicate any critical dates when portions of the work will be completed. If your proposal is accepted, the work plan will become contractually binding. Any slippage in the schedule you propose may jeopardize the contract or cost your organization a considerable amount of money. Therefore, be careful when preparing this section of the proposal. Don't promise to deliver more than you can realistically achieve within a given period.

> Use the work plan to describe the tasks to be completed under the terms of the contract.

■ *Statement of qualifications.* Describes your organization's experience, personnel, and facilities in relation to the client's needs. If you work for a large organization that frequently submits proposals, you can usually borrow much of this section intact from previous proposals. However, be sure to tailor this "boilerplate" to suit the situation. The qualifications section can be an important selling point, and it deserves to be handled carefully.

> In the qualifications section, demonstrate that you have the personnel, facilities, and experience to do a competent job.

■ *Costs.* Typically has few words and many numbers but can make or break the proposal. If your price is out of line, the client will probably reject your bid. However, before you "buy in" with a low bid, remember that you will have to live with the price you quote in the proposal. It's rarely advantageous to win a contract if you're doomed to lose money on the job. Because it is often difficult to estimate costs on experimental projects, the client will be looking for evidence that your cost proposal is realistic. Break down and itemize the costs in detail so that the client can see how you got your numbers: so much for labor, so much for materials, so much for overhead.

> The more detailed your cost proposal, the more credible your estimates.

In a formal proposal, it pays to be as thorough and accurate as possible. Carefully selected detail enhances your credibility. So does successful completion of any task you promise to perform.

Summary

You may want to include a summary or conclusion section; it is your last opportunity to convince the reader to accept your proposal. Summarize the merits of your approach, re-emphasize why you and your firm are the ones to do it, and stress what the benefits will be. The section should be relatively brief, assertive, and confident.

SUMMARY

Preparing formal reports and proposals requires a team effort. Be sure to allow enough time for the various phases in the preparation process, from planning the document to reproducing the final copy.

In typing the final version, be sure to use the correct format, following company-approved guidelines. Long formal reports have a greater number of separate elements than do short ones. The text of the report (introduction, body, and final summary/conclusions/recommendations) is usually prepared first. Visual aids are frequently included to support the text. Various prefatory and supplementary parts—such as the cover, title page, table of contents, appendixes, and bibliography—are added as needed, depending on the length and formality of the document.

Formal proposals are prepared in much the same way as other formal reports, although they differ somewhat in prefatory parts, text elements, and supplementary parts.

CHECKLIST FOR FORMAL REPORTS AND PROPOSALS

A. Quality of the Research
- [ ] 1. Define the problem clearly.
- [ ] 2. State the purpose of the document.
- [ ] 3. Identify all relevant issues.
- [ ] 4. Accumulate evidence pertaining to each issue.
- [ ] 5. Check evidence for accuracy, currency, and reliability.
- [ ] 6. Justify your conclusions by the evidence.
  - [ ] a. Do not omit or distort evidence in order to support your point of view.
  - [ ] b. Identify and justify all assumptions.

B. Preparation of Reports and Proposals
- [ ] 1. Choose a format and length that are appropriate to your audience and the subject.
- [ ] 2. Prepare a sturdy, attractive cover.
  - [ ] a. Label the cover clearly with the title of the document.
  - [ ] b. Use a title that tells the audience exactly what the document is about.
- [ ] 3. Provide all necessary information on the title page.
  - [ ] a. Include the full title of the document.
  - [ ] b. Include the name, title, and affiliation of the recipient.
  - [ ] c. Give the name, title, and affiliation of the author.
  - [ ] d. Provide the date of submission.
  - [ ] e. Balance the information in blocks on the page.
- [ ] 4. Include a copy of the letter of authorization or request for proposal, if appropriate.
- [ ] 5. Prepare a letter or memo of transmittal.
  - [ ] a. Use a memo format for internal documents.
  - [ ] b. Use a letter format for external documents.
  - [ ] c. Include the transmittal letter in only some copies if it contains sensitive or personal information suitable for some but not all readers.
  - [ ] d. Place the transmittal letter right before the table of contents.
  - [ ] e. Use the good-news plan for reports and solicited proposals; use the persuasive plan for unsolicited proposals.
  - [ ] f. Word the letter to "convey" the document officially to the readers; refer to the authorization; and discuss the purpose, scope, background, sources and methods, and limitations.
  - [ ] g. Mention any special points that warrant readers' attention.
  - [ ] h. If you use direct order, summarize conclusions and recommendations (unless they are included in a synopsis).
  - [ ] i. Acknowledge all who were especially helpful in preparing the document.
  - [ ] j. Close with thanks, offer to be of further assistance, and suggest future projects, if appropriate.
- [ ] 6. Prepare the table of contents.
  - [ ] a. Include all first-level headings (perhaps include all second-level headings and perhaps even all third-level headings).
  - [ ] b. Give the page number of each heading included.
  - [ ] c. Word all headings exactly as they appear in the text.
  - [ ] d. Include the synopsis (if there is one) and supplementary parts in the table of contents.
  - [ ] e. Number the table of contents and all prefatory pages with lower-case roman numerals centered at the bottom of the page.
- [ ] 7. Prepare a list of illustrations if you have more than four visual aids.
  - [ ] a. Put the list in the same format as the table of contents.
  - [ ] b. Identify visual aids either directly beneath the

table of contents or on a separate page under the heading "List of Illustrations."

☐ **8.** Develop a synopsis or an executive summary if the document is long and formal.

   ☐ a. Tailor the synopsis to the document's length and tone.

   ☐ b. Condense the main points of the document, using either the informative approach or the descriptive approach, according to the guidelines in this chapter.

   ☐ c. Present the points in the synopsis in the same order as they appear in the document.

☐ **9.** Prepare the introduction to the text.

   ☐ a. Leave a 2-inch margin at the top of the page, and center the title of the document.

   ☐ b. In a long document (ten pages or more), type the first-level heading "Introduction" three lines below the title.

   ☐ c. In a short document (fewer than ten pages), begin typing three lines below the title of the document without the heading "Introduction."

   ☐ d. Discuss the authorization (unless it's covered in the letter of transmittal), purpose, scope, background, sources and methods, definitions, limitations, and text organization.

☐ **10.** Prepare the body of the document.

   ☐ a. Carefully select the organizational plan (see Chapter 11).

   ☐ b. Use either a personal or an impersonal tone consistently.

   ☐ c. Use either a past or a present time perspective consistently.

   ☐ d. Follow a consistent format in typing headings of different levels, using a company format guide, a sample proposal or report, or the format in this textbook as a model (see Appendix B).

   ☐ e. Express comparable (same-level) headings in any given section in parallel grammatical form.

   ☐ f. Group ideas into logical categories.

   ☐ g. Tie sections together with transitional words, sentences, and paragraphs.

   ☐ h. Give ideas of equal importance roughly equal space.

   ☐ i. Avoid overly technical, pretentious, or vague language.

   ☐ j. Develop each paragraph around a topic sentence.

   ☐ k. Make sure all ideas in each paragraph are related.

   ☐ l. Double-space if longer than ten pages.

   ☐ m. For reports and proposals bound on the left, number all pages with arabic numerals in the upper right-hand corner (except for the first page, where the number is centered 1 inch from the bottom); for top-bound documents, number all pages with arabic numerals centered 1 inch from the bottom.

☐ **11.** Incorporate visual aids into the text.

   ☐ a. Number visual aids consecutively throughout the text, numbering tables and figures (other visual aids) separately if that style is preferred.

   ☐ b. Develop explicit titles for all visual aids except in-text tables.

   ☐ c. Refer to each visual aid in the text, and emphasize the significance of the data.

   ☐ d. Place visual aids as soon after their textual explanations as possible, or group them at the ends of chapters or at the end of the document.

☐ **12.** Conclude the text of reports and proposals with a summary and, if appropriate, with conclusions and recommendations.

   ☐ a. In a summary, recap the findings and explanations already presented.

   ☐ b. Place conclusions and recommendations in order of their importance or logic, preferably in list format.

   ☐ c. To induce action, explain in the recommendations section who should do what, when, where, and how.

   ☐ d. If appropriate, point up the benefits of action in order to leave readers with the motivation to follow recommendations.

☐ **13.** Document all material quoted or paraphrased from secondary sources, using a consistent format (see Appendix C).

☐ **14.** Include appendixes at the end of the document to provide useful and detailed information that is of interest to some but not all readers.

   ☐ a. Give each appendix a title, such as "Questionnaire" or "Names and Addresses of Survey Participants."

   ☐ b. If there is more than one appendix, number or letter them consecutively in the order they're referred to in the text.

   ☐ c. Type appendixes in a format consistent with the text of the document.

☐ **15.** Include a bibliography if it seems that readers would benefit or that the document would gain credibility from it.

   ☐ a. Type the bibliography on a separate page headed "Bibliography" or "Sources."

   ☐ b. Alphabetize bibliography entries.

   ☐ c. Use a consistent format for the bibliography (see Appendix C).

ON THE JOB:
Solving a Communication Dilemma at Penn State

When Rodney Erickson set out to assess the impact of football on State College's economy, he assumed that he would come up with a pretty big number, but he didn't know *how* big. After surveying some 1,974 season-ticket holders, he discovered—to his amazement—that the average home game is worth almost $3 million in extra revenue to local businesses. Adding the ripple effect of those dollars flowing through the economy, Erickson calculates that the seven-game season enriches the town to the tune of $40.3 million per year. That boils down to roughly $1,300 for each of the community's 30,000 permanent residents.

In fact, the economic impact of football on State College may be even bigger than Erickson's figures indicate; his study excluded spending by local fans and spending associated with the annual Blue and White preseason scrimmage, which draws a big crowd. He looked only at the 54,000 fans who come from outside the immediate area to see each of the seven regular-season home games. Those fans travel an average of 186 miles to attend the games and spend approximately $54 apiece while they're in town.

How do the fans spend their money? Let us count the ways. First, there are hotel bills. All the local hotels and motels enforce a two-day minimum stay on football weekends, and most of them jack up their room rates by 20 to 40 percent, depending on the quality of the competing team. Many of the hotels also stage special events—dances, musical performances, and the like—which boost their revenues still further.

Meals, of course, are another expense. The Sub Shop on Beaver Street is a popular source of provisions for tailgate picnics. The Sub Shop's owner, Ralph Petrino, figures that on a football Saturday, he sells 480 subs, twice the normal number. Business also generally doubles at fancier spots like the Tavern Restaurant, where, after one Penn State–Notre Dame game, the chef prepared a record-breaking 792 meals, 50 to 60 percent more than his usual Saturday night quota.

As you might expect, shopping also picks up. Football fans flock to the Lions Pride, a store that stocks 500 to 700 Penn State items ranging from sweatshirts to telephone cords decorated with Nittany Lions. According to Jim Styer, the store's manager: "On a football Saturday, you're talking at least triple normal business. At least. It's wall to wall in here. Front to back. Side to side. Everything goes. They clean us out." And it's not just souvenirs that sell. The jewelry stores and the dress shops also do plenty of business, since some of the folks who come along for the weekend prefer to spend Saturday shopping rather than watching the football game.

Gasoline is another item that pumps faster on football weekends. Cars clog every road leading into town, and the University Park Airport is crammed with private airplanes. Sometimes as many as 60 planes crowd into the little airport, and most of them slurp up a tank of fuel before departing. Add it all up, and it makes a big difference to a little town like State College. As Rodney Erickson says, "It's a pretty amazing phenomenon."

Your Mission: You are an aide to Rodney Erickson at Penn State's Center for Regional Business Analysis. He has asked you to help finalize his report about the economic impact of college football on the local economy. Handle each of the following situations to the *best* of your ability.

1. The text of Erickson's report is 15 pages long. Which of the following prefatory parts should he include?
   a. Cover
   b. Title fly
   c. Title page
   d. Letter of authorization
   e. Letter of acceptance
   f. Letter/memo of transmittal
   g. Table of contents
   h. List of illustrations
   i. Synopsis or executive summary

2. Which of the following titles is the best choice for the report?
   a. A Quantitative Analysis of the Economic Impact of The Pennsylvania State University's Home Football Games on Businesses Located in State College, Pennsylvania
   b. Touchdown! Local Economy Wins When Penn State Scores
   c. The Impact of Penn State's Home Football Games on the Local Economy
   d. College Football: What Does It Do for Business?

3. Erickson has decided to send a copy of the report to the chamber of commerce, the president of the alumni association, head football coach Joe Paterno, and several members of Penn State's administration. He has asked you to draft a letter of transmittal. How should you proceed?
   a. Using the good-news organizational plan, develop a brief form letter that can be sent to all the recipients.
   b. Using the good-news plan, develop a form letter but customize the first paragraph so that it is slanted specifically to each of the recipients.

c. Since each recipient has different interests and needs, write a separate letter for each and use the most appropriate organizational plan, given your objective in each case.

4. Erickson has asked you to draft the introductory section of the text. Which of the following versions is superior?
   a. Version one

INTRODUCTION

State College is a town of 30,000 located in the rolling hills of central Pennsylvania. Since 1871, the community has been a "college town." During the school year, 34,000 students swell the local population, providing an important boost to the economy. The magnitude of that boost is especially great during football season, when the Nittany Lions draw big crowds to Beaver Stadium.

This report, prepared by The Pennsylvania State Center for Regional Business Analysis, attempts to quantify the economic impact of the Lions' seven home games on the local business community. The information is intended to provide perspective on the importance of football to the city and the university.

The analysis deals specifically with the impact of out-of-town fans who travel 25 miles or more to attend the regular-season home games. The figures presented in the report do not reflect spending by students or local fans who attend the games, nor do the figures reflect spending associated with preseason scrimmages. The information presented in the report is based on a mail survey of 1,974 season-ticket holders who live at least 25 miles away from State College, 86 percent of whom responded.

The report opens with an overview of the impact of football on the local economy and then reviews the impact of spending for various types of goods and services: hotels and motels, restaurants, retailing, personal services, and other businesses. The final section summarizes the data.

   b. Version two

INTRODUCTION

This report attempts to calculate how much college football is worth to the economy of State College, Pennsylvania. The report was prepared by The Pennsylvania State University's Center for Regional Business Analysis with the objective of providing local businesses, government officials, and university personnel with accurate information on the financial impact of football on the town.

The report is based on the results of a mail survey of 1,974 out-of-town season-ticket holders, 86 percent of whom responded. The analysis tends to understate the importance of football to local businesses because the figures do not reflect spending by students and local fans or spending associated with the preseason scrimmage.

As the following pages indicate, local businesses are the big winners when the Nittany Lions take on their rivals at Beaver Stadium. For a typical Saturday afternoon game, some 54,000 out-of-town fans travel to State College and spend an average of $54 apiece while they're here. Over the course of the regular seven-game home season, these fans spend $20.3 million on lodging, food, merchandise, personal services, and miscellaneous items. If the ripple effect of this spending is taken into consideration, it is safe to say that the total impact of the football season is $40.3 million, or $5.7 million per game.

   c. Version three

INTRODUCTION

If you shudder when football season rolls around and Nittany Lions' fans descend on State College like a plague of locusts, devouring every available parking space, you might want to count your blessings instead of grumbling about the "tourists." After surveying some 1,974 out-of-town season-ticket holders, The Pennsylvania State University Center for Regional Business Analysis has concluded that college football gives the local community a $40.3 million boost every year. That amounts to $1,300 for every man, woman, and child who lives in State College.

The following pages provide the details on how the fans spend their money, to the benefit of hotel keepers, restaurateurs, retailers, hair dressers, and even baby-sitters.

5. Erickson has asked your opinion on whether to include in his report (1) a copy of the direct-mail survey that was used to collect the data for the report and (2) a computer printout quantifying the responses to each question. The survey document is two pages long; the computer compilation of results is five pages long. Without the documents, the report has 15 pages. What do you think?
   a. Include both the survey and the computer compilation of responses in the text of the report.
   b. Include a copy of the survey in the text of the report, and put the computer compilation of responses in an appendix.

c. Describe both the survey and the computer compilation in the text, but put the actual documents in an appendix.

d. Describe both the survey and the computer compilation in the text, but do not include copies of either document.

e. Include a copy of the survey in an appendix, but do not include the computer compilation of results.

6. Erickson has compiled the following statistics on spending by the 54,000 nonresident fans who attended the seven Penn State home football games: stadium, $8,283,600; restaurants, $2,693,100; lodging, $2,075,100; retail goods, $1,793,500; private auto, $984,800; clothing and equipment used in stadium, $801,700; bars and nightclubs, $743,200; retail groceries and beverages, $588,100; commercial transportation, $247,800; donations, $105,100; admission fees, $103,400; personal and health, $41,300; baby-sitters, $25,100; equipment rentals, $17,900; and other, $1,944,900—for a total of $20,448,600. What format is best for presenting this information in the report?

a. The figures should be displayed in a table.

b. The figures should be shown in a pie chart.

c. The figures should be shown in a horizontal bar chart.

d. The figures should be shown in a line chart.

e. The figures should be explained in several paragraphs in the text.

7. Erickson is debating how to handle the final section of the text. Given the purpose of the report (see question 4), which of the following statements would you advise him to include?

a. To capitalize on the opportunities presented by Penn State football games, local merchants should conduct direct-mail advertising aimed at alumni during the football season.

b. Without Penn State football games, many local businesses would probably fail.

c. Penn State football games are a major source of revenue for many local businesses.[2]

QUESTIONS FOR DISCUSSION

1. What are the distinguishing characteristics of a formal report?

2. How should you decide whether to use a synopsis or an executive summary?

3. In what ways might visual aids help people overcome some of the barriers to communication discussed in Chapter 1?

4. How does the information shown in flow charts, organization charts, and diagrams differ from the information shown in line, bar, and pie charts?

5. How do the prefatory parts of a solicited proposal differ from the prefatory parts of an unsolicited proposal?

6. How does the text of a formal proposal differ from the text of other formal reports?

EXERCISES

1. Present the following information in three separate visual aids: a table, a line chart, and a bar chart. Assets of international banks (in billions of dollars): 1982—47.6; 1983—55.0; 1984—59.8; 1985—46.5; 1986—34.1; 1987—42.2; 1988—47.6; 1989—45.0; 1990—44.9; 1991—49.3; 1992—58.3

2. For each of the following types of information, what form of visual aid would you choose?

a. Data on annual sales for FretCo Guitar Corporation for the past 20 years

b. Comparison of FretCo Guitar sales, product by

product (electric guitars, bass guitars, amplifiers, acoustic guitars), for this year and last year

c. Explanation of how a FretCo acoustic guitar is manufactured

d. Comparison of FretCo sales figures to sales figures for three other major guitar makers over the past ten years

3. Based on the information available to you in this chapter's On-the-Job simulation, can you think of any objections readers might raise to Erickson's report?[3]

CASES

SHORT FORMAL REPORTS

1. Picking the better path: Report assisting a client in a career choice
You are employed by Open Options, a career counseling firm, and your main function is to help clients make career choices. Today a client with the same name as yours (a truly curious coincidence!) came to your office and asked for help in deciding between two careers that you yourself had been interested in (an even greater coincidence!).

Your task: Do some research on the two careers, and then prepare a short report that your client can study. Your report should compare at least five major areas, such as salary, working conditions, and education required. Interview the client to understand her or his personal preferences regarding each of the five areas; for example, what is the minimum salary the client will accept? By comparing the client's preferences with the research material you collect, such as salary data, you will have a basis for concluding which of the two careers is best. The report should end with a recommendation.

2. Is anyone out there listening? Report on radio advertising
Martha McCreary is a vice president at Knowles-Mead, a small stock brokerage house in your city. In order to increase its clientele, the firm has decided to run a series of radio advertisements designed to catch the attention of potential investors.

Knowing your interest in local radio, Martha asks your advice. Of the local stations, which one or two would be best for the low-key, factual advertisements that her firm has in mind? At what time during the day and the week might these spots be most effective?

Your task: Listen systematically to three or four radio stations in your area to determine (a) what types of products their advertisers generally are selling, (b) what their programming generally consists of, and (c) what type of listener they seem to appeal to. You should listen to each station at several different times during the day and at different times during the week. Chart your findings.

Then draft a formal report for Martha that contains the results of your research and your conclusions and recommendations. If the report is successful, Knowles-Mead should be able to choose the appropriate times and stations for a series of advertisements that would win new clients.

LONG FORMAL REPORTS REQUIRING ADDITIONAL RESEARCH

3. Group effort: Report on a large-scale topic
The following topics may be too big for any one person, and yet they need to be investigated.

  a. A demographic profile (age, gender, socioeconomic status, residence, employment, educational background, and the like) of the students at your college or university
  b. The best part-time employment opportunities in your community
  c. The best of two or three health clubs or gyms in your community
  d. Actions that can be taken in your community or state to combat alcohol (or drug) abuse
  e. Improvements that could be made in the food service at your college or university
  f. Your college's or university's image in the community and ways to improve it
  g. Your community's strengths and weaknesses in attracting new businesses

Your task: Because these topics require considerable research, your instructor may wish to form groups to work on each. If your group writes a report on the first topic, summarize your findings at the end of the report. For all the other topics, reach conclusions and make recommendations in the report.

4. Secondary sources: Report based on library research
Perhaps one of the following questions has been keeping you awake at night:

  a. What's the best way for someone with your financial status to invest $5,000?
  b. What should be done about parking problems on campus?
  c. How do other consumers regard a product that you use frequently?
  d. Which of three cities that you might like to live in seems most attractive?
  e. What's the surest and easiest route to becoming a millionaire?

Your task: Answer one of these questions, using secondary sources for information. Be sure to document your sources in the correct form. Give conclusions and recommendations in your report.

5. Business problem: Report relating to business
In the business or profession that you are in or are studying for, there are undoubtedly some issues that have not been resolved.

Your task: Choose one of these problems and write a long formal report on it, complete with your own conclusions and recommendations.

FORMAL PROPOSALS

6. Top dogs: Proposal to furnish puppies to Docktor Pet Centers
You are the business manager for Sandy's Kennels of Alma, Kansas, one of the country's largest dog-breeding operations. Every year, you sell 7,500 puppies (for an average price of $130 per dog) to pet shops around the country. The pet stores then sell the dogs for $225 to $300, depending on the breed.

Your business involves both breeding and reselling animals. In your own kennels, you raise 52 kinds of dogs; in addition, you buy dogs from other breeders at approximately $60 per dog and resell them to pet stores. Your dogs are all pedigreed animals with American Kennel Club papers. In addition, they come with all the required puppy vaccinations and are guaranteed to be healthy.

For several years, you have been trying to win a long-term contract to supply puppies to Docktor Pet Centers, the country's largest pet store chain. Finally, you have been invited to submit a proposal to provide 2,000 dogs per year to Docktor's 220 retail outlets. The specifications stipulate that you will ship approximately 150 dogs per month from January through October and 250 dogs in November and in December. The puppies should be eight to ten weeks old at the time of shipment and should have all the necessary shots and AKC papers. Docktor is willing to accept a variety of breeds but has requested that each shipment contain a mix of large and small dogs and males and females. The chain is willing to pay from $115 to $130 per dog, depending on the breed.[4]

Your task: Using your imagination to supply the details, write a proposal describing your plan to provide the dogs.

7. Cruising out to sea: Proposal to host an American Medical Association convention
The marketing department for Miami-based Carnival Cruise Lines, of which you are a member, is responsible for making sure that your firm's cruise ships are fully booked. The job has become increasingly challenging since several rival cruise lines added new ships. The surge in capacity has prompted companies in the industry to scramble for passengers.

As part of your marketing program, you are trying to encourage large groups to book conventions on board your ships. You have recently purchased two new vessels that are particularly suitable for such functions, and each one is capable of carrying 1,900 passengers.

The ships are essentially floating hotels with meeting rooms, restaurants, lounges, pools, and other recreational facilities. Staffed with a crew of 500, each vessel offers outstanding food, entertainment, and service. The ships can be scheduled for three- or seven-day cruises. The price per passenger for shorter cruises ranges from $325 to $855, depending on accommodations and the group's choice of menu and activities. The average price per passenger for week-long cruises is $1,250. Both ships sail from Miami and cruise either the Caribbean or the Gulf of Mexico.

The Southeast Region of the American Medical Association is soliciting proposals for hosting a convention from February 8 through 11. An estimated 1,800 delegates and spouses are expected to attend the convention, which will feature lectures on medical topics as well as recreational activities. The AMA will be responsible for planning the medical portions of the program, but the hotel or convention center that gets the contract will be in charge of organizing recreational activities and planning food and beverage service. The AMA is prepared to pay $1,100 per person for food, lodging, and recreation for the four-day convention, a sum acceptable to Carnival management.[5]

Your task: Develop a proposal that describes how Carnival Cruise Lines can meet the AMA's needs. Emphasize the advantages of booking the convention on board a ship as opposed to holding it in a hotel or convention center. Use your imagination to flesh out the details of the proposal.

8. Tennis anyone? Proposal to convince the Chicago Unified School District to adopt a tennis program
Back in the late 1970s, tennis was the "in" sport. Racquets were selling like hotcakes, and people were reserving court time three weeks in advance. But in recent years, enthusiasm for the sport has waned. The number of players has declined by 40 percent. According to industry analysts, one reason for the declining popularity of tennis is its elitist reputation. To a great extent, the industry has ignored the 71 percent of all players who use public courts and has focused instead on the affluent players who belong to private tennis clubs.

To broaden the appeal of the game, the United States Tennis Association (USTA) is now making a concerted effort to bring tennis to the average person. Part of this effort involves teaching young people to play the game. The USTA has allocated $1 million per year to run the Schools Program, which encourages local schools to provide tennis instruction for elementary and junior high school students. Some 2 million students at over 4,000 schools currently participate in the program.

You have been hired by the USTA as one of 17 regional coordinators for the Schools Program. Your job is to call on schools in Illinois, Wisconsin, Michigan, and Indiana to explain how the program works.

You recently met with the superintendent of schools for the Chicago Unified School District. You explained that the USTA could help participating schools convert their gymnasiums and basketball courts for use as temporary tennis courts. You also explained that the USTA works with equipment manufacturers to obtain free racquets and balls for students. In addition, you described how the district's physical education teachers would be trained by USTA officials to teach tennis to schoolchildren.

The superintendent was enthusiastic about your suggestions, particularly when you explained that the cost to the district would be minimal. He asked you to submit a formal written proposal that could be acted on by the school board.[6]

Your task: Write the proposal, using your imagination to develop specific details.

■ PART FIVE

EMPLOYMENT MESSAGES

Chapter Thirteen:

WRITING RESUMES AND APPLICATION LETTERS

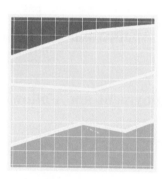

ON THE JOB:
Facing a Communication Dilemma at The Coca-Cola Company
Gulp! It's the Real Thing

As the vice president of black and Hispanic consumer markets for Coca-Cola USA, Charles E. Morrison has opened plenty of doors for minorities eager to make it in the business world. In the process of promoting Coke's various brands with black and Hispanic consumers, Morrison has built bridges to minority communities. He gets around. He meets people. He does what he can to help those who need it. And while he's at it, he reminds blacks and Hispanics that Coke cares about them.

Building Coke's presence in minority communities demands a mix of marketing activities. Morrison and his subordinates get involved in developing media plans, creating promotional programs, and sponsoring community and public relations events. Their activities range from sponsoring scholarships for minority students to brainstorming advertising campaigns aimed at minority markets. Essentially, Morrison's goal is to convey the message that Coke's products are "the real thing" for black and Hispanic consumers. To do the job, Morrison recognizes that he needs a strong team that understands the attitudes and interests of minority consumers. He's always on the lookout for talented people who have the perception and background to help him get his message across.

What qualities does Morrison look for in a job applicant? How does he evaluate the resumes and application letters that land on his desk? What constitutes a good resume? A good application letter? If you were Morrison, on what basis would you choose the candidates to invite for an interview?[1]

WRITING A RESUME

The Coca-Cola Company

As the professionals at Coca-Cola know, many people who are new to the job market have some misconceptions about resumes (see Figure 13.1). The fact is that a resume is a form of advertising designed to help you get an interview. As in all forms of advertising, your objective is to call the reader's attention to your best features and to downplay your disadvantages, without distorting or misrepresenting the facts.

CONTROLLING THE FORMAT AND STYLE

The reader's initial reaction to your resume will be based on its appearance, not its content. For an impressive-looking resume, use clean, black type on letter-size white bond paper. Leave ample margins all around for easy reading. Corrections should be unnoticeable. To make duplicate copies, use offset printing or photocopying.

As a rule of thumb, try to write a one-page resume. But if you have a great deal of experience and are applying for a higher-level position, you may wish to prepare a somewhat longer resume. The important thing is to give yourself

FIGURE 13.1
Fallacies and Facts About Resumes

Fallacy: The purpose of a resume is to list all your skills and abilities.

Fact: The purpose of a resume is to kindle employer interest and generate an interview.

Fallacy: A good resume will get you the job you want.

Fact: Hundreds of thousands of good resumes cross employers' desks every working day.

Fallacy: Your resume will be read carefully and thoroughly by an interested employer.

Fact: Your resume probably has less than ten seconds to make an impression.

Fallacy: The more good information you present about yourself in your resume, the better.

Fact: By including too much information, a resume may actually kill the reader's appetite to know more.

Fallacy: If you want a really good resume, have it prepared by a resume service.

Fact: Many resume services use undistinguished standard formats, so you should prepare your own—unless the position you're after is very high level and you choose the service very carefully.

enough space to present a fair and persuasive portrait of your accomplishments and capabilities.

Skillful layout and graphic design make the resume visually appealing and easy to follow. Break up the text by using headings that call attention to various aspects of your background, such as your work experience and education. Underline or capitalize key points, or set them off in the left margin. Use indented lists to itemize your most important qualifications. Leave plenty of white space, even if doing so forces you to use two pages rather than one.

Pay attention to mechanics. Check the headings and itemized lists to make sure they're grammatically parallel. Be sure that your grammar, spelling, and punctuation are correct.

Your resume has only seconds to make an impression, so keep the writing style simple and direct. Instead of whole sentences, use short, crisp phrases starting with action verbs. Choose these verbs carefully to suggest the kinds of activities required by the job you're applying for. For example, you might say, "Coached a Little League team to the regional playoffs" or "Supervised a fast-food restaurant and four personnel."

> The key characteristics of a good resume are
> - Neatness
> - Simplicity
> - Accuracy
> - Honesty

Martina L. Bradford is vice president of external affairs at AT&T, overseeing one of the largest and most profitable regions of the United States. Bradford targeted the high-growth company as a potential employer only after studying the industry thoroughly. She advises that you analyze where your skills fit in best and target your efforts toward that company.

TAILORING THE CONTENTS

Most potential employers have certain preconceived notions about what belongs in the resume. The bare essentials are your name and address, your academic credentials, and your employment history.

Otherwise, your resume should present your strongest, most impressive qualifications and skirt the areas that might raise questions. Don't exaggerate, alter the past, or claim to have skills you don't have. But don't dwell on negatives, either. For example, you may want to leave out any reference to the brief part-time job that just didn't seem to work out; potential employers for full-time jobs are likely to overlook such a small gap. Or if you've changed jobs rather frequently, you may want to "bury" the dates of employment instead of drawing attention to them with your format. By focusing on your strengths, you can tell the truth and still sound like a winner.

Name and address

The first thing an employer needs to know is who you are and where you can be reached: your name, address, and phone number. If you have an address and a phone number at school or work and also at home, you may include both. By the same token, if you have a work phone and a home phone, list both and indicate which is which.

Many resume headings are nothing more than the name and address centered at the top of the page. But you may also feature the title "Resume" or something more attention-getting. For example:

> The opening section of your resume should show at a glance who you are, how to reach you, and what kind of job you're interested in.

Qualifications of Craig R. Crisp for Insurance Sales Representative

Data Sheet of Jean Gray, an Experienced Retail Fashion Buyer

Public Relations Background of Bradley R. (Brad) Howard

Susan Lee Selwyn's Qualifications
for the Position of Teaching Assistant
in the Dade County School District

Profile of Michael de Vito for Entertainment Management

Whatever heading you use, make sure the reader can tell in an instant who you are and how to communicate with you.

Career objective

There are two schools of thought on stating a career objective on your resume. Some experts argue that your objective will be obvious from your qualifications. They also point out that such a statement is counterproductive (especially if you would like to be considered for any suitable openings) because it labels you as being interested in only one thing. Other experts point out that employers will undoubtedly try to categorize you anyway, so you might as well be sure they attach the right label.

On balance, stating your objective is probably a good idea, because it provides the reader with a frame of reference for reviewing your qualifications. Be as specific as possible about what you want to do, but avoid making a narrow statement that will severely limit your prospects. The statement should indicate any special qualifications that pertain to your objective. Here's an example of this double-barreled type of career objective:

> A junior accounting position in the aerospace industry in which 1-1/2 years of computer programming experience would be valuable

Your objective should indicate what you want to do and why you are qualified to do it.

It is no simple matter to state in one short phrase both your objective and the reasons you are qualified for the job. But it can be done. Start by asking yourself these questions:

- *What specific position do I want?* Think in terms of the functions that the position might have. "Creating copy for a public relations firm" is much more meaningful than such vague wording as "A job in which I can use my creative talents."

- *What especially qualifies me for this job?* In a few brief words, focus on your key strengths and skills.

If you have various types of qualifications (such as a certificate in secretarial science and two years' experience in retail sales), prepare separate resumes, each with a different objective. If your immediate objective differs from your ultimate one, combine both objectives in a single statement:

> A marketing position in a major communications company with an opportunity for eventual management status

> To serve your organization as a proposal writer with the ultimate goal of becoming a contracts administrator

Summary of qualifications and date of availability

Summarize your strongest qualifications to focus and simplify the employer's evaluation.

If your resume is long and your experience is varied, you might want to summarize your qualifications in a brief statement that highlights your strongest points. Use a short, simple heading such as "Preparation for Financial Management" or "Significant Advertising Experience." Then summarize your strongest job-related qualifications. As a convenience for the prospective employer, you may also list your date of availability. State the month and, if you know it, the day you will be available to start work.

Education

If you're still in school, education is probably your strongest selling point. So present your educational background in depth. Give this section a heading, such as "Education," "Professional College Training," or "Academic Preparation." Then, starting with the postsecondary school you most recently attended, list for each school the name and location, the term of your enrollment (in months and years), your major and minor fields of study, significant skills and abilities you developed in your course work, and the degree(s) or certificate(s) you earned. List courses that have directly equipped you for the job sought, and indicate any scholarships, awards, or academic honors you have received.

The education section should also include off-campus training sponsored by business, industry, or government. Indicate any relevant seminars or workshops you have attended, as well as the certificates or other documents you have received. Mention high school or military service here only if your achievements are pertinent to your career goals.

Whether you should list your grades depends on the nature of the work you want and whether they are favorable or unfavorable. If you choose to show grade-point averages for your total program or your major, be sure to say whether you're using a 4-point or a 5-point scale.

Education is usually given less emphasis in a resume after you've worked in your chosen field for a year or more. If work experience is your strongest qualification, save the section on education for later in the resume, where you can discuss it in less detail. But even those who have been out of school for several years should include the name and location of each postsecondary school attended, the dates of enrollment, and the degrees or certificates received.

Work experience

In addition to describing your education, your resume should discuss your work experience off and on campus. Emphasize jobs that are relevant to your target field—including any part-time, summer, or volunteer work—to show that you like the type of position you are seeking. If your former jobs have no relation to your present career objective, list them anyway, without going into too much detail. Employers will see that you have the ability to get and hold a job, which is an important qualification in itself. And if you have worked your way through school, say so. Employers interpret this type of experience as a sign of character.

In describing your work experience, list your jobs in chronological order, with the current or last one first. Start each listing with the name and location of the employer. Then, if the reader is unlikely to recognize the organization or its name doesn't reveal what type of business it is, briefly describe what the employer does. When you want to keep the name of your present employer confidential, state "Name of organization (or company) on request," identify the firm by industry only (for example, "a large film-processing laboratory"), or use the name but request confidentiality in the application letter or in an underlined note ("Resume submitted in confidence") at the top or bottom of the resume. If an organization's name or location has since changed, state the present name or location and then "formerly . . ."

Under each job listing, state your functional title, such as "clerk typist" or "salesperson." If you were a dishwasher, say so. Don't try to make your role seem more important by glamorizing your job title or functions.

In the education section, list information about
- Postsecondary schools
- Off-campus workshops, seminars, and so on
- High school (only if pertinent)
- Military service (only if pertinent)
- Grades (only if pertinent and favorable)

William A. Schreyer is chairman and CEO of Merrill Lynch & Company. He urges you to stress summer employment, extracurricular activities, honors, scholarships, and other accomplishments. Moreover, he says that job offers go to those who make the most persuasive presentation of their qualifications—don't just list what you did, show how well you did it.

For each work experience, state
- Name and location of employer
- What the organization does (if not clear from its name)
- Your functional title
- How long you worked there
- Your duties and responsibilities
- Your significant achievements or contributions

Nonpaid activities may provide valuable work-related skills.

You should also state how long you worked on each job, from month/year to month/year. Use the phrase "to present" to denote current employment. If a job was part-time, say so.

One of the most important features to emphasize is how your previous jobs relate to the position you are seeking. If you achieved something significant in a job, be sure to mention it—for example, "Devised a new collection system that accelerated payment of overdue receivables." Facts about your accomplishments are the most important information you can give a prospective employer. And quantify your accomplishments, where possible: "Designed a new ad that increased videotape sales by 9 percent." Figure 13.2 lists some other statements that may help you identify your own accomplishments. Remember to back them up with specific evidence.

Activities and achievements

Employers like Coca-Cola get a better idea about you if on your resume you describe any paid or unpaid activities that demonstrate your abilities. You should list projects that required leadership, organization, teamwork, and cooperation. Include speaking, writing, or tutoring experience; participation in athletics or creative projects; fund-raising or community service activities; and offices held in academic or professional organizations. (However, mention of political or religious organizations may be a red flag to someone with different views, so use your judgment.) Note any awards you have received.

Again, quantify your achievements with numbers wherever possible. Instead of saying that you addressed various student groups, state how many and the approximate audience sizes.

If your activities have been extensive, you may want to group them into divisions like these: "College Activities," "Community Service," "Professional

FIGURE 13.2 Accomplishment Statements for Resumes

Improved morale and teamwork	Improved existing products
Introduced an improved filing system	Devised new products
Improved customer service	Expanded markets
Stepped up work flow	Arranged financing for company
Contributed new ideas	Trained new employees
Reorganized procedures	Reduced inventory
Motivated co-workers	Increased financial reporting
Increased typing speed and accuracy	Found companies to acquire
Solved problems	Reduced taxes
Improved work efficiency	Improved management reporting
Increased sales	Used cost-saving purchasing techniques
Reduced overdue accounts	Planned better meetings
Increased profits	Relieved boss of administrative details
Saved money	Created a more effective advertising theme
Reduced staff	
Increased productivity	

Associations," "Seminars and Workshops," and "Speaking Activities." Or divide them into two categories: "Service Activities" and "Achievements, Awards, and Honors."

Other relevant facts

You may also want to include a section that describes other aspects of your background that pertain to your career objective. For example, if you were applying for a position with a multinational organization, you would mention your command of a foreign language or your travel experience. Other skills you might mention include the ability to operate a computer, word processor, photocopier, or other equipment.

List anything else that might make you attractive to employers.

Personal data

Sometimes included in a resume are references to hobbies, willingness to travel or relocate, and miscellaneous experiences that may help you get a job, such as military service and citizenship. However, civil rights laws prohibit employers from discriminating on the basis of gender, marital or family status, age (although only those 40 to 70 are protected), race, color, religion, or national origin. Thus you should exclude any items that could encourage discrimination and reduce your chances of being considered for the job.

Provide only the personal data that will help you get the job.

Good health warrants mention because it enhances work performance. You may say "Excellent health" or imply it by listing vigorous hobbies. If your health is less than excellent, say nothing. Of course, a physical disability is independent of health. If it has no bearing on your ability to do the job, you are justified in ignoring it in the resume.

If military service is relevant to the position you are seeking, you may list it in this section (or under "Education" or "Work Experience"). List the date of induction, the branch of service, where you served, the highest rank you achieved, any accomplishments related to your career goals, and the date you were discharged.

References

You may want to list the names of three to five people who can provide potential employers with insights into your abilities and personal characteristics. Your list might include the names of former and present employers, business associates, professors, and contacts who can attest to your character. The most convincing references are people who have a good reputation in their field and who are in a position to know a good deal about you. Because relatives are likely to be biased, they should not be used as references.

A list of three to five references may impress the prospective employer.

Experts argue about including the names of references in your resume. In general, you should try to list only names that will have credibility with the employer. But because you may be preparing a resume for distribution to a number of employers, you may not be able to come up with a list of names that will be appropriate in all cases. Or you may not want to bury the people who are your references under an avalanche of requests for information. In either case, simply state "References available on request" at the end of your resume. Another approach is to call on the services of your college placement office, which may have references on file for you. Then you can state in this section "References and supporting documents available from . . ."; be sure to include the exact address of the placement office.

Before you list anyone's name on your resume as a reference, ask for permission. Then get the person's name (correctly spelled), title, address, and telephone number. If you are currently employed and don't want your employer to know that you are seeking another job, omit his or her name from your list of references.

Supporting data

Instead of sending supporting documents with your resume, offer to supply them on request.

If your academic transcripts, samples of your work, or letters of recommendation might increase your chances of getting the job, insert a line at the end of your resume offering to supply these documents on request. But don't include them with your resume. The only thing that should accompany your resume is the letter of application.

CHOOSING THE BEST ORGANIZATIONAL PLAN

Select an organizational pattern that focuses attention on your strengths.

Although you may want to include a little information in all categories, you should emphasize the information that has a bearing on your career objective and minimize or exclude any that is irrelevant or counterproductive. You do this by adopting an organizational plan—chronological, functional, or targeted—that focuses attention on your strongest points. The "right" choice depends on your background and goals, as Table 13.1 illustrates.

TABLE 13.1   How to Choose an Organizational Plan for Your Resume

TYPE OF RESUME	WHEN TO USE	WHEN NOT TO USE
Chronological: Lists work experience or education in reverse chronological order; describes responsibilities and accomplishments associated with each job or educational experience	Your last employer is well known and highly respected You plan to continue along your established career path Your job history shows progressively more responsible positions You are applying to a traditional organization	You have changed jobs frequently You are changing your career goals You have not progressed in your career You have been away from the job market for some time You are applying for your first job
Functional: Lists functional experience separately from employment history	You want to emphasize capabilities not used in recent jobs You are changing careers You are entering the job market for the first time or are reentering after an absence Your past career progression has been disappointing You have held a variety of unrelated jobs Your work has been of a free-lance or temporary nature	You want to emphasize your career progress You have performed a limited number of functions Your most recent employers are well-known and prestigious You are applying to a traditional organization
Targeted: Lists capabilities and accomplishments pertaining to a specific job; briefly lists work experience in a separate section	You are very clear about your job target You have several career objectives and want a separate resume for each You want to emphasize capabilities that you may not have performed for a regular employer	You want to use one resume for several applications You are not clear about your capabilities or accomplishments You are just starting your career and have little experience

BEHIND THE SCENES AT MOBIL CORPORATION
How to Write a Resume with the Winning Edge

Henry Halaiko is manager of recruiting operations for Mobil Corporation, and he's a busy person. Year-round, he coordinates Mobil's college relations and recruiting, and during a recruiting cycle, he provides a strategic framework for the company's interaction with campuses. "I work with the office of Career Planning and Placement," says Halaiko. "In December I reserve space at next fall's on-campus recruiting. In September, we post our openings, list our requirements, and describe the work locations. Interested students submit resumes to the placement office, which forwards them to Mobil for consideration. At Mobil, the line managers who posted the openings screen the resumes. Then we write to those students who match our needs, and we set up an on-campus interview for October or November. The placement office notifies those students we decide not to schedule for an interview. The managers who screened the resumes conduct the on-campus interviews. Finally, when mutual interest extends beyond the initial interview, an on-site day of from four to six interviews is scheduled. These fall interviews result in hiring people who will report to work after their graduation. The whole process, from initial campus interview to an accepted job offer, shouldn't take more than 60 days."

Mobil typically gets (from all sources) around 30,000 resumes a year to review. One large university, for example, forwarded 1,651 resumes in response to Mobil's posting. Of them, 253 students were interviewed. On average, 1 in 12 of those interviewed is offered a position, a total each year of between 700 and 800 students hired. "Seventy-five percent of our new hires are from the campus program," says Halaiko. "We promote largely from within, so there's little room for outside hiring beyond entry-level positions. But because everyone who submits a resume is a potential employee—not to mention a customer, a stockholder, and, through networking, an influence on others—the company is sensitive even to unsolicited resumes. Each one is reviewed, answered, and filed for future consideration."

The obvious question is, How do I make myself stand out in such a crowd? "This is not a science," Halaiko says. "We're looking for whole people. I go through a resume looking for personal standards of excellence in the classroom, at work, and in extracurricular activities; for flexibility, a willingness to try new things; and for strong oral and written communication skills, regardless of major. It's to your advantage not only to list your job responsibilities but also to list your accomplishments and achievements as well. Give some indication of your level of success. Most candidates will say something like, 'I worked in the toy department, replenishing inventory, closing the books.' What I'm looking for is someone who adds, 'I was responsible for increasing sales by 12 percent during such-and-such a promotion.' This conveys to me that he or she is interested in performance and takes pride in accomplishment. People who describe themselves in this way want to do things better, more effectively. The same is true of extracurricular activities. Don't just say, 'I was on the team or in the fraternity.' Add that you accomplished certain objectives in those roles."

The chronological resume

The most traditional way to organize a resume is chronologically. With this approach, the "Related Experience" section dominates the resume and is placed in the most prominent slot, immediately after the name and address and the job objective. You develop this section by listing your jobs in reverse order, beginning with the most recent position and working backward toward earlier jobs. Under each listing, you describe your responsibilities and accomplishments, giving the most space to the most recent positions.

A chronological resume emphasizes your work history.

The chronological approach is the most common way to organize a resume, and many employers prefer it. It is especially appropriate if you have a strong

Should you stress your grade-point average? "We aren't one of those companies who take the posture that we won't consider anyone below, say, a 3.5 GPA. We certainly look for academic excellence, and 2.8 is more or less a threshold because so many students fall above that level. But we look beyond that to roundedness. Did you carry a 3.0 but work full-time to pay for your education? Was your 2.9 earned in a tough course schedule? Have your grades progressed?"

What role do letters have in this process? Usually, submitting a resume to the placement office is the appropriate response to a posting. "But even this early," Halaiko adds, "we welcome a cover letter in several situations. If you have a low GPA but feel it does not adequately reflect who you are, if you took courses outside your major (which is a real plus), if your resume doesn't show how you used your time (that you were going from a part-time job to class, then to an extracurricular activity, then home to care for a family), write to tell me. It shows you have a high capacity for work and learning. We're interested in people who have enthusiasm for work." Once the interview process has begun, several letters are called for. First, acknowledge the letter inviting you to the first interview and confirm your interest. After the interview, write the interviewer a personalized follow-up letter, focusing on something that was specifically discussed in the interview.

As a package, your letters and resume should convey a sincere interest in the work described in the posting. Tailor your resume to that particular position. "You'd probably not be considered if we posted an opening for a job in technical marketing or sales and your resume said you were seeking a career in design engineering. Don't misrepresent what your real interests are just to get an interview," Halaiko points out. "That wastes your time and mine."

Are there any other no-no's? "If there's a classic error on a resume, it's the one-page resume with a half or a third of the page devoted to references. What that shows me is, you haven't done much."

In the end, says Halaiko, "there's no better feeling than having successfully recruited the candidate everyone was after but for whom the Mobil opportunity offered the best match of interests and needs." As an applicant, you should have the same feeling about completing a job search.

APPLY YOUR KNOWLEDGE

1. After the deadline for responding to posted job opportunities, you learned that Mobil Corporation will be recruiting at your school to fill a vacancy for which you'd be perfect. On-campus interviews are to be held in three weeks. What strategies would you employ to try to bring your interest and qualifications to the attention of Halaiko and the Mobil managers who will be conducting the initial interviews? How will you address the fact that you "missed the posting deadline"?

2. Take a copy of your resume. (If you don't yet have a resume, this can be your first step toward creating one.) Highlight each duty or responsibility you've listed for each job you've held. On a separate sheet of paper, list those duties down the right-hand side. To the left of each one, write out the kind of performance statement Halaiko referred to in his toy department example. For each duty/responsibility, select your performance/result that best illustrates your ability. When you are finished, review the list. Does it reveal anything new about your career interests? Does it change your "feeling" for what you are really good at? In what situations will your resume stand out from the pack? Incorporate the achievement statements into your resume.

employment history and are aiming for a job that builds on your current career path. If you are just graduating from college, you can vary the chronological plan by putting your educational qualifications before your experience, thereby focusing attention on your academic credentials.

The chronological approach is a good choice for Roberto Cortez, who has had considerable experience. Notice in Figure 13.3 how Roberto calls attention to his most recent achievements by setting them off in list format with bullets. He includes a section titled "Personal Data" to emphasize his international background and fluency in Spanish, which are important qualifications for his target position.

RESUME

Roberto Cortez
5687 Crosswoods Drive
Falls Church, VA 22044
Home: (703) 987-0086
Office: (703) 549-6624

OBJECTIVE   To obtain a position in accounting management
                where a knowledge of international finance
                will be of value

EXPERIENCE

March 1988   Staff Accountant/Financial Analyst
to present   INTER-AMERICAN IMPORTS   ALEXANDRIA, VA

                Prepare general accounting reports for
                wholesale giftware importer with annual
                sales of $15 million. Audit all financial
                transactions between company headquarters and
                suppliers in 12 Latin American countries.
                * Created a computerized model to adjust
                  accounts for fluctuations in currency
                  exchange rates
                * Represented company in negotiating
                  joint venture agreements with major
                  suppliers in Mexico and Colombia

October 1984   Staff Accountant
to March 1988   MONSANTO AGRICULTURAL CHEMICALS   MEXICO CITY

                Handled budgeting, billing, and credit pro-
                cessing functions for the Mexico City branch
                of Monsanto's Agricultural Chemicals
                division. Audited travel and entertainment
                expenditures for Monsanto's 30-member Latin
                American sales force. Assisted in launching
                an on-line computer system (IBM).

EDUCATION   GEORGE MASON UNIVERSITY   FAIRFAX, VA
                (1988-1991) M.B.A. with emphasis on
                international business

                UNIVERSIDAD NACIONAL AUTÓNOMA DE MEXICO
                MEXICO CITY, MEXICO
                (1980-1984) B.B.A., Accounting

PERSONAL   Born and raised in Mexico City; became U.S.
DATA   citizen in 1989. Fluent in Spanish and
                German. Have traveled extensively in Latin
                America.

REFERENCES   Available on request.

                Resume Submitted in Confidence

The applicant emphasizes his achievements by using an indented list.

The chronological organization highlights the applicant's impressive career progress.

The applicant's special qualifications are presented as personal data.

The functional resume

A functional resume focuses attention on your areas of competence.

In a functional resume, you emphasize your areas of competence by organizing around a list of accomplishments and then identifying your employers and academic experience in subordinate sections. This organizational pattern is useful for people who are just entering the job market or who are trying to redirect their career or minimize breaks in employment.

Figure 13.4 illustrates how a recent graduate used the functional approach to showcase her qualifications for a career in public relations. Although Glenda St. Johns has not held any paid, full-time positions in public relations, she knows a good deal about the profession from doing research and talking with people in the industry. As a result, she was able to organize her resume in a way that demonstrates her ability to handle such a position.

FIGURE 13.4
Functional Resume for a Public Relations Position

Because she is a recent graduate, the applicant describes her education first.

The use of action verbs and specific facts enhances this resume's effectiveness.

The applicant's sketchy work history is described but not emphasized.

```
                              RESUME

    Glenda St. Johns                 Objective:  To obtain a
    Box 6671, College Station        position in corporate
    Iowa City, Iowa 52240            public relations where
    (515) 545-9856                   my experience is of use.

    WRITING/EDITING:
         * Wrote arts and entertainment articles for college
           newspaper
         * Edited University of Iowa Handbook, guidebook
           mailed to all incoming freshmen
         * Published guest editorial on student attitudes in
           Des Moines Register
         * Wrote prize-winning script for sorority skit in
           Fall Follies talent show

    PUBLIC SPEAKING:
         * Participated in over 100 debates as member of
           college debating team
         * Led seminars to teach job-search skills to under-
           privileged teen-agers as part of campus outreach
           program
         * Performed in summer theater productions in Clear
           Lake, Iowa

    MANAGING:
         * Created and administered summer parks and recreation
           program for city of Osage, Iowa
         * Developed budget, schedule, and layouts for college
           handbook; assigned work to photographers and
           copywriters
         * Developed publicity campaign for Fall Follies,
           three-hour talent show that raised $7,000 for The
           University of Iowa's Panhellenic Council

    EDUCATION:
    The University of Iowa, Iowa City, September 1988-June 1993
    B.A. Journalism (3.81 GPA on 4.0 scale)
    Speech minor; two courses in public relations

    EXPERIENCE:
    June 1992-April 1993, Editor, University of Iowa Handbook
    Summer 1991, Director, Summer Recreation Program, Osage, Iowa
    Summer 1989, Actress, Cobblestone Players, Clear Lake, Iowa

    PERSONAL DATA:
    Excellent health; willing to relocate

    REFERENCES AND SUPPORTING DOCUMENTS:  Available from Placement
    Office, The University of Iowa, Iowa City, IA 52242
```

The targeted resume

A targeted resume shows how you qualify for a specific job.

A targeted resume is organized to focus attention on what you can do for a particular employer in a particular position. Immediately after stating your career objective, you list any capabilities that pertain to it. This list is followed by a list of your achievements, which provide evidence of your capabilities. Employers and schools are listed in subordinate sections.

Targeted resumes are a good choice for people who have a very clear idea of what they want to do and who can demonstrate their ability in the targeted area. This approach was very effective for Erica Vorkamp, whose resume appears in Figure 13.5. Instead of using a chronological pattern, which would have focused attention on her lack of work experience, Erica uses a targeted approach, emphasizing her ability to organize events.

FIGURE 13.5
Targeted Resume for a Position as Special Events Coordinator

The capabilities and achievements all relate to the specific job target, giving a very selective picture of the candidate's abilities.

This work history has little bearing on the candidate's job target, but she felt that recruiters would want to see evidence that she has held a paying position.

These high-powered references lend credibility to the candidate's claims.

```
                    ERICA VORKAMP'S QUALIFICATIONS
            FOR THE POSITION OF SPECIAL EVENTS COORDINATOR
                        IN THE CITY OF BARRINGTON

                           993 Church Street
                          Barrington, IL 60010
                            (312) 884-2153

CAPABILITIES

      * Plan and coordinate large-scale public events
      * Develop community support for concerts, festivals, and
        entertainment
      * Manage publicity for major events
      * Coordinate activities of diverse community groups
      * Establish and maintain financial controls for public events
      * Negotiate contracts with performers, carpenters, electricians,
        and suppliers

ACHIEVEMENTS

      * Arranged 1990's week-long Arts and Entertainment Festival
        for the Barrington Public Library, which involved perfor-
        mances by musicians, dancers, actors, magicians, and artists
      * Served as chairperson for the 1990 Children's Home Society
        Fashion Show, a luncheon for 400 that raised $5,000 for
        orphans and abused children
      * Supervised the 1989 PTA Halloween Carnival, an all-day
        festival with game booths, live bands, contests, and food
        service that raised $7,600 for the PTA
      * Organized the 1989 Midwestern convention for 800 members of
        the League of Women Voters, which extended over a three-day
        period and required arrangements for hotels, meals, speakers,
        and special tours

EDUCATION

      * Northwestern University (Evanston, Illinois), September
        1967 to June 1972, B.A. Psychology; Phi Beta Kappa

WORK HISTORY

      * First National Bank of Chicago, June 1972 to October
        1974, Personnel Counselor/Campus Recruiter

      * Northwestern University, November 1969 to June 1972,
        Part-time Research Assistant

REFERENCES

      * John Detweiler, Mayor, Village of Barrington, Barrington,
        Illinois 60010; (312) 884-0100

      * Jan Flapan, Co-President, Midwestern Division, League of Women
        Voters, 332 South Michigan Avenue, Chicago, Illinois 60004;
        (312) 236-0315

      *  Mark Nesbitt, President, Heartland Promotions, Inc.,
         433 W. Grand Avenue, Chicago, Ilinois 60651; (312) 864-9701
```

WRITING THE PERFECT RESUME

Regardless of what organizational plan you follow, the key to writing the "perfect" resume is to put yourself in the reader's position. If you were applying to Charles Morrison of Coca-Cola, you should think about what he needs as the prospective employer and then tailor your resume accordingly.

People who read thousands of resumes every year complain about the following common resume problems:

- *Too long.* The resume is not concise, relevant, and to the point.

- *Too short or sketchy.* The resume does not give enough information for a proper evaluation of the applicant.

Within a year of becoming president of Godfather's Pizza, Herman Cain returned the floundering chain to profitability. Now principal owner (following a leveraged buyout), Cain says his success springs from his love of the restaurant business. Simple ambition isn't enough to succeed in any business, he advises, so send resumes to companies whose business you have a real passion for.

- *Hard to read.* A lack of white space and of such devices as indentions and underlining makes the reader's job more difficult.

- *Wordy.* Descriptions are verbose, with numerous words used for what could be said more simply.

- *Too slick.* The resume appears to have been written by someone other than the applicant, which raises the question of whether the qualifications are exaggerated.

- *Amateurish.* The applicant appears to have little understanding of the business world or of the particular industry, a lack revealed by including the wrong information or presenting it awkwardly.

- *Poorly reproduced.* The print is faint and difficult to read.

- *Misspelled and ungrammatical throughout.* The applicant lacks verbal skills important on the job and shows poor judgment in failing to have another person proofread the resume.

- *Lacking a career objective.* The resume fails to identify the applicant's job preferences and career goals.

- *Boastful.* The overconfident tone makes the reader wonder whether the applicant's self-evaluation is realistic.

- *Dishonest.* The applicant claims to have expertise that he or she does not possess.

- *Gimmicky.* The words, structure, decoration, or material used in the resume depart so far from the usual as to make it ineffective.[2]

Guard against making these mistakes in your own resume, and compare your final version with the suggestions in the accompanying checklist.

WRITING AN APPLICATION LETTER

Follow the AIDA plan in writing your application letter: attention, interest, desire, action.

If you're like most job seekers, you will send your resume to many employers, because the chances of getting an interview from each inquiry are relatively slight. To make the process more efficient, you will probably use the same resume repeatedly but tailor your application for each potential employer by including a cover letter that tells what you can do for that specific organization.

Like your resume, your application letter is a form of advertising, and it should be organized as a persuasive message. You need to stimulate the reader's interest and then show how you can satisfy the organization's needs. The style should project confidence; you can't hope to sell a potential employer on your merits unless you truly believe in them yourself and sound as though you do.

Your letter should also reflect your personal style, so be yourself. But be businesslike too; avoid sounding cute. Don't use slang or a gimmicky layout. The only time to be unusually creative is when the job you're seeking requires imagination, such as a position in advertising.

Finally, showing that you know something about the organization can pay

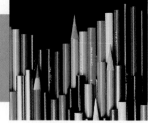

CHECKLIST FOR RESUMES

A. Contents and Style

☐ **1.** Prepare the resume before the application letter to summarize the facts that the letter will be based on.

☐ **2.** Present the strongest, most relevant qualifications first.

☐ **3.** Use short noun phrases and action verbs, not whole sentences.

☐ **4.** Use facts, not opinions.

☐ **5.** Avoid personal pronouns.

☐ **6.** Omit the date of preparation.

☐ **7.** Omit mention of your desired salary, work schedule, or vacation schedule.

B. Heading and Contact Information

☐ **1.** Use a title such as "Resume" as a heading.

☐ **2.** List your name, address, area code, and telephone number—for both home and school or work, if appropriate.

C. Career Objective and Skills Summary

☐ **1.** State the type of work you want (not a job title) and your career objective.

☐   **a.** State a broad and flexible goal to increase the scope of your job prospects.

☐   **b.** Prepare separate resumes if you can do unrelated types of work, such as bookkeeping and nursing.

☐ **2.** Summarize your key qualifications.

☐ **3.** State the month and, if you know it, the day on which you will be available to start work.

D. Education

☐ **1.** List all relevant schooling and training since high school, with the most recent first.

☐   **a.** List the name and location of every postsecondary school you have attended, with the dates you entered and left and the degrees or certificates you obtained.

☐   **b.** Indicate your major (and minor) fields in college work.

☐   **c.** State the numerical base for your grade-point average, overall or in your major, if your average is impressive enough to list.

☐ **2.** List relevant required or elective courses in descending order of importance.

☐ **3.** List any other relevant educational or training experiences, such as job-related seminars or workshops attended and certificates obtained.

---

off. It gets attention. It conveys your desire to join the organization. The more you can learn about the organization, the better you'll be able to write about how your qualifications fit its needs.

WRITING THE OPENING PARAGRAPH

A solicited application letter is one sent in response to an announced job opening. An unsolicited, or "prospecting," letter is one sent to an organization that has not announced an opening. When you send a solicited letter, you usually know in advance what qualifications the organization is looking for. However, you also have more competition because hundreds of other job seekers will have seen the listing and may be sending applications. In some respects, therefore, an unsolicited application letter stands a better chance of being read. Although it may initially be filed away, it will probably be considered eventually, and it may get more individualized attention.

Whether you are sending a solicited or an unsolicited application letter, you should present your qualifications similarly. The main difference is in the opening paragraph. In a solicited letter, no special attention-getting effort is

Unsolicited application letters, which are not designed to respond to a particular opening, must do an especially good job of capturing attention and raising interest.

E. Work Experience

☐ **1.** List all relevant work experience, including paid employment and volunteer work.

☐ **2.** List full-time and part-time jobs, with the most recent one first.

  ☐ a. State the month and year you started and left each job.

  ☐ b. Provide the name and location of the firm that employed you.

  ☐ c. List your job title and describe your functions briefly.

  ☐ d. Note on-the-job accomplishments such as an award or a suggestion that saved the organization time or money.

F. Activities, Honors, and Achievements

☐ **1.** List all relevant unpaid activities, including offices and leadership positions you have held; significant awards or scholarships not listed elsewhere; projects you have undertaken that show an ability to work with others; and writing or speaking activities, publications, and roles in academic or professional organizations.

☐ **2.** In most circumstances, exclude mention of religious or political affiliations.

G. Other Relevant Facts

☐ **1.** List other relevant information such as your typing speed or your proficiency in languages other than English.

☐ **2.** Mention your ability to operate any machines, equipment, or computer software used in the job.

H. Personal Data

☐ **1.** Omit data that could be regarded negatively or used to discriminate against you.

☐ **2.** Omit or downplay references to age if it could suggest inexperience or approaching retirement.

☐ **3.** Describe military service (branch of service, where you served, rank attained, and the dates of induction and discharge) here or, if relevant, under "Education" or "Work Experience."

☐ **4.** List job-related interests and hobbies, especially those indicating stamina, strength, sociability, or other qualities that are desirable in the position you seek.

I. References

☐ **1.** List three to five references, or offer to supply the names on request.

  ☐ a. Supply names of academic, employment, and professional associates—but no relatives.

  ☐ b. Provide a name, title, address, and telephone number for each reference.

  ☐ c. List no name as a reference until you have that person's permission to do so.

☐ **2.** Exclude your present employer if you do not want her or him to know you are seeking another position, or add "Resume submitted in confidence" at the top or bottom of the resume.

needed because you have been invited to apply. The unsolicited letter, however, must start by capturing the reader's attention and interest.

Getting attention

One way to spark attention in the opening paragraph is to show how your strongest work skills could benefit the organization. A 20-year-old secretary with 1½ years of college might begin like this:

When you need a secretary in your export division who can take shorthand at 125 words a minute and type notes at 70--in English, Spanish, or Portuguese--call me.

Another attention-getter consists of describing your understanding of the job's requirements and then showing how well your qualifications fit the job:

From my research, I've learned that the IBM technician needs a diverse array of skills. These include mechanical aptitude, manual dexterity, and public relations skills. Please check the attached resume to see how well my background in telephone repair fits these specifications.

Begin an unsolicited application letter by focusing on one or more of the following:

- Your strongest work skills and how they would help the organization
- The match between job requirements and your qualifications
- The name of someone respected by the reader
- News about the organization that demonstrates your awareness
- A question that reflects your knowledge of the organization's needs
- An imaginative catch phrase
- The source of your knowledge about the job opening

Self-made billionaire H. Ross Perot founded Electronic Data Systems (now owned by General Motors). Known for his patriotic fervor and his single-minded devotion to "rescuing America from the mess it's in," Perot insists that there's no limit to our nation's need for young people with vision. He reminds applicants to get attention by emphasizing how they can help the employer.

Mentioning the name of a person known to and highly regarded by the reader is also bound to capture some attention:

When Janice McHugh of your franchise sales division spoke to our business communication class last week, she said you often add promising new marketing graduates to your sales staff at this time of year.

References to publicized company activities, achievements, changes, or new procedures can also be used to gain attention:

Today's issue of the Detroit News reports that you may need the expertise of computer programmers versed in robotics when your Lansing tire plant automates this spring.

Another type of attention-getting opening uses a question to demonstrate an understanding of the organization's needs:

Can your fast-growing market research division use an interviewer with 1-1/2 years of field survey experience, a B.A. in public relations, and a real desire to succeed? If so, please consider me for the position.

A catch-phrase opening can also capture attention, especially if the job sought requires ingenuity and imagination:

Grande monde--whether said in French, Italian, or Arabic, it still means "high society." As an interior designer for your Beverly Hills showroom, not only could I serve, and sell to, your high-society clientele but I could do it in all these languages. I speak, read, and write them fluently.

In contrast, a solicited letter written in response to a job advertisement usually opens by identifying the publication in which the ad ran and then describing what the applicant has to offer:

Your ad in the April issue of Travel & Leisure for a cruise-line social director caught my eye. My eight years of experience as a social director in the travel industry would allow me to serve your new Caribbean cruise division well.

Notice that all these openings demonstrate the "you" attitude and indicate how the applicant can serve the employer.

Clarifying your reason for writing

The opening paragraph of your application letter should also state your reason for writing: You are applying for a job. It should therefore identify the desired job or job area:

I am seeking an entry-level position in technical writing.

Having had six months of new-car sales experience, I am applying for the fleet sales position advertised by your firm in the Baltimore Sun (March 23, 1993).

Another way to state your reason for writing is to use a title at the opening of your letter. For example:

Subject: Application for bookkeeper position

After this clear signal, your first paragraph can focus on getting attention and indicating how hiring you may benefit the organization.

SUMMARIZING YOUR KEY SELLING POINTS

The middle section of an application letter should
- Summarize those qualifications that are directly related to this job
- Show how you have put your qualifications to use
- Provide evidence of desirable personal qualities
- Tie salary requirements to the benefits of hiring you
- Refer to your resume

The middle paragraph(s) of the application letter should present your strongest selling points in terms of their potential benefit to the organization, thereby creating interest in you and a desire to interview you. If your selling points have already been mentioned in the opening, don't repeat them. Simply give supporting evidence. Otherwise, spell out your key qualifications, together with some convincing evidence of your ability to perform.

To avoid a cluttered application letter, mention only the qualifications that indicate you can do the job. For example, show how your studies and work experience have prepared you for it. Or tell the reader about how you grew up in the business. But be careful not to repeat the facts presented in your resume. Simply interpret them:

Experience in customer relations and college courses in public relations have taught me how to handle the problem-solving tasks that arise in a leading retail clothing firm like yours. Such important tasks include identifying and resolving customer complaints, writing letters that build good customer relations, and above all, promoting the organization's positive image.

When writing a solicited letter in response to a help-wanted advertisement, fully cover each requirement specified in the ad. If you are deficient in any of these requirements, stress other solid selling points to help strengthen your overall presentation.

Stating that you have all the necessary requirements for the job is rarely enough to convince the reader, so back up assertions of your ability by presenting evidence of it. Cite one or two of your key qualifications; then show how you have effectively put them to use. For example:

INSTEAD OF THIS	WRITE THIS
I completed three college courses in business communication, earning an A in each course, and have worked for the past year at Imperial Construction.	Using the skills gained from three semesters of college training in business communication, I developed a collection system for Imperial Construction that reduced its 1992 bad-debt losses by 3.7 percent, or $9,902, over those of 1991. The new collection letters offered discount incentives for speedy payment, rather than time-worn terminology.

This section of the letter should also present evidence of a few significant job-related qualities. For example, the following paragraph demonstrates that the applicant is diligent and hard working:

While attending college full-time, I trained three hours a day with the varsity track team. Additionally, I worked part-time during the school year and up to

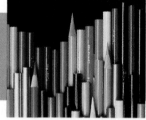

CHECKLIST FOR APPLICATION LETTERS

A. Attention (Opening Paragraph)

☐ **1.** Open the letter by capturing the reader's attention in a businesslike way.

☐ a. *Summary opening.* Present your strongest, most relevant qualifications, with an explanation of how they can benefit the organization.

☐ b. *Name opening.* Mention the name of a person who is well known to the reader and who has suggested that you apply for the job.

☐ c. *Source opening.* When responding to a job ad, identify the publication in which the ad appeared and briefly describe how you meet each requirement stated in the ad.

☐ d. *Question opening.* Pose an attention-getting question that shows you understand an organization's problem, need, or goal and have a genuine desire to help solve, meet, or attain it.

☐ e. *News opening.* Cite a publicized organizational achievement, contemplated change, or new procedure or product, and then link it to your desire to work for the organization.

☐ f. *Personalized opening.* Present one of your relevant interests or views, mention your previous experience with the organization, or cite your present position or status as a means of leading into a discussion of why you want to work for the organization.

☐ g. *Creative opening.* Demonstrate your flair and imagination with colorful phrasing, especially if the job requires these qualities.

☐ **2.** State that you are applying for a job, and identify the position or the type of work you seek.

B. Interest and Desire, or Evidence of Qualifications (Next Several Paragraphs)

☐ **1.** Present your key qualifications for the job, highlighting what is on your resume: job-related education and training; relevant work experience; and related activities, interests, and qualities.

☐ **2.** Adopt a mature and businesslike tone.

☐ a. Eliminate boasting and exaggeration.

☐ b. Back up your claims of ability by citing specific achievements in educational and work settings (or in outside activities).

☐ c. Demonstrate a knowledge of the organization and a desire to join it by citing its operations or trends in the industry.

☐ **3.** Link your education, experience, and personal qualities to the job requirements.

☐ a. Relate aspects of your training or work experience to those of the target position.

☐ b. Outline your educational preparation for the job.

☐ c. Provide proof that you learn quickly, are a hard worker, can handle responsibility, and get along well with others.

☐ d. Present evidence of personal qualities and work attitudes that are desirable for job performance.

☐ e. If asked to state salary requirements, provide current salary or a desired salary range, and link it to the benefits of hiring you.

☐ **4.** Refer the reader to the enclosed resume.

C. Action (Closing Paragraph)

☐ **1.** Request an interview at the reader's convenience.

☐ **2.** Request a screening interview with the nearest regional representative if company headquarters is some distance away.

☐ **3.** To make the interview request easy to comply with, give your phone number (with area code) and the best time to reach you, or mention a time when you will be calling to set up an interview.

☐ **4.** Express appreciation for an opportunity to have an interview.

☐ **5.** To help reinforce the claim that you have something to offer the organization, repeat your strongest qualification.

60 hours a week each summer in order to be totally self-supporting while in college. To your company, I offer these same levels of energetic effort and perseverance.

Other relevant qualities worth noting include the abilities to learn quickly, handle responsibility, and get along with people.

Another matter to bring up in this section is your salary requirements—but only if the organization has asked you to state them. Of course, you should have a reasonable figure in mind and should indicate some flexibility. It is also important to tie your desired salary to the benefits you would provide the organization, as you would handle price in a sales letter. For example:

For the past two years, I have been helping a company similar to yours organize its database. I would therefore like to receive a salary in the same range (the mid-20s) for helping your company set up a more efficient customer database.

Toward the end of this section, refer the reader to your resume. You may do so by citing a specific fact on the resume or by mentioning the references or other information it contains.

WRITING THE CLOSING PARAGRAPH

The "action" section of an application letter should
- Almost always ask for an interview
- Make an interview easy to arrange

The final paragraph of your application letter has two important functions: to ask the reader for a specific action and to make a reply easy. In almost all cases, the action you should ask for is an interview. But don't demand it. Try to sound natural and appreciative. Offer to come to the employer's office at a convenient time or, if the firm is some distance away, to meet with its nearest representative. Make the request easy to fulfill by stating your phone number and the best time to reach you. Refer again to your strongest selling point and, if desired, your date of availability. For example:

After you have reviewed my qualifications, could we discuss the possibility of putting my marketing skills to work for your company? Because I will be on spring break the week of March 8, I would like to arrange a time to talk then. You can reach me by calling (901) 235-6311 during the day or (901) 529-2873 any evening after 5.

An alternative approach is to ask for an interview and then offer to get in touch with the reader to arrange a time for it, rather than requesting a reply. Whichever approach you use, mail your application letter and resume promptly, especially if they have been solicited. Do not enclose a preaddressed, stamped reply envelope unless you are applying for a job with a low-budget employer.

WRITING THE PERFECT APPLICATION LETTER

The "perfect" application letter, like the "perfect" resume, accomplishes one thing: It gets you an interview. But it conforms to no particular model because it's a reflection of your special strengths. Nevertheless, an application letter should contain the basic components. In Figure 13.6, an unsolicited letter for an accounting position, notice how the applicant seeks to gain attention by mentioning a person known to the reader. The letter in Figure 13.7,

FIGURE 13.6
Sample Unsolicited Application Letter

The applicant relates her educational qualifications to the requirements of the position as she understands them.

Knowledge of the company and a specialized capability are sure to interest the reader.

This paragraph emphasizes positive job-related qualities without emphasizing "I."

Mentioning a prominent name calls attention to the enclosed resume.

The "action" paragraph requests an interview and sets up a follow-up phone call.

216 Westview Circle
Dallas, TX 75231
June 16, 1993

Mr. William DuPage, Managing Partner
Grant & Grant Financial Planning Associates
1775 Lakeland Drive
Dallas, TX 75218

Dear Mr. DuPage:

When Roberta Hawley of your personnel department spoke with me today, she indicated that you may be looking for a staff accountant. On the basis of our talk, I believe that my background would benefit Grant & Grant. Four years of college have trained me in accounting and full-charge bookkeeping through trial balance.

My 42 units of college accounting and courses in electronic data processing have equipped me to work with computer-based clients like yours. Training in business writing, human relations, and psychology should help me to achieve solid rapport with them. And advanced studies in tax accounting will enable me to analyze their financial needs from a planning perspective.

Because your company specializes in tax-shelter planning, my work experience could also be beneficial. After two years as a part-time bookkeeper for a securities brokerage firm, I was promoted to full-time financial analyst intern in the corporate investment division. In making recommendations to the firm's corporate clients, I analyzed and selected specific tax-shelter programs. After three months, my accomplishments were acknowledged by a substantial salary increase.

Grant Paul, vice president of Citibank, and other references listed on the enclosed resume will confirm my potential for the staff accountant position.

At a time convenient for you, I would appreciate the opportunity to discuss my qualifications for beginning a career with your company. I will phone you early next Wednesday to see whether we can arrange a meeting at your convenience.

Sincerely,

Diane Fahey

Diane Fahey

Enclosure

written in response to a help-wanted ad, highlights the applicant's chief qualifications.

WRITING OTHER TYPES OF EMPLOYMENT MESSAGES

In your search for a job, you may prepare three other types of written messages: job-inquiry letters, application forms, and application follow-up letters.

WRITING JOB-INQUIRY LETTERS

Some organizations will not consider you for a position until you have filled out and submitted an application form. The inquiry letter is mailed to request such

FIGURE 13.7
Sample Solicited Application Letter

2893 Jack Pine Road
Chapel Hill, NC 27514
February 2, 1993

Ms. Angela Clair
Director of Administration
Cummings and Welbane, Inc.
770 Campus Point Drive
Chapel Hill, NC 27514

Dear Ms. Clair:

Your advertisement in the January 31 issue of the <u>Chapel Hill Post</u> attracted my attention because I believe that I have the "proven skills" you are looking for in an administrative assistant. In addition to having previous experience in a variety of office settings, I am familiar with the computer system that you use in your office.

I recently completed a three-course sequence at Hamilton College on operation of the Beta computer system. I learned how to apply this technology to speed up letter-writing and report-writing tasks. A workshop on "Writing and Editing with the Beta Processor" gave me experience with other valuable applications.

As a result of this training, I am able to compose many types of finished documents, including sales letters, financial reports, and presentation slides.

These specialized skills have proven valuable in my work for the past eight months as assistant to the chief nutritionist at the University of North Carolina campus cafeteria. As my resume indicates, my duties include drafting letters, typing finished correspondence, and handling phone calls. I'm particularly proud of the order-confirmation system I designed, which has sharply reduced the problem of late shipments and depleted inventories.

Because "proven skills" are best explained in person, I would appreciate an interview with you. Please phone me any afternoon between 3 and 5 p.m. at (919) 220-6139 to let me know the day and time most convenient for you.

Sincerely,

Ken Sawyer

Kenneth Sawyer

Enclosure

The opening states the reason for writing and links the writer's experience to stated qualifications.

By discussing how his specific skills apply to the job sought, the applicant shows that he understands the job's responsibilities.

In closing, the writer asks for an interview and facilitates action.

The purpose of a job-inquiry letter is to get you an application form.

a form. To increase your chances of getting the form, include enough information about yourself in the letter to show that you have at least some of the requirements for the position you are seeking. For example:

Please send me an application form for work as an interior designer in your home furnishings department. For my certificate in design, I took courses in retail merchandising and customer relations. I have also had part-time sales experience at Capwell's department store.

Instead of writing a letter of this kind, you may want to drop in at the office you're applying to. You probably won't get a chance to talk to anyone except the receptionist or a personnel assistant while you're there, but you can pick up the form, get an impression of the organization, and demonstrate your initiative and energy.

FILLING OUT APPLICATION FORMS

Some organizations require an application form instead of a resume, and many require both an application form and a resume for all positions. The application form is a standardized data sheet that simplifies comparison of applicants' qualifications. In addition, it provides a convenient one-page source for the information most important to the employer.

> The most important thing about filling out an application form is to be thorough and accurate.

When filling out an application form, make every effort to be thorough and accurate. Use your resume as a reference for such things as dates of employment. If you can't remember something and have no record of it, provide the closest estimate possible. If the form calls for information that you cannot provide because you have no background in it—for example, military experience—write "Not applicable."

Many application forms request that you provide information about the salary you want. Unless you know what other people at the organization are earning in the job you are applying for, the best strategy is to suggest a salary range or to write in "Negotiable" or "Open." You might also prepare for this question by consulting the latest government "Area Wage Survey" at the library; this document presents salary ranges for various job classifications and geographic areas.

Application forms rarely seem to provide the right amount of space or to ask the right kinds of questions to reflect one's skills and abilities accurately. Swallow your frustration, however, and show what a cooperative person you are by doing your best to fill out the form completely. If you get an interview, you'll have an opportunity to fill in the gaps. You might also ask the person who gives you the form whether you may submit a resume and application letter as well.

WRITING APPLICATION FOLLOW-UPS

> The purpose of an application follow-up is to keep your file active and up-to-date.

If your application letter and resume fail to bring a response within a month or so, follow them up with a second letter to keep your file active. This follow-up letter also gives you a chance to update your original application with any recent job-related information:

Since applying to you on May 3 for an executive secretary position, I have completed a course in office management. Also, my typing speed has increased to 75 words per minute.

Please keep my application in your active file, and let me know when you need a skilled executive secretary.

Even if you have received a letter acknowledging your application and saying that it will be kept on file, don't hesitate to send a follow-up letter three months later to show that you are still interested:

Three months have elapsed since I applied to you for an underwriting position, but I want to let you know that I am still very interested in joining your company.

I recently completed a four-week temporary work assignment at a large local insurance agency. There I learned several new verification techniques and gained experience in using the on-line computer system. This experience could increase my value to your underwriting department.

Please keep my application in your active file, and let me know when an opening arises for a capable underwriter.

Unless you tell them otherwise, the personnel office is likely to assume that you've already found a job and are no longer interested in the organization. In addition, organizations' requirements change. Sending a letter like this demonstrates that you are sincerely interested in working for the organization, that you are persistent in pursuing your goals, and that you are upgrading your skills to make yourself a better employee. And it might just get you an interview.

SUMMARY

A resume is a factual report of your qualifications, using action phrases and an abbreviated style. Organizing your resume to emphasize your strong points is entirely acceptable.

A resume should always be accompanied by an application letter, which is a selling piece. Therefore, follow the AIDA plan. The point of writing it is to win yourself an interview.

Other types of employment messages are job-inquiry letters, written to get you an application form; application forms, which should be filled out as completely as possible; and application follow-up letters, written to keep your name on the active list.

ON THE JOB:
Solving a Communication Dilemma at The Coca-Cola Company

Creativity is certainly one of the qualities Charles Morrison looks for in a job candidate. It takes plenty of imagination to build minority awareness of Coke's brands, which include Hi-C, Sprite, Fanta, and Minute Maid soft drinks as well as the Coca-Cola family of sodas. Perhaps the most obvious vehicle for stimulating demand is advertising—one of Morrison's areas of expertise. Before joining Coke, he was an account manager for Burrell Advertising, the agency that has handled Coca-Cola's black-oriented advertising for over 12 years.

Under Morrison's direction, Coca-Cola has created some outstanding ad campaigns aimed at minority consumers. Coca-Cola is one of the few companies to produce Spanish-language commercials, and one of Morrison's most imaginative experiments was a commercial for Sprite, which was produced, directed, and performed by black students from three high schools in Jacksonville, Florida. Morrison also engineered the "Red, White and You" print ad campaign that garnered Coca-Cola and its advertising agency two CEBA (Communications Excellence to Black Audiences) awards for excellence. Hispanic ads feature Mario Morena (known throughout the Hispanic world as "Cantinflas"), and Morrison has also persuaded such well-known black entertainers as Whitney Houston; Earth, Wind, and Fire; and Run DMC to appear in Coke's commercials.

To complement Coca-Cola's minority-oriented advertising, Morrison and his staff arrange a variety of promotional and public relations events. For example, Coke sponsors the "Amateur Night" talent show at the famed Apollo Theater in Harlem—an important proving ground for black musical talent over the past 50 years. Also, Coca-Cola provides entertainment at local Hispanic festivals and gives away samples and premiums.

Sports marketing is another of Morrison's favorite techniques for building demand for Coca-Cola among black and Hispanic youth. Morrison has lined up an impressive roster of sports figures to represent Coca-Cola in commercial and public appearances, including Michael Jordan of the Chicago Bulls, Dominique Wilkins and Spud Webb of the Atlanta Hawks, pro golfer Calvin Peete, Fernando Valenzuela of the Los Angles Dodgers, and Julius Erving, the legendary Dr. J. (who not only appears in Coke promotions but also owns the Philadelphia Coca-Cola Bottling Company, the third-largest black-owned business in the country). Morrison also arranged for Coca-Cola to join with the Jackie Robinson Foundation to sponsor an exhibition commemorating the 40th anniversary of Robinson's entry into the major leagues.

To underscore Coca-Cola's serious side, Morrison and his staff also plan a variety of worthwhile community activities that build goodwill among minority consumers. For example, Morrison worked with the Atlanta Coca-Cola Bottling Company to create the Coca-Cola/Run DMC Anti-Drug Campaign, a summer-long program aimed at providing drug-free fun for young people in Atlanta, including Rap-Off and Slogan contests, free giveaways, and a Run DMC concert. In another goodwill-building effort, Morrison persuaded Coca-Cola to sponsor the Black History Month Sweepstakes, which provides $100,000 in scholarships to students attending predominantly black colleges and universities. Coca-Cola also maintains accounts with Hispanic banks, purchases goods and services from Hispanic vendors, and funds Hispanic scholarships. In addition, Morrison handles Coca-Cola's participation in minority organizations such as the National Conference of Black Mayors, the National Association for the Advancement of Colored People, the United Negro College Fund, and the California Hispanic Chamber of Commerce.

Morrison gives his staff much of the credit for Coca-Cola's success in marketing to black and Hispanic consumers. His team currently includes a veteran in consumer products marketing, a former referee in the National Basketball Association, and two advertising professionals who specialize in Hispanic promotion and marketing.

Your Mission: As a member of Coca-Cola's personnel department, you regularly review resumes that arrive "over the transom." Morrison has asked you to be on the lookout for recent college graduates who might be good candidates for his department. He is looking for a marketing trainee to handle correspondence, schedule activities, and attend to assorted administrative tasks. The person should have the capacity to advance in the marketing function. Give Morrison your *best* advice regarding the various applicants described here:

1. You have received resumes from four people. Based only on the career objectives listed, which of the candidates do you think Morrison would prefer?
   a. Career Objective: An entry-level marketing position in a large, consumer products company
   b. Career Objective: To use my artistic talents and business savvy to develop award-winning television commercials
   c. Career Objective: A marketing position in which a degree in business administration and a personal knowledge of Hispanic culture will be useful
   d. Career Objective: To learn all I can about consumer products marketing in a creative and stimulating environment with a company whose reputation is outstanding

2. On the basis of only the education sections of another four resumes, which of the following candidates would you recommend to Morrison?

   a. EDUCATION
      Morehouse College, Atlanta, GA, 1988-1991. Received B.A. degree with a major in Economics and a minor in Psychology. Graduated with a 3.65 grade-point average. Played varsity football and basketball. Worked 15 hours per week in the library. Coordinated the Invention Convention, a showcase for creative solutions to common problems. Member of Alpha Phi Alpha social fraternity.
   b. Education: I attended Wayne State University in Detroit, Michigan, for two years and then transferred to the University of Michigan at Ann Arbor, where I completed my studies. My major field was physics, but I also took a wide spectrum of liberal arts courses, including cultural anthropology, comparative literature, creative writing, music appreciation, abnormal psychology, and art history. I selected courses based on the professors' reputation for excellence, and I received mostly A's and B's. Unlike many college students, I viewed the acquisition of knowledge--rather than career preparation--as my primary goal. As a consequence, I believe I have received a well-rounded education that has prepared me to think creatively.
   c. ACADEMIC PREPARATION
      Howard University, Washington, D.C. Graduated with a B.A. degree in 1993. Majored in Physical Education. Minored in Business Administration. Graduated with a 2.85 average.
   d. Education: North Texas State University and University of Texas at Tyler. Received B.A. and M.B.A. degrees. I majored in business as an undergraduate and concentrated in marketing during my M.B.A. program. Received a special $2,500 scholarship set aside for academically gifted Hispanic students interested in a career in business. I also won the MEGA award in 1992. Dean's list.

3. Which of the following four candidates would you recommend, based only on the experience sections?
   a. RELATED WORK EXPERIENCE
      McDonald's, Peoria, IL, 1987-1989. Part-time cook. Worked 15 hours per week while attending high school. Prepared hamburgers, chicken bits, and french fries. Received employee-of-the-month award for outstanding work habits.
      University Grill, Ames, IA, 1990-1993. Part-time cook. Worked 20 hours per week while attending college. Prepared hot and cold sandwiches. Helped manager purchase ingredients. Trained new kitchen workers.

b. RELATED EXPERIENCE

Although I have never held a full-time job, I have worked part-time and during summer vacations throughout my high school and college years. During my freshman and sophomore years in high school, I bagged groceries at the A&P store three afternoons a week. The work was not terribly challenging, but I liked the customers and the other employees. During my junior and senior years, I worked at the YMCA as an after-school counselor for elementary school children who were left there while their parents worked. The kids were really sweet, and I still get letters from some of them. During summer vacations while I was in college, I did construction work for a local home builder. The best thing about that job was the pay, but I also learned a lot about carpentry. The guys I worked with were a mixed bag who expanded my vocabulary and knowledge of the world. I also worked part-time in college in the student cafeteria, where I scooped food onto plates. This did not require much talent, but it certainly did teach me a lot about how people behave when standing in line. I also learned quite a bit about life from my boss, Sam "the man" Benson, who has been managing the student cafeteria for 25 years.

c. PREVIOUS WORK EXPERIENCE

The Broadway Department Store, Sherman Oaks, CA, Summers, 1989-1993. Sales Consultant. In my capacity as a sales consultant, I interacted with a diverse group of customers, including suburban matrons, teenagers, and career women. I endeavored to satisfy their individual needs and make their shopping experience memorable, efficient, and enjoyable. Under the direction of the department manager, I arranged merchandise in artistic and eye-catching displays. I also helped manage the inventory, worked the cash register, and handled a variety of returns and complaints with courtesy and aplomb. During the two-week period prior to Christmas 1992, I sold more merchandise than any other part-time clerk in the entire store.

d. EXPERIENCE RELATED TO MARKETING

Belle Fleure, GA, Parks & Recreation Department, June-September 1992. Volunteer on Parks & Recreation Committee.

* Organized and promoted a series of summer concerts for the city of Belle Fleure, GA; persuaded local businesses to finance program; designed, printed, and distributed fliers; wrote and distributed press releases; attracted audience of 1,500 people to final concert
* Designed and wrote copy for ten-page brochure describing park and recreation programs for the city of Belle Fleure
* Conducted a survey of local residents to determine their park and recreation needs; prepared written report for city council and delivered oral summary of findings at town meeting; helped persuade city to fund new community swimming pool

4. What would you do with the following candidate?

Resume of Maria Martin
1124 2nd S.W.
Rhinelander, WI 54501
(715) 369-0098

Career Objective: To build a marketing career in a consumer products company

Summary of Qualifications: As a student at the University of Wisconsin in Madison, carried out various assignments that have required skills related to a career in sales and marketing. For example:

Communication Skills. Wrote over 25 essays and term papers dealing with academic topics. Received an A on all but two of these papers. As a senior, wrote a 20-page analysis of the paper products industry, interviewing the five top executives at the Rhinelander paper company. Received an A+ on this paper.

Planning Skills. As president of the university's foreign affairs forum, organized six lectures and workshops featuring 36 speakers from 16 foreign countries within a nine-month period. Identified and recruited the speakers, handled their travel arrangements, scheduled facilities, and managed the publicity for the events.

Interpersonal Skills. As chairman of the parade committee for homecoming weekend, worked with the city of Madison to obtain approval, permits, and traffic control for the parade. Also encouraged local organizations such as the Lion's Club, the Kiwanis Club, the Boy Scouts, and the Horseman's Club to participate in the parade. Coordinated the efforts of the 15 fraternities and 18 sororities that entered floats in the parade. Recruited 12 marching bands from surrounding communities and coordinated their efforts with the university's marching band and flag team. Also arranged for local auto dealers to provide cars for the ten homecoming queen candidates.

Creativity. Designed the costumes and sets for the university's production of <u>Mandrake</u>, a musical comedy based on a play by Machiavelli. Also served as art editor of the campus literary magazine for two years.

a. Definitely recommend that Morrison take a look at this outstanding candidate.

b. Turn down the candidate. She doesn't give enough information about when she attended college, what she majored in, or where she has worked.

c. Call the candidate on the phone and ask for more information. If she sounds promising, send her an application form that requests more specific information about her academic background and employment history.

d. Consider the candidate's qualifications relative to those of other applicants. Recommend her if you do not have three or four other applicants with more directly relevant qualifications.

5. Which of the following applicants would you recommend to Morrison, based on the application letters shown below?

a. Please consider me as a candidate for employment with the Coca-Cola company. I am particularly interested in a job in your marketing department.

As a devoted Coke fan, I think I can make a real contribution to your organization. I have an M.B.A. degree from the University of Michigan, where I specialized in consumer products marketing. I wrote my graduate thesis on competition in the soft drink industry, and I believe I have a good grasp of the marketing dynamics of the business. In fact, while I was a student, I gained first-hand experience selling soft drinks at the Ann Arbor Drug Store, an old-fashioned pharmacy with a classic soda fountain. To stimulate business, I held Coca-Cola Concoction Conventions, where I mixed up variations on the basic Coca-Cola and then ran taste tests to pick the best formula. My vanilla Cokes were the most popular, but my personal favorite was the Coca-Mocha.

I'd be delighted to share the recipe with you when I'm in Atlanta during spring break, March 21–April 5. I will call sometime next week to arrange a specific appointment to talk with someone, preferably a member of your marketing department.

b. Your Jackie Robinson exhibition is an outstanding contribution to African-American culture. When I saw the display at the New York Historical Society, tears came to my eyes. I think all of us who participate in sports can

appreciate the drama of Robinson's career and share in his racial pride, regardless of our own ethnic background.

As an African-American, I am grateful to Coca-Cola for its efforts to reach out to minority groups. Although many organizations pay lip service to equal opportunity, very few are truly committed to the concept, and most ignore the fact that minorities constitute the most rapidly growing segment of the population and hence represent an important marketing opportunity. I would like to be associated with an organization where people of different racial and ethnic backgrounds are taken seriously. I believe that Coca-Cola is such an organization.

If you are currently looking for people with an interest in marketing or public relations, please consider me as a candidate. As my resume indicates, I have a bachelor's degree in business administration from Bishop College. I believe that my background as an Olympic runner might be useful to you in your sports marketing activities.

c. Barbara Hopkins's recent article about you in <u>Dollars & Sense</u> indicates that you are increasing your commitment to black and Hispanic marketing, a field that interests me for a number of reasons. If you are actively recruiting candidates for entry-level positions in this field, please consider my application.

I am a second-generation Puerto Rican, fluent in Spanish and English, and comfortable in both the Latin and Anglo communities. I have a bachelor's degree from City College of New York, where I majored in mass communications, and a master's degree from the Columbia School of Journalism, where I focused on advertising and public relations. For the past two summers, I have been an intern at Conill Advertising, which specializes in advertising aimed at Hispanic consumers. Although my academic background has been oriented primarily toward advertising, I have a good deal of experience in other facets of marketing, having worked in my family's clothing store in Spanish Harlem for the past four years. I'm particularly proud of a frequent shopper program I created to reward our long-term customers for their loyalty.

Do you have a representative in the New York area who would be available to tell me more about opportunities in your black and Hispanic marketing department? Please write to me at my home address (above) or call me at (212) 998-7698 to schedule an interview.[3]

QUESTIONS FOR DISCUSSION

1. Do you think that employers are justified in reacting to a resume on the basis of its appearance?
2. "A good resume lists all your talents so that potential employers know how versatile you are." Do you agree or disagree? Explain your answer.
3. Studies have found that many people inflate the credentials on their resumes, misrepresenting job qualifications, salaries, and academic credentials. If you were an employer, what would you do to detect resume inflation?

4. If you were a recruiter, would you prefer one organizational pattern for resumes over the others? If so, which one? Why?
5. How do your resume and application letter work together to form a unique sales package targeted to the reader?
6. How does one distinguish between an application letter that's unique (which is good) and one that's cute or gimmicky (which is bad)? Provide examples.

DOCUMENTS FOR ANALYSIS

Read the following documents; then (1) analyze the strengths or weaknesses of each sentence and (2) revise each document so that it follows this chapter's guidelines.

DOCUMENT 13.A

I'm a motivated, experienced professional who can play a key managerial role in helping you become one of the aggressive and recognized leaders in the shopping center industry. As the accountant for a prestigious real estate development company, I have extensive experience in such vital executive activities as:

--Administering and controlling accounting systems, reports, and project costs
--Preparing budgets and cash flow projections
--Managing and supervising a large accounting staff
--Interfacing with a variety of highly skilled development professionals

In addition to offering you ten years of hands-on experience, I offer impressive academic and personal credentials, having both an M.B.A. degree and a C.P.A. certificate. My knowledge of computers and my excellent interpersonal communications skills will be of value to you in your negotiations and transactions, in both the long run and the short run.

Although I am extremely interested in your fine company, let me point out that this self-starter will not be available for long. Five of your competitors in the real estate development industry have also received copies of my resume. It will be advantageous for you to contact me in the immediate future.

DOCUMENT 13.B

Two months ago, I sent you my resume. As I'm sure you remember, you replied that you had no openings for which I was qualified. But you said you would keep my resume in your files in case something turned up. I was wondering whether things had changed there, because I'm still looking for a job and would really like to work in Boston. As you know, looking for a permanent job is not a pleasant task (especially if you've been looking as long as I have).

However, I haven't been completely unemployed since I first wrote you. I've taken a variety of odd jobs: waitress, baby-sitter, door-to-door salesperson. Although none of these positions are in my chosen field of social work, they have increased my understanding of people. I think I have matured considerably in the past two months and would make a better social worker now that I have seen how tough it is to make ends meet when you're making the minimum wage. I'd like to come talk to you about the great things that I can do.

And I have a real commitment to Boston. Because it's one of my favorite cities, I am positive that I would be a real asset to the community.

DOCUMENT 13.C

I saw your ad for a finance major in one of the papers last week, and I'd like to apply for the position. I think I have all the qualifications you're looking for, as you will see when you read my resume (attached).

Let me tell you a little bit about myself. Since I got my B.A. degree in finance (with honors) three years ago from State, I've been working for a little company in Sorrento Valley that makes magnetic tape heads for computers. My title is financial analyst, and I do most of the things you mentioned in your ad: budgeting, cash forecasting, and computer modeling. The work is interesting, but the company is having some problems, and I'd like to get into a more secure situation. Although I don't know much about your outfit, the fact that you are owned by a large company is reassuring.

I'd be grateful if you'd give me an interview. I know you must get a lot of resumes, and I guess mine is pretty much like all the rest, but I have a nice personality and would work hard. You can reach me most of the time by calling 420-4665. Thanks for taking the time to read this.

CASES

WRITING A RESUME AND AN APPLICATION LETTER

1. Applying to Coke: A personal resume You want to apply for a summer internship in Morrison's department at Coca-Cola (see this chapter's On-the-Job simulation).

Your task: Develop a resume and an application letter describing your qualifications.[4]

2. "Help wanted": Application for a job listed in the classified section Among the jobs listed in today's *New Orleans Sentinel* (500 Canal Street, New Orleans, LA 70130) are the following:

ACCOUNTANT/MANAGER

Supervisor needed for 3-person bookkeeping department. Degree in accounting plus collection experience helpful. Contact L. Cichy, Reynolds Clothiers, 1572 Abundance Dr., New Orleans 70119.

ACTIVIST—MAKE DEMOCRACY WORK

The state's largest consumer lobbying organization has permanent positions (full- or part-time) for energetic individuals with excellent communication skills who are interested in working for social change. Reply Sentinel Drawer 973.

ATTENDANT

For video game room, 4647 Almonaster Ave., New Orleans 70216.

CONVENIENCE FOOD STORE MANAGER

Vacancies for managers and trainees in New Orleans area. We are seeking energetic and knowledgeable individuals who will be responsible for profitable operation of convenience food stores and petroleum product sales. Applicants should possess retail sales or

---

managerial training. Interested candidates mail resumes and salary requirements to Prestige Products, Inc., 444 Sherwood Forest Blvd., Baton Rouge, LA 70815. Equal opportunity employer M/F.

Your task: Send a resume and an application letter to one of these potential employers.

3. The goat and the tire: Application letter that shows the writer's creative abilities When Lillian Farmer opened her one-person advertising agency four years ago, it had two small accounts, no name, no office, no reputation. But all that has changed. Now the agency does more than $1 million in annual billings, and it has a name (Notorious, Inc.) and a statewide reputation for placing print and television advertisements that are visible, distinctive, memorable, varied, and compelling.

Her secrets for success are just that—secrets. But Lillian Farmer knows how to find the "heart" of the enterprise, the "drama" in the product, and she knows how to bring these intangibles to life through the color of her words and the bite of her graphics. She makes the ordinary memorable by showing it in unusual combinations or from odd angles, and she makes the extraordinary seem comfortably familiar.

Consider the Roadmaster tire draped around the body of a stuffed goat; almost nobody who saw the ad turned the page without reading the copy, and nobody will ever forget that tire.

Your task: Apply for a job as copywriter with Notorious, Inc. (674 Pellissippi Parkway, Atlanta, GA 30338). By its own example, your application letter must demonstrate your creative ability to write ad copy that gets results. Your resume lists the facts of your academic and professional life; your letter gives you the chance to show off your ability.

WRITING OTHER TYPES OF EMPLOYMENT MESSAGES

4. Crashing the last frontier: Letter of inquiry about jobs in Alaska

Your friend can't understand why you would want to move to Alaska. So you explain: "What really decided it for me was that I'd never seen the Northern Lights."

"But what about the bears? The 60-below winters? The permafrost?"

"No problem. Anchorage doesn't get much colder than Buffalo. Just windier and wetter. But I want to live near Fairbanks, which is near the gold-mining area. And the university is there. Fairbanks has lots of small businesses, like a frontier town in the West about 50 years ago. I think they still have homesteading tracts for people who can do their own building and are willing to stay for a certain number of years."

"Your plans seem a little hasty. Maybe you should write for information before you just take off. How do you know you could get a job?"

Your task: Take your friend's advice and write to the Chamber of Commerce, Fairbanks, AK 99701. Ask what types of employment are available for someone with your education and experience, and ask who specifically is hiring year-round employees.

INTERVIEWING FOR EMPLOYMENT AND FOLLOWING UP

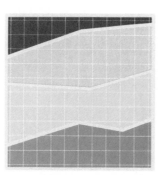

ON THE JOB:
Facing a Communication Dilemma at Herman Miller, Inc.
How to Tell a Good Dancer before the Waltz Begins

Looking for a company that cares about people? You might try Herman Miller, a highly successful establishment that manufactures office furniture in Zeeland, Michigan. Founded in 1923 by D. J. DePree, Herman Miller is justifiably famous for its corporate culture. It may be the only company on the Fortune 500 list that actually has a vice president for people. Participation is the name of the game in this organization. Employees at all levels are consulted about important decisions and reap the rewards if the business does well.

When Herman Miller's recruiters interview a job candidate, they look at the person's education and experience, of course, but they also look for something else: the ability to get along with others. If the candidate's personality is outstanding, the company may be willing to overlook lack of relevant experience. A senior vice president of research was a former high school football coach. The senior vice president of marketing and sales used to be the dean of agriculture at Michigan State. And the vice president for people planned to become a prison warden but joined Herman Miller instead.

On the surface, these people did not seem like good candidates for management jobs in the office furniture business, but Herman Miller looked beyond the superficial to see their true potential. Edward Simon, Jr., president and chief operating officer, notes that the most important quality in a Herman Miller employee is the capacity for teamwork. "To be successful here," he says, "you have to know how to dance."

But how do you know whether someone is a good dancer before you actually begin the waltz? That's the challenge facing Herman Miller's recruiters when they interview job candidates. But what challenges face the candidate? How would you prepare for a job interview? What should you do during an interview? Is there anything you should do after the interview?[1]

INTERVIEWING WITH POTENTIAL EMPLOYERS

Herman Miller, Inc.

The recruiters at Herman Miller know how important it is to find a job that fits. With the right job, you stand to be happy in your work. Thus it pays to approach job interviews with a sound appreciation of their dual purpose. The organization's main objective is to find the best person available for the job; the applicant's main objective is to find the job best suited to his or her goals and capabilities.

HOW TO PREPARE FOR A JOB INTERVIEW

It's perfectly normal to feel a little anxious before an interview. So much depends on it, and you don't know quite what to expect. But don't worry too much; preparation will help you perform well.

Do some basic research

Learning about the organization and the job is important. Figure 14.1 describes some good sources of information and the types of information to look for. You should also try to learn the interviewer's name and title. Knowing these facts shows that you have the interest and initiative to find out things on your own.

Once you have studied the organization, review your resume from the employer's point of view. What aspects of your background are likely to be of greatest interest to this particular organization? Practice relating what you have done and can do to the requirements of the job you want. Let each line of your resume serve as a cue for discussing relevant facts that may not be obvious from the resume.

Be prepared to provide details about your qualifications that will interest the particular organization.

Think ahead about questions

Most job interviews are essentially question-and-answer sessions: You answer the interviewer's questions about your background, and you ask questions of your own to determine whether the job and the organization are right for you. By planning ahead, you can handle these exchanges intelligently.

You can expect to be asked questions about what you have achieved, your interests and hobbies, how you feel about work and school, and your relation-

WHERE
TO LOOK

- *Annual report:* Summarizes year's operations; mentions products, significant events, names of key personnel
- *In-house magazine or newspaper:* Reveals information about company operations, events, personnel
- *Product brochures and publicity releases:* Provide insight into organization's operations and values (obtain from public relations office)
- *Stock research reports:* Help you assess stability and prospects for growth (obtain from local stockbroker)
- *Business and financial pages of local newspapers:* Contain news items about organizations, current performance figures
- *Periodicals indexes:* Contain descriptive listings of magazine and newspaper articles about organizations (obtain from library)
- *Better Business Bureau and Chamber of Commerce:* Distribute information about some local organizations
- *Former and current employees:* Have insight into job and work environment
- *College placement office:* Collects information on organizations that recruit and on job qualifications and salaries

WHAT TO
FIND OUT

About the Organization
- *Full name:* What the organization is officially known as (for example, 3M is Minnesota Mining & Manufacturing Company)
- *Location:* Where the organization's headquarters, branch offices, and plants are
- *Age:* How long the organization has been in business
- *Products:* What goods and services the organization produces and sells
- *Industry position:* What the organization's current market share, financial position, and profit picture are
- *Earnings:* What the trends in the organization's stock prices and dividends are (if the firm is publicly held)
- *Growth:* What changes in earnings and holdings the organization has experienced in recent years and its prospects for expansion
- *Organization:* What subsidiaries, divisions, and departments make up the whole

About the Job
- *Job title:* What you will be called
- *Job functions:* What the main tasks of the job are
- *Job qualifications:* What knowledge and skills the job requires
- *Career path:* What chances for ready advancement exist
- *Salary range:* What the organization typically offers and what pay is reasonable in this industry and geographic area
- *Travel opportunities:* How often, long, and far you'll be allowed (or required) to travel
- *Relocation opportunities:* Where you might be allowed (or required) to move and how often you might be moved

FIGURE 14.1
Finding Out About the Organization and the Job

Types of questions to ask during an interview:
- Warm-up
- Answerable
- Open-ended
- Indirect

ships with friends and family members. For a list of likely questions, see Figure 14.2. Jot down a brief answer to each one. Then read the answers over until you feel comfortable with each one. Or tape-record them, and listen to make sure they sound clear and convincing. This exercise will help you clarify your thinking and equip you with ready answers to even the toughest questions.

The questions you ask in an interview are just as important as the answers you provide. By asking intelligent questions, you can demonstrate your understanding of the organization and steer the discussion into areas where you can present your qualifications to peak advantage. More important, you can get the information you need to evaluate the organization and the job. While recruiters like those at Herman Miller are trying to decide whether you are right

FIGURE 14.2
Twenty-Five Common Interview Questions

1. What courses in school did you like most? Least? Why?

2. What jobs have you held? Why did you leave?

3. What percentage of your college expenses did you earn? How?

4. Why did you choose your particular field of work?

5. Do you prefer to work in any specific geographic location? If so, why?

6. How much money do you hope to earn at age 30? Age 35?

7. Do you think that your extracurricular activities while in college were worth the time you devoted to them? Why or why not?

8. What do you think determines a person's progress in a good organization?

9. What personal characteristics do you feel are necessary for success in your chosen field?

10. Why do you think you would like this particular type of job?

11. Do you prefer working with others or by yourself?

12. What type of boss do you prefer?

13. Tell me a story.

14. Have you served in the military? What rank did you achieve? What jobs did you perform?

15. When did you choose your college major? Did you ever change your major? If so, why?

16. Do you feel you did the best scholastic work you are capable of?

17. Have you ever had any difficulty getting along with other students? With instructors? With co-workers or supervisors?

18. Which of your college years was the toughest?

19. Would you prefer to work in a large or a small organization? Why?

20. What do you think about how this industry operates today?

21. Do you like to travel?

22. How do you feel about overtime work?

23. What are the disadvantages of your chosen field?

24. Do you think grades should be considered by employers? Why or why not?

25. What have you done that shows initiative and willingness to work?

for them, you must decide whether Herman Miller or any other company is right for you.

Before the interview, prepare a list of about a dozen questions, using a mix of formats to elicit various types of information. Start with a warm-up question to help break the ice. For example, you might ask, "Have you already conducted many interviews for this job?" After that, ask only questions that can be answered without difficulty. Interviewers feel good when they have an answer, especially when you acknowledge the answer with a smile. An open-ended question—for example, "How do you see your organization improving on its product sales in the next few years?"—builds rapport by giving the interviewer a chance to express an opinion. Indirect questions are another approach. Comments such as "I'd really like to know more about your space

For 40 years, Colby H. Chandler was chairman and CEO of Eastman Kodak. According to Chandler, the cost of luring a college senior, including recruitment, moving expenses, training, first-year salary, allowances, and benefits, is considerable. So just being asked to an interview should make you feel more confident.

project" or "You must be busy with your new hotel acquisition" show your awareness and interest and may elicit useful information without putting any pressure on the interviewer. For a list of other good questions, see Figure 14.3.

Take your list of questions to the interview on a notepad or clipboard. Don't jot down the interviewer's answers during the meeting, but try to remember the answers and record them afterward. Having a list of questions should impress the interviewer with your organization and thoroughness. It will also show that you are there to evaluate the organization and the job as well as to sell yourself.

Bolster your confidence

By overcoming your tendencies to feel shy, self-conscious, nervous, or uncertain during an interview, you can build your confidence and make a better impression. The best way to counteract these feelings is to identify and deal with their source. For instance, being shy often results from having a real or an imagined deficiency that makes one shrink from contact with others. Here's how to overcome shyness:

- Realize that you are more aware of your seeming drawbacks than others are.

- If an aspect of your appearance makes you uneasy, correct it or offset it by exercising positive traits such as warmth, wit, intelligence, and charm.

FIGURE 14.3
Fifteen Questions to Ask the Interviewer

1. What are this job's major responsibilities?

2. What qualities do you want in the person who fills this position?

3. Do you want to know more about my related training?

4. What is the first problem that needs the attention of the person you hire?

5. What are the organization's major strengths? Weaknesses?

6. Who are your organization's major competitors, and what are their strengths and weaknesses?

7. What makes your organization different from others in the industry?

8. What are your organization's major markets?

9. Does the organization have any plans for new products? Acquisitions?

10. What can you tell me about the person I would report to?

11. How would you define your organization's management philosophy?

12. What additional training does your organization provide?

13. Do employees have an opportunity to continue their education with help from the organization?

14. Would relocation be required, now or in the future?

15. Why is this job now vacant?

- If you feel inferior as a talker, emphasize modes of communication that you're good at, such as writing and researching.

- Make a list of your good points and compare them with your imagined shortcomings.

- Ask yourself this: Of the people you know well, how many would you readily change places with?

- Learn to focus on your strengths so that you can emphasize them to an interviewer.

You must also realize that it is natural to feel self-conscious in the presence of someone you regard as important, such as an interviewer. To conquer self-consciousness, keep this in mind: Everyone is just a person. You and the interviewer may not share all the same experiences and interests, but you are both human. To the extent that you can make the interviewer feel more comfortable, you will lose your own feelings of discomfort.

Many people also feel nervous when they think about being interviewed. Here are some simple ways to overcome nervousness:

- Identify the specific aspect of the interview that is making you feel nervous. Is it the large office building? The busy work atmosphere? The authoritative interviewer? The pressure of having to do well? Once you know what makes you feel uneasy, envision yourself facing it and dealing with it successfully. Repeat this process until you feel your nervousness subside.

- Jot down the reasons you feel anxious about the interview. Then make a list of your positive points. Compare the two. You'll discover that you have more reasons to feel confident than to feel nervous.

- Review your capabilities until you can discuss them readily. Practice doing so aloud in front of a mirror, with a friend, with a tape recorder, or on videotape. Rehearse talking about yourself and selling yourself.

- Use small props during the interview to control nervousness: Keep your resume in front of you to prevent lapses of memory; carry a piece of literature about the organization, such as an annual report that you can refer to; or take along a sample of your work, if appropriate.

- Avoid looking nervous during the interview. Don't chew gum, smoke, tap your fingers on the desk or chair, or play with a key ring or other object. Instead, sit back in the chair, relax, and fold your hands in your lap. This posture will help you look calm and feel calm.

And then there's uncertainty. If you are interviewing for an advertised position and don't feel fully qualified, realize that advertisements often overstate the job requirements. The interviewer may relax the requirements a bit after talking with you. And because such qualities as enthusiasm may overshadow all others, sound and act positive.

Polish your interview style

Confidence helps you walk into an interview, but you'll walk out without a job if you don't also give the interviewer an impression of poise, good manners,

If you feel shy or self-conscious, remember that recruiters are human too.

Ken and Sheryl Dawson own the Houston-based outplacement firm, Dawson and Dawson Management Consultants. Having worked with major corporations around the world, the Dawsons remind you that the interview is a two-way street: Not only does the company want to be sure you're right for it, but you want to be sure that the company is right for you.

Staging mock interviews with a friend is a good way to hone your style.

and good judgment. One way to develop an adept style is to stage mock interviews with a friend. After each practice session, have your friend critique your performance, using the list of interview faults shown in Figure 14.4 to identify opportunities for improvement.

Striking just the right tone in an interview is difficult. You want to avoid any hint of the following flaws:

- *Shrinking in the presence of authority.* Being in awe of the interviewer can reduce you to a quaking ninny, a condition that is unlikely to get you a job offer. To prevent it, project a warm, confident manner from the start. Ask questions and acknowledge answers. Be positive, outgoing, and professional.

- *Seeming "laid back" and flippant.* Perhaps you are so confident of your chances that you'll seem overly relaxed, perhaps even uncaring. To dispel

FIGURE 14.4
Marks Against Applicants (in General Order of Importance)

1. Has a poor personal appearance
2. Is overbearing, overaggressive, conceited; has a "superiority complex"; seems to "know it all"
3. Is unable to express self clearly; has poor voice, diction, grammar
4. Lacks knowledge or experience
5. Is not prepared for interview
6. Has no real interest in job
7. Lacks planning for career; has no purpose or goals
8. Lacks enthusiasm; is passive and indifferent
9. Lacks confidence and poise; is nervous and ill at ease
10. Shows insufficient evidence of achievement
11. Has failed to participate in extracurricular activities
12. Overemphasizes money; is interested only in the best dollar offer
13. Has poor scholastic record; just got by
14. Is unwilling to start at the bottom; expects too much too soon
15. Makes excuses
16. Is evasive; hedges on unfavorable factors in record
17. Lacks tact
18. Lacks maturity
19. Lacks courtesy; is ill-mannered
20. Condemns past employers
21. Lacks social skills
22. Shows marked dislike for schoolwork
23. Lacks vitality
24. Fails to look interviewer in the eye
25. Has limp, weak handshake

this image, try to display real interest during the interview. Learn about the organization in advance, and ask relevant questions. Look alive and attentive. Show enthusiasm. Smile. Comment positively on what the interviewer is saying.

- *Talking too much or too little.* Either one can turn off an interviewer. Ask people close to you about your speaking habits. Do you tend to dominate the conversation? Or do you barely say a word? If you tend to have either problem, try to correct it.

- *Being overwhelming.* If you're a dynamic, exuberant type who talks rapidly, exudes enthusiasm, and sometimes overwhelms others, try to curb your energies during the interview. Sell yourself less assertively. Listen a little more. Promote your ideas a little less vigorously.

Nonverbal behavior has a great effect on the interviewer's opinion of you.

As you stage your mock interviews, pay particular attention to your nonverbal behavior. You are more likely to be invited back for a second interview or offered a job if you maintain eye contact, smile frequently, nod your head, sit in an attentive position, and use frequent hand gestures. These nonverbal signals convince the interviewer that you are alert, assertive, dependable, confident, responsible, and energetic.[2]

The way you speak is almost as important as what you say.

Like other forms of nonverbal behavior, the sound of your voice can have a major impact on your success in a job interview.[3] If you suspect that you are weak in this area, work with a tape recorder to overcome your faults. If you tend to speak too rapidly, practice speaking more slowly. If your voice sounds too loud or too soft, practice adjusting it. Work on eliminating annoying little speech mannerisms such as *you know*, *like*, and *um*, which might make you sound inarticulate. Speak in your natural tone; trying to sound sophisticated may make you seem artificial or affected. But do try to vary the pitch, rate, and volume of your voice to express enthusiasm and energy. If you speak in a flat, emotionless tone, you convey the impression that you are passive or bored.

Plan to look good

You can impress an interviewer just by the way you look. The best policy is to dress conservatively. Wear the best-quality clothing you can. The traditional business colors are dark blue, brown, gray, and maroon, although lighter colors are acceptable if the clothing style is businesslike. At all costs, avoid flamboyant styles, colors, and prints. Before you go to the interview, try to find out what type of clothing is worn by employees at your target job level. By dressing like them, or perhaps a little more conservatively for this special occasion, you'll seem to fit right in.

To look like a winner
- Dress conservatively
- Be well groomed
- Stand and sit up straight
- Smile

Good grooming makes any style of clothing look better. Make sure your clothes are clean and unwrinkled, your shoes unscuffed and well shined, your hair neatly styled and combed, your fingernails clean, your breath fresh. If possible, check your appearance in a mirror before entering the room for the interview. Don't spoil the effect by chewing gum or smoking cigarettes during the interview.

Good posture, another important aspect of appearance, conveys an air of pride and confidence. So avoid slouching during the interview. And avoid crossing your arms and your legs simultaneously. Finally, remember that one of the best ways to look good is to smile.

Van Carlisle is CEO of FireKing International, maker of fire-proof filing cabinets. As such, he tries to perform each task at the optimum level, and he likes working with people who do their homework and who are honest, energetic, and thorough. Carlisle advises applicants to show their own commitment to performance by being well prepared for interviews.

Be ready when you arrive

For the interview, plan to take (perhaps in a neat, compact briefcase) a small notebook, a pen, a list of the questions you want to ask, two copies of your resume protected in a folder, an outline of what you have learned about the organization, and any past correspondence about the position. You may also want to take a small calendar, a transcript of your college grades, a list of references, and if appropriate, samples of your work. Recruiters are impressed by tangible evidence of your job-related accomplishments, such as reports, performance reviews, and certificates of achievement. In an era when many people exaggerate their qualifications, visible proof of your abilities carries a lot of weight.[4]

Finally, be sure that you know when and where the interview will be held. The worst way to start any interview is late. Check the route you will take, even if it means phoning the interviewer's secretary to ask. Find out how much time it takes to get there; then plan to arrive early. And allow a little extra time just in case you run into a problem on the way.

Once you arrive, relax. You may have to wait a little while, so bring along something to read or occupy your time (the less frivolous or controversial, the better). Or if company literature is available, read it while you wait. In either case, be polite to the interviewer's assistant. If he or she doesn't seem too busy, you might ask a few questions about the organization or express enthusiasm for the job. Just keep in mind that anything you do or say while you wait may well get back to the interviewer. So make sure your best side shows from the moment you enter the premises.

HOW TO BE INTERVIEWED

The way to handle the interview itself depends on where you stand in the interview process. Before extending a job offer, most organizations interview an applicant three times: a preliminary screening, an initial evaluation, and a final evaluation. The aim of a screening interview is to narrow the field of applicants. Without resorting to gimmicks, you need to call attention to one key aspect of your background so that the recruiter can say, "Oh yes, I remember Jones—the one who sold encyclopedias door to door in Detroit." Just be sure the trait you accentuate is relevant to the job in question.

Present a memorable "head-line" during a screening interview.

If you have progressed to the initial evaluation interview, you should broaden your sales pitch. Instead of telegraphing the "headline," give the interviewer the whole story. Touch at least briefly on all your strengths, but explain three or four of your best qualifications in depth. At the same time, probe for information that will enable you to evaluate the position objectively. As important as it is to get an offer, it's also important to learn whether the offer is worth taking.

Cover all your strengths during a selection interview.

If you are asked back for a final evaluation, your chances of being offered a position are quite good. At this point, you will be talking to a person who has the authority to make the offer and negotiate terms. This individual may already have concluded that you have the right background for the job, so she or he will be concerned with sizing up your personality. In fact, both you and the employer need to find out whether there is a good psychological fit. Be honest about your motivations and values. If the interview goes well, your objective should be to clinch the deal on the best possible terms.

Emphasize your personality during a final interview.

Regardless of where you stand in the interview process, every interview will proceed through three stages: the warm-up, the question-and-answer session, and the close.

The warm-up

The first minute of the interview is crucial.

Of the three stages, the warm-up is most important, although it may account for only a small fraction of the time you spend in the interview. Psychologists say that 50 percent of the interviewer's decision is made within the first 30 to 60 seconds, and another 25 percent is made within 15 minutes. If you've gotten off to a bad start, it's extremely difficult to turn the interview around.[5]

Body language is important at this point. Because you won't have time to say much in the first minute or two, you must sell yourself nonverbally. Begin by using the interviewer's name if you're sure you can pronounce it correctly. If the interviewer extends a hand, respond with a firm but gentle handshake. Then wait until you are asked to be seated. Let the interviewer start the discussion, and listen for cues that tell you what he or she wants to hear.

The question-and-answer stage

Whether at Herman Miller or elsewhere, you will find that questions and answers consume the greatest part of the interview. During this phase, the interviewer will ask you to restate your qualifications and expand on the points in your resume. You will also be asked whether you have any questions of your own. As questions are asked, tailor your answers to make a favorable impression. Remember that the interviewer will be observing you and noting every word you say. So avoid limiting yourself to yes or no answers, and pause to think before responding if you are asked a difficult question. Consider the direction of the discussion and guide it where you wish with your responses. Another way you can reach your goal is to ask the right questions. If you periodically ask a question or two from the list you've prepared, you will demonstrate interest. Also, form occasional questions by paraphrasing the interviewer's own words.

Effective listening, with your eyes and ears, can help you turn the question-and-answer stage to your advantage.

Paying attention when the interviewer speaks can be as important as giving good answers or asking good questions. Listening should make up about half of the time you spend in an interview. For tips on becoming a better listener, read Chapter 15. Remember to listen with your eyes as well as your ears. The interviewer's facial expressions, eye movements, gestures, and posture may tell you the real meaning of what is being said. If the interviewer says one thing but sends a different message nonverbally, you may want to discount the verbal message. Be especially alert to how your comments are received. For example, does the interviewer nod in agreement or smile to show approval? If so, you're making progress. If not, you might want to introduce another topic or modify your approach.

The close

Like the opening, the end of the interview is more important than its duration would indicate. In the last few minutes, you need to evaluate how well you have done and correct any misconceptions the interviewer might have.

You can generally tell when the interviewer is trying to conclude the session by watching for verbal and nonverbal cues. The interviewer may ask whether you have any more questions, sum up the discussion, change position,

BEHIND THE SCENES AT IBM

Secrets to Winning an Interview

Jim Greenwood is area manager at IBM's National College Recruiting, South, in Atlanta, Georgia. Greenwood, his staff, and IBM managers nationwide work year-round to attract the best students for the company. He arranges career fairs and speaking engagements, and he responds to inquiries. These and other activities assure Greenwood that when recruiting dates are set, interest in IBM will be high. He then coordinates recruiting activity at 40 campuses. In a recent year, of the more than 8,000 entry-level people IBM hired, 2,800 were college graduates—75 percent of them from targeted campuses.

Whether at the IBM Information Day or any other career fair, be aware that the interview process begins when you step up to a company representative. "On that first day, the managers who want to recruit at a given school are there," Greenwood points out, "so bring a resume. Seek out managers in the skill group that is of interest to you. Talk with them about your background and interests. Our managers know their requirements, and if there's a match, they will

sign you up to be interviewed the next day." That will be your second interview, the 30-minute job interview people mistakenly think of as the first interview.

"We do a total assessment," Greenwood says. At the site interview, managers explore technical background and breadth, interests, likes, and dislikes. "We're looking for people who can communicate. When you get into an environment, say a lab or a marketing department, you have to relate to people, sell your ideas, explain how things are to be done."

Greenwood listens for your level of interest. "If you did an internship at Hewlett-Packard, I might say, 'Tell me about your job.' Then I'll ask, 'What did you do? What did you like about it? What didn't you like? What kind of programming did you do? What languages? How proficient are you in those languages? Which do you like the best? Why? Do you like to program? Do you like to write code?'"

Greenwood also listens to the types of questions you ask. "They tell me how well informed you are, what you have done to prepare yourself for the inter-

---

Conclude the interview with courtesy and enthusiasm.

or indicate with a gesture that the interview is over. When you get the signal, respond promptly. Trying to prolong the interview will frustrate the recruiter and work to your disadvantage. But by the same token, don't rush. Be sure to thank the interviewer for the opportunity and express an interest in the organization. If you can do so comfortably, try to pin down what will happen next, but don't press for an immediate decision.

If this is your second or third visit to the organization, the interview may culminate with an offer of employment. You have two options: Accept it, or request time to think it over. The best course is usually to wait. If no job offer is made, the interviewer may not have reached a decision yet. But you may tactfully ask when you can expect to know the decision.

If you do receive an offer during the interview, you will naturally want to discuss salary, but let the interviewer raise the subject. If asked your salary requirements, say that you would expect to receive the standard salary for the job in question. If you have added qualifications, point them out: "With my 18 months of experience in the field, I would expect to start in the middle of the

Don't be afraid to negotiate for a better salary and benefits package, but be realistic in your expectations and diplomatic in your approach.

normal salary range." If you don't like the size of the offer, you might try to negotiate, provided that you are in a good bargaining position and the organization is flexible. You will be in a fairly strong position if your skills are in short supply and you have several other offers. It also helps if you are the favorite candidate and the organization is booming. But many organizations are relatively rigid in their compensation practices, particularly at the entry level. You might just ask, "Is there any room for negotiation?"

view, whether you researched us, whether you know about our products and our corporate culture. But don't try to bluff or tell us what you think we want to hear. Ask questions that matter and that make the right impression. Don't ask the interviewer, 'What do you do?' That shows a lack of preparation and interest. Instead ask about the future: 'What technology are you developing? Where's it going?' You should also raise legitimate concerns—the size of a company like IBM, for example. Ask, 'How are you structured? How do I get my ideas across? How do I interact with other departments?'"

Greenwood's goal is for you to leave the interview feeling positive about IBM and knowing when you will learn the outcome. He wants you to feel "that you were given a good, courteous interview." So, what about follow-up? "Don't write for the sake of writing," says Greenwood. "But if you want to stress special interests or reinforce skills, or if you feel you blew the interview and want to be reconsidered, write to the department manager."

Regarding that much-discussed situation of needing experience to get a job but needing a job to get experience, Greenwood offers this advice: "Getting experience is important, whether it's work-study, a cooperative education program, or work you did over the summers, maybe a pre-professional internship.

Experience helps you focus your academic choices, prepares you for your job search, and lets you sift and sort out what you do and don't want. That shows in the interview—you have a sharper focus on your wants and needs." Not the usual answer? Perhaps. But to come across well in an interview, you have to stress what experience you have and relate it to what you can do once you're employed.

APPLY YOUR KNOWLEDGE

1. Should you be expected to immediately accept or decline a position when it is offered during the interview? If you answered yes, what advantages and disadvantages do you see in doing so? What image is the quick response going to communicate? If you say no, what is a reasonable length of time to take to reach a decision? Why?

2. How would you handle this situation: A company—your first choice both as a career and as a place to work—has offered you a position. However, the starting salary you've been offered is below your expectation and below what you've already been offered by another firm (your third choice as a career and as a workplace). What should you do? Lay out a strategy that you think will get you both the position you most desire and the salary you expect.

Even if you can't bargain for more money, you might be able to win some concessions on benefits and perquisites. The value of negotiating can be significant because benefits often cost the employer 25 to 45 percent of your salary. In other words, if you're offered an annual salary of $20,000, you'll ordinarily get an additional $5,000 to $9,000 in benefits: life, health, and disability insurance; pension and savings plans; vacation time; tuition reimbursement; club memberships; or use of a car.[6] If you can trade one benefit for another, you may be able to enhance the value of the total package. For example, life insurance may be relatively unimportant to you if you are single, whereas extra vacation time might be very valuable indeed. Don't inquire about fringe benefits, however, until you know you have a job offer.

Interview notes

Careful record keeping will help you keep organized and will help you become more adept at interviewing.

If yours is a typical job search, you will have many interviews before you accept a final offer. To refresh your memory of each conversation, you should keep a record of your impressions. As soon as the interview ends, jot down the names and titles of the people you met. If you're unsure of any names or their spellings, phone the organization's receptionist for clarification.

Next, write down in capsule form the interviewer's answers to your questions. Then briefly evaluate your performance during the interview, listing what you handled well and what you didn't. Going over these notes can help you improve your performance in the future.

CHECKLIST FOR INTERVIEWS

A. Preparation

☐ **1.** Determine the requirements and general salary range of the job.

☐ **2.** Research the organization's products, structure, financial standing, and prospects for growth.

☐ **3.** Determine the interviewer's name, title, and status in the firm.

☐ **4.** Prepare answers for the questions you are likely to be asked about your qualifications and achievements, your feelings about work and school, and your interests and hobbies.

☐ **5.** Develop relevant questions to ask, such as what training the organization might offer after employment, what type of management system the firm has, whether its executives are promoted from within, and why the position is vacant.

☐ **6.** Plan your appearance.

   ☐ a. Determine the mode of dress that prevails within the organization so that you can copy it.

   ☐ b. Select conservative, good-quality clothing to wear to the interview.

   ☐ c. Check your clothing to make sure it's clean and wrinkle-free.

   ☐ d. Choose traditional footwear, unscuffed and well shined.

   ☐ e. Wear a minimum of jewelry, but wear a wristwatch to keep track of the time.

   ☐ f. Use fragrances sparingly, and avoid excessive makeup.

   ☐ g. Choose a neat, well-groomed, conventional hairstyle.

   ☐ h. Clean and manicure your fingernails.

   ☐ i. Check your appearance just before going into the interview, if possible.

☐ **7.** Take a list of questions, two copies of your resume, and samples of your work (if appropriate) to the interview in a briefcase.

☐ **8.** Double-check the location and time of the interview.

   ☐ a. Map out the route beforehand, and estimate the time you'll need to get there.

   ☐ b. Plan your arrival for 10 to 15 minutes before the interview.

   ☐ c. Add 10 or 15 more minutes to cover problems that may arise en route.

B. Initial Stages of the Interview

☐ **1.** Greet the interviewer by name, with a smile and direct eye contact.

☐ **2.** Offer a firm but gentle handshake if the interviewer extends a hand.

☐ **3.** Take a seat only after the interviewer invites you to be seated or has taken his or her own seat.

☐ **4.** Sit with an erect posture, facing the interviewer.

☐ **5.** Listen for cues that tell you what the interviewer wants to hear.

☐ **6.** Assume a calm and poised attitude.

☐ **7.** Avoid gum chewing, smoking, and other displays of nervousness.

C. Body of the Interview

☐ **1.** Display a genuine, not artificial, smile at appropriate times.

☐ **2.** Convey interest and enthusiasm.

☐ **3.** Listen attentively so that you can give intelligent responses.

☐ **4.** Take no notes, but remember key points and record them later.

☐ **5.** Sell the interviewer on hiring you.

   ☐ a. Relate your knowledge and skills to the position you are seeking.

   ☐ b. Stress your positive qualities and characteristics.

☐ **6.** Answer questions wisely.

   ☐ a. Keep responses brief, clear, and to the point.

   ☐ b. Avoid exaggeration, and convey honesty and sincerity.

   ☐ c. Avoid slighting references to former employers.

☐ **7.** Avoid cocktails if you are interviewed over lunch.

D. Salary Discussions

☐ **1.** Put off a discussion of salary until late in the interview, if possible.

☐ **2.** Let the interviewer initiate the discussion of salary.

☐ **3.** If asked, state that you would like to receive the standard salary for the position in question.

E. Closing Stages of the Interview

☐ **1.** Watch for signs that the interview is about to end.

☐ **2.** Tactfully ask when you will be advised of the decision on your application.

☐ **3.** If you're offered the job, either accept or ask for time to consider the offer.

☐ **4.** With a warm smile and a handshake, thank the interviewer for meeting with you.

FOLLOWING UP AFTER THE INTERVIEW

Touching base with the prospective employer after the interview, either by phone or in writing, shows that you really want the job and are determined to get it. It also brings your name to the interviewer's attention once again and reminds him or her that you are waiting to know the decision. Because few applicants send follow-up letters or call to say thank you, the prospective employer will probably be impressed if you do.

The two most common forms of follow-up are the thank-you and the inquiry. These are generally handled by letter, but a phone call is often just as effective, particularly if the employer seems to favor a casual, personal style. The other four types of follow-up messages—request for a time extension, letter of acceptance, letter declining a job offer, and letter of resignation—are sent only in certain cases. These types of messages are better handled in writing because it is important to document any official actions relating to your employment. However, regardless of whether you are communicating orally or in writing, you always should follow the principles outlined in this chapter.

Six types of follow-up messages:
- Thank-you
- Inquiry
- Request for a time extension
- Letter of acceptance
- Letter declining a job offer
- Letter of resignation

THANK-YOU

Express your thanks within two days after the interview, even if you feel you have little chance for the job. Acknowledge the interviewer's time and courtesy. Convey the idea that you continue to be interested. Then ask politely for a decision.

Keep your thank-you message brief (less than five minutes or a page in length), and organize it like a routine message. Like all good business messages, it should demonstrate the "you" attitude. Although you don't want to sound doubtful about your chances of getting the job, you must also avoid sounding arrogant or too sure of yourself. The following sample thank-you letter shows how to achieve all this in three brief paragraphs:

As senior vice president of personnel at Levi Strauss and Company, Donna J. Goya believes that developing people is vital to successful business management. You want to be in a company that cares about people, says Goya. And you can show that you care about people by expressing your thanks to the interviewer either by phone or in a letter.

After talking with you yesterday, touring your sets, and watching the television commercials being filmed, I remain very enthusiastic about the possibility of joining your staff as a television/film production assistant. Thanks for taking so much time to show me around.

The opening reminds the interviewer of the reasons for meeting and graciously acknowledges the consideration shown to the applicant.

During our meeting, I said that I would prefer not to relocate. But I've reconsidered the matter. If my apartment can be sublet, I would be pleased to relocate wherever you need my skills in set decoration and prop design.

This paragraph indicates the writer's flexibility and commitment to the job if hired. It also reminds the recruiter of special qualifications.

Now that you've explained the details of your operation, I feel quite strongly that I can make a contribution to the sorts of productions you've begun to line up. You can also count on me to be an energetic worker and a positive addition to your crew. Please let me know your decision as soon as possible.

The letter closes on a confident and you-oriented note, ending with the request for a decision.

Even if the interviewer has said that you are unqualified for the job, a thank-you message like that shown in Figure 14.5 may keep the door open. A letter of this type will probably go into the file for future openings because it demonstrates courtesy and interest.

INQUIRY

An inquiry about a hiring decision should follow the plan for a direct request.

If you are not advised of the interviewer's decision by the promised date or within two weeks, you might make an inquiry. An inquiry is particularly appropriate if you have received a job offer from a second firm and don't want to accept it before you have an answer from the first.

The following inquiry letter follows the general plan for a direct request; the writer assumes that a simple oversight, not outright rejection, is the reason for the delay:

FIGURE 14.5
Sample Thank-You Note

The main idea is the expression of thanks for the interviewer's time and information.

The writer specifically refers to points discussed in the interview. Enthusiasm and eagerness to improve skills are qualities that will impress the interviewer.

The letter closes with a specific and cordial request.

585 Montoya Road
Las Cruces, NM 88005
January 16, 1993

Ms. Gloria Reynolds, Editor
Las Cruces News
317 N. Almendra Street
Las Cruces, NM 88001

Dear Ms. Reynolds:

Our conversation on Tuesday about your newspaper's opening for a food-feature writer was enlightening. Thank you for taking time to talk with me about it.

Your description of the profession makes me feel more certain than ever that I want to be a newspaper writer. Following your advice, I am going to enroll in an evening journalism course soon.

After I achieve the level of writing skills you suggested, I would deeply appreciate the chance to talk with you again.

Sincerely,

Michael Espinosa

Michael Espinosa

When we talked on April 7 about the fashion coordinator position in your Park Avenue showroom, you said you would let me know your decision before May 1. I would still like the position very much, so I'm eager to know what conclusion you've reached.

The opening paragraph identifies the position and introduces the main idea.

To complicate matters, another firm has now offered me a position and has asked that I reply within the next two weeks.

The reason for the request comes second. The writer tactfully avoids naming the other firm.

Because your company seems to offer a greater challenge, I would appreciate knowing about your decision before Thursday, May 12. If you need more information before then, please let me know.

The courteous request for a specific action comes last, in the context of a clearly stated preference for this organization.

REQUEST FOR A TIME EXTENSION

A request for a time extension should follow the plan for a direct request, but pay extra attention to easing the reader's disappointment.

If you receive a job offer while other interviews are still pending and you want more time to decide, write to the organization offering the job and ask for a time extension. Such a request can be risky, so be sure to preface it with a friendly opening like the one shown in the following sample letter. Then ask for more time, stressing your enthusiasm for the organization. Conclude by allowing for a quick decision if your request for additional time is denied. And ask for a prompt reply confirming the time extension if the organization grants it.

The customer relations position in your snack foods division seems like an exciting challenge and a great opportunity. I'm very pleased that you offered it to me.

The letter begins with a strong statement of interest in the job.

Because of another commitment, I would appreciate your giving me until August 29 to make a decision. Before our interview, I scheduled a follow-up interview with another company. Frankly, I'm more interested in your organization because of its impressive quality-control procedures and friendly, attractive work environment. I do feel obligated to keep my appointment, however.

The writer stresses professional obligations, not her desire to learn what the other company may offer. Specific reasons for preferring the first job offer help reassure the reader of her sincerity.

If you need my decision immediately, I'll gladly let you know. But if you can allow me the added time to fulfill the earlier commitment, I'd be grateful. Please let me know right away.

The expression of willingness to yield or compromise conveys continued interest in the position.

This type of letter is, in essence, a direct request. But because the recipient may be disappointed, you must temper your request for an extension with statements indicating your continued interest.

LETTER OF ACCEPTANCE

A letter of acceptance should follow the good-news plan.

When you receive a job offer that you want to accept, reply within five days. Begin by accepting the position and expressing thanks. Identify the job that you're accepting. In the next paragraph, cover any necessary details. Conclude by saying that you look forward to reporting for work.

I'm delighted to accept the graphic design position in your advertising department at the salary of $1,575 a month.	The good-news statement at the beginning confirms the specific terms of the offer.
Enclosed are the health insurance forms you asked me to complete and sign. I've already given notice to my current employer and will be able to start work on Monday, January 18.	Miscellaneous details are covered in the middle.
The prospect of joining your firm is very exciting. Thank you for giving me this opportunity for what I'm sure will be a challenging future.	The letter closes with another reference to the good news and a look toward the future.

As always, a good-news letter should convey your enthusiasm and eagerness to cooperate.

Acceptance of a job offer is legally binding.

You should be aware that a job offer and a written acceptance of that job constitute a legally binding contract, for both you and the employer. So before you write an acceptance letter, be sure you want the job.

LETTER DECLINING A JOB OFFER

A letter declining a job offer should follow the bad-news plan.

After all your interviews, you may find that you need to write a letter declining a job offer. The best approach is to open warmly, state the reasons for refusing the offer, decline the offer explicitly, and close on a pleasant note, expressing gratitude. By taking the time to write a sincere, tactful letter like the one shown here, you leave the door open for future contact:

One of the most interesting interviews I have ever had was the one last month at your Durham textile plant. I'm flattered that you would offer me the computer analyst position that we talked about.	The opening paragraph is a buffer.
During my job search, I applied to five highly rated firms like your own, each one a leader in its field. Both your company and another offered me a position. Because my desire to work abroad can more readily be satisfied by the other company, I have accepted that job offer.	Tactfully phrased reasons for the applicant's unfavorable decision precede the bad news and leave the door open.
I deeply appreciate the hour you spent talking with me. Thank you again for your consideration and kindness.	A sincere and cordial ending lets the reader down gently.

The bad-news plan is ideally suited to this type of letter.

LETTER OF RESIGNATION

A letter of resignation should also follow the bad-news plan.

If you get a job offer and are employed, you should write a letter of resignation to maintain good relations with your current employer. Make the letter sound positive, regardless of how you feel. Say something favorable about the organization, the people you work with, or what you have learned on the job. Then state your intention to leave and the termination date.

My sincere thanks to you and to all the other Emblem Corporation employees for helping me learn so much about serving the public these past 11 months. You have given me untold help and encouragement.

An appreciative opening serves as a buffer.

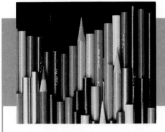

CHECKLIST FOR FOLLOW-UP MESSAGES

A. Thank-you Message
☐ 1. Thank the interviewer by phone or in writing within two days after the interview.
☐ 2. Keep the message to less than five minutes or one page.
☐ 3. In the opening, express thanks, identify the job, and refer to the time and place of the interview.
☐ 4. Use the middle section for supporting details.
   ☐ a. Express your enthusiasm about the organization and the job after the interview.
   ☐ b. Add any new facts that may help your chances.
   ☐ c. Try to undo any negative impressions you may have left during the interview.
☐ 5. Use an action ending.
   ☐ a. Offer to submit more data.
   ☐ b. Express confidence that your qualifications will meet the organization's requirements.
   ☐ c. Look forward to a favorable decision.
   ☐ d. Request an opportunity to prove that you can aid the organization's growth or success.

B. Inquiries
☐ 1. Phone or write an inquiry if you are not informed of the decision by the promised date, especially if another organization is awaiting your reply to a job offer.
☐ 2. Follow the plan for direct requests: main idea, necessary details, specific request.

C. Requests for a Time Extension
☐ 1. Send this type of letter if you receive a job offer while other interviews are pending and you want more time before making your decision.

☐ 2. Open with an expression of warmth.
☐ 3. In the middle section, explain why you need more time and express your continuing interest in the organization.
☐ 4. Conclude by allowing for a quick decision if your request for more time is denied and by asking the interviewer to confirm the time extension if it is granted.

D. Letters Accepting a Job Offer
☐ 1. Begin by stating clearly that you accept the offer with pleasure and by identifying the job you are accepting.
☐ 2. Fill out the letter with vital details.
☐ 3. Conclude with a statement that you look forward to reporting for work.

E. Letters Rejecting a Job Offer
☐ 1. Open a letter of rejection warmly.
☐ 2. Fill out the letter with an explanation of why you are refusing the offer and an expression of appreciation.
☐ 3. End on a sincere, positive note.

F. Letters of Resignation
☐ 1. Send a letter of resignation to your current employer as soon as possible.
☐ 2. Begin with an appreciative buffer.
☐ 3. Fill out the middle section with your reasons for looking for another job and the actual statement that you are leaving.
☐ 4. Close cordially.

You may recall that when you first interviewed me, my goal was to become a customer relations supervisor. Because that opportunity has been offered to me by another organization, I am submitting my resignation. I regret leaving all of you, but I can't pass up this opportunity.

Reasons stated before the bad news itself and tactful phrasing help keep the relationship friendly, should the writer later want letters of recommendation.

I would like to terminate my work here two weeks from today but can arrange to work an additional week if you want me to train a replacement.

An extra paragraph discusses necessary details.

My sincere thanks and best wishes to all of you.

A cordial close tempers any disappointment.

This letter follows the bad-news plan. By sending one like it, you show that you are considerate and mature, and you also help ensure the good feeling that may help you get another job in the future.

SUMMARY

An organization that invites you to an interview wants to find out whether you are the best person to fill a job opening. Your goal is to find out about the job and the organization so that you can make a decision should the job be offered.

You can relieve the anxious and nervous feelings that often accompany interviews by preparing ahead of time. First, analyze the organization, the job, and your own qualifications and needs. Then plan answers to the interviewer's likely questions and devise some questions of your own. The interview itself will go more smoothly if you adopt a relaxed style and an enthusiastic attitude.

Follow-up messages to the interviewer, such as thank-you messages and inquiries, may increase your chances of getting a job offer. Other courteous, well-planned employment letters—whether requesting a time extension, accepting an offer, declining an offer, or resigning—also demonstrate that you are a professional.

ON THE JOB:
Solving a Communication Dilemma at Herman Miller, Inc.

Herman Miller's corporate culture reflects the philosophy of Max DePree, current chairman of the board and son of the firm's founder. DePree bases his management style on his assumptions about human nature. In his view, the idea of motivating people is nonsense. "Employees bring their own motivation," he says. "What people need from work is to be liberated, to be involved, to be accountable, and to reach their potential." DePree believes that good management consists of establishing an environment in which people can unleash their creativity. "My goal for Herman Miller is that when people both inside and outside the company look at all of us, they'll say, 'Those folks have a gift of the spirit.' " He wants the organization, like its products, to be a work of art. And to carry out his philosophy, DePree has created an employee bill of rights, which includes: "The right to be needed, the right to understand, the right to be involved, the right to affect one's own destiny, the right to be accountable, and the right to appeal."

The company's organizational structure reinforces DePree's philosophy. All employees are assigned to work teams. The team leader evaluates the workers every six months, and the workers evaluate the leader as well. Teams elect representatives to caucuses that meet periodically to discuss operations and problems. Through the team structure, employees have a say in decisions that affect them. They also have a vehicle for dealing with grievances. If a problem isn't resolved by the team supervisor, employees can go directly to the next executive level. In fact, Max DePree himself is available to discuss problems with anyone in the organization.

But like all good things, Herman Miller's corporate culture has its downside. Teamwork takes time, and an egalitarian approach to decision making can be frustrating if you're a "take charge" type who likes to get things done as efficiently as possible. It takes a special kind of talent to draw the line between participative management and excessive permissiveness. Finding people who appreciate the distinction is a real challenge.

To identify people who have the right mix of attitudes, Herman Miller uses what it calls "value-based" interviewing. During an initial job interview, the staffing department probes the candidate's work style, likes, and dislikes by posing "what if " questions. By evaluating how the candidate would handle a variety of scenarios, the recruiter gets a good idea of how well the individual would fit into the company. If the fit seems good, the candidate is invited back for follow-up interviews with members of the department where he or she would be working. During these follow-up interviews, the candidate's functional expertise is evaluated along with his or her psychological makeup. By the end of the interview process, Herman Miller has a good idea of whether the candidate "knows how to dance."

Your Mission: As a member of Herman Miller's staffing department, you are responsible for screening job candidates and arranging for interviews between candidates and Herman Miller's professional staff. Your responsibilities include the development of interview questions and evaluation forms for use by company employees involved in the interview process. You also handle all routine correspondence with job candidates. In each of the following situations, choose the *best* alternative:

1. Herman Miller has decided to establish a management training program for recent college graduates. The training program is designed to groom people for careers in finance, strategic planning, marketing, administration, and general management. To recruit people for the program, the firm will conduct on-

campus interviews at several colleges—something it has not generally done. You and the other Herman Miller interviewers will be talking with 30 or 40 applicants on campus. You will have 20 minutes for each interview. Your goal is to identify the candidates who will be invited to come to the office for evaluation interviews. You want the preliminary screening process to be as fair and objective as possible, so how should you approach the task?
   a. Meet with all the Herman Miller interviewers to discuss the characteristics that candidates should exhibit. Allow each interviewer to use his or her own approach to identify these characteristics in applicants. Encourage the interviewers to ask whatever questions seem most useful in light of the individual characteristics of each candidate.
   b. Develop a list of 10 to 15 questions that will be posed to all candidates. Instruct the Herman Miller interviewers to stick strictly to the list so that all applicants will respond to the same questions and be evaluated on the same basis.
   c. Develop a written evaluation form for measuring all candidates against criteria such as academic performance, relevant experience, capacity for teamwork, and communication skills. For each criterion, suggest four or five questions that interviewers might use to evaluate the candidate. Instruct the interviewers to cover all the criteria and to fill out the written evaluation form for each applicant immediately after the interview.

2. During the on-campus screening interviews, you ask several candidates, "Why do you want to work for this organization?" Of the following responses, which would you rank the highest?
   a. "I'd like to work here because I'm interested in the office furniture business. I've always been fascinated by industrial design and the interaction between people and their environment. In addition to studying business, I have taken courses in industrial design and industrial psychology. I also have some personal experience in building furniture. My grandfather is a cabinet maker and an antique restorer, and I have been his apprentice since I was 12 years old. I paid my way through college with the money I've earned working as a carpenter during summer vacations."
   b. "I'm an independent person with a lot of internal drive. I do my best work when I'm given a fairly free reign to use my creativity. From what I've read about your corporate culture, I think my working style would fit very well with your management philosophy. I'm also the sort of person who identifies very strongly with my job. For better or worse, I define myself through my affiliation with my employer. I get a great sense of pride from being part of a first-rate operation, and

I think Herman Miller is first-rate. I've read about the design awards you've won and about your selection as one of America's most admired companies. The articles I've seen all say that Herman Miller is an extremely well-managed company. I think I would learn a lot working here, and I think my drive and creativity would be appreciated."

c. "There are several reasons why I'd like to work for Herman Miller. For one thing, I have family and friends in Zeeland, and I'd like to stay in the area. Also, I have a couple of friends who work for Herman Miller, and they both say it's terrific. I've also heard good things about your compensation and benefits."

d. "My ultimate goal is to start a company of my own, but I realize that first I need to learn more about managing a business. I read in *Fortune* that Herman Miller is one of America's most admired corporations. I think I could learn a lot by being in your management training program and observing your operations."

3. After conducting the screening interviews at the University of Michigan, you and the other Herman Miller recruiters are meeting to select the candidates that you will invite to the office for follow-up interviews. You have already selected five outstanding individuals who appear to meet all your criteria, but you are having trouble deciding what to do with the three candidates described below. What should you do?

a. Anne McKinsey has a 3.5 grade-point average; she majored in business administration and has a minor in industrial design. For the past two summers, she has worked for an interior decorator in Detroit who specializes in office buildings. Her biggest drawback is her appearance. She is 35 pounds overweight, has a poor complexion, and came to the interview in blue jeans and a dirty sweatshirt. The person who interviewed her describes her as being shy and immature, but sweet. Therefore you should invite this candidate back for a follow-up interview.

b. Gary Peterson has a 2.0 grade-point average, and it has taken him five years to graduate. He majored in business but avoided some of the harder quantitative courses. Although Gary is not an outstanding scholar, he has many extracurricular activities to his credit. He played defensive tackle on the football team, was president of his fraternity, performed in a musical comedy, and volunteered as a peer counselor to help freshmen adjust to the pressures of university life. To help finance his education, he also worked 15 hours a week as an aide at the university hospital. During the summers, he works on the family farm in upper Michigan. The interviewer describes him as being "one of the nicest guys I've ever met." You should invite this candidate back for a follow-up interview.

c. Gardner Mandrell has a 3.0 grade-point average with a major in business and a minor in psychology. He was the business manager of the student newspaper for two years and was on the debate squad for four years. He has sold used cars during summer vacations. The interviewer describes him as being "savvy, practical, and highly motivated, but extremely cynical." You should invite this candidate back for a follow-up interview.

d. It's a tough decision, but you should invite all three candidates to visit the company. The extra time spent may be well worth it.

e. Keep all three on hold. You can always invite any or all of them in for a follow-up interview later if you do not fill the trainee slots from the pool of more promising candidates.

4. You are trying to think of questions for the professional staff to use in conducting follow-up interviews at Herman Miller's headquarters. You want a question that will reveal something about the candidates' probable loyalty to the organization. Which of the following questions is the best choice?

a. If you knew you could be one of the world's most successful people in a single occupation, such as music, politics, medicine, or business, what occupation would you choose? If you knew you had only a 10 percent chance of being so successful, would you still choose the same occupation?[7]

b. We value loyalty among our employees. Tell me something about yourself that demonstrates your loyalty as a member of an organization.

c. What would you do if you discovered that a co-worker routinely made personal, unauthorized long-distance phone calls from work?[8]

d. What other companies are you interviewing with?

5. In concluding an evaluation interview, you ask the candidate, "Do you have any questions?" Which of the following answers would you respond most favorably to?

a. "No. I can't think of anything. You've been very thorough in describing the job and the company. Thank you for taking the time to talk with me."

b. "Yes. I have an interview with one of your competitors, Steelcase, next week. How would you sum up the differences between your two firms?"

c. "Yes. If I were offered a position here, what would my chances be of getting promoted within the next 12 months?"

d. "Yes. Do you think Herman Miller will be a better or worse company 15 years from now?"

6. You have interviewed four candidates who all seem equally qualified for the management trainee slot. Each of the four candidates follows up in a different way. Which approach creates the most favorable impression?

a. The first candidate telephones and says: "I wanted to thank you for showing me the facility yesterday and for giving me the chance to present my qualifications. Everything I saw and heard confirms my favorable impression of your organization. I just wanted you to know that I'm extremely interested in working for Herman Miller. I think it's a terrific outfit, and I'd love to be part of your team."

b. The second candidate does not communicate in any way.

c. The third candidate writes the following letter:
I'd like to thank you and the other Herman Miller employees for talking with me yesterday. Seeing the facility made me realize how exciting your organization really is. The atmosphere struck me as being extremely open and creative.

During our conversation, you asked me whether I had any previous experience in the furniture business, and I said no. But I neglected to mention that I do have some experience in space planning and office design. Last summer, my father decided to move his six-person law practice to new quarters. He asked me to locate space, negotiate a lease, and oversee any office improvements that needed to be made. I approached the task by talking with the members of the firm about their space and equipment needs, both now and over the next five years. I then visited 15 potential offices and evaluated the pros and cons of each. After selecting the most suitable site, I oversaw

such tasks as painting, recarpeting, furniture selection, kitchen improvements, and electrical work. This experience opened my eyes to many of the details of space planning that Herman Miller's clients must encounter.

Thank you again for showing me around. I would sincerely welcome the opportunity to join your organization and believe I could make a valuable contribution.

d. The fourth candidate writes:
After seeing Herman Miller in person, I am more convinced than ever that I belong there. My goal is to join your organization and do what I can to make the company even better than it is today.

I think the thing that impresses me most is your team spirit. For a long time, I have felt that companies are the communities of the future. Like the small towns of the past, corporations mold the characters of their members. Without a sense of community, work is merely a means to an end, a way to earn a living. But when an organization is infused with community spirit, work is elevated and attains a spiritually rewarding dimension. The job defines the person, in the best sense. We are what we do.

I want to emphasize my desire to join your organization. Believe me, if you offer me a position, I will take the ball and run with it. I am committed to excellence. Thank you again for sharing your time with me.[9]

QUESTIONS FOR DISCUSSION

1. How should a job applicant answer this question: "What are your greatest weaknesses?"
2. How might an applicant explain a desire to switch jobs because of an inability to work with the current supervisor?
3. What types of questions should an applicant avoid asking?
4. How can an applicant strike a balance between appearing to shrink before the interviewer's authority and appearing to be overconfident?
5. If you felt that you had gotten off to a bad beginning, what would you do to try to save the interview?
6. What are the advantages of thanking an interviewer over the phone instead of writing? What are the disadvantages?

DOCUMENTS FOR ANALYSIS

Read the following documents; then (1) analyze the strengths or weaknesses of each sentence and (2) revise each document so that it follows this chapter's guidelines.

DOCUMENT 14.A
Thank you for the really marvelous opportunity to meet you and your colleagues at Starret Engine Company. I really enjoyed touring your facilities and

talking with all the people there. You have quite a crew! Some of the other companies I have visited have been so rigid and uptight that I can't imagine how I would fit in. It's a relief to run into a group of people who seem to enjoy their work as much as all of you do.

I know that you must be looking at many other candidates for this job, and I know that some of them will probably be more experienced than I am. But I do want to emphasize that my two-year hitch in the Navy involved a good deal of engineering work. I don't think I mentioned all my shipboard responsibilities during the interview.

Please give me a call within the next week to let me know your decision. You can usually find me at my dormitory in the evening after dinner (phone: 877-9080).

DOCUMENT 14.B

I have recently received a very attractive job offer from the Warrington Company. But before I let them know one way or another, I would like to consider any offer that your firm may extend. I was quite impressed with your company during my recent interview, and I am still very interested in a career there.

I don't mean to pressure you, but Warrington has asked for my decision within ten days. Could you let me know by Tuesday whether you plan to offer me a position? That would give me enough time to compare the two offers.

DOCUMENT 14.C

I'm writing to say that I must decline your job offer. Another company has made me a more generous offer, and I have decided to accept. However, if things don't work out for me there, I will let you know. I sincerely appreciate your interest in me.

CASES

INTERVIEWING WITH POTENTIAL EMPLOYERS

1. Interviewers and interviewees: Classroom exercise in interviewing Obviously, interviewing is an interactive process involving at least two people. The best way to practice for interviews is to work with others.

Your task: You and all other members of the class should write letters of application for a management trainee position requiring a pleasant personality and intelligence but a minimum of specialized education or experience. Sign your letters with a fictitious name that conceals your identity. Next, polish (or prepare) a resume that accurately identifies you and your educational and professional accomplishments.

Three members of the class, who volunteer as interviewers, should divide equally among themselves all the anonymously written application letters. Then each interviewer should select for an interview the candidate who seems the most pleasant and convincing in his or her letter. At this time, the selected candidates should identify themselves and give the interviewers their resumes.

Each interviewer should then interview his or her chosen candidate in front of the class, seeking to understand how the items on the resume qualify the candidate for the job. At the end of the interviews, the class may decide who gets the job and discuss why this candidate was successful. Then retrieve your letter, sign it with the right name, and submit it to the instructor for credit.

2. On the spot: Answering a tough interview question You are applying for a position at Herman Miller (see this chapter's On-the-Job simulation). The recruiter asks you, "What important decision in your academic or working life have you based largely on intuition? If you had it to do over again, would you approach the decision more analytically?"

Your task: Draft your response.[10]

FOLLOWING UP AFTER THE INTERVIEW

3. "Dear Mr. Chacon": Follow-up letter to straighten out a possible confusion You have been interviewed for the position of assistant manager of a retail outlet in the In-a-Minute chain, consisting of company-owned stores that sell groceries, some medications, and petroleum products. The chain is successful, with new outlets opening regularly in Missouri, Kentucky, and Tennessee, and you would much appreciate the chance to join the firm.

During the interview, Roger Chacon asked you several questions about your academic record. Your answers, you feel, were somewhat scattered and left Mr. Chacon with no clear understanding of the courses you've taken, your proficiency in several key areas, and the date you expect to graduate—matters that he seemed most interested in.

Your task: Working with your own record, draft a follow-up letter to send to Mr. Chacon with a copy of your college transcript. Describe what you have accomplished in one or two academic areas. Mr. Chacon is with the personnel department at the corporation's headquarters, 99 Litzinger Lane, St. Louis, MO 63124.

4. Job hunt: Set of employment-related letters to a single company Where would you like to work? Pick a real or an imagined company and assume that a month ago you sent your resume and application letter. Not long afterward, you were invited to come for an interview, which seemed to go very well.

Your task: Use your imagination to write the following: (a) a thank-you letter for the interview, (b) a note of inquiry, (c) a request for more time to decide, (d) a letter of acceptance, and (e) a letter declining the job offer.

ORAL COMMUNICATION

■CHAPTER FIFTEEN

After studying this chapter, you will be able to

- Explain the importance of planning and editing your spoken comments
- Discuss the role of listening in oral communication
- Identify the listening skills that suit various situations
- Identify the ingredients of a successful interview
- Explain group dynamics
- Identify the ingredients of effective meetings

LISTENING, INTERVIEWING, AND CONDUCTING MEETINGS

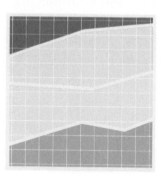

ON THE JOB:
Facing a Communication Dilemma at Du Pont
Paying for Profit

If you wanted people to work harder and feel better about their jobs, would you give them a nice, safe, predictable boost in salary every year, or would you tie their pay to increases in profits? Du Pont's fibers division decided on the latter course when it adopted a new incentive-pay plan. Robert P. McNutt, the plan's architect, believes it will raise efficiency and make workers feel more involved in the organization. Some employees are not so sure.

The plan is aimed at the 20,000 members of Du Pont's fibers division, and it ties employee compensation to profits. If the division exceeds its profit goals, the employees make more money than their counterparts in other divisions. On the other hand, if the fibers division falls short of its profit targets, the employees lose financial ground relative to other Du Pont workers.

Although the majority of the fibers division's employees appear to favor the plan, some are openly skeptical. They argue that the plan pits people against one another and that it will eventually breed widespread cynicism. Their opposition could jeopardize the very team spirit that the plan is supposed to encourage.

If you were Robert McNutt, how would you deal with criticisms of the plan? What factors of oral communication come into play? Would good listening skills help settle things? How might interviews or meetings support the desired team spirit?[1]

COMMUNICATING ORALLY

Du Pont

Du Pont's Robert McNutt knows that speaking and listening are the communication skills we use most. Oral communication has its benefits: Not only does it provide the opportunity for feedback, but when people communicate orally, they are able to interact. They can ask questions and test their understanding of the message; they can share ideas and work together to solve problems. In addition, people can convey and absorb nonverbal information that reveals far more than words alone. By communicating with facial expressions, eye contact, tone of voice, gestures, and postures, people can send subtle messages that add another dimension to their spoken words. Oral communication also makes people feel good. It satisfies one of our deepest needs, the need to be part of the human community. Talking things over helps people in organizations build morale and establish a group identity.

But oral communication also has its dangers. Under most circumstances, it occurs spontaneously: You can't cross out what you just said and start all over, so your dumbest comments may remain etched in the other person's memory, regardless of how much you try to explain that you really meant something else entirely. In addition, if you let your attention wander while someone else is speaking, you miss the point and must either muddle along without knowing what was said or admit you were daydreaming and ask the person to repeat the comment. Finally, oral communication is personal. People tend to confuse your message with you as an individual, and they are likely to judge the content of what you say by your appearance and delivery style. When it comes to oral communication, your goal should be to take advantage of its positive characteristics while minimizing the dangers. To achieve that goal, you must become more adept at two key skills: speaking and listening.

People often judge the substance of a remark by the speaker's style.

SPEAKING

Because speaking is such an ingrained activity, we tend to do it without much thought. But that casual approach can be a problem in business. You must become more conscious of speaking as a tool to accomplish your objectives. The first step is to break the habit of talking spontaneously without planning what you're going to say or how you're going to say it. You must learn to manage the impression you create by consciously tailoring your remarks and delivery style to suit the situation. That's not to say you should become manipulative or dishonest. But you should become aware of what you say, much as you are aware of what you write.

Learn to think before you speak.

With a little effort, you can learn to apply the same process you use in written communication to oral communication. Before you speak, think about your purpose, your main idea, and your audience. Organize your thoughts in a logical way, decide on a style that suits the occasion, and then edit your remarks mentally. As you speak, watch the other person to see whether your message is making the desired impression. If not, revise it and try again.

Adjust your speaking style to suit the situation.

Bear in mind that various situations call for different speaking styles, just as various writing assignments call for different writing styles. Four distinct modes of speech are characterized by changes in vocabulary, voice quality, and sentence structure:

- *Expressive style.* Spontaneous, conversational, and uninhibited. We use it when we are expressing our feelings, joking, complaining, or socializing. For example: "No way am I going to let that nerd force an incentive-pay plan on Du Pont workers!"

- *Directive style.* Authoritative and judgmental. We use this style to give orders, exert leadership, pass judgment, or state our opinions. For example: "I want Mike Romig to explain the new pay plan to each manager."

- *Problem-solving style.* Rational, objective, unbiased, and bland. This is the style most commonly used in business dealings. We use it when we are solving problems and conveying routine information. For example: "Stacy Lee might be able to present the plan more favorably."

- *Meta style.* Used to discuss the communication process itself. Meta language enables us to talk about our interactions. For example: "We seem to be having a hard time agreeing on the specifics of the incentive-pay plan."[2]

Be sure your nonverbal signals are consistent with your words.

As you think about which speaking style is appropriate, think, too, about the nonverbal message you want to convey. People derive less meaning from your words than they do from your facial expressions, vocal characteristics, and body language. Perhaps the most important thing you can do to project yourself more effectively is to remember the "you" attitude. The best way to earn other people's attention and goodwill is to focus on them.

LISTENING

The ability to listen is a vital skill in business.

Listening heads the list of essential managerial skills; it provides most managers with the bulk of the information they need to do their jobs. In addition, lack of listening ability at all levels is a major source of work-related problems.[3] At Du Pont, for example, employees who do not listen to every facet of the new incentive-pay plan are probably less likely to understand it and therefore less likely to accept it. Most of us like to think of ourselves as being good listeners, but research suggests the opposite. The average person remembers only about half of what's said during a 10-minute conversation and forgets half of that within 48 hours.[4]

Most people need to improve their listening skills.

What happens when you listen

Listening involves five steps: sensing, interpreting, evaluating, remembering, and responding.

Listening is a process involving five related activities, which generally occur in this sequence:

1. *Sensing.* Physically hearing the message and taking note of it. Reception can be blocked by interfering noises, impaired hearing, or inattention; you must tune out distractions and focus on registering the message.

When Keith Dunn and his partners started McGuffey's Restaurants, their goals were people oriented—they wanted a restaurant that wouldn't mistreat employees. But it wasn't until Dunn truly began listening to employees that the approach began to work, resulting in increased profits and lowered turnover. Listening is hard, says Dunn, but you have to learn how to do it.

The four forms of listening:
- Content listening enables you to understand and retain the message.
- Critical listening enables you to evaluate the information.
- Empathic listening is used to draw out the other person.
- Active listening helps you understand the other person's point of view and resolve conflicts.

2. *Interpreting.* Decoding and absorbing what you hear. The speaker's frame of reference may be quite different from yours, so you must try to determine what the speaker really means. Paying attention to nonverbal cues often increases the accuracy of your interpretation.

3. *Evaluating.* Forming an opinion about the message. Sorting through the speaker's remarks requires a good deal of effort. It's also tempting to dismiss ideas offered by people who are unattractive or abrasive and to embrace ideas offered by charismatic speakers.

4. *Remembering.* Storing a message for future reference. To retain what you hear, you must take notes or make a mental outline of the speaker's key points.

5. *Responding.* Acknowledging the message by reacting to the speaker in some fashion.

As you can see, listening requires a mix of physical and mental activities, and it is subject to a mix of physical and mental barriers.

The four types of listening

Various situations call for different listening skills. The four types of listening differ not only in purpose but also in the amount of feedback or interaction they entail:

- *Content listening.* The goal is to understand and retain information imparted by a speaker. You may ask questions, but basically, information flows from the speaker to you. Your job is to identify the key points of the message, so you concentrate and listen for clues to its structure: previews, transitions, summaries, and enumerated points. In your mind, you create an outline of the speaker's remarks; afterward, you silently review what you've learned. You may take notes, but you do this sparingly so that you can concentrate on the key points. It doesn't matter whether you agree or disagree, approve or disapprove—only that you understand.

- *Critical listening.* The goal is to evaluate the message at several levels: the logic of the argument, strength of the evidence, and validity of the conclusions; the implications of the message for you or your organization; the speaker's intentions and motives; and the omission of any important or relevant points. But absorbing information and evaluating it at the same time is hard, so reserve judgment until the speaker has finished. Critical listening generally involves interaction as you try to uncover the speaker's point of view. You are bound to evaluate the speaker's credibility as well. Nonverbal signals are often your best clue.

- *Empathic listening.* The goal is to understand the speaker's feelings, needs, and wants in order to help solve a problem; the message is only a vehicle for gaining insight into the person's psyche. However, your purpose is not really to "solve" the problem. By listening, you help the individual vent the emotions that are preventing him or her from dealing dispassionately with the problem. You may be tempted to give advice, but don't. Try not to judge the rightness or wrongness of the individual's feelings. Just let the other person talk.

■ *Active listening.* Psychiatrist Carl Rogers developed this technique to help people resolve their differences,[5] but it can be used in nearly any listening situation. Here's how it works: Before you can reply to another person's comment with a point of your own, you must restate the ideas and feelings behind the comment to the other person's satisfaction. You go back and forth this way, until each of you understands the other's position. The goal is to appreciate the other person's point of view, whether or not you agree.[6]

All four types of listening can be useful in work-related situations, so it pays to learn how to apply them.

How to be a better listener

Regardless of whether the situation calls for content, critical, empathic, or active listening, you can improve your listening ability by following the ten basic guidelines shown in Figure 15.1. In addition, you should put nonverbal skills to work as you listen:

■ Maintain eye contact with the speaker.

■ React responsively with head nods or spoken signals ("Yes," "Uh-huh," "Go on") to confirm continuing attention.

■ Pay attention to body language for signs of stress, excitement, or anxiety.

Effective listening involves being receptive to both information and feelings.

Above all, try to accomplish two things as you listen: (1) the exchange of information that will lead to higher-quality decisions and (2) the open exchange of

FIGURE 15.1 Ten Keys to Effective Listening

TO LISTEN EFFECTIVELY	THE BAD LISTENER	THE GOOD LISTENER
1. Find areas of interest	Tunes out dry subjects	Opportunizes; asks "What's in it for me?"
2. Judge content, not delivery	Tunes out if delivery is poor	Judges content; skips over delivery errors
3. Hold your fire	Tends to enter into argument	Doesn't judge until comprehension is complete; interrupts only to clarify
4. Listen for ideas	Listens for facts	Listens for central themes
5. Be flexible	Takes intensive notes using only one system	Takes fewer notes; uses four to five different systems, depending on speaker
6. Work at listening	Shows no energy output; fakes attention	Works hard; exhibits active body state
7. Resist distractions	Is distracted easily	Fights or avoids distractions; tolerates bad habits; knows how to concentrate
8. Exercise your mind	Resists difficult expository material; seeks light, recreational material	Uses heavier material as exercise for the mind
9. Keep your mind open	Reacts to emotional words	Interprets emotional words; does not get hung up on them
10. Capitalize on the fact that thought is faster than speech	Tends to daydream with slow speakers	Challenges, anticipates, mentally summarizes, weighs the evidence; listens between the lines to tone of voice

feelings that will build understanding and mutual respect. If you do, you'll be well on the way to becoming an effective interviewer and meeting leader, two roles that require especially good listening skills.

CONDUCTING INTERVIEWS ON THE JOB

Interview: any planned conversation with a specific purpose involving two people

Any time two people meet to discuss a particular matter, they are participating in an interview. Thus, from the day you apply for your first job until the day you retire, you will be involved in a wide variety of business interviews. No communication activity is more dependent on oral communication skills.

In a typical interview, the action is controlled by the interviewer, the person who scheduled the session. For example, the director of human resources at Du Pont might schedule interviews with each manager in the fibers division to get an idea of how the new pay plan is being accepted. The director would pose a series of questions designed to elicit information from each manager. Thus the conversation bounces back and forth from interviewer to interviewee. Meanwhile, the interviewee may also seek to accomplish a purpose, perhaps to obtain or provide information, to solve a problem, to create goodwill, or to persuade the other person to take action. If the participants establish rapport and stick to the subject at hand, both parties have a chance of achieving their objectives.

When both the interviewer and the interviewee achieve their purpose, the interview is a success.

The interviewer establishes the style and structure of the session, depending on the purpose of the interview and the relationship between the parties, much as a writer varies the style and structure of a written message to suit the situation.

CATEGORIZING INTERVIEWS

Two types of interviews:
- Those dominated by the exchange of information
- Those involving the exchange of feelings

Not all interviews are alike; thus they do not require the same set of skills. One major difference is that some interviews are dominated by the exchange of information:

- *Job interviews.* The job candidate wants to learn about the position and the organization; the employer wants to learn about the applicant's abilities and experience. Both hope to make a good impression and to establish rapport. Job interviews are usually fairly formal and structured. Content and critical listening skills are especially important.

- *Information interviews.* The interviewer seeks facts that bear on a decision or contribute to basic understanding. Information flows mainly in one direction: One person asks a list of questions that must be covered and listens to the answers supplied by the other person. Content and critical listening skills are dominant.

- *Persuasive interviews.* One person tells another about a new idea, product, or service and explains why the other should act on the recommendations. Persuasive interviews are often associated with, but are certainly not limited to, selling. The persuader discusses the other person's needs and shows how the product or concept is able to meet those needs. Thus persuasive interviews require skill in drawing out and listening to others as well as the ability to impart information.

- *Exit interviews.* The interviewer tries to understand why the interviewee is leaving the organization or transferring to another department or division. A departing employee can often provide insight into whether the business is being handled efficiently or whether things could be improved. The interviewer tends to ask all the questions while the interviewee provides answers. The departing employee should be encouraged to focus on events and processes rather than personal gripes.

Other interviews are geared more toward the exchange of feelings:

As vice president of the home and personal services unit at US West (which provides telephone service over a 14-state region), Jerry Johnson is familiar with interviews: talking with employees in the field, listening to customers' ideas, and discussing competitive strategies with upper management. Whether you're seeking information or providing it, cautions Johnson, listening skills are critical in any interview.

■ *Evaluation interviews.* A supervisor periodically gives an employee feedback on his or her performance. The supervisor and the employee discuss progress toward predetermined standards or goals and evaluate areas that require improvement. They may also discuss goals for the coming year, as well as the employee's longer-term aspirations and general concerns. Content, critical, and empathic listening skills may all be required.

■ *Counseling interviews.* A supervisor talks with an employee about personal problems that are interfering with work performance. The interviewer should be concerned with the welfare of both the employee and the organization and should confine the discussion to business. (Only a trained psychologist should offer advice on such problems as substance abuse, marital tension, and financial trouble.) Critical and empathic listening skills are both important because the employer needs to evaluate the facts of the situation and deal with the human emotions involved.

■ *Conflict-resolution interviews.* Two competing people or groups of people (such as Smith versus Jones, day shift versus night shift, sales versus production) explore their problems and attitudes. The goal is to bring the two parties closer together, cause adjustments in perceptions and attitudes, and create a more productive climate. Empathic and active listening skills are useful in fostering these changes.

■ *Disciplinary interviews.* A supervisor tries to correct the behavior of an employee who has ignored the organization's rules and regulations. The interviewer must not only get the employee to see the reason for the rules and agree to comply but must also review the facts and explore the person's attitude. Because of the emotional reaction that is likely, neutral observations are more effective than critical comments. Active and empathic listening skills are of prime importance.

Notice that all types of interviews deal to some extent in both emotion and fact; although some listening skills predominate in a particular interview, all may come into play.

PLANNING THE INTERVIEW

Plan an interview just as you plan other forms of communication.

Planning an interview is similar to planning any other form of communication. You begin by stating your purpose, analyzing the other person, and formulating your main idea. Then you decide on the length, style, and organization of the interview.

Even as an interviewee, you have some control over the conversation. You need to anticipate the interviewer's questions and then plan your answers so that the points you want to make will be covered. You can also introduce questions and topics of your own. And by your comments and nonverbal cues, you can affect the relationship between you and the interviewer. Think about your respective roles. What does this person expect from you? Is it to your advantage to confirm those expectations? Will you be more likely to accomplish your objective by being friendly and open or by conveying an impression of professional detachment? Should you allow the interviewer to dominate the exchange, or should you try to take control?

The interviewer assumes the main responsibility for planning the interview.

If you are the interviewer, responsibility for planning the session falls on you. On the simplest level, you must schedule the interview and see that it is held in a comfortable and convenient location. You also need to develop a set of interview questions and decide on their sequence. Having a plan will enable you to conduct the interview more efficiently, even if you find it advantageous to deviate from the plan during the interview.

Types of interview questions

The purpose of the interview and the nature of the participants determine the types of questions that should be asked. When you are planning the interview, bear in mind that you ask questions (1) to get information, (2) to motivate the interviewee to respond honestly and appropriately, and (3) to create a good working relationship with the other person.

Four basic types of interview questions:
- Open-ended questions
- Direct open-ended questions
- Closed-ended questions
- Restatement questions

To obtain both factual information and underlying feelings, you will probably want to use various types of questions:

- *Open-ended questions.* Questions like "What do you think your company wants most from its suppliers?" invite the interviewee to offer an opinion, not just a yes or no or a one-word answer. You can learn some interesting and unexpected things from open-ended questions, but they diminish your control of the interview. The other person's idea of what's relevant may not coincide with yours, and you may waste some time getting the interview back on track. Use open-ended questions to warm up the interviewee and to look for information when you have plenty of time to conduct the conversation.

- *Direct open-ended questions.* This type of question suggests a response. For example, "What have you done about . . . ?" assumes that something has been done and calls for an explanation. With direct open-ended questions, you have somewhat more control over the interview, yet you still give the other person some freedom in framing a response. This form is good to use when you want to get a specific conclusion or recommendation from someone.

- *Closed-ended questions.* Closed-ended questions require yes or no answers or call for short responses: "Did you make a reservation for the flight?" "Tell me your age group: 18–25, 26–35, 36–45, 46–55, 56 and over." Questions like these produce specific information, save time, require less effort from the interviewee, and eliminate bias and prejudice in answers. The disadvantage is that they limit the respondent's initiative and may prevent important information from being revealed. They are better for gathering information than for prompting an exchange of feelings.

- *Restatement questions.* Restatement, or mirror, questions invite the respondent to expand on an answer: "You said you dislike completing travel vouchers. Is that correct?" They also signal the interviewee that you are paying attention. Restatements provide opportunities to clarify points and correct misunderstandings. Use them to pursue a subject further or to encourage the other person to explain a statement. You can also use restatement questions to soothe upset customers or co-workers. By acknowledging the other person's complaint, you gain credibility.

The structure of the interview

The various types of questions are tools for developing ideas. They must be arranged in a sequence that will enable you to accomplish your purpose:

Organize an interview much as you would organize a written message, with the interview's purpose and the audience's receptivity shaping the sequence of questions.

- *Informational purpose.* Topical organization, presented in direct order.

- *Analytical or problem-solving purpose.* Organization that allows you to state the problem, review the background and objectives, suggest solutions, evaluate the pros and cons of each, identify the best option, and agree on implementation plans.

- *Persuasive purpose.* Organization based on the other person's receptivity. (If receptive, focus on conclusions or recommendations that highlight the benefits of your ideas; if resistant, focus on a logical argument that gradually builds a convincing case for your position.)

From a practical standpoint, you need to be certain that your interview outline is about the right length for the time you've scheduled. People can speak at the rate of about 125 to 150 words (roughly one paragraph) per minute. Assuming that you are using a mix of question types, you can probably handle about 30 questions in a half-hour (or about the same amount of information that you would cover in a seven- to ten-page document). However, you may want to allow more or less time for each question and response, depending on the subject matter and the complexity of the questions. Bear in mind that open-ended questions take longer to answer than other types do.

Don't try to cover more questions than you have time for.

Like a written message, an interview should have an opening, a body, and a close. The opening should be used to establish rapport and to orient the interviewee to the remainder of the session. You might begin by introducing yourself, asking a few polite questions, and then explaining the purpose and ground rules of the interview.

Use the opening to set the tone and orient the interviewee.

The questions in the body of the interview should reflect the nature of your relationship with the interviewee. For an informational session, such as a market research interview, you may want to prepare a detailed list of specific questions. This approach will enable you to control the interview and use your time efficiently. In addition, it will facilitate repeating the interview with other participants. On the other hand, if the interview is designed to explore problems or persuade the interviewee, you may prefer a less structured approach. You might simply prepare a checklist of general subjects and then let the interview evolve on the basis of the participant's responses. In the body of the interview, use a mix of question types. One good technique is to use closed-ended questions to pin down specific facts that emerge during an open-ended response. For example, you might follow up by asking, "How many people did you contact to get this information?" or "Can we get this product in stock before May 15?"

Use a mix of question types to give the body of the interview rhythm.

The close of the interview is a time for summarizing the outcome, previewing what comes next, and underscoring the rapport that has been established. To signal that the interview is coming to an end, you might lean back in your

Use the close to sum up the interview and leave the interviewee with a cordial feeling.

chair, smile, and use an open, palms-up gesture as you say: "Well, I guess that takes care of all my questions. Would you like to add anything?" If the interviewee has no comments, you might go on to say: "Thank you so much for your help. You've given me all the information I need to finish my report. I should have it completed within two weeks; I'll send you a copy." Then you might rise, shake hands, and approach the door. In parting, you could add a friendly comment to reaffirm your interest in the other person: "I hope you have a nice trip to Yellowstone. I was there when I was a kid, and I've never forgotten the experience."

When you've concluded the interview, take a few moments to write down your thoughts. If it was an information-gathering session, go over your notes. Fill in any blanks while the interview is fresh in your mind. In addition, you might write a short letter or memo that thanks the interviewee for cooperating, confirms understandings between you, and if appropriate, outlines the next steps.

CONDUCTING MEETINGS

Meetings are called to solve problems or share information.

Meetings, like interviews, are vital to the functioning of modern organizations. Rather than interviewing each manager about the new incentive-pay plan, the director of human resources at Du Pont might call a meeting with all of them. Meetings provide a forum for making key decisions and a vehicle for coordinating the activities of people and departments. Whether the meeting is held to solve a problem or to share information, the participants gain a sense of in-

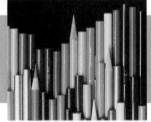

CHECKLIST FOR INTERVIEWS ON THE JOB

A. Preparation
☐ 1. Decide on the purpose and goals of the interview.
☐ 2. Set a structure and format based on your goals.
☐ 3. Determine the needs of your interviewee, and gather background information.
☐ 4. Formulate questions as clearly and concisely as possible, and plot their order.
☐ 5. Project the outcome of the interview, and develop a plan for accomplishing the goal.
☐ 6. Select a time and a site.
☐ 7. Inform the interviewee of the nature of the interview and the agenda to be covered.

B. Conduct
☐ 1. Be on time for the interview appointment.
☐ 2. Remind the interviewee of the purpose and format.
☐ 3. Clear the taking of notes or the use of a tape recorder with the interviewee.

☐ 4. Use your ears and your eyes to pick up verbal and nonverbal cues.
☐ 5. Follow the stated agenda, but be willing to explore relevant subtopics.
☐ 6. At the end of the interview, review the action items, goals, and tasks that each of you has agreed to.
☐ 7. Close the interview on an appreciative note, with thanks to the interviewee for her or his time, interest, and cooperation.

C. Follow-Up
☐ 1. Write a thank-you memo or letter that provides the interviewee with a record of the meeting.
☐ 2. Provide the assistance that you agreed to during your meeting.
☐ 3. Monitor progress by keeping in touch through discussions with your interviewee.

Ineffective meetings are costly in many ways.

volvement and importance from their attendance. Because they share in the decision, they accept it and are committed to seeing it succeed. However, unproductive meetings are frustrating and expensive. Moreover, poor meetings may actually be counterproductive because they may result in bad decisions. When people are pressured to conform, they abandon their sense of personal responsibility and agree to ill-founded plans.

UNDERSTANDING GROUP DYNAMICS

A meeting's success depends not only on what the goal is but also on how the group approaches the task.

A meeting is called for some purpose, and this purpose gives form to the meeting. In addition, however, the interactions and processes that take place in a meeting, the group dynamics, also affect the outcome. On one level, people are assembled to achieve a work-related task; but on another level, each individual has private motives that affect the group's interaction. These "hidden agendas" of the individual members may either contribute to or detract from the group's ability to perform its task.

Role-playing

Members of a group each play a role that affects the outcome of the group's activities.

The roles people play in meetings can be classified into three categories (see Figure 15.2). Self-oriented group members, who are motivated mainly to fulfill personal needs, tend to be less productive than the other two types, who are far more likely to contribute to group goals. Those who assume group-maintenance roles help members work well together. Those who focus on the task facilitate the problem-solving or decision-making process.

To a great extent, the role we assume in a group depends on our status relative to the other members. In most groups, a certain amount of "power politics" occurs as people try to establish their relative status. One or two people typically emerge as the leaders, but often, an undercurrent of tension remains as members vie for better positions in the pecking order. These little power struggles often get in the way of the real work.

Group decision making

Groups usually reach their decisions in a predictable pattern, which can be divided into four phases:

FIGURE 15.2
Roles People Play in Groups

Self-Oriented Roles	Group-Maintenance Roles	Task-Facilitating Roles
Controlling: dominating others by exhibiting superiority or authority	**Encouraging:** drawing out other members by showing verbal and nonverbal support, praise, or agreement	**Initiating:** getting the group started on a line of inquiry
Withdrawing: retiring from the group either by becoming silent or by refusing to deal with a particular aspect of the group's work	**Harmonizing:** reconciling differences among group members through mediation or by using humor to relieve tension	**Information giving or seeking:** offering (or seeking) information relevant to questions facing the group
Attention seeking: calling attention to oneself and demanding recognition from others	**Compromising:** offering to yield on a point in the interest of reaching a mutually acceptable decision	**Coordinating:** showing relationships among ideas, clarifying issues, summarizing what the group has done
Diverting: focusing group discussion on topics of interest to the individual rather than those relevant to the task		**Procedure setting:** suggesting decision-making procedures that will move the group toward a goal

Jennifer C. Smith is assistant vice president of claims at Aetna Life & Casualty. Noted for her ability to interact with top management during meetings, she maintains that the decision-making process can occur more easily if the leader of the group prepares carefully.

1. *Orientation phase.* Group members socialize, establish their roles, and agree on their reason for meeting.

2. *Conflict phase.* Group members begin to discuss their positions on the problem. If group members have been carefully selected to represent a variety of viewpoints and diverse expertise, disagreements are a natural part of this phase. The point is to air all the options and all the pros and cons fully. At the end of this phase, group members begin to settle on a single solution to the problem.

3. *Emergence phase.* The group reaches a decision. Group members who advocated different solutions put aside their objections, either because they are convinced that the majority solution is better or because they recognize that arguing is futile.

4. *Reinforcement phase.* Group feeling is rebuilt, and the solution is summarized. Individual members are given their assignments for carrying out the group's decision, and arrangements are made for following up on these assignments.[7]

By being aware of how small groups of people interact, meeting leaders can take steps to ensure that their meetings are productive.

ARRANGING THE MEETING

Careful planning of four elements—purpose, participants, agenda, and location—is the key to productive meetings. The trick is to bring the right people together in the right place for just enough time to accomplish your goals.

Before calling a meeting, ask yourself whether it is really needed.

- *Determining the purpose.* Before you call a meeting, satisfy yourself that it is the best way to achieve your goal. Then the purpose of a meeting can be categorized as informational or decision making, although many meetings comprise both purposes. An informational meeting is called so that the participants can share information and possibly coordinate actions. This type of meeting may involve individual briefings by each participant or a speech by the leader followed by questions from the attendees. Decision-making meetings are mainly concerned with persuasion, analysis, and problem solving. They often include a brainstorming session followed by a debate on the alternatives, and they tend to be somewhat less predictable than informational meetings.

Limit the number of participants, but include all key people.

- *Selecting the participants.* Try to invite only those whose presence is essential. The number of participants should reflect the purpose of the meeting. If the session is purely informational and one person will be doing most of the talking, you can include a relatively large group. However, if you are trying to solve a problem, develop a plan, or reach a decision, you should try to limit participation to between four and seven people.[8] But be sure to include those who can make an important contribution and those who are key decision makers. Holding a meeting to decide an important matter is pointless if the people with the necessary information aren't there.

- *Setting the agenda.* Although the nature of a meeting may sometimes prevent you from developing a fixed agenda, you should at least prepare

BEHIND THE SCENES AT 3M
The Keys to Masterful Meetings

Virginia Johnson is the manager of 3M's recently established Meeting Management Institute. Among American companies, 3M is known for its role in promoting the importance of effective meetings (as well as for producing such brand names as Scotch cellophane tape and Post-it notes). The company also produces graphics and presentation equipment, which suggests a natural connection between 3M's products and its emphasis on effective meetings. The company finances research, sponsors seminars, and publishes articles and books on the subject.

"We define a meeting as three or more people gathering for an expected outcome," explains Johnson. But top executives spend 17 hours a week in such gatherings and another 6 hours preparing for them: a total of 38 percent of their typical 61-hour week. So, why call meetings at all? Why not put what has to be said in writing and save everybody some time? Johnson says, "You can't accomplish some things without getting your people together—when you want to provide them direct access to an expert, for example, or show that avenues of communication in the company are open. Meetings here at 3M serve other needs too.

They allow us to share information, build teams, brainstorm problems and solutions, reach decisions, and train people. Young companies, especially, and companies in trouble may find meetings indispensable."

To determine whether to hold a meeting, Johnson says she writes "one 25-word sentence stating what I expect people to know, do, and believe after attending. If I can't create that sentence, the need for a meeting isn't apparent." When a meeting is appropriate, she believes that preparation is what makes it successful. "I start by thinking in terms of the agenda. Once it's outlined, I create the visuals that will illustrate the points I want to make.

"Listening is an important skill. Traditionally you help yourself listen by taking notes. We've found that graphics also help people listen, enabling them to visualize and retain information. That's why I plan my graphics early." Johnson finishes by preparing notes containing her main ideas or key phrases. "I never write a speech," she explains. "Speeches are not meetings. My personal style is to be natural and extemporaneous. My agenda, visuals, and notes help me achieve that tone.

Prepare a detailed agenda well in advance of the meeting.

a list of matters to be discussed. The agenda should include the names of the participants and the time, place, and order of business (see Appendix B). Distribute the agenda to the participants several days before the meeting. The more participants know ahead of time about the purpose of the meeting, the better prepared they will be to respond to the issues.

- *Preparing the location.* Decide where you'll hold the meeting, and reserve the location. (For work sessions, morning meetings are usually more productive than afternoon sessions.) Consider the seating arrangements, and give some attention to such details as room temperature, lighting, ventilation, acoustics, and refreshments. Also, if you work for a large organization with teleconferencing capabilities, you may want to use this technology for your meeting. The most common form of electronic meeting is the conference call, using telephone equipment to allow several people at different locations to take part. Videoconferencing, another use of electronic technology, combines long-distance voice and video transmission. In companies where executives would otherwise have to spend countless hours and dollars traveling from one location to another, teleconferencing can be a real boon.

Give attention to the small details that help participants focus on the task at hand.

"For me, the toughest meeting to run is the creative session. Trying to bring out the child in adults, achieving fantasy and free thinking by breaking down management roles, is very demanding." A meeting to generate new ideas in sales training was Johnson's most recent challenge. "I used what I call a 'brain writing' sheet. I asked the eight managers to write down three things about sales training they'd like to see added or changed. They handed their ideas in and took the sheet of another participant. They read that person's suggestions and wrote down three more. After a few rounds of this, they'd forgotten their jobs and titles and were busy scribbling. Each round triggered new ideas."

Johnson is more alert than most to the conduct of meetings, and as a participant, she has the greatest trouble when there is little or no leadership from the meeting facilitator. "My mind wanders," she admits. "If a leader speaks more than 15 or 20 percent of the time, for example, he or she is not being effective. The role of the facilitator is to help other people get their opinions or questions out and responded to." To get the most out of her attendance, Johnson adopts a listening behavior appropriate to the meeting. "If it's a formal meeting, I'll take notes to help me listen and for later recall. At creative sessions I may have to listen intently or shout out my responses. Either way, I want to be free of the technical aspects of meeting attendance." For Virginia Johnson and 3M, planning, conducting, or attending a well-run meeting rewards everyone involved. "If it produces that 'expected outcome,' it's a job well done."

APPLY YOUR KNOWLEDGE

1. You followed Virginia Johnson's advice. For a meeting on the need to improve office telephone techniques, you created 30 visuals to guide you and eight managers through your agenda. En route to the meeting, the case with your visuals was lost. What steps can you take to carry off a productive meeting anyway?

2. Determine the hourly cost of meetings. Create a grid of six vertical columns with these labels: Salary, 2 (executives), 4, 6, 8, and 10. Down the left side, under salary, label five lines with these annual salaries: $20,000, $40,000, $60,000, $80,000, and $100,000. Do the arithmetic and fill in the grid with how much a 1-hour meeting of each group would cost a company (assuming fifty 40-hour weeks to a year). For example, a 1-hour meeting of four executives earning $80,000 a year costs the company $160. Next, determine the cost of an all-morning (3-hour) meeting involving eight executives: one earning $20,000, three earning $40,000, one earning $60,000, two earning $80,000, and one earning $100,000.

RUNNING A PRODUCTIVE MEETING

The meeting leader's duties:
- Pacing the meeting
- Appointing a note taker
- Following the agenda
- Stimulating participation and discussion
- Summarizing the debate
- Reviewing recommendations
- Circulating the minutes

Whether the meeting is conducted electronically or conventionally, its success depends largely on how effective the leader is. If the leader is prepared and has selected the participants carefully, the meeting will generally be productive.

The meeting leader is the person most responsible for keeping the ball rolling. If you're the leader, avoid being so domineering that you close off suggestions, but don't be so passive that you lose control of the group. If the discussion lags, call on those who have not been heard from. Pace the presentation and discussion so that you will have time to complete the agenda. As time begins to run out, interrupt the discussion and summarize what has been accomplished. Another leadership task is either to arrange for someone to record the proceedings or to ask a participant to take notes during the meeting. (Appendix B includes an example of the format for minutes of meetings.)

As the leader, you are expected to follow the agenda; participants have prepared for the meeting on the basis of the announced agenda. However, don't be rigid. Allow enough time for discussion, and give people a chance to raise related issues. If you cut off discussion too quickly or limit the subject too narrowly, no real consensus can emerge.

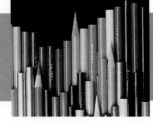

CHECKLIST FOR MEETINGS

A. Preparation
☐ 1. Determine the meeting's objectives.
☐ 2. Work out an agenda that will achieve your objectives.
☐ 3. Select participants.
☐ 4. Determine the location, and reserve a room.
☐ 5. Arrange for light refreshments, if appropriate.
☐ 6. Determine whether the lighting, ventilation, acoustics, and temperature of the room are adequate.
☐ 7. Determine seating needs: chairs only or table and chairs.

B. Conduct
☐ 1. Begin and end the meeting on time.
☐ 2. Control the meeting by following the agenda.
☐ 3. Encourage full participation, and either confront or ignore those who seem to be working at cross-purposes with the group.
☐ 4. Sum up decisions, actions, and recommendations as you move through the agenda, and restate main points at the end.

C. Follow-Up
☐ 1. Distribute notes or minutes on a timely basis.
☐ 2. Take the follow-up action agreed to.

Barbara Walters is co-host of ABC News's *20/20*. She prepares for meetings by doing her homework, reading through all the material she can find, and preparing detailed questions. During the meeting, says Walters, good listening is important, but taking part makes the meeting even more productive.

As the meeting gets under way, you will discover that some participants are too quiet, others too talkative. To draw out the shy types, ask for their input on issues that particularly pertain to them. You might say something like: "Helen, you've done a lot of work in this area. What do you think?" For the overly talkative, simply say that time is limited and others need to be heard from. The best meetings are those where everyone participates, so don't let one or two people dominate your meeting while others doodle on their note pads. As you move through your agenda, stop at the end of each item, summarize what you understand to be the feelings of the group, and state the important points made during the discussion.

At the conclusion of the meeting, tie up the loose ends. Either summarize the general conclusion of the group or list the suggestions. Wrapping things up ensures that all participants agree on the outcome and gives people a chance to clear up any misunderstandings. Before the meeting breaks up, briefly review who has agreed to do what by what date.

As soon as possible after the meeting has taken place, the leader should give all the participants a copy of the minutes or notes, showing recommended actions, schedules, and responsibilities. The minutes will remind everyone of what took place and provide a reference for future actions.

SUMMARY

Oral communication is of primary importance in business. The two key skills are speaking and listening, both of which are augmented by nonverbal communication. Speaking well requires a conscious effort to plan and edit your remarks in light of your audience's needs. Listening also requires conscious effort.

An interview is any planned, purposeful conversation involving two people. Informational interviews require mainly content and critical listening skills; emotion-sharing interviews may require empathic and active listening as well. Various types of interviews require different mixes of the four main types of questions: open-ended, direct open-ended, closed-ended, and restatement. Planning an interview is much like planning a written message. The interview outline should be tailored to the subject, purpose, and audience and should include an opening, a body, and a close.

In business, a great deal of time is spent in meetings. Their effectiveness depends on careful planning and skillful leadership. The personal motives of the participants can affect the outcome of the meeting. The goal is to get all participants to share information or to contribute to a sound decision.

ON THE JOB:
Solving a Communication Dilemma at Du Pont

Tying pay to profits is an increasingly popular concept among American companies. A recent survey of 425 large corporations indicates that 87 percent offer some kind of compensation other than base pay. But Du Pont's new plan involves employees of every rank and is one of the most extensive and innovative plans ever tried at a major U.S. corporation.

The details of the plan are somewhat complicated, but the basic concept is simple: If the division's profits exceed expectations, the employees will make more money than they would if they were getting ordinary cost-of-living and merit increases; if profits stagnate or decline, the employees will get very small raises and will not keep pace economically with workers in other divisions. Under the best of all possible conditions, fibers division employees will earn 12 percent more than their counterparts in other divisions at the end of five years. In the worst-case scenario, they will receive 6 percent less than other Du Pont employees. Theoretically, the incentive-pay plan will motivate people to work harder and become more efficient.

It is still too early to pronounce the program a success, but it does seem to be having the intended effect, at least with some employees. As Jean Tanner, a marketing specialist for Dacron, points out, it's like "becoming a homeowner rather than a renter. You care more about keeping it up. I think more about what's best for the business." To cut costs, for example, Tanner is thinking of trimming the advertising budget for Dacron. She plans to use less expensive forms of promotion, such as talk-show coverage or video news releases.

But even though many workers like the new incentive-pay program, others complain about various aspects of the plan. Perhaps the most pointed criticism is that employees lack the power both to determine the division's profit goal and to track achievement of that goal. Management not only sets the target but also keeps the score.

According to Dean Goad, president of Du Pont's internal union, management set the first year's profit improvement goal at only 2 percent in order to convince people that the goals would be easy to meet. This has created a burst of initial enthusiasm for the program. However, the second year's goal calls for profits to increase by 4 percent—a target that may be more difficult to reach, particularly if a recession hits.

Furthermore, critics contend, management can wipe out an entire year's profits with an accounting change. For example, say that the head of the division decides to take a write-off: There goes the division's profit, and there goes everybody's bonus. Management would suffer too, of course, but not as much as the lower-level workers. Managers participate in another companywide bonus program that the rank and file do not.

Some workers also grumble that the new plan increases conflicts among employees. Wayne Jefferson, a spinning-machine operator and union representative, points out that when a machine broke down recently, some workers complained to management that the operator just stood around waiting for repairs to be made. In another instance, one worker scolded another for throwing away a pair of safety gloves before they were completely worn out. Even though the plan may raise tension on the factory floor, it is even more likely to increase the lower-level employees' resentment of management, according to Goad. Workers wonder why they should worry about saving nickels and dimes when the bosses are able to squander much larger sums.

Despite these criticisms, the incentive-pay plan appears to have more supporters than detractors. At several of the division's 20 locations, up to 60 percent of the nonunion workers have signed up for an optional accelerated version, even though doing so may require a 2 percent pay cut in the short term. Furthermore, 57 percent of the union members who have voted on the program are in favor of it. Robert McNutt is confident that five years from now, everyone will agree that incentive pay is a good deal for both the company and its employees. In the meantime, he is doing all he can to convince people to support the plan.

Your Mission: As a member of the human resources department of Du Pont's fibers division, you are involved in implementing the new incentive-pay program. You hear plenty of talk, pro and con, about the plan. Your goal is to deal with these comments and help make the plan work. Choose the *best* alternative for handling the following situations:

1. One of the spinning-machine operators comes to you with the following complaint: "I told my supervisor that I could do my job better if he would adjust the lighting over my workstation. It's so dark that I can hardly see what I'm doing. I know I could work faster if I could see without squinting and straining my eyes. Now you'd think that with everybody pushing to increase profits, the supervisor would jump at the chance to boost my output, wouldn't you? But what does he do? He says, 'Hey, try bifocals.' Makes a big joke out of it. Well, I can tell you, if my bonus depends on him, I'm going to end up eating peanut butter. I don't think it's fair that people like me have to lose out because people like him are too lazy or too cheap to change the lighting."

   Which of the following remarks is the best way to begin your reply to the machine operator's complaint?
   a. "It sounds as though you and your supervisor don't see eye to eye on this issue."
   b. "I can see why you're provoked. I'd be annoyed too if somebody treated me that way."
   c. "Maybe your supervisor has a good point. I think you should have your eyes checked and see if that might be the problem."
   d. "I'd like to take a look at the situation. Let's go to your workstation right now so I can get a better idea of the lighting conditions there."

2. A union representative from the nylon plant in Seaford, Delaware, has asked you to attend a meeting to address some of the workers' questions about the new incentive-pay plan. The union representative launches the meeting by summarizing the workers' concerns. His comments last about 15 minutes. After responding to these points, you throw the meeting open to additional questions from the audience of roughly 250 union members. An employee in the back of the room stands up and says, "How do we know whether we've reached our goals?" The question seems straightforward, but the employee's tone of voice strikes you as being belligerent. His posture is aggressive, and he has a sneer on his face. How would you interpret his question?
   a. The employee is implying that management will manipulate the financial data to the detriment of the employees.
   b. The employee is simply trying to learn about the process that will be used to inform people of where they stand relative to the goal.
   c. The employee is implying that Du Pont should give the employees frequent "report cards" so that they can adjust their behavior to maximize their chances of meeting the goal.

d. The employee wants to know whether each individual will be assigned a personal goal.

3. Robert McNutt has asked you to explain the incentive-pay program to a new employee who has joined the fibers division as a plant manager. The employee will be involved in administering the plan in his facility, so you want to be sure that he enthusiastically supports the concept and fully understands the details. You are planning your interview with the new plant manager. Which of the following would provide the best structure for the interview?
   a. Version one
      1. Overview of incentive-pay plan and Du Pont's reasons for adopting it
      2. Feature-by-feature description of elements of the plan
      3. Status of implementation
      4. Plant manager's role in administering the plan
      5. Problems plant manager might encounter relative to the plan
      6. Questions plant manager might have about the plan
   b. Version two
      1. Do you have any experience with incentive-pay plans?
      2. What advantages and disadvantages do you see in tying pay to profits?
      3. If you were designing an incentive-pay plan, what features would you include?
      4. What steps will you take to implement the incentive-pay plan at your facility?
      5. How will you deal with resistance to the plan at your facility?
   c. Version three
      1. The problem: Employees are not motivated to care about profits.
      2. Background: Human resources department decides to try incentive-pay plan in fibers division.
      3. Objectives: Plan will tie pay to profits, boost productivity, encourage people to feel more involved.
      4. Alternatives: Various types of incentive-pay plans were evaluated (give a description and the pros and cons of each approach).
      5. Solution: Give key features of selected plan.
      6. Next steps: Discuss plant manager's role in administering plan in his facility.
      7. Answer plant manager's questions.

4. As your meeting with the new plant manager progresses, you get the distinct impression that he has serious reservations about the plan. What should you do?
   a. Give a "sales pitch" for the plan, emphasizing its advantages.

b. Explore his reservations by asking him something like this: "I'm getting the impression that you have some reservations about the plan. What are your concerns?"

c. Continue to explain the plan in an objective, neutral fashion, and hope that the plant manager's reservations will diminish once he hears all the details.

d. Emphasize that the plan has the blessings of Du Pont's senior management, and imply that he had better support the program if he wants to make a good impression.

5. Although employees are generally responding well to the incentive-pay plan, a number of managers have raised an important objection: The plan motivates people to focus too much on short-term results. In an effort to meet annual profit targets, some employees appear to be postponing necessary investments in equipment, research and development, and long-term marketing activities. If people continue to defer these expenditures, the division will eventually suffer a competitive disadvantage. McNutt has decided to call a meeting to discuss this problem. Which purpose should McNutt focus on during the meeting?

a. To redesign the incentive-pay plan so that it encourages long-term profits

b. To determine whether the plan is sending the wrong signal and, if so, to gain agreement on a general approach to solving the problem

c. To inform the key managers of the plan's tendency to promote a short-term focus and to help them counteract that potential problem by reminding their subordinates to consider the future implications of their decisions

d. To persuade top management that the incentive plan does not really reward short-term results at the expense of long-term performance

6. McNutt has invited you to sit in on the meeting and take notes. You notice that one of the department heads repeatedly tries to dominate the discussion. This individual is one of the division's rising stars, and people tend to defer to her because of her organizational power and her forceful personality. Regardless of what other people say, she keeps repeating the same basic comment: The incentive-pay plan rewards the wrong behavior. We ought to scrap the whole thing and start over. You can see that McNutt is worried the group will decide to go along with this person's advice, even though the plan seems to be working very well in most respects.

As a junior member of the fibers division, you have very little power to influence the dynamics of the meeting. However, during a brief break, you have a few minutes alone with McNutt. What would you advise him to do?

a. Adjourn the meeting as soon as possible without reaching any conclusion on the issue; then call another meeting but do not invite the plan's chief critic.

b. Suggest that the division create a special task force to study the issue in more detail.

c. Politely but firmly discourage any further comments from the plan's chief critic. Encourage other people to voice their opinions. Steer the group toward a compromise less extreme than scratching the entire incentive-pay plan.

d. Go along with the dominant individual publicly, but try to work behind the scenes later to salvage the plan.

e. Openly challenge the individual to prove that the existing plan is seriously flawed. Defend the plan by pointing out its advantages. Call for a vote on scrapping the whole plan versus retaining the existing version.[9]

QUESTIONS FOR DISCUSSION

1. Do you feel that you are best at sending written, oral, or nonverbal messages? Why does this particular form of communication appeal to you? When receiving messages, are you best at reading, listening, or interpreting nonverbal cues?

2. What are your major problems as a listener?

3. What are the advantages and disadvantages of the various types of interview questions?

4. How do information-sharing meetings differ from problem-solving or decision-making meetings?

5. How do the goals of various group members affect the ability to achieve group goals?

6. Think of a meeting you have led (or one you have attended). Did the meeting achieve its objectives? What contributed to its success? What could have been done differently to make the meeting more successful?

EXERCISES

1. In your position at Du Pont (see this chapter's On-the-Job simulation), you have been asked to talk with a worker who has repeatedly complained about the injustices of the new incentive-pay plan. This individual is creating tension among his co-workers by constantly grumbling about "greedy managers" and "fat-cat bosses who throw money away on first-class travel, fancy dinners, and endless streams of memos about saving paper clips or some other stupid thing." He gripes that he and his friends in the factory are "supposed to bust a gut to pay for these bozos' designer offices." During your interview with the person, you conclude that his hostility is an ingrained personality trait and that his complaints probably have very little to do with the merits of the incentive-pay plan. What can you do to calm the person down and discourage him from making unfair remarks about the plan to the other employees?[10]

2. What kinds of questions (open-ended, direct open-ended, closed-ended, restatement) are most likely to be asked by the interviewers in these situations? Explain your answers.
   a. Someone conducting an opinion poll
   b. A management consultant evaluating a proposed personnel policy
   c. A job interviewer attempting to solicit additional information from a shy respondent
   d. A travel agent helping a vacationer plan her itinerary
   e. A travel agent firming up dates and times for a client
   f. A teacher preparing an essay-type examination
   g. A personnel counselor probing for more information in a sensitive area

3. Good interviewers and good interviewees plan in advance. In the following situations, think about the interview from the viewpoint of both participants. For each participant, what is the general purpose of the interview? What sequence of conversation might best accomplish this purpose? What type of information should be sought or presented?
   a. A high school debate coach has scheduled an appointment with the school principal in an attempt to obtain $250 to take her debate team to the state finals in Peoria, Illinois. The team is strong, and she feels that it has a good chance of winning some type of award. However, the school activities budget is limited.
   b. A counselor has scheduled an interview with a company employee who has a long, consistent record of excellent work. Recently, however, the employee has been coming to work late and often appears distracted on the job.
   c. As part of the job-evaluation process and in an attempt to have her civil service position upgraded, an employee has submitted a job description of her work. An evaluator from the civil service has scheduled an interview at the job location to discuss the candidate's requested upgrading.

4. Imagine that you have been asked to chair a discussion on a topic that is currently splitting your campus community: whether members of the security department should carry weapons. You know that, with both sides represented, the discussion will be animated. Arriving at any type of consensus is probably impossible, but you have been asked to gather information at the meeting and close it with a vote, which will serve as a recommendation to the campus president. As part of your planning, jot down eight to ten points to keep in mind as the meeting goes on. These may take the form of a proposed agenda, some suggestions to yourself for keeping the discussion on target, or ideas for bringing the meeting to a successful close.

CHAPTER SIXTEEN

After studying this chapter, you will be able to

- Categorize speeches and presentations according to their purpose
- Analyze the audience for speeches and presentations
- Identify the steps required in planning a speech or presentation
- Develop an introduction, a body, and a final summary for a long, formal presentation
- Select, design, and use visual aids
- Deliver your speech or presentation effectively
- Handle questions from the audience

GIVING SPEECHES AND ORAL PRESENTATIONS

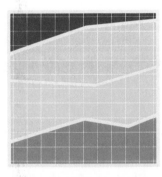

ON THE JOB:
Facing a Communication Dilemma at the Keys Group
Keys's Key

"Acceptance in the community is the key," says Brady Keys. His company—the Keys Group—runs 13 Burger King outlets in Detroit and 11 Kentucky Fried Chicken restaurants in Georgia. With annual sales of more than $14 million, the Keys Group ranks among the largest black-owned businesses in the country.

When Keys started out in the restaurant business more than 20 years ago, he realized that good food was only half the battle. Consumers have hundreds of fast-food outlets to choose from, all with similar menus. If you want the public to come to your store rather than going to the one across the street, you have to do something a little bit extra.

For Brady Keys, the extra ingredient has been personal charisma. A former all-pro defensive halfback for the Pittsburgh Steelers, Keys has used his forceful personality along with expert speaking skills to inspire both investors and employees and to build a presence in the two communities in which he operates: inner-city Detroit and rural Georgia. Today, he is well known and highly respected in both communities, but winning acceptance hasn't been easy.

Keys realized that if he wanted to succeed in business, he'd have to gain people's respect. He'd have to persuade bankers to loan him money and big companies to do business with him. He'd have to convince employees to work hard and customers to trust him. But how? If you were Keys, whether you were addressing a large crowd or an audience of one, what would you need to know about preparing, developing, and delivering speeches? Can improving your speaking skills really lead to the success that Keys has realized?[1]

PREPARING TO SPEAK

Brady Keys, Jr., President, Keys Group

Brady Keys has used his speaking skills effectively because he knows that speeches and oral presentations are much like interviews and meetings: In preparation, you must define your purpose, analyze the audience, and develop a plan for presenting your points. But speeches and presentations differ from interviews and meetings in several important respects. For one thing, speeches and presentations are usually delivered to larger groups, so the nature and amount of interaction between the audience and the speaker are different. Because speeches and presentations are public events, they generally do not deal with emotional issues or personal problems, as some interviews do. Finally, in terms of content and structure, speeches and presentations often have a good deal in common with formal reports; in fact, many of them are oral versions of written documents.

DEFINING THE PURPOSE

The amount of audience interaction varies from presentation to presentation, depending on the speaker's purpose.

Speeches and presentations can be categorized according to their purpose, much as interviews and meetings are categorized. The purpose helps determine content and style; it also affects the amount of audience participation that occurs.

- *To motivate or entertain.* When you are trying to motivate or entertain the audience, you generally do most of the talking. During your speech, the audience plays an essentially passive role, listening to your remarks but providing little direct input in the form of comments or questions. You control the content of the message.

- *To inform or analyze.* When your purpose is to provide information or analyze a situation, you and the audience generally interact somewhat. Basically, a group of people meet to hear the oral equivalent of a written report; then members of the audience offer comments or ask questions.

- *To persuade or collaborate.* The most interaction occurs when you aim to persuade people to take a particular action or to collaborate with them to solve a problem or reach a decision. You generally begin by providing facts and figures that increase the audience's understanding of the subject; you might also offer arguments in defense of certain conclusions or recommendations. But in addition, you invite the audience to participate by expressing their needs, suggesting solutions, and formulating conclusions and recommendations. Because persuasive and collaborative presentations involve so much audience interaction, you have relatively little control of the material. You must be flexible enough to adjust to new input and unexpected reactions; you cannot adhere to a prewritten script.

Often, a speech or presentation accomplishes several of these purposes simultaneously.

ANALYZING THE AUDIENCE

The nature of the audience affects your strategy for achieving your purpose.

Once you have your purpose firmly in mind, you should think about another basic element of your speech or presentation: the audience. Your choice of a strategy for accomplishing your purpose must take into account those who will be attending. First consider the size and composition of the audience. A relatively small group may sensibly be drawn into a decision-making process. But with more than 12 people, it's difficult to manage the give-and-take that is essential to building a consensus, so your approach may lean more toward telling than toward asking. In addition, a homogeneous group (made up, for example, entirely of young engineers or entirely of East Coast sales representatives) benefits from a focused speech or presentation; a diverse group requires a more generalized approach.

You also need to put together some other relevant information about the audience. One very important factor is the likely reaction to your speech or presentation. Brady Keys expects different reactions from various audiences, whether it's one banker considering him for a loan or a hundred employees attending a company picnic. So decide whether your listeners will be hostile, receptive, or indifferent to your point of view: Do they care about the issues you will discuss? You should also learn as much as you can about their level of understanding: How much do they already know about your subject? Finally, you need to take a cold, hard look at their relationship with you: Do they already know you? Do they respect your judgment? The answers will help you decide on the best way to organize your material.

PLANNING YOUR SPEECH OR PRESENTATION

Developing a strategy for delivering an oral message is just as crucial as developing a strategy for a written message. If you can't put information in an easily digestible form, your audience will not only lose patience with you but may also fail to understand some important points. For maximum impact and achievement of your goals, you must define the main idea, construct an outline, estimate the appropriate length, and decide on the most effective style.

Developing a main idea

General H. Norman Schwarzkopf was the military commander of the allied liberation of Kuwait from Iraqi occupation. Now retired, he makes frequent speeches, highlighting his perspective on the Persian Gulf war. A direct and forceful speaker, Schwarzkopf advises you to catch the audience's interest by clearly spelling out your main idea.

The main idea links your subject and purpose to the audience's frame of reference, much as an advertising slogan points out how a product benefits consumers. Your goal in developing a main idea is to make your subject as interesting to the audience as it is to you. Try to state your main idea in one sentence that summarizes the chief argument you will use to convince the audience. Here are a few examples:

Demand for low-calorie, high-quality frozen foods will increase because of basic social and economic trends.

Reorganizing the data-processing department will lead to better service at a lower cost.

The new health plan gives all employees more options for coverage.

The main idea is a you-oriented statement that points up how the audience can benefit from your subject and purpose.	Judy Semmerich has been a dedicated employee, and we are going to miss her when she retires. Notice that each of these statements puts a particular slant on the subject, one that is positive and directly related to the audience's interests. This sort of "you" attitude helps keep the audience's attention and convinces people that your points are relevant.

Developing an outline

<table>
<tr>
<td>Structure a short speech or presentation like a letter or memo.</td>
<td rowspan="1">With a well-crafted main idea to guide you, you can begin to outline the speech or presentation. The structure that you establish should be geared to the subject, the purpose, the audience, and the time allotted for your speech or presentation. If you have ten minutes or less to deliver your message, you should organize your thoughts much as you would a letter or brief memo, using the direct approach if the subject involves routine information or good news and using the indirect approach if the subject involves bad news or persuasion. Figure 16.1 shows the outline of a brief persuasive speech delivered by an art dealer trying to interest a group of executives in investing in corporate art.</td>
</tr>
<tr>
<td>Organize longer speeches and presentations like formal reports.</td>
<td>Longer speeches and presentations should be organized like reports (see Chapters 10–12 for specific suggestions). If the purpose is to entertain, motivate, or inform, use a direct order imposed naturally by the subject. If the purpose is to analyze, persuade, or collaborate, organize around either conclusions and recommendations or a logical argument. Use direct order if the audience is receptive, indirect if you expect resistance. Regardless of the length of your speech or presentation, bear in mind that simplicity of organization is especially useful in oral communication.</td>
</tr>
<tr>
<td>You may use an outline for a speech or presentation as the "script," but prepare some organizational alternatives if you plan to allow considerable audience interaction.</td>
<td>A carefully prepared outline may be more than just the starting point for composing a speech or presentation. If you plan to deliver your presentation from notes rather than from a written text, your outline will also be your final "script." For this reason, the headings on the outline should be complete sentences or lengthy phrases rather than one- or two-word topic headings. Many speakers include notes that indicate where visual aids will be used. You might also want to write out the transitional sentences you will use to connect main points. The excerpt from an outline shown in Figure 16.2 on page 434 is a good example of all these techniques.

Keep in mind, however, that you may have to adjust your organization in response to input from the audience, especially if your purpose is to collaborate. You might want to think of several organizational possibilities, based on "what if " assumptions about the audience's reactions. That way, if someone says something that undercuts your planned approach, you can switch to another argument.</td>
</tr>
</table>

Estimating length

The average speaker can deliver about one paragraph, or 125 to 150 words, in a minute.	Time for speeches and presentations is often strictly regulated. You should learn to tailor your material to the available time so that you can both fill the time allotted to you and keep within the limits. Once you have developed an outline, you can estimate more accurately how long your speech or presentation will take. The average speaker talks at the rate of about 125 to 150 words a minute (or roughly 7,500 to 9,000 words an hour, which corresponds to 20 to 25 double-spaced typed pages of text), and the average paragraph is about 125 to 150 words in length. Thus most of us speak at the rate of about one paragraph per minute.

**FIGURE 16.1
Sample Outline for Brief
Speech**

WHO OWNS THE VAN GOGH?

Purpose: To convince executives that corporate art is a good investment

I. Introduction: On a cold night in March, collectors assembled at
   Christie's auction gallery in London to bid on Van Gogh's Sunflowers.
   Within 5 minutes, the price soared to $39.9 million. The buyer? A
   Japanese insurance company.

II. Corporations are becoming major consumers of art.

   A. Over 1,000 corporations now have art collections.

   B. Companies are motivated by three factors:

      1. Top executives' love of art

      2. Desire to provide public and employees with aesthetic value

      3. Potential for appreciation in the value of the work of art

III. Most corporate collections are conservative.

   A. Corporate collectors tend to avoid the controversial.

   B. The art is generally the work of 20th-century artists.

      1. Moderately priced, compared to Old Masters

      2. In plentiful supply

IV. Several corporate collections have soared in value.

   A. PepsiCo paid $150,000 for a sculpture by Alexander Calder, which is
      worth $1 million today. [slides]

   B. First Bank Systems, Inc.'s collection, acquired for $3 million, has
      doubled in value. [slides]

   C. Sterling Regal's collection of 180 works cost about $2 million and is
      now worth about $4.5 million. [slides]

   D. Domino's Pizza has invested $7.5 million in its collection, which is
      currently valued at $12 million. [slides]

V. Conclusion: Investing in art provides both aesthetic and monetary
   rewards. Corporations are the Medicis of the current art renaissance.

Let's say that you want to make three basic points. In a 10-minute speech,
you could take about 2 minutes to explain each of these points, using roughly
two paragraphs for each point. If you devoted 1 minute each to the introduction and the conclusion, you would have 2 minutes left over to interact with the
audience. If you had an hour, however, you could spend the first 5 minutes
introducing the presentation, establishing rapport with the audience, providing background information, and giving an overview of your topic. In the next
30 to 40 minutes, you could explain each of the three points, spending about 10
to 13 minutes per point (the equivalent of five or six typewritten pages). Your
conclusion might take another 3 to 5 minutes. The remaining 10 to 20 minutes
would then be available for responding to questions and comments from the
audience.

Which is better, the 10-minute speech or the hour-long presentation? The
answer depends on the subject, on the audience's attitude and knowledge, and

**FIGURE 16.2
Sample Outline with
Notes on Delivery**

I. The company's sales growth has flattened in recent years because of weakening demand for cosmetics and our lack of new products.

    A. Consumption of cosmetics has leveled off in the past 3 years. LINE CHART

        1. Working women have more money but less time to spend it.

        2. Recession has dampened demand and prompted a shift to cheaper brands. BAR CHART

    B. Our market share has declined. LINE CHART

        1. Consumers are going to new outlets. PIE CHARTS

        2. Competitors have gained share by introducing cheaper lines for these outlets. TABLE

TRANSITION: Our loss of market share can be reversed.

II. We can regain our position in the cosmetics market if we introduce our own inexpensive line.

---

on the relationship between the audience and the speaker. For a simple, easily accepted message, 10 minutes may be enough. But if your subject is complex or your audience is skeptical, you need more time. The important thing is to use good judgment. Don't try to squeeze a complex presentation into a period that is too brief, and don't draw out a simple talk any longer than necessary.

Be sure that your subject, purpose, and organization are compatible with the time available.

Deciding on the style

Another important element in your planning is determining the style most suitable to the occasion. Is this a formal speech in an impressive setting, with professionally developed visual aids? Or is it a casual working session? The size of the audience, the subject, your purpose, your budget, and the time available for preparation all determine the style.

In general, if you are speaking to a relatively small group, you can often get away with a casual approach that encourages audience participation. A small conference room, with the audience seated around a table, may be appropriate. Use simple visual aids. Invite the audience to interject comments. Deliver your remarks in a conversational tone, using notes to jog your memory if necessary.

Use a casual style for small groups, a formal style for large groups and important events.

On the other hand, if you are addressing a large audience and the event is an important one, you should establish a more formal atmosphere. Hold the presentation in an auditorium or a convention hall, and seat the audience in rows. Show slides or films to dramatize your message. Ask people to hold their questions until after you have completed your remarks. Use detailed notes or a complete script to guide your delivery. Formality is enhanced when you put physical and psychological distance between you and the audience.

DEVELOPING FORMAL SPEECHES AND PRESENTATIONS

Preparing a major speech or presentation is very much like writing a formal report, with one important difference: You must adjust your technique to the oral mode of communication. This is both an opportunity and a challenge. The opportunity lies in the interaction that is possible between you and the audi-

How formal speeches and presentations differ from formal reports:
- More interaction with the audience
- Use of nonverbal cues to express meaning
- Less control of content
- Greater need to help the audience stay on track

ence. When you speak before a group, you can receive information as well as transmit it. As a consequence, you can adjust both the content and the delivery of your message as you go along, editing your speech or presentation to make it clearer and more compelling. Instead of simply expressing your ideas, you can draw out the audience's ideas and use them to reach a mutually acceptable conclusion. You can also capitalize on nonverbal signals to convey information to and from your audience.

However, in order to get the benefits of oral communication, you have to make a few sacrifices. The biggest price you pay is loss of control. Dealing with an audience requires flexibility; the more you plan to interact, the more flexible you must be. Halfway through your presentation, an unexpected comment from someone in the audience may force you to shift to a new line of thought, which requires a good deal of skill. At the same time, you must also accommodate the limitations of listeners. To prevent the audience from losing interest or getting lost, you must use special techniques in developing the various elements of the presentation: the introduction, the body, the final summary, the question-and-answer period, and the visual aids.

THE INTRODUCTION

The introduction should capture attention, inspire confidence, and preview the contents.

You have a lot to accomplish during the first few minutes of your speech or presentation: You need to arouse the audience's interest in your topic, establish your credibility, and prepare the audience for what will follow. That's why the introduction often requires a disproportionate amount of your attention.

Arousing interest

Some subjects are naturally more interesting than others. If you happen to be discussing a matter of profound significance that will personally affect the members of your audience, chances are they will listen, regardless of how you begin. All you really have to do is announce your topic (for example, "Today I'd like to announce the reorganization of the company").

Connect the topic to the listeners' needs and interests.

When you're dealing with an uninterested audience, the best approach is to appeal to human nature. Encourage people to take the subject personally. Show them how they as individuals will be affected. For example, in speaking to clerical employees about a pension program, you might start off with an opening like this:

If somebody offered to give you $200,000 in exchange for $5 per week, would you be interested? That's the amount you can expect to collect during your retirement years if you choose to contribute to the voluntary pension plan. During the next two weeks, you will have to decide whether you want to participate. Although for most of you retirement is many years away, this is an important financial decision. During the next 20 minutes, I hope to give you the information you need to make that decision intelligently.

Make sure that the introduction matches the tone of the speech or presentation. If the occasion is supposed to be fun, you may begin with something light; but if you're talking business to a group of executives, don't waste their time with cute openings. Avoid jokes and personal anecdotes when you're discussing a serious problem. If you're giving a routine oral report, don't be overly dramatic. Most of all, be natural. Nothing turns off the average audience faster than a trite, staged beginning.

As founder of the consulting firm Success Strategies, Lynda R. Paulson addresses the people needs of companies of all sizes. A dynamic speaker, Paulson advises that you establish your credibility early. Everything else depends on it, including your listeners' acceptance of you and their respect for your opinion.

Building credibility

Building credibility is probably even more important than arousing interest. Communication research clearly shows that acceptance of a message depends on the audience's confidence in the speaker.[2] Thus you must establish a good relationship with the audience—and quickly, because people will decide within a few minutes whether you are worth listening to.[3] You want the audience to like you as a person and to respect your opinion.

Establishing credibility is relatively easy if you're speaking to a familiar, open-minded audience. The real difficulty arises when you must earn the confidence of strangers, especially those who are predisposed to be skeptical or antagonistic. One way to handle the problem is to let someone else introduce you. This solution enables you to present your credentials without appearing boastful. Be certain, however, that the person doesn't exaggerate your qualifications. If Brady Keys were to address a group of fast-food franchisees on inner-city operations, some of them might bristle at his being billed as the world's only knowledgeable authority on the subject. If you're introducing yourself, keep your comments simple. But don't be afraid to mention your accomplishments. Your listeners are curious about you. They want to know your qualifications, so tell them very briefly who you are and why you're there:

> I'm Karen Whitney, a market research analyst with Information Resources Corporation. For the past five years, I've specialized in studying high-technology markets. Your director of engineering, John LaBarre, has asked me to brief you on recent trends in computer-aided design so that you'll have a better idea of how to direct your research and development efforts.

Without boasting, explain why you are qualified to speak on the subject.

Notice how this speaker establishes credibility by tying her credentials to the purpose of her presentation. She lets her listeners know immediately that she is qualified to tell them something they need to know. She connects her background to their concerns.

Previewing the presentation

Let the audience know what lies ahead.

Giving your audience a preview of what's ahead adds to your authority and, more important, helps people understand your message. Your introduction should summarize your main idea, identify the supporting points, and indicate the order in which those points will be developed. Once you have established the framework, you can move into the body of the presentation, confident that the audience will understand how the individual facts and figures relate to your main idea.

THE BODY

The body should transmit the three or four most important points you want to make.

The bulk of your speech or presentation should be devoted to a discussion of the three or four main points on your outline. You can use the same organizational patterns that you use in a letter, memo, or report, but strive for simplicity. You want the structure of your speech or presentation to be clear, and you don't want to lose the audience's attention.

Emphasizing structure

To show how ideas are related in an oral presentation, you must rely more on words. For the small links between sentences and paragraphs, one or two transitional words are enough: *therefore, because, in addition, in contrast, moreover, for example, consequently, nevertheless, finally.* But to link major sections of the speech or presentation, you need complete sentences or paragraphs, such as "Now that we've reviewed the problem, let's take a look at some solutions" or "We'll turn now to the three reasons for our loss of market share." Every time you shift topics, stress the connection between ideas; summarize what's been said, and preview what's to come.

The longer the speech or presentation, the more important the transitions become. When you present many facts and ideas, the audience has trouble absorbing them and seeing the relationship among them. Listeners need clear transitions to guide them to the most important points. Furthermore, they need transitions to pick up any ideas they may have missed. If you repeat key ideas in the transitions, you can compensate for lapses in the audience's attention. You might also want to call attention to the transitions by using gestures, changing your tone of voice, or introducing a visual aid.

Help the audience follow your presentation
- By summarizing your remarks as you go along
- By emphasizing the transitions from one idea to the next

Holding the audience's attention

Throughout a speech or presentation, you must continue trying to maintain the audience's interest. Here are a few helpful tips for creating memorable speeches:

- *Relate your subject to the audience's needs.* People are most interested in things that affect them personally. Present every point in light of the audience's needs and values.

- *Use clear, vivid language.* People become bored very quickly when they don't understand the speaker. If your presentation involves abstract ideas, try to show how those abstractions connect with everyday life. Use familiar words, short sentences, and concrete examples.

- *Explain the relationship between your subject and familiar ideas.* By showing exactly how your subject relates to ideas the audience already understands, you give people a way to categorize and remember your points.[4]

Roberto Goizueta is chairman and CEO of The Coca-Cola Company. He is a successful speaker, often relating his accomplishments at Coke and what they've taught him. But to keep the audience's attention, says Goizueta, be sure you show how your subject applies to your industry and to the work of your listeners.

You can also maintain the audience's interest by introducing variety into your speech or presentation. One especially useful technique is to pause occasionally for questions or comments from the audience. Not only do you get a chance to determine whether the audience understands key points before launching into another section, but the audience also gets a chance to switch for a time from listening to participating. Visual aids are another source of both clarification and stimulation. Variety in your tone of voice and gestures will usually help too.

THE ENDING

The ending of a speech or presentation is almost as important as the beginning because audience attention peaks at this point. Plan to devote about 10 percent of the total time to the ending. Begin your conclusion by telling listeners that you are about to finish so that they'll make one final effort to listen intently. Don't be afraid to sound obvious. Say something like "In conclusion" or "To sum it all up." You want people to know that this is the home stretch.

Restating the main points

Summarize the main idea, and restate the main points.

Once you have everyone's attention, repeat your main idea. Be sure to emphasize what you want the audience to do or think. Then state the key motivating factor. Reinforce your theme by repeating the three or four main supporting points. A few sentences are generally enough to refresh people's memories. For example, here's how one speaker ended a presentation on the company's executive compensation program:

> We can all be proud of the way our company has grown. But if we want to continue that growth, we will have to adjust our executive compensation program to reflect competitive practices. If we don't, our best people will look for opportunities elsewhere.
>
> In summary, our survey has shown that we need to do four things to improve executive compensation:
> * Increase the overall level of compensation
> * Install a cash bonus program
> * Offer a variety of stock-based incentives
> * Improve our health insurance and pension benefits
>
> By making these improvements, we can help our company cross the threshold of growth into the major leagues.

Notice how the speaker repeats his recommendations and then concludes with a memorable statement that motivates the audience to take action.

Outlining the next steps

Some speeches and presentations require the audience to reach a decision or to take specific action. In those cases, the final summary must provide a clear wrap-up. If the audience has reached agreement on an issue handled in the speech or presentation, review the consensus in a sentence or two. If not, make the lack of consensus clear by saying something like "We seem to have some fundamental disagreement on this question." You can go on to suggest a method of resolving the differences.

Be certain that everyone agrees on the outcome and understands what should happen next.

If you expect any action to occur, you must explain who is responsible for doing what. One effective technique is to list the action items, with an estimated completion date and the name of the person responsible. This list should be presented in a visual aid that can be seen by the entire audience. Each person on the list should be asked to agree to accomplish his or her assigned task by the target date. This public commitment to action is the best insurance that something will happen.

If the required action is likely to be difficult, make sure everyone understands the problems involved. You don't want people to leave the presentation thinking "This will be easy as pie" only to discover later that the job is a major undertaking. If that happens, they are likely to become discouraged and fail to complete their assignments. You want everyone to have a realistic attitude and be prepared to handle whatever arises. So use the final summary to point up pitfalls; alert people to potential difficulties.

Ending on a positive note

Your final remarks should be enthusiastic and memorable. Even if parts of your speech or presentation have been downbeat, you should try to close on a

The end of your speech should leave a strong and lasting impression.

positive note. For example, you might point up the benefits of action or express confidence in your listeners' ability to accomplish the work ahead. An alternative is to end with a question or with a statement that will leave your audience thinking.

Remember that your final words should round out the presentation. You want to leave the audience with a satisfied feeling, a feeling of completeness. The final summary is not the place to introduce new ideas or to alter the mood of the presentation. Moreover, although you want to close on a positive note, avoid a staged finale. Keep it natural.

THE QUESTION-AND-ANSWER PERIOD

In addition to having an introduction, a body, and a final summary, your speech or presentation should include an opportunity for questions and answers. Otherwise, you might just as well write a report. If you don't plan to interact with the audience, you waste the chief advantage of an oral format.

Encourage questions throughout if you are addressing a small group, but ask a large audience to defer questions until later.

Although you should generally interact with the audience, think carefully about the nature and timing of that interaction. Responding to questions and comments during the presentation interrupts the flow of your argument and reduces your control of the situation. If you are addressing a large group, particularly a hostile or unknown group, questions can be dangerous. Your best bet in this case is to ask people to hold their questions until after you have concluded your remarks. But if you are working with a small group and need to draw out ideas, you should encourage comments from the audience throughout the presentation. Regardless of when you respond to questions, remember that they are one of the most important parts of your presentation. Questions give you a chance to obtain important information, to emphasize your main idea and supporting points, and to build enthusiasm for your point of view.

THE VISUAL AIDS

Visual aids help both the speaker and the audience remember the important points.

Most formal speeches and presentations incorporate visual aids. Whether soliciting funds or outlining a company's strategy, Brady Keys uses visual aids to clarify his ideas. From a purely practical standpoint, visual aids are a convenience for the speaker, who can use them as a tool for remembering the details of the message (no small feat in an hour-long presentation); novice speakers also like visual aids because they draw audience attention away from the speaker. More important, however, visual aids dramatically increase the audience's ability to absorb and remember information.

Designing and presenting visual aids

Two kinds of visual aids:
- Text visuals help listeners follow the flow of ideas.
- Graphic visuals present and emphasize important facts.

Two types of visual aids are used to supplement speeches and presentations. Text visuals consist of words and help the audience follow the flow of ideas. As simplified outlines of your presentation, you can use them to preview and summarize the message and to notify the audience of major shifts in thought. On the other hand, graphic visual aids illustrate the main points. They help the audience grasp numerical data and other types of information that would be hard to follow if presented orally. When designing either type of visual aid, keep in mind that simplicity is the key to effectiveness. Because people cannot read and listen at the same time, the visual aids must be simple enough for the audience to understand them within a moment or two.

Text visuals should consist of no more than six lines, with a maximum of six words per line. They should be typed in large, clear type, using uppercase and lowercase letters, with extra white space between lines of type. Items in list format should be phrased in parallel grammatical form. The wording should be telegraphic ("Compensation Generous," for example) without being cryptic ("Compensation"); you are often better off including both a noun and a verb in each phrase.

Graphic visuals include line, pie, and bar charts, as well as flow charts, organization charts, diagrams, maps, drawings, and tables. Graphic visuals used in oral presentations should be simplified versions of those that appear in written documents. Eliminate anything that is not absolutely essential to the message. To help the audience focus immediately on the point of each graphic visual, use headings that state the message in one clear phrase: "Earnings have increased by 15 percent."

When you present visual aids, you want to give people a chance to read what's there, but you also want them to listen to your explanation. Here are a few tips for handling visual aids effectively:

Visual aids are counterproductive if the audience can't clearly see or understand them within a few moments.

- Be sure that all members of the audience can see the visual aids.

- Allow the audience time to read a visual aid before you begin your explanation.

- Limit each visual aid to one idea.

- Illustrate only the main points, not the entire presentation.

- Do not use any visual aids that conflict with your verbal message.

- Do not read the text of a visual aid word for word; paraphrase it instead.

- When you have finished discussing the point illustrated by the visual aid, remove it from the audience's view.[5]

The visual aids are there to supplement your words—not the other way around.

Selecting the right medium

Visual aids may be presented in a variety of media.

Visual aids for documents are usually limited to paper. But for speeches and presentations, you have a variety of media to choose from:

- *Handouts.* Even in a presentation, you may choose to distribute sheets of paper bearing an agenda, an outline of the program, an abstract, a written report, or such supplementary material as tables, charts, and graphs. Handouts work especially well in informal situations where the audience takes an active role. However, handouts can be distracting because people are inclined to read the material rather than listen to you, so many experienced speakers distribute handouts after completing the presentation.

- *Chalkboards and whiteboards.* When you're addressing a small group of people and want to draw out their ideas, use a board to list points as they are mentioned. Boards provide flexibility, but they are too informal for some situations.

- *Flip charts.* Large sheets of paper attached at the top like a tablet can be propped on an easel; you flip the pages as you speak. Each chart illustrates or clarifies a point. You might have a few lines from your outline on one, a graph or diagram on another, and so on. By using felt-tip markers in various colors, you can highlight ideas as you go along. Flip charts are most effective when you keep them simple. As a general rule, limit each sheet to three or four graphed lines or five or six points written in list format.

- *Overheads.* One of the most common visual aids in business is the overhead transparency, which can be projected on a screen in full daylight. Because you don't have to dim the lights, you don't lose eye contact with the audience.

- *Slides.* The content of slides may be text, graphics, or pictures. If you are trying to create a polished, professional atmosphere, you might find this approach worthwhile, particularly if you will be addressing a crowd and don't mind speaking in a darkened room. However, remember that you may need someone to operate the projector, and that person will need to coordinate the slides with your speech. Check in advance to be sure the equipment works, and practice beforehand with the operator.

- *Other visual aids.* In technical or scientific presentations, a sample of a product or material allows the audience to experience your subject directly. Models built to scale are convenient representations of an object. Audiotapes are often used to supplement a slide show or to present a precisely worded and timed message. Filmstrips and movies are effective for capturing the audience's attention with color and movement. Television and videotapes are good for showing demonstrations, interviews, and other events. However, audiotapes, filmstrips, movies, television, and videotapes require rather elaborate production and presentation equipment.

> Use visual aids to highlight, not just substitute for, the spoken word.

With all visual aids, the crucial factor is how you use them. They should not just substitute for the spoken word but should also save time, create interest, add variety, make an impression, and illustrate things that are difficult to explain in words alone. Let your visual aids highlight your presentation and call attention to points of interest.

MASTERING THE ART OF DELIVERY

> Although some people memorize or read their speeches or presentations, using notes is generally the best way to handle delivery.

When you've planned all the parts of your presentation and have your visual aids in hand, you're ready to begin practicing your delivery. You have a variety of delivery methods to choose from, some easier to handle than others:

- *Memorizing.* Unless you're a trained actor, avoid memorizing an entire speech, particularly a long one. You're likely to forget your lines and botch the whole thing. Furthermore, a memorized speech often sounds stiff and stilted. On the other hand, memorizing a quotation, an opening paragraph, or a few concluding remarks often strengthens your delivery.

- *Reading.* If you're delivering a technical or complex presentation, you may want to read it. Policy statements by highly placed government officials are generally read because the wording is usually critical. If you choose to read your speech, practice enough so that you can still maintain eye contact with the audience. Triple-spaced copy, wide margins,

BEHIND THE SCENES WITH CHARLES OSGOOD
Speaking Out on Public Speaking

As CBS news correspondent, anchor of *CBS Sunday Night News*, and writer and anchor of *Newsbreak* and *The Osgood File* on CBS radio, Charles Osgood is in demand as a public speaker. Also noted for his light verse, he travels throughout the country to address clubs, conferences, and professional organizations. He is well qualified, then, to advise you on relating to your audience.

Here's How It Is with Audiences

> Speakers sometimes overlook the Golden Rule, I
> fear.
> They go ahead and give a speech that they would
> hate to hear.

Like them, and they'll like you. Help them, and they'll help you. Enjoy yourself, and they'll enjoy themselves. Be relaxed, and they'll be relaxed. Lead . . . they'll follow.

Fear

> The audience won't throw things, you will find
> with any luck.
> But if they do, do not despair, just be prepared to
> duck.

Your principal enemy is blind, unreasoning fear. You know that the audience is not going to stone you to death, yet your "fight or flight" instincts are triggered. The adrenaline is pumping. Your mental attitude is that of being attacked by a lion. The last thing you're able to do under these circumstances is relax and speak comfortably to your audience. To put your audience at ease, you have to radiate confidence.

Be Prepared

You don't have to spend weeks preparing. But don't think you can just get up and dazzle everybody by making something up as you go along. Don't confuse worry with preparation. Just because you have been thinking about your speech for a long time and dreading it does not mean that you've been getting ready for it. The more prepared you are, the less worried and the more effective you'll be. Knowing you're going to be effective, you won't worry.

What Are You Going to Say?

> If you know there's a lot you've been wanting to say,
> and forgive me for being a nag,
> All that wisdom and wit but you still cannot fit
> fifty pounds in a twenty-pound bag.

and large type help too. You might even want to include "stage cues" for yourself, such as *pause, raise hands, lower voice.*

- *Speaking from notes.* Making a presentation with the help of an outline, note cards, or visual aids is probably the most effective and easiest delivery mode. It gives you something to refer to and still allows for eye contact and interaction with the audience. If your listeners look puzzled, for example, you can expand on a point or put it another way.

- *Impromptu speaking.* When you're asked to speak without any advance warning, your talk will be impromptu. For example, in a meeting you might be asked to give your opinion as the "resident expert" on something. In these situations, take a moment or two to think through what you're going to say. Then avoid the temptation to ramble.

Regardless of which delivery mode you use, be sure that you are thoroughly familiar with the subject. Your self-confidence will add a great deal to any speech or presentation.

Your audience will come away from your speech with some impression of you and one or two of the main points you'll be talking about. One or two. Not ten. Not twenty. You must decide what those one or two ideas are going to be. Covering too much ground is not going to work. What do you want the audience to feel or to think as a result of hearing you? Concentrate on those things. Forget about everything else. Use only those jokes, anecdotes, and so on that help you set up and make those points. If you cannot express in a sentence or two what it is you intend to get across, your speech is not focused well enough.

Don't Read; Try to Sound Spontaneous

Listening to someone read a prepared text is about as exciting as attending a congressional hearing on interstate commerce. Do not read your statement. Make it. If you're speaking to an audience, speak to them. If you're giving a talk, then talk!

The 12-Minute Secret

The standard length of a vaudeville act was 12 minutes. It was believed that no act, other than the headliner, could sustain interest for longer than that. Consider, then: If all those troupers singing and dancing their hearts out, if all those jugglers and magicians, if all those trained dogs and ponies couldn't go on for more than twelve minutes without boring the customers, what makes you think you can?

The Key to Success

The audience is just like you and me, for goodness' sake.
So relax and be yourself, and give the audience a break.

Be Real

You will probably not get away with trying to be what you are not. The situation magnifies you. If you are being phony, the audience will spot it a mile away. If you don't think a story is funny, the audience won't laugh at it. If you aren't moved by your information, the audience won't be moved either.

APPLY YOUR KNOWLEDGE

1. Select a speech, lecture, or talk you have recently heard that left you disappointed or confused. Make a list of things the speaker did to contribute to your negative reaction. Below each item you list, comment on what you would have done differently to produce a more positive reaction from an audience.

2. Your regional sales manager stops in your office to tell you there will be a staff meeting in one hour to preview your unit's sales results for the quarter. You are the sales representative in charge of new lines, and you are asked to comment on how the new cookies stuffed with pudding are performing. Using Charles Osgood's recommendations as a guide, how would you prepare for the meeting? List ways in which you might involve participants at the meeting to maximize their retention of your material (remember, you have only an hour to prepare).

PREPARING FOR SUCCESSFUL SPEAKING

Before you speak
- Practice
- Prepare the location

Another good way to build self-confidence is to practice, especially if you have not had much experience in public speaking. You may deliver the speech or presentation to nobody but your image in a mirror, but try to visualize a room filled with listeners. Put your talk on tape to check the sound of your voice and your timing, phrasing, and emphasis. If possible, rehearse on videotape to see yourself as your audience will. Go over your visual aids and coordinate them with the talk.

If possible, check the location for your presentation in advance. Know beforehand what the seating arrangements will be, and make sure they are appropriate to your needs. For example, if you want the audience to sit at tables, be sure tables are available. Check the room for outlets that may be needed for your projector or microphone. Locate the light switches and dimmers. If you need a flip-chart easel or a chalkboard, be sure it is on hand. Check for chalk, erasers, extension cords, and any other small but crucial items you might need.

A. Barry Rand is president of the U.S. Marketing Group of the Xerox Corporation. Known as a persuasive and gifted speaker, Rand uses his talents to inspire employees and colleagues. The more familiar you are with your subject, the better, says Rand. Not only will you feel more comfortable during your speech, but your ease will come across as self-confidence.

DELIVERING THE SPEECH

When it's time to deliver the speech, you may feel a bit of stage fright. Most people do, even professional actors. You can overcome your fears, however, by taking a few tips from the professionals:

- Prepare more material than necessary. Extra knowledge, combined with a genuine interest in the topic, will boost your confidence.

- Think positively about your audience, yourself, and what you have to say. See yourself as polished and professional, and your audience will too.

- Be realistic about stage fright. After all, even experienced speakers admit that they feel butterflies before they address an audience. A little nervous excitement can actually provide the extra lift that will make your presentation sparkle.

- Use the few minutes while you are arranging your materials, before you actually begin speaking, to tell yourself you're on and you're ready.

- Before you begin speaking, take a few deep breaths.

- Have your first sentence memorized and on the tip of your tongue.

- If your throat is dry, drink some water.

- If you feel that you are losing your audience during the speech, don't panic. Try to pull them back by involving them in the action.

- Use your visual aids to maintain and revive audience interest.

- Keep going. Things usually get better, and your audience will silently be wishing you success.

Although common, the fear of speaking can be overcome.

Perhaps the best way to overcome stage fright is to concentrate on your message and your audience, not on yourself. When you're busy thinking about your subject and observing the audience's response, you tend to forget your fears. However, as you deliver your presentation, do try to be aware of the nonverbal signals you are transmitting. To a great degree, your effectiveness will depend on how you look and sound. As you approach the speaker's podium, breathe deeply, stand up straight, and walk slowly. Face the audience. Adjust the microphone. Count to three slowly, then survey the room. When you find a friendly face, make eye contact and smile. Count to three again; then begin your presentation.[6] Even if you feel nervous inside, this slow, controlled beginning will help you establish rapport.

Don't rush the opening.

Once your speech is under way, be particularly careful to maintain eye contact with the audience. Pick out several people positioned around the room, and shift your gaze from one to another. Doing this will make you appear to be sincere, confident, and trustworthy, and it will also help you become attuned to the impression you are creating.

Use eye contact, posture, gestures, and voice to convey an aura of mastery and to keep your audience's attention.

Your posture is also important in projecting the right image. Stand tall, with your weight on both feet and your shoulders back. Avoid gripping the podium. Use your hands to emphasize your remarks with appropriate gestures. At the same time, vary your facial expressions to make the message more dynamic.

Also think about the sound of your voice. You should speak in a normal, conversational tone but with enough volume so that everyone in the audience can hear you. Try to sound poised and confident, varying your pitch and speaking rate to add emphasis. Don't ramble or use meaningless filler words such as *um, you know, okay,* and *like.* Speak clearly and crisply, articulating all the syllables and sounds. Try to sound enthusiastic.

HANDLING QUESTIONS

The key to handling this segment effectively is preparation. Before your speech, spend some time thinking about the questions that might arise. Be ready with answers. In fact, some experts recommend that you hold back some dramatic statistics as ammunition for the question-and-answer session.[7]

When someone poses a question, focus your attention on that individual. Pay attention to body language and facial expression to help determine what the person really means. Nod your head to acknowledge the question; then repeat it aloud to confirm your understanding and to ensure that the entire audience has heard it. If the question is vague or confusing, ask for clarification. Then give a simple, direct answer. Don't say more than you need to; you want to have enough time to cover all the questions. If giving an adequate answer would take too long, simply say, "I'm sorry that we don't have time to get into that issue right now, but if you'll see me after the presentation, I'll be

Keep your answers short and sweet.

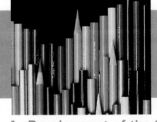

CHECKLIST FOR SPEECHES AND ORAL PRESENTATIONS

A. Development of the Speech or Presentation
- [ ] 1. Analyze the audience.
- [ ] 2. Begin with an attention-getter.
- [ ] 3. Preview the main points.
- [ ] 4. Limit the discussion to no more than three or four points.
- [ ] 5. Explain who, what, when, where, why, and how.
- [ ] 6. In longer presentations, include previews and summaries of major points as you go along.
- [ ] 7. Close by reviewing your main points and making a memorable statement.

B. Visual Aids
- [ ] 1. Use visual aids to show how things look, work, or relate to one another.
- [ ] 2. Use visual aids to highlight important information and create interest.
- [ ] 3. Select appropriate visual aids.
  - [ ] a. Use flip charts, boards, or transparencies for small, informal groups.
  - [ ] b. Use slides or films for major occasions and large groups.
- [ ] 4. Limit each visual aid to three or four graphed lines or five or six points.
- [ ] 5. Use short phrases.
- [ ] 6. Use large, readable type.
- [ ] 7. Make sure equipment works.

C. Delivery
- [ ] 1. Establish eye contact.
- [ ] 2. Speak clearly and distinctly.
- [ ] 3. Do not go too fast.
- [ ] 4. Be sure everyone can hear.
- [ ] 5. Speak in your natural style.
- [ ] 6. Stand up straight.
- [ ] 7. Use gestures in a natural, appropriate way.
- [ ] 8. Encourage questions.
  - [ ] a. Allow questions during the presentation if the group is small.
  - [ ] b. Ask the audience to hold their questions until the end if the group is large or hostile.
- [ ] 9. Respond to questions without getting sidetracked.
- [ ] 10. Maintain control of your feelings in spite of criticism.

happy to discuss it with you." If you don't know the answer, say something like "I don't have those figures. I'll get them for you as quickly as possible."

Don't let any member of the audience monopolize your attention.

Don't allow one or two people to monopolize the question period. Try to give everyone a chance to participate; call on people from various parts of the room. If the same person keeps angling for attention, say something like "Several other people have questions; I'll get back to you if time permits."

Respond unemotionally to tough questions.

Most of the people who ask questions will simply want clarification or additional information. Occasionally, however, you will encounter hostility. When that happens, keep cool. Look the person in the eye, answer the question as well as you can, and try not to show your feelings. Don't get into an argument. Simply state your response, and move on to the next question. Avoid postures or gestures that might seem antagonistic. Don't put your hands on your hips or point your finger in a scolding fashion. Maintain a businesslike tone of voice and a pleasant expression.[8]

When the time allotted for your presentation is up, call a halt to the question-and-answer session, even if more people want to talk. Prepare the audience for the end by saying, "Our time is almost up. Let's have one more question." After you've made your reply, summarize the main idea of the presentation and thank people for their attention. Conclude the way you opened: by looking around the room and making eye contact. Then gather your notes and leave the podium, shoulders straight, head up.

SUMMARY

At some point in your career, you are likely to be called on to give a speech or presentation. Brief speeches (5 to 15 minutes) are organized like letters and short memos. Formal presentations, lasting up to an hour or more, generally involve more complex subjects and require more interaction with the audience. They are organized like formal reports, with an introduction, a body, and a final summary.

Many long speeches and presentations make use of such visual aids as handouts, chalkboards, flip charts, overheads, and slides. These should be selected to suit your purpose and the size and needs of the audience.

Practice your presentation thoroughly in advance. As you address the audience, use nonverbal communication skills to enhance your effectiveness. Be sure to make eye contact and to speak so that everyone can understand you. If you encounter difficult questions, remain unemotional. Respond as well as you can, and then move on.

ON THE JOB:
Solving a Communication Dilemma
at the Keys Group

Brady Keys charged into the fast-food game the same way he charged onto the gridiron—full speed ahead and ready to tackle whatever crossed his path. When he retired from professional football in the late 1960s, he decided to pursue his lifelong dream of owning his own business. When he noticed how well a friend's restaurant was doing, he turned to fried chicken as his business.

His first hurdle was raising enough money to launch the restaurant. Ten banks said "No thanks," but he finally persuaded his former team to loan him $10,000—enough to open his first All-Pro Fried Chicken store. Within three years, he'd presented himself and his ideas to banks and to the government, convincing them to loan him enough capital to open 35 more outlets in Pittsburgh, New York, and

Cleveland. By that time, he was selling a million dollar's worth of fried chicken a year.

He decided it was time to tackle something new—hamburger. He spoke to Burger King President James McLemore and sold him on the idea of giving Keys a shot at turning around a struggling Burger King franchise in Detroit's inner city. Realizing that something had to spark sales, "We introduced a couple of themes that are now universal in the industry," says Keys. "We found that black people didn't want the whopper fixed the usual way, so we made it to order." That concept eventually formed the basis for Burger King's successful "Have It Your Way," advertising campaign. Then as lines began to form for the new customized whopper, Keys stationed a hostess at the end of the lines to take orders and cut the waiting time—a practice that has become standard in many fast-food restaurants. These innovations ultimately transformed the struggling franchise into the top-selling Burger King outlet in the nation. And building on that success, Keys went on to acquire other Burger King outlets in Detroit, using his persuasive speaking powers to negotiate loans with banks and insurance companies.

As Keys points out, "You don't get acceptance by going in and saying 'accept me.' You get it by doing worthy activities." For example, Keys has used his position to help other blacks succeed in franchising: He founded both Burger King's and Kentucky Fried Chicken's Minority Franchise associations; he talked Burger King's management into awarding the construction contract for the company's first inner-city outlet to a black general contractor; and he convinced management to increase the number of minorities on Burger King's roster of franchisees, employees, and vendors.

Selling his All-Pro Fried Chicken stores, Keys became a Kentucky Fried Chicken franchisee. Most of his new outlets were in Albany, Georgia, where worthy activities became even more important. Gaining acceptance in the predominantly white community was more of a challenge than it had been in either Detroit or Pittsburgh. So, says Keys, "I became a philanthropist, I stressed my athletic background, and we brought in the Harlem Globetrotters as a benefit to the Special Olympics." He also served as chairman of the board of the Albany Civic Center Commission, and he is one of the largest individual contributors to the city's March of Dimes fund.

Keys's abilities to speak, to win friends, and to influence people help him deal with employees too. He believes in giving people a chance to live up to their potential. He promotes from within, and he rewards long-term employees with a piece of the ownership. In return, his employees are tremendously loyal, so his turnover is remarkably low—a fact that helps him keep his costs down and his service up. His restaurants actually serve as a "business school" for many young people who eventually move on to more challenging careers. His latest ad campaign features distinguished former "graduates" of the Brady Keys school of practical experience.

Keys's current projects include real estate development, a video game company, a mining and brokering business, and a movie production company. In the process of selling these ideas, he is using his speaking skills to present his ideas to potential investors, to build goodwill in the communities where he operates, and to motivate his employees.

Your Mission: As a member of the Keys Group's public relations department, you help Brady Keys plan some of the many speeches he delivers to company employees and to business, professional, and civic groups. Handle the following assignments to the *best* of your ability:

1. Keys has agreed to give a 20-minute talk in Albany, Georgia, to a group of approximately 35 businesspeople who meet for lunch and networking on a monthly basis. The president of the group has suggested that Keys deal with the topic of franchising. Which of the following purposes do you think he should try to accomplish?
   a. To inform the audience about the history of franchising in America
   b. To inspire members of the audience to buy a franchise
   c. To entertain the audience with stories about Keys's franchising experiences
   d. To analyze the impact of national franchises on small, independently owned local businesses

2. Keys has been invited to give a ten-minute speech during the graduation ceremonies at a predominantly black two-year vocational college in Detroit. Based on his own experience, he expects that many of the students will face daunting obstacles in their efforts to build their careers. He wants to inspire these students to establish a goal and keep on trying to achieve it, regardless of the problems that arise. He has asked you to give him some ideas for developing the speech. Which of the following main ideas would you recommend to him?
   a. Life is like a football game. If you want to win, you have to know where the end zone is and keep on trying to get there, even if the other team is bigger and tougher than your team.
   b. During the darkest days of World War II, Winston Churchill inspired the English people by telling them that England would "never, never, never, never give up." The English eventually won the war, and you can win too if you remember Churchill's advice.
   c. If you can communicate effectively with all types of people, you will eventually succeed in your career.
   d. Despite the difficulties that lie ahead, you can triumph over adversity, just like many other African-Americans who have overcome tough odds and achieved success. These individuals all shared one trait: perseverance.

3. Keys has asked you to help him plan a ten-minute speech that he can give to the employees of his Detroit Burger Kings during the annual summer picnic. He expects between 750 and 1,000 employees to attend the function, which will be held in a park. His topic is "the state of the company." His purpose is to inspire the employees to keep up the good work. His main idea is that the Keys Group is doing an excellent job in meeting the competition, thanks to the efforts of the workers. What general organizational scheme do you recommend for developing this idea?
   a. Chronological: Highlights of company performance over the past year and outlook for the future
   b. Geographical: Performance, problems, and opportunities in each of the 13 Detroit Burger Kings
   c. Topical: Achievements of various types of employees such as store managers, kitchen workers, order takers, maintenance workers, and so on
   d. Comparison and contrast: Burger King versus McDonald's, Wendy's, and other competitors

4. Keys is trying to persuade a group of investors to put some money into his new movie production company. He has prepared a presentation that describes the company's goals, activities, and financial prospects. He is currently wrestling with the introduction to the presentation. Which of the following introductions would you recommend?
   a. Years ago, when I bought my first Burger King Franchise, I knew I had to do something to attract business. So I said to myself, why not try some TV advertising? I was operating on a shoestring at the time, so I decided to write, produce, direct, and star in the commercial myself. If I'd had more money and more sense, I probably wouldn't have taken on the job, but lacking both money and experience, I was willing to try anything. Anyway, once I got started, I discovered that making commercials isn't really all that tricky. All you need is a little money, a little equipment, a little imagination, and a little luck. And Bingo! You're in business. I've made a lot of my own commercials since then, and I've thoroughly enjoyed the process.

   That's one of the reasons I decided to get into the movie business. I said to myself, "Brady, if you can have this much fun making commercials, imagine what a ball you can have making movies." But having fun is only one of my reasons for starting a movie production company. My principal motive is making money. And that's what I want to talk to you about today: how you can make money in the movie business.
   b. In the last ten years, the number of movie screens in the United States has increased by 50 percent, to nearly 25,000. Those screens are all designed to do one thing: show films. But the major studios, such as Warner, Columbia Pictures, and 20th Century Fox, cannot possibly provide enough films to support all the new theaters being built. As a consequence, a new breed of independent film maker is springing up, many of whom are far more profitable than their larger rivals.

   I'd like to talk to you today about how you can participate in this exciting business opportunity. I think you will be intrigued by the magnitude of the potential payoff and the relatively limited risk involved. I'll begin by giving you a little background on the revolution currently under way in the movie industry. Then I'll describe the film production company that I'm forming in partnership with actor Leon Issac Kennedy. After you've had a chance to learn about our strategy and plans, I'll brief you on the financial returns that you could expect on your investment in the business.
   c. When's the last time you went to the movies? And when did you last see a film on HBO or network TV? What about videocassettes? Have you rented any of them lately?

   If you're like most people, you're hooked on movies, whether you see them in theaters or on TV. Somebody is making all those movies, and it isn't necessarily Paramount or Universal Studios or Walt Disney. Many of the films you're seeing are created by independent companies.

   Starting an independent film production company requires relatively little capital, and the financial returns can be considerable. If you're careful, you can whip out a low-budget film and bring it to market for as little as $2 million. Even if you don't do too well at the box office, you can still clear maybe $3 or $4 million from the TV rights and videocassette sales. Multiply that by, say, ten movies per year, and you have a $30- to $40-million business.

5. In his role as chairman of the board of the Albany Civic Center Commission, Keys must give a speech outlining the center's financial position. The audience will include other board members, the mayor and members of the city council, and a group of 15 to 20 influential business and professional people. How should he handle the quantitative financial details?
   a. He should prepare handouts that summarize the financial data in tabular and graphic form. As the audience arrives, he should give everyone a copy of the handout and refer to it during his speech.
   b. Keys should write the information on a blackboard while he delivers the speech.

c. He should prepare simple overhead transparencies to use during the speech. As he concludes his remarks, he should tell the audience that detailed financial statements are available at the door for those who are interested.

d. Given the size and importance of the audience, he should show full-color 35-mm slides that summarize the financial information in tabular and graphic format. The slides should be professionally prepared to ensure their quality.

e. He should explain the financial information by using examples and analogies and a few well-chosen facts and figures.

6. Keys has agreed to deliver a speech at the annual convention of Burger King's Minority Franchise Association. His topic is "the promise and pitfalls of operating in the inner city." The audience will include approximately 250 people, who will be seated at dinner tables scattered around the room. Keys will deliver his remarks from an elevated platform at the front of the room. The speech is supposed to last about 20 minutes. Keys is trying to decide whether to set aside some of that time for questions and answers. How much audience participation do you think he should encourage? At what point during the speech—if any—should he invite comments and questions?

a. Keys should encourage plenty of audience participation. Since many of the members of the audience will have first-hand experience in running inner-city franchises, they can offer useful ideas on the subject. Keys should organize his remarks around three or four major points. After discussing each point for three or four minutes, he should allow another three or four minutes for comments and questions.

b. With such a large audience, Keys should discourage audience participation. If too many people ask questions or make comments, Keys might run over the amount of time allotted for his speech. Furthermore, given the subject of the speech, some of the questions might be hostile. By avoiding a question-and-answer period, Keys may avoid trouble.

c. Keys should encourage a modest amount of participation. At the end of his speech, he should allow five minutes or so for questions and comments from the floor.[9]

QUESTIONS FOR DISCUSSION

1. How do speeches and presentations compare with interviews and meetings?
2. What factors determine the style of a speech or presentation?
3. Why is it important to emphasize transitions in a speech or presentation? What are some of the techniques you can use to emphasize the transitions?
4. What are the advantages and disadvantages of responding to questions from the audience throughout a speech or presentation?
5. What are the benefits and dangers of using various types of visual aids?
6. What should you do when you encounter hostile questions?

EXERCISES

1. Prepare outlines or "scripts" for the following speaking situations:
   a. A 5-minute pep talk to 20 production workers straining to meet a deadline
   b. A 15-minute after-dinner speech on "Your Community in the Year 2000" to an audience of about 100 at the annual meeting of the local chamber of commerce
   c. A 10-minute informative presentation to a 15-member board of directors on the results of a search for a new executive director for a nonprofit organization
   d. A 30-minute sales presentation touting a new textbook to a 5-member teachers' committee
   e. An hour-long presentation to a 6-member group of top executives in which you and two colleagues (1) present the results of marketing studies on trends in the fast-food market and (2) facilitate an executive decision about which new opportunities to pursue
2. Choose a successful professional whom you know, and assume that this person will be speaking to a specific campus group (your choice too). Write a three-minute introduction that relates some of the speaker's accomplishments to the interests of the group. In other words, bring the speaker and the group together. Try to word your introduction as if you were actually speaking to the group.

3. Make a five-minute speech or presentation to your classmates on any business topic. When you finish, ask your audience to comment on your performance. If your instructor prefers, you might prepare evaluation forms for your audience to fill out anonymously.

4. Plan a ten-minute speech that Brady Keys could give to the graduating students at your college (see this chapter's On-the-Job simulation). Using the guidelines in the chapter, analyze the audience to the best of your ability. State the purpose, develop the main idea, and outline the main points. Write the introductory paragraph.[10]

PART SEVEN

SPECIAL TYPES OF BUSINESS COMMUNICATION

■CHAPTER SEVENTEEN

After studying this chapter, you will be able to

- Explain what is meant by *culture*
- Identify potential barriers to international communication
- Begin preparing yourself to do business with people from other cultures

INTERCULTURAL BUSINESS COMMUNICATION

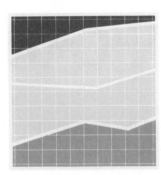

ON THE JOB:
Facing a Communication Dilemma at Procter & Gamble

Translating Pampers to Profits

When Edwin Artzt took over as president of Procter & Gamble's international division, it seemed as though the sun was setting on P&G profits in Japan. P&G entered the Japanese market in the 1970s with a shopping cart full of successful U.S. brands. However, within three years, the firm lost $250 million and still had not captured any significant market share. Determined to succeed, P&G introduced Pampers, Japan's first disposable diaper. Pampers quickly captured 10 percent of the diaper market, but when Japanese rivals brought out competing products, Pampers' popularity plummeted. How could so mighty a company stumble so badly?

Artzt examined the situation and found that P&G marketers had measured the size of the Japanese market but they hadn't really been able to understand the life-style or unique customs of the Japanese people. He realized that P&G faced more than a language barrier; the company also had to get to know its Japanese customers, make products to fit their needs, and then inform customers about the new products. All of this required effective communication.

If you were Artzt, how would you learn about the values and needs of Japanese customers? What messages would you send to persuade Japanese customers to try P&G products? How would you overcome the language barrier and the problems caused by earlier products that were not tailored to the Japanese market?[1]

BASICS OF INTERCULTURAL BUSINESS COMMUNICATION

Procter & Gamble

As Edwin Artzt knows, the first step in learning to communicate with people from other cultures is to become aware of what culture means. Your awareness of intercultural differences is both useful and necessary in today's world of business. For example, the opportunities for conducting business in Eastern Europe are suddenly promising—now that Polish communists are sharing power with the Solidarity movement, now that the Berlin wall has opened, and now that Lithuania and other Baltic states are clamoring for freedom.[2] But what can American businesses expect from these long-isolated regions? Will trading through the parting iron curtain differ from the trade that already exists in Western Europe, South America, or Japan? How does international trade differ from domestic trade with Americans who have a Vietnamese or Hispanic background?

UNDERSTANDING CULTURE

You may not realize it, but you belong to several cultures. The most obvious is the culture you share with all other people who live in this country. But you also belong to other cultural groups, such as an ethnic group, a religious group, a fraternity or sorority, or perhaps a profession that has its own special language and customs.

So what exactly is culture? It is useful to define *culture* as a system of shared symbols, beliefs, attitudes, values, expectations, and norms for behavior. Thus all members of a culture have, and tend to act on, similar assumptions about how people should think, behave, and communicate.

Distinct groups that exist within a major culture are more properly referred to as *subcultures*. Among groups that might be considered subcultures are Mexican Americans in East Los Angeles, Mormons in Salt Lake City, and longshoremen in Montreal. Subcultures without geographic boundaries can be found as well, such as wrestling fans, Russian immigrants, and Harvard M.B.A.s.

Cultures and subcultures vary in several ways that affect intercultural communication:

> Think of *culture* as a system of shared symbols, beliefs, attitudes, values, expectations, and norms for behavior.

- *Stability.* Conditions in the culture may be stable or may be changing slowly or rapidly.

- *Complexity.* Cultures vary in the accessibility of information. In North America information is contained in explicit codes, including words, whereas in Japan a great deal of information is conveyed implicitly, through body language, physical context, and the like.

- *Composition.* Some cultures are made up of many diverse and disparate subcultures; others tend to be more homogeneous.

- *Acceptance.* Cultures vary in their attitudes toward outsiders. Some are openly hostile or maintain a detached aloofness. Others are friendly and cooperative toward strangers.

As you can see, cultures vary widely. It's no wonder that most of us need special training before we can become comfortable with a culture other than our own.

DEVELOPING INTERCULTURAL COMMUNICATION SKILLS

When faced with the need (or desire) to learn about another culture, you have two main approaches to choose from. One is to learn as much as possible—the language, cultural background and history, social rules, and so on—about the specific culture that you expect to deal with. The other is to develop general skills that will help you adapt in any culture.

The first approach, in-depth knowledge of a particular culture, certainly works. But there are two drawbacks. One is that you will never be able to understand another culture completely. No matter how much you study German culture, for example, you will never be a German or share the experiences of having grown up in Germany. Even if you could understand the culture completely, Germans might resent your assumption that you know everything there is to know about them. The other drawback to immersing yourself in a specific culture is the trap of overgeneralization, looking at people from a culture not as individuals with their own unique characteristics, but as instances of Germans or Japanese or black Americans. The trick is to learn useful general information but to be open to variations and individual differences.

The second approach to cultural learning, general development of intercultural skills, is especially useful if you interact with people from a variety of cultures or subcultures. Among the skills you need to learn are the following:

- *Taking responsibility for communication.* Don't assume that it is the other person's job to communicate with you.

- *Withholding judgment.* Learn to listen to the whole story and to accept differences in others.

- *Showing respect.* Learn the ways in which respect is communicated—through gestures, eye contact, and so on—in various cultures.

- *Empathizing.* Try to put yourself in the other person's shoes. Listen carefully to what the other person is trying to communicate; imagine the person's feelings and point of view.

- *Tolerating ambiguity.* Learn to control your frustration when placed in an unfamiliar or confusing situation.

- *Looking beyond the superficial.* Don't be distracted by such things as dress, appearance, or environmental discomforts.

- *Being patient and persistent.* If you want to accomplish a task, don't give up easily.

- *Recognizing your own cultural biases.* Learn to identify when your assumptions are different from the other person's.

- *Being flexible.* Be prepared to change your habits, preferences, and attitudes.

- *Emphasizing common ground.* Look for similarities to work from.

- *Sending clear messages.* Make your verbal and nonverbal messages consistent.

- *Taking risks.* Try things that will help you gain a better understanding of the other person or culture.

Ford Motor Company chairman Harold Pohling says his experience leading a multinational corporation has taught him that intercultural communication helps all parties by bringing forward the best ideas, regardless of their country of origin. Whether you are learning about a specific culture or developing general skills, advises Pohling, remember to keep an open mind.

- *Increasing your cultural sensitivity.* Learn about variations in customs and practices so that you will be more aware of potential areas for miscommunication or misunderstanding.

- *Dealing with the individual.* Avoid stereotyping and overgeneralization.

These are skills that will help you communicate with anybody, whether someone from your own culture or from another.

DIFFICULTIES OF INTERCULTURAL BUSINESS COMMUNICATION

The more differences there are between the people who are communicating, the more difficult it is to communicate effectively. The major problems in intercultural business communication are language barriers, cultural differences, and ethnocentric reactions.

LANGUAGE BARRIERS

If you're doing business in London, you obviously won't have much of a language problem. You may encounter a few unusual terms or accents in the 29 countries in which English is an official language, but your problems will be relatively minor. Language barriers will also be relatively minor when you are dealing with people who use English as a second language (and some 650 million people fall into this category). Some of these millions are extremely fluent; others have only an elementary command of English. Although you may miss a few subtleties in dealing with those who are less fluent in English, you will still be able to communicate. The pitfall to watch for is assuming that the other person understands everything you say, even slang, local idioms, and accents. One group of English-speaking Japanese who moved to the United States as employees of Toyota had to enroll in a special course to learn that "Jeat yet?" means "Did you eat yet?" and that "Cannahepya?" means "Can I help you?"

> When dealing with someone who is less fluent in English, don't assume he or she understands everything you say.

The real problem with language arises when you are dealing with people who speak virtually no English. In situations like this, you have very few options: You can learn their language, you can use an intermediary or a translator, or you can teach them your language. Becoming fluent in a new language (which you must do to conduct business in that language) is time consuming. The U.S. State Department, for example, gives its Foreign Service officers a six-month language training program and expects them to continue their language education at their foreign posts. Even the Berlitz method, which is famous for the speed of its results, requires a month of intensive effort—13 hours a day, 5 days a week. It is estimated that minimum proficiency in another language requires at least 240 hours of study over 8 weeks; more complex languages, such as Arabic and Chinese, require more than 480 hours. Language courses can be quite expensive as well. Unless you are planning to spend several years abroad or to make frequent trips over an extended period, learning another language may take more time, effort, and money than you're able to spend.

A more practical approach may be to use an intermediary or a translator. For example, if your company has a foreign subsidiary, you can delegate the communication job to local nationals who are bilingual. Or you can hire bilingual advertising consultants, distributors, lobbyists, lawyers, translators, and other professionals to help you. P&G's Edwin Artzt knows the importance of overcoming language barriers, and P&G uses professional translators to clarify both oral and written messages.

The option of teaching other people to speak your language doesn't appear to be very practical at first glance; however, many multinational companies do, in fact, have language training programs for their foreign employees. Tenneco, for example, instituted an English-language training program for its Spanish-speaking employees in a New Jersey plant. The classes concentrated on practical English for use on the job. According to the company, these classes were a success: Accidents and grievances declined, and productivity improved.[3]

In general, the magnitude of the language barrier depends on whether you are writing or speaking. Written communication is generally easier to handle.

Barriers to written communication

One survey of 100 companies engaged in international business revealed that between 95 and 99 percent of their business letters to other countries are written in English. Moreover, 59 percent of the respondents reported that the foreign letters they receive are usually written in English, although they also receive letters written in Spanish and French. Other languages are rare in international business correspondence.[4]

Because many international business letters are written in English, North American firms do not always have to worry about translating their correspondence. However, even when both parties write in English, minor interpretation problems do exist because of different usage of technical terms. These problems do not usually pose a major barrier to communication, especially if correspondence between the two parties continues and each gradually learns the terminology of the other.

More significant problems arise in other forms of written communication that require translation. Advertisements, for example, are almost always translated into the language of the country in which the products are being sold. Documents such as warranties, repair and maintenance manuals, and product labels also require translation. In addition, some multinational companies must translate policy and procedure manuals and benefit plans for use in overseas offices. Reports from foreign subsidiaries to the home office may also be written in one language and then translated into another.

Sometimes the translations aren't very good. For example, the well-known slogan "Come alive with Pepsi" was translated literally for Asian markets as "Pepsi brings your ancestors back from the grave," with unfortunate results. Part of the message is almost inevitably lost during any translation process, sometimes with major consequences.

Barriers to oral communication

Oral communication usually presents more problems than written communication. If you have ever studied a foreign language, you know from personal experience that it's easier to write in a foreign language than to conduct a conversation. Even if the other person is speaking English, you're likely to have a hard time understanding the pronunciation if the person is not proficient in English. For example, many foreigners notice no difference between the English sounds *v* and *w*; they say *wery* for *very*. At the same time, many

---

Margin notes:

Foreign letters are usually written in English, Spanish, or French.

Make sure that the translations you use are good ones and that they say what you want them to.

Barriers to oral communication include
- Pronunciation
- Tone of voice
- Idiomatic expressions

As vice president of human resources at Scott Paper Company, Barbara A. Rice is heading the attempt to develop managers who can maintain their balance in the global market. For intercultural exchanges, says Rice, open yourself up to a broader view. You must know more than just your market. You need to know something about the culture you're dealing with.

people from North America cannot pronounce some of the sounds that are frequently used in other parts of the world.

In addition to pronouncing sounds differently, people use their voices in different ways, a fact that often leads to misunderstanding. The Russians, for example, speak in flat, level tones in their native tongue. When they speak English, they maintain this pattern, and Westerners may assume that they are bored or rude. Middle Easterners tend to speak more loudly than Westerners and may therefore mistakenly be considered more emotional. On the other hand, the Japanese are soft-spoken, a characteristic that implies politeness or humility to Westerners.

Idiomatic expressions are another source of confusion. If you tell a foreigner that a certain product "doesn't cut the mustard," chances are that you will fail to communicate. Even when the words make sense, their meanings may differ according to the situation. For example, suppose that you are dining with a German woman who speaks English quite well. You inquire, "More bread?" She says, "Thank you," so you pass the bread. She looks confused, then takes the breadbasket and sets it down without taking any. In German, *thank you* (*danke*) can also be used as a polite refusal. If the woman had wanted more bread, she would have used the word *please* (*bitte* in German).

When speaking in English to those for whom English is a second language, follow these simple guidelines:

- *Try to eliminate "noise."* Pronounce words clearly, and stop at distinct punctuation points. Make one point at a time.

- *Look for feedback.* Be alert to glazed eyes or signs of confusion in your listener. Realize that nods and smiles do not necessarily mean understanding. Don't be afraid to ask, "Is that clear?" and be sure to check the listener's comprehension through specific questions. Encourage the listener to ask questions.

- *Rephrase your sentence when necessary.* If someone doesn't seem to understand what you have said, choose simpler words; don't just repeat the sentence in a louder voice.

- *Don't talk down to the other person.* Americans tend to overenunciate and to "blame" the listener for lack of comprehension. It is preferable to use phrases such as "Am I going too fast?" rather than "Is this too difficult for you?"

- *Use objective, accurate language.* Americans tend to throw around adjectives such as *fantastic* and *fabulous*, which foreigners consider unreal and overly dramatic. Calling something a "disaster" will give rise to images of war and death; calling someone an "idiot" or a "prince" may be taken literally.

- *Let other people finish what they have to say.* If you interrupt, you may miss something important. And you'll show a lack of respect.

CULTURAL DIFFERENCES

Misunderstandings occur more often among people of different backgrounds.

As you know, misunderstandings are especially likely to occur when the people who are communicating have different backgrounds. Party A encodes a message in one context, using assumptions common to people in his or her culture;

Party B decodes the message using a different set of assumptions. The result is confusion and, often, hard feelings. For example, take the case of the computer sales representative who was calling on a client in China. Hoping to make a good impression, the salesperson brought along a gift to break the ice, an expensive grandfather clock. Unfortunately, the Chinese client was deeply offended because, in China, giving clocks as gifts is considered bad luck for the recipient.[5]

Such problems arise because of our unconscious assumptions and nonverbal communication patterns. We ignore the fact that people from other cultures differ from us in many ways: in their religion and values, their ideas of status, their decision-making habits, their attitude toward time, their use of space, their body language, and their manners. We assume, wrongly, that other people are like us. P&G learned this lesson in Japan and now spends a great deal of time focusing on its Japanese customers' cultural preferences.

Religion and values

Although North America is a melting pot of people with different religions and values, the predominant influence in our culture is the Puritan ethic: If you work hard and achieve success, you will find favor in the eyes of God. We tend to assume that material comfort is a sign of superiority, that the rich are a little bit better than the poor, that people who work hard are better than those who don't. We believe that money solves many problems. We assume that people from other cultures share our view, that they dislike poverty and value hard work. In fact, many societies condemn materialism and prize a carefree lifestyle.

Do not assume that other cultures value material comfort or efficiency in achieving goals.

As a culture, we are goal-oriented. We want to get the work done in the most efficient manner, and we assume that everyone else does too. We think we are improving things if we can figure out a way for two people using modern methods to do the same work as four people using the "old way." But in countries like India and Pakistan, where unemployment is extremely high, creating jobs is more important than getting the work done efficiently. Executives in these countries would rather employ four workers than two.

Roles and status

Culture dictates the roles people play, including who communicates with whom, what they communicate, and in what way. In many countries, for example, women still do not play a very prominent role in business. As a result, female executives from American firms may find themselves sent off to eat in a separate room with the wives of Arab businessmen, while the men all eat dinner together.

People have various ways of establishing their credibility.

Concepts of status also differ, and as a consequence, people establish their credibility in different ways. North Americans, for example, send status signals that reflect materialistic values. The big boss has the corner office on the top floor, deep carpets, an expensive desk, and handsome accessories. The most successful companies are located in the most prestigious buildings. In other countries, status is communicated in other ways. For example, the highest-ranking executives in France sit in the middle of an open area, surrounded by lower-level employees. In the Middle East, fine possessions are reserved for the home, and business is conducted in cramped and modest quarters. An American executive who assumes that these office arrangements indicate a lack of status is making a big mistake.

Decision-making customs

In North America, we try to reach decisions as quickly and efficiently as possible. The top people focus on reaching agreement on the main points and leave the details to be worked out later by others. In Greece, this approach would backfire. A Greek executive assumes that anyone who ignores the details is being evasive and untrustworthy. Spending time on every little point is considered a mark of good faith. Similarly, Latin Americans prefer to make their deals slowly, after a lengthy period of discussion. They resist an authoritarian "Here's the deal, take it or leave it" approach, preferring the more sociable method of an extended discussion.

Cultures also differ in terms of who makes the decisions. In our culture, many organizations are dominated by a single figure who says yes or no to every deal. It is the same in Pakistan, where you can get a decision quickly if you reach the highest-ranking executive.[6] In other cultures, notably China and Japan, decision making is a shared responsibility. No individual has the authority to commit the organization without first consulting others. In Japan, for example, the negotiating team arrives at a consensus through an elaborate, time-consuming process (agreement must be complete—there is no majority rule). If the process is not laborious enough, the Japanese feel uncomfortable.[7]

Barbara S. Thomas is senior vice president of international private banking for Bankers Trust Company, where she is noted for making you feel like the most important person in the world, whether you're a customer or an employee. When dealing with international customers, you can't be rigid, says Thomas. You must be aware of potential misunderstandings.

Concepts of time

Differing perceptions of time are another factor that can lead to misunderstandings. An executive from North America or Germany attaches one meaning to time; an executive from Latin America, Ethiopia, or Japan attaches another. Let's say that a salesperson from Chicago calls on a client in Mexico City. After spending 30 minutes in the outer office, the person from Chicago feels angry and insulted, assuming, "This client must attach a very low priority to my visit to keep me waiting half an hour." In fact, the Mexican client does not mean to imply anything at all by this delay. To the Mexican, a wait of 30 minutes is a matter of course.

Or let's say that a New Yorker is trying to negotiate a deal in Ethiopia. This is an important deal, and the New Yorker assumes that the Ethiopians will give the matter top priority and reach a decision quickly. Not so. In Ethiopia, important deals take a long, long time. After all, if a deal is important, it should be given much careful thought, shouldn't it?

The Japanese, knowing that North Americans are impatient, use time to their advantage when negotiating with us. One of them expressed it this way: "You Americans have one terrible weakness. If we make you wait long enough, you will agree to anything."[8]

Concepts of personal space

The classic story of a conversation between a North American and a Latin American is that the interaction may begin at one end of a hallway but end up at the other, with neither party aware of having moved. During the interaction, the Latin American instinctively moves closer to the North American, who in turn instinctively steps back, resulting in an intercultural dance across the floor. Like time, space means different things in different cultures. North Americans stand about five feet apart when conducting a business conversation. To an Arab or a Latin American, this distance is uncomfortable. In meetings with North Americans, they move a little closer. We assume they are pushy and react negatively, although we don't know exactly why.

Body language

Gestures help us clarify confusing messages, so differences in body language are a major source of misunderstanding. We may also make the mistake of assuming that a non-American who speaks English has mastered the body language of our culture as well. It therefore pays to learn some basic differences in the ways people supplement their words with body movement. Take the signal for no. We North Americans shake our heads back and forth; the Japanese move their right hands; Sicilians raise their chins. Or take eye contact. North Americans read each other through eye contact. We may assume that a person who won't meet our gaze is evasive and dishonest. But in many parts of Latin America, keeping your eyes lowered is a sign of respect. It's also a sign of respect among many black Americans, which some schoolteachers have failed to learn. When they scold their black students, saying "Look at me when I'm talking to you," they only create confusion for the children.

Sometimes people from different cultures misread an intentional signal, and sometimes they overlook the signal entirely or assume that a meaningless

> Do not assume that non-Americans who speak English have mastered North American body language.

BEHIND THE SCENES AT PARKER PEN

Do as the Natives Do, But Should You Eat the Roast Gorilla Hand?

If offered, you should eat the roast gorilla hand—so says Roger E. Axtel, vice president of The Parker Pen Company. Axtel spent 18 years living and traveling in the 154 countries where Parker sells pens. He learned that communicating with foreign nationals demands more than merely learning their language. The gorilla hand (served rising from mashed yams) was prepared for a meal in honor of an American family-planning expert who was visiting a newly emerged African nation, and the guest of honor was expected to eat it, so he did. Learning the behavior expected of you as you do business internationally can be daunting if not intimidating. Axtel recommends the following rules to help you get off to a good start without embarrassment.

Basic Rule #1: What's in a Name?

The first transaction between even ordinary citizens—and the first chance to make an impression for better or worse—is an exchange of names. In America, there is not very much to get wrong. And even if you do, so what? Not so elsewhere. In the Eastern Hemisphere, where name frequently denotes social rank or family status, a mistake can be an outright insult, and so can using someone's given name without permission.

"What would you like me to call you?" is always the opening line of one overseas deputy director for an international telecommunications corporation. "Better to ask several times," he advises, "than to get it wrong." Even then, "I err on the side of formality." Another frequent traveler insists his company provide him with a list of key people he will meet—country by country, surnames underlined—to be memorized on the flight over.

Basic Rule #2: Eat, Drink, and Be Wary

Away from home, eating is a language all its own. No words can match it for saying "glad to meet you . . . glad to be doing business with you . . . glad to have you here." Mealtime is no time for a thanks-but-no-thanks response. Accepting what is on your plate is tantamount to accepting host, country, and company. So no matter how tough things may be to swallow, swallow. Often what is offered constitutes your host country's proudest culinary achievements. Squeamishness comes not so much from the thing itself as from your unfamiliarity with it. After all, an oyster has remarkably the same look and consistency as a sheep's eye (a delicacy in Saudi Arabia).

gesture is significant. For example, an Arab man indicates a romantic interest in a woman by running a hand backward across his hair; most Americans would dismiss this gesture as meaningless. On the other hand, an Egyptian might mistakenly assume that a Westerner sitting with the sole of his or her shoe showing is offering a grave insult.

Social behavior and manners

What is polite in one country may be considered rude in another. In Arab countries, for example, it is impolite to take gifts to a man's wife but acceptable to take gifts to his children. In Germany, giving a woman a red rose is considered a romantic invitation, inappropriate if you are trying to establish a business relationship with her. In India, you might be invited to visit someone's home "any time." Being reluctant to make an unexpected visit, you might wait to get a more definite invitation. But your failure to take the Indian literally is an insult, a sign that you do not care to develop the friendship.

Is there any polite way out besides the back door? Most business travelers say no, at least not before taking a few bites. It helps to slice unfamiliar food very thin. This way, you minimize the texture and the reminder of where it came from. Another useful dodge is not knowing what you are eating. What's for dinner? Don't ask.

Basic Rule #3: Clothes Can Make You or Break You

Wherever you are, you should not look out of place. Wear something you look natural in, something you know how to wear, and something that fits in with your surroundings. For example, a woman dressed in a tailored suit, even with high heels and flowery blouse, looks startlingly masculine in a country full of diaphanous saris. More appropriate attire might be a silky, loose-fitting dress in a bright color. With few exceptions, the general rule everywhere, whether for business, for eating out, or even for visiting people at home, is that you should be very buttoned up: conservative suit and tie for men, dress or skirt-suit for women.

Basic Rule #4: American Spoken Here— You Hope

We should be grateful that so many people outside the United States speak English. Even where Americans aren't understood, their language often is. It's when we try to speak someone else's language that the most dramatic failures of communication seem to occur. At times, the way we speak is as misinterpreted as what we are trying to say; some languages are incomprehensible as pronounced by outsiders. But no matter how you twist most native tongues, some meaning gets through—or at least you get an A for effort even if it doesn't. Memorizing a toast or greeting nearly always serves to break the ice, if not the communication barrier.

APPLY YOUR KNOWLEDGE

1. Select a non-English-speaking nation that trades with the United States. With the help of either a foreign language instructor or a translation dictionary, type or print the accepted translation for the following business terms: (1) *contract*, (2) *sale*, (3) *delivery date*, (4) *duplicate copies*, and (5) *negligence*. Separately, show three friends the list of translated terms only. Ask each to pronounce the terms. In your notebook, spell phonetically the pronunciations you hear. When finished, compare the pronunciations. How different are they? Which terms produced the greatest variety? What do your findings suggest about communication problems in the world of global business?

2. Should colleges and universities that offer a business major require a separate degree or certification program for international business? What courses from the curriculum at your school would you require for such a degree/certificate? What new courses can you suggest that would prepare you for doing business on the international level?

Rules of etiquette and politeness may be formal or
informal.

Rules of etiquette may be formal or informal. Formal rules are the specifically taught "rights" and "wrongs" of how to behave in common situations,
such as table manners at meals. Members of a culture can put into words the
formal rule being violated. Informal social rules are much more difficult to
identify and are usually learned by watching how people behave and then
imitating that behavior. Informal rules govern how men and women are supposed to behave, how and when people may touch each other, when it is appropriate to use a person's first name, and so on. Violations of these rules cause a
great deal of discomfort to the members of the culture, but they usually cannot
verbalize what it is that bothers them.[9]

ETHNOCENTRIC REACTIONS

Although language and cultural differences are significant barriers to communication, these problems can be resolved if people maintain an open mind.
Unfortunately, however, many of us have an ethnocentric reaction to people
from other cultures—that is, we judge all other groups according to our own
standards.[10]

An ethnocentric reaction is a
judgment of all other groups
according to the standards of
one culture.

When we react ethnocentrically, we ignore the distinctions between our
own culture and the other person's culture. We assume that others will react
the same way we do, that they will operate from the same assumptions, and
that they will use language and symbols in the "American" way. An ethnocentric reaction makes us lose sight of the possibility that our words and actions
will be misunderstood, and it makes us more likely to misunderstand the behavior of foreigners.

Generally, ethnocentric people are prone to stereotyping and prejudice:
They generalize about an entire group of people on the basis of sketchy evidence and then develop biased attitudes toward the group. As a consequence,
they fail to see people as they really are. Instead of talking with Abdul Karhum, unique human being, they talk to an Arab. Although they have never met
an Arab before, they may already believe that all Arabs are, say, hagglers.
The personal qualities of Abdul Karhum become insignificant in the face of
such preconceptions. Everything he says and does will be forced to fit the
preconceived image.

Bear in mind that Americans are not the only people in the world who are
prone to ethnocentrism. Often, both parties are guilty of stereotyping and
prejudice. Neither is open-minded about the other. Little wonder, then, that
misunderstandings arise. Fortunately, a healthy dose of tolerance can prevent
a lot of problems.

TIPS FOR COMMUNICATING WITH PEOPLE FROM OTHER CULTURES

You may never completely overcome linguistic and cultural barriers or totally
erase ethnocentric tendencies, but you can communicate effectively with people from other cultures if you work at it. Here are some tips for handling
intercultural business communication more effectively.

LEARNING ABOUT A CULTURE

Learning about another culture includes
- Studying the language
- Reading books and articles on the culture
- Finding out about a country's subculture, especially its business subculture

The best way to prepare yourself to do business with people from another culture is to study their culture in advance. If you plan to live in another country or to do business there repeatedly, learn the language. The same holds true if you must work closely with a subculture that has its own language, such as Vietnamese Americans or Hispanic Americans. Even if you end up transacting business in English, you show respect by making the effort to learn the language. In addition, you will learn something about the culture and its customs in the process. If you do not have the time or opportunity to learn the language, at least learn a few words.

You should also read books and articles about the culture and talk to people who have dealt with its members, preferably people who have done business with them. Concentrate on learning something about their history, religion, politics, and customs, but don't ignore the practical details either. In that regard, you should know something about another country's weather conditions, health-care facilities, money, transportation, communications, and customs regulations.

Also find out about a country's subcultures, especially its business subculture. Does the business world have its own rules and protocol? Who makes decisions? How are negotiations usually conducted? Is gift giving expected? What is the etiquette for exchanging business cards? What is the appropriate attire for attending a business meeting? Seasoned business travelers suggest the following:

- In Spain, let a handshake last five to seven strokes; pulling away too soon may be interpreted as a sign of rejection. In France, however, the preferred handshake is a single stroke.

- Never give a gift of liquor in Arab countries.

- In England, never stick pens or other objects in your front suit pocket; doing so is considered gauche.

- In Pakistan, don't be surprised when businesspeople excuse themselves in the midst of a meeting to conduct prayers. Moslems pray five times a day.

- Allow plenty of time to get to know the people you're dealing with in Africa. They're suspicious of people who are in a hurry. If you concentrate solely on the task at hand, Africans will distrust you and avoid doing business with you.

- In Arab countries, never turn down food or drink; it's an insult to refuse hospitality of any kind. But don't be too quick to accept, either. A ritual refusal ("I don't want to put you to any trouble" or "I don't want to be a bother") is expected before you finally accept.

- Stress the longevity of your company when dealing with the Germans, Dutch, and Swiss. If your company has been around for a while, the founding date should be printed on your business cards.

These are just a few examples of the variations in customs that make intercultural business so interesting.

HANDLING WRITTEN COMMUNICATION

Intercultural business writing falls into the same general categories as other forms of business writing. How you handle these categories depends on the subject and purpose of your message, the relationship between you and the reader, and the customs of the person to whom the message is addressed.

Letters

Letters are the most common form of intercultural business correspondence. They serve the same purposes and follow the same basic organizational plans (direct and indirect) as letters you would send within your own country. Unless you are personally fluent in the language of the intended readers, you should ordinarily write your letters in English or have them translated by a professional translator. If you and the reader speak different languages, be especially concerned with achieving clarity:

Strive for clarity in letters.

- Use short, precise words that say exactly what you mean.

- Rely on specific terms to explain your points. Avoid abstractions altogether, or illustrate them with concrete examples.

- Stay away from slang, jargon, and buzz words. Such words rarely translate well. Nor do idioms and figurative expressions. Abbreviations, acronyms (such as NORAD and CAD/CAM), and North American product names may also lead to confusion.

- Construct sentences that are shorter and simpler than those you might use when writing to someone fluent in English.

- Use short paragraphs. Each paragraph should stick to one topic and be no more than eight to ten lines.

- Help readers follow your train of thought by using transitional devices. Precede related points with expressions like *in addition* and *first, second, third.*

- Use numbers, visual aids, and preprinted forms to clarify your message. These devices are generally understood in most cultures.

People in other countries use different writing techniques.

Your word choice should also reflect the relationship between you and the reader. In general, be somewhat more formal than you would be in writing to people in your own culture. In many other cultures, people use a more elaborate, old-fashioned style, and you should gear your letters to their expectations. However, do not carry formality to extremes, or you will sound unnatural.

In terms of format, the two most common approaches for intercultural business letters are the block style (with blocked paragraphs) and the modified block style (with indented paragraphs). You may use either the American format for dates (with the month, day, and year, in that order) or the European style (with the day before the month and year). For the salutation, use *Dear (Title/Last Name).* Close the letter with *Sincerely* or *Sincerely yours,* and sign it personally.

If you correspond frequently with people in foreign countries, your letterhead should include the name of your country and cable or telex information. Send your letters by air mail, and ask that responses be sent that way as well.

Check the postage too; rates for sending mail to most other countries are not the same as rates for sending it within your own.

In the letters you receive, you will notice that people in other countries use different techniques for their correspondence. If you are aware of some of these practices, you will be able to concentrate on the message without passing judgment on the writers. Their approaches are not good or bad, just different.

The Japanese, for example, are slow to come to the point. Their letters typically begin with a remark about the season or weather. This is followed by an inquiry about your health or congratulations on your prosperity. A note of thanks for your patronage might come next. After these preliminaries, the main idea is introduced. If the letter contains bad news, the Japanese begin not with a buffer, but with apologies for disappointing you.

Letters from Latin America look different too. Instead of using letterhead stationery, Latin American companies use a cover page with their printed seal in the center. Their letters appear to be longer than ours because they use much wider margins.

Memos and reports

Memos and reports sent overseas fall into two general categories: those written to and from subsidiaries, branches, or joint venture partners and those written to clients or other outsiders. When the memo or report has an internal audience, the style may differ only slightly from that of a memo or report written for internal use in North America. Because sender and recipient have a working relationship and share a common frame of reference, many of the language and cultural barriers that lead to misunderstandings have already been overcome. However, if the reader's native language is not English, you should take extra care to ensure clarity: Use concrete and explicit words, simple and direct sentences, short paragraphs, headings, and many transitional devices.

When writing long, formal reports for an external audience, discuss reporting requirements and expectations, and submit a preliminary draft for comments.

If the memo or report is written for an external audience, the style of the document should be relatively formal and impersonal. If possible, the format should be like that of reports typically prepared or received by the audience. In the case of long, formal reports, it is also useful to discuss reporting requirements and expectations with the recipient beforehand and to submit a preliminary draft for comments before delivering the final report.

Other documents

Many international transactions involve shipping and receiving goods. A number of special-purpose documents are required to handle these transactions: price quotations, invoices, bills of lading, time drafts, letters of credit, correspondence with international freight forwarders, packing lists, shipping documents, and collection documents. Many of these documents are standard forms; you simply fill in the data as clearly and accurately as possible in the spaces provided. Samples are ordinarily available in a company's files if it frequently does business abroad. If not, you may obtain descriptions of the necessary documentation from the United States Department of Commerce, International Trade Administration, Washington, D.C., 20230. (For Canadian information, contact the Department of External Affairs, Trade Division, Ottawa, Ontario, K1A 0G2.)

When preparing forms, pay particular attention to the method you use for stating weights and measures and money values. The preferred method is to use the other country's system of measurement and its currency values for documenting the transaction; however, if your company uses U.S. or Canadian weights, measures, and dollars, you should follow that policy. Check any conversion calculations carefully.

HANDLING ORAL COMMUNICATION

Oral communication with people from other cultures is more difficult to handle than written communication, but it can also be more rewarding, from both a business and a personal standpoint. Some transactions simply cannot be handled without face-to-face contact.

When engaging in oral communication, be alert to the possibilities for misunderstanding. Recognize that you may be sending signals you are unaware of and that you may be misreading cues sent by the other person. To overcome language and cultural barriers, follow these suggestions:

- Keep an open mind. Don't stereotype the other person or react with preconceived ideas. Regard the person as an individual first, not as a representative of another culture.

- Be alert to the other person's customs. Expect him or her to have different values, beliefs, expectations, and mannerisms.

- Try to be aware of unintentional meanings that may be read into your message. Clarify your true intent by repetition and examples.

- Listen carefully and patiently. If you do not understand a comment, ask the person to repeat it.

- Be aware that the other person's body language may mislead you. Gestures and expressions mean different things in different cultures. Rely more on words than on nonverbal communication to interpret the message.

- Adapt your style to the other person's. If the other person appears to be direct and straightforward, follow suit. If not, adjust your behavior to match.

- At the end of a conversation, be sure that you and the other person both agree on what has been said and decided. Clarify what will happen next.

- If appropriate, follow up by writing a letter or memo summarizing the conversation and thanking the person for meeting with you.

When communicating orally, be alert to the possibilities for misunderstanding.

In short, take advantage of the other person's presence to make sure that your message is getting across and that you understand his or her message too.

Speeches are both harder and simpler to deal with than personal conversations. On the one hand, speeches don't provide much of an opportunity for exchanging feedback; on the other, you may either use a translator or prepare your remarks in advance and have someone who is familiar with the culture check them over. If you use a translator, however, be sure to use someone who is familiar not only with both languages but also with the terminology of your field of business. Experts recommend that the translator be given a copy of the speech at least a day in advance. Furthermore, a written translation given to members of the audience to accompany the English speech can help reduce communication barriers. The extra effort will be appreciated and will help you get your point across.

SUMMARY

In your capacity as a business communicator, you, too, will have opportunities for dealing with people from other cultures. You may need to travel to another country to do business, or you may do business with foreigners who are traveling or living here. In this country, you may work for a foreign-owned firm or have dealings with other citizens who have cultural backgrounds distinctly different from your own. You will thus find an awareness of intercultural differences useful.

ON THE JOB:
Solving a Communication Dilemma at Procter & Gamble

Looking at Japan, Edwin Artzt saw a communicator's dream: 99.7 percent literacy and a compact geographical area that supports 4 national newspapers, 250 local papers, 20,000 magazines, and 5 national broadcasting networks. Thanks to this comprehensive network of media, advertisers in Japan can efficiently blanket the entire country with a single message—a sharp contrast to the situation in most countries, where few national media exist and many separate messages must be sent in a variety of media to cover an entire region or country. But despite this winning combination of effective media, literate customers, and top-quality products, P&G's Pampers were losing market share in Japan.

Importing Pampers from the United States had seemed like a good way to jump into the market, but locally made products were quickly luring customers away. These local competitors recognized that Japanese parents liked the convenience of disposable diapers, but they also found ways of adapting the product to the unique demands of the Japanese market. As parents flocked to the local products, P&G's share of the Japanese diaper market plummeted.

To reverse the slide, P&G marketers began looking more closely at their customers. They soon realized that their initial assumptions about the needs and values of Japanese parents had been incorrect. Through months of careful market research, P&G learned that the giant cartons of bulky Pampers took up too much of the limited storage space in typical Japanese households. P&G also learned that Japanese parents were extremely concerned about cleanliness, so they changed their babies' diapers more often than U.S. parents do. Whereas Pampers had been designed to let U.S. parents avoid frequent diaper changes, Japanese parents didn't want or need that benefit. In addition, by studying customer reaction to various advertising approaches, P&G managers uncovered considerable resistance to the hard-sell method that the company had been favoring in its commercials.

Armed with this knowledge of customer life-style, values, and behavior, P&G revamped the product and the promotional communications. Product developers reworked Pampers with a new superabsorbent material and eventually created a diaper one-third as thick as the original. The improved diapers fit better and were more effective in preventing leaks. They also took up less storage space, and they featured convenient reclosable tapes.

But an improved product was only part of the solution. Artzt had to do more than sell the new product; he had to overcome the image that the original Pampers had created in the minds of Japanese consumers. At the same time, he wanted to communicate P&G's commitment to meeting customer needs and its increased sensitivity to the culture and customs of Japan.

To accomplish these goals, P&G launched an advertising campaign specially tailored for the Japanese market. Research indicated that Japanese audiences do not like ads that are too aggressive or that directly compare one company's products with its competitors' products. So the new campaign took a more indirect approach and featured a talking diaper celebrating the intimate relationship between the Japanese mother and child. This talking diaper campaign, which used both print and television media, was completely different from P&G's previous ads. It delivered a subtle but sincere message, more in tune with the preferences of the Japanese audience. The talking diaper quickly won the hearts—and pocketbooks—of Japanese parents. The campaign was so successful that the television commercial ran for more than six years, becoming the longest-running ad in Japan.

Within 30 months, Pampers' market share climbed to 28 percent, then to 30 percent. P&G again dominated the Japanese disposable diaper market. But Artzt didn't stop there. Having reformulated Pampers to meet the high standards of Japanese customers, he believed that he could adapt the new product to satisfy customer needs in other countries. As a result, P&G created Ultra Pampers and Ultra Pampers Plus, both based on the slim superabsorbent Japanese model, for the European and the North American markets.

P&G now offers more than 20 products in Japan, ring-ing up $1 billion in annual sales. No longer a burden on profits, Japan has become one of the jewels in Edwin Artzt's thriving international empire. Artzt became CEO in 1990, and he is looking to Japan—and to 140 other countries—for the profits to ensure P&G's future.

Your Mission: You have been named special assistant to P&G president John E. Pepper, who now heads the company's international division. Pepper wants to build sales and profits in Japan, and he has asked you to study the market. You want to stay in touch with the needs of your customers, and you also want to consider the interests of the retailers who sell your products. Although your knowledge of Japan and the Japanese language may be limited, use your skill in intercultural communication to determine the *best* response to each of the following situations:

1. P&G's Japanese subsidiary is starting a training program in which newly hired managers spend three months in the corporate headquarters in Cincinnati to learn about the parent company. You are working with one of these trainees, who learned English in high school and college, but you are not sure whether he understands everything you say. Each time you discuss something with him, the trainee smiles shyly and nods. How can you be sure your message is getting through?
   a. Speak slowly and distinctly, and ask whether the trainee understands specific phrases or instructions. Also, pause frequently and repeat or write down anything he doesn't understand.
   b. You need feedback, so ask the trainee to repeat word for word what you've said. That way, you'll know that he understands.
   c. To be sure the trainee receives your message, write everything down. He can refer to the written explanation later to check his comprehension.
   d. You will be better able to convey your message if you talk loudly and use larger hand gestures to clarify your meaning and to keep the listener's interest.

2. You want to improve sales of Camay soap in Japan, so you invite managers from your new Japanese advertising agency to meet with the product managers in Cincinnati. One ad agency manager transferred to Japan from the United States, so he is fluent in English, but the others are not. Which of the following is the most effective way to explain Camay's background so that the agency can develop new advertising?
   a. Use videotape to overcome the language barrier. Prepare a tape showing the product when it was first launched in Japan, and include clips from every Camay commercial previously used. Use narration or subtitles in both Japanese and English.

   b. Use videotape as suggested in (a), but also include a report, in Japanese and in English, showing Camay's sales history, customer information, and a profile of the Japanese soap market.
   c. Videotape can't adequately convey the tradition and quality of Camay. Write a detailed report (translated into Japanese) that describes Camay's global history, and include the changes in chemical formulation that resulted in the improved product sold in Japan today.
   d. To avoid possible misunderstanding, stick to oral rather than written communication. Make a speech in English that covers sales history and customer information, and show slides of Camay commercials used in the past. At the end of the speech, offer to answer any questions that the ad agency people have.

3. To learn more about the role of retailers in the Japanese market, you plan to travel to Tokyo, Osaka, and Yokohama to visit several supermarket and drugstore chains. You'd like to see how P&G products are displayed, and you'd also like to gain a better understanding of the retail system. What is the best way to arrange these store visits?
   a. Before you go, write a brief but formal letter in English to the head of each chain, introducing yourself as Pepper's assistant and requesting permission to tour a few stores. Stress your interest in learning more about their needs as retail customers, and ask when it would be convenient for you to visit.
   b. Your boss, John Pepper, knows many of the key retailers in Japan, so you should carry a letter of introduction from him (translated into Japanese), which you can show when you get to each store. This personal introduction will open doors for you, and it will explain your visit and your objective once you get to Japan.
   c. Instead of taking the time to write and then waiting for an answer, it would be quicker to telephone the heads of each chain. Through an interpreter, you can stress that you are interested in their views of the market for P&G products and in learning how the Japanese retail system operates. Let them know that you are eager to see them as soon as possible, and press for a definite date on which you can visit their stores.
   d. To get the background you need to discuss P&G products with Japan's leading retailers, make an unannounced visit to several stores. Look at how P&G products are arranged on the shelves, and then visit the executive offices to meet with top managers.

4. The managing director of Meidi-ya, a Japanese supermarket chain known for its large selection of im-

ported foods and household products, has written to ask about the possibility of offering more foreign-made P&G products in Japan. He asks whether any other Japanese chains are testing this idea, and he wants help in determining which P&G products to stock. Your research shows that Tokyo and other major cities are attracting a growing contingent of foreigners, and you believe that this group would welcome the opportunity to buy the same brands they bought at home, whether home is the United States, Germany, or any other country where P&G products are sold. Pepper asks you to reply to this request by writing a letter to the Meidi-ya executive. Choose the best response from the following alternatives:

a. We are in receipt of your correspondence of May 7, in which you raised the possibility of importing Procter & Gamble products to sell in stores located in neighborhoods with a large expatriate population. We at P&G concur whole-heartedly with your conclusion that people who have become accustomed to buying a particular brand in their homeland would be likely to purchase it when they are living in another country. We would like to support your endeavor in any way we can. Much to our regret, however, we are unable to comply with your request for information regarding competitive experiments in this type of activity. Even if we were aware of the experiences of other Japanese stores that stock large quantities of imported P&G products, we would not be able to reveal this data to you, nor would we divulge information of this type to other stores interested in learning about Meidi-ya's activities.

Regarding your request for help in determining an appropriate assortment of P&G's food and household products suitable for import to Japan, we enclose a list of our best-selling brands in the United States and in Europe. Among the foods, Jif peanut butter and Crisco shortening are especially popular in the United States, and among the laundry products, Lenor fabric softener is a top seller in Germany. With respect to the exact products your chain might stock, we recommend that you start with a small group of products made in the United States. Once you have monitored customer response, you will be able to ascertain which products are most attractive, and then you have a firm foundation upon which to build a more ambitious import program. Again, we want to apologize for any inconvenience that our rejection of your request for competitive information may have caused, and we want to reaffirm our desire to help you in

any way we can. We trust you will be successful in your new endeavor.

b. Thanks for dropping us a note about importing P&G products. You're right, people living abroad would probably jump for joy at the sight of the brands they enjoyed at home. You can count on us to give you a hand in establishing this new endeavor. But please understand that our lips are sealed about any plans of other Japanese retailers to import our products. However, if we get word about a store in another country that is trying something similar, we'll let you know.

So that you can pick the cream of the crop from the P&G lineup of products, we enclose a run-down of our number one products in the United States and in Europe. These products fly off the shelves in their own countries, but we don't know for sure whether they'll be as popular with your customers. How about starting with a small group of products and keeping an eye on the results? Then you can reorder the best sellers and think about plunging ahead with other imports.

Please let us know if we can help in any way as you get this new project off the ground. Good luck!

c. Thank you for your interest in importing Procter & Gamble products. We agree that people living abroad would probably be eager to buy familiar brands, and we will gladly help you in this new endeavor. Just as we will not reveal any details of your plans, we ask you to understand that we are unable to tell you about what other Japanese retailers may be doing. However, if we learn about a retailer in another country that has tried importing P&G products, we will ask whether that store is interested in exchanging information with you.

To help you select the products that your customers will recognize and buy, we enclose a list of our best-selling brands in the United States and in Europe. These products are very popular in their native countries, but we can't predict whether your customers will want to buy them in Japan. So we suggest that you start with a small group of products and see how your customers react. Then you can reorder the best sellers and perhaps test other P&G imports in Meidi-ya stores.

Please don't hesitate to contact us if we can be of further assistance. Good luck in your new endeavor.[11]

QUESTIONS FOR DISCUSSION

1. What are the general goals of intercultural business communication? Why are they especially difficult to achieve?
2. What are some of the advantages and disadvantages of delegating your intercultural communication to intermediaries or translators?
3. Why is written communication less of a problem in intercultural interactions than oral communication is?
4. How would you characterize the "national personality" of people from your own country?
5. What are some of your own stereotypes and prejudices? For example, what are your beliefs and attitudes with respect to Germans? Japanese? Saudi Arabians? Cubans? Ethiopians? Mexicans? Tahitians?
6. What are some of the issues to consider in deciding whether to accept a job overseas?

EXERCISES

1. A Procter & Gamble product manager (see this chapter's On-the-Job simulation) has asked you to review a letter that will be sent to the president of a Japanese retail chain, a man named Yuji Kobayashi. Here are the greeting and the first paragraph; how would you improve them?

   Hi Yuji,
   It's hard not to be disappointed with the slow sales growth of our new line of detergents throughout Japan. I haven't seen the specific numbers for your stores, but I assume your sales are as slow as everyone else's in Japan. Here in the U.S., the new line captured 20 percent of the market within six months of its introduction. I've analyzed why we were so successful here, and I'd like to give you some ideas for improvements.[12]

2. Imagine that you have been assigned to host a group of Japanese students who are visiting your campus for the next two weeks. They have all studied English since they were 10 years old and speak the language well. What things should you tell them that will help them fit into the culture on your campus and in your town? Make a list of behavioral rules they should know about.

3. Choose a specific foreign country, such as India, Brazil, China, Thailand, Malaysia, or Nigeria. The less familiar you are with it, the better. Research the business subculture of the country, and write a report summarizing what an American would need to know to conduct business successfully there (business etiquette, roles and status, decision-making customs, concepts of time, nonverbal communication styles, and so on).

4. Locate someone, preferably a businessperson, who has spent some time in another country, and interview him or her about the experience. What preparation did the person have before going to the country? In what ways was the preparation adequate? Inadequate? In hindsight, how might he or she have prepared differently? Ask for anecdotes about particular communication problems or mistakes.

■ CHAPTER EIGHTEEN

After studying this chapter, you will be able to

- Categorize the various types of office machines used in business today and understand their functions
- Explain what constitutes an electronic office

BUSINESS COMMUNICATION TECHNOLOGY

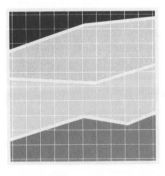

ON THE JOB:
Facing a Communication Dilemma at Metropolitan Life Insurance Company
Taming the Paper Tiger

Picture the insurance business for a minute. What do you see? William D. Livesey sees paper, piles and piles of paper: policies, responses to claims, statements of benefits, descriptive booklets. As Metropolitan Life Insurance Company's vice president of group insurance, national accounts, Livesey is ultimately responsible for producing hundreds of thousands of words per year. He supervises roughly 75 employees who provide administrative services to support Metropolitan Life's group insurance accounts. His department handles group life, health, and disability coverage for major corporations like General Electric, AT&T, Rockwell International, and Mobil Oil.

Every time one of these major customers revamps its insurance benefits, Metropolitan Life faces many tasks, among them that of revising the descriptive booklets used by each corporate customer to explain its benefits package to its employees. That may not sound like too much trouble, but try producing or revising 125 booklets a month. Throw in all the other documents the insurance business ordinarily generates, and it all adds up to being a pretty big job. If you were William Livesey, how would you manage this problem of paper? Are there machines that might help? What innovations have been made in office technology that could reduce the sea of paper faced by businesses like Metropolitan?[1]

A SURVEY OF OFFICE TECHNOLOGY

Metropolitan Life Insurance Company

In addition to the machines needed by Metropolitan Life to reduce paper, technology now provides businesses with faster, more efficient equipment for every aspect of communication. However, it's no easy task to describe in a limited space the wide variety of office machines that now exist. Anyone who sets out to make a comprehensive list would be stymied by the rapidly changing marketplace for office equipment. This section is therefore divided according to the general functions that office machines fulfill: origination, production, reproduction, distribution/transmission, and storage. It includes a description of some of the most common equipment available for performing these tasks. With the help of this framework, you can categorize the equipment currently used in most organizations and still understand new developments.

ORIGINATION EQUIPMENT

Origination equipment includes
- Dictation machines
- Adding machines and calculators
- Typewriters, word/information processors, and microcomputers

Pens and pencils applied to paper constitute a simple technology that may be used by someone writing in longhand; it may also be used by someone writing in shorthand while someone else dictates a message. Such personal dictation has a certain elegance, but it does require coordinating the time of two employees. However, a *dictation machine*, which is like a tape recorder (see Figure 18.1), is frequently more efficient. The transcriber uses a similar machine (but with headphones instead of a microphone) to play back the message and put it in written form, at his or her convenience.

Adding machines and calculators may also be considered origination equipment because they can be used to generate the numbers for a letter, memo, or report. Moreover, the microchip revolution has made electronic calculators very compact; one model can even be worn like a wristwatch.

Messages may also be originated on keyboard devices such as *typewriters, word/information processors*, and *microcomputers*, which are discussed more

FIGURE 18.1
Dictation Equipment

thoroughly in the next section. They are quick and easy to use for composing messages, as long as you know your way around a keyboard. Word/information processors and computers have an extra benefit: At the touch of a key (or keys) you can rearrange words, sentences, paragraphs, or pages.

PRODUCTION EQUIPMENT

Once the message has been composed, it must be put into polished form. That old standby, the *typewriter*, is the basic tool for transforming a draft into final copy. In the hands of a trained typist or secretary, a typewriter can produce a document that looks supremely professional. A somewhat more sophisticated tool is the *electronic typewriter*, which has a memory unit that can display what has been typed before any characters are printed on the page. Typewriters with larger memories—usually augmented with separate magnetic disks, tape cassettes, or magnetic cards—can store addresses, entire letters, or selected paragraphs or sentences for replay when needed or for putting together "customized" letters. The other main advantage of electronic typewriters is that they make it much easier for a typist to underline words, center titles, set up tables, and justify lines on a page (that is, space characters so that all lines end at the same place on the right).

An electronic typewriter and a word/information-processing unit are very similar. The major difference is that a *word/information processor* usually has a large display screen, a separate printing device, and greater memory and computing power (see Figure 18.2). A word/information processor may also be linked to other word/information processors. The advantage of such links is that one person can review what another has typed by simply looking at the display screen on his or her desk, thereby eliminating the need for producing a

Susan Mersereau is vice president and general manager of Weyerhaeuser Information Systems. As such, Mersereau heads the group responsible for the company's worldwide telecommunications program, linking voice and data communications, electronic mail, facsimile, and videoconferencing facilities. To manage change, says Mersereau, you must control vast amounts of information, which is something technology can help you do.

FIGURE 18.2
Word-Processing Center

hard, or paper, copy. *Microcomputers* and *computer terminals* linked in a network, perhaps with minicomputers and mainframe computers, serve much the same function.

Organizations like Metropolitan Life—which produce a lot of documents for outside distribution, such as annual reports, brochures, and magazines—may also have *photo-typesetting equipment* that produces a fully justified, precisely spaced page with all the indentions and headings automatically placed where they belong, just like a page of this book.

REPRODUCTION EQUIPMENT

Most business messages are copied in some way before they are sent to their intended receivers. If nothing else, it is often important to have a copy in the files for future reference. For many years, *carbon paper* was considered an indispensable aid for creating multiple copies. Now *carbonless copy sets*, made of several layers of coated paper, are also popular, especially for preprinted forms such as memos, order forms, and sales reports.

Reproduction equipment includes
- Photocopiers
- Offset printing machines
- Audiotapes, videotapes, and videodiscs
- Computer printers

The most common type of reproduction equipment is the *photocopier*, which uses light and chemicals to produce, in essence, a photo of a document on paper (see Figure 18.3). Some photocopiers can feed originals into the machine one page at a time, freeing the operator to do something else; some copiers can also reduce or enlarge images. When hooked up to a computer, a photocopier may even be commanded to produce different kinds of copies by someone sitting at a keyboard in a distant room. Extra equipment is available for collating (sorting multiple copies of a multipage document into the proper order).

The *offset printing machine* has become popular for making a large number of copies. Photographs are made of the document, and the image is transferred to a metal or paper printing plate. The plate is then attached to a drum, which transfers the image to paper with ink as it rotates.

To reproduce a speech or presentation with all the intonation and gesture that might enhance its literal meaning, the business communicator can produce

FIGURE 18.3
Photocopier

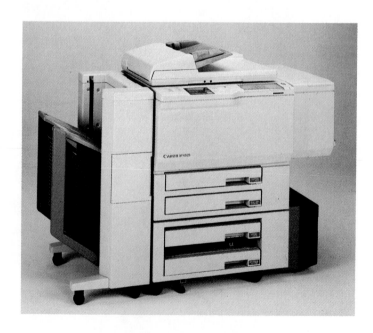

audiotapes, *videotapes*, and laser-read *videodiscs*, which are compact and easy to use. Some organizations use audio cassettes for motivational messages to the sales force, for example. Others use videotapes or videodiscs to pass along company information. Equipment similar to that used by the music industry permits multiple copies to be made and sent to widely scattered branch offices.

The computer, the jack-of-all-trades of the modern office, can also be used to reproduce documents. Once a message has been perfected, the *computer printer* can be switched on to generate multiple copies of what looks like a hand-typed letter—and in a fraction of the time a human typist would take.

DISTRIBUTION/TRANSMISSION EQUIPMENT

This category of office equipment is probably the most diverse and fastest growing. Given the dynamic status of this equipment, it is difficult to make a comprehensive list. The simplest way to categorize distribution and transmission equipment is to label it as either a physical delivery system or an electronic delivery system.

Physical delivery systems

A message can always be delivered from *hand to hand*, of course. In a large organization, or when many people are to receive a document, a company mail room may do the distributing (*interoffice mail*). In a sense, a *meeting* is also a physical distribution system because the speaker delivers the message directly to the audience without the help of any other devices.

The largest and best-known physical delivery system in the United States is the *U.S. Postal Service*. (In Canada, it's the *Canada Post Corporation*.) Each year, billions of messages are passed from one person to another by the friendly mail carrier in blue. Few of these messages get lost, and most arrive in a reasonable amount of time. The Postal Service does have rules and conventions that its users must follow, however, a few of which are detailed in Appendix B. For the most part, these guidelines were developed to allow the Postal Service to handle most business mail by machine.

> Physical delivery systems include public services such as the U.S. Postal Service and private services such as UPS.

Special mail-handling devices fall somewhere between the physical and electronic categories (see Figure 18.4 on page 476). However, they have been designed to aid in the physical delivery of mail, and so they're included here. *Mail conveyors* and *automated delivery carts* are machines for transporting mail from one spot to another. *Postage meters*, which are leased from the manufacturer and serviced by the Postal Service, weigh letters and imprint them with the appropriate amount of postage. *Mail sorters* help categorize mail mechanically by, say, ZIP code or department code. *Optical character readers* (OCRs) scan a piece of paper, change the information to an electronic code, and then store or sort the information in a computer. The Postal Service uses OCRs to sort mail by ZIP code.

Given the inevitable inefficiencies of an organization as large as the U.S. Postal Service, it is no wonder that such *private delivery services* as Federal Express and United Parcel Service (UPS) have sprung up. Some guarantee faster delivery (for a premium price, of course); some guarantee lower rates, especially for bulky or heavy packages. Another alternative for sensitive messages or for deliveries within a city is *messenger services*, which put someone in a car, on a motorcycle, or even on a bicycle to hand-deliver messages for a fee.

Self-Propelled Delivery Cart

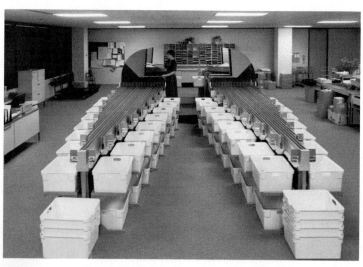

Horizontal Conveyor

FIGURE 18.4
Physical Distribution
Equipment

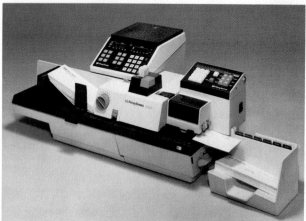

Postage Meter

Electronic delivery systems

Electronic delivery systems
include
- Telephones
- Teletypewriters
- Telegrams
- Mailgrams
- Electronic mail
- Data phones
- Fax equipment
- Communicating word/
  information processors
- Video players and film
  projectors
- Public-address systems
- Closed-circuit television
  systems
- Teleconferencing facilities

It is hard to imagine how the world economy could have developed to its present extent without the *telephone* being widely available to speed communication. Now even very small offices may have *multiple-line telephones*. Callers can be put on hold by pushing a button; pushing another button allows the phone to function as an intercom so that people in the same building can talk to each other without leaving their desks; calls can be transferred from one office to another; and someone in one office can cover the phone for someone absent from another office.

On a large scale, these functions are handled by a *PBX (private branch exchange) system*, shown in Figure 18.5. In many companies, a PBX operator screens and routes all calls. In others, telephone operations are computerized so that most calls (except those requesting general information) are handled automatically. *Centrex* and *PABX (private automatic branch exchange) systems* eliminate the need for a company operator because callers can dial each phone directly.

The wires and satellites that make the phone system work can also be used to transmit purely electronic information (unlike the telephone, which transmits voice messages). *Teletypewriters* are used, like a regular keyboard, to produce letters and numbers that are coded electronically and sent over tele-

FIGURE 18.5
Electronic Distribution
Equipment

PBX System, AT&T

Fax (Facsimile) Machine

Katherine M. Hudson is vice president and director of corporate information systems at Eastman Kodak Company. Hudson and her worldwide team lead the corporate information-systems division, which is responsible for Kodak's global computing and telecommunications. Such networks allow us to exchange ideas more readily, says Hudson, but people still have to dream up the ideas to communicate.

phone lines for printout on teletypewriters in other locations. *Telegrams* are similar but are used more often by organizations that do not send a lot of electronic messages and therefore do not need an in-house teletypewriter. If the message is not urgent, the organization may choose instead to send a *mailgram,* which is transmitted from one telegraph office to another and then converted to a paper format that can be delivered with the regular mail. In general, teletype messages and telegrams are less expensive than phone calls, especially if the message must be transmitted a long way.

A modern development is called *electronic mail.* In brief, two or more computers are linked by telephone, and they send oral or written messages back and forth. *Data phones* are similar, but instead of linking the computer terminals of two users, they link a user with a data source. *Fax (facsimile) equipment,* one of the fastest-spreading distribution systems, uses a device like a photocopier to send copies of a document via telephone lines and radio waves (see Figure 18.5). *Communicating word/information processors* are likewise linked by telephone lines to a computer memory; but instead of putting the message on a screen, the message is typed out on the printer.

The major advantage of all these modern technologies is that messages can be encoded during the working day or at the sender's convenience, accumulated by the computer, sent when telephone rates are low or when transmission channels are less crowded, and decoded at a time convenient to the receiver. However, besides being used to conduct normal business, technology has also been used in unforseen ways. For example, when the Chinese government withheld from its people the news of the Tiananmen Square massacre, the truth was smuggled in from America by Chinese students who faxed photos and news accounts to any fax number they could get hold of.[2] Thus the government's blackout of one technology was defeated by the students' creative use of another.

Audiovisual equipment can distribute such messages as speeches and presentations. *Video players* and *film projectors* are necessary when a prerecorded message needs to be delivered. For simultaneous delivery of a speech or presentation to many people, businesses may use a *public address system*, consisting of a microphone and speakers, or a *closed-circuit television system*, consisting of a video camera and television monitors.

Via telephone lines or satellites, *teleconferencing facilities* use video equipment and telephones or computers to link meeting participants in two or more locations. Participants in a videoconference must gather in a specially equipped room at a prearranged time. With computers, however, conferencing is conducted from regular terminals, and participants individually receive and transmit messages at their convenience. The disadvantage of computer conferencing is that the computer is less efficient than video and telephone equipment when it comes to conveying individual expressions of feeling.

STORAGE EQUIPMENT

Messages often need to be saved for later reference or for piecemeal distribution of copies over time. The most common and least complicated form of storage equipment is the *file cabinet*, though such devices as *card files*, *rotary files*, *disk files*, and *horizontal files* serve the same purpose: to categorize documents so that they can readily be found (see Figure 18.6). As you might guess, the computer revolution has left its imprint on this sort of equipment too. *Magnetic disks*, *tapes*, and *cards* store information for use on a computer or word/information processor and may themselves be stored in special cabinets or folders according to some classification scheme. Some information may also be stored in the computer itself.

> Storage equipment includes
> - Magnetic disks, tapes, and cards
> - Audio and video recordings
> - Micrographic equipment

Magnetic and laser technology now make it possible to store *audio and video recordings* too. Important meetings and telephone conversations and significant events in the organization are likely prospects for storage. However, these recordings are sensitive to heat, dust, and magnetism, so they must be handled carefully.

In organizations with vast files of information, *micrographic equipment* is often used. Document pages are reproduced in miniature on film (microfilm) and then viewed with a special machine when someone needs to see the information (see Figure 18.6). The main advantage of both microfilm and magnetic computer disks is that they take up much less space than paper would.

THE ELECTRONIC OFFICE

> The electronic office transmits information electronically rather than by paper.

To the extent that an office (or even an entire company) is transmitting information electronically rather than by paper, it may be considered an electronic office. The advantages are many and central to better business: faster access to data, hence faster response to customers' needs, competitors' actions, and other developments in the business environment; greater accuracy in analysis; and elimination of many of the most routine and boring tasks, freeing a company's employees for more creative and interesting work.[3]

FIGURE 18.6
Storage Equipment

Motorized Rotary File

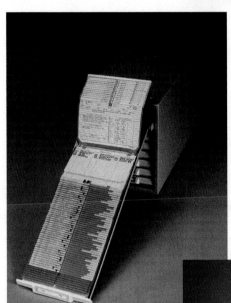

Visible Card File

Horizontal File

Floppy Disk File

Microfilm Reader/Printer

SuperStation TBS founder Ted Turner is a pioneer in the cable TV industry. The challenge of technology, says Turner, is managing it to create our world—instead of merely being dragged along by it.

In a sense, the development of office technology is coming full circle. Long ago, a mind and a hand putting pen to paper were all a businessperson needed to communicate with someone in another place or time. Then specialized machines were developed to handle specific parts of the communication process, such as producing a message and sending it. Now, however, the electronic office has fewer pieces of equipment, most related to the computer and telephone transmission lines, but they perform multiple functions.

DESKTOP COMPUTING

Companies of every size have emphatically joined the computer age. Some companies provide each employee with a terminal that is connected to a large *mainframe computer* or a somewhat smaller *minicomputer*, allowing a number of people to have access to the same data. Some companies put a separate *microcomputer* on each desk, allowing employees to work independently. And still other companies have intelligent *workstations* that provide users with a more powerful computing system. Computers can integrate the office environment, linking individual employees with each other, with other companies, and even with the rest of the world through distribution services and information networks.

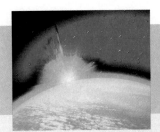

BEHIND THE SCENES AT MIKE'S VIDEO
Video Club Thrives on Office Technology

Mike's Video, Inc., in State College, Pennsylvania, serves the students of Penn State University and the surrounding community. Since opening in 1984, the company has grown from one club to four clubs and has opened a TV and appliance store. In the process, owners Mike Negra, Alan Abruzzo, and Wanda White have learned to communicate using a wide and constantly changing array of office technology products. "Retailing is a people business," Negra points out. "If you don't like interacting with people, you're in the wrong place. On day one, there were just the three of us standing there waiting on people."

Mike's Video has been successful because it communicates effectively with its club members, employees, and suppliers. And technology has had an impact on every aspect of the company's communication, from auto-dial telephones to electronic mail, from word processing on a Macintosh Plus with laser printer to faxing newsletter articles to their publisher in Arkansas. Something that has to go out fast is hand-written and faxed, not typed and mailed.

Wanda White manages operations: "The PC does our letters, puts together our club newsletter, and does our signs, business cards, stationery, forms, anything that needs printing. To draw more attention to our fax messages, we designed a cover sheet on the computer." And if the computer gives them problems? "We page our programmer on his beeper and he calls in." Alan Abruzzo purchases videos (14,000 copies of 3,800 titles at last count), TVs, VCRs, and stereos. The telephone and fax machine are his tools: "I order all the movies from seven distributors through telemarketers. Appliance manufacturers send their specials overnight on the fax machine, and I can call in an order the next day. If we're planning a large purchase, I solicit bids by telephone, then get responses and send out the contract and order by fax." As president, Negra travels for the company and oversees appliances. He uses a cellular phone to help him keep on top of things: "With our Centrex system, I can call one store and be switched to any phone in our company."

John L. Sims is vice president of strategic resources for Digital Equipment Corporation, which leads the world in computer network technology. At Digital, employees stay on-line with the company's own VAXstations, a family of computerized workstations. Machines can't do it alone, says Sims. It takes good people to use them.

The main uses for these computers range from word and data processing to design and decision support. In *word processing*, documents are drafted, polished, and produced on the computer. In *data processing*, raw numbers—sales, costs, inventories, and so on—are entered into the database, manipulated, analyzed, and transformed into information that the organization can use to produce more efficiently and market more effectively. In *design and decision support*, modeling of products, organizations, and operations can be simulated to help designers and managers see what might happen under various circumstances.

Software is what makes a computer so versatile. For example, with the insertion of various diskettes, a single microcomputer can be used to draft and produce letters, calculate statistics from raw data, and keep mailing lists. A great selection of ready-to-use software is now available for microcomputers. Minicomputers and mainframe computers often use software that is specially designed to meet the organization's unique needs.

The most recent business function for computers is called *desktop publishing*. A combination of word processing and graphics, desktop publishing allows the production of polished newsletters, catalogs, and reports. Blocks of text, special headlines, and diagrams can be laid out together on-screen so that the user can see exactly what will come out on the printer (WYSIWYG—"wizzywig," or what you see is what you get). *Laser printers* produce pages

Most important, technology gives Mike's Video the ability to create and to deliver service to its customers. "Our club members are amazed at how efficient we are," says White. "Our computer system and telephones allow us to be on top of the service details in a timely and expedient way." Negra adds: "When you call a club to buy a TV, you are switched to the appliance store without having to redial. When you call your club to rent a certain movie, our computer can tell us which store has it. Then if you return it to another of our clubs while you're out running around, your club knows instantly that you've returned it, so there are no delays when you show up to rent a new movie."

All of this does have drawbacks. Abruzzo believes it's less personal than face-to-face communication: "I've done business with some people almost daily for five years, and I've never met them." For Negra, the struggle is keeping the problems of a small business on the minds of large manufacturers: "To a distributor in Pittsburgh, our success was important. We had a rep visiting us, and if we bought $100,000 in TVs from her, that made us important to her. But now the distributor is gone. We deal directly with the manufacturer in, say, St. Louis. To him, our $100,000 doesn't look so big, so we don't get the attention we need." To White, who handles personnel, there is the danger of missed communication: "When I put a message out on our system, the club reps logging on get their mes-

sages all right, but there's no body language, tone, or inflection to measure. Its just black words on a white screen." All agree there's overdependence on technology, to the point that if one system malfunctions, it generally affects all the other operations.

"But don't forget," says Negra, "technology is merely a tool. We can train people to operate it. When we hire students for part-time work or a salesperson for our store, we need people with good communication skills. To make the technology work for us, our people have to understand the communication process. All you basically need to know about the technology is how to use it."

APPLY YOUR KNOWLEDGE

1. Suggest as many ways as you can for the people at Mike's Video to personalize their use of the technology described. How might they give some identity to their technologically driven communications?

2. How would the following problems affect operations at Mike's Video: (1) An employee tampers with the movie inventory database. (2) A fire destroys one club. (3) Power fails throughout State College. (4) A customer insists, "The computer is wrong; I did return the five movies." (5) Telephone company employees go on strike. If you were running the business, which problem would you devise a plan for first? Why?

that look much more like professionally typeset material than the "connect the dot" computer printouts of the past. Although a desktop publishing system cannot yet substitute for the artistic expertise of a professional designer or match the quality of professional typesetting equipment, it does give organizations like Metropolitan Life a quick and relatively inexpensive alternative to typesetting.

ELECTRONIC NETWORKS

Computers are certainly versatile, but they are even more versatile when linked together electronically. Within a building, computer terminals and microcomputers can be hard-wired (linked directly) to minicomputers and mainframe computers. *Local-area networks* (LANs) permit microcomputers to be linked together, along with such accessories as printers. With either arrangement, employees share access to computing power, data, and a wide variety of equipment, saving the company money and space. The computer connections among employees also give them another channel for communicating.

LANs allow microcomputers to be linked to one another as well as to devices such as printers.

Such links are no longer limited to employees within a single building either. Telecommunication gives anyone at the end of a telephone line the potential to communicate by computer with anyone else on the line. One popular use for this link is *electronic mail* (sometimes called an electronic bulletin board when confined to the organization): One user types or speaks a message into the computer, coded for access only by the intended receiver or receivers, and the message is stored in the computer at the other end until the receiver is ready to look at it or listen to it. A pilot study of electronic mail at a large office equipment corporation found that it reduced paper memos by 50 percent, interoffice mail by 94 percent, photocopying by 60 percent, and time on the phone by 80 percent.[4]

Small laptop, or portable, computers take the concept one step further; they not only allow information processing almost anywhere but also let someone out in the field tap into a central database back at headquarters. And if the organization's own database isn't big enough, telecommunication allows any subscriber to consult the large databases maintained by such information networks as CompuServe and The Source.

In addition to written messages, electronic networks can transmit visual and spoken messages.

Computer messages have typically been written messages. But visual messages and spoken messages can now be transmitted through electronic networks too. *Voice mail* is similar to electronic mail, except that (1) it doesn't require each user to have a computer (only a Touch-Tone phone) and (2) it permits the sending, storage, and retrieval of spoken messages. *Teleconferencing* is a way of conducting a meeting when the participants are in scattered locations but all near a phone. *Videoconferencing* uses phone lines too; but with cameras and special viewing equipment, it allows participants to be seen as well as heard.

The overall social and economic effect of these new communication links remains to be seen. Some speculate that *telecommuting*—working at home and keeping in touch with fellow employees, customers, and suppliers through computer and telephone networks—will become much more prevalent. One source estimates that 10,000 Americans working for 300 companies already telecommute every day and that 10 million workers may telecommute by the end of the century.[5]

SUMMARY

Computers and electronic networks now serve employees at almost every level of the organization, from executive suite to production line. Word and data processing, electronic mail, and video conferencing put businesses in touch with one another more quickly than ever before, and decisions are more likely to be based on the most accurate information available.

ON THE JOB:
Solving a Communication Dilemma at Metropolitan Life Insurance Company

The primary objective motivating William Livesey to produce employee benefit booklets for corporate accounts is satisfying the customer. He wants to provide clear, attractive booklets in the minimum amount of time so that Metropolitan's corporate customers always have up-to-date explanations of their insurance coverage for their employees. Livesey assigns 20 people to handle the workload of roughly 125 booklets a month.

Until recently, the job of producing the booklets involved a division of labor between Metropolitan's internal employees and the outside typesetting and printing services. This arrangement, however, introduced inevitable delays. As Livesey points out, "the Ping-Pong effect" was inherently inefficient, with paper bouncing back and forth between Metropolitan and its contractors for typesetting, proofreading, revisions, and printing.

A few years ago, when Metropolitan decided to reorganize its national accounts activities and move to new quarters, Livesey pounced on the opportunity to overhaul the procedures for producing the booklets. He invested in an electronic publishing system, including personal computers and laser printers, that enables Metropolitan to create professionally styled documents internally.

With the new system, Metropolitan has cut three to four weeks off the time required to produce new and revised booklets. As Livesey says, "We have regained control of the process, eliminated the time delays caused by the middlemen, and greatly improved the responsiveness to customers." Not only that, Metropolitan is saving money. Livesey estimates that the system will more than pay for itself in 18 months.

Although creating and revising descriptive booklets is the main application for the system, it is also used for other purposes. "We're now producing some of our financial reports, charts, and forms," Livesey says. "Those have been an unexpected bonus of having this system at our disposal."

Your Mission: You supervise the 20-person department that produces employee benefits booklets. Your responsibilities involve everything from writing the text to laying out pages and reproducing the booklets. Handle the following situations to the *best* of your ability:

1. One of Metropolitan's major customers has revised its group insurance benefits. The salesperson handling the customer has asked you to provide details on how you will handle the revisions of that company's benefits booklet, which is bound in a loose-leaf three-ring binder. You estimate that roughly half the pages in the existing booklet will be affected by the changes. What will you tell the salesperson you are going to do?
   a. Ask the customer to return all existing employee benefits booklets and then take out the old pages and insert the new pages.
   b. Enter the changes to the existing text on Metropolitan's electronic publishing system and then print as many completely new booklets as the customer requires.
   c. Revise the pages in question and then send copies of those pages to the customer for insertion into the benefit booklets.
   d. Describe the changes in a cross-referenced addendum that supplements the existing booklet. Then print and ship enough copies of the addendum so that all the customer's employees can have their own copy.

2. Livesey has asked you to shop for some new software that can be used with the electronic publishing system to make transparencies for oral presentations. What is the first step you should take in approaching this task?
   a. Buy an assortment of magazines that cover the subject of computer software, and read articles on the various programs available.
   b. Contact the company that manufactures the hardware Metropolitan is currently using, ask for a listing of compatible software programs for making transparencies, and write to all the software companies for sales literature.

c. Talk to the people at Metropolitan who use transparencies in their oral presentations, and determine what they are looking for in the way of graphics capabilities, clip art, color, and various types and sizes of print.

d. Attend a trade show that features electronic publishing hardware and software so that you can see the alternatives firsthand.

e. Hire a consultant who specializes in developing customized software for corporations.

3. Although the electronic publishing system has streamlined Metropolitan's document production process, you would like to take additional steps to save time. Which of the following options might be worth a closer look?

a. Buy a new, high-speed photocopy machine.

b. Distribute booklets to customers via the fax machine.

c. Study the time spent on various steps in the booklet production and distribution process to identify possible bottlenecks.

d. Invest in software that checks for spelling, punctuation, and style problems.

4. As Metropolitan's business grows, Mr. Livesey anticipates that the department will need to increase its booklet production capacity. What is the best way to prepare for expansion?

a. Hire one or two additional writers, and train them to use the electronic publishing system.

b. Analyze the capacity of the electronic publishing system, and determine how many more workstations it can handle. Add machine capacity and workstations as needed to support the department's increasing workload.

c. Analyze how current employees are spending their time, and then determine how much additional work each person can handle. Increase the work load of each employee so that everyone is turning out as many booklets as possible. Hire new workers when all existing employees reach the limits of their capacity.

d. Redesign the booklets so that they can be produced in less time.

e. Analyze the capacity of both the electronic publishing system and the employees to determine how much excess capacity the department currently has. Add new people and equipment as needed to handle the growing work load.

5. Livesey has asked you to look into the possibility of supplementing the descriptive booklets with videotapes that explain each customer's group insurance benefits. What is the first step you should take in conducting your investigation?

a. Develop a rough outline for such a videotape; then call up a cross section of the customers and ask them what they think of the idea.

b. Find out whether Metropolitan's competitors provide videotape explanations of group insurance benefits.

c. Take a course on how to produce videotapes.

d. Develop a rough outline for such a videotape, and then ask some outside producers to give you an idea of how much it would cost to produce and update tapes for each of your major customers.

e. Attend a videotape equipment show to determine what equipment Metropolitan would need to purchase to produce its own training films.

6. The sales and marketing department has persuaded Metropolitan Life to install a toll-free hot line that allows group insurance customers to call with questions during business hours. Livesey has asked you to recommend the best way to keep the hot-line operators informed on the details of each customer's insurance benefits coverage. What would you propose?

a. Give each hot-line operator a copy of the benefits booklet for each of Metropolitan's group insurance customers.

b. Provide each hot-line operator with a computer terminal that has access to the texts of all the insurance booklets created on the electronic publishing system. Program the computers so that the operators can quickly access the appropriate information for each group insurance customer. (Set up a read-only safeguard so that the operators cannot inadvertently alter the text.)

c. Prepare a fact sheet that provides answers to the most frequently asked questions. Instruct the hot-line operators to direct questions not covered by the fact sheet to the sales representative who handles that customer's account.

d. Have a fax machine at the telephone service center to allow the hot-line operators to provide the inquiring customers with copies of the appropriate pages from the benefits booklet when questions arise.

7. One of your most experienced booklet writers has notified you that her spouse has been relocated to another city by his employer. Rather than quit, the employee has proposed setting up a home office in the city where she and her spouse will be living so that she can "commute" to Metropolitan Life via long-distance phone lines. What pieces of equipment would you need to provide to enable the employee to continue to make a productive contribution to your department?

a. A typewriter and a generous supply of envelopes and postage stamps.

b. A computer and draft-quality printer linked by telephone to Metropolitan Life's electronic publishing system, together with the software required to produce the booklets.

c. A duplicate of the entire electronic publishing system, including a computer terminal, laser printer, color plotter, photocopy machine, and fax machine, along with the related software.

d. A complete teleconferencing setup to allow the employee to attend meetings at Metropolitan's headquarters, together with all the input and output devices required to tie into the electronic publishing system.[6]

QUESTIONS FOR DISCUSSION

1. Given the importance of keyboards in today's office, should everyone studying business be required to learn keyboarding? Why or why not?
2. In a small office, what sort of production equipment would be most versatile?
3. What is an electronic office, and how does it help the conduct of business? What are its disadvantages?
4. What are the main components of the electronic office, and how do they break down into the five categories of office equipment (origination, production, reproduction, distribution/transmission, storage)?
5. What makes a computer so versatile?
6. How does the electronic office affect business communication? What communication skills are most important in an electronic office? Be specific.

EXERCISES

1. Visit two or three types of businesses in your area, such as an insurance company, a school, and a car dealership. Interview the office managers about each company's system for handling and storing records. Prepare a report comparing the systems and perhaps making recommendations for upgrading or improving them.
2. Visit the word-processing center at a large company or at your school. Develop a flow chart of how the word-processing system works, from origination to distribution and storage. Be sure to indicate the approximate time required at each step for various types of documents.
3. Consider any two types of office equipment designed to perform the same function, and compare their advantages and disadvantages. Take into account the purchase and operating costs of each, their ease of operation, their flexibility in handling varied assignments, their dependability, and other relevant matters. Remember to consider the time lost while staff members attend training programs to learn how to operate sophisticated equipment.
4. See this chapter's On-the-Job simulation. As your department has grown in size and importance, you and Livesey have agreed that it is time for you to hire and train an assistant supervisor. Outline the steps you would take to train and develop the person you hire so that he or she can assist you daily as well as stand in for you when you are away from the office.[7]

FUNDAMENTALS OF GRAMMAR AND USAGE

Grammar is nothing more than the way words are combined into sentences, and usage is the way words are used by a network of people—in this case, the community of businesspeople who use English. You will find it easier to get along in this community if you know the accepted standards of grammar and usage.

What follows is a review of the basics of grammar and usage, things you have probably learned but may have forgotten. Without a firm grasp of these basics, you may be misunderstood, damage your company's image, lose money for your company, and possibly even lose your job.

1.0 GRAMMAR

The sentences below look innocent, but consider the bombs they contain:

> We sell tuxedos as well as rent.

> (You might sell rent, but it's highly unlikely. Whatever you are selling, some people will ignore your message because of a blunder like this.)

> Vice President Eldon Neale told his chief engineer that he would no longer be with Avix, Inc., as of June 30.

> (Is Eldon or the engineer leaving? No matter which side the facts are on, the sentence can be read the other way. You may have a hard time convincing either person that your simple mistake was not a move in a game of office politics.)

Now look at this sentence:

> The year before we budgeted more for advertising sales were up.

Confused? Perhaps this is what you meant:

> The year before, we budgeted more for advertising. Sales were up.

Or did you mean this?

> The year before we budgeted more for advertising, sales were up.

The meanings of language fall into bundles called sentences. A listener or reader can take only so much meaning before filing a sentence away and getting ready for the next one. So writers have to know what a sentence is. They need to know where one ends and the next one begins.

But anyone who wants to know what something is has to find out what goes into it, what its ingredients are. Luckily, the basic ingredients of an English sentence are simple. They are called the parts of speech. The content-bearing parts of speech are nouns, pronouns, verbs, adjectives, and adverbs. They combine with a few functional parts of speech to convey meaning. Meaning is also transmitted by punctuation, mechanics, and vocabulary.

1.1 NOUNS

A noun names a person, place, or thing. Anything you can see or detect with one of your other senses has a noun to name it. Some things you can't see or sense are also nouns—ions, for example, or space. And so are things that exist as ideas, such as accuracy and height. (You can see that something is accurate or that a building is tall, but you can't see the idea of accuracy or the idea of height.) These names for ideas are known as abstract nouns. But the simplest nouns are the names of things you can see or touch: car, building, cloud, brick.

1.1.1 Proper nouns and common nouns

So far, all the examples of nouns have been common nouns referring to general classes of things. The word *building*, for example, refers to a whole class of structures. Common nouns are not capitalized.

But if you want to talk about one particular building, you might refer to the Glazier Building. Notice that the name is capitalized, indicating that *Glazier Building* is a proper noun. Here are three sets of common and proper nouns for comparison:

COMMON	PROPER
city	Kansas City
company	Blaisden Company
store	Books Galore

1.1.2 Plural nouns

Nouns can be either singular or plural. The usual way to make a plural noun is to add *s* to the singular form of the word:

SINGULAR	PLURAL
rock	rocks
picture	pictures
song	songs

But many nouns have other ways of forming the plural. For example, letters, numbers, and words used as words are sometimes made plural by adding an apostrophe and an *s*. As a rule, *'s* is used with abbreviations that have periods, lowercase letters that stand alone, and capital letters that might be confused with other words when made into plurals:

Spell out all *St.*'s and *Ave.*'s.

He divided the page with a row of *x*'s.

Sarah will register the *A*'s through *I*'s at the convention.

In other cases, however, the apostrophe may be left out:

They'll review their ABCs.

The stock market climbed through most of the 1980s.

Circle all *the*s in the paragraph.

Observe in the preceding examples how letters and words used as words are italicized.

Other nouns, like those below, are so-called irregular nouns; they form the plural in some way other than simply adding *s*:

SINGULAR	PLURAL
tax	taxes
specialty	specialties
cargo	cargoes
shelf	shelves
child	children
woman	women
tooth	teeth
mouse	mice
parenthesis	parentheses
son-in-law	sons-in-law
editor-in-chief	editors-in-chief

Rather than memorize a lot of rules about forming plurals, use a dictionary. If the dictionary says nothing about the plural of a word, it is formed the usual way—by adding *s*. If the plural is formed in some irregular way, the dictionary will show the plural or have a note something like this: pl. *-es*.

1.1.3 Possessive nouns

A noun becomes possessive when it is used to show the ownership of something. Then you add *'s* to the word:

the man's car   the woman's apartment

But ownership does not need to be legal:

the secretary's desk   the company's assets

And ownership may be nothing more than an automatic association:

a day's work   a job's prestige

An exception to the rule about adding *'s* to make a noun possessive occurs when the word is singular but already has two *s* sounds at the end. In cases like the following, an apostrophe is all that is needed:

crisis' dimensions   Mr. Moses' application

When the noun has only one *s* sound at the end, however, retain the *'s*:

Chris's book   Carolyn Nuss's office

With hyphenated nouns (compound nouns), add *'s* to the last word:

HYPHENATED NOUN	POSSESSIVE NOUN
mother-in-law	mother-in-law's
mayor-elect	mayor-elect's

Forming the possessive of plural nouns may at first seem confusing, but it is really rather simple. Just begin by following the same rule as with singular nouns: add *'s*. But if the plural noun already ends in an *s* (as most do), drop the one you have added, leaving only the apostrophe:

the clients's complaints   employees's benefits

1.2 PRONOUNS

A pronoun is a word that stands for a noun; it saves having to repeat the noun.

> *Drivers* have some choice of weeks for vacation, but *they* must notify this office of *their* preference by March 1.

The pronouns *they* and *their* stand in for the noun *drivers*. The noun that a pronoun stands for is called the antecedent of the pronoun; *drivers* is the antecedent of *they* and *their*.

When the antecedent is plural, the pronoun that stands in for it has to be plural; *they* and *their* are plural pronouns because *drivers* is plural. Likewise, when the antecedent is singular, the pronoun has to be singular:

We thought the *contract* had been signed, but we soon learned *it* had not been.

1.2.1 Multiple antecedents

Sometimes a pronoun has a double (or even triple) antecedent:

> *Kathryn Boettcher and Luis Gutierrez* went beyond *their* sales quotas for January.

Kathryn Boettcher, if taken alone, is a singular antecedent. So is *Luis Gutierrez*. But when both are the antecedent of a pronoun, they are plural and the pronoun has to be plural. Thus the pronoun is *their* instead of *her* or *his*.

1.2.2 Unclear antecedents

In some sentences, the pronoun's antecedent is not clear:

> Sandy Wright sent Jane Brougham *her* production figures for the previous year. *She* thought they were too low.

To whom does the pronoun *her* refer? Someone who knew Sandy and Jane and knew their business relationship might be able to figure out the antecedent for *her*. But even with such an advantage, a reader still might receive the wrong meaning. And it would be nearly impossible for any reader to know which name is the antecedent of *she*. The best way to clarify an ambiguous pronoun is usually to rewrite the sentence, repeating nouns when needed for clarity:

> Sandy Wright sent her production figures for the previous year to Jane Brougham. *Jane* thought they were too low.

But repeat the noun only when the antecedent is unclear.

1.2.3 Gender-neutral pronouns

The pronouns that stand for males are *he*, *his*, and *him*. The pronouns that stand for females are *she*, *hers*, and *her*. But you will often be faced with the dilemma of choosing a pronoun for a noun that refers to both females and males:

> Each manager must make up (his, her, his or her, its, their?) own mind about stocking this item and about the quantity that (he, she, he or she, it, they?) can sell.

This sentence calls for a pronoun that is neither masculine nor feminine.

The issue of gender-neutral pronouns has arisen in response to efforts to treat females and males evenhandedly. Here are some possible ways to deal with this issue:

Each manager must make up *his* . . .
(But not all managers are men.)

Each manager must make up *her* . . .
(Nor are all managers women.)

Each manager must make up *his or her* . . .
(This solution is acceptable but becomes awkward when repeated more than once or twice in a document.)

Each manager must make up *her* . . . Every manager will receive *his* . . . A manager may send *her* . . .
(A manager's gender does not alternate like a windshield wiper!)

Each manager must make up *their* . . .
(The pronoun can't be plural when the antecedent is singular.)

Each manager must make up *its* . . .
(*It* never refers to people.)

The best solution is to make the noun plural or to revise the passage altogether:

Managers must make up *their* minds . . .

Each manager must decide whether . . .

But be careful not to change the original meaning.

1.2.4 Case of pronouns

The case of a pronoun tells whether it is acting or acted upon:

She sells an average of five packages each week.

In this sentence, *she* is doing the selling. Because *she* is acting, *she* is said to be in the nominative case. But consider what happens when the pronoun is acted upon:

After six months, Ms. Browning promoted *her*.

In this sentence, the pronoun *her* is acted upon. The pronoun *her* is thus said to be in the objective case. Contrast the nominative and objective pronouns in this list:

NOMINATIVE	OBJECTIVE
I	me
we	us
he	him
she	her
they	them
who	whom
whoever	whomever

Objective pronouns may be used either as the object of a verb (like *promoted*) or as the object of a preposition (like *with*):

Rob worked with *them* until the order was filled.

In this example, *them* is the object of the preposition *with*, because Rob acted upon—worked with—them.

Here is a sample sentence with three pronouns, the first one nominative, the second the object of a verb, and the third the object of a preposition:

He paid *us* as soon as the check came from *them*.

He is nominative; *us* is objective because it is the object of the verb *paid*; *them* is objective because it is the object of the preposition *from*.

Every writer sometimes wonders whether to use *who* or *whom*:

(Who, Whom) will you hire?

Because this sentence is a question, it is difficult to see that *whom* is the object of the verb *hire*. You can figure out which pronoun to use if you rearrange the question and temporarily try *she* and *her* in place of *who* and *whom*: "Will you hire *she*?" or "Will you hire *her*?" *Her* and *whom* are both objective, so the correct choice is "*Whom* will you hire?" Here's a different example:

(Who, Whom) logged so much travel time?

Turning the question into a statement, you get:

He logged so much travel time.

Therefore, the correct question is:

Who logged so much travel time?

1.2.5 Possessive pronouns

Possessive pronouns are like possessive nouns in the way they work: They show ownership or automatic association.

her job	their preferences
his account	its equipment

But possessive pronouns are different from possessive nouns in the way they are written; that is, possessive pronouns never have an apostrophe:

POSSESSIVE NOUN	POSSESSIVE PRONOUN
the woman's estate	her estate
Roger Franklin's plans	his plans
the shareholders' feelings	their feelings
the vacuum cleaner's attachments	its attachments

Note that *its* is the possessive of *it*. Like all possessive pronouns, *its* does not have an apostrophe. Some people confuse *its* with *it's*, the contraction of *it is*. Contractions are discussed later, but remember this point.

1.3 VERBS

A verb describes an action:

> They all *quit* in disgust.

Or it describes a state of being:

> Working conditions *were* substandard.

The English language is full of action verbs. Here are a few you will often run across in the business world:

verify	perform	fulfill
hire	succeed	send
leave	improve	receive
accept	develop	pay

You could undoubtedly list many more.

The most common verb describing a state of being instead of an action is *to be* and all its forms:

I *am, was,* or *will be*   you *are, were,* or *will be*

But other verbs describe a state of being too:

> It *seemed* like a good plan at the time.

> She *sounds* impressive at a meeting.

These verbs link what comes before them in the sentence with what comes after; no action is involved. (See Section 1.7.5 for a fuller discussion of linking verbs.)

1.3.1 Verb tenses

English has three simple verb tenses: present, past, and future.

Present: Our branches in Hawaii *stock* fewer cold-weather items.

Past: When we *stocked* Purquil pens, we received a great many complaints.

Future: Rotex Tire Stores *will stock* your line of tires when you begin a program of effective national advertising.

With most verbs (the regular ones), the past tense ends in *-ed;* the future tense always has *will* or *shall* in front of it. But the present tense is a little more complex:

SINGULAR	PLURAL
I stock	we stock
you stock	you stock
he, she, it stocks	they stock

Notice that the basic form, *stock*, takes an additional *s* when *he, she,* or *it* precedes it.

In addition to the three simple tenses, there are three perfect tenses, using forms of the helping verb *have*. The present perfect tense uses the past participle (regularly the past tense) of the main verb, *stocked*, and adds the present-tense *have* or *has* to the front of it:

> (I, we, you, they) *have stocked.*

> (He, she, it) *has stocked.*

The past perfect tense uses the past participle of the main verb, *stocked*, and adds the past-tense *had* to the front of it:

> (I, you, he, she, it, we, they) *had stocked.*

The future perfect tense also uses the past participle of the main verb, *stocked*, but adds the future-tense *will have:*

> (I, you, he, she, it, we, they) *will have stocked.*

Keep verbs in the same tense when the actions occur at the same time:

> When the payroll checks *came* in, everyone *showed* up for work.
>
> We *have found* that everyone *has pitched* in to help.

Of course, when the actions occur at different times, you may change tense accordingly:

> A shipment *came* last Wednesday, so when another one *comes* in today, please return it.
>
> The new employee *had been* ill-at-ease, but now she *has become* a full-fledged member of the team.

1.3.2 Irregular verbs

Many verbs do not follow in every detail the patterns already described. The most irregular of these verbs is *to be:*

	SINGULAR	PLURAL
Present:	I *am*	we *are*
	you *are*	you *are*
	he, she, it *is*	they *are*
Past:	I *was*	we *were*
	you *were*	you *were*
	he, she, it *was*	they *were*

The future tense of *to be* is formed the same way the future tense of a regular verb is formed.

The perfect tenses of *to be* are also formed as they would be for a regular verb, except that the past participle is a special form, *been*, instead of just the past tense:

Present Perfect:	you *have been*
Past Perfect:	you *had been*
Future Perfect:	you *will have been*

Here's a sampling of other irregular verbs:

PRESENT	PAST	PAST PARTICIPLE
begin	began	begun
shrink	shrank	shrunk
know	knew	known
rise	rose	risen
become	became	become
go	went	gone
do	did	done

Dictionaries list the various forms of other irregular verbs.

1.3.3 Transitive and intransitive verbs

Many people are confused by three particular sets of verbs:

lie/lay   sit/set   rise/raise

Using these verbs correctly is much easier when you learn the difference between transitive and intransitive verbs. Transitive verbs convey their action to an object; they "transfer" their action to an object. Intransitive verbs do not. Here are some sample uses of transitive and intransitive verbs:

INTRANSITIVE	TRANSITIVE
We should include in our new offices a place to *lie* down for a nap.	The workers will be here on Monday to *lay* new carpeting.
Even the way an interviewee *sits* is important.	That crate is full of stemware, so *set* it down carefully.
Salaries at Compu-Link, Inc., *rise* swiftly.	They *raise* their level of production every year.

The workers *lay* carpeting, you *set* down the crate, they *raise* production—each action is transferred to something. But in the intransitive sentences, one *lies* down, an interviewee *sits*, and salaries *rise* without (at least grammatically) affecting anything else. Intransitive sentences are complete with only a subject and a verb; transitive sentences are not complete unless they also include an object, or something to transfer the action to.

Tenses are a confusing element of the *lie/lay* problem:

PRESENT	PAST	PAST PARTICIPLE
I *lie*	I *lay*	I have *lain*
I *lay* (something down)	I *laid* (something down)	I have *laid* (something down)

Notice that the past tense of *lie* and the present tense of *lay* look and sound alike, even though they are different verbs.

1.3.4 Voice of verbs

Verbs have two voices, active and passive:

Active: The buyer *paid* a large amount.

Passive: A large amount *was paid* by the buyer.

Notice that the passive voice uses a form of the verb *to be*.

Notice also that the passive-voice sentence uses eight words, whereas the active-voice sentence uses six words to say the same thing. Thus the words *was* and *by* are unnecessary to convey the meaning of the sentence. In fact, extra words usually clog meaning. So always opt for the active voice when you have a choice.

At times, however, you have no choice:

Several items *have been taken*, but so far we don't know who took them.

The passive voice becomes necessary when the writer does not know (or doesn't want to say) who performed the action. But the active voice is bolder and more direct.

1.3.5 Mood of verbs

You have three moods to choose from, depending on your intentions. Most of the time, you use the indicative mood to make a statement or ask a question:

The secretary *mailed* a letter to each supplier.

Did the secretary *mail* a letter to each supplier?

When you wish to command or request, use the imperative mood:

Please *mail* a letter to each supplier.

Sometimes, especially in business, a courteous request is stated like a question; in that case, however, no question mark is required.

Would you *mail* a letter to each supplier.

The subjunctive mood, most often used in formal writing or in presenting bad news, expresses a possibility or a recommendation. Usually, it is signaled by a word such as *if* or *that*. Notice in these examples that the subjunctive mood uses special verb forms:

If the secretary *were to mail* a letter to each supplier, we might save some money.

I suggested that the secretary *mail* a letter to each supplier.

Although the subjunctive mood is not used very often anymore, it is still found in such expressions as *Come what may* and *If I were you*.

1.4 ADJECTIVES

An adjective modifies (tells something about) a noun or pronoun:

an *efficient* staff   a *heavy* price

brisk trade   *poor* you

Each of these phrases says more about the noun or pronoun than the noun or pronoun says alone. Adjectives should always tell us something we would not know without them. So avoid using adjectives when the noun alone, or a different noun, will give the meaning:

a *company* employee
(An employee ordinarily works for a company.)

a *crate-type* container
(*Crate* gives the entire meaning.)

At times, adjectives pile up in a series:

It was a *long*, *hot*, and *active* workday.

Such series are acceptable as long as each adjective conveys a different part of the phrase's meaning.

Verbs in the *-ing* form can be used as adjectives:

A *boring* job can sometimes turn into a *fascinating* career.

So can the past participle of verbs:

A freshly *painted* house is a *sold* house.

Adjectives modify nouns more often than they modify pronouns. But when adjectives do modify pronouns, the sentence usually has a linking verb:

They were *attentive.*   It looked *appropriate.*

He seems *interested.*   You are *skillful.*

Most adjectives can take three forms: simple, comparative, and superlative. The simple form modifies a single noun or pronoun. Use the comparative form when comparing two items. When comparing three or more items, use the superlative form.

SIMPLE	COMPARATIVE	SUPERLATIVE
hard	harder	hardest
safe	safer	safest
dry	drier	driest

Notice that the comparative form adds *-er* to the simple form and the superlative form adds *-est.* (The *y* at the end of a word changes to *i* before the *-er* or *-est* is added.)

But a small number of adjectives are irregular, including these:

SIMPLE	COMPARATIVE	SUPERLATIVE
good	better	best
bad	worse	worst
little	less	least

When the simple form of an adjective is two or more syllables, you must usually add *more* to form the comparative and *most* to form the superlative:

SIMPLE	COMPARATIVE	SUPERLATIVE
useful	more useful	most useful
exhausting	more exhausting	most exhausting
expensive	more expensive	most expensive

The only exception might be a two-syllable adjective that ends in *y:*

SIMPLE	COMPARATIVE	SUPERLATIVE
happy	happier	happiest
costly	costlier	costliest

If you choose this option, change the *y* to *i,* and tack *-er* or *-est* onto the end.

1.5 ADVERBS

An adverb modifies a verb, an adjective, or another adverb:

Modifying a Verb:	Our marketing department works *efficiently.*
Modifying an Adjective:	She was not dependable, although she was *highly* intelligent.
Modifying Another Adverb:	His territory was *too* broadly diversified, so he moved *extremely* cautiously.

Notice that most of the adverbs mentioned are adjectives turned into adverbs by adding *-ly,* which is how many adverbs are formed:

ADJECTIVE	ADVERB
efficient	efficiently
high	highly
extreme	extremely
special	specially
official	officially
separate	separately

But some adverbs are made by dropping or changing the final letter of the adjective and then adding *-ly:*

ADJECTIVE	ADVERB
due	duly
busy	busily

Other adverbs do not end in *-ly* at all. Here are a few examples of this type:

often	fast	too
soon	very	so

1.6 OTHER PARTS OF SPEECH

Nouns, pronouns, verbs, adjectives, and adverbs carry most of the meaning in a sentence. But four other parts of speech link them together in sentences: prepositions, conjunctions, articles, and interjections.

1.6.1 Prepositions

Prepositions are words like these:

of	to	for	with
at	by	from	about

They most often begin prepositional phrases, which function like adjectives and adverbs by telling more about a pronoun, noun, or verb:

of a type   *by* Friday

to the point   *with* characteristic flair

1.6.2 Conjunctions, articles, and interjections

Conjunctions are words that usually join parts of a sentence. Here are a few:

and	but	because
yet	although	if

The use of conjunctions is discussed in Sections 1.7.3 and 1.7.4.

Only three articles exist in English: *the*, *a*, and *an*. These words are used, like adjectives, to specify which item you are talking about.

Interjections are words that express no solid information, only emotion:

Wow!	Well, well!
Oh no!	Good!

Such purely emotional language has its place in private life and advertising copy, but it only weakens the effect of most business writing.

1.7 WHOLE SENTENCES

Sentences are constructed with the major building blocks, the parts of speech.

Money talks.

This two-word sentence consists of a noun (*money*) and a verb (*talks*). When used in this way, the noun works as the first requirement for a sentence, the subject, and the verb works as the second requirement, the predicate. Now look at this sentence:

They merged.

The subject in this case is a pronoun (*they*), and the predicate is a verb (*merged*). This is a sentence,

then, because it has a subject and a predicate. Here is yet another kind of sentence:

The plans are ready.

This sentence has a more complicated subject, the noun *plans* and the article *the*; the complete predicate is a state-of-being verb (*are*) and an adjective (*ready*). Without these two parts—the subject (who or what does something) and the predicate (the doing of it)—no collection of words is a sentence.

1.7.1 Commands

In commands, the subject is only understood, not stated. It is always *you*:

(You) Move your desk to the better office.

(You) Please try to finish by six o'clock.

1.7.2 Longer sentences

More complicated sentences have more complicated subjects and predicates. But they still have a simple subject and a predicate verb. In the following examples, the simple subject is underlined once, the predicate verb twice:

Marex and Contron enjoy higher earnings each quarter.
(Marex [and] Contron did something; enjoy is what they did.)

My interview, coming minutes after my freeway accident, did not impress or move anyone.
(Interview is what did something. What did it do? It did [not] impress [or] move.)

In terms of usable space, a steel warehouse, with its extremely long span of roof unsupported by pillars, makes more sense.
(Warehouse is what makes.)

These three sentences demonstrate several things. First, notice that in all three sentences the simple subject and predicate verb are the "bare bones" of the sentence, the parts that carry the core idea of the sentence. When trying to find the simple subject and predicate verb, disregard all prepositional phrases, modifiers, conjunctions, and articles.

Second, notice in the third sentence that the verb is singular (*makes*) because the subject is singular (*warehouse*). Even though the plural noun *pillars* is closer to the verb, *warehouse* is the real subject.

So *warehouse* determines whether the verb is singular or plural. Subject and predicate must agree.

Third, notice that the subject in the first sentence is compound (*Marex* [and] *Contron*). A compound subject, when connected by *and*, requires a plural verb (*enjoy*). Notice, also, in the second sentence that compound predicates (*did* [not] *impress* [or] *move*) are possible.

Fourth, notice that the second sentence incorporates a group of words—*coming minutes after my freeway accident*—containing a form of a verb (*coming*) and a noun (*accident*). Yet this group of words is not a complete sentence for two reasons:

■ *Accident* is not the subject of *coming*. Not all nouns are subjects.

■ A verb that ends in *-ing* can never be the predicate of a sentence unless preceded by a form of *to be* (as in *was coming*). Not all verbs are predicates.

Because it does not have a subject and a predicate, the group of words *coming minutes after my freeway accident* (called a phrase) cannot be written as a sentence. That is, it cannot stand alone, beginning with a capital letter and ending with a period. Because a phrase cannot stand alone, it must always be part of a sentence.

Sometimes a sentence incorporates two or more groups of words that do contain a subject and a predicate; these word groups are called clauses.

> My interview, because it came minutes after my freeway accident, did not impress or move anyone.

The independent clause is the portion of the sentence that could stand alone without revision:

> My interview did not impress or move anyone.

But the other part of the sentence could stand alone only by removing *because*:

> (because) It came minutes after my freeway accident.

This part of the sentence is known as a dependent clause; although it has a subject and a predicate, as an independent clause has, it is linked to the main part of the sentence by a word (*because*), thus showing its dependence.

To summarize, the two types of clauses—dependent and independent—both have a subject and a predicate. But dependent clauses do not bear the main meaning of the sentence and must therefore be linked to an independent clause. Nor can phrases stand alone; phrases lack a subject and predicate. Only independent clauses can be written as sentences without revision.

1.7.3 Sentence fragments

When an incomplete sentence (a phrase or dependent clause) is written as though it were a complete sentence, it is called a fragment. Consider the following sentence fragments:

> Marilyn Sanders, having had pilferage problems in her store for the past year. Refuses to accept the results of our investigation.

This serious error can easily be corrected by putting the two fragments together:

> Marilyn Sanders, having had pilferage problems in her store for the past year, refuses to accept the results of our investigation.

> Not all fragments can be corrected so easily:

> Employees a part of it. No authority or discipline.

Only the writer knows the intended meaning of these two phrases. Perhaps the employees are taking part in the pilferage. If so, the sentence should read:

> Some employees are part of the pilferage problem.

On the other hand, it is possible that some employees are helping with the investigation. Then the sentence would read:

> Some employees are taking part in our investigation.

But it is just as likely that the employees are not only taking part in the pilferage but are also being analyzed:

> Those employees who are part of the pilferage problem will accept no authority or discipline.

In fact, even more meanings could be read into these

fragments. Because fragments like these can mean so many things, they mean nothing. No well-written memo, letter, or report should ever demand that the reader be an imaginative genius.

One more type of fragment exists, the kind represented by a dependent clause. Notice what *because* does to what was once a unified sentence:

Our stock of sprinklers is depleted.

Because our stock of sprinklers is depleted.

Although it contains a subject and a predicate, the second version is a fragment because of *because*. Words like *because* form a special group of words called subordinating conjunctions. Here is a partial list:

since	though	whenever
although	if	unless
while	even if	after

When a word of this type begins a clause, the clause is dependent and cannot stand alone as a sentence. But if a dependent clause is combined with an independent clause, it can convey a complete meaning. The independent clause may come before or after the dependent clause:

We are unable to fill your order because our stock of sprinklers is depleted.

Because our stock of sprinklers is depleted, we are unable to fill your order.

Another remedy for a fragment that is a dependent clause is to remove the subordinating conjunction. That solution leaves a simple but complete sentence:

Our stock of sprinklers is depleted.

The actual details of a transaction will determine the best way to remedy a fragment problem.

There is one exception to the ban on fragments. Some advertising copy contains sentence fragments, written knowingly to convey a certain rhythm. However, advertising is the only area of business in which fragments are acceptable.

1.7.4 Fused sentences and comma splices

Just as there can be too little in a group of words to make it a sentence, there can also be too much:

All our mail is run through a postage meter every afternoon someone picks it up.

There are two sentences here, not one. But the two have been blended so that it is hard to tell where one ends and the next begins. Is the mail run through a meter every afternoon? If so, the sentences should read:

All our mail is run through a postage meter every afternoon. Someone picks it up.

But perhaps the mail is run through a meter at some other time (morning, for example) and is picked up every afternoon:

All our mail is run through a postage meter. Every afternoon someone picks it up.

The order of words is the same in all three cases; sentence division makes all the difference. Either of the last two cases is grammatically correct. The choice depends on the facts of the situation.

Sometimes these so-called fused sentences have a more obvious point of separation:

Several large orders arrived within a few days of one another, too many came in for us to process by the end of the month.

Here the comma has been put between two independent clauses in an attempt to link them. When a lowly comma separates two complete sentences, the result is called a comma splice. A comma splice can be remedied in one of three ways:

- Replace the comma with a period, and capitalize the next word: ". . . one another. Too many . . ."

- Replace the comma with a semicolon, but do not capitalize the next word: ". . . one another; too many . . ." This remedy works only when the two sentences have closely related meanings.

- Change one of the sentences so that it becomes a phrase or a dependent clause. This remedy often produces the best writing, but it takes more work.

The third alternative can be carried out in several ways. One is to begin the blended sentence with a subordinating conjunction:

Whenever several large orders arrived within a few days of one another, too many came in for us to process by the end of the month.

Another way is to remove part of the subject or the predicate verb from one of the independent clauses, thereby creating a phrase:

> Several large <u>orders</u> <u>arrived</u> within a few days of one another, too <u>many</u> for us to process by the end of the month.

Finally, you can change one of the predicate verbs to its *-ing* form:

> Several large <u>orders</u> <u>arrived</u> within a few days of one another, too <u>many</u> coming in for us to process by the end of the month.

At other times, a simple coordinating conjunction (such as *or*, *and*, or *but*) can separate fused sentences:

> You can fire them, *or* you can make better use of their abilities.

> Margaret drew up the designs, *and* Matt carried them out.

> We will have three strong months, *but* after that sales will taper off.

The use of coordinating conjunctions calls for caution: They should be used only to join simple sentences that express similar ideas.

Coordinating conjunctions should not be overused, because they say relatively little about the relationship between the two clauses they join: *and* is merely an addition sign; *but* is just a turn signal; *or* only points to an alternative. Subordinating conjunctions such as *because* and *whenever* tell the reader a lot more.

1.7.5 Sentences with linking verbs

Linking verbs were discussed briefly in the section on verbs (Section 1.3). Here you can see more fully the way they function in a sentence. The following is a model of any sentence with a linking verb:

> A (verb) B.

Although words like *seems* and *feels* can also be linking verbs, let's assume that the verb is a form of *to be:*

> A *is* B.

In such a sentence, A and B are always nouns, pronouns, or adjectives. When one is a noun and the other's a pronoun, the sentence says that one is the same as the other:

> She is president.

When one is an adjective, it modifies or describes the other:

> She is forceful.

Remember that when one is an adjective, it modifies the other as any adjective modifies a noun or pronoun, except that a linking verb stands between the adjective and the word it modifies.

1.7.6 Misplaced modifiers

The position of a modifier in a sentence is important. Notice how the movement of *only* changes the meaning in the following sentences:

> *Only* we are obliged to supply those items specified in your contract.

> We are obliged *only* to supply those items specified in your contract.

> We are obliged to supply *only* those items specified in your contract.

> We are obliged to supply those items specified *only* in your contract.

In any particular set of circumstances, only one of these sentences would be accurate. The others would very likely cause problems. To prevent misunderstanding, modifiers like *only* must be placed as close as possible to the noun or verb they modify.

For similar reasons, whole phrases that are modifiers must be placed near the right noun or verb. Mistakes in placement create ludicrous meanings:

> Antia Information Systems has bought new computer chairs for the programmers *with more comfortable seats*.

The anatomy of programmers is not normally a concern of business writing. Obviously the comfort of the chairs was the issue:

> Antia Information Systems has bought new computer chairs *with more comfortable seats* for the programmers.

Here is another example:

I asked him to file all the letters in the cabinet *that had been answered.*

In this ridiculous sentence, the cabinet has been answered, even though no cabinet in history is known to have asked a question. *That had been answered* is too far from *letters* and too close to *cabinet.* Here's an improvement:

I asked him to file in the cabinet all the letters *that had been answered.*

Notice that in some cases, instead of moving the modifying phrase closer to the word it modifies, the best solution is to move the word closer to the modifying phrase.

2.0 PUNCTUATION

On the highway, signs tell you when to slow down or stop, where to turn, when to merge. In similar fashion, punctuation helps readers negotiate your prose. The proper use of punctuation keeps readers from losing track of your meaning.

2.1 PERIODS

Use a period (1) to end any sentence that is not a question, (2) with certain abbreviations, and (3) between dollars and cents in an amount of money.

2.2 QUESTION MARKS

Use a question mark after any direct question that requests an answer:

Are you planning to enclose a check, or shall we bill you?

Do not use a question mark with commands phrased as questions for the sake of politeness:

Will you send us a check today.

2.3 EXCLAMATION POINTS

Use exclamation points after highly emotional language. But because business writing almost never calls for emotional language, you should almost never use exclamation points.

2.4 SEMICOLONS

Semicolons have three main uses. The first is to separate two independent clauses when they are closely related:

The outline for the report is due within a week; the report itself is due at the end of the month.

A semicolon should also be used instead of a comma when the items in a series have commas within them:

Our previous meetings were on November 11, 1991; February 20, 1992; and April 28, 1992.

Finally, a semicolon should be used to separate independent clauses when the second one begins with a word such as *however, therefore,* or *nevertheless* or a phrase such as *for example* or *in that case:*

Our supplier has been out of part D712 for 10 weeks; however, we have found another source that can ship the part right away.

His test scores were quite low; on the other hand, he has a lot of relevant experience.

Section 4.4 tells more about using transitional words and phrases like these.

2.5 COLONS

Use a colon (1) after the salutation in a business letter and (2) at the end of a sentence or phrase introducing a list, a quotation, or an idea:

Our study included the three most critical problems: insufficient capital, incompetent management, and inappropriate location.

In some introductory sentences, *the following* or *that is* is implied by use of the colon.

A colon should not be used when the list, quotation, or idea is a direct object or part of the introductory sentence:

We are able to supply

staples	wood screws
nails	toggle bolts

2.6 COMMAS

Commas have many uses, the most common being to separate items in a series:

He took the job, learned it well, worked hard, and succeeded.

Put paper, pencils, and paper clips on the requisition list.

Be aware that company style often dictates omitting the final comma in a series. If you have a choice, however, use the final comma. It is often necessary to prevent misunderstanding.

The second place to use a comma is between clauses. A comma should separate independent clauses (unless one or both are very short):

She spoke to the sales staff, and he spoke to the production staff.

I was advised to proceed and I did.

A dependent clause at the beginning of a sentence is also separated from an independent clause by a comma:

Because of our lead in the market, we may be able to risk introducing a new product.

But a dependent clause at the end of a sentence is separated from the independent clause by a comma only when the dependent clause is unnecessary to the main meaning of the sentence:

We may be able to introduce a new product, although it may involve some risk.

A third use for the comma is after an introductory phrase or word:

Starting with this amount of capital, we can survive in the red for one year.

Through more careful planning, we may be able to serve more people.

In short, the move to Tulsa was a good idea.

Yes, you may proceed as originally planned.

However, with short introductory prepositional phrases and some one-syllable words (such as *hence* and *thus*), the comma is often omitted:

Before January 1 we must complete the inventory. Thus we may not need to hire anyone.

Fourth, commas are used to surround parenthetical phrases or words, which can be removed from the sentence without changing the meaning:

The new owners, the Kowacks, are pleased with their purchase.

Fifth, commas are used between adjectives modifying the same noun:

She left Monday for a long, difficult recruiting trip.

To test the appropriateness of such a comma, try reversing the order of the adjectives: "a difficult, long recruiting trip." If the order cannot be reversed, leave out the comma ("a good old friend" isn't the same as "an old good friend"). Neither is a comma used when one of the adjectives is part of the noun. Compare these two phrases:

a distinguished, well-known figure

a distinguished public figure

The adjective-noun combination of *public* and *figure* has been used together so often that it has come to be considered a single thing: *public figure*. Thus no comma is required.

Sixth, commas should surround *Jr., Sr., Inc.,* and the like:

Cloverdell, Inc.   Daniel Garcia, Jr.

In a sentence, a comma should also follow the abbreviation:

Belle Brown, Ph.D., is the new tenant.

Seventh, commas are used both before and after the year when writing month, day, and year:

It will be sent by December 15, 1993, from our Cincinnati plant.

Some companies write dates in another form: 15 December 1993. No commas should be used in this case. Nor is a comma needed when only the month and year are present (December 1993).

Eighth, a comma may be used after an informal salutation in a letter to a personal friend. (In business letters, however, salutations are followed by colons.)

Ninth, a comma is used to separate a quotation from the rest of the sentence:

> Your warranty reads, "These conditions remain in effect for one year from date of purchase."

However, the comma is left out when the quotation as a whole is built into the structure of the sentence:

> He hurried off with an angry "Look where you're going."

Finally, a comma should be used whenever it is needed to avoid confusion or an unintended meaning. Compare the following:

> Ever since they have planned new ventures more carefully.

> Ever since, they have planned new ventures more carefully.

2.7 DASHES

Use a dash to surround a parenthetical comment when the comment is a sudden turn in thought:

> Membership in the IBSA—it's expensive but worth it—may be obtained by applying to our New York office.

A dash can also be used to emphasize a parenthetical word or phrase:

> Third-quarter profits—in excess of $2 million—are up sharply.

Finally, use dashes to set off a phrase that contains commas:

> All our offices—Milwaukee, New Orleans, and Phoenix—have sent representatives.

Do not confuse a dash with a hyphen. A dash separates words, phrases, and clauses more strongly

than a comma does; a hyphen ties two words so tightly that they almost become one word. When typing a dash, type two hyphens with no spacing before, between, or after.

2.8 HYPHENS

Hyphens are used in three main ways. The first is to separate the parts of compound words beginning with such prefixes as *self-*, *ex-*, *quasi-*, and *all-*:

self-assured	quasi-official
ex-wife	all-important

But hyphens are usually left out and the words closed up when using such prefixes as *pro-*, *anti-*, *non-*, *un-*, *inter-*, and *extra-*:

prolabor	nonunion
antifascist	interdepartmental

An exception occurs when the prefix occurs before a proper noun and sometimes when the vowel at the end of the prefix is the same as the first letter of the root word:

pro-Republican	anti-American
anti-inflammatory	extra-atmospheric

If in doubt, consult your dictionary.

Hyphens are also used in some compound adjectives, which are adjectives made up of two or more words. Specifically, you should use hyphens in compound adjectives that come before the noun:

a first-rate company	well-informed executives

But do not hyphenate when the adjective follows a linking verb:

> This company is first rate.

> Their executives are well informed.

You can shorten sentences that list similar hyphenated words by dropping the common part from all but the last word:

> Check the costs of first-, second-, and third-class postage.

Finally, hyphens may be used to divide words at

the end of a typed line. Such hyphenation is best avoided, but when you have to divide words at the end of a line, do so correctly (see Section 3.4). A dictionary will show how words are divided into syllables.

2.9 APOSTROPHES

Use an apostrophe in the possessive form of a noun (but not in a pronoun):

> On *his* desk was a reply to *Bette Ainsley's* application for the *manager's* position.

Apostrophes are also used in place of the missing letter(s) of a contraction:

WHOLE WORDS	CONTRACTION
we will	we'll
do not	don't
they are	they're

2.10 QUOTATION MARKS

Use quotation marks to surround words that are repeated exactly as they were said or written:

> The collection letter ended by saying, "This is your third and final notice."

Notice two things: (1) When the quoted material is a complete sentence, the first word is capitalized; (2) the final comma or period goes inside the closing quotation marks.

Quotation marks are also used to set off the title of a newspaper story, magazine article, or book chapter:

> You should read "Legal Aspects of the Collection Letter" in *Today's Credit*.

Notice that the book title is in italics. When typewritten, the title is underlined. The same treatment is proper for newspaper and magazine titles. (Appendix C explains documentation style in more detail.)

Quotation marks may also be used to indicate special treatment for words or phrases, such as terms that you are using in an unusual or ironic way:

> Our management "team" spends more time squabbling than working to solve company problems.

When using quotation marks, take care to put in both sets, the closing marks as well as the opening ones.

Although periods and commas go inside any quotation marks, colons or semicolons go outside them. A question mark goes inside the quotation marks only if the quotation is a question:

> All that day we wondered, "Is he with us?"

If the quotation is not a question but the entire sentence is, the question mark goes outside:

> What did she mean by "You will hear from me"?

2.11 PARENTHESES

Use parentheses to surround comments that are entirely incidental:

> Our figures do not match yours, although (if my calculations are correct) they are closer than we thought.

Parentheses are also used in legal documents to surround figures in arabic numerals that follow the same amount in words:

> Remittance will be One Thousand Two Hundred Dollars ($1,200).

Be careful to put punctuation (period, comma, and so on) outside the parentheses unless it is part of the statement in parentheses.

2.12 ELLIPSES

Use ellipsis points, or dots, to indicate that material has been left out of a direct quotation. But use them only in direct quotations and only at the point where material was left out. Notice how the first sentence is quoted in the second:

> The Dow Jones Industrial Average, which skidded 38.17 points in the previous five sessions, gained 4.61 to end at 2213.84.

> According to the Honolulu *Star Bulletin*, "The Dow Jones Industrial Average . . . gained 4.61" on June 10.

The number of dots in ellipses is not optional; always use three. Occasionally, the points of ellipsis come at the end of a sentence, where they seem to grow a fourth dot. But don't be fooled: One of the dots is a period.

2.13 UNDERSCORES AND ITALICS

Usually a line typed underneath a word or phrase either provides emphasis or indicates the title of a book, magazine, or newspaper. If possible, use italics instead of an underscore. Italics (or underlining) should also be used for defining terms and for discussing words as words.

> In this report, *net sales* refers to after-tax sales dollars.

> The word *building* is a common noun and should not be capitalized.

3.0 MECHANICS

The most obvious and least tolerable mistakes that a business writer makes are probably those related to grammar and punctuation. However, a number of small details, known as writing mechanics, demonstrate the writer's polish and reflect on the company's professionalism.

3.1 CAPITALS

You should, of course, capitalize words that begin sentences:

> *Before* hanging up, he said, "*We'll* meet here on Wednesday at 10 a.m."

A quotation that is a complete sentence should also begin with a capitalized word.

The names of particular persons, places, and things (proper nouns) are also capitalized:

> We sent *Ms. Larson* an application form, informing her that not all *applicants* are interviewed.

> Let's consider opening a branch in the *West*, perhaps at the *west* end of *Tucson, Arizona*.

> As *office buildings* go, the *Kinney Building* is a pleasant setting for *TDG Office Equipment*.

Notice that Ms. Larson's name is capitalized because she is a particular applicant, whereas the general term *applicant* is left uncapitalized. Likewise, *West* is capitalized when it refers to a particular place but not when it means a direction. In the same way, *office* and *building* are not capitalized when they are general terms (common nouns) but are capitalized when they are part of the title of a particular office or building (proper nouns).

Titles within families, governments, or companies may also be capitalized:

> My *Uncle David* offered me a job, but I wouldn't be comfortable working for one of my *uncles*.

> We've never had a *president* quite like *President* Sweeney.

In addition, always capitalize the first word of the salutation and complimentary close of a letter:

> *Dear* Mr. Andrews:

> *Yours* very truly,

Finally, capitalize the first word after a colon when it begins a complete sentence:

> Follow this rule: When in doubt, leave it out.

Otherwise, the first word after a colon should not be capitalized.

3.2 ABBREVIATIONS

Abbreviations are used heavily in tables, charts, lists, and forms. They are used sparingly in prose paragraphs, however.

Here are some abbreviations often used in business writing:

ABBREVIATION	FULL TERM
b/l	bill of lading
ca.	circa (about)
dol., dols.	dollar, dollars
etc.	et cetera (and so on)
FDIC	Federal Deposit Insurance Corporation
Inc.	Incorporated
L.f.	Ledger folio

Ltd.	Limited
mgr.	manager
NSF or N/S	not sufficient funds
P&L or P/L	profit and loss

Notice that *etc.* contains a word meaning *and;* therefore, never write *and etc.*

3.3 NUMBERS

Numbers may correctly be handled many ways in business writing, so follow company style. In the absence of a set style, however, you should generally spell out all numbers from one to ten and use arabic numerals for the rest.

But there are some exceptions to this general rule. First, never begin a sentence with a numeral:

> *Twenty* of us produced *641* units per week in the first *12* weeks of the year.

Second, use numerals for the numbers one through ten if they are in the same list as larger numbers:

> Our weekly quota rose from *9* to *15* to *27.*

Third, use numerals for percentages, time of day (except with *o'clock*) and dates, and dollar amounts.

> We are responsible for *7* percent of total sales.
>
> The meeting is at *8:30* a.m. on August *2.*
>
> Add *$3* for postage and handling.

Numbers with four digits should use a comma (*1,257*) unless the company specifies another style.

When writing dollar amounts, use a decimal point only if cents are included. In lists of two or more dollar amounts, use the decimal point either for all or for none:

> He sent two checks, one for *$67.92* and one for *$90.00.*

3.4 WORD DIVISION

In general, you should avoid dividing words at the ends of lines. But when you must, follow these rules:

- Do not divide one-syllable words, such as *since, walked,* and *thought*; abbreviations (*mgr.*); contractions (*isn't*); or numbers expressed in numerals (*117,500*).

- Divide words between syllables, as specified in a dictionary or word-division manual.

- Make sure that at least three letters of the divided word are moved to the second line: *sin-cerely* instead of *sincere-ly.*

- Do not end a page or more than two consecutive lines with hyphens.

- Leave syllables consisting of a single vowel at the end of the first line (*impedi-ment* instead of *imped-iment*), except when the single vowel is part of a suffix like *-able, -ible, -ical,* or *-ity* (*respons-ible* instead of *responsi-ble*).

- Divide between double letters (*tomor-row*), except when the root word ends in double letters (*call-ing* instead of *cal-ling*).

- Divide hyphenated words after the hyphen: *anti-independence* instead of *anti-inde-pendence.*

4.0 VOCABULARY

Use of the right word in the right place is a crucial skill in business communication. However, many pitfalls await the unwary.

4.1 FREQUENTLY CONFUSED WORDS

Because the following sets of words sound similar, you must be careful not to use one when you mean to use the other:

WORD	MEANING
accede	to comply with
exceed	to go beyond
accept	to take
except	to exclude
access	admittance
excess	too much
advice	suggestion
advise	to suggest

WORD	MEANING	WORD	MEANING
affect	to influence	lead	a metal
effect	the result	led	guided
allot	to distribute	lean	to rest at an angle
a lot	much or many	lien	claim
all ready	completely prepared	levee	embankment
already	completed earlier	levy	tax
born	given birth to	loath	reluctant
borne	carried	loathe	to hate
capital	money, chief city	loose	free, not tight
capitol	a government building	lose	to mislay
cite	to quote	material	substance
sight	a view	materiel	equipment
site	a location	miner	mineworker
complement	complete amount, to go well with	minor	under-age person
compliment	to flatter	moral	virtuous, a lesson
corespondent	party in a divorce suit	morale	sense of well-being
correspondent	letter writer	ordinance	law
council	a panel of people	ordnance	weapons
counsel	advice, a lawyer	overdo	to do in excess
defer	to put off until later	overdue	past due
differ	to be different	peace	lack of conflict
device	a mechanism	piece	a fragment
devise	to plan	pedal	a foot lever
die	to stop living, a tool	peddle	to sell
dye	to color	persecute	to torment
discreet	careful	prosecute	to sue
discrete	separate	personal	private
envelop	to surround	personnel	employees
envelope	a covering for a letter	precedence	priority
forth	forward	precedents	previous events
fourth	number four	principal	sum of money, chief, main
holey	full of holes	principle	general rule
holy	sacred	rap	to knock
wholly	completely	wrap	to cover
human	of people	residence	home
humane	kindly	residents	inhabitants
incidence	frequency	right	correct
incidents	events	rite	ceremony
instance	example	write	to form words on a surface
instants	moments	role	a part to play
interstate	between states	roll	to tumble, a list
intrastate	within a state	root	part of a plant
later	afterward	rout	to defeat
latter	the second of two	route	a traveler's way

WORD	MEANING
shear	to cut
sheer	thin, steep
stationary	immovable
stationery	paper
than	as compared to
then	at that time
their	belonging to them
there	in that place
they're	they are
to	a preposition
too	excessively, also
two	the number
waive	to set aside
wave	a swell of water, a gesture
weather	atmospheric conditions
whether	if

In the preceding list, only enough of each word's meaning is given to help you distinguish among the words in each group. Several meanings are left out entirely. For more complete definitions, consult a dictionary.

4.2 FREQUENTLY MISUSED WORDS

The following words tend to be misused for reasons other than their sound. A number of reference books (including *The Random House College Dictionary*, Revised Edition, Follett's *Modern American Usage*, and Fowler's *Modern English Usage*) can help you with similar questions of usage.

a lot: When the writer means many, *a lot* is always two separate words, never one.

correspond with: Use this phrase when you are talking about exchanging letters; use *correspond to* when you mean "similar to." Either *with* or *to* may be used to mean "relate to."

disinterested: This word means fair, unbiased, having no favorites, impartial. If you mean bored or not interested, use *uninterested*.

etc.: This is the abbreviated form of a Latin phrase, *et cetera*. It means "and so on" or "and so forth." The current tendency among business writers is to use English rather than Latin.

imply/infer: Both refer to hints. Their great difference lies in who is acting. The writer *implies*; the reader, in seeing between the lines, *infers*.

lay: This is a transitive verb. Never use it for the intransitive *lie*. (See Section 1.3.3.)

less: Use *less* for uncountable quantities (such as amounts of water, air, sugar, and oil). Use *fewer* for countable quantities (such as numbers of jars, saws, words, pages, and humans). The same distinction applies to *much* and *little* (uncountable) versus *many* and *few* (countable).

like: Use *like* only when the word that follows is just a noun or pronoun. Use *as* or *as if* when a phrase or clause follows:

> She looks *like* him.
>
> She did just *as* he had expected.
>
> It seems *as if* she had plenty of time.

many/much: See *less*.

regardless: The *-less* ending is the negative part. No word needs two negative parts, so it is incorrect to add *ir-* at the beginning.

to me/personally: Use these phrases only when personal reactions, apart from company policy, are being stated (not often the case in business writing).

try: Always follow with *to*, never *and*.

verbal: People in the business community who are careful with language frown on those who use *verbal* to mean *spoken* or *oral*. Many others do say "verbal agreement." But strictly speaking, *verbal* means "of words" and therefore includes both spoken and written words. Be guided in this matter by company usage.

4.3 FREQUENTLY MISSPELLED WORDS

All of us, even the world's best spellers, sometimes have to check a dictionary for the spelling of some words. But people who have never memorized the spelling of commonly used words have to look up so many of them that they often become exasperated and give up on spelling words correctly.

You should not expect perfection, nor need you surrender. If you can memorize the spelling of just the words listed below, you will need the dictionary far less often and will write with more confidence.

absence	advantageous	analyze
absorption	affiliated	apparent
accessible	aggressive	appropriate
accommodate	alignment	argument
accumulate	aluminum	asphalt
achieve	ambience	assistant

asterisk
auditor

bankruptcy
believable
benefited
brilliant
bulletin

calendar
campaign
canceled
category
ceiling
changeable
clientele
collateral
committee
comparative
competitor
concede
congratulations
connoisseur
consensus
convenient
convertible
corroborate
criticism

definitely
description
desirable
dilemma
disappear
disappoint
disbursement
discrepancy
dissatisfied
dissipate

eligible
embarrassing
endorsement
exaggerate
exceed
exhaust
existence
extraordinary

fallacy
familiar
flexible
fluctuation
forty

gesture
grievous

haphazard
holiday

illegible
immigrant
incidentally
indelible
independent
indispensable
insistent
intermediary
irresistible

jewelry
judgment
judicial

labeling
legitimate
leisure
license
litigation

maintenance
mathematics
mediocre
minimum

necessary
negligence
negotiable
newsstand
noticeable

occurrence
omission

parallel
pastime
peaceable
permanent
perseverance

persistent
personnel
persuade
possesses
precede
predictable
preferred
privilege
procedure
proceed
pronunciation
psychology
pursue

questionnaire

receive
recommend
repetition
rescind
rhythmical
ridiculous

salable
secretary
seize
separate
sincerely
succeed
suddenness
superintendent
supersede
surprise

tangible
tariff
technique
tenant
truly

unanimous
until

vacillate
vacuum
vicious

4.4 TRANSITIONAL WORDS AND PHRASES

The following two sentences don't communicate as well as they might because they lack a transitional word or phrase:

Production delays are inevitable. Our current lag time in filling orders is one month.

A semicolon between the two sentences would signal a close relationship between their meanings, but it would not even hint at what that relationship is. Here are the sentences, now linked by means of a semicolon, with a space for a transitional word or phrase:

Production delays are inevitable; _____, our current lag time in filling orders is one month.

Now read the sentence with *nevertheless* in the blank space. You are receiving one of many meanings that the writer may have had in mind. Now try *therefore*, *incidentally*, *in fact*, and *at any rate* in the blank. Each changes the meaning of the sentence.

Here are some transitional words (called conjunctive adverbs) that will help you write more clearly:

accordingly	furthermore	moreover
anyway	however	otherwise
besides	incidentally	still
consequently	likewise	therefore
finally	meanwhile	

The following transitional phrases are used in the same way:

as a result	in other words
at any rate	in the second place
for example	on the other hand
in fact	to the contrary

When one of these words or phrases joins two independent clauses, it should be preceded by a semicolon and followed by a comma, as shown here:

The consultant recommended a complete reorganization; moreover, she suggested that we drop several products.

■ APPENDIX B

FORMAT AND LAYOUT OF BUSINESS DOCUMENTS

An effective letter, memo, or report does more than store words on paper. It must get to the right person, make an impression, and tell the recipient who wrote it and when it was written. The sender may also need to find out later how and by whom the document was processed. Over the centuries, certain conventions for formatting and laying out business documents have developed. As with most matters of style, however, few hard-and-fast rules exist. Certain styles—namely, those described here—are more common than others.

In addition, organizations often develop a variation of the standard style to suit their own needs. Each writer or organization should use a style that best conveys the types of messages it sends. In most organizations, secretaries are expected to know how to put documents into the proper form and how to make them attractive to readers. But you should also be familiar with these conventions, if only to be sure you provide all the information that the secretary needs.

FIRST IMPRESSIONS

A letter or other written document is often the first or only contact that a person has with your organization. Thus it is important for documents to look neat and professional and to be easy to read. Several elements—the paper you use, the letterhead, and the typing—tell readers a lot about you and your company's professionalism.

PAPER

Your own experience should tell you that a flimsy, see-through piece of paper gives a much less favorable impression than a richly textured piece. But you may not know that the quality of paper is measured in two ways. The first method is by weight, specifically, the weight of four reams (each a 500-sheet package) of letter-size paper. The quality most commonly used by business organizations is 20-pound paper, but 16- and 24-pound weights are also used. The second measure of quality is the percentage of cotton in the paper. Cotton does not yellow over time the way wood pulp does, and it is simultaneously strong and soft. In general, paper with a 25-percent cotton content is an appropriate quality for letters and outside reports. For memos and other internal documents, lighter-weight paper with a lower cotton content may be used.

The standard size of paper for business documents is 8½ by 11 inches. But legal documents are presented on paper that measures 8½ by 14 inches. And sometimes executives have heavier 7-by-10-inch paper on hand (with matching envelopes) for such personal messages as congratulations and recommendations.[1] Executives may also have a box of correspondence note cards imprinted with their initials and a box of plain folded notes for condolences or for acknowledging formal invitations.

Stationery may also vary in color. White is the usual standard for business purposes, although neutral colors like gray and ivory are also used. Memos are sometimes produced on pastel-colored paper so that they can more easily be distinguished from outside letters; sometimes memos are typed on different colors of paper for routing to various departments. Light-colored papers are distinctive and often appropriate; bright or dark colors, however, are difficult to read and may convey too frivolous an impression.

CUSTOMIZATION

For letters to outsiders, businesses commonly use letterhead stationery printed with the company's name and address, usually at the top of the page but sometimes along the left side or even at the bottom of the page. Other information may be included in the letterhead as well: the company's telephone number, cable address, product lines, date of establishment, officers and directors, slogan, and symbol (logo). The idea is to give the recipient of the letter pertinent reference data and a better idea of what the company does. But the letterhead should be as simple as possible; too much information gives the page a cluttered look, cuts into the space needed for the letter, and may become outdated before all the letterhead has been used. Company letterhead should always be used for the first page of a letter. Successive pages should be typed on a plain sheet of paper that matches the letterhead in color and quality or on a specially printed second-page letterhead bearing only the company's name.

Many companies also design and print standardized forms for memos and for reports that are written frequently and that always require the same types of information (such as sales reports and expense reports). These forms may be printed in sets for use with carbon paper or in carbonless copy sets that produce multiple copies automatically with the original.

TYPING

Most business documents should be typed or printed on a typewriter-quality computer printer. Typing is usually easier to read than handwriting and is smaller, so more words fit into less space. Some short, informal memos are handwritten, however, and it is appropriate to handwrite a note of condolence to a close business associate. The envelope should be handwritten or typed to match the document.

Even a letter on the best-quality paper with the best-designed letterhead may look unprofessional if it is poorly typed. All documents (but especially those that leave the company) should be centered on the page, with margins of at least an inch all around. This balance can be achieved in one of two ways: by establishing a standard line length or by establishing a "picture frame."

Most commonly, the standard line length is about 6 inches wide. Lines should usually not be justified (aligned exactly with both margins) because a justified letter is hard to read and looks too much like a form letter. Variations in line length look more personal and interesting. If the typewriter or word processor has larger, pica type, each line will have 60 characters; if smaller, elite type is used, each line will have 72 characters. Sometimes a guide sheet, with the margins and the center point marked in dark ink, is used as a backing when typing a page. The number of lines between elements of the document (such as the date line and inside address in a letter) can be adjusted to ensure that the document fills the page vertically or, if it's a longer document, extends to at least three lines of body on the last page.

Fitting type into a picture frame with even margins all around requires more skill. First the length of the document is estimated; then the number of characters for each line is determined. Table B.1 gives the most commonly used guidelines for estimating line length; however, tables, set-off quotations, and exceptionally long or short opening and closing elements all affect the size of the margins.

Another important aspect of a professional-looking document is the proper spacing after punctuation. For example, you should always leave two spaces at the ends of sentences and after colons; single spaces are used after commas and semicolons. Each letter in a person's initials is followed by a period and a single space. Abbreviations for organizations, such as U.S.A., may or may not have periods,

TABLE B.1
Guidelines for Establishing Line Lengths Using the "Picture Frame" Method

LENGTH OF LETTER	NUMBER OF WORDS	LINE LENGTH		
		INCHES	ELITE CHARACTERS	PICA CHARACTERS
Short	Under 100	4	50	40
Medium	100–200	5	60	50
Long	200–300	6	70	60
Two pages	Over 300	6	70	60

but they should never have internal spaces. Dashes should be typed as two hyphens with no space between or on either side of the dash. Other details of this sort are provided in most secretarial handbooks.

Most business documents should be cleanly typed. Electric/electronic typewriters, word processors, and some computer printers produce a clearer, more regular impression than manual typewriters do. In addition, a carbon or plastic ribbon produces a darker, more uniform image than a cloth ribbon. Finally, messy corrections are dreadfully obvious; a letter, an outside report, or a memo to a higher-up that requires a lot of corrections should simply be retyped. This sort of mess can be avoided by using a self-correcting typewriter or a word processor that can produce correction-free documents at the push of a button.

LETTERS

For a very long time, written messages from one person to another have begun with some type of phrase in greeting and have ended with some sort of polite expression and the writer's signature. In fact, books printed in the sixteenth century prescribed letter formats for writers to follow. Styles have changed some since then, but all business letters still have certain elements in common. Several of these parts appear in every letter; others appear only when desirable or appropriate. In addition, these parts are usually arranged in one of three basic letter formats.

STANDARD LETTER PARTS

All business letters typically include seven elements, in the following order:

1. Heading
2. Date
3. Inside address
4. Salutation
5. Body
6. Complimentary close
7. Signature block

The letter in Figure B.1 shows the placement of these standard letter parts (see page 510). Because it's a personal business letter, it includes a typed heading instead of a printed letterhead.

Heading

Letterhead, the usual heading, shows the organization's name, full address, and (almost always) telephone number. Executive letterhead bears the name of an individual within the organization as well. If letterhead stationery is not available, the heading consists of a return address (but not a name) starting 13 lines from the top of the page, which leaves 2 inches between the return address and the top of the page.

Date

If you are using letterhead paper, the date on which the letter is typed should be placed at least one blank line beneath the lowest part of the letterhead. Without letterhead, the date is typed immediately below the return address.

When you're typing the date, the full name of the month (no abbreviations) is followed by the day (in numerals), a comma, and then the year: July 14, 1993. This is the standard method of writing the date. In some industries and in government, how-

FIGURE B.1
Standard Letter Parts

Heading

Date

Inside Address

Salutation

Body

Complimentary Close

Typewritten Name

```
                              *
                              *
                              *
                              *
                              *
                              *
                              *

   6412 Belmont Drive
   New Weston, OH 45348
   June 22, 1993


   Mr. Richard Garcia
   Director of Franchises
   Snack Shoppes
   2344 Western Avenue
   Seattle, WA 98123

   Dear Mr. Garcia

   Last Monday, my wife and I were on our way home from
   a long weekend, and we stopped at a Snack Shoppe for
   a quick sandwich.  A sign on the cash register gave
   your address in the event customers were interested
   in operating a franchise of their own somewhere
   else.  We talked about the idea all evening and into
   the night.

   Although we talked about changing jobs--I'm an
   administrative analyst for a utility company and my
   wife sells real estate--the thought of operating a
   franchised business had never occurred to us.  We'd
   always thought in terms of starting a business from
   scratch.  But owning a Snack Shoppe is an intriguing
   idea.

   We would appreciate your sending us full details on
   owning our own outlet.  Please include the names and
   telephone numbers of other Snack Shoppe owners so
   we can talk to them before we make any decision
   to proceed further.  We're excited about hearing
   from you.  Please write soon.

   Cordially


   Peter Simond

   Peter Simond
```

□   One blank space

*   Variable spacing, depending on length of the letter, except for the top margin,
    which should be two inches

---

ever, the date is typed with the day (in numerals) first, followed by the month (unabbreviated), followed by the year—with no comma: 14 July 1993. In this country, the date is rarely typed all in numerals. Also, it is considered old-fashioned to include *rd* or *th* after the numeral representing the day at the top of a letter.

Inside address

The inside address, which identifies the recipient of the letter, is typed one or more lines below the date, depending on how long the letter is.

The addressee's name is preceded by a courtesy title, such as *Dr.*, *Mr.*, or *Ms*. The accepted courtesy title for women in business is *Ms.;* however, a woman who is known to prefer the title *Miss* or *Mrs.* should be accommodated. Any other titles, such as *Professor* or *General*, should not be abbreviated. Table B.2 shows the proper forms of address for various dignitaries.

The person's organizational title, such as *Director*, may also be included on this first line (if it is short) or on the line below; the name of a department may follow. If the name of a specific person is unavailable, the letter may be addressed to the department or to a specific position within the department.

This example shows all the information that may be included in the inside address and its proper order:

Ms. Linda Coolidge, Director
Corporate Planning Department
Midwest Airlines
Kowalski Building, Suite 21-A
7279 Bristol Avenue
Toledo, OH 43617

Canadian addresses are similar:

Dr. H. C. Armstrong
Research and Development
Commonwealth Mining Consortium
The Chelton Building, Suite 301
585 Second Street SW
Calgary, Alberta T2P 2P5

Salutation

The salutation of a letter should use the person's name if at all possible. Your relationship with the addressee affects the formality of the salutation. If you would say "Mary" in conversation, your letter's salutation should be *Dear Mary* followed by a colon. Letters to people you do not know well enough to address personally should use the courtesy title and last name followed by a colon. Presuming to write *Dear Lewis* instead of *Dear Professor Chang* demonstrates a disrespectful familiarity that a stranger will probably resent.

TABLE B.2 Forms of Address for Dignitaries

PERSONAGE	NAME IN ADDRESS	SALUTATION
President of the United States	The President	Dear Mr. or Madam President
Cabinet member	The Honorable [first and last name]	Dear Mr. or Madam Secretary
Attorney General	The Honorable [first and last name]	Dear Mr. or Madam Attorney General
U.S. Senator	The Honorable [first and last name]	Dear Senator [last name]
U.S. Representative	The Honorable [first and last name]	Dear Mr. or Ms. [last name]
Governor	The Honorable [first and last name]	Dear Governor [last name]
State senator or representative	The Honorable [first and last name]	Dear Mr. or Ms. [last name]
Mayor	The Honorable [first and last name]	Dear Mayor [last name] or Dear Mr. or Madam Mayor
Judge	The Honorable [first and last name]	Dear Judge [last name]
Lawyer	Mr. or Ms. [first and last name]	Dear Mr. or Ms. [last name]
University president	Dr. [first and last name], President	Dear Dr. [last name]
Dean	Dr. [first and last name], Dean of [school or college]	Dear Dr. [last name]
Professor	Professor [first and last name]	Dear Professor [last name]
Rabbi	Rabbi [first and last name]	Dear Rabbi [last name]
Protestant clergy	The Reverend [first and last name]	Dear Dr., Mr., or Ms. [last name]
Roman Catholic priest	The Reverend Father [first and last name]	Reverend Father or Dear Father [last name]
Roman Catholic nun	Sister [name]	Dear Sister

Don't overlook an especially important point with personalized salutations: Whether you choose an informal or a formal style, make sure you spell names right. A misspelled name is glaring evidence of carelessness, and it belies the personal interest you are trying to express.

Choosing a salutation for a letter addressed to a group or to an unknown person is one of the least-settled issues related to salutations. Several choices are available:

- *Ladies and Gentlemen*—unless it is known that the group is made up entirely of women or men or unless your organization dictates the use of *Gentlemen* for mixed groups
- *Dear Sir or Madam*—again, unless the gender of the recipient is known or company policy requires the use of *Sir*
- *Dear Colleague*—or *Dear Policyholder, Dear Customer*, or some other appropriate title
- *To Whom It May Concern*

Dear Sir (or *Dear Madam*) and *To Whom It May Concern* are quite stiff and formal; use them only when you wish to establish a polite barrier.

In an attempt to avoid the awkwardness of a salutation, some letter writers use a salutopening on the salutation line. A salutopening omits *Dear* but includes the first few words of the opening paragraph along with the recipient's name. After this line, the sentence continues a double space below as part of the body of the letter, as in these examples:

Thank you, Mr. Brown,	Salutopening
for your prompt payment of your bill.	Body
Congratulations, Ms. Lake!	Salutopening
Your promotion is well deserved.	Body

Body

The body of the letter is the message. Almost all letters are typed single-spaced, with double spacing (one blank line) before and after the salutation or salutopening, between paragraphs, and before the complimentary close. The body may include indented lists, entire paragraphs indented for emphasis, and even subheadings. If so, all similar elements should

be treated in the same way. A department or company often selects a format to be used for all letters.

Complimentary close

The complimentary close is typed on the second line below the body of the letter. A number of alternatives for wording are available, but currently, the trend seems to be toward using one-word closes, such as *Sincerely* and *Cordially*. In any case, the complimentary close should reflect the relationship between the writer and the recipient of the letter. Be wary of closes that are too cute, such as *Yours for bigger profits;* if the recipient doesn't know you well, your sense of humor may be misunderstood.

Signature block

After leaving three blank lines for a written signature below the complimentary close, the sender's name is typed (unless it appears in the letterhead). The person's title may appear on the same line as the name or on the line below:

Cordially,

Raymond Dunnigan
Director of Personnel

Use of letterhead indicates that the writer is representing the company. But if the letter is typed on plain paper or runs to a second page, the writer may want to emphasize that she or he is speaking legally for the company. The accepted way to do that is to type the company's name in capital letters a double space below the complimentary close and the sender's name four lines below that, with the title following:

Sincerely,

WENTWORTH INDUSTRIES

(Mrs.) Helen B. Taylor
President

If the writer's name could be taken for either a man's or a woman's, a courtesy title indicating gender should be included in the typewritten name, with parentheses or without. Also, women who prefer a particular courtesy title should include it.

ADDITIONAL LETTER PARTS

Letters vary greatly in subject matter and thus in the identifying information they need and the format they adopt. The following elements may be used in any combination, depending on the requirements of the particular letter, but generally in this order:

1. Addressee notation
2. Attention line
3. Subject line
4. Second-page heading
5. Company name
6. Reference initials
7. Enclosure notation
8. Copy notation
9. Mailing notation
10. Postscript

The letter in Figure B.2 shows how these additional parts should be arranged (see pages 514 and 515).

Addressee notation

Letters that have a restricted readership or that must be handled in a special way should include such addressee notations as *Personal*, *Confidential*, or *Please Forward*. This sort of notation appears two lines above the inside address in capital letters.

Attention line

Although an attention line is not commonly used today, you may find it useful if you know only the last name of the person you are writing to. An attention line can also be used to direct a letter to a position title or department. An attention line may take any of the following forms or variants of them: *Attention Dr. McHenry*, *Attention Director of Marketing*, or *Attention Marketing Department*. You may place the attention line on the first line and use the company name as the second line of the inside address.

Some companies prefer an alternative approach in which the attention line is placed a double space below the inside address. It may be typed against the left margin (the most common procedure), indented as the paragraphs in the body of the letter are, or centered. The word *Attention* or the whole line may also be underlined.

With either approach, the address on the envelope should always match the style of the inside address shown in Figure B.2, in order to conform to postal specifications.

Subject line

The subject line is a device to let the recipient know at a glance what the letter is about; it also helps indicate where to file the letter for future reference. It is usually typed below the salutation—against the left margin, indented as the paragraphs in the body of the letter are, or centered on the line. Sometimes the subject line is typed above the salutation or at the very top of the page. The subject line may take a wide variety of forms, including the following:

Subject:　RainMaster Sprinklers

About your February 2, 1993, order

FALL 1993 SALES MEETING

Reference Order No. 27920

Sometimes the subject line (or the last line of a long subject "line") is underscored. And some writers omit the word *Subject* and put the other information all in capitals to distinguish it from the other parts of the letter.

Second-page heading

If the letter is long and an additional page is required, a second-page heading must be used. Some companies have second-page letterhead, with the company name and address on one line and in smaller type than the regular letterhead. In any case, the second page must bear the name of the person (preferably) and organization receiving the letter, the page number, and the date of the letter; a reference number may also be included. All the following are acceptable:

Ms. Melissa Baker
May 10, 1993
Page 2

Ms. Melissa Baker, May 10, 1993, Page 2

Ms. Melissa Baker -2- May 10, 1993

FIGURE B.2
Additional Letter Parts

Addressee Notation

Attention Line

Subject Line

☐

* * *

☐

☐

☐

☐

Worldwide Talent Agency
2314 Hollywood Boulevard
Hollywood, California 90021-1654
(213) 695-2864

November 18, 1993

CONFIDENTIAL

Peachtree Lecture Bureau
Attention Mr. Trevino
2920 S. Bennett Parkway
Albany, GA 31702-1324

Ladies and Gentlemen:

Subject: Contract No. 27-83176

I have put together some additional information for
you to consider. Please note especially the dates

☐ One blank space
* Variable spacing, depending on length of the letter

Triple-space (leave two blank lines) between the second-page heading and the body.

Company name

The company's name, if included in the signature block, is typed all in capital letters a double space below the complimentary close. The company's name is usually included in the signature block only when the writer is serving as the company's official spokesperson or when letterhead has not been used.

Reference initials

It is very common in business for one person to dictate or write a letter and another person to type it. Reference initials show who helped prepare the letter, and they always appear at the left margin a double space below the last line of the signature block. When the writer's name has been typed in the signature block, only the typist's initials are necessary. But if only the department name appears in the signature block, both sets of initials should appear, usually in one of the following forms:

RSR/sm

RSR:sm

RSR:SM

The first set of initials is the writer's; the second is the typist's.

Sometimes the writer and the signer of a letter are different people. In that case, at least the file copy of a letter should bear both their initials as well as those of the typist: JFS/RSR/sm (signer, writer, typist).

Enclosure notation

Enclosure notations also appear at the bottom of a letter, one or two lines below the reference initials. Some common forms:

Enclosure

Enclosures (2)

Enclosures: Resume
             Photograph

Attachment

FIGURE B.2
Additional Letter Parts (continued)

Second-Page Heading

Company Name

Reference Initials

Enclosure Notation

Copy Notation

Mailing Notation

Postscript

```
Peachtree Lecture Bureau
November 18, 1993
Page 2


This information should clarify our commitment
to you.  I look forward to good news from you in
the near future.

Sincerely,

WORLDWIDE TALENT AGENCY


J. Elizabeth Spencer
J. Elizabeth Spencer
President

nt

Enclosures:  Talent Roster
             Commission Schedule

Copy to Everett Cunningham, Chairperson of
the Board, InterHosts, Inc.

Special Delivery

PS:  The lunch you treated me to the other day
was a fine display of Southern hospitality.
Thanks again.
```

☐   One blank space

*   Variable spacing, depending on length of the letter

Copy notation

Copy notations may follow reference initials or enclosure notations. They indicate who is receiving carbon copies or photocopies (*cc* or *pc* or just *c*) of the letter, preferably in order of rank or in alphabetical order. Among the forms used:

c: David Wentworth

pc: Martha Littlefield

Copy to Hans Vogel

Addresses may be included, along with notations about any enclosures that are being sent with the copies.

Sometimes it is desirable to keep the sending of copies a secret from the person who receives the original copy of the letter. In that case, the notation *bc*, *bcc*, or *bpc* (for blind copy, blind carbon copy, or blind photocopy) appears with the name—but only on the copy, not on the original—where the copy notation would normally appear.

Mailing notation

A mailing notation, such as *Special Delivery* or *Registered Mail*, may be placed after reference initials, enclosure notations, and copy notations at the bottom of the letter; or it may be placed at the top of the letter, either above the inside address on the left-hand side or just below the date on the right-hand side. For greater visibility, mailing notations may be typed in capital letters.

Postscript

Letters may also bear postscripts, which are afterthoughts to the letter, messages that require emphasis, or personal notes. The postscript is usually the last thing on any letter and may be preceded by *P.S.*, *PS.*, *PS:*, or nothing at all. A second afterthought would be designated *P.P.S.*, meaning post postscript. Postscripts are usually avoided because they indicate poor planning. However, they are commonly used in sales letters, not as an afterthought but as a punch line to remind the reader of a benefit in taking advantage of the offer.

LETTER FORMATS

Although the basic letter parts have remained the same for centuries, ways of arranging them do

FIGURE B.3
Block Letter Format

Mattel Toys

> Mattel, Inc.
> 5150 Rosecrans Avenue
> Hawthorne, CA 90250-6692
> Telephone 213 978 5150
> TELEX 188155 or 188170

September 5, 1993

Mr. Clifford Hanson
General Manager
The Toy Trunk
356 Emerald Drive
Lexington, KY 40500

Dear Mr. Hanson:

You should receive your shipment of Barbie dolls and accessories within two weeks, just in time for the holiday shopping season. The merchandise is being shipped by United Parcel Service. As the enclosed invoice indicates, the amount due is $352.32.

In preparing to ship your order, I noticed that this is your 15th year as a Mattel customer. During that period, you have sold over 3,750 Barbie dolls! We sincerely appreciate the part you have played in marketing our toys to the public.

Your customers should be particularly excited about the new Barbie vacation outfits that you have ordered. Our winter advertising campaign will portray Barbie trekking through the jungle in her safari suit, climbing mountains in her down parka, and snorkeling off a coral reef in her skin diving gear.

Next month, you'll be receiving our spring catalog. Notice the new series of action figures that will tie in with a TV cartoon featuring King Arthur and the Knights of the Round Table. As a special introductory incentive, you can receive a 15 percent discount on all items in this line until the end of January. Please send your order soon.

Sincerely,

Rhonda Rogers

Ms. Rhonda Rogers
Customer Service Representative

jhb

Enclosure

☐ One blank space   * Variable spacing, depending on the length of the letter

change. Sometimes a company adopts a certain format as its policy; sometimes the individual letter writer or secretary is allowed to choose the format most appropriate for a given letter or to settle on a personal preference. Today, three major letter formats are commonly used:

- Block format (Figure B.3)
- Modified block format (Figure B.4)
- Simplified format (Figure B.5)

The major differences among these formats are the way that paragraphs are indented, the placement of letter parts, and some of the punctuation. However, the elements are always separated by at least one blank line, and the typewritten name is always separated from the line above by at least three blank lines to allow space for a signature. If paragraphs are indented, the indention is normally five spaces.

In addition to these three letter formats, letters may also be classified according to the style of punctuation they use. *Standard*, or *mixed*, *punctuation* uses a colon after the salutation (a comma if the letter is social or personal) and a comma after the complimentary close. *Open punctuation* uses no colon or comma after the salutation or the complimentary close. Either style of punctuation may be used with

FIGURE B.4
Modified Block Letter Format

June 3, 1993

Ms. Clara Simpson, President
League of Women Voters of Miami
P.O. Box 112
Miami, FL 33152

Dear Ms. Simpson:

Thank you for inviting us to participate in the League of Women Voters' Spring Fashion Show. We will be delighted to provide some clothing samples for the May 15 event.

You indicated that you would like us to supply about 12 outfits from our designer collection, all in a size 6. We can certainly accommodate your request. To give your audience a representative overview of our merchandise, I suggest we provide the following: three tailored daytime dresses or suits, two dressy dresses, one formal ball gown, four casual weekend outfits, and two active sports outfits.

Please give me a call to schedule a "shopping" trip for you and your committee members. Together, I'm sure we can find exactly what you need to stage a well-rounded show. In the meantime, you might enjoy looking through the enclosed catalog. It will introduce you to some of the options.

Sincerely,

Vera O'Donnell

(Mrs.) Vera O'Donnell
Director, Public Relations

bcg

Enclosure

J. C. Penney Company, Inc., 1301 Avenue of the Americas, New York, New York 10019

☐ One blank space   * Variable spacing, depending on the length of the letter block or modified block letter formats. But because the simplified letter format has no salutation or complimentary close, the style of punctuation is irrelevant.

Block format

As you can see in Figure B.3, each part of a letter typed in block format begins at the left margin (see page 516). The main advantage of this format is that letters can be typed quickly and efficiently.

Modified block format

The modified block format is similar to the block format. However, as Figure B.4 shows, the date, com-

plimentary close, and signature block start near the center of the page (see page 517). Although the letter in Figure B.4 does not show indented paragraphs, the modified block format does permit indention as an option. This format mixes speed of typing with traditional placement of some letter parts. It also looks more balanced on the page than the block format does.

Simplified format

Instead of a salutation, the simplified version of the block format sometimes works the recipient's name into the first line or two of the body and often includes a subject line in capital letters (see Figure

FIGURE B.5
Simplified Letter Format

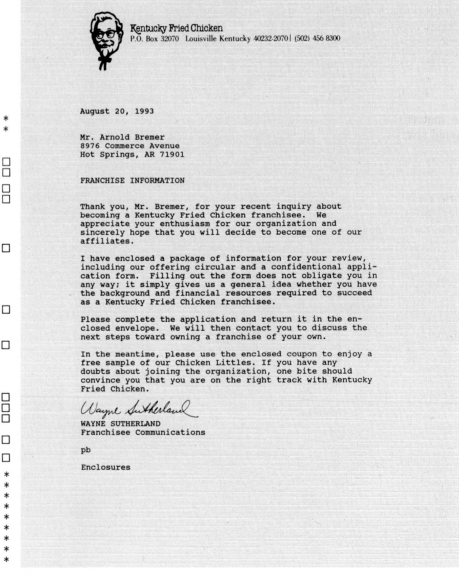

□ One blank space   * Variable spacing, depending on the length of the letter

B.5). It also omits the complimentary close; the writer signs between the body of the letter and the typewritten name. Because no salutation is required, the simplified format is convenient when you don't know the reader's name. On the other hand, some people object to this format because it seems mechanical and impersonal (a drawback that may be overcome with a warm writing style, however). In Figure B.5, the elimination of certain letter parts changes some of the spacing between lines.

ENVELOPES

The quality of the envelope is just as important to first impressions as the quality of the stationery. In fact, letterhead and envelopes should be of the same paper stock, have the same color ink, and be imprinted with the same address and logo. Most envelopes used in business are No. 10 envelopes (9½ inches long), which are sized to contain an 8½-by-11-inch piece of paper folded in thirds. Some occasions call for a smaller, No. 6¾ envelope or for envelopes proportioned to fit special stationery. Figure B.6 shows the two most common sizes used in business.

ADDRESSING THE ENVELOPE

No matter what size an envelope is, the address should always be typed in block form—that is, with all lines aligned on the left—and the lines should be single-spaced. The inside address on the letter and the address on the envelope should be in the same style and present the same information. The order to follow is from the smallest division to the largest:

1. Name and title of recipient

2. Name of department or subgroup

3. Name of organization

4. Name of building

5. Street address and suite number, or post office box number

6. City, state or province, and ZIP code or Postal Code

7. Name of country (if the letter is being sent abroad)

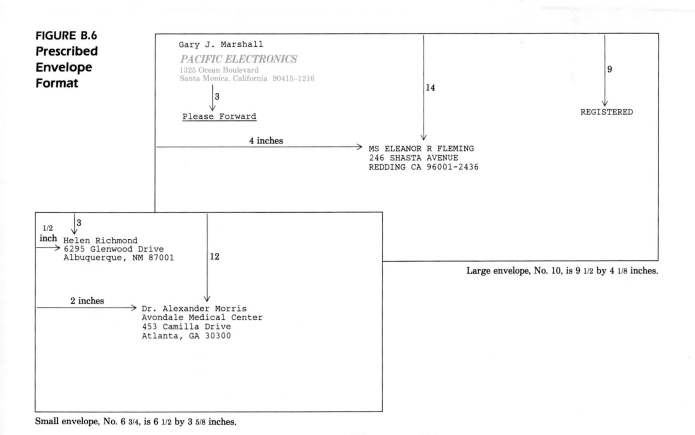

FIGURE B.6 Prescribed Envelope Format

Gary J. Marshall
PACIFIC ELECTRONICS
1325 Ocean Boulevard
Santa Monica, California 90415-1216

Please Forward

4 inches

MS ELEANOR R FLEMING
246 SHASTA AVENUE
REDDING CA 96001-2436

REGISTERED

Large envelope, No. 10, is 9 1/2 by 4 1/8 inches.

1/2 inch
Helen Richmond
6295 Glenwood Drive
Albuquerque, NM 87001

2 inches

Dr. Alexander Morris
Avondale Medical Center
453 Camilla Drive
Atlanta, GA 30300

Small envelope, No. 6 3/4, is 6 1/2 by 3 5/8 inches.

Because the post office uses optical scanners to sort mail, envelopes for quantity mailings, in particular, should be addressed in the prescribed format. In the top example of Figure B.6, everything is typed in capital letters, no punctuation is included, and all mailing instructions of interest to the post office are placed above the address area. (Canada Post requires a similar format, except that only the city is typed all in capitals and the Postal Code is placed on the line below the name of the city.) The post office scanners read addresses from the bottom up, so if a letter is to be sent to a post office box rather than a street address, the street address should appear on the line above the box number.

The U.S. Postal Service and the Canada Post Corporation have published lists of two-letter mailing abbreviations for states, provinces, and territories (see Table B.3), to be used without periods or commas. But some executives prefer that state and province names be typed out in full and that a comma be used to separate the city and state or province names. Thus the use of a comma between the name of the city and the two-letter abbreviation is an unresolved issue. Most commonly, the comma is included; however, the comma is sometimes eliminated to conform with the post office standards.

Quantity mailings should follow post office requirements. But for letters that are not mailed in quantity, a reasonable compromise is to use traditional punctuation with uppercase and lowercase letters for names and street addresses and with two-letter state or province abbreviations, as shown here:

Mr. Kevin Kennedy
2107 E. Packer Drive
Amarillo, TX 79108

For all out-of-office correspondence, you should use ZIP codes and Postal Codes, which have been assigned in an attempt to speed the delivery of mail. The U.S. Postal Service has divided the United States and its territories into ten zones, each represented by a digit from 0 to 9; this digit comes first in the ZIP code. The second and third digits represent smaller geographic areas within a state, and the last two digits identify a "local delivery area." Canadian Postal Codes are alphanumeric, with a three-digit

TABLE B.3 Two-Letter Mailing Abbreviations for the United States and Canada

STATE/TERRITORY/PROVINCE	ABBREVIATION	STATE/TERRITORY/PROVINCE	ABBREVIATION	STATE/TERRITORY/PROVINCE	ABBREVIATION
UNITED STATES					
Alabama	AL	Michigan	MI	Utah	UT
Alaska	AK	Minnesota	MN	Vermont	VT
Arizona	AZ	Mississippi	MS	Virginia	VA
Arkansas	AR	Missouri	MO	Virgin Islands	VI
American Samoa	AS	Montana	MT	Washington	WA
California	CA	Nebraska	NE	West Virginia	WV
Canal Zone	CZ	Nevada	NV	Wisconsin	WI
Colorado	CO	New Hampshire	NH	Wyoming	WY
Connecticut	CT	New Jersey	NJ		
Delaware	DE	New Mexico	NM		
District of Columbia	DC	New York	NY		
Florida	FL	North Carolina	NC		
Georgia	GA	North Dakota	ND	**CANADA**	
Guam	GU	Northern Mariana Islands	CM	Alberta	AB
Hawaii	HI	Ohio	OH	British Columbia	BC
Idaho	ID	Oklahoma	OK	Labrador	LB
Illinois	IL	Oregon	OR	Manitoba	MB
Indiana	IN	Pennsylvania	PA	New Brunswick	NB
Iowa	IA	Puerto Rico	PR	Newfoundland	NF
Kansas	KS	Rhode Island	RI	Northwest Territories	NT
Kentucky	KY	South Carolina	SC	Nova Scotia	NS
Louisiana	LA	South Dakota	SD	Ontario	ON
Maine	ME	Tennessee	TN	Prince Edward Island	PE
Maryland	MD	Trust Territories	TT	Quebec	PQ
Massachusetts	MA	Texas	TX	Saskatchewan	SK
				Yukon Territory	YT

FIGURE B.7
Letter Folds for Standard-Size Letterhead

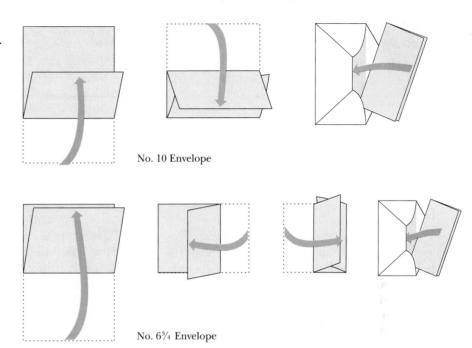

No. 10 Envelope

No. 6¾ Envelope

"area code" and a three-digit "local code" separated by a single space (for example, K2P 5A5). ZIP codes and Postal Codes should be separated from state and province names by one space. As an alternative, a Canadian Postal Code may be put on the bottom line of the address all by itself.

The U.S. Postal Service has introduced ZIP + 4 codes, which add a hyphen and four more numbers to the standard ZIP codes. The first two of the new numbers may identify an area as small as a single large building, and the last two digits may identify one floor in a large building or even a specific department of an organization. The ZIP + 4 codes are therefore especially useful for business correspondence. The Canada Post Corporation achieves the same result with special postal codes assigned to buildings and organizations that receive a large volume of mail.

FOLDING TO FIT

Trivial as it may seem, the way a letter is folded also contributes to the recipient's overall impression of your organization's professionalism. A standard-size piece of paper sent in a No. 10 envelope should be folded in thirds, with the bottom folded up first and then the top folded down over it (see Figure B.7); the open end should be at the top of the envelope and facing out. Smaller stationery should fit neatly into the appropriate envelope simply by folding it in half or in thirds. But when standard-size letterhead must be sent in a No. 6¾ envelope, it should first be folded in half from top to bottom and then in thirds from side to side.

MEMOS

Interoffice memos are not distributed outside the organization and thus may not need to be typed on the best-quality paper. But they nevertheless convey important information. Clarity, careful arrangement, and neatness are therefore important. As with letters, the guidelines that have developed for formatting memos help recipients understand at a glance what they have received and from whom.

Many organizations have memo forms printed, with labeled spaces for the date, the recipient's name (or sometimes a checklist of all departments in an organization or persons in a department), the sender's name, and the subject (see Figure B.8 on page 522). If such forms do not exist, memos are typed on plain paper or sometimes on letterhead.

Memos typed on plain paper or on letterhead

FIGURE B.8
Preprinted Memo Form

MEMO

DATE: _____

TO: _____   FROM: _____

DEPT: _____   TELEPHONE: _____

SUBJECT: _____

For your
☐ APPROVAL ☐ INFORMATION ☐ COMMENT

Message, Comment, or Reply

should always have a title like *Memo* or *Interoffice Correspondence* (all in capitals) centered at the top of the page or aligned with the left margin. The words *Date, To, From,* and *Subject*—followed by the appropriate information—should also appear at the top with a blank line between, as shown here:

MEMO

DATE:

TO:

FROM:

SUBJECT:

Sometimes the heading is organized like this:

MEMO

TO: DATE:

FROM: SUBJECT:

These four pieces of information may be arranged in almost any order, as long as they are present. Sometimes the date is typed without the heading *Date*; the subject may also be presented without the heading, but in that case, it is typed in capital letters so that it stands out clearly. A file or reference number, introduced by the word *File*, may also be included at the top.

If the memo is to be sent to a long list of people, the notation *See distribution list* or *See below* goes into the *To* position at the top, and the names are placed at the end of the memo. Alphabetical arrangement of such a list is usually the most diplomatic course, although high-ranking officials may deserve more prominent placement. Sometimes memos are addressed to groups of people—for example, *All Sales Representatives, Production Group, Assistant Vice Presidents.*

Courtesy titles need not be used anywhere on a memo; in fact, first initials and last names, first names, or even initials alone are sometimes sufficient. As a general rule, however, you should use a courtesy title if you would use one in face-to-face encounters with the person.

The subject line of a memo helps busy colleagues find out quickly what the memo is about. Although the subject "line" may overflow onto a second line, it is most helpful when it is short but still informative.

The body of the memo starts on the second or third line below the heading. Like the body of a letter, it is usually single-spaced. Paragraphs are separated by blank lines but may or may not be indented. Lists, important passages, and subheadings may all be handled as they are in letters. If the memo is very short, it may be double-spaced.

If the memo carries over to a second page, the second page is headed just as the second page of a letter is.

Unlike a letter, a memo does not require a complimentary close or a signature, because the writer's name is already prominent at the top. However, the memo writer may initial the memo—beside the name typed at the top or at the bottom of the memo—or even sign his or her name at the bottom, particularly if the memo deals with money or confidential matters. All other elements—reference initials, enclosure notations, and copy notations—are treated as they would be in a letter.

Memos may be delivered by hand, by the post office (when the recipient doesn't work at the same location as the memo writer), or through interoffice mail. Interoffice mail may require the use of special reusable envelopes that have spaces for noting the recipient's name and department or room number; the name of the previous recipient is simply crossed out. If a regular envelope is used, the words *Interoffice Mail* should be typed where the stamp normally goes so that it isn't accidentally stamped and mailed with the rest of the office correspondence.

Many times, informal, routine, or brief reports for distribution within a company are presented in memo form (see Chapter 10). Such report parts as a table of contents and appendixes are not included, but the body of the memo report is written just as carefully as a formal report.

TIME-SAVING MESSAGES

In the business world, time is money. So if there's a way to speed up the communication process, the organization stands to gain. Telephones and electronic mail systems are very quick indeed, as are mailgrams, telegrams, facsimiles, and the like. In addition, organizations have developed these special formats that reduce the amount of time spent writing and typing short messages:

- *Memo-letters.* Printed with a heading somewhat like a memo's, although they provide a space for an inside address so that the message may be sent outside the company (see Figure B.9). Folded properly, the address shows through a window in the envelope, thereby eliminating the need to address the envelope separately. Memo-letters often include a space for a reply message as well so that the recipient will not

FIGURE B.9
Memo-Letter

MEMO

TO: Green Ridge Gifts
            1786 Century Road
            Nashua, NH 03060
            USA

FROM: Whiteside Import/Export, Ltd.
            1601 Ronson Drive
            Toronto, Ontario M9W 5Z3
            CANADA

SUBJECT: Order for Royal Dorchester china
            completer sets

DATE: October 11, 1993

MESSAGE:

The six Wellington pattern completer sets that you ordered by telephone October 9 are on their way and should reach your shop by October 18.

The three Mayfield pattern completer sets are coming from the factory, however, and will not arrive here until October 26 or 27. That means you will get them around November 2 or 3.

Do you still want the Mayfield sets? Or would you like us to bill you for the Wellington sets only, so you can place the Mayfield order at a later date? Please add your reply below, retain the yellow copy for your records, and send us the white and pink copies.

SIGNED: *Barbara Hutchins*

REPLY: PLEASE SEND THE MAYFIELD SETS AS SOON AS POSSIBLE. YOU MAY BILL FOR BOTH MAYFIELD AND WELLINGTON SETS

DATE: Oct. 15, 1993

SIGNED: *William L. Smith*

have to type a whole new letter in response; carbonless copy sets allow sender and recipient to keep on file a copy of the entire correspondence.

- *Short-note reply technique.* Used in many organizations, even without a special form. The recipient of a memo (or sometimes a letter) simply handwrites a response on the original document, makes a copy for the files, and sends the annotated original back to the person who wrote it.

- *Letterhead postcards.* Another time-saving device, ideal for short, impersonal messages. Organizations that often deal by mail with individuals (such as mail-order companies and government agencies) frequently have postcards and sometimes letters preprinted with a list of responses; the "writer" merely checks the appropriate response(s) and slips the postcard into the mail.

The important thing to realize about these and all message formats is that they have developed over time to meet the need for clear communication and to speed responses to the needs of customers, suppliers, and associates.

REPORTS

The way a report is laid out and typed may enhance its effectiveness. Therefore, pay careful attention to the margins, headings, spacing, indention, and page numbers of a report.

MARGINS

Each prefatory part and supplementary part of a report and the first page of its text should have a two-inch top margin. All remaining pages of the report should start one inch from the top of the page. For very long reports, you may wish to start each major section or chapter on a new page; the first-level headings for each new section should then be typed two inches from the top of the page.

The side and bottom margins for all pages of a report should be at least an inch wide. If you are going to bind your report, at the left or at the top, add half an inch to the margin on the bound edge (see Figure B.10). Because of the space taken by the binding on left-bound reports, the center point of the typed page is a quarter inch to the right of the center of the paper. Be sure that centered headings are centered over the typed portion, not centered on the paper. Other guidelines for typing a report can be found in the sample report near the end of Chapter 12.

FIGURE B.10
Margins for Formal Reports

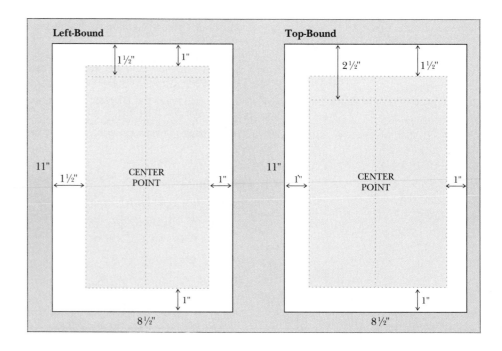

HEADINGS

Headings of various levels provide visual clues to a report's organization. Figure 10.8 illustrates one good system for showing these levels, but many variations exist. No matter which system you use, be sure to be consistent.

SPACING AND INDENTIONS

The spacing and indention of most elements of a report are relatively easy. If your report is double-spaced (and long or technical reports probably should be, for reading ease), all paragraphs should be indented five spaces. In single-spaced reports, the paragraphs are usually blocked (without paragraph indentions) and one blank line is left between paragraphs.

Properly spacing the material on the title page is more complicated, however. For reports that will be bound on the left, start a quarter inch to the right of center. From that point, backspace once for each two letters so that the line will appear centered once the report is bound.

To correctly place lines of type on the title page, first count the number of lines in each block of copy, including blank lines. Subtract the total from 66 (the total number of lines on an 11-inch page) to get the number of unused lines. To allocate these unused lines equally among the spaces between the blocks of copy, divide the number of unused lines by the number of blank areas (always one more than the number of blocks of copy). The result is the number of blank lines to devote to each section. The title page of the sample report in Chapter 12 shows how this procedure produces a balanced-looking page.

PAGE NUMBERS

Remember that every page in the report is counted but that not all pages have numbers shown on them. For instance, the first page of the report, normally the title page, is not numbered. But all other pages in the prefatory section are numbered with a lower-case roman numeral, beginning with ii and continuing with iii, iv, v, and so on. The unadorned (no dashes, no period) page number is centered one inch from the bottom of the page.

The first page of the text of the report carries the unadorned arabic numeral 1, centered one inch from the bottom of the page. In left-bound reports, the following pages, including the supplementary parts, are numbered consecutively with unadorned arabic numerals (2, 3, and so on), placed one inch from the top edge of the page at the right-hand margin. For top-bound reports, these page numbers are typed one inch from the bottom of the page and at the center.

MEETING DOCUMENTS

Meetings are an important forum for business communication. But the success of any meeting depends on the preparation of the participants and on the follow-up measures they take to implement decisions or to seek information after the meeting. Meeting documents—agendas and minutes—aid this process by putting the meeting plan and results into permanent, written form.

Small, informal meetings may not require a written agenda, but any meeting involving a relatively large number of people or covering a lot of ground will run more smoothly if an agenda is distributed in advance. The advantage of having a written agenda is that it helps participants prepare by telling them what will be discussed, and it helps keep them on track once the meeting begins.

The typical agenda format (shown in Figure B.11 on page 526) may seem stiff and formal, but it helps structure a meeting so that as little time as possible is wasted. At the same time, it provides opportunities for discussion, if that's what is called for.

The presentation, a special form of meeting that allows for relatively little group interaction, may also require an agenda or a detailed outline. Special visual aids such as flip charts help attendees grasp the message, and copies of the charts are often provided for future reference.

After a meeting, the secretary who attended prepares a set of minutes for distribution to all attendees and to any other interested parties. The minutes are prepared in much the same format as a memo or letter, except for the heading, which takes this form:

MINUTES

PLANNING COMMITTEE MEETING

TUESDAY, AUGUST 21, 1993

FIGURE B.11
Agenda Format

AGENDA

PLANNING COMMITTEE MEETING
TUESDAY, AUGUST 21, 1993
10:00 A.M.
EXECUTIVE CONFERENCE ROOM

I. Call to Order

II. Roll Call

III. Approval of Agenda

IV. Approval of Minutes from Previous Meeting

V. Chairperson's Report

VI. Subcommittee Reports

    A. New Markets

    B. New Products

    C. Finance

VII. Unfinished Business

VIII. New Business

    A. Carson & Canfield Data

    B. Reassignments

IX. Announcements

X. Adjournment

Present: [All invited attendees are listed here, generally by rank, in alphabetical order, or in some combination.]

Absent:

The body of the minutes, which follows the heading, should note the times at which the meeting started and ended, all major decisions reached at the meeting, all assignments of tasks to meeting participants, and all subjects that were deferred to a later meeting. In addition, the minutes should objectively summarize important discussions, noting the names of those who contributed major points. Outlines, subheadings, and lists help organize the minutes, as in letters, memos, and reports. Additional documentation, such as tables or charts submitted by meeting participants, should be noted in the minutes and attached.

At the end of the minutes, the words *Submitted by* should be added, followed by a couple of blank lines for a signature and then the preparer's typed name and title (if appropriate). If the minutes have been prepared by one person and typed by another, the typist's initials should be added, as in the reference initials on a letter or memo

An informal meeting may not require minutes. Attendees simply pencil their own notes onto their copies of the agenda. Follow-up is then their responsibility, although the meeting leader may need to remind them through a memo, phone call, or face-to-face talk.

APPENDIX C

DOCUMENTATION OF REPORT SOURCES

Documenting a report through source notes and a bibliography is too important a task to undertake haphazardly. When you provide information about your sources, the facts and opinions that you present gain credibility. By documenting your work, you also give readers the means for checking your findings and pursuing the subject further. Finally, documentation is the accepted way to give credit to the people whose works you have drawn on.

The specific style you use to document your report may vary from the style recommended here.

Not only do experts disagree on the "correct" form, but you may also find that your company or organization has adopted a form somewhat different from any suggested by the experts. Don't let this discrepancy confuse you. If your employer specifies a form, use it; the standardized form is easier for colleagues to understand. If the choice of form is left to you, however, adopt a style like one of those described here. Just be consistent within any given report, using the same order, punctuation, and so on, from one source note or bibliographic entry to the next.

SECONDARY SOURCES

Chapter 11 describes the difference between primary data and secondary data and tells how to gather both kinds. Most of this appendix describes how the results of secondary research are reported in source notes and bibliographies. (However, studies and surveys that you conduct yourself as the basis for a report are usually documented through descriptions of your methods and findings within the text of the report.) But before reviewing documentation formats, you must know how to get enough information. Most business research depends on secondary sources, which are traditionally stored in libraries.

A LIBRARY'S RESOURCES

"Just go to the library and look it up." That isn't as straightforward a proposition as it may sound. The

American Library Directory lists more than 30,000 public, college, university, and special libraries in the United States and 3,000 in Canada. In addition, many companies have their own libraries. Today, the first hurdle in getting information is to figure out which library to visit or to phone with your query. Most libraries, however, have the same types of information sources.

Basic references

Once you've decided which library to use, you should head for the reference section. A librarian with specialized knowledge of general sources of information can direct you to the appropriate dictionaries, encyclopedias, almanacs, atlases, biographical reference books, handbooks, manuals, directories of companies and associations, and perhaps even a collection of corporations' annual reports. In the absence of a knowledgeable reference librarian, consult *Reference Books: A Brief Guide* or *Business Information Sources*. Or refer to Figure C.1, which lists the major reference books used by business researchers.

Books and articles

Both books and articles provide in-depth coverage of specific topics. Although articles are more timely than books, books have a broader focus. A combination of the two often provides the best background for your report.

So many books and articles are published every year that a library must be selective in choosing those to put on its shelves. For specialized information, therefore, a public library is not very useful. You will have better luck finding books and articles on technical subjects at college libraries (assuming the college offers courses in those subjects) and in company libraries.

All libraries provide bibliographies of the books and back issues of publications they stock. The traditional card catalog contains vast numbers of index cards organized by subject, title, and author; a code on each card directs you to the shelf where the book or publication is located. Some libraries have con-

FIGURE C.1 Major Reference Works

- *Biography Index:* Indexes biographical data from more than 2,400 periodicals as well as from English-language books.

- *Books in Print:* Lists more than 425,000 books in 62,000 subject categories currently available from over 6,000 U.S. publishers. Also indexes books by author and by title.

- *Business Periodicals Index:* Lists articles from about 280 business-related periodicals; companion is *Canadian Business Index.*

- *Current Biography:* Features biographical data about individuals who have achieved fame during the period covered.

- *Directory of Directories:* Indexes several thousand business, industrial, and professional directories.

- *Dun & Bradstreet, Inc., Million Dollar Directory:* Lists more than 120,000 U.S. companies by net worth. Includes names of officers and directors, goods and services, approximate sales, and number of employees.

- *Encyclopedia of Associations:* Indexes thousands of associations by broad subject category, by specific subject, by name of association, and by geographic location.

- *Moody's Manuals:* In a series of publications for specific industries—such as banks and financial institutions, public utilities, and international companies—lists financial data of the sort found in corporate annual reports.

- *Reader's Guide to Periodical Literature:* Indexes articles in some 190 popular periodicals by subject and author.

- *Standard & Poor's Register of Corporations:* Indexes more than 37,000 U.S., Canadian, and major international corporations. Lists officers, products, sales volume, and number of employees.

- *Standard Periodical Directory:* Describes more than 66,000 U.S. and Canadian periodicals.

- *Statistical Abstract of the United States:* Presents U.S. economic, social, political, and industrial statistics.

- *Survey of Current Business:* Features national business statistics on construction, real estate, employment and earn-

ings, finance, foreign trade, transportation, communication, and other key topics.

- *Thomas Register of American Manufacturers:* Presents information on thousands of U.S. manufacturers, indexed by company name and product.

- *U.S. Government Publications: Monthly Catalog:* Lists titles of more than 1,000 new U.S. government publications in each issue.

- *Who's Who in America:* Summarizes the achievements of living U.S. citizens who have gained prominence in their fields; *Canadian Who's Who* and *Who's Who in Business and Finance* are similar.

- *World Almanac and Book of Facts:* Presents statistical information about many events, people, and places. Index contains both general subject headings and specific names. Similar information is available in the *Canadian Yearbook* and the *Corpus Almanac of Canada.*

- Other indexes of articles in newspapers, magazines, and journals:

    Accountants' Index
    Applied Science and Technology Index
    Art Index
    Biological and Agricultural Index
    Computer Literature Index
    Education Index
    Engineering Index
    General Science Index
    Humanities Index
    Index Medicus
    Index to Legal Periodicals
    The New York Times Index
    Predicasts (U.S. and international editions)
    Public Affairs Information Bulletin
    Social Sciences Index
    The Wall Street Journal Index

verted their card catalogs to microfilm or microfiche, which takes up far less space. Inserted in a special viewing device, microfilm and microfiche tell you where to find what you want. Other libraries now have computerized information about their holdings.

Abstracts

One way to find out a lot relatively quickly is to consult abstracts. Instead of just supplying a categorized list of article titles, as indexes do, abstracts summarize each article's contents as well. Many fields are served by abstracts that regularly review articles in the most useful periodicals. Here are the names of a few abstracts that may prove useful:

ABS Guide to Recent Publications in the Social and Behavioral Sciences

Book Review Digest

Business Publications Index and Abstracts

Computer Abstracts

Dissertation Abstracts International

Educational Research Information Center (ERIC)

Personnel Management Abstracts

Psychological Abstracts

Sociological Abstracts

Government documents

When you want to know the exact provisions of a law, the background of a court decision, or population and business patterns, you can consult the government documents section of a library. The ins and outs of this sort of research are rather complicated, but a librarian can direct you to the information you need. Just know what government body you're interested in (for example, U.S. Congress, Ninth Court of Appeals, or Department of Labor) and some sort of identification for the specific information you need (such as the Safe Drinking Water Act of 1974, *Price v. Shell Oil Co.*, or *1990 Census*). If you have a date and the name of a publication containing the document, so much the better.

COMPUTERIZED DATABANKS

One resource available in some companies is a computerized database (referred to as a management information system), containing company-generated statistics on sales and expenses, product specifications, inventory status, market research data, and perhaps reports and correspondence as well. Employees can often tap into that information directly through the computers or terminals on their desks, or they may be able to ask the data-processing department to get them a printout of the information they need.

Your access to information expands greatly when you also subscribe to one of the commercial databases, such as Management Contents, National Newspaper Index, and Trade and Industry Index. (More and more libraries are also database subscribers.) Their extensive files are continuously updated, thoroughly indexed, and readily accessible over standard telephone lines.

NOTE CARDS

Many people check books out of the library. Or they make photocopies or printouts of articles and other documents so that they can study them more carefully in their own offices. (Good researchers carefully note all necessary bibliographic information so that they don't have to go back to the library or supply incomplete documentation.) Photocopying is legal as long as you are not doing so to avoid buying the publication or to resell the information.

Sometimes, however, you just need to note a point or two from a document; you don't need to have the whole document. In such cases, you will find note cards useful. You should make a separate note card for each fact, quotation, or general concept you want to record. Summarize in your own words unless you think specific data or quotations may be useful.

Bear in mind that the reason for using note cards is to help you remember and retrieve useful information for your report. As a practical matter, then, you should write the author's name, the book's or article's title, and other necessary bibliographic information at the top of each card. (As an alternative when you're collecting several pieces of information from each source, you might prepare a bibliography card for each, number the cards, and then use these numbers to cross-reference your note cards.) It is also helpful to note at the top of the card the general subject of the material, in a simple phrase or with identifying numbers from your preliminary outline so that you can sort your notes more easily when it comes time to write your report. Figure C.2 on page 530 shows a sample note card.

FIGURE C.2
Sample Note Card

> II-B-2a
>
> William Hoffer, "Businesswomen:
> Equal but Different," *Nation's Business*
> August 1987, 46-47.
> Liz Claiborne, Inc., launched by
> Elisabeth Claiborne Ortenberg,
> Arthur Ortenberg, & Leonard Boxer
> w/ $250,000 initial funding (p. 47)

COPYRIGHT AND FAIR USE

There is an important reason for carefully documenting the sources you consult during secondary research: Although ideas belong to no one person, the way they are expressed provides the livelihood for many scholars, consultants, and writers. To protect their interests, most countries have established copyright laws. Transgress those laws, and you or your company could be sued, not to mention embarrassed.

In addition to printed materials like books and magazines, copyright law covers audiovisual materials, many forms of artistic expression, computer programs, maps, mailing lists, and even answering machine messages. However, copyright law does not protect

- Titles, names, short phrases, and slogans
- Familiar symbols or designs
- Listings of ingredients or contents
- Ideas, procedures, methods, systems, processes, concepts, principles, discoveries, or devices (although it does cover their description, explanation, or illustration)

A work is considered copyrighted as soon as it is put into fixed form, even if it has not been registered.[1]

How do you avoid plagiarism (presenting someone else's work as your own)? Here are a couple of guidelines:

- Whenever you quote another person's work, whether published or unpublished, tell where you found the statement. This rule applies to books, articles, tables, charts, diagrams, song lyrics, scripted dialogue, letters, speeches, anything that you take verbatim (word for word) from someone else. Even if you paraphrase (change the wording somewhat), you should give credit to the person who has found an effective way to express an idea.

- You do not, however, have to cite the source of general knowledge or specialized knowledge generally known among your readers. For example, everyone knows that Franklin Roosevelt was elected to the presidency of the United States four times. You can say so on your own authority, even if you have read an article in which the author said the same thing.

Merely crediting the source is not always enough, however. The fair use doctrine says that you can use other people's work only as long as you do not unfairly prevent them from benefiting as a result. For example, if you reproduce someone else's copyrighted questionnaire in a report you are writing (and identify the source thoroughly), you are preventing the author from selling a copy of that questionnaire to your readers. It is generally best to avoid relying to such a great extent on someone else's work. But when it can't be avoided, you must write to the copyright holder (usually the author or publisher) for permission to reprint. You will usually be asked to pay a fee.

Fair use is decided in the courts on a case-by-case basis. Thus you will not find any hard-and-fast rules about when you must get permission and when permission is unnecessary. In general, however, you should probably get permission to use

- More than 250 words quoted from a book

- More than 50 words from a magazine or journal article

- Any reproduction of a piece of artwork (including fully reproduced charts and tables) or excerpt from commercially produced audiovisual material

- Any dialogue from a play or line from a poem or song

- Any portion of consumable materials, such as workbooks

- Multiple copies of copyrighted works that you intend to distribute widely or repeatedly, especially for non-educational purposes

You do not need permission to use materials published before 1907, news articles more than three months old, or materials originally published by the government. Nor do you need permission to use copies as the basis for "criticism, comment, news reporting, teaching (including multiple copies for one-time classroom use), scholarship, or research." [2]

In deciding whether you may use someone else's work without permission, remember that the courts (if they get involved) will consider the length of your quotation in relation to the total length of the work from which it is taken, the type of work you are taking it from, your purpose, and the effect your action has on the original author's efforts to distribute the work. If you think you may be infringing on the author's rights, write for permission and provide a credit line. In any case, be sure to acknowledge the original author's work with a source note.

SOURCE NOTES

Source notes have traditionally been presented as footnotes at the bottom of report pages. But endnotes, typed at the end of each chapter or at the end of the report (just before the bibliography), have become quite common. Each practice has pluses and minuses. Footnotes, for instance, are harder to type within the margins of the page, but they are handier for the reader. Endnotes, on the other hand, are much easier to type, but the reader may become annoyed at having to flip to the end of the report.

The solution to the dilemma may lie, in part, in distinguishing between two types of notes. *Source notes* are used to document quotations (word-for-word selections from another work), paraphrased passages (someone else's ideas stated in your own words), and visual aids. Any information taken from another source requires a source note. *Content notes* are used from time to time to supplement your main text with asides about a particular issue or event, to provide a cross-reference to another section of your report, or to direct the reader to a related source (explaining the connection between one thing and the other). Any note that contains more than a simple reference to another work is a content note.

For the reader's convenience, content notes are often presented at the bottom of the page they refer to, and source notes are placed at the end of the document, where they are less distracting. Or you might consider which type of note is most common in your report and then choose whether to present them all as endnotes or all as footnotes. However, regardless of the method you select for references to textual information, remember that both content and source notes pertaining to visual aids are placed on the same page as the visual aid.

MECHANICS

Notes of all varieties are single-spaced and separated from one another by a double space. In footnotes to text information, the identifying number is indented five spaces, placed on the line, and followed by a period. Two spaces are left after the period before the entry begins (see the section containing examples). Endnotes, however, are typed beginning at the left margin. Notes referring to visual aids are handled differently too: A source note, preceded by the underlined (italicized) word *Source* and a colon, is placed at the bottom of the visual aid; content notes, if any, are listed below the source note. Figure 12.2 shows the placement of these notes on visual aids.

When using footnotes, you must plan carefully to leave enough space for the footnote at the bottom of the page and still maintain the standard margin. A line about 1½ inches long (15 spaces in pica type, 20 in elite), made with the underscore key on a typewriter, separates the footnote(s) from the text.

Reference marks

Content and source notes pertaining to text are signaled with superscripts, which are arabic numerals placed just above the line of type. Usually, superscripts come at the end of the sentence containing the referenced statement; but occasionally, to avoid confusion, a superscript is placed right after the referenced statement:

Rising interest rates put a damper on third-quarter profits in all industries,[1] and profits did not pick up again until the Federal Reserve loosened the money supply.[2]

Notice that the first superscript in the example comes after the comma. Superscripts follow all punctuation marks except the dash, which is placed after the superscript.

Reference marks are numbered consecutively throughout the report. (In very long reports, they may be numbered consecutively throughout each chapter.) If a note is added or deleted, all the reference marks that follow must be changed to maintain an unbroken sequence. If you change the reference marks, be sure to renumber the notes as well.

In visual aids, content notes are marked with asterisks and other symbols (or italicized small letters if the visual aids contain many numbers).

Quotations

Quotations from secondary sources must always be followed by a reference mark. However, quotations may appear in one of two forms, depending on their length. A brief quotation (three lines or less) can be typed right into the main body of the text. Quotation marks at the beginning and end of the quotation separate the other person's words from your own. A longer quotation must be set off as an extract, which begins on a new line with both right and left margins indented five to seven spaces. No quotation marks are needed. Although the main text may be single- or double-spaced, an extract is always single-spaced.

Often, you will want to leave out some part of a quotation. Ellipsis points (or dots) are the three periodlike punctuation marks that show something is missing:

Brant has demonstrated . . . a wanton disregard for the realities of the marketplace. His days at the helm are numbered. . . . Already several lower-level executives are jockeying for position.[3]

In this example, you can see how ellipsis points are handled between sentences: A period is followed by the three dots. Note also that ellipsis points are typed with spaces between them.

FORM

Many schemes have been proposed for organizing the information in source notes. But all break the information into two main parts: (1) information about the author and the work and (2) publication information. The first part includes the author's name, the title of the work, and such other identifying information as the edition and volume number. The second part includes the place of publication, the publisher, and the date of publication, followed by relevant page numbers. A few details about these elements are described in the sections that follow.

Author's name

If the author of the work is only one person, her or his name is spelled out and followed by a comma. Two authors are listed similarly, with *and* separating their names. For three authors, you should separate the names with commas and insert *and* before the last author's name. But four or more authors may be handled more concisely. After the first author's name, you simply insert *et al.* or *and others*, with no preceding comma.

Title of the work

Titles are usually typed using uppercase and lowercase, which means that the first and last words start with a capital letter, as do all nouns, pronouns, verbs, adverbs, and adjectives. However, prepositions, conjunctions, and articles start with a lowercase letter; exceptions are prepositions that are an inseparable part of an expression (as in "Looking Up New Words") and, often, prepositions and conjunctions with more than four letters.

When works have a two-part title, a colon should be used to separate the two parts:

Managerial Communications: A Strategic Approach

Leave two spaces after the colon, and capitalize the letter that comes right after the colon.

Titles of books, periodicals (journals and magazines published at regular intervals), and other major works are usually printed in italics, which means that when using a typewriter you should underline them. Sometimes, however, they are typed all in capitals with no underlining to make the typing task easier and to make the title stand out more. Titles of articles, pamphlets, chapters in books, and the like are placed in quotation marks.

Publication information

Source notes referring to periodicals do not usually include the publisher's name and place of business (see sample source notes 7, 12, and 13), but source notes for books, pamphlets, and other hard-to-find works do. Such publication information is set off in parentheses.

In a reference to a book, the first item following the opening parenthesis is the city where the publisher is located. If the city is large and well known and if there are no other well-known cities by the same name, its name can appear alone. But if necessary for proper identification, the state, province, or country should also be indicated. Abbreviations (the standard kind, not the two-letter postal abbreviations) are used for states and provinces, but the names of countries are spelled out. A colon follows the name of the place.

The publisher's name comes after the colon, often in a shortened form. For example, McGraw-Hill, Inc., can easily be identified when shortened to McGraw-Hill. If you begin with shortened publishers' names, be sure to carry through with the same short forms throughout your source notes and bibliography. But use a publisher's full name if it is not well known or might be confused with some other organization.

The publication date you should use is the most recent year on the copyright notice. Ignore the dates of printing. After the date, close the parentheses.

A source note often refers to a specific page number. If so, the closing parenthesis is followed by a comma, which in turn is followed by the page number(s).

Repeated source notes

You may need to cite the same reference more than once in the course of your report. When you do, you can save time and effort by using a full citation for the first source note and a shortened form for later references to the same work. If your report has a comprehensive alphabetical bibliography, you may opt to use the short form for all your source notes, not just first citations.

The information in repeated source notes can be handled in two ways. One is a formal, traditional style; the other is informal. The formal style uses Latin abbreviations to indicate certain information; the informal style uses shortened versions of that information instead.

Here are some repeated source notes using the formal style:

4. Thomas W. Horn, Business Valuation Manual (Lancaster, Penn.: Charter Oak Press, 1985), 59-60.

5. Ibid., 130. [refers to page 130 in the Horn book]

6. Robert Levering, Milton Moskowitz, and Michael Katz, The 100 Best Companies to Work For in America (New York: New American Library, 1985), 9.

7. Steven Fink, "Planning for a Crisis," Nation's Business, April 1986, 49.

8. Levering, Moskowitz, and Katz, op. cit., 28. [refers to a new page in the book cited in note 6]

9. Fink, loc. cit. [refers to page 49 of Fink]

Ibid. means "in the same place"—that is, the same reference mentioned in the immediately preceding entry but perhaps a different page (indicated by giving the page number). *Op. cit.* means "in the work cited"; because it is used when at least one other reference has come between it and the original citation, you must include the last name of the author. You must also use a new page number; otherwise, you would use *loc. cit.* ("in the place cited") and omit the page number.

The informal style, which is commonly used today, avoids Latin abbreviations by adopting a shortened form for the title of a reference that is repeated. In this style, the previous list of source notes would appear as follows:

4. Thomas W. Horn, Business Valuation Manual (Lancaster, Penn.: Charter Oak Press, 1985), 59-60.

5. Horn, Valuation Manual, 130.

6. Robert Levering, Milton Moskowitz, and Michael Katz, The 100 Best Companies to Work For in America (New York: New American Library, 1985), 9.

7. Steven Fink, "Planning for a Crisis," Nation's Business, April 1986, 49.

8. Levering, Moskowitz, and Katz, 100 Best Companies, 28.

9. Fink, "Planning for a Crisis," 49.

Notice that only the author's last name, a short form of the title, and the page number are used in this style of repeated source note.

EXAMPLES

With these few general guidelines in mind, take a closer look at how the form of a source note depends on the type of reference being cited. You'll find some additional examples in the sample report in Chapter 12.

Books

In their simplest form, references to books look like source notes 4 and 6 in the preceding set of examples. Sometimes, however, you will want to note the edition of a book:

10. William Strunk, Jr., and E. B. White, <u>The Elements of Style</u>, 3d ed. (New York: Macmillan, 1979), 27.

When you need to cite a volume number, place *vol. 3* (or the correct number) after the title or edition number and before the publication data.

On other occasions, you'll need to use the name of an editor instead of an author:

11. Warren K. Agee, Phillip H. Ault, and Edwin Emery, eds., <u>Perspectives on Mass Communications</u> (New York: Harper & Row, 1982).

Periodicals

The typical periodical reference looks like source note 7 in the previous examples. The article author's name (if there is one) is handled as a book author's is, but the title of the article appears in quotation marks. Like the title of a book, the title of the magazine or journal appears either in italics (underlined) or in all capital letters.

The rest of the periodical note can be tricky, however. For popular and business magazines, you need include only the date and page number(s) after the title. (Note that the date is inverted, unlike dates used in text.)

12. "Now Introducing Son of Greenmail," <u>Time</u>, 8 June 1987, 62.

But for scientific or academic journals, you should include the volume number and treat the page number as shown here:

13. John A. Quelch and Kristina Cannon-Bonventre, "Better Marketing at the Point of Purchase," <u>Harvard Business Review</u> 61 (November-December 1983): 165. [volume 61, page 165]

As a rule of thumb, you should use the more scholarly style of source note 13 if your report is weighted heavily toward serious research in professional journals; if popular and trade magazines dominate your references, you may stick with the simpler style that leaves out the volume number. Your guiding principle in choosing a style should be to provide the information that your readers need to find your source easily.

Newspapers

When a newspaper article does not have an author, the citation begins with the name of the article. The name of the newspaper is treated like the title of a book or periodical. Many of the best-known newspapers—for example *The New York Times*, *The Wall Street Journal*, and *The Christian Science Monitor*—cannot be mistaken for other newspapers, but many smaller newspapers are not so easily identified. If the name of the city (plus the state or province for obscure or small cities) does not appear in the title of these newspapers, you should put the place name in brackets after the title. Finally, a newspaper reference should specify the date of publication in the same way a magazine does, and it should end with a section name or number (if appropriate) and a page number:

14. "In the U.S. Today, 'Common Courtesy' Is Contradictory Phrase," <u>The Wall Street Journal</u>, 12 March 1987, sec. 1, 1.

Public documents

Government documents and court cases are often useful in business reports, but source notes referring to them are hard to construct. As you struggle with a complex set of "authors" and publication data, remember that the goal is to provide just enough information to identify the work and to distinguish it from others.

Here are some examples of source notes for government and legal documents:

15. U.S. Department of Commerce, Task Force on Corporate Social Performance, <u>Corporate Social Reporting in the United States and Western Europe</u> (Washington, D.C.: Government Printing Office, July

1979), 3. [identifies the group issuing the document as specifically as possible]

16. U.S. Congress, House Committee on Labor, An Investigation Relating to Health Conditions of Workers Employed in the Construction and Maintenance of Public Utilities, 74th Cong., 2d sess., 16-29 January 1936.

17. Simpson v. Union Oil Co. of California, 377 U.S. 13 (U.S. Sup. Ct. 1964). [provides the name of the case, the volume and page numbers of the law report, the name of the court that decided the case (the U.S. Supreme Court here), and the date of the decision]

For more information on documenting specialized sources like these, consult the librarian in the documents section or one of the style books cited at the end of this appendix.

Unpublished material

Theses, dissertations, and company reports—which are usually prepared for a limited audience of insiders—are handled similarly. The title, like an article title, is in quotation marks, and "publication" data that will help the reader find the work are put in parentheses:

18. John Peter Randolph, "Development and Implementation of Public Access Through Cable Television" (Master's thesis, San Diego State University, 1989), 73-74.

19. Frances Asakawa, "Recommendations for Replacing the Sales Fleet Based on a Comparison of Three Midsize Automobiles" (Report to Daniel Standish, Director of Sales, Midwest Marketing, Inc., 17 November 1992), 17.

This format can be used for any written source that doesn't fall into one of the other categories, such as a sales brochure or a presentation handout. Identify the author, title, and place and date of publication as completely as you can so that your readers have a way to refer to the source.

Letters, speeches, interviews, and other types of unprinted references should also be identified as completely as possible to give readers some means of checking the source. Begin with the name, title, and

affiliation of the "author"; then describe the nature of the communication, the date and possibly the place, and if appropriate, the location of the files containing the document:

20. Nancy Sjoberg, President, Del Mar Associates, welcoming address at CRM Reunion, San Diego, California, 15 August 1991.

21. Victor Schoenberg, letter to Barbara Parsons, 10 February 1992.

22. Dorothy Gabbei, interview with the writer, Emporia, Kansas, 14 July 1993.

You may want to weave references to such sources into the text of your report. If you have many of them, however, you may just as well put them into notes so that they won't be distracting to readers.

Electronic media

Television and radio programs, films, computer programs, and the like, should also be documented. It may be more difficult for a reader to refer to these media (especially television and radio programs), but you should at least acknowledge ideas and facts borrowed from someone else. Many times, you can weave references to electronic media into the text of your report. When you prefer to use source notes, however, your citations should look something like this:

23. Mike Wallace, "60 Minutes," CBS-TV, 25 March 1993.

24. Group Productivity (Del Mar, Calif.: CRM/ McGraw-Hill Films, 1985), videotape, 22 min.

25. WordPerfect Version 5.1 (Orem, Utah: WordPerfect Corporation, 1990), software for IBM Personal Computers.

The exact information you provide depends on your subject and audience and on the context of the reference. For example, in citing a film, it may be appropriate to note the scriptwriter or director. When it comes to electronic media, which are rather new sources of information for business researchers, you must use good judgment in constructing source notes.

BIBLIOGRAPHIES

The reason for including a bibliography in a report is to give your readers a complete list of the sources

you consulted. In addition, a bibliography serves as a reading list for readers who want to pursue the subject of your report further. The bibliography should therefore present, in alphabetical order, every source that appears in the notes and perhaps additional references that you didn't specifically refer to in the body of your report. If all your sources are listed in endnotes, you may find that a bibliography is unnecessary. However, the longer and more formal the report, the greater the need for a separate bibliography.

Because a bibliography may serve as a reading list, you may want to annotate each entry—that is, comment on the subject matter and viewpoint of the source, as well as its usefulness to your readers:

Baldrige, Letitia. Complete Guide to Executive Manners. New York: Rawson Associates, 1985. Thorough review of etiquette as it relates to the business world. Two parts: Human Relations at Work and Business Protocol; 499 pages.

Annotations may be written in either complete or incomplete sentences.

MECHANICS

Depending on the length of your report and the complexity and number of your sources, you may either put the entire bibliography at the end of the report (after the endnotes) or put relevant sections at the end of each chapter. Another way to make a long bibliography more manageable is to subdivide it into categories (a classified bibliography), either by type of reference (such as books, articles, and unpublished material) or by subject matter (such as government regulation, market forces, and so on).

When typing the bibliography, each entry should start at the left margin, with the author's last name first. In general, the content of the entries and the order of the elements are the same as in source notes. Like source notes, bibliographic entries are single-spaced, with a double space between them. However, some of the punctuation is different, and bibliographic entries are indented after the first line (hanging indent). The sample report in Chapter 12 includes a complete bibliography.

EXAMPLES

To point up the differences between source notes and bibliographic entries, the following examples use the same works as sample source notes 10 through 19. The major content difference is that bibliographic

entries do not include page numbers (unless they are articles or chapters in books), because the reader is being referred to the work as a whole.

To be sure you have all the information you need when it comes time to construct a bibliography, use this same format during your research. Many writers use a separate index card for each work consulted, which makes alphabetizing the entries relatively painless.

Books

Note that only the first author's name is typed in reverse order and that parentheses are not used around the publication data:

Agee, Warren K., Phillip H. Ault, and Edwin Emery, eds. Perspectives on Mass Communications. New York: Harper & Row, 1982.

Strunk, William, Jr., and E. B. White. The Elements of Style. 3d ed. New York: Macmillan, 1979.

For more than one work by the same author, use six hyphens in place of the author's name. But repeat the name if one of the books is by a single author and another is by that author with others.

Periodicals

Use the same information that appears in the source note, but use inclusive page numbers (page numbers for the whole article):

"Now Introducing Son of Greenmail." Time, 8 June 1987, 62-63.

Quelch, John A., and Kristina Cannon-Bonventre. "Better Marketing at the Point of Purchase." Harvard Business Review 61 (November-December 1983): 162-169.

Note the differences in punctuation between bibliographic style and source note style.

Newspapers

Again, the major difference is in the punctuation:

"In the U.S. Today, 'Common Courtesy' Is Contradictory Phrase." The Wall Street Journal, 12 March 1987, sec. 1, 1.

Because no author is listed, this entry would be alphabetized by the first word of the article title (In) instead of by author's name.

Public documents

Here, in alphabetical order, are bibliographic entries for sample source notes 15, 16, and 17:

Simpson v. Union Oil Co. of California. 377 U.S. 13 (U.S. Sup. Ct. 1964).

U.S. Congress. House Committee on Labor. An Investigation Relating to Health Conditions of Workers Employed in the Construction and Maintenance of Public Utilities. 74th Cong., 2d sess., 16-29 January 1936.

U.S. Department of Commerce. Task Force on Corporate Social Performance. Corporate Social Reporting in the United States and Western Europe. Washington, D.C.: Government Printing Office, July 1979.

Legal cases are often not listed in bibliographies, just mentioned in the text or cited in source notes.

Unpublished material

Letters, casual interviews, and telephone conversations are rarely included in bibliographies. But theses, dissertations, company reports, and formal interviews may be if the source is accessible to readers. Here are two examples, in alphabetical order:

Asakawa, Frances. "Recommendations for Replacing the Sales Fleet Based on a Comparison of Three Midsize Automobiles." Report to Daniel Standish, Director of Sales, Midwest Marketing, Inc., 17 November 1992.

Randolph, John Peter. "Development and Implementation of Public Access Through Cable Television." Master's thesis, San Diego State University, 1989.

Electronic media

Here, in alphabetical order, are bibliographic entries for sample source notes 23 through 25:

Group Productivity. Del Mar, Calif.: CRM/McGraw-Hill Films, 1989. Videotape, 22 min.

Wallace, Mike. "60 Minutes." CBS-TV, 25 March 1993.

WordPerfect Version 5.1. Orem, Utah: WordPerfect Corporation, 1990. Software for IBM Personal Computers.

The information provided in these entries is sufficient to give readers a clear idea of the works you consulted, but more information may be needed if they are to easily consult the works themselves.

REFERENCE CITATIONS

Another method of documenting report sources has become popular in recent years. In an attempt to eliminate the need for separate source notes and bibliography, references are listed at the ends of chapters or at the end of the report, in much the same format as a regular bibliography; however, superscripts and source notes are eliminated. Three popular ways of handling so-called reference citations are explained here. All three were designed to streamline the report and to eliminate some of the tedium of preparing both source notes and bibliography.

AUTHOR-DATE SYSTEM

One simple system uses regular bibliographic style for the list of references. However, if the reference list has many instances of multiple works by one author or if the report writer wants to highlight the currency of the research, the date of publication may be moved to the spot just after the author's name. This is the style recommended by the American Psychological Association.

In the text, reference to a given work is documented mainly with the author's last name and the date of publication (with a page number added when necessary):

. . . a basic understanding of the problem (Randolph 1989, 67).

An alternative is to weave the name of the author into the sentence:

According to Randolph (1989), no solution is likely to come . . .

When no author is named, use a short form of the title of the work. If the "author" is an organization, then shorten the name of the organization. In either case, make sure a reader can easily find the entry in the bibliography:

. . . with an emphasis on environmental matters (U.S. Department of Commerce, 1979).

If this entry were identified as "Department of Commerce," a reader would be searching the *D*'s instead of the *U*'s for the correct reference.

In listing more than one work by the same author, rely on the year of publication to distinguish between them. A lowercase letter (*a*, *b*, and so on) after the year differentiates two works by the same author published in the same year.

KEY-NUMBER SYSTEM

The second approach numbers each bibliography entry in sequence, with an arabic numeral followed by a period. Sometimes the "bibliography" is arranged in order of the appearance of each source in the text instead of in alphabetical order.

In the text, references are documented with numbers. The first is the number assigned to the source, the second is the page number:

. . . a basic understanding of the problem (12:7).

This reference cites page 7 of item 12 in the reference list.

MLA SIMPLIFIED STYLE

Like the author-date system, the documentation system recommended by the Modern Language Association lets you weave references into the text. However, instead of using the author's name with the date of publication, MLA simplified style uses the author's name and a page reference:

. . . giving retailers some additional options (Quelch and Cannon-Bonventre 166).

Often parenthetical references can be reduced to just the page number or eliminated entirely (when you refer to the work as a whole instead of specific pages):

In her chapter on international business manners, Baldrige emphasizes Japanese customs (171-76).

Strunk and White offer a few simple guidelines that cover most writing problems.

The reference list at the end of the report (usually labeled "Works Cited" or, when uncited works are included, "Works Consulted") is arranged alphabetically in a format much like the bibliography format recommended in this appendix. The main difference is that publication information—especially the names of months, the names of easily recognized periodicals, and portions of publishers' names—is often abbreviated:

United States Dept. of Commerce. Task Force on Corporate Social Performance. Corporate Social Reporting in the United States and Western Europe. Washington: GPO, 1979.

In addition, punctuation is minimized in newspaper and periodical citations:

"In the U.S. Today, 'Common Courtesy' Is Contradictory Phrase." The Wall Street Journal 12 Mar. 1987, sec. 1: 1.

"Now Introducing Son of Greenmail." Time 8 June 1987: 62-63.

The goal, as in other methods of using reference citations, is to simplify the traditional documentation style.

FURTHER INFORMATION ON DOCUMENTATION

As mentioned earlier, a wide variety of style books provides information on constructing source notes and bibliographies. These are a few of the guides most commonly used:

Achtert, Walter S., and Joseph Gibaldi. *The MLA Style Manual.* New York: Modern Language Association, 1985.

Basis for the note and bibliography style used in much academic writing and recommended in many college textbooks on writing term papers; provides lots of examples in the humanities.

American Psychological Association. *Publication Manual of the American Psychological Association.* 3d ed. Washington, D.C.: American Psychological Association, 1983.

Details the author-date system, which is preferred in the social sciences and often in the natural sciences as well.

Campbell, William Giles, Stephen Vaughan Ballou, and Carole Slade. *Form and Style: Theses, Reports, Term Papers.* 6th ed. Boston: Houghton Mifflin, 1982.

Compares documentation styles recommended by the Modern Language Association and by *The Chicago Manual of Style.*

The Chicago Manual of Style. 13th ed. Chicago: University of Chicago Press, 1982.

Known as the *Chicago Manual* and widely used in the publishing industry; detailed treatment of documentation in Chapters 15, 16, and 17.

Shields, Nancy E., and Mary E. Uhle. *Where Credit Is Due: A Guide to Proper Citing of Sources—Print and Nonprint.* Metuchen, N.J.: Scarecrow Press, 1985.

Invaluable for its exhaustive treatment of troublesome sources, such as pamphlets, reports, oral messages, and electronic media.

Turabian, Kate L. *A Manual for Writers of Term Papers, Theses, and Dissertations.* 4th ed. Chicago: University of Chicago Press, 1973.

Based on the *Chicago Manual,* but smaller and limited to matters of concern to report writers; many examples of documenting nonstandard references.

U.S. Government Printing Office Style Manual. Rev. ed. Washington, D.C.: Government Printing Office, 1984.

Known as the *GPO Manual;* particularly useful for styling references to government documents.

APPENDIX D

CORRECTION SYMBOLS

Instructors often use these short, easy-to-remember correction symbols and abbreviations when evaluating students' writing. You can use them too, to understand your instructor's suggestions and to revise and proofread your own letters, memos, and reports. Refer to Appendix A for additional information on grammar and usage.

CONTENT AND STYLE

Acc	Accuracy. Check to be sure information is correct.
ACE	Avoid copying examples.
ACP	Avoid copying problems.
Adp	Adapt. Tailor message to reader.
Assign	Assignment. Review instructions for assignment.
AV	Active verb. Substitute active for passive.
Awk	Awkward phrasing. Rewrite.
BC	Be consistent.
BMS	Be more sincere.
Chop	Choppy sentences. Use longer sentences and more transitional phrases.
Con	Condense. Use fewer words.
CT	Conversational tone. Avoid using overly formal language.
Depers	Depersonalize. Avoid attributing credit or blame to any individual or group.
Dev	Develop. Provide greater detail.
Dir	Direct. Use direct approach; get to the point.
Emph	Emphasize. Develop this point more fully.
EW	Explanation weak. Check logic; provide more proof.
Fl	Flattery. Avoid flattery that is insincere.
FS	Figure of speech. Find a more accurate expression.
GNF	Good news first. Use direct order.
GRF	Give reasons first. Use indirect order.
GW	Goodwill. Put more emphasis on expressions of goodwill.
H/E	Honesty/ethics. Revise statement to reflect good business practices.
Imp	Imply. Avoid being direct.
Inc	Incomplete. Develop further.
Jar	Jargon. Use less specialized language.
Log	Logic. Check development of argument.
Neg	Negative. Use more positive approach or expression.
Obv	Obvious. Do not state point in such detail.
OC	Overconfident. Adopt more humble language.
OM	Omission
Org	Organization. Strengthen outline.
OS	Off the subject. Close with point on main subject.
Par	Parallel. Use same structure.

Plan	Follow proper organizational plan. (Refer to Chapter 4.)	Stet	Let stand in original form.
		Sub	Subordinate. Make this point less important.
Pom	Pompous. Rephrase in down-to-earth terms.	SX	Sexist. Avoid language that contributes to gender stereotypes.
PV	Point of view. Make statement from reader's perspective rather than your own.		
		Tone	Tone needs improvement.
RB	Reader benefit. Explain what reader stands to gain.	Trans	Transition. Show connection between points.
Red	Redundant. Reduce number of times this point is made.	UAE	Use action ending. Close by stating what reader should do next.
Ref	Reference. Cite source of information.	UAS	Use appropriate salutation.
Rep	Repetitive. Provide different expression.	UAV	Use active voice.
RS	Resale. Reassure reader that he or she has made a good choice.	Unc	Unclear. Rewrite to clarify meaning.
		UPV	Use passive voice.
SA	Service attitude. Put more emphasis on helping reader.	USS	Use shorter sentences.
Sin	Sincerity. Avoid sounding glib or uncaring.	V	Variety. Use different expression or sentence pattern.
SL	Stereotyped language. Focus on individual's characteristics instead of on false generalizations.	W	Wordy. Eliminate unnecessary words.
		WC	Word choice. Find a more appropriate word.
Spec	Specific. Provide more specific statement.	YA	"You" attitude. Rewrite to emphasize reader's needs.
SPM	Sales promotion material. Tell reader about related goods or services.		

GRAMMAR, USAGE, AND MECHANICS

Ab	Abbreviation. Avoid abbreviations in most cases; use correct abbreviation.	Exp	Expletive. Avoid expletive beginnings, such as *it is*, *there are*, and *there is*.
Adj	Adjective. Use adjective instead.	F	Format. Improve layout of document.
Adv	Adverb. Use adverb instead.	Frag	Fragment. Rewrite as complete sentence.
Agr	Agreement. Make subject and verb or noun and pronoun agree.	Gram	Grammar. Correct grammatical error.
		HCA	Hyphenate compound adjective.
Ap	Appearance. Improve appearance.	lc	Lowercase. Do not use capital letter.
Apos	Apostrophe. Check use of apostrophe.	M	Margins. Improve frame around document.
Art	Article. Use correct article.	MM	Misplaced modifier. Place modifier close to word it modifies.
BC	Be consistent.		
Cap	Capitalize.	NRC	Nonrestrictive clause. Separate from rest of sentence with commas.
Case	Use cases correctly.		
CoAdj	Coordinate adjective. Insert comma between coordinate adjectives; delete comma between adjective and compound noun.	P	Punctuation. Use correct punctuation.
		Par	Parallel. Use same structure.
		PH	Place higher. Move document up on page.
CS	Comma splice. Use period or semicolon to separate clauses.	PL	Place lower. Move document down on page.
		Prep	Preposition. Use correct preposition.
DM	Dangling modifier. Rewrite so modifier clearly relates to subject of sentence.	RC	Restrictive clause. Remove commas that separate clause from rest of sentence.

RO	Run-on sentence. Separate two sentences with comma or semicolon.	S-V	Subject-verb pair. Do not separate with comma.
SC	Series comma. Add comma before *and*.	Syl	Syllabification. Divide word between syllables.
SI	Split infinitive. Do not separate *to* from rest of verb.	WD	Word division. Check dictionary for proper end-of-line hyphenation.
Sp	Spelling error. Consult dictionary.	WW	Wrong word. Replace with another word.
Stet	Let stand in original form.		

PROOFREADING MARKS

SYMBOL	MEANING	SYMBOL USED IN CONTEXT	CORRECTED COPY
=	Align horizontally	meaningful result	meaningful result
‖	Align vertically	1. Power cable 2. Keyboard	1. Power cable 2. Keyboard
(uc)	Capitalize	(uc) Do not immerse.	DO NOT IMMERSE.
≡	Capitalize	Pepsico, Inc.	PepsiCo, Inc.
◡	Close up	self- confidence	self-confidence
ℓ	Delete	harrassment and abuse	harrassment
(STET)	Restore to original	all of the STET	all of the
∧	Insert	tirquoise and white shirts	turquoise and white shirts
⋏	Insert comma	a, b and c	a, b, and c
⊙	Insert period	Harrigan et al	Harrigan et al.
/	Lowercase	TULSA, South of here	Tulsa, south of here
⊏	Move left	Attention: Security	Attention: Security
⊐	Move right	February 2, 1993	February 2, 1993
⊔	Move down	Sincerely,	Sincerely,
⊓	Move up	THIRD-QUARTER SALES	THIRD-QUARTER SALES
⊐ ⊏	Center	Awards Banquet	Awards Banquet
⌐ ¬	Start new line	Marla Fenton, Manager, Distribution	Marla Fenton Manager, Distribution
∼	Run lines together	Manager, Distribution	Manager, Distribution
¶	Start paragraph	The solution is easy to determine but difficult to implement in a competitive environment like the one we now face.	The solution is easy to determine but difficult to implement in a competitive environment like the one we now face.
#	Insert space	real estate testcase	real estate test case
◯	Spell out	(COD)	cash on delivery
(SP)	Spell out	(SP) Assn. of Biochem. Engrs.	Association of Biochemical Engineers
∿	Transpose	airy, light, casual tone	light, airy, casual tone

REFERENCES

CHAPTER 1

1. Adapted from Mark Bittman, "Ben & Jerry's Caring Capitalism," *Restaurant Business,* 20 November 1990, 132; Jim Castelli, "Management Styles: Finding the Right Fit," *HR Magazine,* September 1990, 38; Steven S. Ross, "Green Groceries," *Mother Jones,* February–March 1989, 48; Bill Kelley, "The Cause Effect," *Food and Beverage Marketing,* March 1990, 20; Ellie Winninghoff, "Citizen Cohen," *Mother Jones,* January 1990, 12; Erik Larson, "Forever Young," *Inc.,* July 1988, 50; Jeanne Wegner, "This Season, Sharp-Dressed Dairy Products Are Wearing Green," *Dairy Foods,* September 1990, 72; "Soda, Milk Bottles Lead the Way," *Plastics World,* 22 April 1990, 7; Therese R. Welter, "Industry and the Environment: A Farewell to Arms," *Industry Week,* 20 August 1990, 36; Daniel Seligman, "Ben & Jerry Save the World," *Fortune,* 3 June 1991, 247; Fleming Meeks, "We All Scream for Rice and Beans," *Forbes,* 30 March 1992, 20.
2. David Givens, "You Animal! How to Win Friends and Influence Homo Sapiens," *The Toastmaster,* August 1986, 9.
3. Mark L. Hickson III and Don W. Stacks, *Nonverbal Communication: Studies and Applications* (Dubuque, Iowa: Brown, 1985), 4.
4. Dale G. Leathers, "The Impact of Multichannel Message Inconsistency on Verbal and Nonverbal Decoding Behaviors," *Communication Monographs* 46: 88–100.
5. Dale G. Leathers, *Successful Nonverbal Communication: Principles and Applications* (New York: Macmillan, 1986), 13.
6. Stuart Berg Flexner, "From 'Gadzooks' to 'Nice,' the Language Keeps Changing," *U.S. News & World Report,* 18 February 1985, 59.
7. Phillip Morgan and H. Kent Baker, "Building a Professional Image: Improving Listening Behavior," *Supervisory Management,* November 1985, 35, 36.
8. Irwin Ross, "Corporations Take Aim at Illiteracy," *Fortune,* 29 September 1986, 49.
9. See note 1.
10. See note 1.

CHAPTER 2

1. Adapted from "An Interview with General Motors' Alvie Smith," *Communication World,* June 1984, 19–21; Jerry Flint, "A Year for Living Dangerously," *Forbes,* 4 March 1991, 84–85; Paul Ingrassia and Joseph B. White, "GM Posts Record '91 Loss of $4.45 Billion, Sends Tough Message to UAW on Closings," *Wall Street Journal,* 25 February 1992, A3, A6; Andrea Gabor, "General Motors Reinvents the Wheel," *U.S. News & World Report,* 21 August 1989, 40–41; Bruce Goodsite, "General Motors Attacks Its Frozen Middle," *Communication World,* October 1987, 20–23; S. C. Gwynne, "The Right Stuff," *Time,* 29 October 1990, 74–84; S. C. Gwynne, "Two Sides of a Giant," *Time,* 19 February 1990, 68–70; Michelle Krebs, "Satellite System to Link GM, Dealers," *Automotive News,* 21 May 1990, 1, 55; Patrick McKeand, "GM Division Builds a Classic System to Share Internal Information," *Public Relations Journal,* November 1990, 24–26, 41; M. M. Petty, James Cashman, Anson Seers, Robert Stevenson, Charles Barker, and Grady Cook, "Better Communication at General Motors," *Personnel Journal,* September 1989, 40–49; John H. Sheridan, "A Star in the GM Heavens," *Industry Week,* 18 March 1991, 50–54; Alex Taylor III, "The New Drive to Revive GM," *Fortune,* 9 April 1990, 52–61; James B. Treece, "Will GM Learn from Its Own Role Models?" *Business Week,* 9 April 1990, 62.
2. J. Michael Sproule, *Communication Today* (Glenview, Ill.: Scott, Foresman, 1981), 327.
3. Walter D. St. John, "You Are What You Communicate," *Personnel Journal,* October 1985, 40.
4. Thomas J. Peters, "In Search of Communication Excellence," *Communication World,* February 1984, 12–15; Thomas J. Peters and Robert H. Waterman, Jr., *In Search of Excellence* (New York: Warner Books, 1984), 220.
5. "Employees Rate Company Information," *Small Business Report,* December 1986, 15.
6. Michael Brody, "Listen to Your Whistle Blower," *Fortune,* 24 November 1986, 77.
7. Sproule, *Communication Today,* 329.
8. Donald B. Simmons, "The Nature of the Organizational Grapevine," *Supervisory Management,* November 1985, 40.
9. Simmons, "Organizational Grapevine," 40.
10. David E. Sanger, "Challenger's Failure and NASA's Flaws," *New York Times,* 2 March 1986, sec. 4.
11. "Hands-Off Managers Need a Firm Grasp: Four Basic Methods of Management," *San Diego Union,* 10 March 1987, C-1.
12. James C. Shaffer, "Seven Emerging Trends in Organizational Communication," *IABC Communication World,* February 1986, 18.
13. Dianna Booher, "Don't Put It in Writing," *Training and Development Journal,* October 1986, 46.
14. Lynn Asinof, "Copious Copies," *Wall Street Journal,* 28 August 1986, A1.
15. John S. Fielden, Jean D. Fielden, and Ronald E. Dulek, *The Business Writing Style Book* (Englewood Cliffs, N.J.: Prentice-Hall, 1984), 7.
16. "1987 Business Letter Cost Tops $9.00," *Dartnell Target Survey,* Dartnell Institute of Business Research, 1987, 1.
17. Lloyd Shearer, "Intelligence Report," *Parade,* 1 January 1983, 9.
18. Dan Cook, "Why Gerber Is Standing Its Ground," *Business Week,* 17 March 1986, 50–51.
19. Edwin McDowell, "In a Crisis, 'Tell It All and Tell It Fast,'" *New York Times,* 28 December 1986, sec. 3.
20. Bruce Harrison with Tom Prugh, "Assessing the Damage," *Public Relations Journal,* October 1989, 40–45; Alex Stanton, "Crisis '89: Lessons Learned—On the Home Front," *Public Relations Journal,* September 1989, 15–18.
21. William J. Seiler, E. Scott Baudhuin, and L. David Schuelke, *Communication in Business and Professional Organizations* (Reading, Mass.: Addison-Wesley, 1982), 7.
22. See note 1.
23. See note 1.

CHAPTER 3

1. Adapted from Michelle Green and Denise Gellene, "As a Tiny Plastic Star Turns 30, the Real Barbie and Ken Reflect on Life in the Shadow of the Dolls," *People,* 6 March 1989, 186–189; Denise Gellene, "Forever Young," *Los Angeles Times,* 29 January 1989, D1, D4; Ann Hornaday, "Top Guns: The Most Powerful Women in Corporate America," *Savvy,* May 1989, 57, 60; Jennifer Roethe, "Dolls and Dollars Go Together like Ken and Barbie," *Cincinnati Business Courier,* 10 July 1989, 1.
2. Mary Munter, *Guide to Managerial Communication* (Englewood Cliffs, N.J.: Prentice-Hall, 1982), 9.
3. William P. Dommermuth, *Promotion: Analysis, Creativity, and Strategy* (Boston: Kent Publishing, 1982), 282.
4. Morgan W. McCall, Jr., and Robert L. Hannon, *Studies of Managerial Work: Results and Methods,* Technical Report no. 9 (Greensboro, N.C.: Center for Creative Leadership, 1978), 6–10.
5. Ernest Thompson, "Some Effects of Message Structure on Listener's Comprehension," *Speech Monographs* 34 (March 1967): 51–57.
6. See note 1.
7. See note 1.

CHAPTER 4

1. Adapted from Diane Cole, "What's New in Outplacement," *New York Times,* 14 February 1988, sec. 4, 15; Dana Bottorff, "The Velvet Boot," *New England Business,* 19 October 1987, 24–28; Lisa Spooner, "Outplacement Eases Termination Woes," *Savings Institutions,* March 1986, 99, 101; Blayne Cutler, "Corporate Victims," *American Demographics,* May 1989, 19.
2. Carol S. Mull, "Orchestrate Your Ideas," *The Toastmaster,* February 1987, 19.
3. Bruce B. MacMillan, "How to Write to Top Management," *Business Marketing,* March 1985, 138.
4. MacMillan, "How to Write to Top Management," 138.
5. Based on the Pyramid Model developed by Barbara Minto of McKinsey & Company, management consultants.
6. John S. Fielden, Jean D. Fielden, and Ronald E. Dulek, *The Business Writing Style Book* (Englewood Cliffs, N.J.: Prentice-Hall, 1984), 7.
7. See note 1.
8. See note 1.

CHAPTER 5

1. Adapted from Dyan Machan, "Great Hash Browns, but Watch Those Biscuits," *Forbes,* 19 September 1988, 192–196; Brian Bremner, "The Burger Wars Were Just a Warmup for McDonald's," *Business Week,* 8 May 1989, 67, 70; Richard Gibson and Robert Johnson, "Big Mac Plots Strategy to Regain Sizzle; Besides Pizza, It Ponders Music and Low Lights," *Wall Street Journal,* 29 September 1989, B1; Penny Moser, "The McDonald's Mystique," *Fortune,* 4 July 1988, 112–116; Thomas N. Cochran, "McDonald's Corporation," *Barron's,* 16 November 1987, 53–55; Lenore Skenazy, "McDonald's Colors Its World," *Advertising Age,* 9 February 1987, 37.
2. Robert Half International, "Message Lost in Some Memos," *USA Today,* 25 March 1987, 1A.

3. Portions of this section are adapted from Courtland L. Bovée, *Techniques of Writing Business Letters, Memos, and Reports* (Sherman Oaks, Calif.: Banner Books International, 1978), 13–90.
4. Judy E. Pickens, "Terms of Equality: A Guide to Bias-Free Language," *Personnel Journal*, August 1985, 24.
5. Alinda Drury, "Evaluating Readability," *IEEE Transactions on Professional Communication* PC28 (December 1985): 12.
6. See note 1.
7. See note 1.

CHAPTER 6

1. Carlin Romano, "Don't Pan His Bookstores," *Philadelphia Inquirer*, 20 December 1991, D1; John Blades, "Bookstores Expand Table of Contents: To Survive, Merchants Are Making Room for Sweat Shirts and Show Biz," *Chicago Tribune*, 12 May 1991, C1; "B. Dalton Turns New Page—To Superstores," *Chicago Tribune*, 6 September 1990, C3; Guy Halverson, "Big and Little Booksellers Succeed: Demographics, Technological Advances, and Innovative Services Allow Booksellers to Press On," *Christian Science Monitor*, 14 February 1990, 12; PRNewswire, "B. Dalton Acquires 'Scribner's Bookstore' Name; Plans to Open Additional Stores," 11 May 1989; Bill Vlasic, "Burning Competition in Books," *USA Today*, 30 July 1990, B4; Deirdre Donahue, "Bookstore Chains Boost Serious Works," *USA Today*, 1 May 1991, D1; George F. Will, "Few Adults Read Literature, So Give Thanks that a Serious Book Chain Succeeds," *Philadelphia Inquirer*, 7 June 1991, A16; Jessica Rosenthal Benson, "Bookstore Chains Become More 'Reader-Friendly'," *Philadelphia Inquirer*, 29 July 1990, 12; Eddie Olsen, "Bookstore Chains Offer Deals to Win Repeat Customers," *Philadelphia Inquirer*, 22 April 1990, G29; Linda Owen, "Book Chain's Superstore Seen as Challenge to Independents," *St. Paul Pioneer Press Dispatch*, 6 September 1990, B1.
2. See note 1.
3. Adapted from *Music Design Wholesale Catalog and Price List*, Fall 1991.
4. Adapted from Lynn Simross, "Something Extra at the Auto Shows," *Los Angeles Times*, 15 January 1992, E4.
5. Adapted from Wendy Lowe, "Sales Are Roaring at Jungle Stores," *USA Today*, 22 May 1986, 1B; Henry Weil, "Keeping Up with the (Indiana) Joneses," *Savvy*, February 1986, 43–46; *Banana Republic Travel & Safari Clothing Co. Catalog*, no. 30, Holiday 1986, 51.
6. See note 1.
7. Adapted from Steven Greenhouse, "The Big Bucks in Knees and Elbows," *New York Times*, 1 February 1987, sec. 3, 1.
8. Debora Toth, "What's New in Fragrances: To Relax or Stay Alert, New Mood-Altering Scents," *New York Times*, 24 September 1989, sec. 3, 15.
9. Adapted from *Trek USA 1992 Bicycles, Specialized Bicycles and Accessories*, and *Schwinn 92* catalogs; Champion International Corporation advertisement, *Wall Street Journal*, 13 September 1991, A2.
10. Rick Christie, "When It Doesn't Have to be There Fast," *Wall Street Journal*, 28 June 1989, B1.
11. Adapted from Associated Press, "Flood of Imports into Argentina Delights Shoppers, Riles Local Industry," *Los Angeles Times*, 6 January 1992, D4.
12. Adapted from Rose-Marie Turk, "Just a Touch," *Los Angeles Times*, 20 December 1991, E20; Business Notes, "Lipstick with a Conscience," *Time*, 7 October 1991, 45.
13. Adapted from Business Technology, "Portable Registers to the Rescue of Red-Hot Spenders," *New York Times*, 15 January 1992, Sec. d, 5.

CHAPTER 7

1. Joseph Weber, "Campbell Is Bubbling, But for How Long?" *Business Week*, 17 June 1991, 56–57; Joseph Weber, "From Soup to Nuts and Back to Soup," *Business Week*, 5 November 1990, 114, 116; "Here Are the Women to Watch in Corporate America," *Business Month*, April 1989, 40; Alix Freedman and Frank Allen, "John Dorrance's Death Leaves Campbell Soup with Cloudy Future," *Wall Street Journal*, 19 April 1989, A1, A14; Claudie H. Deutsch, "Stirring Up Profits at Campbell," *New York Times*, 20 November 1988, sec. 3, 1, 22; Bill Saporito, "The Fly in Campbell's Soup," *Fortune*, 9 May 1988, 67–70; 1990 Campbell Soup Company Annual Report; Biography of Zoe Coulson from *Marquis Who's Who*, accessed on-line, 24 May 1992.
2. Adapted from Arthur G. Sharp, "See You in Court," *Supervision*, April 1986, 3–5; Arthur G. Sharp, "The Revenge of the Fired," *Newsweek*, 16 February 1987, 46–47.
3. Susan Stobaugh, "Watch Your Language," *Inc.*, May 1985, 156.
4. John Schwartz, "You Deserve a Pizza Today," *Newsweek*, 11 November 1989, 46.
5. See note 1.
6. Adapted from Hilary Appelman, "Xerox Breaks Into the Japanese Market," *Los Angeles Times*, 3 February 1992, D3.
7. Adapted from Eben Shapiro, "The Sincerest Form of Rivalry," *New York Times*, 19 October 1991, 17, 29; Martha T. Moore, "Body Shop: Profits with Principles," *USA Today*, 10 October 1991, 8B; The Body Shop By Mail catalogs, brochures, and leaflets, 1991–92.
8. Adapted from Jeanne Wright, "Another Lifetime of Worry Over DES," *Los Angeles Times*, 11 February 1992, E1.
9. Michael Manges, "Hotel Ads Criticized as Short-Sighted," *Wall Street Journal*, 10 August 1989, B1.
10. Adapted from Andrew Pollack, "It's Asians' Turn in Silicon Valley," *New York Times*, 14 January 1992, sec. d, 1, 5.
11. See note 1.
12. Adapted from Anthony Ramirez, "Hot-Wiring Overseas Telephone Calls," *New York Times*, 9 January 1992, sec. d, 1, 6.
13. Adapted from George Russell, "Where the Customer Is Still King," *Time*, 2 February 1987, 56.
14. Adapted from Bill Montague, "Crayola Cleans Up Kids' Act," *USA Today*, 3 February 1992, 1A; Ellen Neuborne, "Crayola Fans Have Old Colors Back," *USA Today*, 2 October 1991, 2B; "Just Color Us Tickled Pink," *Newsweek*, 14 October 1991, 54; "Return of the Crayola Eight," *Time*, 14 October 1991, 33; Elaine Underwood, "Retro Brands," *Adweek's Marketing Week*, 14 October 1991, MK9.
15. Adapted from Glenn Rifkin, "Digital Back in PC Market with Bold Mail-Order Plans," *New York Times*, 14 January 1991, sec. d, 1, 3; "Digital Equipment Cuts PC Prices," *New York Times*, 7 February 1992, sec. c, 3.
16. Louis Uchitelle. "The Stanley Works Goes Global," *New York Times*, 23 July 1989, sec. 3, 1

CHAPTER 8

1. Adapted from Michael Barrier, "Working for 'Peanuts,'" *Nation's Business*, November 1988, 64–67; William Scobie, "Happiness Is . . . Snoopy," *Reader's Digest*, May 1986, 99–104; Carla Lazzareschi, "Fortune Grows from 'Peanuts' for Schulz, a Reluctant Tycoon. Good Grief!" *Los Angeles Times*, 29 November 1987, D1; Thomas R. King, "Ad Frenzy Is Planned to Mark 40th Birthday of Peanuts Gang," *Wall Street Journal*, 25 October 1989, B6; Craig Wilson, "He's a Good Man, Mr. Schulz," *USA Today*, 4 October 1989, 1D.
2. Rod Riggs, "Damage May Top $1 Billion; Most Lack Quake Insurance," *San Diego Union*, 19 October 1989, A-7.
3. See note 1.
4. Adapted from Beth Ann Krier, "Still Fishing for Compliments," *Los Angeles Times*, 10 January 1992, E5; Ralph Marlin & Company 1992 catalog.
5. Adapted from Zachary Schiller, "At Rubbermaid, Little Things Mean a Lot," *Business Week*, 11 November 1991, 126.
6. Adapted from Mark Maremont, "They're All Screaming For Haagen-Dazs," *Business Week*, 14 October 1991, 121; Carla Rapoport, "No Sexy Sales Ads, Please—We're Brits and Swedes," *Fortune*, 21 October 1991, 13.
7. See note 1.
8. Adapted from Thomas R. King, "Doctors Vow to Proscribe Infant-Formula Ad Plans," *Wall Street Journal*, 24 August 1989, B1.
9. Adapted from John M. Glionna, "Owner of Julian Surfing Store Makes Waves with 14-Foot Sign," *Los Angeles Times*, 6 January 1992, B1, B3; Bob Rowland, "Surfing Sign Makes Big Waves in Julian," *San Diego Union*, 10 January 1992, B-1, B-4.
10. Adapted from Janet Guyon, "Fairness Issue: Inequality in Granting Child-Care Benefits Makes Workers Seethe," *Wall Street Journal*, 23 October 1991, A1, A7.
11. Adapted from Susan Spillman, "Tell-all Previews Rile Movie Fans," *USA Today*, 21 November 1991, 1D; Susan Spillman, "The Delicate Art of Hooking Moviegoers," *USA Today*, 21 November 1991, 5D; Tom Green, "Rating the Previews for Some Holiday Films," *USA Today*, 21 November 1991, 5D; Susan Spillman, "Thumbs Down from Fans," *USA Today*, 21 November 1991, 5D.
12. Adapted from Barbara Foley, "Stepping into Something, Um, Ugly," *Los Angeles Times*, 18 December 1991, E1, E8.
13. Adapted from Fleming Meeks, "Shakespeare, Dickens & Hillegass," *Forbes*, 30 October 1989, 206, 208, 209.
14. Adapted from "I.R.S. Error of $40 Million," *New York Times*, 7 February 1992, sec. c, 4.

CHAPTER 9

1. Adapted from Ed Bean, "Small Rural Hospitals Struggle for Survival Under Medicare Setup," *Wall Street Journal*, 4 January 1988, A1, A6.
2. Jeanette W. Gilsdorf, "Executives' and Academics' Perceptions on the Need for Instruction in Written Persuasion," *Journal of Business Communication* 23 (Fall 1986): 67.
3. "FDA Plans New Curbs on Unchecked Health Claims," *San Diego Union*, 31 October 1989, A-1, A-7.
4. William North Jayme, quoted in Albert Haas, Jr., "How to Sell Almost Anything by Direct Mail," *Across the Board*, November 1986, 50.
5. Direct Mail Marketing Association, New York, 1989.

6. Bob Stone, *Successful Direct Marketing Methods*, 3d ed. (Lincolnwood, Ill.: Crain Books, 1987).
7. See note 1.
8. Adapted from Claudia H. Deutsch, "Rewarding Employees for 'Wellness,'" *New York Times*, 15 September 1991, 21; Hilary Stout, "Paying Workers for Good Health Habits Catches On as a Way to Cut Medical Costs," *Wall Street Journal*, 26 November 1991, B1, B5.
9. Adapted from Jacqueline Mitchell, "Volvo Creates a Stir Again with TV Ads," *New York Times*, 18 November 1991, sec. b, 1, 6; Micheline Maynard and James R. Healey, "Volvo Defends Ad Slamming Minivans," *USA Today*, 18 November 1991, 3B.
10. Adapted from Joanne Lipman, "Consumers Rebel Against Becoming a Captive Audience," *Wall Street Journal*, 13 September 1991, B1.
11. Adapted from David A. Avila, "Mentally Ill Find Health in Flowers," *Los Angeles Times*, 15 January 1992, B2.
12. Adapted from John H. Cushman, Jr., "Makers of Small Planes Wait for Brighter Skies," *New York Times*, 18 January 1992, 37, 39.
13. Adapted from Tim Friend, "Health Care That's Also Fiscally Fit," *USA Today*, 5 December 1991, 1D, 2D.
14. Adapted from Roger Thurow, "Seeing the Light," *Wall Street Journal*, 20 September 91, R1, R2; Erin Kelly, "Business School in Prague Trains Future Capitalists," *Los Angeles Times*, 12 January 1992, D3.
15. See note 1.
16. Adapted from "This Mannequin Watches You," *The San Diego Union*, 8 July 1989, E-1.
17. Adapted from M. P. Dunleavey, "It's a Bird. A Plane! A Blimp?" *New York Times*, 1 September 1991, sec. f, 5.
18. Adapted from Lawrence J. Magid, "Computer File: Software That Helps You Play Piano," *Los Angeles Times*, 19 December 1991, D3.
19. Adapted from Anthony Ramirez, "Consumer Videophone by AT&T," *New York Times*, 7 January 1992, sec. d, 1, 4; A. Michael Noll, "Videophone: A Flop That Won't Die," *New York Times*, 12 January 1992, sec. 3, 13.
20. Mark Robichaux, "Dealing with Deadbeats: Call Early and Often to Collect," *Wall Street Journal*, 18 July 1989, B7.

CHAPTER 10

1. Adapted from Christopher Vaughn, "Pumping Up the Jam for Profits," *Black Enterprise*, December 1991, 51–67; David Mills, "Jheryl Busby and the Fight for Motown's Soul," *Washington Post*, 2 June 1991, sec. g, 1; Paul Farhi, "MCA Marketing Misses Hits, Motown Records Suit Alleges," *Washington Post*, 15 May 1991, sec. g, 1; Bruce Britt, "Motown Ready for a Brand-New Heat," *Daily News of Los Angeles*, 27 January 1992, sec. 1, 18; Richard Turner, "The Motown Rift," *Daily News of Los Angeles*, 26 September 1991, sec. b, 1; Richard W. Stevenson, "Putting Motown Back on the Map," *New York Times*, 19 February 1989, sec. 3, 4; David Lieberman, "Now Playing: The Sound of Money," *Business Week*, 15 August 1988, 86–90; "For the Record: Diana Ross Becomes a Motown Owner," *Wall Street Journal*, 14 February 1989, B5; Amy Dawes, "Motown Label Going to MCA at $61 Million," *Variety*, 29 June 1988, 1; Kevin D. Thompson, "The Motown Lament: Where Did Our Company Go?" *Black Enterprise*, August 1988, 17.

CHAPTER 11

2. Roger P. Wilcox, *Communication at Work: Writing and Speaking* (Boston: Houghton Mifflin, 1977), 49–51.
3. See note 1; Kevin Maney, "Production Costs Keep Band in Hock," *USA Today*, 28 August 1987, 1B, 2B.
4. See note 1.

CHAPTER 11

1. Adapted from James B. Shuman, "Easy Rider Rides Again," *Business Tokyo*, July 1991, 26–30; Vaughn Beals, "Harley-Davidson: An American Success Story," *Journal for Quality and Participation*, June 1988, A19–A23; Vaughn Beals, "Quality and Productivity: The Harley-Davidson Experience," *Survey of Business*, Spring 1986, 9–11; Sharon Brady, "School of Hard Knocks," *Software Magazine*, April 1988, 37–44; Shirley Cayer, "Harley's New Manager-Owners Put Purchasing Out Front," *Purchasing*, 13 October 1988, 50–54; Claudia H. Deutch, "Now Harley-Davidson Is All Over the Road," *New York Times*, 17 April 1988, F12; Holt Hackney, "Easy Rider," *Financial World*, 4 September 1990, 48–49; Roy L. Harmon and Leroy D. Peterson, "Reinventing the Factory," *Across the Board*, March 1990, 30–38; John Holusha, "How Harley Outfoxed Japan with Exports," *New York Times*, 12 August 1990, F5; Peter C. Reid, "How Harley Beat Back the Japanese," *Fortune*, 25 September 1989, 155–164.
2. Rudolf Flesch, "How to Say It with Statistics," *Marketing Communications*, 8 December 1950, 23–24.
3. Flesch, "How to Say It with Statistics," 23–24.
4. See note 1.
5. See note 1.

CHAPTER 12

1. Adapted from N. R. Kleinfield, "Penn State's $20 Million Touchdown," *New York Times*, 13 September 1987, sec. 3, 1, 8; Bruce Walker, "The Demand for Professional League Football and the Success of Football League Teams: Some City Size Effects," *Urban Studies*, June 1986, 209–219; "The Way We Were: The Tenuous Economics of the Gridiron," *Canadian Business*, September 1988, 118; Glen Waggoner, "Money Madness: The True Story about the Crazy Economics of Professional Sports," *Esquire*, June 1982, 49; John Merwin, "Dumb Like Foxes," *Forbes*, 24 October 1988, 703–724.
2. See note 1.
3. See note 1.
4. Adapted from Nicholas E. Lefferts, "What's New in the Pet Business," *New York Times*, 28 July 1985, sec. 3.
5. Adapted from Justine Kaplan, "What's New in Cruises," *New York Times*, 3 August 1986, sec. 3, F17.
6. Adapted from David Tuller, "What's New in the Tennis Business," *New York Times*, 7 June 1987, sec. 3, F21.

CHAPTER 13

1. Adapted from Barbara C. Hopkins, "Charles E. Morrison, Marketing Executive Is on Target," *Dollars & Sense*, August–September 1988, 16–22; Asra Q. Nomani, "Steeped in Tradition, 'Step Dance' Unites Blacks on Campus," *Wall Street Journal*, 10 July 1989, A1; Joel Kotkin, "Selling to the New America," *Inc.*, July 1987, 44–52; Alfred Edmond, Jr., "These Guys Don't Blink," *Black Enterprise*, June 1987, 310–316; Carol Kenton, "Market-

ing to Blacks," *Incentive Marketing*, February 1986, 22–30; Rick Blake, "Minorities: Reaching the World's Ninth Largest Market," *Public Relations Journal*, June 1985, 30–31; Candace Campbell, "Adding Some Fizz to Soft Drink Sales," *Advertising Age*, 27 February 1986, 24–26; Dorothy Townsend, "Coca-Cola Plans Program to Aid Latino Community," *Los Angeles Times*, 16 November 1983, D2; Sonia L. Nazario, "Coke Plans Program to Improve Its Links with Hispanic Firms," *Wall Street Journal*, 15 November 1983, A24; Ray Rivas, "Hispanic Marketing: Translating Goals into Results," *Marketing Communications*, July 1985, 23–28..
2. Adapted from Burdette E. Bostwick, *How to Find the Job You've Always Wanted* (New York: Wiley, 1982), 69–70.
3. See note 1.
4. See note 1.

CHAPTER 14

1. Adapted from Kenneth Labich, "Hot Company, Warm Culture," *Fortune*, 27 February 1989, 74–78; Tom Peters and Nancy Austin, *A Passion for Excellence* (New York: Random House, 1985), 204–205; George Melloan, "Herman Miller's Secrets of Corporate Creativity," *Wall Street Journal*, 3 May 1988, A31; Beverly Geber, "Herman Miller: Where Profits and Participation Meet," *Training*, November 1987, 62–66; Robert J. McClory, "The Creative Process at Herman Miller," *Across the Board*, May 1985, 8–22.
2. Robert Gifford, Cheuk Fan Ng, and Margaret Wilkinson, "Nonverbal Cues in the Employment Interview: Links Between Applicant Qualities and Interviewer Judgments," *Journal of Applied Psychology* 70, no. 4 (1985): 729.
3. Dale G. Leathers, *Successful Nonverbal Communication* (New York: Macmillan, 1986), 225.
4. Shirley J. Shepherd, "How to Get That Job in 60 Minutes or Less," *Working Woman*, March 1986, 119.
5. Shepherd, "How to Get That Job," 118.
6. Marilyn Moats Kennedy, "Are You Getting Paid What You're Worth?" *New Woman*, November 1984, 110.
7. Questions adapted from Gregory Stock, *The Book of Questions* (New York: Workman Publishing, 1987), 39.
8. Stock, *The Book of Questions*, 196.
9. See note 1.
10. See note 1.

CHAPTER 15

1. Adapted from Laurie Hays, "All Eyes on Du Pont's Incentive-Pay Plan," *Wall Street Journal*, 5 December 1988, B1; George Ruben, "Du Pont Adopts Pay Incentive Plan," *Monthly Labor Review* 3 (December 1988): 51; Bernard A. Rusch, "Du Pont Transforms a Division's Culture," *Management Review* 78 (March 1989): 37.
2. J. Michael Sproule, *Communication Today* (Glenview, Ill.: Scott, Foresman, 1981), 167–170.
3. James J. Floyd, *Listening: A Practical Approach* (Glenview, Ill.: Scott, Foresman, 1985), 5–6.
4. Phillip Morgan and H. Kent Baker, "Building a Professional Image: Improving Listening Behavior," *Supervisory Management*, November 1985, 35–36.
5. Sproule, *Communication Today*, 69.
6. Sproule, *Communication Today*, 55–70.

7. B. Aubrey Fisher, *Small Group Decision Making: Communication and the Group Process*, 2d ed. (New York: McGraw-Hill, 1980), 145–149.
8. "Successful Meetings: Management's Ongoing Challenge," *Small Business Report*, January 1987, 77.
9. See note 1.
10. See note 1.

CHAPTER 16

1. Adapted from Trudy Gallant-Stokes, "Brady Keys Does Franchising Right," *Black Enterprise*, September 1988, 56–62; Cynthia Legette, "The New Entrepreneur: Nobody Does It Better," *Black Enterprise* 19 (December 1988): 56–60; Bill Carlino, "Keys Opens Doors for Minorities," *Nation's Restaurant News* 22 (10 October 1988): 1; Marsha Westbrook, "Burger King Honors a Pioneering Food Franchisee," *Black Enterprise* 18 (February 1988): 40.
2. H. C. Kelman and C. I. Hovland, "'Reinstatement' of the Communicator in Delayed Measurement of Opinion Change," *Journal of Abnormal and Social Psychology* 48 (1953): 327–335.
3. Walter Kiechel III, "How to Give a Speech," *Fortune*, 8 June 1987, 180.
4. *Communication and Leadership Program* (Santa Ana, Calif.: Toastmasters International, 1980), 44, 45.
5. *How to Prepare and Use Effective Visual Aids*, Info-Line series, Elizabeth Lean, managing ed. (Washington, D.C.: American Society for Training and Development, October 1984), 2.
6. Judy Linscott, "Getting On and Off the Podium," *Savvy*, October 1985, 44.
7. Sandra Moyer, "Braving No Woman's Land," *The Toastmaster*, August 1986, 13.
8. Robert L. Montgomery, "Listening on Your Feet," *The Toastmaster*, July 1987, 14–15.

9. See note 1.
10. See note 1.

CHAPTER 17

1. Adapted from Kaori Shoji, "Custom-Made Campaigns," *Business Tokyo*, March 1991, 18–22; William J. Best, "Western Companies in Japan: Relearning the Basics," *Directors & Boards*, Summer 1990, 29–32; Edwin Artzt, "Winning in Japan: Keys to Global Success," *Business Quarterly*, Winter 1989, 12–16; Brian Dumaine, "P&G Rewrites the Marketing Rules," *Fortune*, 6 November 1989, 35–36, 38, 40, 42, 46, 48; Thomas Olson, "Japanese Culture Initially Stymied Mighty P&G," *Cincinnati Business Courier*, 23–29 April 1990, 18.
2. Stephen J. Simurda, "Opening in the East," *Adweek's Marketing Week*, 20 November 1989, 2–4.
3. Vern Terpstra, *The Cultural Environment of International Business* (Cincinnati: South-Western, 1979), 19.
4. Retha H. Kilpatrick, "International Business Communication Practices," *Journal of Business Communication* 21 (Fall 1984): 36.
5. Kathleen K. Reardon, "It's the Thought That Counts," *Harvard Business Review*, September–October 1984, 141.
6. "Pakistan: A Congenial Business Climate," *Nation's Business*, July 1986, 50.
7. Herschel Peak, "Conquering Cross-Cultural Challenges," *Business Marketing*, October 1985, 139.
8. Edward T. Hall, "The Silent Language of Overseas Business," in *Dimensions of Communication*, Lee Richardson, ed. (New York: Appleton-Century-Crofts, 1969), 442.
9. Sharon Ruhly, *Intercultural Communication*, 2d ed., MODCOM (Modules in Speech Communication) (Chicago: Science Research Associates, 1982), 14.
10. Ruhly, *Intercultural Communication*, 28.

11. See note 1.
12. See note 1.

CHAPTER 18

1. Adapted from Lura K. Romei, "Publishing Pays Off," *Modern Office Technology*, October 1988, 59–62; Patricia M. Fernberg, "Putting the 'E.T.' in Met Life," *Modern Office Technology*, November 1988, 72, 74; Darlane Hoffman, "Have You Compressed Your Data Today?" *Best's Review*, May 1988, 48–54; Marilyn Gasaway and Anna Welke, "How Leading Insurers Use Technology to Compete," *ICP Insurance Software*, Autumn 1986, 14–23; "The Automated Office: Waging a Paper War," *ICP Insurance Software*, Spring 1984, 8.
2. Larry Martz, "Revolution by Information," *Newsweek*, 19 June 1989, 28–29.
3. David J. Rachman, Michael H. Mescon, Courtland L. Bovée, and John V. Thill, "Computers and Information Technology," *Business Today*, 6th ed. (New York: McGraw-Hill, 1990), 417.
4. International Data Corporation, "Office Systems for the Eighties: Automation and the Bottom Line," White Paper to Management, *Fortune*, 3 October 1983, 142.
5. "Telecommuting," *Openline: For the Pacific Bell Customer*, August 1986, 1–2.
6. See note 1.
7. See note 1.

APPENDIX B

1. Patricia A. Dreyfus, "Paper That's Letter Perfect," *Money*, May 1985, 184.

APPENDIX C

1. Dorothy Geisler, "How to Avoid Copyright Lawsuits," *IABC Communication World*, June 1984, 34–37.
2. Robert W. Goddard, "The Crime of Copying," *Management World*, July–August 1986, 20–22.

ACKNOWLEDGMENTS

TEXT, FIGURES, AND TABLES

5 (Figure 1.1): From Philip I. Morgan et al., "Building a Professional Image: Improving Listening Behavior." Reprinted, by permission of the publisher, from *Supervisory Management*, November 1985. © 1985 American Management Association, New York. All rights reserved. 6–7 "Behind the Scenes at Federal Express—When It Absolutely, Positively Has to Be Perfect": Jon Sutton, personal interview, June 1989. Used with permission. 12 (Figure 1.2): From *Communicating on the Job* by Allan D. Frank, p. 20. Used with permission of Allen D. Frank. 28 (Figure 2.1): From David J. Rachman and Michael H. Mescon, *Business Today*, 5th edition. © 1987 McGraw-Hill Publishing Company. Reprinted with permission. 31 (Figure 2.3): From David J. Rachman and Michael H. Mescon, *Business Today*, 5th edition. © 1987 McGraw-Hill Publishing Company. Reprinted with permission. 38–39 "Behind the Scenes at Amtrak—Keeping an Image on Track": John Jacobsen and Sue Martin, personal interview, June 1989. Used with permission. 50–51 "Behind the Scenes at Allstate Insurance—Editing for Action: Fine Print that Insures Success": Patrick Williams, personal interview, June 1989. Used with permission. 78–79 "Behind the Scenes at General Electric—The Making of an Annual Report": David Warshaw, personal interview, June 1989. Used with permission. 91, 114–116 From Dyan Machan, "Great Hash Browns, but Watch Those Biscuits" from the September 19, 1988 issue of *Forbes*. Reprinted by permission of *Forbes* magazine. © Forbes Inc., 1988. 94–95 "Behind the Scenes at the La Jolla Playhouse—Greasepaint, Bright Lights, and Rewrites": Constance Harvey, personal interview, May 1992. Used with permission. 130–131 "Behind the Scenes at the Phoenix Symphony—Orchestrating Direct Requests": Gail Warden, personal interview, April 1992. Used with permission. 150–151 "Behind the Scenes at Citibank—Solving Problems, Saving Business": Jane Wolchonok, personal interview, June 1989. Used with permission. 167 (Figure 7.4): Letterhead courtesy of TWA. 180, 198–202 From Michael Barrier, "Working for 'Peanuts.'" Adapted with permission, *Nation's Business*, November 1988. Copyright 1988, U.S. Chamber of Commerce. 186–187 "Behind the Scenes at America West—Navigating Bad News": Daphne Dicino, personal interview, March 1992. Used with permission. 209–210, 233–236 From Ed Bean, "Small Rural Hospitals Struggle for Survival Under Medicare Setup," *The Wall Street Journal*, January 4, 1988, p. 1. Adapted by permission of *The Wall Street Journal*, © Dow Jones & Company, Inc. 1988. All rights reserved worldwide. 226–227 "Behind the Scenes with John Keil—The Case of the Rat's Guillotine": adapted from John M. Keil, *The Creative Mystique*. (New York: Wiley, 1985), 46–48. Copyright © 1985. Reprinted by permission of John Wiley & Sons, Inc. 252–253 "Behind the Scenes at the San Diego Zoo—Even Tapirs Leave a Paper Trail": Rick Barongi, personal interview, May 1992. Used with permission. 293 (Figure 11.4): From David J. Rachman and Michael H. Mescon, *Business Today*, 5th edition. © 1987 McGraw-Hill Publishing Company. Reprinted with permission. 296–297 "Behind the Scenes at Gannett Company—Getting the Scoop on a Media Giant": Sheila J. Gibbons, personal interview, June 1989. Used with permission. 308–309 "Behind the Scenes at the Rocky Mountain Institute—Energy Efficiency: Getting the Word to the World": Adapted from L. Hunter Lovins, personal interview, April 1992. Used with permission; James R. Udall, "Prophets of an Energy Revolution," *National Wild-*

life, December–January 1992, 10–13; *Water Efficiency: A Resource for Utility Managers, Community Planners, and Other Decisionmakers*, Rocky Mountain Institute, November 1991.   317   (Figure 12.4): From Gene Zelanzy, *Say It with Charts*, Richard D. Irwin, Inc., © 1984, p. 112. Reprinted with permission.   318   From David M. Kroenke and Kathleen A. Dolan, *Business Computer Systems: An Introduction*, © 1987 McGraw-Hill Publishing Company. Reprinted with permission.   319   (Figure B): Data from *Nation's Restaurant News*, 3 August 1987, 7. Copyright *Nation's Restaurant News*.   319   (Figure C): From *Psychology Today*, May 1980, 72. Reprinted with permission from *Psychology Today* Magazine. Copyright © 1980 (Sussex Publishers, Inc.).   320   (Figure E): Courtesy of Paladin Press, Boulder, Colorado, from *Life After Doomsday*, Dr. Bruce Clayton, 1980.   322   (Figure 12.6): From Robert Lefferts, *How to Prepare Charts and Graphics for Effective Reports*. Copyright © 1981 by Robert Lefferts.   354–355, 377–380   From Barbara C. Hopkins, "Charles E. Morrison, Marketing Executive Is on Target," *Dollars & Sense*, August-September 1988, 16–22. Adapted from *Dollars & Sense* magazine, Chicago, Il 60649; and from Asra Q. Nomani, "Steeped in Tradition, 'Step Dance' Unites Blacks on Campus," *Wall Street Journal*, 10 July 1989, A1. Reprinted by permission of *The Wall Street Journal*, © Dow Jones & Company, Inc. 1989. All rights reserved.   355   (Figure 13.1): From Tom Jackson, *Guerilla Tactics in the Job Market*, Bantam Books, a division of Bantam, Doubleday, Dell Publishing Group, Inc. Reprinted by permission.   361   (Table 13.1): Excerpts from *The Perfect Resume* by Tom Jackson, copyright © 1981 by Tom Jackson. Used by permission of Doubleday, a division of Bantam, Doubleday, Dell Publishing Group, Inc.   362–363   "Behind the Scenes at Mobil Corporation— How to Write a Resume with the Winning Edge": Henry Halaiko, personal interview, June 1989. Used with permission.   394–395   "Behind the Scenes at IBM—Secrets to Winning an Interview": Jim Greenwood, personal interview, June 1989. Used with permission.   410–411, 425–427   From Laurie Hays, "All Eyes on DuPont's Incentive-Pay Plan," *The Wall Street Journal*, December 5 1988, p. B1. Adapted by permission of *The Wall Street Journal*, © 1988 Dow Jones & Company, Inc. All Rights Reserved Worldwide.   414   (Figure 15.1): Adapted from material prepared by Dr. Lyman K. Steil, President, Communication Development, Inc., St. Paul, Minnesota, for the Sperry Corporation. Reprinted with permission of Dr. Steil and the Unisys Corporation.   420   (Figure 15.2): From J. Michael Sproule, *Communication Today*, copyright © 1980 by J. Michael Sproule. Reprinted by permission of the author.   422–423   "Behind the Scenes at 3M—The Keys to Masterful Meetings": Virginia Johnson, personal interview, June 1989. Used with permission.   429–430, 446–449   From Trudy Gallant-Stokes, "Brady Keys Does Franchising Right," *Black Enterprise*, September 1988, 56–62. Copyright September 1988 The Earl G. Graves Publishing Co., Inc., 130 Fifth Avenue, New York, NY 10011. All rights reserved.   442–443   "Behind the Scenes with Charles Osgood—Speaking Out on Public Speaking": adapted from Charles Osgood, *Osgood on Speaking* (New York: Morrow, 1988), 10, 11, 21–23, 25–27, 34–35, 41, 89–90, 95. Copyright © 1988 by the author. By permission of William Morrow & Co.   460–461   "Behind the Scenes at Parker Pen—Do as the Natives Do, But Should You Eat the Roast Gorilla Hand?": Roger Axtel, personal communication, June 1989. Used with permission.   471, 483–485   From Lura K. Romei, "Publishing Pays Off." Adapted from the October 1988 issue of *Modern Office Technology*, and copyrighted 1988 by Penton Publishing, Subsidiary of Pittway Corporation.   480–481   "Behind the Scenes at Mike's Video—Video Club Thrives on Office Technology": Mike Negra, Alan Abruzzo, and Wanda White, personal communication, June 1989. Used with permission.   509   (Table B.1): Adaptation of figure from *The Secretary's Handbook*, 3d edition, by Doris H. Whalen, copyright © 1978 by Harcourt Brace Jovanovich, Inc., reprinted by permission of the publisher.   511   (Table B.2): Excerpt(s) from *The Amy Vanderbilt Complete Book of Etiquette by Amy Vanderbilt*, revised by Letitia Baldrige, copyright © 1978 by Curtis B. Kellar and Lincoln G. Clark as executors of the estate of Amy Vanderbilt and Doubleday. Used by permission of the publisher.   516   (Figure B.3): Letterhead courtesy of Mattel Toys.   517   (Figure B.4): Letterhead courtesy of J. C. Penney.   518   (Figure B.5): Letterhead courtesy of Kentucky Fried Chicken.

PHOTO CREDITS

Logo for Behind the Scenes Steven Hunt/The Image Bank   **Logo for Checklist** Lou Jones/The Image Bank   **Logo for Report Writer's Notebook** David Frazier/The Stock Market

iv (**top**) E. J. Camp/Outline Press   iv (**bottom**) Courtesy General Motors   v (**top**) Lynda Finch, courtesy of Mattel Toys   v (**bottom**) Mark Sherman/Bruce Coleman   vi (**top**) Michael L. Abramson/Woodfin Camp & Associates   vi (**bottom**) Geri Engberg/The Stock Market   vii (**top**) McGraw-Hill Photo   vii (**bottom**) Reprinted by permission of UFS, Inc.   viii (**top**) Deangelo McDaniel/The Moulton Advertiser   viii (**bottom**) Courtesy of Motown Historical Museum   ix (**top**) Courtesy of Harley Davidson   ix (**middle**) Wide World Photos   ix (**bottom**) Courtesy of The Coca-Cola Company   x (**top**) Courtesy of Herman Miller Co.   x (**bottom**) Courtesy of Du Pont   xi (**top**) Courtesy of Keys Group Company   xi (**middle**) Caroline Parsons   xi (**bottom**) Courtesy of Metropolitan Life Insurance Company   3 E. J. Camp/Outline Press   9 Carol Halebian/Gamma Liaison   12 Courtesy of Avon Products, Inc.   13 Robert McElroy/Woodfin Camp & Associates   14 Courtesy of Ameritech   25 Courtesy General Motors   27 Courtesy of McDonald's, Inc.   30 Courtesy of General Electric   32 Wide World Photos   35 Courtesy of Mrs. Fields Cookies, Busath Photography   47 Lynda Finch, courtesy of Mattel Toys   48 Wally McNamee/Woodfin Camp & Associates   49 Courtesy of General Motors Corp.   52 Courtesy of Reebok International Ltd.   53 Courtesy of Nynex Service Co.   68 Mark Sherman/Bruce Coleman   72 Courtesy of Ford Plastic Products Division   73 Jack Mitchell/Outline Press   83 Reuters/Bettman Newsphoto   85 J. Zimberoff/Gamma Liaison   92 (**top**) Michael L. Abramson/Woodfin Camp & Associates   92 (**bottom**) Courtesy of Walt Disney Company   95 John Biever/Picture Group   97 Courtesy of CBS News   98 Courtesy of Allied Signal, Inc.   123 Geri Engberg/The Stock Market   124 Wide World Photos   126 Courtesy of AT&T   132 Bill O'Leary/The Washington Post   135 Courtesy of Lorraine Scarpa   148 McGraw-Hill Photo   149 Reuters/Bettman Newsphoto   158 Courtesy of Colonial Mortgage Company   164 Courtesy of Avon Products, Inc.   166 Mark Thomas, courtesy of Hal Riney & Partners   181 Reprinted by permission of UFS, Inc.   182 Louis Psihoyos/Matrix   185 Newsweek   186 Courtesy of Metropolitan Life Insurance Company   193 Courtesy of American Express Company   210 Deangelo McDaniel/The Moulton Advertiser   211 Courtesy of Mary Kay Cosmetics   212 Courtesy The Black & Decker Corporation   214 Roger Ressmeyer/Starlight   217 Courtesy of the National Easter Seal Society   247 Courtesy of Motown Historical Museum   250 Courtesy of the United States Supreme Court   257 Courtesy of Simpson/Bruckheimer Productions   260 Courtesy of Liz Claiborne   270 Tim Naprestek   280 (**top**) Courtesy of Harley Davidson   280 (**bottom**) Courtesy of Capitol Cities/ABC, Inc.   286 Federal Express Corporation   288 Elfriede Riley/Random House   291 Wide World Photos   305 Wide World Photos   308 Bill Ray   311 Doug Menuez/Picture Group   313 Werner Wolf/Black Star   343 Courtesy of Computer Associates International, Inc.   355 Courtesy of The Coca-Cola Company   356 Courtesy of AT&T   358 Courtesy of Merrill Lynch   367 Courtesy of Godfather's Pizza   370 C. Thatcher/Woodfin Camp & Associates   385 Courtesy of Herman Miller Co.   388 Courtesy of Eastman Kodak Co.   389 Courtesy of Gittings   392 Courtesy of FireKing International, Inc.   395 Courtesy of Levi Strauss   411 Courtesy of Du Pont   413 Courtesy of McGuffy's Restaurant   416 Courtesy of US West Communications   421 Courtesy of Aetna Life & Casualty   424 Courtesy of Capitol Cities/ABC, Inc.   430 Courtesy of Keys Group Company   431 Reuters/Bettmann Newsphotos   436 Courtesy of Success Strategy, Inc.   437 Bill Weems/The Coca-Cola Company   444 Peter Steiner/Xerox Corporation   453 Caroline Parsons   454 Gwendolen Cates/Outline   457 Courtesy of Scott Paper   459 Courtesy of Bankers Trust Company   463 Robert McElroy/Woodfin Camp & Associates   466 Courtesy of Eastern Airlines   472 (**top**) Courtesy of Metropolitan Life Insurance Company   472 (**bottom**) Courtesy of Dictaphone   473 (**top**) Courtesy of Weyerhaeuser   473 (**bottom**) Courtesy of Xerox Corporation   474 Courtesy of Cannon USA, Inc.   476 (**top left**) Courtesy of Bell & Howell Mailmobile Co.   476 (**top right**) The Novak Company   476 (**bottom**) Courtesy of Pitney Bowes Business Systems   477 (**top left**) Courtesy of AT&T Archives   477 (**top right**) Courtesy of Xerox Corporation   477 (**bottom**) Courtesy of Eastman Kodak Company   479 (**top**) Courtesy of Delco Associates   479 (**center left**) Courtesy of Acme Visible Records   479 (**center**) Courtesy of Isabel Stacor Corp.   479 (**center right**) Courtesy of Ring King Visibles, Inc.   479 (**bottom**) Courtesy of Bell & Howell   480 Courtesy of TBS   481 Courtesy of Digital Equipment

ORGANIZATION INDEX

SUBJECT/PERSON INDEX